❧ 93D CONGRESS, 1ST SESSION . . HOUSE DOCUMENT NO. 93–111 ❧

MEMORIAL SERVICES IN THE

CONGRESS OF THE UNITED STATES

AND TRIBUTES IN EULOGY OF

Lyndon Baines Johnson

LATE A PRESIDENT OF THE

UNITED STATES

Compiled Under the Direction of
the Joint Committee on Printing

UNITED STATES GOVERNMENT PRINTING OFFICE
WASHINGTON : 1973

House Concurrent Resolution No. 109

(Mr. PATMAN submitted the following concurrent resolution)

IN THE HOUSE OF REPRESENTATIVES,

February 5, 1973.

Resolved by the House of Representatives (the Senate concurring), That there be printed, with illustrations, as a House document and bound, under the direction of the Joint Committee on Printing, all of the speeches and remarks which constitute tributes to the life, character, and public service of the late President of the United States, Lyndon Baines Johnson, and which were delivered on January 24 and 25, 1973, in the rotunda of the Capitol of the United States where the remains of the late President lay in state, at his funeral service held at the National City Christian Church, Washington, District of Columbia, and at his burial service in Texas, together with such additional explanatory matter as the joint committee may deem pertinent, and all speeches and remarks of tribute to the late President delivered in the Halls of Congress.

SEC. 2. There shall be printed and bound, as directed by the Joint Committee on Printing, thirty-two thousand four hundred additional copies of such documents, of which twenty-two thousand one hundred copies shall be for the use of the House of Representatives and ten thousand three hundred copies shall be for the use of the Senate.

Senate Concurrent Resolution No. 9

(Mr. BENTSEN submitted the following concurrent resolution)

IN THE SENATE OF THE UNITED STATES,

February 5, 1973.

Providing for the printing of remarks of tribute to the late President of the United States, Lyndon Baines Johnson.

Resolved by the Senate (the House of Representatives concurring), That there be printed, with illustrations, as a Senate document and bound, under the direction of the Joint Committee on Printing, all of the speeches and remarks which constitute tributes to the life, character, and public service of the late President of the United States, Lyndon Baines Johnson, and which were delivered on January 24 and 25, 1973, in the rotunda of the Capitol of the United States where the remains of the late President lay in state, at his funeral service held at the National City Christian Church, Washington, District of Columbia, and at his burial service in Texas, together with such additional explanatory matter as the joint committee may deem pertinent, and all speeches and remarks of tribute to the late President delivered in the Halls of Congress.

SEC. 2. There shall be printed and bound, as directed by the Joint Committee on Printing, thirty-two thousand four hundred additional copies of such document, of which twenty-two thousand one hundred copies shall be for the use of the House of Representatives and ten thousand three hundred copies shall be for the use of the Senate.

A compilation of addresses and tributes as given in the United States Senate and House of Representatives plus such additional materials, including the texts of eulogies, messages, prayers, and scriptural selections delivered at the funeral services held in Washington, D.C., and in Johnson City, Tex., on the life, character, and public service of the late President Lyndon Baines Johnson.

Lyndon Baines Johnson

(1908-1973)

LYNDON BAINES JOHNSON, a Representative and a Senator from Texas and a Vice President and 36th President of the United States; born on a farm near Stonewall, Gillespie County, Tex., on August 27, 1908; moved with his parents to Johnson City, in 1913; attended the public schools of Blanco County, Tex.; was graduated from the Johnson City (Tex.) High School in 1924 and from the Southwest Texas State Teachers College at San Marcos in 1930; attended the Georgetown University Law School, Washington, D.C., 1934; teacher in Cotulla, Tex., 1928–1929, and in Houston, Tex., high school in 1930–1931; served as secretary to Congressman Richard M. Kleberg 1931–1935; State director of the National Youth Administration of Texas 1935–1937; elected as a Democrat to the Seventy-fifth Congress to fill the vacancy caused by the death of James P. Buchanan; reelected to the Seventy-sixth and to the four succeeding Congresses and served from April 10, 1937, to January 3, 1949; served as lieutenant commander in the United States Navy from December 9, 1941, to July 27, 1942; delegate to the Democratic National Conventions in 1940, 1950, and 1960; was an unsuccessful candidate for election to the United States Senate in 1941; was not a candidate for renomination to the Eighty-first Congress in 1948; elected to the United States Senate in 1948 for the term commencing January 3, 1949; reelected in 1954 and again in 1960 for the term ending January 3, 1967; majority whip 1951–1953; minority leader 1953–1955; majority leader 1955–1961; nominated for the office of Vice President of the United States by the Democratic Party at the convention in Los Angeles in 1960; elected Vice President of the United States on November 8, 1960, for the term beginning January 20, 1961; resigned from the United States Senate January 3, 1961; on the death of President Kennedy was sworn in as President of the United States on November 22, 1963; elected to the Presidency November 3, 1964, for the term commencing January 20, 1965, and served until January 20, 1969; did not seek reelection in 1968; retired to his ranch near Johnson City, Tex.; died on January 22, 1973, enroute to Brooke General Hospital, San Antonio, Tex.; interment in the family cemetery at the LBJ ranch.

Contents

THE STATE FUNERAL OF

Lyndon Baines Johnson

1908-1973

THE STATE FUNERAL OF
LYNDON BAINES JOHNSON

(1908–1973)

CAPITOL ROTUNDA

Congressman J. J. Pickle
Honorable Dean Rusk

NATIONAL CITY CHRISTIAN CHURCH

Honorable W. Marvin Watson
Dr. George Davis

Hymns: "Take My Hand, Precious Lord"   Leontyne Price
"Onward Christian Soldiers'   Leontyne Price
"In Christ There Is No East or West"   Congregation
"Once To Every Man And Nation"   Sanctuary Choir

GRAVESIDE SERVICES—LBJ RANCH

Reverend Wunibald Schneider
Honorable John B. Connally
Reverend Dr. Billy Graham
Hymn: "Battle Hymn of the Republic" Anita Bryant

Remarks by Congressman J. J. PICKLE

Services at the Capitol Rotunda

LYNDON BAINES JOHNSON

January 24, 1973

Mr. President, Mrs. Johnson and Family, my Colleagues, and Fellow Americans:

Lyndon Baines Johnson was a President for the people. Working for the people came easily and naturally to his Presidency. It was the fulfillment of a career as Texas National Youth Administrator, Congressman, Senator, and Vice-President.

When I was elected in 1963 to the 10th Congressional District seat of Texas that Lyndon Johnson filled in 1937, I sought his advice. He gave me one guiding principle: "Congressman, when you vote, vote for the people."

It was the same principle that guided Lyndon Johnson's public life.

Wherever he served, we were struck by the bigness of this man, his energy, his drive, his ambition, his quest for perfection in all he did and in all he asked us to do.

His demand for the best within us was relentless. He persuaded, cajoled, and drove us until we fulfilled potentials we never knew we had. And, when we did our best, he wrapped his long arms around us—for he loved us and he loved to see us at our best.

To those of us who were closest to him from the start, we understood him for we were "his boys." He meant to us what the great Sam Rayburn meant to him and what Franklin Roosevelt meant to both of them.

We could sense the reach for greatness deep within this man. We were joined by dozens, then hundreds, of young men and women that Lyndon Johnson gathered around him over the course of his public life—not simply to serve him, but to help him achieve his vision of America.

His ambition for himself was as nothing compared to his ambition for America. As hard as he drove America toward this vision and asked us to work for the Great Society, he gave more of himself to that goal than he ever asked of any of us.

As a young man, he experienced poverty and witnessed discrimination. He learned first-hand about drought and parched earth, about stomachs that weren't full and sores that weren't healed. He brought water and electricity and housing to the Congressional district which he served. As a Congressman, he knew what it was like to be a poor farmer, a working man without a job, a Black or a Mexican-American, and he set about changing life for the disadvantaged among his constituents.

As Senator and Vice-President, he saw that it was just as difficult to be poor or unemployed, or Black or Mexican-American, in the big cities of the Northeast and the West Coast as it was in Central Texas.

His Presidency changed America for the good and America will never be the same again.

In 1964, the people gave him the greatest vote of confidence any President has ever received in our history. In turn, he voted his Presidency for the people. Medicare became the right of every older American rather than a dream. He authored the first Elementary and Secondary Education Act in our Nation's history and the Head Start program to give every American child the opportunity to go to school and develop his talents to the fullest. He saw the landscape ravaged by American technology and he moved to clean our air and our water, to protect our land, and to turn the brilliance of that technology to the restoration of our natural environment.

He knew well what that technology could do, for he guided our space program as Senator, Vice-President, and President until America placed the first man on the moon.

Lyndon Johnson was proudest of his achievements in the field of civil rights:

the 1964 Civil Rights Act, which opened public accommodations and jobs to all Americans regardless of color; and

the 1968 Fair Housing Act which gives every American, regardless of his color, the right to live in any house he can afford.

By his own testimony, Lyndon Johnson's greatest achievement in civil rights was the Voting Rights Act of 1965. As he said shortly before he left the White House:

"It is . . . going to make democracy real. It is going to correct an injustice of decades and centuries. I think it is going to make it possible for this Government to endure, not half slave and half free, but united."

He waged the war he loved—the War on Poverty—with more energy and imagination than all the Presidents who preceded him. He gave even more of himself to his efforts to end the war he hated—the war in Vietnam. Before he left office, he opened the negotiations in Paris which last night culminated in the peace agreement he wanted so much.

However history may judge Lyndon Johnson's foreign policy, that, too, was directed by his desire to help all the people. He saw foreign assistance not as a military program, but as a program to feed and clothe, heal and educate, the disadvantaged people of the world. His concern in Southeast Asia was for the people of Vietnam, North as well as South, and he offered the resources of this Nation to help rebuild both countries.

He devoted his life "to working toward the day when there would be no second-class citizenship in America, no second-quality opportunity, no second-hand justice at home, no second-place status in the world for our ideals and benefits."

Theodore Roosevelt once said:

"It is far better to dare mighty things and to enjoy your hour of triumph even though it may be checkered occasionally by failure, than to take stock with those poor souls who neither enjoy much nor suffer much because they live in a gray twilight that knows neither victory nor defeat."

Lyndon Johnson never lived in a gray twilight.

He experienced and appreciated the joy of the Democratic process when it served to enrich the lives of the people. And he suffered with the people when that process did not serve them soon or well enough.

His was a time of turbulence because it was a time of dramatic change. But he never saw that change as a time of collapse or deterioration. He put it best himself when he said:

"The old is not coming down. Rather, the troubling and torment of these days stems from the new trying to rise into place."

His closest friend and wisest advisor was his wife. She inspired his concern for our environment. Most of all, Lady Bird Johnson understood her husband and he understood her as few men and women dare hope to understand and love each other. It is no wonder that their daughters, Lynda Bird and Luci, brought so much credit to their family and to our country, for they came out of this beautiful bond and were privileged to share in this close and loving relationship.

Lyndon Johnson was a President who came from the land, from the hill country of Texas, where sun and rain are the most precious values a man can tie to; and where God's will is seen and felt and gaged by the sky and the wind.

It was from this land that Lyndon Johnson drew his strength. It was from his family that he rekindled the love he gave to his country. And it was from the potential he saw in the people that he drew his vision of America. And he knew—as no other man—that human dignity and economic justice were essential to our people to set them free and to achieve that vision.

This was a man who saw his purpose in life and lived his creed:

"Throughout my entire career, I have followed the personal philosophy that I am a free man, an American, a public servant, and a member of my party—and in that order."

He saw also his Presidency and his vision of America when he told the Congress and this Nation:

"I do not want to be the President who built empires or sought grandeur or extended dominion.

"I want to be the President who educated young children to the wonders of their world.

"I want to be the President who helped to feed the hungry and to prepare them to be taxpayers instead of taxeaters.

"I want to be the President who helped to end hatred among his fellow men and who promoted love among the people of all races and all regions and all parties.

"I want to be the President who helped to end war among the brothers of this earth."

From his "Vantage Point," the President will rest in his beloved hill country, where he has told us his father before him said he wanted to be home, "where folks know when you're sick and care when you die."

Two hundred million Americans care, Mr. President. We care—and we love you.

Honorable DEAN RUSK

Services for LYNDON BAINES JOHNSON

Capitol Rotunda

January 24, 1973

A home on the bank of the Pedernales in the beautiful hill country of Texas, surrounded by his beloved family and the friends with whom he so fully shared his warm and generous spirit.

A home in this place where we are gathered today, in the Congress, which was his life for so long, filled with friendships and livened by that political debate which is the lifeblood of a free society, but friendships cemented by the common task of insuring that the public business somehow would go forward at the end of the day.

A home for more than five years at the summit of responsibility, of responsibility and not necessarily of power—for he, as other Presidents, understood that many expectations and demands were addressed to him which were beyond his constitutional reach or, indeed, beyond the reach of our Nation in a world community where we might persuade but cannot command. These were years of awesome burdens, but burdens lightened by the fine intelligence and the natural grace and the personal devotion of the First Lady who was always at his side.

And now he returns to the Pedernales to a home among the immortals, the goodly company of men and women whom we shall forever cherish because they were concerned about those matters which barred the path to our becoming what we have in us to become.

More than a thousand years ago, in a simpler and more robust age, perhaps we might have known him as Lyndon the Liberator, for he was determined to free our people in body, mind and spirit.

A few strokes of the brush cannot portray this man to whom we offer our affection and respect today. As for me, I would begin with his deep compassion for his fellowman, a com-passion which was shared by the Congress and resulted in the most extraordinary legislative season in our history.

Who can forget that remarkable evening of March 15, 1965, when President Johnson addressed a joint session of Congress on voting rights and other civil rights? It was perhaps his finest single message.

You will remember that, after recalling his days as a teacher of poor Mexican-American children back in 1928, he said, "It never even occurred to me in my fondest dreams that I might have the chance to help the sons and daughters of those students and to help people like them all over the country."

And then, with eyes which bored into the conscience of all who heard him, he said, "But now I do have that chance, and I'll let you in on a secret—I mean to use it. And I hope you will use it with me."

And then he went on to disclose in a very frank way what some of his deepest hopes were. Congressman Pickle has already quoted those hopes. One may give these ideas any name or epithet one might choose. They did not evolve out of some empty intellectual exercise. They were not the product of shrewd political calculation. His colleagues knew them as a volcanic eruption from the innermost being of his soul when the responsibility for leadership finally became his own.

Many have said that Lyndon Johnson was demanding upon his colleagues and personal staff. Indeed he was. And demanding upon the Congress and the American people and many a foreign leader as well. But he was most demanding upon himself and stubbornly resisted the admonitions of his associates to slow down.

xvii

There was so much to do, and there was so little time in which to get it done.

President Johnson sometimes deprecated his own background in foreign affairs. Actually, he brought great talents and a rich experience to this aspect of the Presidency in November 1963. As Senate Majority Leader throughout most of the Eisenhower years, he was necessarily and deeply involved in the widest range of legislation affecting foreign and defense policy.

When he became Vice President, President Kennedy asked him frequently to make foreign visits and consult with foreign leaders on matters of major importance—not merely a tourist's visit.

He absorbed briefings in a most expert fashion, and with a powerful intellect went directly to the heart of the issues under discussion. And as many present know, he was always formidable in negotiation or persuasion.

He had a special ability, perhaps learned in the Senate, to begin his consideration of a problem by putting himself in the other fellow's shoes, in an attempt to understand which answers might be possible.

He had a personal code of relations among political leaders which did not permit him or his colleagues to engage in personal vilification aimed at foreign leaders, however deep the disagreement might appear to be.

Today's writers are inclined to discuss Lyndon Johnson almost solely in terms of Vietnam, and such questions as whether he did too much or too little in that tragic struggle. The historian will take a broader view and weigh such things as the Consular and Civil Air Agreements with the Soviet Union, the Non-proliferation Treaty, our space treaties, his East-West trade bill, the beginnings of SALT talks, and many other initiatives aimed at building the peace.

He had a very special and affectionate feeling for the nations of the western hemisphere. He used to say to us, "This hemisphere is where we live, this is our home, these are our neighbors. We must start with our own neighborhood."

Mr. President, last evening you made some moving remarks about President Johnson in your brief address to the American people. We congratulate you on the substance of that address and give you our best wishes for the weeks and months ahead. I mention two points which you made about Lyndon Johnson. That President Johnson was a man of peace and would have welcomed the peace which seems now to be opening up in Southeast Asia. How true. And he would, indeed, have joined you, Mr. President, in paying tribute to those millions of gallant and dedicated men in uniform whose service and sacrifice opened the way for the peace which is before us. In his last State of the Union Message to the Congress, his final sentence was, "But I believe that at least it will be said that we tried." Ah, yes, he tried, with reckless disregard for his own life.

And then, in the final chapter of his book, when he was reflecting upon how it looked to him as he returned to that ranch which he loved so much, his final sentence was, "And I knew also that I had given it everything that was in me."

As time passes, the world will increasingly acknowledge that the "everything" that was in him was a very great deal, and that men and women all over the earth are forever in his debt.

PRESIDENT LYNDON B. JOHNSON

A Eulogy by W. Marvin Watson

National City Christian Church, Washington, D.C.

January 25, 1973, 10:00 a.m.

He was ours, and we loved him beyond any telling of it.

We shared his victories and his defeats.

In victory he taught us to be magnanimous . . . in defeat he taught us to be without hate . . . to learn . . . to rally . . . to accept the challenge and to try again.

He believed that good men together could accomplish anything, even the most impossible of dreams. No matter who his opponent, he constantly sought to find that touchstone within the soul of every man which, if discovered, would release the impulse for honest and fair solution. Hate was never in this man's heart.

Each of you has your own memories of this man who served for 37 years in this city. I had the honor of being with him through the final four years of his Presidency . . . in those great moments of triumph when the American people endorsed him so strongly . . . in those magnificent hours when he stood before the Congress of the United States and led the way to the passage of laws long overdue that would lead to justice long denied . . . and in that darkening twilight when, as a man seeking peace, he was forced to continue a bitter war to honor our country's commitment to a small, far-off ally.

I watched the gray come into his hair.

I saw each deep line etch itself into his face as he gave all at his command to lead our country through the turmoil which surged around us.

I watched him as he used his great gift of persuasion to convince a Southern Senator that the time had come for the Civil Rights Act . . . I watched him formulate, secure passage and sign into law the most comprehensive legislative program in education, housing, conservation and health of any President in history . . . I watched him in the Situation Room at the time of crisis during the Six Day War when only his ability, his knowledge, and his sheer courage helped to keep that conflict from erupting into a wider confrontation.

I sat with him through those long nights as he endured the agony of Vietnam, as he sought the key to peace, and as he waited for word of men whom he had ordered into battle. Each was a human being to him, not a statistic; each was a name linked with wives and parents and children—he cared for people, not for numbers.

So desperately did he want a just and lasting peace . . . so much did he want us to reason together . . . so much did he yearn that man's goodness would triumph over man's evil . . . so often as friend turned to political foe, did he nod with sad understanding and pray that in the years to come, the sacrifices he was making would be worthy of the American people and serve ultimately as a firm platform on which to build a better world.

And through it all, I saw him earnestly seek God's wisdom for his decisions, for this was a man with a strong belief in the Almighty.

President Nixon, as you so eloquently stated in your message informing Congress of President Johnson's death, it was his "noble and difficult destiny to lead America through a long, dark night of necessity at home and abroad." If he could have chosen other circumstances in which to be President, perhaps he would have. But, America has a capacity to call forth the leadership it must have in those hours of

xix

its greatest need. We had Abraham Lincoln when he was needed. We had Franklin Roosevelt when he was needed. History will record that in the seventh decade of the 20th century, America had Lyndon Johnson when he was needed.

When you remember him, remember him please for two things—his devotion to his country . . . and his restraint.

So often in his Presidency, dissension escalated into violence. Yet always, no matter how critical the situation, his inner faith in the people came to the fore and his restraint in the uses of power permitted the people to confront each situation and overcome it utilizing the inherent rights of free men.

Those of us who loved him take comfort in the knowledge that before he died, he could see the dawn of domestic tranquility and of foreign peace which he gave so much of his great heart to bring about. The structure of peace which President Nixon, with great distinction and determination, is building in the world today will rest upon a foundation laid in loneliness and stubborn courage by Lyndon Johnson.

This man's restless, searching heart began to give out long before January 22d. He gave so much of himself to so many that it is wondrous that God, in His grace, granted him four years to enjoy his retirement in the hill country he so deeply treasured.

Not for him the easy way.

Not for him any halfway measures.

He was a tall man of giant character, and when he committed himself, he committed himself totally. And he asked his countrymen to do the same.

He asked those who had much to be concerned for those who had least.

He asked us to live up to our national promise.

He asked us to be worthy of our heritage.

He asked us to be true to ourselves.

But, he never asked more than he was willing to give . . . and what he gave was good enough to confirm and advance the progress of the Nation he served.

Lyndon Johnson loved a woman, and she was his greatest joy and his greatest comfort. He loved his children and his grandchildren and to see them together was a heartwarming experience, for it transcended normal family devotion.

And coupled with that he loved each of us, sometimes with wry amusement at our failures, often with sharp words at our imperfections, but always with a sweeping and generous understanding of our frailties. The dimension of this man were vast.

He is gone from us now . . . and this afternoon we shall take him home and he will be forever a part of the hill country.

Last September, I had the opportunity to be with him when he spoke of America and of the future.

He knew then that he might not see another autumn, but this was not a man who welcomed or needed sympathy.

Years from now, when historians appraise him, his speech that day could serve as the cornerstone of their research—for it reflected the true Lyndon Johnson. He gave much of himself to it, and it might well be his epitaph. He said:

"With the coming of September, each year, we are reminded as the song says, that the days are dwindling down to a precious few . . . the green leaves of summer will begin to brown . . . the chill winds of winter will begin to blow . . . and before we are ready for the end to come, the year will be gone.

"As it is with the calendar, so it sometimes seems to be with our country and our system. For there are those among us who would have us believe that America has come to its own September . . . and that our Nation's span as mankind's last best hope will be done."

President Johnson continued:

"But I live by the faith that with each passing day we are always approaching nearer to the beginning of a new springtime and it is by that perspective that I see our country now.

"No nation can be more than the visions of its people. America cannot be more than we believe ourselves capable of becoming.

"I want to open the soul of America to the warm sunlight of faith in itself . . . faith in the principles and precepts of its birth . . . and faith in the promise and potential of its people."

That was Lyndon Baines Johnson, the 36th President of the United States of America.

The years will be lonely without him.

Devotional Message and Eulogy Given at the Funeral and Memorial Service for President Lyndon Baines Johnson by Dr. George Davis, Minister, National City Christian Church, January 25, 1973

Devotional Message and Eulogy

I stand in a unique relationship in this pulpit, as I stood across the years in a unique relationship. I was not the political advisor of President Johnson. I have no expertise in this field. He never asked my opinion about what he should do in this policy or that. I was not his emissary. He never sent me on a mission to secure information or to share with him my insights into the international picture. Around him, as with President Nixon, there were men and women qualified in their fields. I was his minister and his friend. What more could a man ask? I was his minister in that he knew if he wanted my spiritual service, I was at his command, but he never asked me for anything at a time I was committed to something he felt would be an imposition upon me. I was his friend because he trusted me and knew that I would never, with friend or foe, betray him. But he was my minister and friend. You see, lay people are ministers too. I learned from him many lessons. I learned first of all how to deal with the pressures of life. And how to live within this city, which drives men to insanity, and to early graves. As President Truman so eloquently said, although in a strange way, "If you can't stand the heat, get out of the kitchen." From Lyndon Johnson I have learned that men can live within the heat, and bear it. I learned what prayer means, from him. I was often in prayer with him, but never with a man in desperation grasping at a straw as if a ship were going down. He wanted prayer as if he were talking to the Friend of the Universe. And then I watched him wheeled down corridors of hospitals, to surgery, laughing with the nurses and the interns. For to him, religion was no phony business. Religion was life, and you could best work it out in your profession and he felt, as I am sure President Nixon does, that in the political field and arena, there he could best express God's will for his life and his help to humankind.

I was his minister and friend. He was my minister and friend. Briefly I want to leave a text with you from the Old Testament, from a word God gave when Moses died. Now Lyndon Johnson—and I never called him Lyndon, always President Johnson—would abhor being compared to any character in the Bible. He would consider this a vast presumption. For he was so human— that's what I liked about him—one of the things I liked about him. I think one of the things he liked about me was that he thought I wasn't a "stuffed shirt" ecclesiastical leader. When Moses died, and there were likenesses, the hardness of discipline, great decisions, sitting on top of a volcano you didn't create trying to control it, when Moses died, people began to wonder, "What on earth are we to do?" And God said to Joshua, and to the people of Israel, "Moses my servant is dead. Now therefore arise." There is time for sorrow. I shall cry about this in private, when I am alone, and feel no shame, for I loved him, with profound devotion. There is a time for mourning. But the word America needs today, the word Lyndon Johnson would speak today if he were speaking, the word God says to us I believe, "Lyndon, my servant, is dead. Now therefore arise." Arise first of all to memory. To the memory of his vast accomplishments, and you name the area he strove. He said, whether it was original with him, I don't know, but he said it, "It isn't hard to do right. It's hard to know what is right to do." Let us arise and stand in exaltation to remember what this man did in his human way, for Moses was human. He was not even allowed to enter the Promised Land, but he was God's man. I think God uses men, not angels. Angels frighten me. God uses men on earth to do His will, human men with frailties, and sins, and weaknesses. Lyndon my servant is dead. Therefore arise to the great memory and heritage that he has left. Let us arise to memory. Let us arise to rededication. The task is unfinished.

In Moses' case he was unable to enter the Promised Land due to some fault or flaw which God understood. He could only stand and look into the Promised Land while Joshua led the people in. Sometimes people do not enter the Promised Land for which they have yearned and to which they had a right due to other causes than a fault of their own and all of this we must trust to God, but one thing surely may be said of Moses, he had so much to do with leading the people out of bondage toward the Promised Land. Not all of us live to see our dreams accomplished. Why do we have to? Why can't we let the future accomplish some of them? Why can't we let our children and our grandchildren do something? Why do we have to worry ourselves to death believing we have to accomplish all the tasks? And that we've failed if somehow we didn't achieve all of our dreams? My father never did. My mother never did. Nobody ever did. Lyndon my servant is dead, therefore, arise, and be to the task. Lyndon my servant is dead, therefore the call to renewal. To a rebirth of faith, personal and deep and profound. The newspapers reported that President Johnson died alone. Oh, oh no! Oh, no: Not alone. No man ever dies alone. Men die lonely deaths in ghettos, on battlefields, in loneliness, but never alone. For they that wait upon the Lord shall renew their strength. They shall mount up with wings as eagles, they shall run and not be weary. They shall walk and not faint.

I plan to see President Johnson someday again. I do not know how in the mystery of God this will be accomplished, I don't even know how I got into this world. I don't understand how my grandchildren were born, how this miracle of human birth is achieved. I therefore do not understand what heaven is or where it is or how we get there. I believe deep within me I shall cross his path again. And that he is alive. Lyndon Johnson is dead but alive. Therefore arise to the age in which we live committed to the tasks in which he believed and in which you believe. And one of the most magnificent things he ever accomplished was in that great crises following the assassination of President Kennedy when he assumed the leadership, and with his wonderful wife helped to hold this Nation together. And never in all of our history has a more gracious exchange of power been made than between President Nixon and President Johnson. It will stand out through all the years of American history as one of the most gracious acts on the part of two men in the exchange of power and place.

Arise! Arise! Onward Christian soldiers.

"TAKE MY HAND, PRECIOUS LORD"

Sung by Miss Leontyne Price

The National City Christian Church

Services for Lyndon Baines Johnson

January 25, 1973

Precious Lord, take my hand
Lead me on, let me stand,
I am tired, I am weak,
I am worn, Thru the storm
thru the night Lead me on to
the light, Take my hand,
precious Lord, Lead me home.

1st Verse

When my way grows drear precious Lord
Linger near when my life is almost gone
Hear my cry, hear my call,
Hold my hand lest I fall
Take my hand, precious Lord,
Lead me home

Precious Lord, take my hand
Lead me on, let me stand,
I am tired, I am weak,
I am worn, Thru the storm
thru the night Lead me on to
the light, Take my hand,
precious Lord, Lead me home.

2nd Verse

When the darkness appears
and the night draws near
and the day is past and gone
At the river I stand,
Guide my feet, hold my hand
Take my hand, precious Lord,
Lead me home.

"ONWARD CHRISTIAN SOLDIERS"

Sung by Miss Leontyne Price

The National City Christian Church

Services for Lyndon Baines Johnson

January 25, 1973

1st Verse

Onward Christian Soldiers
Marching as to War
With the Cross of Jesus
Going on Before

Christ the Royal Master
Leads Against the Foe
Forward Into Battle
See His Banners Go

Refrain: Onward Christian Soldiers
Marching as to War
With the Cross of Jesus
Going on Before

2nd Verse

Like a Mighty Army
Moves the Church of God
Brothers we are treading
Where the Saints have trod
We are not divided
All one body we
One in Hope and doctrine
One in charity

Refrain: Onward Christian Soldiers
Marching as to War
With the Cross of Jesus
Going on Before

3rd Verse

Crowns and thrones may perish
Kingdoms rise and wane
But the Church of Jesus
Constant will remain

Gates of Hell can never gainst
That church prevail
We have Christ on promise
And that cannot fail

Refrain: Onward Christian Soldiers
Marching as to War
With the Cross of Jesus
Going on Before

4th Verse

Onward then ye people
Join our happy throng
Blend with ours your voices
In the triumph song
Glory laud and honor
Unto Christ the King
This through countless ages
Men and angels sing

Refrain: Onward Christian Soldiers
Marching as to War
With the Cross of Jesus
Going on Before

"IN CHRIST THERE IS NO EAST OR WEST"

As Sung by the Congregation

At the National City Christian Church

Services for Lyndon Baines Johnson

January 25, 1973

1st Verse

In Christ there is no East or West
In him no South or North
But one great fellowship of love
Throughout the whole wide earth.

2nd Verse

In him shall true hearts everywhere
Their high communion find
His service is the golden cord
Close-binding all mankind

3rd Verse

Join hands then brothers of the faith
What e'er your race may be
Who serves my Father as a son
Is surely kind to me

4th Verse

In Christ now meet both East and West
In him meet South and North
All Christly souls are one in him
Throughout the whole wide earth
Amen.

"ONCE TO EVERY MAN AND NATION"

As Sung by the Sanctuary Choir

The National City Christian Church

Services for Lyndon Baines Johnson

January 25, 1973

1st Verse

Once to every man and Nation
Comes the moment to decide
In the strife of truth with falsehood
For the good or evil side
Some great cause God's new messiah
Offering each the bloom or blight
And the choice goes by forever
Twixt that darkness and that light

2nd Verse

By the light of burning marty
Jesus bleeding feet I track
Toiling up new Calvaries ever
With the cross that turns not back

New Occasions teach new duties
Time makes ancient good uncouth
They must upward still and onward
Who would keep abreast of truth

3rd Verse

Through the cause of evil prosper
Yet tis truth alone is strong
Truth forever on the scaffold
Wrong for ever on the throne
Yet that scaffold sways the future
And behind the dim unknown
Standeth God within the shadow
Keeping watch above his own

Remarks of REVEREND WUNIBALD SCHNEIDER

Services for Lyndon Baines Johnson

January 25, 1973, LBJ Ranch

The book of Ecclesiastes tells us, "Mourn but a little for the dead for they are at rest." We pray, Eternal God and our Father we realize our great need of strength and courage. Help us that we look to you for guidance and wisdom at this time of sorrow and loss of President Lyndon Baines Johnson. We, who have been privileged of knowing and having this forthright man; this stalwart President; we suffer his loss. A man who had the patriotism of George Washington. Today as we bid our final farewell to him we pray to God Almighty that we always remember his loveableness, his generosity, and his loyalty.

President Johnson was an ordinary man, but he had this extraordinary love for each and every one of us. In his generosity he was concerned for everybody. His loyalty to his family, to us, to all Americans, and to his native land for which he dedicated his life, was outstanding. We pray that his soul is now happy with God. And may his memory be always in our hearts as a symbol of love for country and all mankind. We all have lost a dear friend and benefactor. All of a sudden he has been taken from us. We all miss him. Lord, God, give us the strength to bear this heavy cross of loss patiently. Heavenly Father, bless and assist the loved ones at this time of grief. We will remember him and all the family at the altar of God. *Amen.*

Remarks of JOHN B. CONNALLY

Services for Lyndon B. Johnson

January 25, 1973

We lay to rest here a man whose whole life embodied the spirit and hope of America.

How can a few words eulogize a man such as he?

Not in a purely personal way, although President and Mrs. Johnson had a profound effect on my life, on Nellie's and the lives of our children, just as they had on the lives of many of you within sound of my voice.

Not in a dispassionate way, because none who knew him could speak dispassionately of him.

And not in words of great elegance and adornment, simply because he would not have wanted that.

Lyndon Johnson spoke plainly all of his life. He spoke to the hearts of people. The wellspring of his thoughts and words and deeds was always the fundamental character of the plain people he loved and whose dreams and aspirations he tried so hard to bring to reality.

Eloquent praise and heartfelt words of sympathy rave poured forth since last Monday afternoon when we learned this great heart had stilled. The world has a fallen leader and owes him much honor.

But I feel today it is these plain people he loved—the silent people—who mourn him the most.

He gave them all he had for forty years.

He gave them his incredible energy, his matchless legislative mind, and his restless devotion to the ideal that his country's grasp should always exceed its reach . . . that nothing was impossible where there was a determined will.

He was one of them. He never forgot it, and they will never forget him.

Lyndon Johnson was one of three Presidents to be born in this century. But this hill country in 1908 was not much different from the frontier his father and mother had known.

The comforts and amenities were few, the educational opportunities were determined by the quality of a single teacher or a handful of teachers, and man's fortunes were dictated by the amount of rain or the heat of the sun or the coldness of the north wind.

Yet a child's dreams could be as wide as the sky and his future as green as the winter oats, because this, after all, was America.

Lyndon Johnson made his dreams come true because he saw the real opportunity of this land and this political system into which he was born. He never doubted he could do it, because he always knew he could work harder than anyone else, sustain his dedication longer than anyone else, and renew his spirit more completely than anyone else no matter how serious the setback or even the defeat.

Thus he rose from these limited beginnings to the zenith of power, and as he so often said with a mixture of awe and pride, "I guess I've come a long way for a boy from Johnson City, Texas."

But with all of his strengths, Lyndon Johnson cannot be viewed as a man above men, a mythical hero conquering all before him.

In a sense, his life was one of opposites—of conflicting forces within him trying to emerge supreme.

The product of simple rural surroundings, he was thrust by his own ambition into an urbane and complicated world.

Born into a Southwestern, Protestant, Anglo-Saxon heritage, he found his native values challenged constantly in the political and social climate which enveloped him.

Reared and educated without benefit of a more worldly existence, he thirsted for the knowledge that would propel him to the heights in the life he chose for himself.

Some criticized him for being unlettered and unsophisticated when in truth he was incredibly wise and incredibly sophisticated in ways his critics never understood, perhaps because he always dealt not with things as they should have been, but as they were.

He dealt with basic human qualities and basic human reactions.

He was uninhibited by hypocrisy or false pride. He was not afraid to let his feelings show.

It is said that in some ways he was an insecure man. Of course he was. He knew he was not endowed with the kingly virtues of always being right; he tried merely to do his best to discover what was right.

He recognized his own shortcomings far more than many of his detractors recognized theirs. He never hesitated to ask for help and he understood better than most the meaning of loyalty and mutual affection among friends and associates.

The same insecurities existed in Lyndon Johnson that exist in all of us. His strengths and his weaknesses were universally human qualities, shared by people everywhere who have also dreamed of the mountaintop, each in his own way.

President Johnson cared for people, no matter where they lived in this world or their color or their heritage.

He showed this in public ways too numerous to list. What is more important he showed it in private ways when the world was not looking.

Not long ago he visited the ranch of a friend in Mexico and discovered a small rural schoolhouse for children in the depths of poverty.

When he returned to Austin he and Mrs. Johnson gathered dozens of small wind-up toys, medicine, clothing and other items for those children, and when he went back to Mexico he took those things with him and he had his own Christmas celebration with those children.

So we have the vision of a former President of the United States, perhaps down on his knees, surrounded by youngsters from another land, whose language he did not speak, demonstrating for them how to wind up a 25-cent toy.

Somehow, I think that's how Lyndon Johnson would like best for us to remember him.

The tens of thousands who have filed past his bier and the tens of millions who mourn him from afar—these are the people who understand who he was and what he was and how he thought, because he was one *of* them.

I think they would know of his frustrations of leadership, his impatience, the occasional temper, sometimes the sharp tongue, but always the overriding courage and determination of this complex man.

Surely they would know of his anguish over sending men to war when all he wanted was peace and prosperity and freedom. It seems ironic on this day that his predecessors began the war in Southeast Asia and his successor ended it. It

xxvii

was his fate to be the bridge over the intervening chasm of conflict that swept this country and the world. But he accepted that role without flinching, and no one would be happier today, no one would be more appreciative of the beginning of peace and the President who achieved it, than the President who worked so long and so unselfishly for the tranquility that eluded him.

It is fashionable among some to refer to Lyndon Johnson as a tragic President.

But I believe history will describe his Presidency as tragic only in the sense that it began through tragedy, for his service was not one of tragedy but one of triumph.

It was a triumph for the poor, a triumph for the oppressed, a triumph for social justice, and a triumph for mankind's never-ending quest for freedom.

Along this stream and under these trees he loved he will now rest.

He first saw light here. He last felt life here. May he now find peace here.

Funeral of
PRESIDENT LYNDON B. JOHNSON
Order of Graveside Service
Officiated by the Rev. Dr. Billy Graham
LBJ Ranch, Stonewall, Texas
Thursday, January 25, 1973

LET US WORSHIP GOD

"I am the resurrection, and the life; he that believeth in Me, though he were dead, yet shall he live:

"And whosoever liveth and believeth in Me shall never die." (John 11: 25–26)

"Let not your heart be troubled: ye believe in God, believe also in Me.

"In My Father's house are many mansions: if it were not so, I would have told you. I go to prepare a place for you.

"And if I go and prepare a place for you, I will come again, and receive you unto Myself; that where I am, there ye may be also." (John 14: 1–3)

THE MEDITATION

Few events touch the heart of every American as profoundly as the death of a President—for the President is our leader and every American feels that he knows him in a special way because he hears his voice so often, glimpses at his picture in the paper, sees him on television, and so we all mourn his loss and feel that our world will be a lonelier place without him. But to you who were close to him, this grief is an added pain because you wept when he wept and you laughed when he laughed. When he was misunderstood you felt his pain and wondered why others had no heart to feel or no eyes to see, but such is the burden, the anguish and the glory of the Presidency.

Here amidst these familiar hills and under these expansive skies his earthly life has come full circle. It was here that Lyndon Baines Johnson was born and reared and his life molded. But the Scripture teaches that there is a time to be born and a time to live and a time to die. Lyndon Johnson's time to die came last Monday. The absence of his vibrant and dominant personality seem so strange as we gather on this site. There was a mass of manhood in Lyndon Johnson. "He was a mountain of a man with a whirlwind for a heart." He loved this hill country. He often said, "I love this country where people know when you are sick, love you while you are alive, and miss you when you die."

Not long ago President Johnson brought me here to this very spot and said, "One day you are going to be asked to preach my funeral. You'll come right here under this tree and I'll be buried right there." In his homespun way he continued, "You'll read the Bible and preach the Gospel and I want you to." And he said, "I hope you'll tell the people about some of the things I tried to do."

History will not ignore him for he was history in motion. He will stand tall in the history books that future generations will study. The great events of his life have already been widely recounted by the news media this week. I think most of us have been staggered at the enormous things he accomplished during his lifetime. His thirty-eight years of public service kept him at the center of the events that have shaped our destiny. During his years of public service, Lyndon Johnson was on center stage in our generation. To him the Great Society was not a wild dream but a realistic hope. The thing nearest to his heart was to harness the wealth and knowledge of a mighty nation to assist the plight of the poor. It was his destiny to be involved in a tragic war. It is a mysterious act of Providence that his death came during the same week that a peace agreement was reached. As President Nixon said Tuesday night: "No one would have welcomed this peace more than he."

However, there was another more personal, more intimate, and more human side to Lyndon Johnson—that his family, neighbors and friends that are gathered here today would know. For example, some of you have seen him load his car or station wagon with children of various racial and ethnic backgrounds and take then on rides or to see the deer running across the ranch. There were hundreds of little things that he did for little people that no one would ever know about. He had a compassion for the underdog.

No one could ever understand Lyndon Johnson unless they understood the land and the people from which he came. His roots were deep in this hill country. They were also deep in the religious heritage of this country. President Johnson often pointed with pride to a faded yellow letter on the wall of his office written to his great grandfather by Sam Houston. His great grandfather, like many of his forebears, was a preacher and had led Sam Houston to a personal faith in Jesus Christ. Symbolically it says that Lyndon Baines Johnson had respect for "the faith" that has guided his family, his state and his nation through generations. Lyndon Johnson's mother Rebekah Baines Johnson, who lies here, often read the Bible to her young son.

Within weeks of the time he became President of the United States he said, "No man can live where I live now, nor work at the desk where I work now, without needing and seeking the strength and support of earnest and frequent prayer."

He could have had more excuses than most for not attending church on Sunday. But one of the things for which he will be remembered is that he probably went to church more than any other President.

Some months ago my wife and I were visiting the Johnsons here at the ranch. Lyndon Johnson brought me out to this spot and reminded me again that I was to participate in this service. We spoke of the brevity of life and the fact that every man will someday die and stand before his Creator. There is a democracy about death. John Donne said: "It comes equally to us all and makes us all equal when it comes." The Bible says: "It is appointed unto men once to die, but after this the judgment." (Hebrews 9: 27)

For the believer who has been to the Cross, death is no frightful leap in the dark, but is the entrance into a glorious new life. The Apostle Paul said: "For to me to live is Christ, and to die is gain" (Phil. 1: 21). For the believer the brutal fact of death has been conquered by the historical resurrection of Jesus Christ. For the person who has turned from sin and has received Christ, as Lord and Savior, death is not the end. For the believer there is "hope" beyond the grave. There is a future life! As the poet has written:

God writes in characters too grand
For our short sight to understand;
We catch but broken strokes, and try
To fathom all the mystery
Of withered hopes, of death, of life,
The endless war, the useless strife,
But there, with larger, clearer sight,
We shall see this—God's way was right.

John Oxenham

We do not say goodbye to Lyndon today. The French have a better way of saying it. They say, "Au revoir!"—till we meet again. To you Mrs. Johnson, Lynda, Luci, and other members of the family, it is my prayer that God's grace will be sufficient for you in the days to come. May God grant to each of you a deep satisfaction in the life of one who served his country with such complete dedication. May the God and Father of our Lord Jesus Christ, the Father of all Mercies and the God of all comfort, sustain you now and in the days to come.

What he once said about another President we can now say about him: "A great leader is dead. A great nation must move on. Yesterday is not ours to recover but tomorrow is ours to win or lose."

PRAYER FOR THE FAMILY

Our Heavenly Father, who art the dwelling place of Thy people in all generations, have mercy upon us as we are here today under the shadow of great affliction; for in Thee alone is our confidence and our hope.

God of all comfort, in the silence of this hour we ask Thee to sustain this family and these loved ones and to deliver them from loneliness, despair and doubt. Fill their desolate hearts with Thy peace and may this be a moment of rededication to Thee.

Our Father, those of us who have been left behind have the solemn responsibilities of life. Help us to live according to Thy will and for Thy glory—so that when Thou dost call us that we will be prepared to meet Thee.

We offer our prayer in the Name of Him who is the resurrection and the life, even Jesus Christ our Lord. *Amen.*

BENEDICTION

"Unto Him that loved us; and washed us from our sins in His own blood,
"And hath made us kings and priests unto God and His Father; to Him be glory and dominion for ever and ever. *Amen.*" (Revelation 1: 5–6)

"BATTLE HYMN OF THE REPUBLIC"

As Sung by Anita Bryant

Services for Lyndon Baines Johnson

January 25, 1973, LBJ Ranch

1st Verse

Mine eyes have seen the Glory
  of the coming of the Lord
He is trampling out the vintage
  where the grapes of wrath are stored

He hath loosed the fateful lightning
  of His terrible swift sword

His truth is marching on

  Glory Glory Hallelujah
  Glory Glory Hallelujah
  Glory Glory Hallelujah
  His Truth is marching on

2nd Verse

He has sounded forth the trumpet
  that shall never call retreat

He is sifting out the heart of men
  before His judgment seat
Oh be swift my soul to answer Him
  be jubilant my feet
Our God is marching on

  Glory Glory Hallelujah
  Glory Glory Hallelujah
  Glory Glory Hallelujah
  His Truth is marching on

3rd Verse

In the beauty of the lilies Christ
  was born across the sea
With a glory in His bosom that
  transfigures you and me
As he died to make men holy
  let us live to make men free
While God is marching on

Memorial Tributes

IN THE

House of Representatives
of the United States

IN EULOGY OF

Lyndon Baines Johnson

96-333 O - 73 -- 3

In the House of Representatives
of the United States

JANUARY 23, 1973

The House met at 12 o'clock noon.

The Chaplain, Rev. Edward G. Latch, D.D., offered the following prayer:

Yea, though I walk through the valley of the shadow of death, I will fear no evil, for Thou art with me.—Psalm 23: 4.

O God and Father of us all, in deep sadness of heart we lift our spirits unto Thee as we journey through the valley of the shadow of death with the family of our beloved LYNDON BAINES JOHNSON. We thank Thee for his long and distinguished service to his State and our country, for his contribution as a Member of this body, as Senator, as Vice President, and for his leadership as President of our Republic.

We are grateful for his integrity of mind, his sincerity of heart, his seeking the best ways to do the best things, for his dedication to freedom among men and to justice for men and for his efforts on behalf of peace in our world.

Grant unto his family and friends the comfort of Thy presence and the assurance of Thy love. Strengthen them with courage and faith for the days that lie ahead.

O Lord, we are most grateful for the coming peace to our world. May it continue forever and ever and ever. Amen.

The Speaker laid before the House the following message from the President of the United States:

To the Congress of the United States:

It is my sad duty to inform you officially of the death of LYNDON BAINES JOHNSON, the thirty-sixth President of the United States.

His loss is especially poignant for all of us who knew him and worked with him in the House and Senate. It was there that he first became a legend and there that he began to influence our destiny as a great Nation.

Yet LYNDON JOHNSON's legacy extends far beyond his years in the Congress. He was a man of fierce devotion and love. He was devoted to his family. He was devoted to the cause of freedom and equality for his fellow man. And as President, he was devoted in a very special way to the land he loved.

The whole story of the Johnson years in the White House remains to be told, and history has yet to make its judgment. But millions of Americans will always remember a bitter day in November, 1963, when so many of our people doubted the very future of this Republic, when so many were stunned at the very idea that an American Chief of State could be assassinated in this age, and so many abroad were fearful about the future course of the American democracy. And LYNDON JOHNSON rose above the doubt and the fear to hold this Nation on course until we rediscovered our faith in ourselves.

If he had done no more, his place in history would have been assured. But he did much more, and his role then was not a high-water mark but a hallmark. For it was his noble and difficult destiny to lead America through a long, dark night of necessity at home and abroad. He had the courage to do what many of his contemporaries condemned him for, but what will surely win warm praise in the history books of tomorrow.

RICHARD NIXON,
THE WHITE HOUSE, *January 23, 1973.*

1

Mr. O'Neill. Mr. Speaker, I offer a concurrent resolution (H. Con. Res. 90) and ask for its immediate consideration.

The Clerk read the concurrent resolution as follows:

HOUSE CONCURRENT RESOLUTION 90

Resolved by the House of Representatives (the Senate concurring), That in recognition of the long and distinguished service rendered to the Nation and to the world by LYNDON B. JOHNSON, Thirty-sixth President of the United States, his remains be permitted to lie in state in the rotunda of the Capitol from January 24 to January 25, 1973, and the Architect of the Capitol, under the direction of the Speaker of the House of Representatives and the President pro tempore of the Senate, shall take all necessary steps for the accomplishment of that purpose.

The concurrent resolution was agreed to.

A motion to reconsider was laid on the table.

Mr. Gonzalez. Mr. Speaker, indeed today is a day of sorrow and grief, not only to those of us who were Members during the time of this great President and great giant of a man, LYNDON B. JOHNSON, but, I think, to every Texan and every American who has had a chance to understand recent American history.

It was not too long ago that I had the great good fortune to visit briefly with President JOHNSON. It was with expectation and hope that we were wishing that the Lord in His wisdom would have permitted him to remain in this earthly existence a bit longer.

Mr. Speaker, as he lived he died, and I believe that history will surely record his greatness. But there is one aspect that perhaps history never can quite record.

There was a human, plain, down-to-earth LYNDON JOHNSON that some of us had the brilliant opportunity to know.

The last time I spoke with him he mentioned the fact that the main and principal reason why he had not sought office again was simply because he had been told on good medical authority that, if he did and if he had the approval of the American people, the chances were against his surviving another 4 years. I think events proved that.

Mr. Patman. Will the gentleman yield?

Mr. Gonzalez. I yield to the gentleman.

Mr. Patman. May I suggest to the gentleman that the Speaker has arranged to have a special order set later on this week or next week for this occasion and we did not expect to have any speeches on this subject today. If you yield to one, you will have to yield to all.

I have a resolution to be introduced later and also a program for the final rites.

Mr. Gonzalez. I thank the distinguished chairman.

It is my expectation to join with the others when the official time for that purpose arises, but I think here I should take the privilege of this 1 minute to say this:

The greatest shrine to the memory of LYNDON JOHNSON is that which enshrines him in the hearts of every one of us, particularly those who have been designated members of the minorities of the United States, who will forever remember with gratitude his constant remembrance and the fact that when in higher office he never forgot them.

Mr. Patman. Mr. Speaker, on yesterday the people of our entire Nation were saddened by the announcement of the death of LYNDON B. JOHNSON, former President of the United States.

At this point, Mr. Speaker, I place in the Record the schedule of arrangements for the final services for our late President, LYNDON B. JOHNSON:

TUESDAY, JANUARY 23, 1973

At 12 noon: Lie in state at The L. B. J. Library until 8 a.m., Wednesday, January 24, 1973. Full honor guard.

WEDNESDAY, JANUARY 24, 1973

At 8:30 a.m.: Proceed to Bergstrom Air Force Base.

At 9:15: Depart Bergstrom Air Force Base via Presidential aircraft.

At 1 p.m.: Arrive at Andrews Air Force Base, Md.

At 1:20 p.m.: Depart Andrews Air Force Base to 16th and Constitution Avenue where President JOHNSON will be transfered to a horse-drawn caisson for procession to the U.S. Capitol. There will be a flyover by the U.S. Air Force at Fourth Street as the caisson passes. Procession arrives at the U.S. Capitol, and President JOHNSON is placed in the rotunda.

At 2:30 p.m.: Ceremony in the rotunda. President JOHNSON will lie in state in the rotunda until 8 a.m. Thursday.

THURSDAY, JANUARY 25, 1973

From 9 to 9:30 a.m.: Departure from U.S. Capitol. Motorcade to National City Christian

Church. Route: West on Constitution Avenue to Pennsylvania Avenue; northwest on Pennsylvania Avenue to 14th Street; north on 14th Street to Thomas Circle.

At 10: Funeral service at National City Christian Church.

From 11 a.m. to 12 noon: Motorcade to Andrews Air Force Base.

12:30: Depart Andrews Air Force Base for direct flight to L. B. J. Ranch.

At 3 p.m.: Arrive L. B. J. Ranch via U.S. Air Force aircraft.

At 3:10 p.m.: Depart L. B. J. Ranch to family cemetery.

At 3:30 p.m.: Final rites at the family cemetery.

The Speaker assures me that he will sometime in the near future arrange for a special day and a special time for memorial services here in the Chamber so that Members may deliver eulogies concerning the life and services of the late President LYNDON B. JOHNSON.

Mr. Speaker, I offer a resolution.

The Clerk read the resolution as follows:

HOUSE RESOLUTION 152

Resolved, That the House of Representatives has learned with profound regret and sorrow of the death of LYNDON BAINES JOHNSON, former President of the United States of America.

Resolved, That in recognition of the many virtues, public and private, of one who served with distinction as a Representative, Senator, Vice President, and President, the Speaker shall appoint committees of the House to join with such Members of the Senate as may be designated, to attend the funeral services of the former President.

Resolved, That the House tenders its deep sympathy to the members of the family of the former President in their sad bereavement.

Resolved, That the Sergeant at Arms of the House be authorized and directed to take such steps as may be necessary for carrying out the provisions of these resolutions, and that the necessary expenses in connection therewith be paid out of the contingent fund of the House.

Resolved, That the Clerk communicate these resolutions to the Senate and transmit a copy of the same to the family of the deceased.

Resolved, That as a further mark of respect to the memory of the former President, this House do now adjourn.

The resolution was agreed to.

Mr. Collins. Mr. Speaker, the death of LYNDON B. JOHNSON marks the end of the trail of one of America's greatest Presidents. This man who came from the heart of Texas has left his L. B. J. brand on American history.

Whether you were for or against LYNDON B. JOHNSON, you were bound to admire him. And I am one who admired this man of action.

Back in 1948, we only had one party in Texas and LYNDON B. JOHNSON was making a bid for the U.S. Senate. As the runoff headed to election day, he looked like a hopeless second. I remember as we worked in Dallas on that campaign, and I remember his drive and enthusiasm. In an uphill fight his tremendous energy led the way as he came through the winner.

The untiring energy was the JOHNSON trademark. He worked hard and he expected everyone around him to work hard. He was in action every minute of the day.

He understood Congress. He came up through the ranks. He knew how the wheels turned. But even more he knew every wheel in Congress. As the Senate leader, as the President, he kept the wheels rolling. He talked, he listened, and one of L. B. J.'s greatest statements was "Come and reason together."

But I remember President JOHNSON most as a friendly man. He loved people. He had a warm handshake. The JOHNSON smile was always a friendly smile. And the warm pat he gave you on the back was a sincere friendly greeting.

Just a short time ago, Dee and I attended the opening of the great Lyndon B. Johnson Library at the University of Texas in Austin. This was undoubtedly the best organized and most impressive dedication of any building in this country. With all the dignitaries, with all the precision of the program, with all the pomp and ceremony, the thing that stood out above all else was the friendly hospitality of the Lyndon B. Johnson family.

Dee and I extend our deepest sympathy to Lady Bird Johnson. She has spent her life with President JOHNSON through turbulent politics. And in all those years, I have never heard an unkind word raised about this lovely lady. The Nation admires her, Texas loves her, and we all share in her sorrow at the loss of our great President.

Texas has raised many great leaders for the Democratic Party. From my position on the other side of the aisle, I can objectively state that LYNDON B. JOHNSON will go down in history as the greatest Democrat of them all.

Texas will always be proud of her great traditions and her sons and daughters. And none will stand higher or prouder than the legend of the son Texas gave to the United States as its President, LYNDON B. JOHNSON.

Mr. Teague of Texas. Mr. Speaker, the United States of America has lost one of its greatest citizens and one of the most courageous leaders of its history, through the death of LYNDON BAINES JOHNSON.

And through the death of LYNDON BAINES JOHNSON, many of us—and I am proud to count myself among them—have lost a loyal and devoted friend.

It is ironic that our two surviving former Presidents—Harry S Truman and LYNDON B. JOHNSON—should have died within a few weeks of each other. They had so much in common. Both were men of the people, rising from the most discouraging poverty to the highest office in the Nation. Both were suddenly catapulted into the Presidency to succeed men almost totally different from them in style of thought and action.

Through circumstances beyond their control, neither man was totally popular in the White House. But both men had the integrity and courage to scorn easy popularity in search of more lasting and worthwhile goals.

Harry S Truman lived to see much of his record vindicated and to hear men who once scorned him, call him great. And I am convinced that history, eventually, will take a generous and approving backward look at the Presidency of LYNDON B. JOHNSON.

Certainly no man can doubt LYNDON JOHNSON's courage in office. No man can doubt his burning desire to serve the American people as well, if not better, than any man who ever occupied the White House. Nobody can doubt his sincere passion to build a truly great society in which all men would be at peace, and hunger, poverty and ignorance would be banished from the earth.

He wanted desperately to be remembered as a great President.

Some of us—including myself—disagreed with the methods he chose or with particular segments of the future society that he envisaged.

On many occasions I found it necessary to disagree with his philosophy—sometimes quite vigorously. But I did so always with great respect for his courage and his intentions. I am proud to say I never lost his friendship or his trust.

Mr. Speaker, LYNDON JOHNSON was a child of Capitol Hill. He was a distinguished Member of this House and an even more distinguished leader of the other body. I do not think he was ever as happy in any other capacity as he was while serving in the Congress of the United States. And few men have served here as effectively as he served.

With the death of LYNDON BAINES JOHNSON, every citizen is diminished a little. Indeed, the entire Nation is diminished a little, for he served us well and he served his country well. With our sorrow today we should mingle both gratitude and pride that we produced from our soil a citizen of his magnitude, a leader of his stature and vision.

I would like to extend the most sincere sympathy of Mrs. Teague and myself to his wonderful widow, Lady Bird, and to his two fine daughters, Luci and Lynda.

Mr. Koch. Mr. Speaker, today the country mourns the death of a great leader and a great American President.

In this hour of LYNDON JOHNSON's passing, let us put aside the disagreement that many of us had with him over Vietnam. He was a man with great courage and fortitude, a man who did what he thought was right, misguided though some of his decisions may have been.

At home LYNDON JOHNSON had the courage and compassion to grapple with some of the most difficult problems of our times: poverty and racial discrimination. He did not retreat from these challenges; indeed, he pursued them with great vision and determination. History will most fondly remember LYNDON JOHNSON for his civil rights legislation and for the commitment the Federal Government made under his leadership to improving the quality of life for all Americans.

LYNDON JOHNSON was a big man in every regard: in stature, in energy, in vision, in capacity, and in compassion. He was a man who embodied almost every human quality in such magnitude that he will be remembered not only for what he did but for the man he was and the dimensions of his leadership.

We all remember the many pictures of the man in the Oval Office who often looked tired and haggard. But, that craggy face reassured us that a man was in the White House who knew and cared about what was going on in the Federal Government and in the country.

It is tragic that LYNDON JOHNSON should have died before the signing of a peace accord settling the Vietnam conflict that through the months of his administration had become so personally consuming and finally his political nemesis.

Within the past month we have lost two great men our country has known. Let this be a period in which we reaffirm our resolve to meet the ideals on which our country was founded.

Mr. Speaker, in remembering President JOHNSON today, my sympathy goes to Lady Bird, Lynda, and Luci and the rest of the Johnson family who gave him such support and comfort during his years in Washington and in his retirement.

WEDNESDAY, *January 24, 1973.*

Mr. McFall. Mr. Speaker, I take this time to make a brief announcement with respect to the funeral arrangements for former President JOHNSON.

Members who plan to attend the services in Washington, at 10 a.m., Thursday, at the National City Christian Church should contact the Sergeant at Arms with respect to tickets and transportation. Only a limited number of tickets are available for the House delegation. Bus transportation to these services will depart from New Jersey Avenue, between the Longworth and Cannon Office Buildings, at 9:10 tomorrow morning and will return to the Capitol after the services.

Members appointed to attend the services in Texas should also contact the Sergeant at Arms with respect to transportation. I understand that the scheduling of transportation to Texas is such that it will not be possible for Members going on that flight to attend the services at the National City Christian Church.

The Speaker. The Speaker appoints himself and the entire membership of the House to attend the funeral services for former President LYNDON BAINES JOHNSON which are to be held this afternoon, at 2:30 p.m., in the rotunda of the Capitol.

The Chair suggests that all Members attending these services should take their places in that portion of the rotunda set aside for the House delegation not later than 2:15 p.m.

The Chair appoints the entire membership of the House to attend the funeral services for former President LYNDON BAINES JOHNSON which are to be held in the National City Christian Church, Washington, D.C., on Thursday morning, at 10 a.m.

The Speaker. The Chair appoints the following Members of the House to attend the funeral services for former President LYNDON BAINES JOHNSON which are to be held in Texas on Thursday afternoon: The Speaker, Mr. McFall, Mr. Gerald R. Ford, Mr. Arends, Mr. Patman, Mr. Mahon, Mr. Poage, Mr. Fisher, Mr. Teague of Texas, Mr. Burleson of Texas, Mr. Brooks, Mr. Wright, Mr. Young of Texas, Mr. Casey of Texas, Mr. Gonzalez, Mr. Roberts, Mr. Pickle, Mr. E de la Garza, Mr. White, Mr. Eckhardt, Mr. Kazen, Mr. Price of Texas, Mr. Collins, Mr. Archer, Miss Jordan, Mr. Milford, Mr. Steelman, Mr. Charles Wilson of Texas, Mr. Rooney of New York, Mr. Hays, Mr. Steed, Mr. Dorn, Mr. Fountain, Mr. Landrum, Mr. Sisk, Mr. Brademas, Mr. Randall, Mr. Taylor of North Carolina, Mr. Anderson of Illinois, Mr. Pepper, Mr. Rooney of Pennsylvania, Mr. Foley, Mr. Hanley, Mr. Stokes, and Mr. Jones of Oklahoma.

Hon. Antonio Borja Won Pat
OF GUAM

Mr. Speaker, the American people have lost a great public servant and a distinguished legislator with the passing of our beloved former President LYNDON B. JOHNSON.

Truly a product of this country's heritage of self-made men, President JOHNSON came from a humble beginning, rose through adversity to become an astute legislator, and ended his proud career by serving as one of the most compassionate Presidents America has ever known.

Born in a poor section of Texas, President JOHNSON grew up fully aware of what the evils of poverty and racial discrimination meant to the Mexican-Americans, the blacks, and other minority groups in our country.

It was this sense of great morality which elevated President JOHNSON from being merely a good Chief Executive to being the equal of some of our most compassionate Presidents, as were Franklin Roosevelt and Abraham Lincoln.

As the delegate from the territory of Guam, I speak from firsthand knowledge of our late President's sensitivities to his fellow man. During his term in office, our fellow Americans on Guam became eligible for inclusion in more Federal programs than ever before in the territory's history. Much of the credit for our legislative success was due to the new era of good will and sympathetic legislation which President JOHNSON and Members of Congress urged at every opportunity.

The late President also focused an important measure of attention on Guam when he came to our island to hold the first in a continuing round of peace talks with South Vietnam's leaders, and thus became the first President to ever visit the territory.

And, when President JOHNSON affixed his signature to the Guam elective Governor bill, on September 11, 1968, he characteristically said:

It is high time that the people of Guam were accorded this basic right. I am pleased and proud to sign a bill which will permit them to elect their own Chief Executive.

History will remember President Johnson for many reasons, including his unfortunate involvement in the Vietnam war. But, I am certain that history will best remember our late President for the extraordinary and unlimited understanding and sympathy which he felt for the common man. And the Great Society which he strove so mightily for, will continue to live on in the hearts and minds of his fellow man as a lasting tribute to Lyndon Baines Johnson.

Hon. J. Herbert Burke
OF FLORIDA

Mr. Speaker, when any national leader, especially a former President passes away, there is certainly a feeling of great loss in the Nation, and I feel this loss. Nevertheless, I cannot be a hypocrite and praise Mr. Johnson's record, for there were too many instances where we disagreed on issues.

Still, it takes a certain kind of dedication and love for one's country to run for elective office, and former President Johnson had this in abundance. Although, I did not agree in toto with Mr. Johnson's proposals, I greatly admired his dedication to public life.

Idealistically I am a conservative and former President Johnson was a liberal. Yet, good government needs a balance of equal quantities of both. The adversary system is used to bring justice in our courts, and it is used in Congress to ascertain proper avenues for government. President Johnson was a liberal warrior and we differed in our views. However, I can honestly say that I had a tremendous respect for his ability and his love of country.

Hon. Charles E. Chamberlain
OF MICHIGAN

Mr. Speaker, the death of President Lyndon B. Johnson marks the first time since 1933 that this Nation has been without the wisdom and counsel of a living former Chief Executive. As we mourn our great loss, however, I think the American people can take comfort in the knowledge that President Johnson gave fully of his heart, his mind, and physical being to serve our Nation both through periods of crises and time of significant progress.

The editorial in the State Journal of Lansing, Mich., of January 24, 1973, points out that he may best be remembered for the calm and self-confident leadership he provided in the days and weeks following that grim day in November of 1963 when President John F. Kennedy was assassinated.

The editorial follows:

[From the State Journal, Lansing, Mich., Jan. 24, 1973]

JOHNSON: A CAREER OF COURAGE

For the second time in a month, the nation mourns the passing of a former President, Lyndon B. Johnson, who died Monday of an apparent heart attack.

Mr. Johnson, like Harry S Truman, was thrust into office upon the death of an incumbent chief executive during a most turbulent period in American history.

While Truman faced the staggering problems of the post-World War II era, Johnson was burdened with what some historians view as the most serious domestic crisis of the century, complicated by massive entanglement in a grim and devisive war in Southeast Asia.

It was ironic that during his early years in office Lyndon Johnson emerged as one of the most popular Presidents in decades, winning a smashing, landslide re-election in 1964. Unlike his fallen predecessor, John F. Kennedy, he marshalled the support of a balky U.S. Congress to push through the most significant domestic reform and civil rights legislation in a century.

But by the time he left office in 1968 he was the target of widespread attack and vilification because of a deepening and seemingly hopeless involvement in the quagmire of Vietnam.

History will decide whether Mr. Johnson was the victim of poor judgment or perhaps bad advice in his decision to stand and fight the Communist tide in Indochina, or whether that decision, in the long run, may prove a decisive one for preventing future conflicts.

Mr. Johnson was a master at the science of politics and compiled an outstanding record in Congress. But he may best be remembered for the calm and self-confident leadership he provided in the days and weeks following that grim day in November of 1963 when Kennedy was shot.

With the nation still in a state of shock following the assassination of its youthful president, Mr. Johnson emerged as a takecharge leader who, with his famous Texas drawl, appealed for unity to carry on the programs of his predecessor.

This story was not kind to Lyndon Johnson in the turbulent years that followed. But in the task of grappling with the immense problems of his office he demonstrated great courage and determination in fighting for what he believed to be the best interests of his country. And his hallmark efforts in behalf of minority peoples changed the course of the nation.

He was an American first and last. We are grateful for his service and saddened by his death.

Hon. Thaddeus J. Dulski
OF NEW YORK

Mr. Speaker, the sudden passing of former President LYNDON BAINES JOHNSON takes from the American scene our only living former President.

He will be greatly missed.

Within less than 1 month, our last two former Presidents have been called by their Maker. Indeed, when President JOHNSON died, the flags still were flying at half-mast around our country in mourning for former President Harry S Truman.

President JOHNSON played an outstanding role as a legislator and leader in the Congress before he moved into the Vice Presidency and then the Presidency.

His record in the executive branch may take precedence in history, but those who know and were a part of that era recall with great respect and admiration his legislative ability. There can be no doubt that his legislative experience and leadership served him well in the White House.

His dedication to his country and his sense of responsibility toward its citizens are unquestioned. As with anyone in public life, he had his detractors as well as his supporters.

But no one can dispute his compassion for the impoverished, his concern for the realization of the highest goals and opportunities for Americans, and his commitment for using the highest office in our land for the betterment of the quality of life for all men.

I had the opportunity on numerous occasions to meet with President JOHNSON at the White House and my recollections are of a man who would listen intently to the visitor, a man who was friendly and relaxed, a man who was indeed a leader.

The particular occasion I recall was when I was invited to the White House for the signing of a bill which I had sponsored of interest to philatelists. Postmaster General Marvin Watson was present with me and we found the President very relaxed. A photographer took an excellent series of pictures which now form a montage on my office wall along with the pen he used to sign the bill.

After the bill signing, the President settled back in his chair for a leisurely chat. In the course of the conversation, he asked me if there was anything he could help me with.

I had not expected the question, but I answered quickly that, yes, there was one. I said that we in Buffalo need another $1.5 million in Federal funds to get work started on our new Federal office building.

The President's response was immediate—and favorable. It was the last clearance we needed for the long-pending project which since has been completed in downtown Buffalo.

The job of President is a lonely one and, as President Truman always said, it is where the buck stops. President JOHNSON was a distinguished and dedicated public servant who served his country well.

The Nation's history is enriched by the long public service of LYNDON BAINES JOHNSON and its future is enhanced—perhaps more than any of us can comprehend fully at this time—by his initiative, tenacity, and foresight.

I join my colleagues in extending deepest sympathy to his family at this difficult time. I also join in expressing sincere gratitude to them for having shared his talents and his life with us.

President JOHNSON could well be described as "one who loved his fellowman."

LYNDON BAINES JOHNSON will be greatly missed.

Hon. Garner E. Shriver
OF KANSAS

Mr. Speaker, it is with a great deal of sorrow that I join with my colleagues today in mourning the loss of former President LYNDON B. JOHNSON. We are shocked and deeply saddened by his sudden passing.

LYNDON JOHNSON was a skilled and powerful statesman. His incredible stamina, both intellectual and physical, made him a driving force throughout all his years in Washington.

Some have said that LYNDON JOHNSON was the most powerful and successful majority leader the Senate has had in recent years. His long and successful career in the Senate gave him a keen understanding of the legislative process, and an awareness of the importance of close communication with the Congress, when he moved to the White House.

I believe that LYNDON JOHNSON was one of the political giants of our times. He had a brilliant career of public service. He was a hardworking, sincere President, who tried to do what he believed to be right for our country. He was a towering strength, in a divisive and tragic period in our history.

LYNDON JOHNSON sought to make this country a place where all were equal. He cared for the people of this Nation, and worked hard for them. President JOHNSON always contended that the people of this Nation, and of the world, should "reason together."

It is sad for all of us to remember how LYNDON JOHNSON's dream of a Great Society seemed shattered at times by strife at home and abroad, and even sadder for us to realize that the peace he strove for so desperately may be only days away and he will not see it. It would be a great day for the man who has said:

No man living ever wanted peace as much as I did.

LYNDON JOHNSON's place in history will be an important one, and he will be sorely missed. Our heartfelt sympathy goes out to Mr. JOHNSON's wife and family.

Hon. Lawrence Coughlin
OF PENNSYLVANIA

Mr. Speaker, it is with profound sorrow that I learned of the death of former President LYNDON B. JOHNSON at a relatively young age.

Mr. JOHNSON's long and distinguished career was marked, above all, by his legislative craftsmanship. From his tenure in the House and Senate through his years in the White House, he provided legislative leadership almost unparalleled in our history. Certainly there has not been a more effective, more dynamic Senate majority leader in the last half century.

During his years as President, more far-reaching domestic legislation was enacted than under any other President with the possible exception of Franklin D. Roosevelt. Mr. JOHNSON's humanitarian consideration for people was evidenced in the major legislation his Presidency produced, particularly in civil rights, medicare, housing, and environmental legislation.

I wish to express my sympathy to Mrs. Lady Bird Johnson and her family on their loss. Indeed, Mr. JOHNSON's death is a great loss for us all.

Hon. Yvonne Brathwaite Burke
OF CALIFORNIA

Mr. Speaker, it is with a deep sense of loss and bereavement that I extend to the family of the late President LYNDON BAINES JOHNSON my sympathy. The loss is one that will be felt by his loved ones and by our Nation.

It is indeed fitting that Mrs. Johnson should say that the best way to extend sympathy to the family would be by doing something to help others because this was the example he leaves as his legacy for the Nation and especially for the downtrodden and those who have not enjoyed the full benefits of the riches of our Nation.

History will herald this great President because of his ability to provide leadership in its truest sense. Leadership in times of tranquility is not always easy, but, leadership during times of turbulence is the true test. President JOHNSON exhibited the caliber of leadership seen on rare occasions in our history. He turned the turbulent sixties into an example of social change. The courage of his convictions gave courage to others in the legislative and judicial branches of government to overturn the impediments of obsolete tradition and to move forward with full recognition of the rights of all men. Only during his term of office did the constitutional guarantees of the right to vote, equal access to housing and accommodations start to take shape.

Today, we see more and more blacks in elective positions, more than at any time since reconstruction. The emergence of greater participation by blacks in our governmental process is the direct outgrowth of his willingness to demand full voting rights for all Americans and his leadership in carrying out administratively, the necessary steps to implement the legislation.

President JOHNSON was not a person that allowed himself to be hindered by regionalism, party or pressures from political and economic forces. He gave hope to those that had lost their faith in the ability of our legislative process to recognize the less fortunate and the disenfranchised.

No moment in his life will stand out like the dedication of the Johnson Library in Austin, Tex. The compiling of the documents that embodied the civil rights legislation and all of the works that contributed to the partial fulfillment of the civil rights movement represented a tribute to the President that is largely responsible for those accomplishments.

President JOHNSON ended his speech at that dedication with the words "we shall overcome". We will overcome the inequities that exist in our society, we will overcome racial injustice and bigotry. We will overcome because a great President resolved that this land was for all Americans and that he would make whatever sacrifice necessary to accomplish that goal.

Hon. Wm. Jennings Bryan Dorn
OF SOUTH CAROLINA

Mr. Speaker, Ernest Cuneo wrote a spendid column prior to the passing of President LYNDON B. JOHNSON. This very timely and factual article appeared in a number of publications including the Greenville, S.C. News. I was very much impressed by the record of President JOHNSON's aid to education. His massive educational program already has improved the standard of living and the opportunities for so many Americans. I commend Mr. Cuneo's article to the attention of all Americans.

EDUCATION AND L. B. J.

(By Ernest Cuneo)

WASHINGTON.—The Census Bureau released a factual comparison of national educational attainment in 1940 with that of 1972. In rough figures, in 1940, about 15 per cent of a population of 74 million Americans over the age of 25 had had some college or more. In 1972, 35 per cent of 111 million in the same age group had had the same educational benefit.

In front-paging this remarkable record of national achievement, The New York Times opined:

"These signs of change, covering the whole adult population, mask still sharper gains in schooling among young adults. For example, the median educational level among those aged 20 to 21 is 12.8 years—almost a year of college. Among persons aged 65 to 74, the median is 9.1 years—just over a year in high school."

What this means, in plain language, is that the census figures are misleading. It means that there was no steady growth between 1940 and 1972; that, on the contrary, what is "masked" is that higher education and population of the United States has doubled in the past 10 years.

This indeed is a "mask," as The Times indicates; and what it masks is that President LYNDON BAINES JOHNSON launched the greatest educational program in recorded history—and it has paid off.

This is a doubly serious matter. It is serious in that most Americans insist on fair play and even those who may not be among LBJ's warmest admirers would not stand for an admittedly monumental work being "masked" by going back to 1940 when, in fact, the figures have doubled since LBJ revolutionized the American educational system. The second serious matter is that what is front page news now was available and reportable news while it was happening and which this column did in fact report.

The current report continues: "The new census report demonstrates striking gains for blacks in an absolute sense. Among all blacks, educational attainment has nearly doubled since 1940. Then it was 5.7 years of schooling. Now it is 10.3 years."

The fact is that practically all of this took place because of LBJ's massive educational broadening, encompassing among other things, the greatest building program since the Pharaohs.

Declares The Times account: "The report, like earlier studies, also found a strong relationship between schooling and income."

Under these circumstances, fairminded Americans among this column's readers will recall that it reported that President JOHNSON's 1967 expenditures contained grants of $1.508 billion for elementary and secondary schools as against none in 1960.

PRESIDENT JOHNSON's expenditures included $429 million in grants and loans for construction of college classrooms as against not one dime in 1960.

In 1967, LBJ pushed through loans to 1,028,000 college students, as against 93,000 in 1960. He told then Sen. Wayne Morse that he hoped to see $7 billion out on loans to students by 1972. In the same year, $260 million went to vocational education; as against only $45 million in 1960.

As to the correlation between education and earning power, while this columnist has not seen the final census figures, these are a rough prognosis which appeared in a reputable business magazine: In 1960, there were 20,000 black families with an income of over $15,000. In 1972, there are about 400,000. In 1960, there were 200,000 black families with an income between $10,000 and $15,000. In 1972 there are 700,000.

More importantly in hard terms, is that President Johnson cut the two million black families living below the poverty level down to 100,000. Today, 60 per cent of all black males between the ages of 25 to 29 have been through high school.

All in all, this black advance marks the most spectacular progress of any one group of people in all of history in such a short space of time.

Since, as indicated, the census figures represent not a steady growth, but a doubling, expansion, it is perfectly obvious that the racial equality problem is much closer to solution than those who have a vested interest in prolonging it would like to believe.

Inaccurate though the 1972 census comparison is, the heartwarming news is that the "news" is far better than it indicates, because the speed of development is doubling.

Hon. James A. Burke
OF MASSACHUSETTS

Mr. Speaker, the Nation is shocked and saddened by the sudden and untimely death of former President LYNDON B. JOHNSON. His masterful assumption of the reins of our American government upon the unfortunate assassination of our President John F. Kennedy and the almost unbelievably smooth transition that he led should be remembered with gratitude by the American people.

LYNDON JOHNSON to many may have seemed a complex and complicated man. A commanding figure, big in physical stature, forceful, and toughminded, he was at the same time warm and understanding, a compassionate man. Known to be stubborn at times he was nevertheless capable of compromise and concession when he felt it to be in the best interest of his country. He was a leader of world stature yet completely at home with the less fortunate and underprivileged, wherever he met them.

It is generally acknowledged that LYNDON JOHNSON accomplished some of the greatest legislative victories in behalf of the people in our Nation's history. Medicare, medicaid, the historic landmark Civil Rights Act of 1964, massive Federal aid to education, housing, mental health, child welfare, conservation, and worked constantly for the general well-being of the average working man and woman, and those in our society who sometimes had no other champion. It is with reverence that LYNDON JOHNSON may truly be called the "President of the Poor."

Mr. JOHNSON believed in America; in America's dedication and ability to provide justice for all, in America's role as a world leader, and most importantly, he believed in the people of America. His hopes and dreams for these people will only be fully appreciated in the years to come.

Our heartfelt sympathy goes out to Mrs. Johnson, her two daughters, and other members of the family upon their great personal loss.

Hon. Robert Price
OF TEXAS

Mr. Speaker, the American people have witnessed a most remarkable month—first with the passing of former President Harry S Truman on December 26, followed by the reinauguration of President Richard Nixon on January 20, and now again with the passing of another former President, LYNDON B. JOHNSON.

This has been a month of mixed emotions— Americans have both celebrated and mourned. We have looked with anticipation to the future and yet paused to contemplate the past.

LYNDON B. JOHNSON was no ordinary man. Regardless of whether one agreed or disagreed with his policies, JOHNSON was a man of incredible strength and endurance. His steadfastness which was often a target for his detractors nevertheless gave Americans a sense of security and continuity during a time so wrought by strife and emotion.

Although ascending to the Presidency through an act of fate not expected or awaited, LYNDON B. JOHNSON carved his own record, and set into motion the most comprehensive domestic legislative program in history. LYNDON B. JOHNSON, a fellow Texan and political protege of the immortal Sam Rayburn, will have a place in history. We today are too close in time as his contemporaries to truly measure the significance of his presence upon the course of national and world affairs.

But LYNDON B. JOHNSON can never be doubted in his great faith in the American system. To all citizens, regardless of political party, he beckoned to the call of a task yet unfinished. And of that work which is good, he said, "Let us continue."

Hon. John E. Hunt
OF NEW JERSEY

Mr. Speaker, it is both tragic and ironic that former President LYNDON B. JOHNSON passed away yesterday, on the eve of peace in Vietnam. It was during his administration that the United States brought power to bear on the North Vietnamese in an effort to bring them to the bargaining table. It was during President JOHNSON's administration that Paris became the center of attention when it was announced that peace talks would begin.

One could not help but feel while watching the news last night that it was ironical that the Majestic Hotel in Paris was being prepared for the signing of the peace treaty ending the conflict in Vietnam. It was in this same hotel, in that very room shown last night, that the first hurdle to clear in the talks was the seating arrangement. This was just the first of many frustrations President JOHNSON would suffer in bargaining with the North.

He was indeed a casualty of the war.

Because of his efforts to deal with the Communists and the war with a strong hand, he was snubbed by his own party at the convention in 1968. But now, in retrospect, he, more than anyone else at the time, knew the best way to deal with his adversaries was through strength not weakness.

The war reached its fullest fury under JOHNSON, but it was he, and he alone who had to assume the consequences of difficult decisions, decisions which can only be made by the Commander in Chief.

History may yet prove him right.

Hon. William S. Cohen
OF MAINE

Mr. Speaker, I would like to join my colleagues in expressing the sorrow we all feel in mourning the untimely death of former President LYNDON B. JOHNSON.

Throughout his long career in public service, LYNDON JOHNSON served with distinction. He gave himself totally to the duties of the Presidency and will long be remembered for landmark accomplishments, especially in the field of civil rights. It is tragic and ironic that President JOHNSON could not live to experience the joy we all now feel as the Vietnam war is brought to a final conclusion.

The former President's love of his country, respect for the ideals upon which it was founded, and his complete dedication to public life have and will continue to serve as an inspiration to all of us. While only history can ultimately judge his deeds, those of us who have been fortunate enough to live in his lifetime will honor his memory with admiration and respect.

Hon. Frank Annunzio
OF ILLINOIS

Mr. Speaker, the death on January 22 of Hon. LYNDON BAINES JOHNSON, 36th President of the United States, is a tremendous loss to our Nation and to freedom-loving peoples throughout the world.

In my own city of Chicago, Mayor Richard J. Daley called a special meeting of the Chicago City Council where a memorial service was held on Wednesday, January 24, at 10 a.m.

The hour-long city council service was attended by many leaders of politics, business, labor, and religion, who came to pay their last respects to former President JOHNSON.

During the service, the fire department, American Legion post presented the colors, the Chicago Children's Choir and the Bluejacket Choir of Great Lakes Naval Training Station participated, and John Cardinal Cody, archbishop of Chicago, gave the invocation.

At the conclusion of the service in Chicago, Mayor Daley, Mrs. Daley, and Col. Jack Reilly, director of special events for the city of Chicago, came to Washington, D.C., and attended the ceremony in honor of our former President in the rotunda of the Capitol Building and the memorial service at the National City Christian Church.

The program for the Chicago City Council memorial service follows:

MEMORIAL SERVICES FOR FORMER PRESIDENT LYNDON B. JOHNSON, CHICAGO CITY COUNCIL, SPECIAL MEETING, WEDNESDAY, JANUARY 24, 1973, AT 10 A.M.

Call to order: Mayor Richard J. Daley.

Call for meeting read: John C. Marcin, city clerk.

Posting of colors: Color Guard—Chicago Fire Department Post, the American Legion.

The National Anthem: Louis Sudler.

Invocation: His Eminence John Cardinal Cody, Archbishop of Chicago.

Selection: "Salvation Is Created," Chicago Children's Choir, Christopher Moore and Joseph Brewer—Leaders.

Reading of resolution adopted on death of former President LYNDON B. JOHNSON.

Alderman Thomas E. Keane moves for adoption of resolution.

Alderman Jack I. Sperling seconds motion for adoption.

Mayor Daley introduces for prayers: Rabbi Ralph Simon, Rodfei Zeded Congregation; Reverend Richard Keller, Beth Eden Baptist Church.

Mayor Daley presents distinguished guests who have joined the city council to pay tribute to the memory of former President JOHNSON.

Benediction: Father Severino Lopez, Claretian Fathers.

Selection: "The Navy Hymn," Blue Jacket Choir, Great Lakes Naval Station.

Sounding of Taps.

Retirement of Colors: Fire Department Post of American Legion Color Guard.

Benediction.

Adjournment.

Hon. Wright Patman
OF TEXAS

Mr. Speaker, since the news flashed around the world last Monday afternoon of President LYNDON JOHNSON's death, people who knew him have been recounting the achievements of this great leader. The newspapers and the television screens and the radio airwaves have been filled with the recounting of his long and dedicated services to the people as a Congressman, a U.S. Senator, Vice President, and President.

It is fitting that we do whatever possible to keep the memory of this public service alive and before the people of the world. As we all know, President JOHNSON's work covered a fantastically wide range, but he was extremely proud of the leadership which he provided to our highly successful space program. His efforts to push the U.S. space program forward began while he served in the Senate and continued while he was Vice President and President. Many of the major milestones of the space program were accomplished during this period.

Therefore, I am proposing that the Manned

Spacecraft Center in Houston, Tex., be renamed the Lyndon Baines Johnson Space Center.

A joint resolution to accomplish this has been introduced in the U.S. Senate by our distinguished colleague from Texas, Senator Lloyd Bentsen. I shall introduce an identical resolution in the House on the next legislative day.

Mr. Speaker, I place in the Record at this point a copy of remarks which Senator Bentsen made when he proposed this new honor for our late President.

I also place in the Record a copy of the text of the resolution which Senator Bentsen introduced and which I shall introduce on the next legislative day in the House:

REMARKS OF THE HONORABLE LLOYD BENTSEN

Mr. President, I am today introducing a joint resolution to change the name of the Manned Spacecraft Center in Houston, Texas to the Lyndon B. Johnson Space Center.

No President has been more closely identified with the creation and the operation of America's space program than LYNDON JOHNSON.

His interest in space started during his years in the Senate, long before America put its first satellite in orbit.

As Chairman of the Senate Armed Services Preparedness Subcommittee in the late fifties, he chaired hearings on the appropriate American response to the Russian sputnik. As a result of these hearings, the Senate Special Committee on Science and Astronautics was established. LYNDON JOHNSON served as Chairman of that Committee from January 1958 through August, 1958 and conducted hearings which led to the establishment of the permanent Senate Committee on Aeronautical and Space Sciences.

He served as Chairman of that Committee from August of 1958 until he left the Senate to become Vice President in January of 1961.

John F. Kennedy recognized the Vice President's long association with the space program and appointed him the Chairman of the National Aeronautics and Space Council, a creature of the Executive Branch, which was responsible for coordinating all of the aeronautical and space activities of our executive agencies.

President Kennedy also asked his Vice President to be in charge of a panel to determine what could be done to close the "missile gap", a major issue during the campaign of 1960.

From the studies on this issue came a recommendation from the Vice President that the United States should make an effort to go to the moon in the 1960's. And, of course, the Apollo Program, which landed an American on the moon, led to the establishment of the Manned Spacecraft Center in Houston.

During his Presidency, LYNDON JOHNSON continued his keen interest in the space program. The entire series of Gemini flights was flown during the Johnson years, and the Apollo program, through Apollo 8 was successfully completed.

When LYNDON JOHNSON left the White House, Frank Borman and his crew had already completed their flight around the moon, setting the stage for the manned landing in July, 1969.

Mr. President, LYNDON JOHNSON, knew the space program from its early beginnings and he lived to see his vision of that program accomplished.

I believe that his interest in space grew from his sense of challenge and his absolute belief in America's destiny. He believed that this country could do aything it set out to do, and, with his support America marshalled the greatest scientific team the world has ever known and harnessed its talents to achieve one of mankind's greatest adventures.

But he did not see space as something "out there", unrelated to life on this planet. As with most men of vision, he had the ability to see beyond the spectacular, momentary achievements of space exploration to the time when the knowledge we gain from space can be put to use in improving the quality of life on Earth.

Mr. President, LYNDON JOHNSON is one of the Fathers of our space program. The legislation I introduce today seeks to honor him for his role in that great effort.

JOINT RESOLUTION TO DESIGNATE THE MANNED SPACE CRAFT CENTER IN HOUSTON, TEXAS, AS THE LYNDON B. JOHNSON SPACE CENTER IN HONOR OF THE LATE PRESIDENT

Resolved by the Senate and House of Representatives of the United States of America in Congress assembled,

Whereas, President LYNDON B. JOHNSON was one of the first of our National leaders to recognize the long-range benefits of an intensive space exploration effort;

Whereas, President LYNDON B. JOHNSON was one of the first of our National leaders Chairman of the Special Committee on Science and Astronautics which gave the initial direction to the U.S. space effort;

Whereas, President JOHNSON as Vice President of the United States, served as Chairman of the National Aeronautics and Space Council which recommended the goals for the manned space program;

Whereas, President JOHNSON for five years as President of the United States, bore ultimate responsibility for the development of the Gemini and Apollo programs which resulted in man's first landing on the moon;

Be it enacted by the Senate and House of Representatives of the United States of America in Congress assembled, that the Manned Space Craft Center. located in Houston, Texas, shall hereafter be known and designated as the Lyndon B. Johnson Space Center. Any reference to such facility in any law, or other paper of the United States shall be deemed a reference to it as the Lyndon B. Johnson Space Center.

Hon. Samuel S. Stratton
OF NEW YORK

Mr. Speaker, the sudden and untimely passing of President JOHNSON last week came as a heavy blow to me. He was more than a leader and a President to me. He was a personal friend. I first met him over 32 years ago when I came to Washington to serve as a congressional secretary and he was a young, third-term Congressman from Texas. Since then I have had the opportunity to watch his progress through the leadership channels in Washington to the White House.

As a President no man did more than LYNDON JOHNSON to maintain close and continuing consultation with Congress. In the Johnson days Members of Congress were in the White House repeatedly and many of us flew with him on important occasions in Air Force One. He was dynamic and persuasive, most effective in small groups. But somehow this charm never came across on television, unfortunately.

I believe that history will be much kinder to LYNDON JOHNSON than his contemporaries have been. His actions in Vietnam were most courageous and prevented a dangerous shift in the balance of world power in Asia. His legislative record on domestic issues is almost without parallel, especially in civil rights.

The last time I saw President JOHNSON was 3 weeks ago at the memorial mass in New Orleans for our beloved majority leader, Hale Boggs. Mr. JOHNSON looked tired then and his pace had slowed. But he had not hesitated to fly halfway across the country to pay tribute to a great friend and a very loyal supporter. It was characteristic of a big heart and a great man. That was LYNDON JOHNSON.

Hon. John M. Murphy
OF NEW YORK

Mr. Speaker, under the leave to extend my remarks in the Record, I include the following:

THE LEGACY OF LYNDON BAINES JOHNSON—A TRIBUTE

(By John M. Murphy)

"He was a man, take him for all in all,
 I shall not look upon his like again."
—Hamlet, Act 1 Scene 2

With a heart crippled by the ravages of disease, until his dying moments LYNDON BAINES JOHNSON was battling for the have-nots of society. His last major public appearance was as a mediator at a civil rights dispute in Austin, Texas. When the program was threatened by a violent outbreak, JOHNSON "obviously sick and tired," took command and according to the President of the University of Texas, his "chest expanded and his eyes flashed, and he calmed the situation down. He said exactly the right thing, extemporaneously. You could see a great man at the top of his power."

The President told the ominous and troubled audience:

"To be black—to one who is black—is to be proud, to be worthy, to be honorable. But to be black in a white society is not to stand on level ground.

"While the races may stand side by side, whites stand on history's mountain and blacks stand in history's hollow.

"Unless we overcome unequal history, we cannot overcome unequal opportunity. That is not—nor will it ever be—an easy goal to achieve."

Within days of his death in what must have been moments of acute pain, LYNDON JOHNSON rose with one last burst of his rapidly failing energy and spoke as eloquently as he ever had on the meaning of being a minority American.

President JOHNSON brought the same fire, the same drive and the same love of the American people to everything he did. Forged in the desperate poverty and spirit-killing depression that engulfed his beloved Texas during the 1930's he projected his burning desire to change things for the better from the banks of his rural Perdenales to the ghettos of America's cities.

Heeding the call of the deprived, the disadvantaged and the disenfranchised, he spread his philosophy of a great society for all to his foreign policy thinking. And believing in the right of weaker people to self-determination and a place in the sun, LYNDON JOHNSON applied his philosophy to the people of South Viet Nam. But between the journey from the banks of the Perdenales to the banks of the Mekong River, President JOHNSON's dream—for a time—turned into his own personal nightmare.

So, despite his unprecedented success in putting through Congress and into operation the new frontier program of the slain John F. Kennedy, and despite the sometimes tenuous, but always progressing, successes of his own programs—his own domestic wars against discrimination, against poverty and against the corruptors of our environment—he was to reach a point where he was haunted by the spectre of the Vietnam War that bedeviled him like Banquos' ghost.

His torment was not so much the result of defeats on the field or in the sputtering truce negotiations which he initiated. His torment was largely attributable to his anguish over and devotion to the "grunts" in that tragic effort, the G.I.'s who were bearing the brunt of the battle in the face of what seemed at time futile efforts to end the war. From General Westmoreland to the lowliest private, LYNDON JOHNSON could not conceal from friends and reporters a compassion that betrayed his innermost turmoil over the lives—and deaths—of the American fighting men. While he was concerned for the victims of that war-torn nation, his concern for the American soldier was so great that he gave up the Presidency he had gotten by the most incredible vote of confidence from the people in American history so that their chances for survival might be increased.

It was perhaps symbolic that the news of the success of the peace negotiations that he so fervently sought should come to him hours before he left us.

The wounds of war will heal and the perspective of history will, I am certain, record LYNDON JOHNSON's role in it with compassion for the people of Vietnam, North *and* South, and his desire to rebuild both nations, that was the real goal of the 36th President of the United States.

And while the Vietnam controversy swirled around his head, President JOHNSON's domestic programs of change were not without their attendant disruptions. When Americans of the future remember LYNDON JOHNSON, they will think about his revolutionary ideas—and that revolutionary ideas sometimes bring about revolutions of a sort. I remember the ashes of Watts, Newark, Detroit—and Washington, D.C. But out of these ashes this country and the world have witnessed the rebirth of a new America, an America where the oppressed people President JOHNSON loved so much are finding new freedom, new dignity, new life and a rebirth of the human spirit. Observing the turbulent mid-sixties, LYNDON JOHNSON did not view it as America coming apart at the seams. He described it as:

"The old . . . not coming down. Rather the troubling and torment of these days stems from the new trying to rise into place."

When LYNDON JOHNSON was thrust into the presidency by that fatal burst of gunfire in Dallas, one of his first major moves was to begin what was to be the passage of the most sweeping civil rights legislation in America's history. Of this achievement President JOHNSON was to say, "It's going to make democracy real. It is going to correct an injustice of decades and centuries."

If he had done nothing else, LYNDON JOHNSON had begun to make his great society available to everyone. And for this all Americans could be grateful. But he wanted more for the needy of America so he designed and put into operation the Office of Economic Opportunity to eliminate poverty; he developed plans to cope with our urban crisis; and, President JOHNSON's Administration gave greater support to the educational needs of our people than any government in history.

This record of achievement is the real legacy of LYNDON JOHNSON. It wasn't easy, but he had the courage to see that the die was cast for freedom and this country— and the world—are bearing the fruits of his labors.

The legacy of LYNDON JOHNSON will not be the memory of the nightmare of Vietnam, but the renewed dedication to his dream of a great society which I am convinced will inspire Democrats and Republicans alike.

His legacy will herald a renewed commitment to an America where he worked to guarantee no second-class citizenship, no second-quality opportunity, no second-hand justice at home, and no second-place status in the world for our ideals and benefits.

While he was untimely ripped from our midst, all Americans can rejoice in the fact that he *was* here; in the fact that, as a close friend eulogized, in the seventh decade of the 20th Century, this country had LYNDON BAINES JOHNSON.

This country will not look upon his like again.

Hon. Glenn M. Anderson

OF CALIFORNIA

Mr. Speaker, the Nation has lost a great and patriotic citizen, one whose passing has deeply saddened the Nation.

The American people loved, respected, and admired the 36th President of the United States—LYNDON BAINES JOHNSON.

They knew he was their friend, they had confidence in him and they knew he was, without question, a man of the people and for the people.

LYNDON JOHNSON has returned to the Texas hills, the place where he spent most of his life, and the land he loved the most. However he will not be forgotten by the Nation and the world,

who loved and respected him, not only as a leader, but as a man.

As a Congressman, Senator, Vice President, and President of the United States, Mr. JOHNSON's accomplishments and achievements are numerous.

He put his principles into action with the greatest amount of energy and enthusiasm. As chairman of the Senate Space Committee, he initiated the great strides made in the national space program.

LYNDON JOHNSON's accomplishments in the areas of civil rights, medicare, poverty, and housing are unmatchable. They were truly a victory for him and a victory for the Nation as a whole.

I am extremely proud to join my colleagues in paying homage to LYNDON B. JOHNSON. I feel honored to have known him—a man with the deepest compassion for all mankind and a true American.

He will be remembered in the hearts of all who knew him and of those who had the great privilege of his friendship.

The United States has lost a fine citizen and public servant.

We shall all miss him. Mrs. Anderson joins me in expressing our deepest sympathy to Mrs. Johnson and their two daughters, Lynda, and Luci.

Hon. Carl Albert

OF OKLAHOMA

The Speaker laid before the House the following communications from the Ambassador of Turkey:

JANUARY 29, 1973.

Hon. CARL ALBERT,
The Speaker of the House of Representatives, Washington, D.C.

DEAR MR. SPEAKER: I have the honor to enclose herewith the message of His Excellency Sabit Osman Avci, the President of the National Assembly of Turkey, to Your Excellency on the occasion of the death of His Excellency LYNDON B. JOHNSON, former President of the United States.

In sharing the sentiments expressed in the message, please accept, Mr. Speaker, in behalf of my wife and myself, our heartfelt condolences.

MELIH ESENBEL,
Ambassador of Turkey.

&

Hon. CARL ALBERT,
The Speaker of the House of Representatives, Washington, D.C.:

I am deeply grieved by the news of the death of H.E. LYNDON B. JOHNSON, former President of the United States of America.

On this very sad occasion I wish to convey to your excellency my sincere feelings of sympathy and condolences.

SABIT OSMAN AVCI,
Speaker of the National Assembly of Turkey.

Hon. William G. Bray

OF INDIANA

Mr. Speaker, it is a privilege to include in the Record at this point the following tributes to the late President LYNDON B. JOHNSON which appeared in the Indianapolis Star and News.

The first was written by Mr. Eugene C. Pulliam, publisher of the Star and News, and a long-time personal friend of the Johnson family. Following are the special tributes written by Ben Cole, of the Star, and Lou Hiner, of the News, as well as the editorials appearing in both newspapers:

"A TRULY LOVABLE MAN," EUGENE C. PULLIAM SAYS

"LYNDON B. JOHNSON was one of my dear personal friends for more than 30 years. Ours was a unique friendship. The public didn't know it, but he was a truly lovable man. We disagreed on many things political, but it never affected our friendship. I don't know how many times when I have introduced him to a small group of friends or to a large audience he prefaced his remarks by saying 'Gene Pulliam is my dear friend. A long time ago when I was still a senator we learned we could disagree without being disagreeable.' And that statement from President JOHNSON was an inspiring and deeply rewarding gift of our friendship.

"It was just about the same with dear Lady Bird and my wife, Nina, when they met for the first time. It was like old friends greeting each other after a long separation.

"We had had many letters from both Mr. and Mrs. Johnson, the last one just last week. They always expressed the feeling that they looked forward to seeing us soon again.

"I am not trying to write a eulogy to a great President. The cup of tributes and praise will run over from every state in the Union. But I do want to express our deepdown affection for a man we both knew and loved as a true and wonderful friend. And to let dear Lady Bird know our sympathy and understanding come from the bottom of loving and saddened hearts."

EUGENE C. PULLIAM, *Publisher.*

❧

L. B. J. CONQUERED WASHINGTON WITH TEXAS-STYLE
VITALITY

(By Ben Cole)

WASHINGTON.—The vitality that LYNDON BAINES JOHNSON gave to everything he did was the hallmark of his style, and it will be a long time before the nation's capital sees his equal.

His presence began to be felt almost as soon as he moved from the House of Representatives to the United

States Senate in 1949 after his 87-vote hair's breadth landslide of 1948.

The Senate was his milieu. He took to its mysteries as a duck takes to water, and he set about instantly to make himself known and his ability and ambition understood.

David E. Botter, later to become a McGill School of Journalism professor before his death, had come up from Dallas the year Mr. JOHNSON moved to the Senate as a correspondent for the Dallas Morning News. His senior colleague, Walter C. Hornaday, preferred the commoner clay of the House and Botter covered the Senate—which pretty much meant LYNDON JOHNSON.

In the late summer, probably at Mr. JOHNSON's suggestion, Botter arranged an evening with the tall Texas freshmen for a handful of his newspaper colleagues. The Indianapolis Star's correspondent, as new to Washington as Botter, fortunately was included in that company.

All the issues of the day were discussed and Senator JOHNSON did the discussing. His performance was a revelation to the newsmen—he ranged easily over foreign trade, oil and gas problems, the Southerners' problems with civil rights.

What he said that night is forgotten, but not the style. Among the reporters on hand was William S. White, now a syndicated columnist but then of the New York Times. White became the best interpreter of Mr. JOHNSON among the Washington press, and the two men were fast friends.

It wasn't long before the senator from Texas was given the chair of leadership. One of his first moves was to hire out of the press gallery a big, bushy-haired Hoosier, pipe-smoking George Reedy, the son of an old Chicago front-page type newsman of the same name. As deliberate and careful as Mr. JOHNSON was mercurial, Reedy was a happy choice for the senator from Texas.

During his majority leader days, Mr. JOHNSON wore loose-fitting, brightly colored silk suits, and he loved to jangle coins or keys in his pockets while his haberdashery rippled in the light.

Majority leader JOHNSON never lost his publicity sense, and he knew a good story when he had one to give the press. One day this reporter was sitting in an inordinately dull Appropriations Committee hearing, hoping to get a few notes on the fate of an immigration office at Tucson, Ariz. Some of the committee staff joined the lone reporter at the press table just to keep him company.

Mr. JOHNSON strode into the hearing, glanced at the press table and noted that several persons were seated there. He almost immediately attacked the then-commissioner of immigration for having gone to Juarez, Mexico, to hire a maid.

The story appeared in one newspaper, but next day it became a sensation.

Mr. JOHNSON's influence on young people was pronounced. When he was Vice-President, he spoke each summer to the students doing intern work in the Federal service. A University of Virginia student who later took up a government career returned home from one of Mr. JOHNSON's speeches with eyes alight.

"Mr. JOHNSON told us that the one thing that distinguishes the American system from any other system in the world is that a young man who is willing to work hard may hope to succeed," he said. It became the young man's article of faith in America.

During the summer and autumn of 1964, when he was completing the term of President Kennedy and before he was elected in his own right, Mr. Johnson enjoyed his happiest moments in office. The Vietnam war had not yet become a fester, his election prospects were good and the country was solidly with him.

Going to the White House every Saturday was an adventure, because most of the time the President would call the press into his oval office and conduct a give-and-take news conference. Then he would adjourn to the White House lawn and walk for miles around the circular driveway, thoroughly enjoying the gaggle of reporters jostling each other to get closer to him.

The routine became established: If you had something special to ask the President, you lagged behind the main body of his infantry and allowed him to catch up with you. Then you could ask your question, and usually get an answer before the herd engulfed you and you were pushed away.

The campaign that year was a romp for the big Texan. He loved to turn the press out at dawn, take off for a day or so of frantic campaigning that could cover all of New England or sweep the South or cover the Middle West. His face was alight when he leaped into the crowds to shake hands. Once, in Brooklyn, he became so ebullient that he simply hauled an ecstatic woman into his open car and hauled her along in his caravan for a mile or two.

President and Mrs. Johnson, unlike some first families, always included members of the working press in the social lists for state dinners. There is no thrill like attending a state dinner for the first time, and President Johnson was aware of the fact. He didn't forget the men and women in the press gallery who shared the story of his fabulous career.

One of his favorites in the press corps was Mrs. Elizabeth May Craig, the grandmotherly little woman who appeared often on the TV show, "Meet the Press." At Portland, Me., during a campaign trip, President Johnson turned a city hall rally into a May Craig appreciation event. Mrs. Craig, by the way, had sent Mr. Johnson a note every day that he was hospitalized with his 1955 heart attack, and he never forgot her thoughtfulness.

When he entertained the press at his ranch in Texas the day after the 1963 election, there was an auction of some of the campaign paraphernalia. Among the items sold was the bull horn that the President had used in haranguing the crowds along the campaign trail. A joyous May Craig bid it in.

A week later she received a phone call from the President of the United States, imploring her to return his treasure. He hadn't intended to let his bull horn get away, he said, and May would be doing him a big favor to return it. She did.

As the bitterness over Vietnam closed in on him, and his own worry for the men he was committing to battle deepened, the President became withdrawn from the press and there were no more walks around the White House driveway.

Once he held a news conference in the White House rose garden, and while the preliminaries were in progress he appeared prematurely and asked for George Reedy, his trusted press secretary. George was engaged in answering queries from a group, of reporters, and the President groused, "Reedy thinks he works for you-all instead of for me."

In a light-hearted way, this reporter suggested, "Well, Mr. President, there are more of us than there are of you." But the President wasn't in the mood for light banter with an Indiana newspaperman, and the little jest fell flat.

The final years of his administration were saddened by the hostility that was heaped upon President Johnson, often by men who owed their political lives to his skill and generosity. Bill White, now a syndicated columnist, was one of the voices raised in defense of the President and Bill was chagrined when, during the 1972 campaign, Mr. Johnson allowed Senator George McGovern (D–S.D.) to visit the ranch along the Pedernales, giving a modicum of indorsement to the Democratic nominee's campaign.

Any newsman who lived in Washington for that golden span of years between 1949 and the end of the Johnson administration has a storehouse of memories that come alive this day. Lyndon Baines Johnson, for all the criticism some elements of the press found it convenient to heap upon him, was a newspaperman's President. He made the front page exciting every single day.

Down-to-Earth: L. B. J. Noted for His Wit and Humor

(By Lou Hiner, Jr.)

Among many things, the late President Lyndon B. Johnson will be remembered for his wit and humor.

He liked a good belly laugh himself and he often provided the same to those in his company. Many of his stories were ribald but mostly his was a down-to-earth humor.

When the American Society of Newspaper Editors met in Washington in April 1964, Johnson invited the editors and their wives to drop in for a visit at the White House but he received them instead in the Rose Garden.

He explained: "The reason I wanted you in the Rose Garden is simply because if we had gone inside the White House, Lady Bird would have insisted that I turn on all the light. We are going in shortly to the White House, so you can pick up your candles in a box over there."

(LBJ at the time was on a turn-off-the-lights kick.)

In May 1964 he let Washington correspondents bring their families to the White House grounds for an outdoors news conference. After the 30-minute session before the wives and children, Johnson announced:

"Friends and reporters—I hope you are the same—and children of reporters. I am so glad so many of you youngsters are here today . . . I want to ask all the children to come up here and pose with me for a group picture. Let's don't have any mamas or papas. They are always crowding into pictures, anyway."

After being introduced with lavish remarks at a meeting in Nashville, Johnson responded:

"I honestly believe that is the second best introduction I ever had in my life. The best one was when the governor was supposed to introduce me one time at Memphis but his legislature was in session and he didn't make it and I had to introduce myself."

Sen. Barry M. Goldwater, R-Ariz., was one of LBJ's favorite friends. Even so, he said of Goldwater during the 1964 presidential campaign: "He wants to repeal the present and veto the future." He invited the Goldwaters to a White House dinner before the GOP convention, and after dancing with Mrs. Goldwater he quipped: "I have to be nice to Peggy. I might want to get invited back here next year."

JOHNSON often liked to tell the story of Rep. Magnus Johnson, D-Minn.: "One day, Magnus Johnson rose in the House and declared, 'What we have to do is to take the bull by the tail and look the situation in the face.'"

He called the late President Truman in Independence when Truman was celebrating his 8oth birthday anniversary in 1964. He began the conversation: "I wanted to call collect but Lady Bird wouldn't let me."

Truman and the late House Speaker Sam Rayburn, D-Texas, were men he greatly admired and respected. He often recalled the advice Rayburn gave Truman after Truman became President: "Harry, they'll try to put you behind a wall down here. There will be people that will surround you and cut you off from any ideas but theirs. They'll try to make you think that the President is the smartest man in the world. And, Harry, you know he ain't, and I know he ain't."

୬

LYNDON B. JOHNSON

The death of LYNDON JOHNSON has taken the last of the nation's former living presidents, barely a month after the passing of Harry Truman.

JOHNSON will be deeply missed by political friends and foes alike. In a way he was the most American of our presidents, a figure larger than life, embodying within himself all the fantastic energy of a sprawling and powerful nation. A son of the South Texas prairie, JOHNSON worked his way from humble beginnings through the many stages of political endeavor to assume the highest office in the land. And like the state which nurtured him, he was cast on a gigantic scale.

The former President's career spanned the epoch of modern politics—from his early congressional service in the days of Franklin Roosevelt to his own White House tenure in the '6o's. When he was majority leader in the U.S. Senate, stories abounded of his fabulous energy, ability to reconcile conflicting views, and aptitude for practical results. He was a worker for the causes in which he believed, and seldom has a legislative leader accomplished so much under a president of another party as did JOHNSON under Dwight D. Eisenhower.

Perhaps the most memorable single moment in JOHNSON's career was his ascension to the presidency in the aftermath of the Kennedy assassination. At that time of national pain and confusion, the man from Texas provided the nation with a steady hand and effected a quiet but surefooted transition. He was able to unite the country in an hour when healing leadership was needed, and that leadership was confirmed by an enormous margin in the election of 1964.

Most assessments of JOHNSON's career will praise his domestic record while asserting that he foundered on the subject of Vietnam. While the record on both these topics can be read in various ways, we tend to think the verdict of history will be the reverse of current assessments. The domestic initiatives of the JOHNSON presidency, indeed, have already begun to be reevaluated; it was in his repeated statements that the nation must stand firm against the tide of Communist aggression that JOHNSON came closest to striking to the core of historical reality in the 20th century.

LYNDON JOHNSON was a big man who embodied within himself the many impulses that are America, and whose life was itself a continuing chronicle of modern American statecraft. Our politics will be infinitely the poorer for his passing.

୬

LYNDON B. JOHNSON

LYNDON BAINES JOHNSON became the 36th president of the United States against a background of national grief and shock, and left office in a time of strife and questioning of the things he stood for and the things he did.

But history may prove to be a fairer judge and a more honest one than some contemporaries in whose eyes disillusionment with the recent past seems overwhelming.

Born on a farm near Stonewall, Texas, he was also born to politics, his father and grandfather having served in the Texas state legislature. As a young man he taught school and as a teacher, learned much about how everyday Americans lived.

In 1937 he won a contest for a vacancy in the United States House of Representatives in which he was to serve five full terms, and after serving as a Navy lieutenant commander in World War II was elected to the Senate, becoming Democratic leader in 1953. His brilliance as a parliamentary tactician and strategist carried him to the top level of leadership and put him in line for the vice-presidency in 1960.

It was not only his Great Society programs, launched after he became President, that aroused whirlwinds of controversy that would rage beyond his days in the White House, but the escalating U.S. involvement in Vietnam, which in spite of a heavy cost in the lives and wealth, came more and more to seem like a futile, unendable conflict.

His welfare, civil rights, and anti-poverty legislation produced mixed results and sharp differences of opinion, as to their merit, among the people. The high cost and expanding bureaucracy, in the view of many, were not justified by the debatable effects. Yet on the whole the care of the aged and poor and improvement in the rights of minorities made undeniable strides.

The war aroused the hottest, bitterest debate of all. Yet hindsight has conferred upon JBJ's sharpest critics a vision which most lacked in the early stages of the war. And despite the war's out-of-focus grand strategy, it has not yet been demonstrated conclusively to the majority of Americans that the defense of the perimeters of the free world is possible without recourse to arms, or that freedom and U.S. national interests are not worth defending.

LYNDON BAINES JOHNSON has been characterized by his bitterest enemies as an inept and evil president, but we think the record shows he was a good-hearted man, often struggling against terrible odds, who did his best—which was not inconsiderable—in behalf of what he and most of his fellow countrymen considered the best interests of the nation as he understood them.

And history may well judge that he was among those presidents who helped to defend freedom in its hour of greatest peril and made possible for many millions of whom it had been hitherto denied a greater measure of realization of what is often called "the American dream."

Hon. John Brademas
OF INDIANA

Mr. Speaker, the late President LYNDON B. JOHNSON wanted to be known as the "Education President."

I am confident that he will, for no President in American history worked so hard to provide opportunities for a good education to so many.

As a member of the House Committee on Education and Labor during President JOHNSON's service as President, I know from my own experience the dedication and energy he brought to achieving the goal of improving the quality of education in our country and widening access to education.

Mr. Speaker, I include at this point in the Record from the January 29, 1973, issue of the Chronicle of Higher Education, an article entitled: "LYNDON B. JOHNSON, 1908–1973: 'Education President'":

LYNDON B. JOHNSON, 1908–73:
"EDUCATION PRESIDENT"

(By Philip W. Semas)

During his term as President of the United States, LYNDON BAINES JOHNSON signed 60 laws providing federal aid to education.

He often said he, wanted to be known as the "Education President." Many observers believe he earned that title, since most of the legislation authorizing the first large-scale federal effort to aid education was passed by Congress under his prodding.

"We're very much in his debt," said Roger W. Heyns, president of the American Council on Education, after Mr. JOHNSON died last week at the age of 64. "His commitment to education has benefitted millions of our young people."

Before Mr. JOHNSON became President, attempts to provide extensive federal aid to education had run up against the stone wall of the church-state controversy. The Johnson Administration went around that wall by proposing large-scale aid for specific programs, rather than general aid to colleges and schools.

In higher education, President JOHNSON's greatest accomplishment was the Higher Education Act of 1965, which established such programs as guaranteed student loans, educational opportunity grants for needy students, and aid to developing colleges—programs that still form the foundation for much federal aid to higher education today.

He also signed the Higher Education Facilities Act of 1963, which authorized federal aid for construction of classroom and library buildings. He got Congress to pass the Sea-Grant Act which provided money for marine research; the International Education Act, which has never been funded; and the Education Professions Development Act, which provided funds for the education of educators.

Mr. JOHNSON, who once taught public speaking in a Texas high school, liked to be called "the teacher in the White House."

He had an almost religious faith in the value of education. Although his mother had to persuade him to go to college, he believed his attendance at Southwest Texas State Teachers College saved him from a life of drifting.

But in the end Mr. JOHNSON's accomplishments in education—like his accomplishment in civil rights and other domestic areas—ran afoul of the Vietnam war.

By the end of his term, he had stopped proposing huge increases in appropriations for aid to education, as the cost of the war took an ever-larger share of the federal budget. He also rejected proposals from within his administration to initiate new programs in education, some of which have since been enacted.

And the President who hoped to be hailed on college campuses for his contributions to higher education was instead the object of bitter denunciations from many students and professors for his prosecution of the war.

After he retired from the Presidency in 1969, Mr. JOHNSON supervised the building of a Presidential library and school of public affairs, both of which bear his name, at the University of Texas.

The first set of his Presidential papers to be made public at the library were the documents on education, almost exactly a year ago. At that time he said, "I take great pride that I was referred to, when people tried to be generous, as the education President."

MAJOR JOHNSON-ERA EDUCATION MEASURES

Dec. 16, 1963—The Higher Education Facilities Act, which provided for grants and loans for classroom and library construction.

Aug. 20, 1964—The Economic Opportunity Act, which authorized work-study aid for needy students and created Project Upward Bound.

Nov. 8, 1965—The Higher Education Act of 1965, which authorized federal funds for guaranteed student loans, for colleges to buy instructional equipment, for educational opportunity grants to needy students, for library materials and librarian training, for the Teacher Corps, for aid to developing colleges, and for colleges to become involved in community service.

Oct. 15, 1966—The National Sea-Grant Program and College Act, which provided for aid to marine research at designated colleges.

Oct. 29, 1966—The International Education Act, which authorized federal funds for centers for international studies and for improving undergraduate studies of international affairs.

June 29, 1967—The Education Professions Development Act, which authorized funds for the training of educational personnel from grade school teachers to college administrators.

Oct. 16, 1968—The Higher Education Amendments of 1968, which refined student-aid programs and created new programs of aid for college use of educational technology, for cooperative education, for law schools, and for graduate education, as well as extending earlier legislation.

Mr. Speaker, former President LYNDON B. JOHNSON left us a legacy of many bold and innovative new programs.

One of the late President's interests that enriched all our lives was his commitment to support the creative and performing arts in America.

This commitment found voice in his support of the National Foundation for the Arts and Humanities, the John F. Kennedy Center for the Performing Arts, the Corporation for Public Broadcasting, and the National Museum Act of 1966, to mention only a few of President JOHNSON's most noteworthy achievements.

Mr. Speaker, Richard L. Coe, the distinguished critic of the Washington Post, recently published an account of the arts under the stewardship of LYNDON JOHNSON.

I include Mr. Coe's story, for the benefit of my colleagues, at this point.

L. B. J. AND ART

(By Richard L. Coe)

LBJ did more for the arts than all his 35 presidential predecessors combined. The irony was that the most vocal members of the arts community derided him and mocked his "style."

In the four eventful years from 1964 to '68, President JOHNSON guided into reality at least a dozen projects which the arts community had dreamed of vaguely for years. Even now many in that community are unaware such programs exist. They were:

The National Council on the Arts, authorized to develop a plan for the federal role in all the arts.

The National Foundation on the Arts and Humanities, the first agency in our history specifically designed to support the growth of all the arts throughout the nation.

The John F. Kennedy Center for the Performing Arts.

The National Museum Act of 1966, providing for programs of museum training, research, surveys and publications.

The Corporation for Public Broadcasting to encourage the development of noncommercial radio and TV.

Acquisition of the Joseph H. Hirschhorn collection, its building now nearing completion on the Mall.

Realization, through Arts Endowment funds and private sources, of the American Film Institute.

Grants through the Office of Education, making possible funding for artists to visit elementary and secondary schools under the Education Act of 1965.

Programs in 16 major cities to provide summer arts programs for young people.

Creation of the National Collection of Fine Arts and the National Portrait Gallery in the old Patent Building at 8th and F Sts.

Reclaiming the old Court of Claims at the corner of Penn. Ave. and 17th St., now the Renwick Gallery.

Grants-in-aid programs both to regional theaters, music and dance groups and, as well, individual awards to painters, sculptors and writers.

These accomplishments had a trusted strategic planner and field commander, Roger L. Stevens, who for much of the Johnson years had three titles: White House con-

sultant on the arts, chairman of the National Council on the Arts and Chairman of the Board of the Kennedy Center, a title Stevens still holds by vote of the board.

In the late '50s even tentative mention of such projects was deemed visionary. In the early '60s both Sens. Kennedy and Nixon, then running for the presidency, spoke virtually unanimously about more government relationship to the arts but three years after taking the oath of office President Kennedy answered a criticism of mine that no advances had been made with the promise: "Cheer up. We'll get them done." Ten months later he was dead.

President JOHNSON waded into the challenge with a vengeance. Within a week after he assumed office he went along with Sen. Fulbright and Rep. Thompson in altering their bill for a "National Cultural Center" into a "living memorial" for his predecessor. At the same time he urged Honolulu to name its new East-West Theater for President Kennedy. On a chillingly cold, rainy December morning of 1964, President JOHNSON broke ground for the Center. He looked on the project with a visionary vigor, but on his several post-White House visits to the area, never got around to visiting the building.

But he saw to it that the cream of American artists visited the White House both as guests and as performers on the elegant little stage Rebekah Harkness, his wife's friend, contributed from the design of famed Jo Mielziner. This portable stage repeated the East Room's hand-crafted panels, fluted pilasters and neo-classic capitals, so that the stage seemed a part of the room itself, not a make-shift that had been shoved into place.

Hardly an American artist of distinction refused an invitation to perform for the dinner guests assembled honoring world leaders. Here, for Morocco's Hassan II, the late Jose Limon danced his geat work, "The Moor's Pavanne," his "Othello" variation. Marian Anderson, Dorothy Maynor, and Duke Ellington were recognized as peerless black artists. Carol Channing's "Hello, Dolly!" was given its fourth birthday performance on Mrs. Harkness' stage and at its end President JOHNSON wheeled on a huge birthday cake for the star who'd spent the '64 campaign singing "Hello, LYNDON."

The most famous day—and it was all-out Texas style— was the Johnson's Festival for the Arts, June 15, 1965. It began in the morning, lasted till after midnight and was a day spread all over the house and grounds, embracing sculpture, painting, photography, literature, films, drama, dance and music, an amazingly vast panorama of American arts. Everyone trekked over with Mrs. Johnson for lunch at the National Gallery and dinner was served under the trees of the White House south lawn, LBJ table-hopping.

If it was an expansive day it was also an abrasive one. In advance Robert Lowell had refused to attend on the grounds that "we are in danger of imperceptibly becoming an explosive and suddenly chauvenistic nation." Invited to read, John Hersey stated he would contribute sections from his "Hiroshima." He did so and was welcomed. Mark Van Doren introduced him and Ambassador George Kennan faced the topic of government and the arts:

"Art is not a political weapon but much of what the artist does is profoundly political in helping to dissolve barriers of hatred and ignorance. In this way you work toward peace, not the peace which is simply the absence of war, but the peace which liberates man to reach for the finest fulfillment of his spirit."

LBJ said: "Amen to that" and then smiled, a bit

sadly I thought, at his guests, some of them visibly signing the protest against the Vietnam war which guest Dwight MacDonald was circulating for all to sign and leave behind for their host.

The man who did much to organize the day, Princeton Prof. Eric Goldman would later write a book about that experience and it would prove to be almost as abrasive a work as the controversy itself.

I doubt that LBJ read Goldman's book, though very likely Mrs. Johnson at least read its magazine excerpts. She read everything about the arts, saw all the plays from her earliest days as a Washington congressman's wife and unquestionably influenced LBJ's actions for the arts. One big occasion, a "Salute to Congress" in the fall of '65, lost most of its audience because the House was then debating, far into the night, Mrs. Johnson's national beautification bill. The President kidded Lady Bird that their spoiled party was her own fault.

What one remembers from all the gregarious gatherings is the top quality of the guests, all leaders in the arts. There was Catherine Drinker Bowen talked of how she researched her biographies, Hume Cronyn and Jessica Tandy collecting words about the Great Society, Eugene Ormandy chatting with Satchmo Armstrong, tiny Beatrice Lillie looking up at her Marine escort. There was Gregory Peck laughing about reports he was going to run for Congress. There was Charlton Heston, invited to the unveiling of Franklin D. Roosevelt's portrait and playing a scene from "Sunrise at Campobello" and Alice Roosevelt Longworth telling him: "I'm here today not because I was a close friend of Franklin but because I was a close critic."

Mrs. Johnson's interest over-ruled such obstacles as health. She'd arranged for presentation of the Margo Jones Award in the upstairs Oval Room but when the time came she was in bed with the flu. But she talked to each of the honorees on the phone to make them feel welcome and as they were leaving they had a glimpse of LBJ leaving his oval office. There was the night a company of "You're A Good Man, Charlie Brown" came in from Shady Grove to serenade Lynda Robb and her new baby, Lucinda, with an East Room performance and LBJ looked in on the small, youngish group to say goodnight to his grandchild.

Roaming restlessly among his guests, sometimes hundreds of them, sometimes only a few, was the tall Texan, often not talking as you'd expect that man to do, but listening, it sometimes seemed, with his eyes; taking in all the details about his particular segment of his Great Society, the artists, finding them very different from himself but not, for that reason, to be despised. It was as though they were a luxury he'd missed along his way to the top and he wanted to grasp all he could about this colorful, assertive breed. He used his energetic know-how on their behalf and if he was puzzled at their ingratitude he was too proudly sensitive to mention it.

Hon. John A. Blatnik

OF MINNESOTA

Mr. Speaker, Congress and the Nation have said goodby to LYNDON BAINES JOHNSON, our former colleague in the House and Senate, and 36th President of the United States. We have joined his family in mourning his passing; we have reflected, publicly and privately among ourselves, on his tremendous impact on this Nation and the world.

The media have had their say, too, but none have spoken of L. B. J. more eloquently than Walter Cronkite, on CBS Radio, the evening following his death. It was broadcast January 23, 1973.

Mr. Cronkite had been taping a series of television interviews with L. B. J., and less than 2 weeks before his death spoke with the former President on his civil rights legacy, surely the crowning achievement of this restless, compassionate giant.

I would like to insert Mr. Cronkite's radio commentary in the Record, so that the Nation may have the benefit of his most recent insights, and personal perceptions, of the man who dominated the legislative landscape for so long, both as Representative, Senator, and President of the United States.

The commentary follows:

LYNDON JOHNSON was a man of incredible contradictions. A man who became President with a prime commitment to domestic reform, yet ultimately saw his domestic program tainted by controversy aboard. A man who won the biggest Presidential landslide in U.S. history, yet could not try again just four years later because his stock had sunk so low. A Southerner who championed the greatest civil rights advances in the nation's history. A man who hobnobbed with Texas conservatives, and yet fathered the war on poverty and pushed Medicare through Congress. And certainly not least, a man who gloried publicly in acquiring and manipulating political power while repressing grave private doubts if the power was properly his to hold.

He certainly didn't become any less complex a man when you got to know him personally. I had been going down to the LBJ Ranch at irregular intervals ever since Mr. JOHNSON left the White House to interview him before TV cameras on various aspects of his controversial Presidential years. The most recent installment, devoted mainly to the civil rights issue, took place less than two weeks ago. Clearly, it was more congenial for Mr. JOHNSON to talk about civil rights than about Vietnam, which we'd discussed earlier. Perhaps this was one reason why he seemed to have mellowed somewhat. He even occasionally acknowledged making a mistake or two while in office. Before, he'd seemed much more petulant and defensive; and mistakes or misunderstandings were by his adversaries or critics—not by him.

Yet, with this unbelievably restless, energetic man, mellowness was at best a relative condition. He obviously was not in the best of health. At least twice during our formal interview, he suffered chest pains; one of these times, he had to interrupt the filming to recover and take a pill. Yet his conversation made no concession to infirmity. His style was as animated and vigorous as ever. He talked of future plans—private, not public, ones—dealing in part with cattle and land sales. As he had done now and then in the past—despite his poor heart—he once more appeared to be neglecting his health. He smoked a great deal. Apparently, he was so nervous and cantankerous when not smoking that he was told to go ahead and smoke again, as a lesser evil. He also seemed to be ignoring his diet. At one meal, when dessert was rice pudding with whipped cream, he not only demolished one portion but then, as the conversation continued, leaned over and started eating his neighbor's portion as well.

Undisciplined zestfulness—conduct that others often considered crude—were of course one part of LYNDON JOHNSON's public record. There were other traits the public could not see, parts of Mr. JOHNSON that unfortunately froze up and disappeared during formal occasions, such as speeches or news conferences. One such trait was the personal warmth that emanated from this big, blustering Texan when you met him face to face. Another was the depth of his commitment to the have-nots in life. He made mistakes with his head. Whatever one thought of his Vietnam policy, there was no condoning his misleading the public about it as he did in '64 and '65; but at the same time, he was a man with a big heart. He learned about underprivileged minorities from teaching Mexican children in public school; about unemployment from his back-country neighbors; about poverty from his own youthful experiences. The lessons stuck. Publicly, he may have impressed some as an ambitious, self-serving wheeler-dealer. Actually, he was a man with genuine, lasting compassion for others.

So, it was nice to learn from him, during this last encounter, that a few days before, he'd received another phone call from President Nixon, who reportedly said that this time a cease-fire agreement really was in the works. If Mr. JOHNSON had to die without knowing the war that hurt him so badly was over, he at least passed on reasonably certain it was about to end. One may hope he also left us reassured of his own place in history, to be recalled, despite his imperfections, as a zealous public servant with a compelling dream of a better America—who made enormous strides to make that dream come true.

Hon. Joseph G. Minish
OF NEW JERSEY

Mr. Speaker, we have all heard many outstanding and well-deserved tributes to the memory of our recently departed Presidents, Harry S Truman and LYNDON B. JOHNSON.

The governing body of the township of Maplewood, N.J., which I am privileged to represent in the Congress, conducted memorial services for both President Truman and President JOHNSON. During these services, eulogies were delivered by Maplewood Mayor Robert Grasmere for President Truman and by Maplewood Commissioner Robert C. Klein for President JOHNSON.

I should like to share with my colleagues two of the most moving statements I have encountered on the lives and times of these great American leaders:

TRIBUTE TO PRESIDENT TRUMAN ON THE OCCASION
OF HIS DEATH

(By Mayor Grasmere)

The Presidency of the United States carries with it the most awesome responsibility of any position which the world's work has yet devised.

That Harry Truman bore this responsibility well and decisively, on occasion even jauntily, the pens of historians have, in the years since his retirement, begun to recognize. They are more accurately sketching the dimensions of a greatness which, at the time of his presidency was often hidden somewhat by the modest exterior and very human qualities of the man.

This somewhat reluctant titan of deed and decisions was drawn to the world's stage by the sudden death of President Roosevelt, but went on to secure the office in his own right in a campaign which is still a classic. He disregarded the critics, the press, the overwhelming odds and took his case to the people.

The people perhaps saw in him what one writer described as "Everyman". Most people could perceive his essential likeness to them and they took heart, for, in place of the sophistication which appeared to have totally pre-empted the presidency, there was once again the plainness and simplicity of an unmistakable man of the people—a man with very human faults and rather precious flaws.

A family man who would fly to his beloved daughter's defense with energy and salty language when he felt the press was overly critical and harsh toward her concert singing career.

A man who enraged great chefs on two continents by liberally salting and peppering prior to tasting culinary creations which had long and nerve wracking hours in preparation.

A man who appreciated Bourbon and Missouri Branch water and played the piano inexpertly.

A man who replied to a famous writer who had described his father as a failure saying, "My father was not a failure, he was the father of the President of the United States".

A man of immense loyalties and deep friendships who, nevertheless, didn't fear to incur the wrath of millions by removing from command perhaps the most capable military genius of this century when it appeared that presidential orders were being grudgingly carried out in Korea.

To this very human being were given some of the most soul-wracking decisions ever necessitated: Atomic warfare to prevent the predicted slaughter of a half-million G.I.'s had we, instead, engaged the non-surrendering Japanese on their home islands. The decision to save the eastern Mediterranean countries from the postwar pattern of communist subjugation through the Marshall Plan aid. The formation of NATO in Europe, and countless other decisions. He said and meant: "The buck" (often passed) "stops here".

During a Presidents term of office, the criticism which surrounds him is an inescapable and healthy fact of our national political life. Equally inescapable is the respect, often grudging, which we all have for the office and the man who bears its burden, inconceivable heavy to most of us. It is no accident that there are never more than one or two ex-presidents alive.

There is now only one, and we in Maplewood join Americans everywhere regardless of political affiliation in tribute to the man and the prodigious labors he performed for his nation and mankind.

That a man of such modest background could become a distinguished President is a particularly American story. When the story was unfolding, it gave many a pleased chuckle to Mr. Average Citizen, not the least of whom was Harry S. Truman of Independence, Missouri, 33rd President of these United States.

To paraphrase one of his pungent sayings which has become part of America—"He could—and did—stand the heat, and has now left us for other kitchens."

❧

TRIBUTE TO PRESIDENT JOHNSON ON THE OCCASION OF
HIS DEATH

(By Hon. Robert C. Klein)

LYNDON JOHNSON gave a lifetime of faithful and effective service to his State, his Nation and the World. As an individual, his energy and drive were sources of constant amazement to those around him, thriving on work with eighteen-hour days being the norm rather than the unusual. He developed an expertise as a political master that has seldom been equaled: Yet he remained a man who loved and needed people.

At one point he analyzed himself this way: "I am a Free man, an American, a United States Senator, and a Democrat, in that order. I am also a Liberal, a Conservative, a Consumer, a Parent, a Voter and not as young as I used to be nor as old as I expect to be—and I am all those things in no fixed order."

He proposed, fostered, persuaded, and eventually signed into Law, legislation in the areas of Health Care, Aid to Education, Immigration Reform, Poverty and Pollution Control.

He was the only President from a Southern State since Zachary Taylor yet he embraced the problems of the Negro and the poor. JOHNSON's Presidency touched the lives of millions in need of better Health Care, better Education, and expanded Civil Rights in such a way that the promise of America was more of a reality for more of our people than ever in our History.

President JOHNSON put it this way: The Negro says "No". Others say "Never". The voice of responsible Americans . . . Says, "Together". There is no other way. Until justice is blind to color, until education is unaware of race, until opportunity is unconcerned with the color of men's skins, emancipation will be a proclamation and not a fact. "Unfortunately many Americans live on the outskirts of hope—some because of their poverty, some because of their color, and all too many because of both. Our task is to help replace their despair with opportunity".

He was sworn in as the Thirty-Sixth President of the United States under the most adverse conditions confronting any American President at a time when even the stability of the Republic was questioned. His domestic reforms won him the admiration of the people and he was reelected with the widest margin of vote of any prior President.

Ironically the Vietnam War, in which he played so large a roll, frustrated many of his goals and overshadowed many of his accomplishments in the latter years of his Presidency. Yet he had a yearning desire to bring the War to a conclusion and achieve Peace. Unfortunately his passing occurred just hours before peace was announced. He always did what he conceived to serve the greatest good, for the greatest number. It remains for History to judge his performance but I believe the judgment will be overwhelmingly favorable and that his great domestic legislation and strong leadership will form an unforgettable monument in the Annals of History.

Hon. Richard Bolling
OF MISSOURI

Mr. Speaker, a thoughtful evaluation of the Johnson Presidency was published by the Economist on January 27, It follows:

A BETTER DAY FOR L. B. J.

(If LYNDON JOHNSON could have lived 24 hours longer he would have known that he was on the way to getting his true value in history)

It was LYNDON JOHNSON's last piece of bad luck that he died before the revival of his reputation was complete, and a single day before the event that could do more than anything else to complete it. Harry Truman had 20 years after he left the White House until his death in December for the historians to start to get a clear view of his presidency. Even Dwight Eisenhower had eight years. But LYNDON JOHNSON, who died on Tuesday, would still have been in the White House until last weekend but for the war whose end President Nixon announced on Wednesday night. Four years, in which the war was still dividing America, were not long enough for his contemporaries to reach a dispassionate reckoning of this remarkable man. LYNDON JOHNSON would have liked to know that the war was over at last, on terms he would have been glad to settle for. He would have liked even better to have lived to hear people eating even more of the savage things they said about him four or five years ago.

As it is, what has been written about him this week has been far more generous than would have been conceivable in 1968. Forgotten is the entirely personal dislike of his style and his manners that colored so much of the opposition to his policies. JOHNSON was a child of his background, the old south and the old west: he was ruthless in the pursuit of what he thought to be right, he could be as brutal with other men's feelings as he was sensitive about his own, he never had much time for people who tried to stand on the middle ground between right and wrong. And there was something even more damaging for his effectiveness while he was in the presidency. He was a man from an America that was ceasing to exist, trying to cajole and exhort and jolly along, in his own way, the new America that was growing up in the university-educated suburbs. He was a non-intellectual, non-middle-class survival of the frontier spirit in an increasingly middle-class half-intellectualized United States. There was not much communication between them. The things he said in public were rarely memorable; the memorable things he said pungently in private were too often unprintable. He was, for the politics of his time, and in the jargon he loathed, a disadvantaged man. But the personal disadvantages he carried with him have fallen into proportion even in these four years. It is no longer held against him that he was the sort of person he was.

Forgotten, too, is the accusation that he was responsible for the whole three-layered time of troubles that came upon America in the 1960s—the convergence of three separate crises that fed upon one another, but would each have happened even if the others had not.

It was JOHNSON who ordered the American army to take over the fighting in Vietnam in 1965. But he was not responsible for the fact that the early 1960s found America's blacks sufficiently aroused in their expectations of equality, and sufficiently self-confident at last, to turn to violence to make sure they got what they wanted. He was not responsible for the fact that in the later 1960s the long erosion of the Christian basis of morality, and the long dying of certainty in the two great political ideas of the nineteenth century, liberalism and marxism, brought about an explosion of desire for new certainties among the middle-class young all over the western world. The blacks and the young made Vietnam one of their issues, to be sure, and they carried some of the non-young, non-black with them, especially liberal America; but these were three separate movements of history, and it was just JOHNSON's bad luck to be there when they came together. It is not easy, or pleasant, to remember how fashionable it once was to blame him for everything: even among some people, to hint that the assassination of John Kennedy was not what the facts said it was. There was a good deal of hysteria in American politics throughout the 1960s, which came to the surface on that day in Dallas, and the Johnson presidency took the brunt of it.

THE FEAT, AND THE DOUBT

The United States has grown calmer since then, and the removal of what is irrelevant in the charges against JOHNSON has let the magnitude of his social reforms stand out unobscured. His legislative programs of 1964 and 1965—the anti-poverty program and civil rights act in the first year, and the measures the next year to get fuller voting rights for blacks, and to bring federal money to the help of poor schools and the aged sick—remain a monument to the ideas that dominated a third of a century of American politics. They were the last great act, and the justification, of the Democratic coalition that Roosevelt created in 1932. The curious thing is that the growing recognition of what JOHNSON achieved in getting those laws through Congress is now matched by a growing doubt about their effectiveness. It no longer seems as evident as it did to the Rooseveltians that these problems should, and will, yield to the application of federal willpower and federal money; the causes of inequality and discrimination may lie deeper than governments can reach. The politics of communal compassion, for the moment at any rate, have given ground to the politics of individual responsibility. But that change in the intellectual climate is not peculiar to America, and it takes nothing away from JOHNSON's achievement.

There remains the argument of the "fatal flaw," the decision about Vietnam that "destroyed" him, as this week's headlines have put it. Of course, JOHNSON knew that he had made serious mistakes over Vietnam. He underestimated the communists' resistance, and therefore the length of the war and the damage it would do to American morale; he authorized his army to use unnecessarily and, as it turned out, ineffectually brutal tactics in trying to find and beat its enemy. But he also saw the terrible weakness in the argument of the neo-isolationists—that the United States had no business to be even trying to fight such a war, because it ought to be concentrating on removing the flaws in its own society. The problems of poverty and oppression were far greater outside America, he would have replied; and the richest country in the world, the ultimate guarantor of the liberal idea, could not escape the responsibilities such a world imposed on it.

THE GREAT IF

Whether or not the United States has succeeded in doing what it wanted to do when JOHNSON dispatched that army in 1965, and whether it was worth doing at the cost it has turned out to involve, are still questions without clear answers. The previous article suggests that the terms Mr. Nixon has now achieved, on the basis of LYNDON JOHNSON's refusal to accept Hanoi's original terms, could make history's eventual answer very different from the glib assumption implied in so many of this week's headlines.

At least JOHNSON knew that the decision he took in 1965 came straight out of the body of liberal ideas that shaped his political life, in what he did both within America and toward the world. He knew before he died that if he had not acted in 1965 the verdict of events would already have gone the other way. There would be a communist-controlled government in South Vietnam, imposed without any test of its subjects' wishes; there would be the same sort of government in Laos, and a client state in Cambodia; China would probably not now have swung over to the relative moderation of Chou En-lai; and the rulers of countries south, east and west of Hanoi and Peking would be accommodating themselves to the demonstration of success flowing outward from those capitals. That is what the domino theory means. It it because of LYNDON JOHNSON that that has not happened by now. Harry Truman brought America out of the innocence of its power into the time of its maturity, when decisions were harder. And then LYNDON JOHNSON had to take the most difficult of all the decisions that confronted America in its maturity. His irreverent ghost will be content to see what history says about it.

Hon. Wright Patman
OF TEXAS

Mr. Speaker, the Members of the House are today privileged to honor and pay tribute to the memory of the 36th President of the United States, the Honorable LYNDON BAINES JOHNSON, once a Representative in this Chamber, a U.S. Senator, Vice President of the United States and thereafter the leader of this Nation from November 22, 1963, until January 20, 1969, during the tenure of the 88th, 89th, and 90th Congresses. President JOHNSON died suddenly at the age of 64 on January 22, 1973, deeply mourned and universally respected. My own association with President JOHNSON goes back over half a century when I was desk mate in the Texas Legislature with his father, Sam Houston Johnson, a rancher and former teacher from Johnson City, Tex. Young LYNDON visited his father frequently at Austin and although he was only 12 years of age he already stood 6 feet tall. He was a serious and purposeful young fellow interested even then in legislative procedures.

LYNDON JOHNSON's growth and early stature are particularly significant to me in view of the recurrent theme in a number of recent editorials and oral discussions and tributes that, in retrospect, President JOHNSON looms "larger than life," and I would like to comment on the meaning that can be attached to this widespread observation by knowledgeable people.

For those of us who knew him personally, there was his overwhelming physical presence, his vitality, his dynamic forceful energy, his straight-out eyeball-to-eyeball courage, and forthright, even aggressive demeanor—like a folk hero out of a saga from our frontier days—larger than life, like Davy Crockett or one of the storied martyrs who died at the Alamo. I suspect that for many Americans, LYNDON became a legend during his lifetime because here was a man who believed in America with his whole heart, the America he grew up in, not too far removed from the days of raw rampaging growth when there was no guilt attached to being strong or successful, before it was necessary to think too much about pollution; when the smoke that spewed from chimneys was less noted than the goods delivered to factory loading docks; when, in brief, America was bursting out all over, a great country, when the proudest thing you could imagine was to be a U.S. citizen. I am speaking of LYNDON JOHNSON the patriot, who could say with an earlier American, and I paraphrase—our country, may she always be in the right, but right or wrong, our country. Yes, LYNDON JOHNSON was bigger than life.

When the young JOHNSON departed Texas for his first term in Congress in 1937, he was relatively inexperienced, but he had good advice from his father. It soon became clear, however, that LYNDON could land on his feet like a cat under any circumstances and it was not long before he was considered one of the most able Members of Congress. In fact, stemming from his 11 years as a Representative he grew to love the House as the instrument of government closest to the people, and even when he became a Senator for Texas and then Vice President and President he never lost touch with House Members. It was during these years that he began his close association with Speaker Sam Rayburn, that other giant from Texas who served as Speaker longer than any other man.

It can be said to LYNDON JOHNSON's credit that there were two great Americans to whom he was particularly devoted, Franklin Delano Roosevelt and Sam Rayburn, and from each he learned about our Government, and that its one purpose is service to the people. As a further indication of his special regard for the House, I would like to relate an incident that occurred a year ago last Christmas when Mrs. Patman and I were weekend guests at the LBJ Ranch. We drove from there to the LBJ Library at Austin and the President used the car telephone to call his daughter, Luci Nugent, and had her meet us at the library with her young son, Lyn. When we got there the President said to his grandson:

Little Lyn, I've asked Mr. Patman to help you be elected to Congress when you grow old enough, and to prepare you to be ready for it, and I want you to go to Congress.

This is a pledge I will certainly keep if I am given the opportunity, and I think the President's wish for Lyn reflects his feeling that the House is closest of all to the people and that there is more pleasure to be derived from helping others than from any other walk of life.

Loving America and being proud of his heritage, LYNDON JOHNSON would not accept anything less than full citizenship for all the people, and because of him we have laws on the books that mean decent living for the greatest number of people in the history of mankind—his Great Society was more than a slogan, it was a workable "New Deal," the high watermark for the American education system, low-cost housing for the poor, assistance for the underprivileged, health services for the elderly—what has been called a physical and spiritual rebirth for all America. This was the definitive answer to FDR's battle call. You remember President Roosevelt's description of one-third of the Nation as ill-housed, ill-clothed, and ill-fed. It is my hope that we will not recede from the high standard of living that LBJ cajoled, schemed, and demanded for the people of this country—the greatest improvement in living conditions in the shortest period of time ever achieved by anyone. Is it possible to do too much good too fast? What ethic can condemn an ambition that is humble for itself and demanding only for others?

A great deal of LYNDON JOHNSON can be understood in the light of his deep religious feeling. LYNDON JOHNSON was a churchgoing man—he believed in the existence of a power for good and also that there is a power for evil. He stood foursquare against the forces in this world that would overthrow and pervert our democracy. From the official announcement of the peace agreement for Vietnam released just 3 days after President JOHNSON's death, I read the following:

Let us be proud of the two and a half million young Americans who served in Vietnam, who served with honor and distinction in one of the most selfless enterprises in the history of nations.

This bears repeating: "One of the most selfless enterprises in the history of nations." It is a point that is too frequently overlooked. There was absolutely no self-interest in our involvement in South Vietnam, and from this standpoint, it is probably the most altruistic of all wars. I quote again from a Washington editorial:

Perhaps when time and distance have restored a little perspective, another generation of Americans will look back and remember that we came to the aid of a small nation whose freedom was threatened and that, at the cost of much blood and gold, we sustained that freedom. Perhaps with the benefit hindsight they will recognize that because we fought in Vietnam we did not have to fight in Germany or in Burma.

And perhaps LYNDON JOHNSON will then be universally praised for his patriotic vision that looked so truly and so far into the future.

The people of this country had only one rival in the affections of President JOHNSON—his great and abiding love for the members of his family. When he had dark hours there was his wife, Lady Bird, a lovely and truly remarkable life partner to whom this country will ever be in debt for the composure, grace, and charm she brought to her home in the White House, and the splendid rearing of her fine daughters, Lynda and Luci. This strong family atmosphere was a great force for good in this country and served as a shining example for the fifty million other families that constitute this great Nation.

There are many people, and not all of them are Texans, who find there is no need to toll the years for a just appraisal of LYNDON JOHNSON's service to the Nation. We feel we know him

and his accomplishments. We know he was an intensely loyal man, loyal to family and friend, loyal to State and country, a Texan born and bred, true to the land, true to the people.

The editorials and news media continue their thousands of words attempting to define his place in history. I stand by the thoughts I wrote just 4 years ago as L. B. J. left the highest office in the land:

The Honorable LYNDON BAINES JOHNSON, President of the United States from November 22, 1963 to January 20, 1969, in my opinion stands among the honored few whose thoughts, words and actions have had a special significance in making this country productive, powerful and preeminent among nations; he shares the mantle of greatness with Presidents Lincoln, Wilson, Franklin Roosevelt, and Truman, with whom there is special reason to compare his five difficult years in the Nation's highest office. And I believe that Mrs. Johnson, whom we in East Texas know so well, fully merits the observation by Life Magazine that: "Quite possibly she is the best First Lady we have ever had." Last Thursday (January 16, 1969) on the floor of the House of Representatives, as Dean of the Texas Delegation, I was privileged to salute President and Mrs. Johnson, stating my absolute belief that history will accord high honor to their great accomplishments.

LBJ will, I know, in the years ahead work meaningfully in the best interests of the people. And I fully anticipate that Lady Bird will continue to give, particularly to Texans, her fine example and leadership in those special fields of beautification, conservation, and historic preservation which already bear the imprint of her tremendous interest and expert knowledge.

My predictions were borne out by President JOHNSON's devoted service after leaving the White House, and there can be no doubt that Lady Bird will continue to be an influential and inspirational force for good for many years to come. At this point, I would like to introduce for the Record the text of a statement made by LYNDON B. JOHNSON at Temple, Tex., in September 1972:

AS THE DAYS DWINDLE DOWN

(By Lyndon B. Johnson)

TEMPLE, TEX.—With the coming of September each year, we are reminded, as the song says, that the days are dwindling down to a precious few. By the calendar, we know that soon the green leaves of summer will begin to brown; the chill winds of winter will begin to blow; and—before we are ready for the end to come— the year will be gone.

If we permit our thoughts to dwell upon this perspective, days can become a melancholy season.

As it is with the calendar, so it sometimes seems to be with our country and its system. For there are those among us who would have us believe that America has come to its own September. That our days are dwindling down to a precious few. That the green leaves of our best season are turning brown and will soon be falling to the ground. That before long we will feel the first chill wind of a long American winter—and that our nation's stand as mankind's "last best hope" will be done.

For those who preach this prophecy—and for those who believe it—this period of our affairs can only be a melancholy season. But it is to that mood—and to the perceptions which foster it—that I want to address my remarks today.

Over the course of a long, full and gratifying life, I have seen many Septembers and have known many autumns. In public service—and in private life—I have experienced a full measure of unwelcome winters. Yet melancholy is not a mood which I have ever allowed to weigh for long upon my spirits.

I live—as I have always worked—by the faith that with each passing day, we are always approaching nearer to the beginning of a new springtime. It is by perspective I see our country now.

If I believe anything of this land—if I know anything of its people and their character—I believe and I know that we have not come to and are not approaching America's September.

On the contrary, it is my conviction—a conviction which deepens every day—that this land and its people are quickening with the new life and new potential of what will become the springtime of a new America.

I do not say this merely to offer reassurance in anxious times. Far from it. I intend what I say to be taken as a challenge—a challenge to every citizen of every age.

No nation can be more than the visions of its people. Americans cannot be more than we believe ourselves capable of becoming. Thus we are directly challenged to choose between two different perceptions of what we are and what we can make of America itself.

On the one hand, we can choose to guide our course by the light of the bright perceptions—of America the beautiful, America the just, America the land of the free and the home of the brave.

Or, on the other hand, we can choose to move toward the shadows of what some have called "the dark perception" of America the unclean, America the unjust, America the unworthy.

For myself—as, I am sure, for many of you—there is no real choice. I want to open the soul of America to the warm sunlight of faith in itself, faith in the principles and precepts of its birth, faith in the promise and potential of its resources and skills and people. Yet I know that, in these times, that is not easy.

For too long, we have permitted the dark perception to pervade our midst. Day after day, month after month, the portrayal of America as unclean, unjust and unworthy has been ground into the consciousness of our people.

We no longer see the blooming flowers for we are searching for the litter. We no longer celebrate the many fresh triumphs of justice for we are lingering over the residue of yesterday's shortcomings. We no longer measure the miles we have come toward a more humane, civil and peaceful world for we are too busy calibrating the remaining inches of times we are trying to escape and leave behind.

This is our clear and present challenge.

When we permit these dark perceptions to dominate us, we are allowing our future to be shaped by visions that are small and mean and diminishing to our potential. We are, in simple terms, dooming those who come after us to know what could only be a second-rate America.

This is a future which I am unwilling to accept.

I have devoted my time on this earth to working toward the day when there would be no second-class citizenship in America, no second-quality opportunity, no second-hand justice at home, no second-place status in the world for our ideals and benefits.

I do not intend now that second-rate visions shall set our course toward settling for a second-rate America. That is why I speak as I do now.

All through the pages of history we read the heart-rending stories of those who set out in quest of great goals and discoveries, yet when they were almost to the edge of success, they hesitated—not knowing or understanding how near they were to their aims. Out of that moment of hesitation, all too often they lost forever their opportunity to succeed.

In many respects, that seems to me to be a pattern we ourselves are in danger of repeating.

Over all the years of our nation's existence, we have been setting goals for ourselves and striving tirelessly to reach them. Those goals have been both the slogans and the substance of national affairs for generation after generation.

Full employment. Decent wages. Adequate housing. Education for everyone. Opportunity for all. Good health, good medical care, good hospitals for even the least among us. Above all, equal justice under the law for all our fellow men. America's goals have been simple and basic.

They have permeated and motivated all our institutions—churches and schools, professions and labor unions and corporations and foundations—as well as our government at every level.

All our American resources and strengths—private and public—have been committed to the effort and we have come very close to success.

Nowhere—over all the globe—have any people, under any other system, come nearer to fulfillment of such aspirations than we have under our system.

Yet, at the very moment we were near to realization, we have allowed our effort to go slack, our momentum to slow and we have entered a season of hesitation. Why?

Basically, I believe, it is because we have not understood—and still do not fully comprehend—where we are or what we are about.

Whatever may be your own perception of where we are and where we may be heading, let me say for myself that I see little today suggesting that our system is failing—but I see all too much which convincingly argues that by our doubts and hesitation we may be failing the promise and potential of our system.

We are not living in times of collapse. The old is not coming down. Rather, the troubling and torment these days stems from the new trying to rise into place.

With our nation's past efforts, with our long and faithfully kept commitments, with our infinite successes in so many fields, we have brought into being the materials, as it were, with which to construct a new America.

Faced with the task of such great dimensions, we have no time for melancholy. We have no cause for moroseness. We have work to be done—the greatest work any generation of Americans has ever faced. Believing that, I say—let's be on with our labors.

The essentials of a new America—a better America—

are all on hand and within our reach. It is our destiny—and, I believe, our duty—to take up our appointed positions and commence the labors that will change what needs change among us.

Our real challenge lies not in suppressing change but utilizing it to vitalize and energize our society. Change is not our enemy. On the contrary, this society has no deadlier danger than refusal to change.

That is what I believe our young Americans are trying—and have been trying—to communicate to us. With their fine young minds, fresh new learning and clear new vision, they are seeing many segments of our society as it needs to be seen and understood.

The most freightening thing that could happen to us today would be for us to close our eyes to new ideas, and to close our ears to those—particularly the young, in whom we have invested so much hope and effort through the years of our existence—who are trying to tell us how they would go about perfecting the visions of America.

It is just such spirit that we honor on this occasion. It is by restoring that spirit to our lives and our nation's life that we can honor our own trust as Americans.

Again, I return to the theme "larger than life," and I accept the thought that LYNDON JOHNSON was big—as America is big, that LYNDON JOHNSON was good—as America is good, and that with the help of God, some day our country will be all that he wished it to be.

Hon. Carl Albert

OF OKLAHOMA

Mr. Speaker, where have all the giants gone? In the month of January 1973, America interred two great former President, Harry S Truman and LYNDON BAINES JOHNSON. Old Glory flies at half-mast for two of the greatest leaders America—and the world—have ever known. But we are not bankrupt—their legacies will enrich this Nation for years to come.

LYNDON BAINES JOHNSON devoted all of his vigor, his vision, his productive years to the service of his country. Having known him intimately as Congressman, Senate majority leader, as Vice President, and as President, I know that LYNDON BAINES JOHNSON lived and breathed in the work rhythm of America. He was the original American. His view of his country was similar to that of the frontiersman which in many respects he was. He had a Southwesterner's unrestricted view of the panorama of his homeland. He challenged America's greatest problems—civil rights, poverty, education, housing, health. All things seemed possible to him. He made them seem possible to much of America, those Americans who gave him his historic election victory in 1964.

America recognized greatness in the President who entered the oval room in the sorrowing, uncertain days which followed the assassination of John F. Kennedy. This country can never be anything but grateful for the perfect manner in which he carried out the change of command under such terrible duress. Could any man fault his stability, his compassion, his vision? He held the Nation on a steady course; he opened the Johnson era with the burden of melancholy, but also with determination to achieve the goals of an administration of which he had been a part. He branded them as his own, and he breathed life into them.

The plight of the common man lay deep in his understanding. He set out to assure that every American could go to the polls and vote, that every American would be able to find an exit from the pit of poverty, have decent housing, the opportunity to be educated to the limit of his abilities, the means with which to maintain his health and cure his ills, a fighting chance in the marketplace to get a dollar in value for his hard earned paycheck dollar. LYNDON JOHNSON did not simply talk about the problems of the minorities, the poor, the sick, the elderly, the young uneducated, and the old untrained. He called Congress to the White House: He discussed these problems with us, we exchanged information, we planned programs, we passed them and he signed them into law. Today those statutes are his epitaph. They will endure longer than all the tributes which will be heaped above his bier and written into his obituary.

LYNDON BAINES JOHNSON was a giant-sized President. Where faint-hearted men might have hesitated, he acted, letting the chips fall where they may. He knew that above all things the man in the White House must endure the loneliness, perhaps the blame, of having had the last word.

As his great predecessor, Harry S Truman, LYNDON JOHNSON accepted the philosophy that a man who could not bear the heat must get out of the kitchen. They were much alike in their philosophy of government. They were great leaders, born leaders and trained, and while they sought counsel and aid from Government heads and advisers, and called for the confidence and support of the people, they were prepared to make hard decisions based on their own conscience and their own judgment, and particularly their understanding of the philosophy of our Constitution, the commitment and mission of the greatest possible republic on earth.

LYNDON JOHNSON was the most experienced public servant ever to have occupied the White House. There was no arm of Government, person, program, agency a stranger to him. He could not have begun to set down the entire range of information, insights, and knowledge he had acquired over a lifetime, even in his formative years, of observing and being a part of National Government. He held every high elective office in the land at the Federal level—Congressman, Senator—chosen also by his own party as majority leader of the Senate—Vice President and President.

LYNDON BAINES JOHNSON was without peer in his strength, without peer in his dedication, without peer in his ability to produce solid results, without peer in his determination to make America better than he found it when he entered 1600 Pennsylvania Avenue. The great disappointment of his life, of course, and perhaps the fact which accounts for his early demise as surely as it did those of the returning American servicemen whose loss broke his heart, was his inability to end the war. None can say he did not seek an honorable withdrawal from Indochina with the same diligence that he pursued successfully the great domestic programs with which he is credited. He laid the groundwork for peace before he left the White House. It was his misfortune that the flow of events toward peace did not run their course within his term of office. In the words of Shakespeare:

There is a tide in the affairs of men which when taken at the flood, leads on to fortune.

The crest did not come, and the President did not have the opportunity to claim the peace he so assiduously sought. It is comforting to me to know that President Nixon had advised him of the imminent announcement of the truce prior to his death.

No President soared to greater heights in his attainments. Perhaps none stirred such strong feelings both of opposition and support. How could it be otherwise in a period when divisions were springing up on every side, when values were changing, when society and government were under challenge, and all Americans suffered trauma and uncertainty? It was President JOHNSON's dream to lead a united people in the creation of the Great Society. He certainly left a better society.

I cannot believe other than that the judgment of history will say LYNDON BAINES JOHNSON was one of the greatest most courageous, most American Presidents, of all time.

In a personal vein, may I conclude by saying that President JOHNSON's death was not only a great national loss. I have had to say "good-bye" to a personal friend with whom I have served and worked for many years, one who has always been on my side in every moment of triumph and difficulty. So has his wonderful wife, Lady Bird. She and her two daughters, Linda and Lucy, will always be numbered among my friends and helpers. To them and their fine husbands and children and to all the host of friends and relatives of the late President, my wife, Mary, and my children, Mary Frances and David, extend our deepest sympathy and love.

Mr. Speaker, among all those who knew and worked with LYNDON BAINES JOHNSON during his long career in the Capitol and in the White House, none was closer to him than former Speaker John W. McCormack of Massachusetts. John W. McCormack was in the House of Representatives every day that LYNDON JOHNSON served in the House of Representatives. John W. McCormack was a member of the House leadership every day that LYNDON JOHNSON was a member of the Senate leadership. John W. McCormack was Speaker of the House of Representatives every day during the Presidency of LYNDON BAINES JOHNSON.

The Honorable John W. McCormack has made a statement on his friend, his close co-worker, the late President JOHNSON, and I ask the indulgence of the House to listen to me as I read this statement of our former beloved Speaker:

STATEMENT OF HON. JOHN McCORMACK

The recent death of former President LYNDON BAINES JOHNSON took from our midst one of the great Presidents of American history. President JOHNSON was very kind in his relationships with other people, but he was very firm in performing the duties of his office. He met every responsibility which came his way as a Member of the House of Representatives, as Majority Leader of the Senate, as Vice President and, particularly, as President of the United States.

The sudden and tragic death of President John Fitzgerald Kennedy thrust the Presidency, with all its challenges and problems upon LYNDON JOHNSON. Our people soon recognized that in President JOHNSON the country had an outstanding leader. During his active term of office, he manifested the great qualities of leadership with which he was possessed.

The eminent role played by our late beloved President in that critical part of the world is history, his firm desire that peace and justice with honor should prevail in the world will insure his place of prominence in history. Time has clearly shown his courageous decision in relation to the crisis in the Dominican Republic was sound and in the national interest of our country. Time will also show his decisions in relation to Viet Nam, and more broadly all of Southeast Asia, including our Far Eastern defenses were sound and, in light of existing circumstances, were consistent with the national interest of the United States.

LYNDON JOHNSON was not only a great man, he was a good man, with an intense love of all human beings, particularly the poor, the sick, the handicapped, the underprivileged, and those against whom discrimination in any way was directed. He recognized in a most vital way the importance of education.

While he was President over 400 major pieces of legislation recommended by him were enacted into law. These laws make America a stronger nation and a better place in which to live. Laws recommended by President Johnson and enacted into law have favorably affected every phase of life and liberty in this nation. He has enriched the lives of each and every one of us.

President JOHNSON gave to our country a leadership in thought, action and accomplishment that will always be a monument to his memory.

For many years I enjoyed a very close friendship with President JOHNSON. I am deeply saddened by his death.

I extend to Mrs. Johnson and to her daughters, Lynda and Lucy and their loved ones my deep sympathy in their great loss and sorrow.

Hon. Gerald R. Ford
OF MICHIGAN

Mr. Speaker, literally millions of words have been written and spoken in recent weeks about the late President LYNDON B. JOHNSON. For this reason it is extremely difficult to add anything that has not already been said except perhaps on a personal basis, but at this time I do want to pay my very personal respects to his memory.

There have been 10 Presidents of the United States in my lifetime, and five during the years I have been a Member of Congress. They have all been extremely different personalities, from very different backgrounds, so it is very hard to compare them and it is too early to say how history will finally rate them. About all we can say is that the problems facing the world and this country following World War II have been infinitely greater and more complex than previous Presidents had to deal with in safer and saner times, when we did not have nuclear weapons and instant communications and worldwide commitments.

By any standard President JOHNSON did his best, as I think all Presidents do, but he became

President under especially trying circumstances, perhaps more overwhelming than have faced any Vice President since the previous President Johnson took the oath upon the assassination of President Lincoln. It would be my judgment at this time, Mr. Speaker, that history will undoubtedly record that LYNDON B. JOHNSON met the test of that difficult period.

My first close contact with LYNDON JOHNSON as President was when he appointed me and six others in late November of 1963 to what has come to be known as the Warren Commission. He gave Chief Justice Warren and the six others on that commission a responsibility to dig out the facts and to come to conclusions concerning the tragic death of President John F. Kennedy. When our report was concluded, President JOHNSON commended us for our efforts and thanked each and every member of the Warren Commission for the job that he had assigned us. All of us who had that serious responsibility were grateful for the support he gave us at that time and also after the report was published when many critics were attacking our conclusions.

Time has dimmed the memory of how manfully President JOHNSON took up the reins of leadership and held a shocked and grief-stricken nation together during those dark hours in late 1963, and he did so despite the reservations of some within his own party as well as others. It is a tribute to him that he retained many key officials from his predecessor's administration as his top advisers.

President JOHNSON inherited a nasty war which was already unpopular and which he was unable to resolve even at the high price of declining to seek another term in office. As one of the leaders of the "loyal opposition" in Congress during the elected term of President LYNDON JOHNSON, I know firsthand how much anguish the Vietnam War caused him and how desperately he longed for peace under honorable conditions.

Mr. Speaker, a few days before he left office in 1969, I was called to the White House one weekend for what I supposed was another crisis briefing of the bipartisan leadership. Instead, Mr. Speaker, I found myself ushered upstairs to the Lincoln bedroom and alone with President JOHNSON. We talked for quite awhile casually about many things—our differences as well as our many areas of agreement during the previous 4 years.

Mr. Speaker, it was obvious to me that he seemed to be in no hurry, for once. Before I left, he thanked me for my firm support of his hard decisions as Commander in Chief, and said that while we had had our little differences in the political arena, he wanted to leave Washington without any enemies left behind.

Let me assure you, Mr. Speaker, I am deeply grateful for such an experience with a President I greatly respected, a man I admired, and a friend for whom I learned to have a wonderful affection.

Mr. Speaker, after he returned to Texas, President LYNDON JOHNSON wrote me on several occasions very warm and very friendly letters, which I shall cherish as mementos of our fine relationship.

Finally, Mr. Speaker, I want to repeat a comment that I heard often during the memorial services for the late President. Most appropriately, people would say as they watched Mrs. Johnson and her family, that any man with such a truly great wife and two such lovely daughters must have contained goodness and greatness in his character. He had both, and many more outstanding characteristics.

He was a complex individual, surely, and certainly a controversial one, but I know he loved his country and his family and his friends.

We are all poorer for his passing.

Hon. Thomas P. O'Neill, Jr.
OF MASSACHUSETTS

Mr. Speaker, at this time I place in the Record following my own remarks, the remarks of U.S. Representative J. J. Pickle.

He made these remarks at the memorial service in the U.S. Capitol for the late President, LYNDON BAINES JOHNSON.

As a Member of Congress, I know I express the sentiments of so many of his colleagues when I say that the inspiring words of Mr. Pickle really moved a mournful nation that particular day.

Mr. Speaker, our Nation deeply mourns the untimely passing of an eminent leader and distinguished American, President LYNDON JOHNSON. It is with the greatest respect and admiration that I pay tribute today to my former colleague and dear friend.

LYNDON BAINES JOHNSON was a man who clearly placed America first and foremost in his list of priorities, evidenced by his constant hard work and sacrifice even at the expense of his physical well being.

Born of humble origins, he rose to the highest position in our Nation's Government. After attending high school in Johnson City, LYNDON worked for several years before attending Texas State Teachers College, from which he was graduated in 1930.

Two years later, he came to Washington assisting Representative Richard Kleberg of Texas. From that time until his retirement from public office in 1969, President JOHNSON continued to serve our Nation with great dedication and purpose. His personal courage and integrity are well known by all who worked with him.

As he moved up the political ladder from Representative to Senate majority leader to President, LYNDON JOHNSON continued his unrelenting devotion to each succeeding task. For President JOHNSON, no legislation received too much attention. Diligence and resourcefulness marked JOHNSON's years in Washington.

Party affiliations were least important among his priorities. He once said:

I have followed the personal philosophy that I am a free man, an American, a public servant, and a member of my party, in that order always and only.

He was partisan only in the sense of his unswerving devotion to the important and necessary causes which he championed throughout his career: education, medical care, and civil rights. In his own words, he believed that—

Until justice is blind to color, until education is unaware of race, and until opportunity is unconcerned with the color of men's skins . . . emancipation will be a proclamation . . . which falls short of assuring freedom to the free.

And against doctor's orders, LYNDON BAINES JOHNSON made his last public speech calling for a greater national effort to provide equal opportunity for blacks.

President JOHNSON did not want a good society. He aspired for a great society. In his years as President he did more for the minorities of this country through his great society programs than anyone else in the history of the United States. He was a man who made a vital distinction in assessing the benefits of our national domestic commitments. He asked:

Not how much, but how much good, not only how to create wealth, but how to use it, and not only how fast we are going but where we are going. The great society proposes as the first test of a nation: the quality of its people.

Under his leadership, an extraordinary number of bills aimed at eliminating some of the severe problems crippling our Nation's welfare were passed. Our debt to LYNDON JOHNSON for his accomplishments on the domestic front has not yet been realized.

And in the realm of foreign affairs, JOHNSON acted without regard for his own personal ambitions, but in what he believed were the interests of America.

Few men if any desired peace more than LYNDON JOHNSON. Acting with courage and conviction in an attempt to realize that peace, he was greatly disturbed when he failed. If historians are to judge LYNDON JOHNSON by his own motto:

A President's hardest task is not to do what is right, but to know what is right.

Then he must be remembered as one of our greatest Presidents. He saw injustice and tried to right it, and he saw peace and desired to achieve it.

It was ironic that his father, Samuel Johnson, whose ambition it was that his son achieve political prominence, should have died shortly before his son attained that goal. Similarly, it is ironic that President JOHNSON, who so desired peace, should pass away before his desire could be fulfilled.

The Nation has lost another great leader, and I have lost a dear friend. Mrs. O'Neill joins me in extending our deepest sympathies to Mrs. Johnson and the Johnson family.

The remarks of Mr. Pickle follow:

REMARKS OF U.S. REPRESENTATIVE J. J. PICKLE DURING MEMORIAL SERVICES FOR THE HONORABLE LYNDON B. JOHNSON IN THE U.S. CAPITOL

Mr. President, Mrs. Johnson and Family, my colleagues and Fellow Americans:

LYNDON BAINES JOHNSON was a President *for the people*. Working *for the people* came easily and naturally to his Presidency. It was the fulfillment of a career as Texas National Youth Administrator, Congressman, Senator, and Vice President.

When I was elected in 1963 to the 10th Congressional District seat of Texas that LYNDON JOHNSON filled in 1937, I sought his advice. He gave me one guiding principle: "Congressman, when you vote, just vote *for the people*."

This was the same principle that guided LYNDON JOHNSON's public life.

Wherever he served, we were struck by the bigness of this man, his energy, his drive, his ambition, his quest for perfection in all he did and in all he asked us to do.

His demand for the best within us was relentless. He persuaded, cajoled and drove us until we fulfilled potentials we never knew we had. And, when we did our best, he wrapped his long arms around us—for he loved us and he loved to see us and our country at our best.

To those of us who were closest to him from the start, we understood him for we were "his boys." He meant to us what the great Sam Rayburn meant to him and what Franklin Roosevelt meant to both of them.

We could sense even then the reach for greatness deep within this man. We were joined by dozens, then hundreds of young men and women that LYNDON JOHNSON gathered around him over the course of his public life—not simply to serve him, but to help him achieve his vision of America.

His ambition for himself was as nothing compared to his ambition for America. As hard as he drove America toward this vision, and asked us to work for a Great Society, he *gave more* of himself to that goal than he ever asked of any of us.

As a young man, he experienced poverty and witnessed discrimination. He learned first-hand about drought and parched earth, about stomachs that weren't full and sores that weren't healed. He brought water and electricity and housing to the Congressional District which he served. As a Congressman, he knew what it was like to be a poor farmer, a working man without a job, a Black or a Mexican-American, and he set about changing life for the disadvantaged among his constituents.

As Senator and Vice-President, he saw that it was just as difficult to be poor or unemployed, or Black or Mexican-American in the big cities of the Northeast and West Coast as it was in Central Texas.

His Presidency changed America for the good, and America will never be the same again.

In 1964, the people gave him the greatest vote of confidence any President has ever received in our history. In turn, he voted his Presidency *for the people*. Medicare became the right of every older American, rather than a dream. He authored the first Elementary and Secondary Education Act in our nation's history, and the Head Start Program which bears the imprint of Mrs. Johnson so vividly, to give every American child the opportunity to go to school and develop his talents to the fullest. He saw the landscape ravaged by American technology and he moved to clean our air and our water, to protect our land, and to turn the brilliance of that technology to the restoration of our natural environment.

He knew well what that technology could do, for he guided our space program as Senator, Vice-President, and President until America placed the first man on the Moon.

LYNDON JOHNSON was proudest of his achievements in the field of civil rights:

The 1964 Civil Rights Act, the grand-daddy of them all, which opened public accommodations and jobs to all Americans regardless of color; and

The 1968 Fair Housing Act which gives every American regardless of his color, the right to live in any house he can afford.

By his own testimony, LYNDON JOHNSON's greatest achievement in civil rights was the Voting Rights Act of 1965. As he said shortly before he left the White House:

"It is . . . going to make democracy real. It is going to correct an injustice of decades and centuries. I think it is going to make it possible for this Government to endure, not half slave and half free, but united."

He waged the war he loved—the War on Poverty—

with more energy and imagination than all the Presidents who preceded him. He gave even more of himself to his efforts to end the war he hated—the War in Vietnam. Before he left office, he opened the negotiations in Paris which last night culminated in the peace agreement he wanted so much.

However history may judge LYNDON JOHNSON's foreign policy, that, too, was directed by his desire to help all the people. He saw foreign assistance not as a military program, but as a program to feed and clothe, heal and educate the disadvantaged people of the world. His concern in Southeast Asia was for the people of Vietnam, North as well as South, and he offered the resources of this nation to help rebuild both countries.

He devoted his life "to working toward the day when there would be no second-class citizenship in America, no second-quality opportunity, no second-hand justice at home, no second-place status in the world for our ideals and benefits."

Theodore Roosevelt once said:

"It is far better to dare mighty things and to enjoy your hour of triumph even though it may be checkered occasionally by failure, than to take stock with those poor souls who neither enjoy much nor suffer much because they live in a gray twilight that knows neither victory nor defeat."

LYNDON JOHNSON never lived in a gray twilight.

He experienced and appreciated the joy of the Democratic process when it served to enrich the lives of the people. And he suffered with the people when that process did not serve them soon or well enough.

His was a time of turbulence because it was a time of dramatic change. But he never saw that change as a time of collapse or deterioration. He put it best himself when he said:

"The old is not coming down. Rather, the troubling of torment of these days stems from the *new* trying to rise into place."

His closest friend and wisest advisor was his wife. She inspired his concern for our environment. Most of all, Lady Bird Johnson understood her husband and he understood her as few men and women dare hope to understand and love each other. It is no wonder that their daughters, Lynda Bird and Luci, brought so much credit to their family, *and to our country*, for they came out of this beautiful bond and were privileged to share in this close and loving relationship.

LYNDON JOHNSON is a President who came from the land, from the Hill Country of Texas, where sun and rain are the most precious values a man can tie to; and where God's will is seen and felt and gauged by the sky and the wind.

It was from this land that LYNDON JOHNSON drew his strength. It was from his family that he rekindled the love he gave to his country. And it was from the potential he saw in the people that he drew his vision of America. And he knew—as no other man—that human dignity and economic justice were essential to our people to set them free to achieve that vision.

This was a man who saw his purpose in life and lived his creed:

"Throughout my entire career, I have followed the personal philosophy that I am a free man, an American, a public servant, and a member of my Party—and in that order."

He saw also his Presidency and his vision of America when he told the Congress and this Nation:

"I do not want to be the President who built empires or sought grandeur or extended dominion.

"I want to be the President who educated young children to the wonders of their world.

"I want to be the President who helped to feed the hungry and to prepare them to be taxpayers instead of tax-eaters.

"I want to be the President who helped to end hatred among his fellow men and who promoted love among the people of all races and all regions and all parties.

"I want to be the President who helped to end war among the brothers of this earth."

And he did all these things.

From his new "Vantage Point," the President will rest in his beloved Hill Country, where he has told us his Daddy before him said he wanted to come home. Come home—"where folks know when you're sick and care when you die."

Two hundred million Americans care, Mr. President. We care—and we love you.

Hon. John Young
OF TEXAS

Mr. Speaker, with the passing of the 36th President of the United States a great void was left in the country, in the world, and, of course, in the dear family he loved so much.

A void was left with those of us who had the privilege and honor of being somewhat close to him.

The area that I represent in Texas feels especially close to LYNDON JOHNSON and to his memory. As a youth he worked in a cotton gin down in Robstown, Tex., where he earned a part of the money he needed to get his college education.

Then some years later his first public experience in Washington was gained through his position as administrative assistant to the distinguished Richard M. Kleberg, Congressman from the 14th Congressional District of Texas, which I have the honor to represent here now.

So, Mr. Speaker, we all lament more than anybody can say over the passing of this man, which means so much to us. We all feel a great gratification and pride, in that we know he had the great faculty that wherever he went his presence was felt.

People understood him. People knew him well. Those who knew him well knew him favorably.

I suppose there is no man in the history of this country who has had a greater career in the legislative field than our distinguished friend LYNDON JOHNSON.

Of course, Presidents do not avoid history. Presidents like LYNDON JOHNSON make history. When history is written, history will tell what happened.

Time here does not permit me or anyone else, for that matter, to enumerate or to chronicle the many, many great accomplishments of this great American President, this great American individual.

But I must say that particularly in the field of civil justice, in the field of education, and in the field of human dignity this President not only did more than any other President in the history of this country, but in this field of justice and education and dignity he did more than all of the previous Presidents combined.

And by that measure, Mr. Speaker, I will add that LYNDON JOHNSON in the field of justice and dignity and education did more than any other man in the history of the world.

So it is no wonder, aside from the grave personal feeling of vacancy that we will all have, then, that this country will miss our friend, and it is no wonder that his presence in the world will be missed.

Mr. Speaker, I suppose no greater compliment could be paid to anybody than simply to say that our country and our world was better off for his having been in it.

Hon. George H. Mahon
OF TEXAS

Mr. Speaker, I have been pleased to observe the deep feeling which has been apparent in the remarks made here today about LYNDON JOHNSON. This is not hard to understand. It is all because LYNDON JOHNSON meant so much to so many of us personally, aside from what he meant to the Nation and to the world.

It is hard to know what one should say about this warm and devoted friend who has left us— this great American. I shall not speak at length. Others will recount many things about this man but we all have so many cherished memories of our association with him over so many years we know not where to start or what to say.

LYNDON JOHNSON was much beloved but he was much criticized in certain quarters prior to his departure from the White House and thereafter.

All Presidents receive a full measure of criticism. It is often not easy for a public official to

deal with criticism. All public officials long to be loved by the people, and certainly LYNDON JOHNSON yearned for the support and good will, and shall I say, the love of his fellow man. And I must say he had it in large measure.

Mr. Speaker, Mrs. Mahon and I spent a couple of days and nights at the Johnson ranch with the Johnsons in late October of last year. At that time I talked to him about the criticism he suffered and as we talked it became obvious to me that he considered this to be a matter of little consequence. He was not disturbed or embittered. He was most tolerant. It was clear to me that LYNDON JOHNSON was so convinced he had done the right thing, insofar as he knew the right that he could not be bothered by the criticisms which were made of him.

Furthermore, Mr. Speaker, LYNDON JOHNSON knew that he had a place in history. I feel certain that the Members of Congress agree with me that LYNDON JOHNSON's place in history is secure. He earned it. None of the critics can ever take away from him his shining record of achievement.

LYNDON JOHNSON had great respect for our institutions and for our system of government. This was nowhere more evident than in the great respect he showed for the Office of the President.

The relations between the Republican Party and the Democratic Party are naturally characterized at times by spirited partisanship. That is our system. But, when President JOHNSON laid down the responsibility of the Presidency, he did everything he could to provide for a smooth transition and to remove stumbling blocks from the path of his successor. He felt his successor should have the fullest opportunity to address himself to the awesome responsibilities of the Presidency—and no one was as acutely aware of the responsibilities and problems confronting Richard Nixon as was President JOHNSON. President JOHNSON was most considerate of his successor and President Nixon extended to him great respect and friendship.

I have heard President JOHNSON say many times we cannot have but one President at a time. In office President JOHNSON conducted himself in an exemplary way. When he departed from the Presidency he conducted himself in the most commendatory and gracious manner as a former President.

With pride I join in the salute being given today to his memory. My wife Helen joins me in sentiments of warmest affection for Lady Bird and for his wonderful and talented daughters and loved ones who meant so much to him. They all have our deepest sympathy.

Hon. W. R. Poage
OF TEXAS

Mr. Speaker, there have been but a few men who have changed the history of nations. LYNDON JOHNSON was one of these men. Certainly he was President of the United States. Thirty-six other men have been President of the United States. We can all probably name no more than six who have greatly influenced the history of the United States. LYNDON JOHNSON was one of those.

He did not guide our country to independence; he did not expand our boundaries; he did not establish the sovereignty of the Federal Government over the States; nor did he lead us into a world war. But he did establish the responsibility of the Federal Government for meeting the needs and the aspirations of our people in their everyday activities.

I was not one who agreed with all of his reforms. He held a somewhat more liberal philosophy than that which I accept. He believed that the Government could and should do for the individual many of those things which to me seem to be both improper and impossible for the Government to achieve. At the same time I never questioned his sincere belief that what he proposed was going to be beneficial to the people whom he loved. There have always been, and there are now, individuals in our Government who have, and do hold, his views relative to the power of Government to change the attitude of individuals, but these officials have never been able to translate their views into action as LYNDON JOHNSON did.

When he saw suffering he looked to the Government for a cure and in most cases he provided, if not a cure, an improvement, because he was a compassionate man. He was not so concerned with the perpetuation of our form of government as he was with using it to provide immediate relief where he felt a change was needed. And he never refused to take a part of what he felt was needed because he could not get all of what he sought, because he was a practical man.

LYNDON JOHNSON loved the people of America and he secured for them every benefit which he could grasp. He was a man of great intellect and of great ability, but a still greater heart. He was impatient with those of us who sometimes questioned the method he suggested for giving aid to our people. He was concerned almost entirely with results and he got results. He fed the hungry; he protected the weak; and he gave dignity to those who had been denied recognition. He was willing to sacrifice what some of us felt were important principles of government and of economics. At times he found it necessary to sacrifice his friends when they stood in the way of what he believed to be essential for the American people. But he proved his sincerity through his unhesitating willingness to sacrifice himself for the same causes. He only asked of others what he himself was willing to give.

I think it is clear that LYNDON JOHNSON would have been reelected by an overwhelming vote had he run for a second full term, and I have no doubt but what he wanted that second term most desperately. But he was convinced that his withdrawal from the Presidency would enhance the possibility of peace in Southeast Asia. He never whimpered. He saw his duty and he did it. He stepped aside. He applied the same harsh rule to his own ambitions that he so often applied to others.

LYNDON JOHNSON loved his associates and all people of his country. He wanted to be loved in return but it was inevitable that a man with such strong views and such resolute action would make outspoken enemies and indeed his enemies were vocal. I think LYNDON JOHNSON overestimated the number of his enemies and I think he was prone to mistakingly include among that category all those who disagreed with his policies. As a matter of fact, he had remarkably few enemies. Most of the American people admired the man and respected him even when they disagreed with him.

To most of the American people, LYNDON JOHNSON's life was entirely political. They knew him only as a statesman. In this field those who were not blinded by prejudice certainly knew him as one who demanded much and who gave much. "No greater love hath any man that he lay down his life for a friend." Politically, LYNDON JOHNSON laid down his life for his friends when he refused to run for reelection because he believed by so doing he could save the lives of both American and Vietnamese boys. But LYNDON JOHNSON was not simply a politician or even simply a statesman. He was one of the greatest politicians that the country has ever known, but he was also a husband, a father, and a citizen of a frontier community. He built a home and reared a family on a remote Texas ranch. He was always just as proud of his home and his family, of his wife, his daughters, and his grandchildren as he was of his achievements as President. He had a right to be, because his was an outstanding family.

We in Texas are proud of all of the Johnson family and, while we in the Texas congressional delegation miss our personal friend, we are fully aware of his great impact on our country and on the lives of our people. But at the same time we share in the pride which his family has and which this Nation has in his accomplishments.

Hon. Jack Brooks
OF TEXAS

Mr. Speaker, America has lost a great leader and I have lost a longtime personal friend.

LYNDON JOHNSON was a man of rare capability, compassion, and understanding, who wanted to be remembered as the President who did the most for the well-being and dignity of our citizens. History will reflect he was a great President and, as time passes, America will become increasingly grateful for all he did.

I have known President JOHNSON and his lovely wife, Lady Bird, throughout my years in public office. We served together in the Congress and I worked with him to get his programs enacted when he was in the White House.

Some of America's greatest moments in history occurred because LYNDON JOHNSON was President. All Americans live better because of his concern for people, for equality, for health care for the elderly, for opportunity for the poor, for the sanctity of the American democratic system.

I shall be forever grateful that he was my friend. Although he had the greatest power that man had ever known, he never lost his humanity. He could be abrupt and overbearing when he needed to get things done in a hurry, but he was never petty or mean. He somehow always found time to think of his family, his friends, and those who needed his help.

Just last month, I visited with him in New Orleans and a few weeks before, he had Charlotte, my children, and me as his guests at the ranch. He seemed to be enjoying the chance he finally had to visit with his family and his friends. He took Jeb and Kate to see his ranch,

the cattle, and some of the game he kept there. He thoroughly enjoyed himself and the children returned his warm affection.

I regret that he did not live longer to enjoy this leisure and time to indulge himself in some of the pleasures we take as common but that duty denied him—a quiet family life—undisturbed visits with his wife, children, and grandchildren—time to relax and reflect on his accomplishments.

His lovely wife, Lady Bird, is a most gracious lady and to her and her fine children and grandchildren I extend my deepest sympathy.

I had hoped that he would live another 30 years. Although this could not be, I am grateful that I knew him, I am grateful for his advice and counsel, I am grateful that we had him as our President. Time will honor this man in a way that no amount of public acclaim ever could during his lifetime.

Hon. O. C. Fisher
OF TEXAS

Mr. Speaker, I share with my colleagues the sadness and lament concerning the death on last January 22 of LYNDON B. JOHNSON, 36th President of the United States.

It happened that the late President lived much of his life and died at his beloved LBJ Ranch, located in the district in Texas which I represent. That area, through which coursed the beautiful spring-fed Pedernales River, was very much a part of the life of the man whose loss we mourn here today. He loved the verdant hillsides that abound there. It was a source of strength and inspiration for the man who rose from the ranks of humble origin to become the Nation's leader during one of the most turbulent periods in American history.

I recall that during the time he was convalescing from his first heart attack I was invited to visit him and spend the night at the LBJ Ranch. As an indicator of his personal concern for others, after dinner that evening I accompanied him on a visit he made to neighboring homes. He stopped at several places to inquire about the health and well-being of families and express his concern and solicitude. He wanted to know what he might be able to do for them. It will be recalled that he was at that time majority leader of the U.S. Senate.

Throughout the time he served in the Congress, as Vice President, as President, and right down to the time of his death, LYNDON JOHNSON took a very active interest in problems associated with the livestock industry in that area. When I would see him he would often inquire about the current prices of cattle, sheep, and goats. And he would want to know what problems needed the attention of those of us who represented the growers.

It goes without saying that the "Sage of the Pedernales" enjoyed many friendships among those who made their homes in the "LBJ country," as it came to be known. To many he was a pioneer in terms of progress and achievement in the area of State, national, and world affairs. Shortly after JOHNSON's death, an admirer, Mrs. Judy Poe of nearby Bandera, wrote this poem to his memory:

FAREWELL, O PIONEER

Across the land a tolling bell
Peals a song of sad farewell.

Each wind-swept hill with cedar head
Nods in grief above his bed.

The live oaks twist their naked hands
While lonely sheep roam overland.

On the range, the moan of cattle
In the barn an empty saddle.

Farewell, farewell, O Pioneer
Farewell, O mighty friend

Farewell, farewell, O Pioneer
Who loved his fellow-men.

Already assessments are being made of LYNDON B. JOHNSON's place in history. Perhaps at a later time, with a wider perspective, a better judgment can be formed. As I see it, his handling of the war in Vietnam will loom as a lasting and significant achievement.

Devoted as he was to the cause of human freedom and the freedom and independence of both people and nations, his courageous decisions during the war in Vietnam, tragic though that conflict was, figured in the ultimate outcome of that war. The enemy was defeated and a peace settlement was agreed upon the day following the death of President JOHNSON.

Hon. Henry B. Gonzalez
OF TEXAS

Mr. Speaker, 2 weeks ago the life and era of LYNDON JOHNSON ended.

The last ceremony is over. The last funeral

notes, the last salutes, have long since echoed and faded away in the hills of Texas to be lost forever in the winds of time, and he is at rest—and we somehow are amazed, disbelieving that a man of such intensity and restless, endless energy, could ever be at rest.

But social conscience did not die with him, and if he were here, he would be reminding us how much is left undone.

I do not think there was any problem, any injustice, any human need, that escaped his concern or failed to draw his attention. No problem, no human dilemma, no matter how far removed, no matter how intractable, would be too much for him to contend with. If he were standing here today, he would be telling us how high we could reach, how far we had to go, if we only dared and cared enough.

No one who ever knew or met LYNDON JOHNSON could come away without being impressed; he confounded his enemies and his friends alike; he never faltered or failed; never took the easy way out; and if he fell far, he reached higher than any other man ever dared.

And as he would remind you of things left undone, so will I—not that I have his powers of persuasion, but because we cannot deny nor refuse to recognize those problems and concerns that moved him, and ought to move us. They did not die when he did, nor did they fade away with a change of Government; nor will they.

Hon. Walter Flowers
OF ALABAMA

Mr. Speaker, today we are honoring the memory of former President LYNDON B. JOHNSON.

L. B. J. was no ordinary man. Whether one agreed or disagreed with his politics, JOHNSON was a man of incredible strength and endurance.

He was a master at the science of politics and his record in Congress bears this out. But he may best be remembered for the calm and confident leadership he provided in the time following that tragic day in November 1963 when President Kennedy was shot and killed.

Most of LYNDON JOHNSON's adult life was spent in service to his country culminating in his being called upon first by circumstances and then by a great majority of voters to serve as

President of the United States. Throughout his entire career he worked tirelessly and with great dedication for the good of the country as he perceived it.

While only history can ultimately judge his deeds, those of us who lived in his lifetime honor his memory with the utmost respect.

Hon. Joseph M. Gaydos
OF PENNSYLVANIA

Mr. Speaker, history will remember LYNDON BAINES JOHNSON. From the time he assumed the awesome responsibilities of the Presidency, 99 minutes after the assassination of President John F. Kennedy, until he left that office in 1969, his administration was studded with monumental decisions and dramatic actions.

It was an administration that spanned an era of turbulence that America will never forget. The mid-1960's saw our country locked in conflict abroad and wrenched apart by violence at home. It was an era where the clarion call for civil rights echoed over the land and the stain of civil disorder spread from coast to coast. It was an era which saw two leaders of our Government murdered—President Kennedy and his brother, Senator Robert Kennedy. It was an era which Americans saw grow bitter and take sides against our involvement in Vietnam. It was an era which would have drained the physical and moral strength of any man and it was LYNDON JOHNSON's destiny to be the man tested. He was not found wanting.

History, unquestionably, will link President JOHNSON with Vietnam. His policies regarding the war have been and will be questioned by many people. I believe, however, that his critics, if they be honest and reasonable, will bring peace to that land, to America, and to the world. I deeply regret he did not live to see it happen.

But, if war is to be LYNDON JOHNSON's footnote on the pages of history, then let history also remember his other wars. Let it remember LYNDON JOHNSON's war against poverty, his war against the lack of decent housing for poor Americans, his war for expanded educational opportunities for young Americans, and his war for increased medical and health benefits for older Americans.

Let history remember that when President JOHNSON took office he promised nothing more than to do his best and asked for the help of his people and his God in this quest. Who could promise more?

Hon. Floyd V. Hicks
OF WASHINGTON

Mr. Speaker, LYNDON JOHNSON was at the same time one of the most capable, promising, and yet tragic Presidents in American history.

He held the capacity for greatness. When the Great Society programs tackled all of our problems—race, poverty, public education, medical care, and housing—we all felt we were a part of changes that would shake the world.

The tragedy was that these programs withered on the vine. In his years in office President JOHNSON was obsessed with the war in Vietnam. His tremendous promise for a better world was killed by an unpopular war in a strange land.

I have no doubt that the trials and turmoil of his last years in the White House hastened his death. He will be missed by his many friends in Congress. And, if history is kind, he will be remembered by all Americans for his desire to make our country a better place to live.

Hon. Joe D. Waggonner, Jr.
OF LOUISIANA

Mr. Speaker, in the untimely passing of the late President LYNDON BAINES JOHNSON, the United States has lost a great man who was deeply respected by his colleagues, his friends, and those he lead and served so devotedly during his Presidency. Just as all Americans shared with Mrs. Johnson and her daughters the warmth and wisdom of their loving husband and father for so many years, we share with them now the sadness they feel.

I was honored to serve in the Congress during the Johnson years, and I will treasure and remember those years for the rest of my life. While the two of us disagreed from time to time, I respected and admired L. B. J. for the firmness of his dedication to the ideals and convictions he believed in. History will record and men will long remember LYNDON BAINES JOHNSON and the Great Society he sought so diligently to create. While his efforts took so much from him, he thought it worthwhile and necessary no matter what the cost.

I can appreciate and understand his wanting to return to the hill country, for I, too, feel a special closeness to a section of the country very similar to the hills and the ranch that he called home. The peacefulness and simplicity of the hills, coupled with the family which meant so much to him and knowledge of the achievement of the peace which had so successfully eluded him, provided L. B. J. with contentment and happiness during his last days; and I am sure he would have wanted it to end in no other way, for finally he had what he wanted most—peace.

Hon. Richard H. Ichord
OF MISSOURI

Mr. Speaker, the sudden death of former President LYNDON JOHNSON less than a month after the death of former President Truman has filled the entire Nation as well as those of us who serve in the Congress with a great sense of sadness. Two devoted public servants have been taken from our midst leaving us with no living former Presidents. Such an occurrence reminds us all of our own mortality and of the fleeting nature of life itself.

The writer of the book of Ecclesiastes reminds us that there "is a season for everything"—a time to be born, weep, laugh, mourn, dance, a time to speak and a time to remain silent, and finally a time to die. It is rather interesting that the time to die for Presidents Truman and JOHNSON came so close together because there were great similarities in the terms they served as President. They both served as Vice President and took office upon the death of the President. They both served one elected term and chose not to run for reelection. Both men left office with great controversies surrounding their terms in office.

LYNDON JOHNSON, like Harry Truman, understood and loved politics, knew how to use power and was not hesitant to make a decision. I did not always agree with President JOHNSON but I always respected and admired him. LYNDON JOHNSON's devotion to his principles can be very cleary seen in the decision he made in March of 1968. He believed so strongly that the course he pursued in Vietnam was just that he was willing to give up the opportunity to serve another term as President rather than alter his Vietnam policy. History may judge him right or wrong in this decision if it is ever able to render a clear verdict but it will have to recognize the fact that he made a decision and stuck by it.

One of the tragic aspects of the timing of President JOHNSON's death is the fact that it came just a few hours before the public announcement of a cease-fire in Vietnam. It is my opinion that no person in America desired to see a just and lasting peace in Vietnam more than LYNDON JOHNSON.

I can only conclude by saying that another great and dedicated leader has been taken from us and we will miss his presence and his guidance as time passes.

Hon. Benjamin A. Gilman
OF NEW YORK

Mr. Speaker, the untimely death of President LYNDON JOHNSON is not only a great loss to his family and friends, but to the entire Nation and to the world.

Mr. JOHNSON, who gave more than half of his 64 years in service to his country, assumed the extremely difficult role of President following the abrupt and tragic death of President Kennedy. Throughout his term in office President JOHNSON, saddled by the additional burden of an unpopular war, proved his ability not only as an outstanding executive but as a staunch, highly respected leader of legislators.

Some solace to those who mourn his death can be found in that Fate was kind enough to have allowed LYNDON JOHNSON knowledge of the Vietnam cease-fire prior to his death. This welcome news must have been a great comfort to the man who sought so long for peace.

The death of our 36th President, a sad event for our entire Nation, will be brought to mind in the next 30 days by the flying of our Nation's flags at half-mast—a symbolic tribute to LYNDON BAINES JOHNSON and a reminder to all Americans of the earnest and powerful man who served his country faithfully and well in some of her most troubled times.

Hon. Mendel J. Davis
OF SOUTH CAROLINA

Mr. Speaker and my fellow colleagues. I did not know LYNDON JOHNSON—either as a Member of this House, as a Senator, or as the President. In fact, there is only one time that I talked with him, but that memory will remain with me as long as I live.

I have read and heard a lot about LYNDON JOHNSON—the rough edged, hard-riding LYNDON JOHNSON—the folksy LYNDON JOHNSON and the unbendingly, patriotic LYNDON JOHNSON. I have heard about the LYNDON JOHNSON of civil rights fame and Great Society fame, but the LYNDON JOHNSON that I know and remember is the one of deep compassion and concern.

Mr. JOHNSON had been gone from the Presidency for 2 years, from the Senate for 11 years, and this House of Representatives for 23 years. Yet on a cold night in December of 1971, LYNDON JOHNSON took the time himself to call Birmingham, Ala., to inquire how my boss, the late Congressman Mendel Rivers, was doing. Mr. Rivers had undergone heart surgery. Mr. JOHNSON told me on the phone that night:

I just wanted to call and see if everything is all right. I hope you don't mind if we keep calling the next few days.

Then he went on to explain:

You see, Mr. Rivers is an old friend of mine from our days together in the House.

Every day for the next few days, either he or Mrs. Johnson would call and get a report on the Congressman's condition. This touching tribute to an old friend told me all I ever have to know about LYNDON JOHNSON. Here was true compassion—away from the glare of publicity—genuine concern for an old friendship. That is the mark of a true leader and man. One who can relate to the everyday problems of his fellow man. One who can take the time to care about a friendship kept.

Mr. Speaker, I express the thanks of a grateful Nation, that LYNDON JOHNSON was the right man for the right time. LYNDON JOHNSON gave this country a heritage that will be well remembered in the history books tomorrow. Thousands of Americans today—and millions in the future—will live better because LYNDON JOHNSON was a caring President. LYNDON JOHNSON was many things to many people, but he was above all a very human being—and while this Nation today mourns the death of our 36th President, we can feel thankful indeed that a man like LYNDON JOHNSON occupied the residence at 1600 Pennsylvania Avenue. We can be thankful that LYNDON JOHNSON was on hand to step in and lead the American people through one of the most trying times of our history.

Hon. Thomas N. Downing
OF VIRGINIA

Mr. Speaker, I have had the privilege of serving with four great Presidents. Of the four, I probably spent more time in the presence of the late President JOHNSON than any of the others. My memory of those experiences will not soon fade.

LYNDON B. JOHNSON was a strong man in every respect. He was a natural-born leader. He was a leader in the House; a leader in the Senate; and he certainly led our Nation with strength and ability. Our country has been fortunate indeed to have such leaders at the ready in time of crisis.

I wish he could have lived to have seen this agonizing war come to its end. Certainly he did everything within his enormous power to extricate this country from her morass—but to no avail. Finally with calm resolve, the President, who loved his country more than the prestige of being its leader, chose to refuse certain reelection in an effort to restore peace. History will probably recall that his action did indeed cause peace to be possible.

The late President should go down in history as one of our great Presidents. A grateful Nation says goodbye.

Hon. Thomas E. Morgan
OF PENNSYLVANIA

Mr. Speaker, it is with deep regret and sorrow that I reflect upon the untimely passing away of LYNDON BAINES JOHNSON, the 36th President of the United States.

Of all the leaders of our country during these momentous times, I have known him, and worked with him, the longest: First, when we were both Members of the House, with offices in the Cannon Building; then when he became Senator; later, when he ascended to the Vice Presidency; and, finally, when he became the Chief Executive of our Government.

It was a long association, and one which I shall always treasure. For although President JOHNSON may have made some mistakes, he was also a great man who came from the Congress, who loved it, and who knew how to work with it for the benefit of our Nation.

During his tenure as Senate majority leader, and as the President of the United States, our country had made more difficult and far-reaching decisions than probably during any other comparable period in our history.

Most of those decisions will affect the character of this country, and the condition of life of the American people, for decades to come.

And they will affect them for the better.

For LYNDON BAINES JOHNSON has done more than any other single man to bring about a profound change in the relationship between the Government and the people of the United States—a change which made the Government an active champion of the right to equal opportunity, and a better standard of life, for all Americans.

Some people may tend to forget this, and to judge President JOHNSON's stewardship of the highest office in this land by our tragic military involvement in Vietnam.

I believe that history will show that the initiatives which he undertook in the field of foreign policy, whether they were based on sound or on questionable advice, did not come from a narrow motive but were intended to strengthen the cause of freedom, and of peace, in the world.

Moreover, history will show that in a time of crisis, President JOHNSON had the courage to make the most difficult decision of all: to reverse himself, and to renounce the office of the Presidency, for the sake of reaching peace.

Nearly 5 years later, as he rests in his beloved Texas soil, the results of that momentous decision are at hand: a cease-fire has been signed in Vietnam and, hopefully, the cause of peace in Indochina is gaining momentum.

It is sad indeed that the man who turned our involvement in the direction of peace is not here to see the fruition of his hopes.

The singular courage which President JOHNSON displayed in March of 1968 was characteristic of his approach to the basic and controversial issues of our age.

Time and again, he withstood public rancor and abuse, risking his political career for the sake of the poor, the forgotten, and the dispossessed.

As chairman of the Committee on Foreign Affairs, and as a Representative of a district which has experienced its share of sorrow and hardship, I have admired his compassion for the less fortunate at home and abroad; his deep sense of fairness and justice; and his full commitment to the highest principles for which the United States has stood for nearly two centuries.

These parts of his record, these outstanding achievements, shall serve as the finest testament that any President could leave to his countrymen.

We are fortunate that LYNDON B. JOHNSON lived in our time; and we sorrow at his passing.

To Mrs. Johnson, and to the members of our late President's family, Mrs. Morgan and I wish to extend our sincerest condolences.

Hon. Martha W. Griffiths
OF MICHIGAN

Mr. Speaker, there was a man among us. And now he is gone.

He stood taller, reached wider, worked and fought harder, talked and cajoled and persuaded and listened better than the rest.

His thoughts, his ideas, his plans were greater and more generous than most. And his energy, his pounding, driving energy, it was as the strength of ten.

And there were those—some in admiration, some in mockery—who said he was larger than life.

And now he is gone. His body lies in the ground, in unaccustomed stillness. His mind, his heart, his energy no longer churn with thoughts, feelings, and action. He is at rest.

But even in death, he stands tall. And now there are many—all in admiration, none in mockery—who say he is larger than life.

For LYNDON JOHNSON has not left the company of his fellow Americans. His life was too big to be circumscribed by a day of birth at one end and a day of death at the other. His life and his spirit live on not just in our memory, but in the real world he did so much to build and in the millions of men and women who inhabit his structure.

Other Presidents gave us the words of emancipation and the promise of reconstruction. LYNDON JOHNSON gave us its reality.

Other Presidents gave us the hope of health protection and better education. LYNDON JOHNSON gave us its actuality.

Other Presidents gave us eloquence and agendas. LYNDON JOHNSON gave us hospitals, and houses, and national parks, and schools, and roads, and better cities, and dignity in our old age and opportunity in our youth.

And when we partake in any of these promises he made into reality, he shall live on in us.

He was an alchemist of dreams, transmuting the fragile stuff on which dreams are made into the tough, pragmatic substance of which Federal law and Federal policy is built. It may not be perfect but you can see it, touch it, use it, test it, live with it or improve it.

These are two sentences of LYNDON JOHNSON's that I shall never forget. They are plain words rather than poetry. But, how moving they were when he said them and how timely they are now. And both reflect what was really his favorite pronouns—not "I" and "me," but "us" and "we."

"Let us continue." He said that when he assumed the leadership of this Nation.

"We shall overcome." He said that when he assumed the role of its conscience.

And now he is gone. And we are left to carry on. But we are not alone. We are not without him.

For he is the rock upon which we shall build a greater society.

Let us continue. And surely we shall overcome.

Hon. Harold T. Johnson
OF CALIFORNIA

Mr. Speaker, we are going to miss LYNDON JOHNSON probably more than we realize today.

Those of us who knew him and worked with him and supported him will miss his vision, his compassion, his legislative institution and skills that moved ideas into reality.

But even more, our citizens will miss him— the poor, the sick, the old, the disadvantaged— all of those who had a friend as President who was determined to do what he could to turn the vast resources of our country toward doing what is right for the people.

I only wish that the tribute of today, the vast outpouring of recognition of the man he was, of the things he achieved, could have been expressed in his lifetime.

Harry Truman, who left the Presidency some 20 years before his death, benefited from the study and evaluation and finally, the general recognition that he indeed was one of our great Presidents.

I have no doubt that 20 years from now the scholars and historians who evaluate the Johnson years will give him the highest marks as a man and as a leader during most trying times.

President JOHNSON confronted the critical and fast-moving events of his day with the determination to make the decisions that would serve the greatest good for the greatest number of people.

I am glad that I was able to support him during these critical years and I remember with pride his letting me know on more than one occasion that I was one of those he could depend on and rely on.

Mrs. Johnson and I will miss him. We extend our affection and best wishes to his family.

Hon. Neal Smith
OF IOWA

Mr. Speaker, I am glad to join in this tribute. While anything I could say at this point would be redundant because our Speaker, majority leader, minority leader, and members of the Texas delegation, have already most appropriately expressed the feeling of Americans. However, I also want to take this occasion to announce that I am today introducing a bill to designate the Interstate Highway System as the Rayburn-Johnson Highway System. These great leaders were responsible for devising a method and a means for building this system which is almost completed and links all of the United States today.

There were many proposals under which most of the money would have gone for interest payments, and periodic infusions of money followed by slowdowns would have amounted to a no-plan plan. But these great leaders, Sam Rayburn as Speaker of the House and LYNDON JOHNSON as leader of the Senate, saw the need and in a great exercise of leadership devised a successful plan for accomplishing the objective, using the resources of the Federal and State Governments as well as great private expertise. Both great leaders have now passed on and I think it is most appropriate at this time that the system be named the Rayburn-Johnson Highway System.

Hon. Ray J. Madden
OF INDIANA

Mr. Speaker, I wish to commend Congressman Wright Patman, the dean of the House of Representatives for securing this time on the House floor today for himself and other Members to pay tribute to our former colleague and departed President LYNDON BAINES JOHNSON.

During the 79th Congress, which was my second term, I served on the Naval Affairs Committee with Congressman LYNDON JOHNSON. I became acquainted with him as a co-member of this committee and have always admired his ability, not only as a legislator but also his great service in the U.S. Senate, particularly as leader of the Senate. LYNDON JOHNSON's leadership in the Senate was outstanding. His ability as legislative leader was recognized by all Members of that body, as well as Members of the House. He was a master in the art of legislative compromise which resulted in the passage of many legislative bills for the benefit of humanity and the Nation.

At the 1960 Democratic Convention, when John F. Kennedy was nominated, he greatly aided the Democratic ticket nationally by becoming a candidate for Vice President which resulted in a great Democratic victory throughout the Nation.

After the unfortunate tragedy to President Kennedy, at Dallas, Tex., Vice President JOHNSON was sworn in as President and carried on the various programs which President Kennedy had sponsored during his one and one-half years as our Executive and he enacted many additional legislative programs. He exhibited the same outstanding ability as an Executive that he displayed as a legislative leader of the Senate.

During his almost two terms as President of the United States, he accomplished more than any President in history with the possible exception of President Franklin Roosevelt in successfully placing upon the Federal statute books more progressive legislation than any President in the history of our country.

The Civil Rights legislation which had been debated, postponed, stalled, filibustered, and neglected for generations was enacted into law through the extraordinary persuasion and finesse of LYNDON JOHNSON. Housing legislation, social security expansion, medicare, health, rural, and labor bills were enacted and expanded during his regime in the White House.

His patriotism and dedication to his country and his sense of sincerity and responsibility toward all segments of our citizenry was unquestioned. I, along with other members of congressional committees was invited to the White House by President JOHNSON to participate in his ceremonies of signing many important bills for the benefit of the impoverished and the middle- and low-income population of the United States.

LYNDON JOHNSON was a common man who could occupy the highest office in the world with dignity, ability, and not lose the common touch because he as a youngster and student in grade school, high school and college mingled with all stratas of society in his native Texas. Even as President of the United States when meeting friends in the White House or at State functions he always had time to stop and converse and greet old-time friends from all segments of life.

The Nation for generations to come will be enriched and benefited by the long public service of LYNDON BAINES JOHNSON through his sagacity and foresight in fighting for principles that would be beneficial to all segments of our Nation's population.

When President JOHNSON's casket was flown to Washington and placed in the rotunda of the Capitol tens of thousands of his adoring public marched by and paid tribute to his memory during the afternoon and night after the ceremonial tribute. I wish to join with all our citizens in extending this farewell tribute to a great leader and extend sympathy to his wife, family, and relatives in their bereavement.

Hon. Leonor K. Sullivan
OF MISSOURI

Mr. Speaker, in 1952 when the Democrats had a fine candidate for President of the United States in Gov. Adlai Stevenson of Illinois, the attacks on President Harry S Truman had become so bitter and mean that those who were masterminding the Stevenson campaign decided to make a particular point of disassociating the Stevenson candidacy from the Truman administration, on the assumption that Mr. Truman was an unpopular President. But regardless of what was being said about him at the time by his political enemies, President Truman had deeply impressed the American people with his sincerity and his compassion and his courage, and as the years went by history more and more accorded him the greatness he had earned in office. Had he run for reelection in 1952, I am sure he would have won.

And if LYNDON B. JOHNSON had run for reelection in 1968, I am sure he would have won, too, despite the attacks which were then being made upon him and his administration. For he, like Truman, had had the courage to fight for the kind of legislation which the people of the United States wanted and needed, and his achievements in the fields of health, safety, consumer protection, economic opportunity, civil rights, natural resource development, transportation, conservation, and economic expansion were of such vast scope that it will take us years to appreciate their real significance.

His decision not to run for reelection reflected his consuming desire to find a way to terminate the tragic war in Vietnam, since his own efforts in this respect had succeeded only in bringing the Paris peace talks into existence but with no prospect at that time of any agreement. So he relinquished an office in which he was a superb practitioner of the art and science of government—an office he filled with great distinction and effectiveness—in the hope that his stepping down would enable his successor to achieve the peace which eluded him. The bitterness over the war so clouded the political atmosphere of 1968 that to many articulate Americans, LYNDON JOHNSON was a failure as a President and a man to be vilified. But the outpouring of genuine grief which marked his premature death demonstrated the deep regard in which he was held as a President and as a man by the millions upon millions of Americans of every race, creed, color, and economic station who recognized the tangible results of his unprecedented achievements as a President of and by and for the people. Presidents Truman and JOHNSON had much in common in that respect.

A few days before President JOHNSON left office, an attempt was made to bring into focus the remarkable achievements of "The Johnson Years" in a book presented to President JOHNSON at a dinner in New York City on January 13, 1969. I felt deeply honored to be the only Member of Congress to contribute to this presentation volume. My assignment was to discuss in a few short paragraphs the contributions made by the Johnson Presidency to the protection of the American consumer.

Now, in looking over that volume of capsule evaluations of the Johnson Presidency; by a score or so of prominent Americans who were closely associated with Johnson administration objectives but including many who were not a part of the Federal Government themselves, I am struck by the incisiveness of the judgments expressed 4 years ago as to what his great achievements really were.

TRIBUTE BY JAMES MAC GREGOR BURNS

The historian, James MacGregor Burns of Williams College, summed up the stature of the man in this overview of the Johnson Presidency which began the volume:

OVERVIEW

(By James MacGregor Burns)

Last winter I stepped out onto the balcony of the White House in the company of the President of the United States. In the distance the figure of Thomas Jefferson gleamed like a jewel in his marble pantheon—and I thought of the greatness of the first democratic President of the United States and of the littleness of some of those who attacked him. We were standing on "Truman's balcony"—and I remembered the absurd criticism by those who were dead set against any kind of change, whether of architecture or of policy.

History has a way of siphoning into oblivion the petty and the irrelevant and of measuring up the real stature of a man. History does not supply one final verdict but many assessments. Those assessments add up to as final a judgment as a man can receive on earth.

Some historians will remember LYNDON B. JOHNSON as the man who declared total war on poverty, deprivation, disease, and ignorance—and who threw himself, day and night, into the leadership of that battle with every ounce of energy he possessed.

Other historians will remember him as the man who—like Jackson and Wilson and Truman—suffered criticism because he stuck to the course that he believed was right; a man who endured attacks with the patience and tolerance of a Lincoln; and as a man who risked the consensus he cherished because he put duty and conscience over an easy popularity.

Still other historians will remember him as the man from the South and from the Senate who made a personal and political commitment to full opportunity for black Americans—a commitment that stamped him as truly the President of all the people and a symbol of hope for the whole nation.

Students of government, like myself, will remember LYNDON JOHNSON for a further and special reason. He was the first President to recognize fully that our basic social ills are so rooted in encrusted attitudes and stubborn social structures that no single solution or dramatic crusade will solve them; the first President to see clearly that only a total attack across the widest front, with every possible weapon, would bring a breakthrough; and the first President to propose basic institutional changes to make a total attack possible.

No one defined the problem better than the President himself: "Our democracy cannot remain static, a prisoner to the past . . . Government itself has the continuing obligation—second to no other—to keep the machinery of public participation functioning smoothly and to improve it where necessary so that democracy remains a vital and vibrant institution."

OTHER CONTRIBUTORS TO THE "JOHNSON YEARS"

Mr. Speaker, there followed then a series of summarizations of JOHNSON administration achievements in many different fields, accompanied by a list of landmark laws enacted at President JOHNSON's request and with his vigorous participation.

Those who contributed short chapters for the presentation volume and their affiliations at the time were:

Foreign Affairs—McGeorge Bundy, president of the Ford Foundation; National Defense—Robert S. McNamara, President of the International Bank for Reconstruction and Development; The Economy—Walter Heller, University of Minnesota; Civil Rights—Ralph Ellison; Poverty— Carl B. Stokes, Mayor of Cleveland; Education— John W. Gardner, Chairman, the Urban Coalition; Health—Michael E. DeBakey, Baylor College of Medicine; Housing and Urban Development—Edgar F. Kaiser, chairman of the board, Kaiser Industries Corp.; Farming and Rural America—Herschel D. Newsom, past master of the National Grange; Older Americans—Wilbur J. Cohen, Secretary of Health, Education, and Welfare; Transportation—Ben W. Heineman, president, Northwest Industries, Inc.; Law and Justice—Tom C. Clark, Associate Justice of the Supreme Court of the United States, 1949–67; Excellence in Government— Kermit Gordon, President, the Brookings Institution; Federal State Partnership—Nelson A. Rockefeller, Governor of New York; Business Government Partnership—Henry Ford II, chairman of the board, Ford Motor Co.; Labor Government Partnership—George Meany, President of the American Federation of Labor and Congress of Industrial Organizations; Quality of the Environment—Laurance S. Rockefeller, Chairman, Citizens' Advisory Committee on Recreation and Natural Beauty; Protecting the Consumer—Leonor K. Sullivan, Member of Congress, chairman, Subcommittee on Consumer Affairs, House Committee on Banking and Currency; Space—James E. Webb, former Administrator, National Aeronautics and Space Administration; The Arts and Humanities—Roger L. Stevens, Chairman, National Council of the Arts.

A FEW OF THE LANDMARK JOHNSON LAWS

Mr. Speaker, the mere listing in this book of the remarkable laws and administrative actions taken during the Johnson years in the White House in each of these fields is almost overpowering. Included among the consumer protection listings are:

The Truth in Securities Act of 1965; the Traffic and Highway Safety Act of 1966; the Fair Packaging and Labeling Act of 1966; the Child Protection Act of 1966; the Flammable Fabric Amendment of 1967; the Product Safety Commission Act of 1967; the Fire and Safety Research Act of 1967; the Truth in Lending Act of 1968; the Meat and Poultry Inspection Act of 1968; the Gas Pipeline Safety Act of 1968; the Hazardous Radiation Act of 1968; and establishment of consumer representation in the White House and Justice Department.

Many, many more consumer measures are listed under other headings in the volume, such as medicare, the food stamp program, the Water Quality and Clean Air and Solid Waste Disposal Acts, innovative new housing programs, the Law Enforcement Assistance and the Safe Streets Acts, and numerous others. The Johnson record in office matches or exceeds that of any other administration in the history of our Nation in working effectively for the well-being of all citizens.

President JOHNSON not only built upon the accomplishments of such illustrious predecessors as Franklin D. Roosevelt, Harry S. Truman, Dwight D. Eisenhower, and John F. Kennedy but blazed new paths in many areas of economic improvement and the health of the American people.

LAWS IN WHICH ALL AMERICANS CAN TAKE PRIDE

In the consumer field particularly, President JOHNSON was outstandingly successful. In my tribute to his administration's consumer record, in my contribution to the book presented to him on January 13, 1969, I stated:

From the standpoint of the well-being of the American people as consumers, the past five years have been the most dramatic and productive in our entire history. And the credit for this remarkable change in the consumer's long-neglected status belongs entirely to President LYNDON B. JOHNSON. The results will stand always as a tribute to his deep concern for people, and his determination to assure a better, safer, healthier, happier life for all Americans.

From his first days in the White House, President JOHNSON initiated a drive for far-reaching and long-needed consumer laws which was as effective as it was unrelenting. Furthermore, through establishment of the White House office of Special Assistant to the President for Consumer Affairs, he brought the Voice of the Consumer into the highest counsels of government. To this office, he named first Esther Peterson and then Betty Furness, dynamic women of outstanding ability, who succeeded in creating throughout the Federal Government, and in the States as well, a new sense of public agency awareness of government's obligations to consumers.

As one who has made consumer causes my main concern in the Congress, I am convinced that without President JOHNSON's wholehearted leadership in this field, the impressive catalogue of landmark consumer laws of the past five years could never have been achieved. These are laws in which all Americans can take pride.

LEONOR K. SULLIVAN,
Member of Congress, Chairman, Subcommittee on Consumer Affairs, House Committee on Banking and Currency.

Mr. Speaker, I shall always treasure the inscription in the volume he sent to me, thanking me for helping to "give the consumer a voice." Had it not been for the vigor with which he galvanized his entire administration into support of the Food Stamp Act of 1964 and the Consumer Credit Protection Act of 1968 and other measures which I sponsored which were bitterly opposed at the time, I know they would never have become law, or would have been so watered down as to be virtually nothing more than shells.

Franklin D. Roosevelt once said the American people had a "rendezvous with destiny." LYNDON B. JOHNSON exemplified that concept in his untiring drive to make this a better country for every citizen. We and those who come after us will all be in his debt for the achievements of his Presidency.

Hon. Edward P. Boland

OF MASSACHUSETTS

Mr. Speaker, I join with my colleagues in the House and with Americans everywhere in mourning the loss of a great American President, LYNDON BAINES JOHNSON, whose passing on January 22 came within a month of the death of another great President, Harry S. Truman, on December 26, 1972.

Both former Presidents will long be remembered for the role they played in providing medical care for the needy in America; President Truman for his proposal of a medical aid program to the Congress in 1949 and President JOHNSON, who fought for the enactment of medicare by the Congress and signed it into law in 1965 with President Truman by his side.

Historians of the future cannot escape linking the names of these two former great Presidents, Harry S Truman and LYNDON B. JOHNSON, to the epoch leadership they played in placing the first meaningful civil rights law on the statute books since President Abraham Lincoln signed the Emancipation Proclamation one century earlier.

Harry S. Truman, as President, had the courage to propose civil rights to the Congress in 1948; and LYNDON B. JOHNSON, as Senate majority leader, floor managed the first voting rights legislation onto the lawbooks in 1957, and as President saw the fulfillment of that goal by signing the Civil Rights Act of 1964.

Mr. Speaker, PRESIDENT JOHNSON was indeed one of America's great public servants, as a congressional secretary, as a Member of this House, as a Senator from Texas and Senate majority leader, as Vice President and President of the United States. All of his years in Washington were devoted to helping the poor, the sick, the uneducated, the oppressed, and those whom society had forgotten or ignored. His public life was filled with controversy because he was a man of decision, and a man who cared.

One of LYNDON B. JOHNSON's close friends and confidantes on the Washington scene for many years, former Supreme Court Associate Justice Abe Fortas, summed it up eloquently when he said of the former President:

Above all, let us remember that he was a large man, of enormous strength and intense dedication. He was a man alive, vital, eager, restless, warm and passionate. He was America. He was America's frontier, without which America is just another tired, retreating society, headed towards mankind's end and not towards the fulfillment of its dreams.

Let us not lose our way. Let us honor him by continuing the ascent which he began.

Mr. Speaker, the ascent to which former Justice Fortas refers reads like a litany of LYNDON BAINES JOHNSON's legislative accomplishments: civil rights, medicare, Elementary and Secondary Education Act, Higher Education Act, Older Americans Act, the War on Poverty, the Immigration Act abolishing discriminatory national origins quota system, Mental Health, Heart, Cancer, and Stroke Acts, housing programs and model cities, the Water and Air Pollution Acts, the Truth in Packaging Act, Auto and Highway Safety Acts, Child Protection Act, minimum wage and social security liberalization, increased veterans benefits and a new GI Education Act, the Wholesome Meat Act, the Flammable Fabrics Act, the Age Discrimination Act, Vocational Training Act, and the Library Services and Construction Act.

President Nixon aptly said in his tribute that President JOHNSON's concept of the American dream was no catch phrase to LYNDON BAINES JOHNSON:

He believed in America—in what America could mean to all of its citizens and what America could mean to the world. In the service of that faith, he gave himself completely.

Mr. Speaker, the many accomplishments of LYNDON BAINES JOHNSON speak for themselves.

It must have been gratifying for him to know before his untimely death that in the 4 short years since he left the White House, his long-sought quest for peace in Southeast Asia was coming to fruition as a result of the Paris peace talks he initiated; and that his fellow countrymen were favorably viewing his Presidency with a new perspective as one of enlightenment, progress, and compassion for less-fortunate Americans.

As we mourn the passing of this physically large and dynamic leader of unshakeable courage, we are grateful for the life God gave him and for the useful purposes to which he channeled his every breath and ounce of energy for the benefit of his fellow man. I join my colleagues in offering profound sympathy on behalf of myself and the citizens of the Second Congressional District of Massachusetts to President JOHNSON's beloved wife, Lady Bird, and to their daughters, Lynda and Luci, in their great hour of sorrow.

Mr. Speaker, I include with my tribute at this time editorials from the Springfield, Mass., Daily News of January 23, and the Boston Globe of January 24, and former Justice Fortas' tribute to President JOHNSON in the New York Times of January 25, 1973:

[From the Springfield (Mass.) Daily News, Jan. 23, 1973]

LYNDON JOHNSON FOUGHT FOR RIGHTS

It is fitting that, in his last public speech little more than a month ago, LYNDON BAINES JOHNSON spoke out once more for civil rights—the area of human need in which the 36th President of the United States made his greatest contribution to our society.

Pictures of that civil rights symposium at the LBJ Library in Austin gave the initial impression that Mr. JOHNSON had aged suddenly—faster than his 64 years should allow. But the lasting impression was that the passage of time and withdrawal from public life had not dimmed Mr. JOHNSON's abiding passion for equal rights for his fellow Americans.

He spoke softly but with deep conviction as he appealed for a unified effort to advance new civil rights programs and told opposing factions at that symposium: "We shall overcome!"

Indeed, the tall Texan with the Southern drawl and the down-to-earth manner did overcome. If the time was ripe in the mid-1960s for passage of the first meaning-ripe in the mid-1960's for passage of the first meaning-President JOHNSON's great credit that he was the unifying and moving force responsible for getting this historic legislation through Congress.

Mr. JOHNSON's social legislation, the outgrowth of his Great Society policies, was unquestionably the distinguishing feature of his administration—just as, in contrast, the war in Vietnam was his political albatross.

Without Vietnam, history would, most likely, rank Mr. JOHNSON as one of America's greatest Presidents. Despite Vietnam, historians will, in assessing his White House years, have to consider that Mr. JOHNSON's record of legislative accomplishment in Congress is unequaled in recent times.

LYNDON JOHNSON was a consummate politician. No President was more adept at maneuvering Congress into doing his bidding—a mastery of the high political art of compromise developed in his days as a congressman and senator and refined during his eight years as Senate majority leader.

Unfortunately, Mr. JOHNSON's skills in behind-the-scenes political maneuvering were not translated to his public image. He was not a good public speaker. And it was easy to let the recited speeches and the Texas drawl divert attention from the significance of his message, and even obscure his deep sense of dedication to the achievement of a better society for all Americans.

LYNDON JOHNSON developed his political skills early on. It seemed that politics and LBJ were a natural combination. In contrast to Harry S Truman who labored for years in the political vineyards before achieving recognition and success, LYNDON JOHNSON first appeared on the Washington scene, as a secretary to a congressman, at age 23. He became a congressman before he was 30 and advanced to the U.S. Senate slightly more than a decade later. He was only 46 when he was chosen by his colleagues for the most prestigious and powerful Senate job, majority leader.

But if his early political brilliance and his legislative accomplishment as Democratic lealer in the Senate eminently qualified him for advancement to the presidency, this advancement came under tragic circumstances—the assassination in Dallas of President John F. Kennedy on Nov. 23, 1963.

Again, it is to Mr. JOHNSON's credit that, recognizing the depth of the nation's loss and the very painful transition of power in the White House, he devoted his efforts first to carrying on President Kennedy's unfinished programs.

LYNDON JOHNSON will be remembered for many things during his five years and two months as President. He fashioned his own Great Society. He instituted a national War on Poverty. He carried on the Peace Corps, the Job Corps, and put the full weight of the federal government behind an effort to improve the lot of millions of Americans who had never before been given the opportunity for better rchools, better housing, participation in the election process, and, in fact, equal rights in all areas of American life.

On July 2, 1964, President JOHNSON signed the civil rights bill—opening up to blacks all hotels, motels, restaurants and other businesses serving the public. This historic law also guaranteed equal job opportunities for all.

But, LYNDON BAINES JOHNSON will also be remembered as the President who got America deeper and deeper into an increasingly unpopular war in Vietnam and, try as he might, could not get us out.

Under mounting criticism and attack, even from his own Democratic party, Mr. JOHNSON did not seek reelection to a second full term, opting instead to devote his final months in office to efforts to achieve peace in Vietnam.

This peace never came. And it will remain a paradox of history that this man who labored so hard and so successfully to advance human and humane causes at home was, to reverse the saying, a prophet without honor in Vietnam. He was a man of peace who was hailed for his concern for the needs of Americans, and, simultaneously, a man of war—reviled by many for his hard-line war policies in a distant land.

History may record that this skilled politician's greatest triumph was his smashing election victory over Sen. Barry M. Goldwater in 1964. And history will doubtless point to his summit meeting at Glassboro in 1967 with Russian Premier Kosygin as a highpoint of the Johnson presidential years.

But, the thought persists that the finest hour for LYNDON BAINES JOHNSON came last Dec. 12 in that civil rights symposium in Austin when—his shoulders stooped, his hair graying, and his steps almost hesitating—he returned to the rostrum to mediate a civil rights dispute and appeal for a cause in which he believed so deeply and so sincerely.

Americans and the entire world are shocked by President JOHNSON's sudden and premature death at age 64.

We mourn his passing. And we pay tribute to this man who fought so courageously and untiringly for civil rights, and for a better America.

ఎ

[From the Boston Globe, Jan. 24, 1973]

L. B. J.—WE SHALL OVERCOME

The entire nation has reason to mourn the death of LYNDON B. JOHNSON, which has come so soon after the passing of our only other former President, Harry S. Truman.

We say this notwithstanding the fact that Mr. JOHNSON presided over the most unpopular war in American history, the one about which President Nixon addressed the nation last night.

But there was also another LYNDON JOHNSON. He played a leading role—and we were surprised to find no reference to it in the pages of print about him yesterday—in keeping us out of war in Vietnam back in April of 1954. He was Senate Majority Leader then, and John Foster Dulles called eight congressional leaders before Adm. Arthur W. Radford, chairman of the Joint Chiefs of Staff, and told him President Eisenhower wanted a joint resolution permitting air and naval attacks.

JOHNSON vigorously opposed it, and we stayed out of war for seven or eight more years. Then, tragically, it came. He did not start it, but might have stopped it. To his great credit he did finally stare down his generals in March of 1968 and refuse the massive reinforcement of U.S. troops they were seeking.

But then he had lost the majority that in 1964 had given him what still stands today after President Nixon's recent landslide as the largest percentage of the popular vote ever given to a presidential candidate. And by the time of his decision not to run again, he had accomplished much with the support that vote gave him in Congress.

It was this other LYNDON JOHNSON who, even before that, persuaded Congress to enact in 1964 the most meaningful Civil Rights Law in a century. And there were other major accomplishments of his campaign for a

"Great Society," such as laws giving massive Federal aid to our schools, medical care for the aged and funds for his war on poverty.

He tried to mix the two wars, and they wouldn't mix, any more than guns and butter. This was his tragedy.

Yet there is great hope for the country in much of what he said and did. And surely one of the best farewell addresses was his impromptu speech only last Dec. 12, before a heated audience in Austin, Texas:

"I believe that the essence of government lies with unceasing concern for . . . every individual . . . regardless of color, creed, ancestry, sex or age. . . . To be black, I believe—to one who is black or brown—is to be proud, to be worthy, to be honorable. But to be black in a white society is not to stand on level ground. While the races may stand side by side, whites stand on history's mountain and blacks stand in history's hollow. . . . We must get down to the business of trying to stand black and white on level ground."

It was a most moving speech right down to his very last sentence and very last words: "And if our efforts continue, if our will is strong, if our hearts are right and if courage remains our constant companion then, my fellow Americans, I am confident we shall overcome."

ఎ

[From the New York Times, Jan. 25, 1973]

He Was America

(by Abe Fortas) [1]

Let us remember LYNDON JOHNSON's greatness. Let us remember his love for people. To him, people were not statistics. Each of them was a warm, real, living human being, endowed with the spark of immortality. He could not believe that any of them was less deserving than any other of dignity, of compassion, of a position in the world of mankind.

Let us remember the totality of his dedication of his role, unsparing and unflagging.

Let us remember the fullness of his understanding of his nation, of its roots, its meaning, its mission. Let us remember that he was determined that his nation should fulfill and not frustrate its destiny.

Let us remember that it was he who, risking constituency and traditional friends, vowed faithfulness to the impossible dreams of President Kennedy; and that it was he who made them come true.

Let us remember that he led and drove the nation to a new plateau of humanity; that it was LYNDON JOHNSON who breathed life and vitality into the mutilated body of our Constitution's noble principles; that it was he who destroyed the ideological ghetto left by slavery's habits, that it was he who insisted that twenty million black people, too, are entitled to a jury of their peers, to a vote, and to equality of opportunity; that it was he who marshalled the nation's forces in an assault upon a disgraceful poverty; that it was he who committed the nation to the cure of illness and the cause of health; that it was he who dedicated the nation's resources to providing education for all.

LYNDON JOHNSON transformed his nation. He saw to it that the forgotten people of the New Deal, the blacks and abjectly poor, are no longer forgotten—and this is LYNDON JOHNSON's achievement.

---

[1] Abe Fortas was a close friend of President JOHNSON and an Associate Justice of the Supreme Court.

Let us remember his sad, heartbreaking words about the misery of Vietnam which he inherited: "Peace has eluded me." He sought peace, not victory, in Vietnam; and when the successive application of force did not bring the enemy to the peace table, he gave himself to the cause. In March of 1968 he sacrificed his career and his future; as an earnestness of good faith, to further the cause of peace. It was this, as much as any other event, that marked the beginning of the long and agonizing road to an agreement in Vietnam.

Above all, let us remember that he was a large man, of enormous strength and intense dedication. He was a man alive, vital, eager, restless, warm and passionate. He was America. He was American's frontier, without which America is just another tired, retreating society, headed towards mankind's end and not towards the fulfillment of its dreams.

Let us not lose our way. Let us honor him by continuing the ascent which he began.

Hon. James J. Delaney
OF NEW YORK

Mr. Speaker, like multitudes of people throughout the world, I was deeply saddened by the untimely death of former President LYNDON B. JOHNSON.

As Congressman, Senator, Vice President, and President of the United States, his name will long be remembered for the numerous legislative proposals which were enacted because of his dedication and skill.

LYNDON JOHNSON was preeminently a legislator. As a protege of the late Speaker, Sam Rayburn, he learned the legislative process thoroughly, and developed a unique and exceptional ability to guide complex and difficult proposals through the Congress.

For some years, Mr. JOHNSON, as Senate majority leader, and Mr. Sam, as Speaker of the House, performed as a legislative team whose effectiveness is unlikely to ever be surpassed.

LYNDON JOHNSON was a man of the people. He rose from humble origins to become President of the United States, a position which the people of this Nation have entrusted to only 36 others.

During his Presidency he worked day and might with dynamic intensity to make America a better place in which to live. He was particularly concerned about civil rights, education, public health, and improving conditions for the poor. He was a man of great compassion, who was devoted to improving the condition of our less fortunate citizens.

Those of us who had the privilege of knowing him and working with him will long cherish our association and friendship.

Texas has lost a favorite son. The United States has lost a great leader and a devoted public servant.

I extend my deepest sympathy to Mrs. Johnson, and their two daughters, Lynda and Lucy.

Hon. Peter W. Rodino, Jr.
OF NEW JERSEY

Mr. Speaker, yes, I served under L. B. J.—I, along with many of my distinguished colleagues here in this Chamber today. I knew him, however, not only as my President, but also as my friend. He, himself, told me so, during the 1964 Presidential campaign, while driving with me through my home town of Newark, N.J. "I can tell what's in a man's heart," our 36th President would often say, "by looking straight into his eyes." "And you," he said, "I'm looking at you straight, right here," pointing a finger directly at my nose and right between my eyes—"I can tell that you are my friend."

President LYNDON JOHNSON had a way of saying something which really got through to us. He had a way of making one feel really close, of really drawing one in. He sought loyalty, and at the same time, he gave loyalty. As a great leader, he had the ability to bring together other leaders, to work out together his blueprint to overcome the crippling legacy of bigotry and injustice, which had been plaguing, for too long his people. His style, his nature, his character was strong, intense, tempestuous, earthy. He was a mover and a doer. In a sense, he was overwhelming—so electric, so extremely powerful, yet so compassionate and so filled with great visions and great dreams.

I remember him telephoning in 1966 to congratulate me upon the successful passage of his Open Housing bill in the House. "Pete, this is LYNDON," he said, "LYNDON" . . . No matter when I would come to the White House, he would always make it a point to stop, to introduce me to whomever he was with, and to ask me to come along with him for awhile. I often recall his declaration that first he was a citizen of the world, a human being, then he was an American, and finally he was a Democrat—all in that order. His ability to make each of us feel very special, to make each of us feel we had a most important part to play in the progress of our world, was indeed a most remarkable gift.

On Wednesday, January 24, Haynes Johnson shared his impressions of our late President, with the readers of the Washington Post. Because the "Recollections" of Haynes Johnson touch deeply the hearts of all of us who knew L. B. J. over these many years and because the experience of this author could easily have been our experience had we lunched with President JOHNSON along with the rest of the Post press corps that Tuesday, April 7, 1970, I would like to enter, at this time, Haynes Johnson's remarks into the body of this Record:

RECOLLECTIONS

(By Haynes Johnson)

Perhaps the most poignant aspect of LYNDON JOHNSON's death is that this most public man, who was in his element when surrounded by cheering crowds, died alone, calling for help.

His wife, who had stood by him in every crisis and on whom he relied so much, was away. His daughters, grandchildren, cronies and friends whom he loved to regale with his inimitable stories were absent.

He reached for a phone in his bedroom at 3:50 p.m., we are told, and asked for the head of his Secret Service detail. The agent was in a car at the time, so another agent answered the call. Mr. JOHNSON asked him to come immediately to the bedroom without saying why.

When the agents arrived, they found the 36th President lying on the floor next to his bed, apparently dead.

His death came quietly, in lonely seclusion after a stormy life played out so largely in public view.

It is that vibrant life that Washington is recalling today as LYNDON JOHNSON's body is borne back to the Capitol he once dominated.

While memories are fresh, and before the stories pale, let one last recollection be recorded. It is an account of the last time many of us at The Washington Post saw LYNDON JOHNSON.

He came to lunch that Tuesday, April 7, 1970. Nearly five hours later he left us all drained, fascinated, enthralled and full of questions that never could be answered or resolved.

Probably none of us present that day could successfully capture or reconstruct all the moods, the language, the mobile expressions or the specific points made. It was, at the least, a virtuoso performance. He was soft, sarcastic, crisp, commanding, anecdotal, colorful—and in the end confounding as always.

LYNDON JOHNSON was telling us his story, and speaking to his place in history. He was a salesman, and the ex-President came prepared with the goods in the form of stacks of papers marked Top Secret and Top Secret Sensitive. Over and over, he read from the various memoranda, letters and other documents to back up his positions.

In retrospect what was most memorable about his performance was not what he said about the war or other

aspects of his presidency. It was the two sides of LYNDON JOHNSON displayed that day that made the most lasting impression.

It was a subdued, somber LYNDON JOHNSON who first appeared. He had only recently recovered from a stay in a San Antonio hospital, where he had been admitted suffering from chest pains, and his initial conversation was all about his health. He had aged dramatically.

"He came in a little after 12:30" Richard Harwood wrote immediately after the long luncheon, "looking less tall, less bulky than I had remembered him. His hair was almost completely white and was growing long in the back in the old-fashioned Southern senator style, the way Mendel Rivers wears it.

"His illness showed in his face, I thought, and from the side his skin had the yellowish-gray look you find on extremely sick men. His hands were mottled with crimson splotches; there was a scab on the back of one finger and lots of freckles, all of which brought images of an old man."

LYNDON JOHNSON's own manner reinforced the impression. He seemed tired, withdrawn, quiet, and appeared preoccupied with problems of his health. He was on a diet of 850 calories a day, he said, and he was getting back his strength gradually. There had been quite a bit of pain this time, he said. His trouble really had begun the previous spring when he was working on his ranch.

He liked to get out and take his exercise, but he went on slowly. One day he was laying lengths of pipe, lifting and placing them in the mud. Suddenly he became short of breath and began to experience slight pains in his chest. He remembered stopping his work without realizing quite why.

For nearly the next hour at the luncheon, he continued in the same vein. He was the elder statesman, above partisanship.

There was none of the old remembered JOHNSON fire and flash, none of the earthy, anecdotes about men and events. He would not comment on Richard Nixon. He preferred to speak philosophically, it seemed, to talk about the memoirs on which he was working each day, to reflect on the higher problems of the presidency (he favored a single six-year term, and he didn't think being a lame-duck President necessarily reduced a chief executive's power).

But gradually his manner and mood changed. He began talking about Vietnam, and suddenly he was more vigorous and assertive. He folded and unfolded his napkin, began leaning forward, rocking back and forth in his chair, speaking first softly and then loudly. Now he was, clearly, LBJ.

To quote Harwood's recollections—one of many we all composed that day—"As he talked he seemed to take on another appearance. The pallor and signs of sickness went away and all of a sudden you were sitting with a vigorous, commanding, strong man whose mind was so clear, so well-organized, so quick that you instantly became aware of the power of his personality, of the ability to dominate and persuade and overwhelm."

Much of what he said that day about Vietnam has since appeared in his book. But what was most fascinating was not what he said about the war and other problems, but how he said it.

LBJ was overpowering. He thumped on the table, moved back and forth vigorously, grimaced, licked his lips, gestured with his arms, slumped back into his seat, switched from a sharp to a soft story, and kept the conversation going from the moment he sat down at the dining table until hours later when his wife called The Post and sent in a note reminding him he should come home and rest.

As he reminisced, going back into his childhood and then on through his entire political career, he became more colloquial and more Texan. His Daddy used to whip him with a razor strop, he said, and "It hurt him more than it hurt me. But that's the kind of thing you have to do in a family." In a way, it was the same as being President: there were certain things you had to do that were unpopular, but you did them for the public benefit.

His language, and phrases, were picturesque:

"So I took a cold belly buster . . ."

"Anyone who's smart enough to pour water from a boot . . ."

"And Dick Russell said, 'I've been to the duck blind with the man. I know him. I may not agree with him on everything, but he's a good man, he cares for the people, and he'll try to do what's right (referring to his plans to nominate his friend, Judge Homer Thornberry of Texas, to the Supreme Court)."

"Those Laotians can't stop anybody. They just stand around throwing water at each other . . ."

"MacArthur pinned a medal on me for heroism. It looks good on my chest"—here, he fingered the Silver Star citation in his coat lapel—"but it's a good thing they couldn't see what that flight did to my pants."

"Now, I don't want you good people to have a heart attack here at this good table eating this good food. And if any of you has heart trouble, you better take nitroglycerine now, because the first person to urge me to halt the bombing was Walt Rostow . . ."

He mentioned his wife, Lady Bird, and said, "She always knew how to handle me." Then he told how he had decided, in advance of the 1964 Democratic convention, that he was going to announce publicly that he would not be a candidate *that* year. But Bird, he said, talked him out of it. She told him she knew he would like to leave the White House, but that he would miss being where things were happening, and where he had a chance to accomplish everything he had worked for in 30 years of politics.

But that wasn't why he should run, he said she told him. "It would make it seem as though you were running away. Your friends would hang their heads in shame, your enemies would dance and rejoice."

He recalled a story from his early days as a young Texas congressman. Elliott Roosevelt, the President's son, came to him on behalf of electrical power interests in Texas, he said. This was at a time when LBJ was fighting the power companies there.

"I always liked Elliott," he said. "He was a good boy. But they'd got to him, and so he came down there to see me and asked me to ease up on them.

"He said he had talked with his Daddy and his Daddy wanted him to tell me that he agreed. So I said, 'All right, I'll do that, Elliott. But before I do, I want you to do one thing for me. I want you to go back to your Daddy and tell him I'll do it if he wants me to, but ask him to write me a letter, in his own hand, saying what he wants, and then sign it.' Well, I could see Elliott wasn't expecting that. I'd kind of roughed him up. So he said, 'Why

do you want father to write you a letter? I've already seen him, and he wants you to do this.'

"And I told him, Well, Elliott, it's this way: when I do what your Daddy wants and I come back to Texas they're going to run me out of the state. Now the nearest border is 150 miles away and that's over the bridge to Mexico. And I figure I can get to that bridge before they get me, and when I'm half way over, and on the Mexican side, I want to be able to turn around and stop and hold up that letter showing the signature of Franklin Delano Roosevelt so everyone can read it. Like this'."

He held up an imaginary piece of paper, relishing the role he was playing and the laughter it inspired.

LBJ was full of such performances. He acted out various roles. He mimicked people: Clark Clifford sitting up straight and dignified like this (he sat up very straight and very solemnly in his chair and folded his arms over his chest); Hubert Humphrey and HHH's reaction to the news LBJ was going to renounce the presidency in 1968: "I told him not to go off to Mexico, but I guess he didn't believe me." LBJ gave a "hee-hee-hee-hee-hee" rendition to show how silly Humphrey thought the idea.

Finally, after nearly five hours, Lady Bird's note was sent into the dining room asking him to come home. LYNDON JOHNSON became serious. "I want you to know," he said, "no matter how we differ about things, I feel I am at the table of friends, and I want to thank you for letting me come and visit with you."

Here he was, he went on, in the twilight of his years, among good friends. He had one more story to tell. It was one Sam Rayburn used to tell about a small Texas town.

Once, when Rayburn was just beginning as a politician, everyone important in that town had turned him down when he was looking for a place to spend the night—the banker, the newspaper editor, the judge. Finally a little old blacksmith said he would be glad to take Rayburn in for the night. Years later, after Rayburn had become famous and powerful, he came back to that town. Everyone clamored for him, the banker, the newspaper editor, the judge. They all wanted the honor of his staying with them.

No, Rayburn told each to his face, he didn't want to stay with them. But was that little old blacksmith still there. Yes, he was. Bring him to me, Rayburn commanded. When the blacksmith came, Rayburn told him: "Jeeter, I'd like to spend the night at your house if you'll have me. The blacksmith did, and kept Rayburn up all night talking. When Rayburn said he had to go to sleep, for he had a busy day ahead of him, tears welled up in the blacksmiths eyes.

"Mr. Sam, I'd just like to talk to you all night."

And that, LYNDON BAINES JOHNSON said, was the way he felt about his friends at The Post.

There were some bitter-end Johnson critics among those of us around that dining table, but when LBJ stood up to begin shaking each person's hand to say good-bye we all spontaneously burst into applause. Some of us had tears in our eyes.

We thought we might never see his likes again. And perhaps we were right.

Mr. JOHNSON stated:

The problem of an American President is not the problem of doing what's right. The President's problem is knowing what's right.

President JOHNSON felt he had "so much to preserve, so much to protect and so much to believe in." "I love this country," he would often say. And, all who heard his words were affected by this sincerity and this love. He wrote, as we well know, one of the greatest chapters of social legislation in our history. Now that the chapter has been written, it is left in our hands to breathe life into his words. In the Choices We Face, written by L. B. J. after he had left the White House, he reminded us:

None of what we have achieved is self executing. Programs that express commitment to people must be funded. An education act cannot teach a single child. A housing act cannot give shelter to a single family, nor can a manpower act provide a single job, nor can a civil rights act give one human being the dignity and respect he deserves. The real test of our commitment is whether we are willing to achieve over a period of years what those acts only promise. The certain fact is that there is no turning back. No closing that door. We can weather our troubles now because the kind of America we seek is right and because the alternative, denying just hopes and risking a divided and hostile nation is intolerable.

Thus, President LYNDON BAINES JOHNSON, in these words, let us know that he knew what was right. Ours is now the task to keep these promises, to make his vision of the Great Society live. For if his legacy of social, economic, and racial justice is to have any real meaning and any great effect on the people of this Nation, ours is now the task to do what is right.

Hon. David R. Obey
OF WISCONSIN

Mr. Speaker, much has been written and said about a great President who left us recently, the 36th President of the United States. LYNDON BAINES JOHNSON.

Every American will carry in his own mind's eye his personal reminiscences of the Johnson Presidency. To me, the equality that marked the Johnson Presidency more than any other was a passionate concern for the little people of America. I am firmly convinced that LYNDON JOHNSON will be regarded by history as one of the great domestic Presidents of all time. True, some of the programs pushed by President JOHNSON have had administrative problems, but those programs defined the Nation's purpose to make available to all Americans opportunities which have not been equally shared in the past.

I think the one sentence which best sums up the Johnson administration in domestic affairs was uttered by one of LYNDON JOHNSON's political heroes President Franklin D. Roosevelt who said in 1936:

Better the occasional faults of a government living in the spirit of charity than the consistent omissions of a government frozen in the ice of its own indifference.

LYNDON JOHNSON's record shows that he remembered that statement. Let us hope that as we go about our work in this next session of Congress we will remember them as well.

Hon. Spark M. Matsunaga
OF HAWAII

Mr. Speaker, LYNDON BAINES JOHNSON will undoubtedly be recorded in history as one of our truly great Presidents. More than any other President, he advanced the causes of civil rights and aid to the poor and downtrodden. During his administration, older Americans saw medicare become a reality to save them from crushing medical expenses. Headstart gave disadvantaged preschool children a chance to compete with others on a more nearly equal basis. The Elementary and Secondary Education Act of 1965 bears monumental witness to President JOHNSON's concern that all young Americans be afforded the chance to learn.

His proudest accomplishments were in the field of civil rights, where he fought for the enactment of law after law—the Civil Rights Act of 1964, the Voting Rights Act of 1965, the Fair Housing Act of 1968—all calculated to eradicate what he called "an injustice of decades and centuries."

Mr. Speaker, the name of LYNDON B. JOHNSON will always have a special meaning for Hawaii and its people, for without his leadership in the U.S. Senate when he was majority leader, Hawaii's bid for statehood would not have succeeded when it did. The East-West Center on the University of Hawaii campus will stand as a special living monument to President JOHNSON for it was he who almost single-handedly enacted legislation for its creation after being convinced of its desirability by Hawaii's then Delegate to Congress, John A. Burns.

As I stood at his graveside at the L.B.J. Ranch in Texas, listening to the singing of the Battle Hymn of the Republic, I recalled my accompanying President JOHNSON on his first visit to Hawaii on Air Force One as President. He was so grateful to the people of the Island State for having given him one of the greatest pluralities of all the 50 States in the 1964 election, that he kept repeating to me, "Sparky, I love your people." I kept responding, "They all love you too, Mr. President." The people of Hawaii loved LYNDON JOHNSON and will miss him dearly. As one who was fortunate enough to experience the warmth of his friendship, I feel the emptiness which follows the loss of a dear friend.

All America will miss LYNDON JOHNSON. His irresistible manner, his commitment to equality for all Americans, his personal anguish over a war that eventually caused him to step down in order to bring peace, make him a man deserving of admiration and praise.

At Temple, Tex., last September 16, Mr. JOHNSON delivered a speech that may stand as his final farewell to the Nation he served—a deeply moving reaffirmation of faith. The following article from the January 23, 1973, Honolulu Star-Bulletin is adapted from that speech and I believe my colleagues will find it inspiring.

To Lady Bird Johnson and other members of the Johnson family, I extend my deepest condolences. They can be sure that their personal loss is shared by millions of people around the world.

[From the Honolulu Star-Bulletin, Jan. 23, 1973]

As the Days Dwindle Down

(NOTE.—At Temple, Tex., last Sept. 16 LYNDON JOHNSON delivered a speech that may stand as his final farewell to his nation—a deeply moving reaffirmation of faith. The following article is adapted from it.)

TEMPLE, TEX.—With the coming of September each year, we are reminded, as the song says, that the days are dwindling down to a precious few. By the calendar, we know that soon the green leaves of summer will begin to brown; the chill winds of winter will begin to blow; and—before we are ready for the end to come the year will be gone.

If we permit our thoughts to dwell upon this perspective, these days can become a melancholy season.

As it is with the calendar, so it sometimes seems to be with our country and its system. For there are those among us who would have us believe that America has come to its own September. That our days are dwindling down to a precious few. That the green leaves of our best season are turning brown and will soon be falling to the ground. That before long we will feel the first chill wind of a long American winter—and that our nation's stand as mankind's "last best hope" will be done.

For those who preach this prophecy—and for those who believe it—this period of our affairs can only be a melancholy season. But it is to that mood—and to the perceptions which foster it—that I want to address my remarks today.

Over the course of a long, full and gratifying life, I have seen many Septembers and have known many autumns. In public service—and in private life—I have experienced a full measure of unwelcome winters. Yet melancholy is not a mood which I have ever allowed to weigh for long upon my spirits.

I live—as I have always worked—by the faith that with each passing day, we are always approaching nearer to the beginning of new springtime. It is by that perspective I see our country now.

If I believe anything of this land—if I know anything of its people and their character—I believe and I know that we have not come to and are not approaching America's September.

On the country, it is my conviction—a conviction which deepens every day—that this land and its people are quickening with the new life and new potential of what will become the springtime of a new America.

I do not say this merely to offer reassurance in anxious times. Far from it, I intend what I say to be taken as a challenge—a challenge to every citizen of every age.

No nation can be more than the visions of its people, Americans cannot be more than we believe ourselves capable of becoming. Thus we are directly challenged to choose between two very different perceptions of what we are and what we can make of America itself.

On the one hand, we can choose to guide our course by the light of the bright perceptions—of America the beautiful, America the just, America the land of the free and the home of the brave.

Or, on the other hand, we can choose to move toward the shadows of what some have called 'the dark perception of America the unclean, America the unjust, America the unworthy.

For myself—as, I am sure, for many of you—there is no real choice. I want to open the soul of America to the warm sunlight of faith in itself, faith in the principles and precepts of its birth, faith in the promise and potential of its resources and skills and people. Yet I know that, in these times, this is not easy.

For too long, we have permitted the dark perception to pervade our midst. Day after day, month after month, the portrayal of America as unclean, unjust and unworthy has been ground into the consciousness of our people.

We no longer see the blooming flowers for we are searching for the litter. We no longer celebrate the many fresh triumphs of justice for we are lingering over the residue of yesterday's shortcomings. We no longer measure the miles we have come toward a more humane, civil and peaceful world for we are too busy calibrating the remaining inches of times we are trying to escape and leave behind.

This is our clear and present challenge.

When we permit these dark perceptions to dominate us, we are allowing our future to be shaped by visions that are small and mean and diminishing to our potential. We are, in simple terms, dooming those who come after us to know what could only be a second-rate America.

This is a future which I am unwilling to accept.

I have devoted my time on this earth to working toward the day when there would be no second-class citizenship in America, no second-quality opportunity, no second-hand justice at home, no second-place status in the world for our ideals and benefits.

I do not intend now that second-rate visions shall set our course toward settling for a second-rate America. That is why I speak as I do now.

All through the pages of history we read the heart-rending stories of those who set out in quest of great goals and discoveries, yet when they were almost to the edge of success, they hesitated—not knowing or understanding how near they were to their aims. Out of that moment of hesitation, all too often they lost forever their opportunity to succeed.

In many respects, that seems to me to be a pattern we ourselves are in danger of repeating.

Over all the years of our nation's existence, we have been setting goals for ourselves and striving tirelessly to reach them. Those goals have been both the slogans and the substance of national affairs for generation after generation.

Full employment. Decent wages. Adequate housing. Education for everyone. Opportunity for all. Good health, good medical care, good hospitals for even the least among us. Above all equal justice under the law for all our fellow men. America's goals have been simple and basic.

They have permeated and motivated all our institutions—churches and schools, professions and labor unions and corporations and foundations—as well as our government at every level.

All our American resources and strengths—private and public—have been committed to the effort and we have come very close to success.

Nowhere—over all the globe—have any people, under any other system, come nearer to fulfillment of such aspirations than we have under our system.

Yet, at the very moment we were near to realization we have allowed our effort to go slack, our momentum to slow and we have entered a season of hesitation.

Why?

Basically, I believe, it is because we have not understood—and still do not fully comprehend—where we are or what we are about.

Whatever may be your own perception of where we are and where we may be heading, let me say for myself that I see little today suggesting that our system is failing—but I see all too much which convincingly argues that by our doubts and hesitation we may be failing the promise and potential of our system.

We are not living in times of collapse. The old is not coming down. Rather, the troubling and torment these days stem from the new trying to rise into place.

With our nation's past efforts, with our long and faithfully kept commitments with our infinite successes in so many fields, we have brought into being the materials, as it were, with which to construct a new America.

Faced with the task of such great dimensions, we have no time for melancholy. We have no cause for moroseness. We have work to be done—the greatest work any generation of Americans has ever faced. Believing that, I say—let's be on with our labors.

The essentials of a new America—a better America—are all on hand and within our reach. It is our destiny—and, I believe, our duty—to take up our appointed positions and commence the labors that will change what needs changing among us.

Our real challenge lies not in suppressing change but utilizing it to vitalize and energize our society. Change is not our enemy. On the contrary, this society has no deadlier danger than refusal to change.

This is what I believe our young Americans are trying—and have been trying—to communicate to us. With their fine young minds, fresh new learning and clear new vision, they are seeing many segments of our society as it needs to be seen and understood.

The most frightening thing that could happen to us today would be for us to close our eyes to new ideas, and to close our ears to those—particularly the young, in whom we have invested so much hope and effort through the years of our existence—who are trying to tell us how they would go about perfecting the visions of America.

It is just such spirit that we honor on this occasion. It is by restoring that spirit to our lives and our nation's life that we can honor our own trust as Americans.

Hon. Charles J. Carney
OF OHIO

Mr. Speaker, all of us have been deeply saddened by the death of our former leader and President, LYNDON BAINES JOHNSON.

We knew him not only as President—in his words—"of all the people," but also as a friend. No man worked harder for the causes he believed in than LYNDON JOHNSON. His major accomplishments were in the fields of civil rights and antipoverty programs, and his triumphant battle to secure a greater measure of justice for all Americans regardless of race, color, or ethnic origin, will live on as testimony to the greatness of the man.

He was a friend of labor, and he never lost sight of the needs of America's working men and women. He fought for a higher minimum wage so that the workers of our Nation might better share in the fruits of their labor. He saw the need for new health programs and he signed into law the program known as medicare.

Mr. JOHNSON called the 89th Congress "the fabulous 89th," because during that time some 86 administration measures were passed and sent to the White House for his signature. These measures were indicative of the man, LYNDON BAINES JOHNSON, for they were destined to have far-reaching and beneficial effects on the whole quality of life in America.

It is difficult to take the measure of such a giant among men, or to express our feelings about him, in mere words. Perhaps the best way to describe LYNDON JOHNSON is by means of the words he himself spoke at his inauguration in 1965:

We aspire to nothing that belongs to others. We seek no dominion over our fellowman, but man's dominion over tyranny and misery.

He now belongs to the ages. But surely history, with its widened perspective and wisdom, will accord him a place as one of our greatest Presidents.

Hon. Alan Steelman
OF TEXAS

Mr. Speaker, LYNDON BAINES JOHNSON was a many-faceted man. No words will be able to pin him down—no descriptions will aptly fit the man who served his country publicly for 41 years. He was a superior congressional leader and an able Chief Executive.

History will be kinder to LYNDON JOHNSON than many of his contemporaries were. His label as a warmonger will be exchanged for that of a man who was caught by circumstances in a superhuman situation. Vietnam will fade as JOHNSON is remembered as a President of the people—of all the people.

Where LYNDON JOHNSON was cursed for his foreign entanglements, he will be praised for his domestic achievements and legislative skill. He took the half-completed concepts of previous administrations and turned them into realities for the underprivileged. He was the champion of the minorities—a fighter who did battle for those people who could not fight for themselves.

Above all, LYNDON BAINES JOHNSON was a Texan. A man of drive, compassion, insight, determination, and pride. Those of us who are Texans share a special sense of loss with his passing. But we can be proud that we come from the same background and heritage. We will miss him.

Hon. George A. Goodling
OF PENNSYLVANIA

Mr. Speaker, I join with my colleagues in expressing my deep sorrow in the passing of our late President, LYNDON B. JOHNSON.

LYNDON JOHNSON was a dedicated public servant, having served in many official capacities in his lifetime, the ultimate of which was the Presidency.

He had a deep love for his country, a patriot in the deep sense of the word. He adhered assiduously to plans and programs which he felt would advance the best interests of America, and he had a passion for providing opportunities for the physically and economically poor to lift themselves above their adversities.

Mr. JOHNSON was a big man physically, built in the standard of men of the frontier period of this country's history. In addition to this, he was highly active and very deliberate in his pursuit of what he judged right. He was also very compassionate, for it is reported that during some dark days of the Vietnam conflict, he brooded in the quiet of his White House quarters, mourning the loss of lives in Vietnam.

LYNDON JOHNSON met with fortitude the challenges that confronted him in the Presidency. His presence will be missed, but there can be no denying that in his absence, he will leave an impressive mark on American history.

Hon. E de la Garza
OF TEXAS

Mr. Speaker, the Lyndon Johnson span in the history of the United States holds so many fond remembrances among those privileged to know him well—there is so much can be said about this great Texan—so many things a person remembers so vividly about the leadership that was part of him—but the first impressions that came to me after we lost LYNDON JOHNSON I wrote in my weekly newsletter which I introduce here so that all who knew him may share these thoughts conveyed to my south Texas constituency:

WASHINGTON, D.C.—LYNDON JOHNSON had a special place in his heart for South Texas. As U.S. Senator and as President, he visited our area often and he knew our people, knew their problems and hopes and needs. His lifelong concern for the poor and disadvantaged grew out of his knowledge, which he began to acquire as a young school teacher in Cotulla. As State Administrator of the National Youth Administration during the economic depression of the 1930s, he came face to face with the anxieties of young people who wanted and needed jobs when few jobs were to be had. As Congressman, Senator, Vice President and President, he remembered and he cared.

MY PERSONAL FRIEND

LYNDON JOHNSON had many friends in South Texas, and I am proud that I was among them—I and members of my family. Memories flood my mind. For some time he kept on his desk in the White House a little ceramic Beagle puppy given to him by my children. When I first came to Washington as a member of Congress and attended a reception at the White House, as I reached the President in the receiving line he threw his long arms around me in a bear hug and yelled, "Kika." I never felt more warmly welcomed in my life, and I shall always treasure the picture sent from the White House recording that event.

When the people of South Texas staged a great Appreciation Day for me on September 21, 1971 (a date I shall never forget), LBJ was there to be welcomed by thousands of folks who knew him as their friend. He was at his best—in great good humor, laughing, talking informally, clearly enjoying himself. And in speaking of me, he said something that I will always cherish in my mind and heart—that Kika de la Garza is "a man who has never forgotten his beginnings." All my life I will be proud of that tribute from a man who certainly never forgot *his* beginnings and who carried into the highest office in our land the attributes of character that had been formed in his early life in the Hill Country of Texas.

After I entered Congress, the President time and again was helpful to me in my efforts to give the best possible service to the 15th Congressional District.

I recall that after Hurricane Beulah had devastated much of our area and LBJ had personally come down for a personal inspection I was having trouble with the Federal bureaucracy about disaster relief. The Farmers Home Administration and the Small Business Administration were tossing the ball back and forth, each claiming the other was the agency responsible for extending help to the victims of the hurricane.

Being invited to a reception at the White House, I prepared a memorandum outlining the situation. Against all precedent, so I am told, I passed the memo to the President when he greeted me at the reception. LBJ did not tell me that this kind of thing simply was not done. No, he glanced at my memo, then handed it over to his trusted aide, Marvin Watson, and said, "Whatever Kika asks here, have it done".

The logjam was promptly broken to the benefit of South Texas.

I miss my friend, our friend, South Texas' friend.

AN INTERNATIONAL LEADER

Persons far more skilled with the written word than I have set down their appraisals of the former President. In passing, it is interesting to note that many persons now see LYNDON JOHNSON's presidency in a different light from that they focused upon it in his lifetime. The Eastern press was rarely able to get rid of its prejudices in viewing LBJ the President. It was frequently unfair, often malicious.

The fact remains, and I believe history will bear me out, that LYNDON JOHNSON exerted outstanding leadership not only in the nation but in this world as well. For the past week, newspapers and television commentators have been listing the great accomplishments of his Administration. Even with the U.S. caught up in a cruel war during most of the time he was President, he was able to get through Congress a large crop of constructive legislation. Much of it was designed to improve the lives of the disinherited and dispossessed of our land.

LBJ was preeminently a mass of the people in the tradition of other great Presidents. He loved America and Americans and his life was devoted to their service. His place in history is assured. His place in the hearts of his friends is secure and everlasting. And those friendly hearts are today warm with sympathy for Lady Bird Johnson, a great lady indeed, and her two fine daughters. May God give them solace and our never ending gratitude for the many times they unselfishly shared LBJ with us.

Hon. John Melcher
OF MONTANA

Mr. Speaker, I join in this tribute to LYNDON B. JOHNSON, the Nation's 36th President who I am certain will go down in history as an architect of far-reaching social legislation for the people of the United States.

It is indeed unfortunate that efforts are being made to dismantle some of his Great Society programs that have proven their worth. We need to keep them alive for the benefit of the poor, the downtrodden, and minorities.

While I was not a Member of this body while President JOHNSON was in the White House or the Congress, I followed his career closely. He was a strong and able majority leader of the Senate and an equally strong and able Chief Executive.

Mr. Speaker, LYNDON B. JOHNSON understood, better than most, the legislative process. And he used this know-how with a Texan's flare and forthrightness to persuade others to understand and follow his compassion for civil rights, poverty, and health laws. He was a true man of the people.

Hon. Edith Green
OF OREGON

Mr. Speaker, one of the most singular and appealing characteristics of President JOHNSON was his robust involvement in life. When such a person leaves us, it is particularly depressing because he contributed so much to our own sense of vitality and interest in the world around us. His energy was infectious and though he sometimes stirred our anger, he never, never bored us.

He was genuine in his desire to alleviate the burdens of poverty, in his commitment to education and in his commitment to make real the promises of our Constitution to millions of black Americans. It would be hypocritical of me to leave the impression that I agreed with all his policies, for neither I nor many others did. But his goals were worthy and in his essential humanness and courage, his disposition to dare greatly, accepting both risks and responsibilities, he represented the American character as perhaps few other Chief Executives in modern times have because he embodied the essence of the American character: plainspoken in the homespun accents of rural America, hard-working, hard-bargaining, possessed of visions and dreams for America and her potential for greatness that more erudite and polished statesmen would shrink from articulating, let alone, as he did, consciously strive to attain.

No brief assessment is possible. He was "larger than life." With my fellow citizens, I mourn his passing with especially poignant regret at this moment when the dawn of an era of peace— peace such as he earnestly believed his personal efforts would lead to—has at least begun to shed a glimmer over a nation and a world.

Hon. Henry Helstoski
OF NEW JERSEY

Mr. Speaker, in this day of mass communication, as we grow somewhat callous to the sad news that floods broadcasts and newspapers, platitudes for passing statesmen become more and more meaningless. There is, of course, still some initial shock, but after that we tend to be numb as we await the next hero's death. Yesterday's hero is as readily forgotten as yesterday's headline.

I doubt if this will be the fate of LYNDON BAINES JOHNSON. The memory of him will not fade from this earth or into the remote pages of history books. His image lends itself to the most resplendent of platitudes.

On Capitol Hill, LYNDON JOHNSON will long be remembered for his leadership as a Representative, Senator, Vice President, and President of the United States. It is a widely accepted fact that he was among the most effective legislators ever to serve. But this is not where his immortality will carry its greatest weight.

What Mr. JOHNSON did for the United States and the world will be fully realized only as we mature in the ways of history and begin to reflect with an objective eye; however, some glimpse of the basis for his real immortality can be comprehended even now.

While at times accused of turning the country increasingly outward, President JOHNSON urged upon this Nation a seriously needed time of introspection and internal repairs. He dared to challenge problems as old and as complex as man himself.

Making wise use of the power of the country's highest office, he attacked poverty; not only the poverty of material want, but the poverty of mind

and spirit which lingered stubbornly throughout this Nation.

He did not totally eradicate it, but he did begin an erosion of that poverty, an erosion which is still gaining momentum today. If we allow this momentum to take its natural course, the Nation and the world will truly be the Great Society for which Mr. JOHNSON so anxiously yearned.

The poverty of material want was stormed through President JOHNSON's war on it, a war that, if nothing else, made America aware of the hungry and poor millions still living in our Nation during the jet age. He showed people that starvation and malnutrition were not phenomena of the outside world alone. It was a problem existing right here at home. And not only did the President make us aware, he acted. In the historic 89th Congress, he drove through welfare reforms and programs that filled us with fresh hope and astonishment at their sweeping scope.

The poverties of mind and spirit were pressed into retreat by Mr. JOHNSON's bold leadership in the cause of human rights. A southerner, he dared beckon Americans to support the black man's struggle for equality. "We shall overcome," he cried, and the Nation thundered forward with dynamic reforms in the Civil Rights Act of 1964 and the firmer foundations of the Voting Rights Act of 1965 which followed.

President JOHNSON saw to it that his Justice Department made every effort to uphold that legislation. It was a frustrating battle against a disease deeply imbedded in the attitudes of far too many Americans. Yet the President continued to fight. Courageously, he appointed a black man to the Supreme Court and another as the top official in the Department of Housing and Urban Development.

A former schoolteacher, he encouraged higher education and held students dear to his heart. He clamored to achieve the American ideal of an education for all, and held to the belief that better education would mean a greater people.

Clearly conscious of the generations to come and the welfare of all, he formed cabinet departments to deal with the problems of our burgeoning cities.

And he did not abandon America's forgotten generation over 65. Its greatest advocate, he guided medicare in its thrust through Congress.

Zealously, LYNDON JOHNSON sought to rid this Nation and the world of all their ills. His campaigns against the poverties of spirit, mind, and material want were all carried out with a dedication to all he thought was right and just.

He was a man with a vision, a compassionate man who loved all the peoples of the world, not as children under his wing, but as brothers and sisters, individuals all. And, perhaps, his greatest frustration was his inability to use his office to make them all eternally happy.

Yet, through all the frustration, he remained in the forefront, carrying the burdens of the world on his broad shoulders. He caused us to pause and reflect. He offered us hope. He convinced us that there was a way to find happiness on this planet.

He taught us to question, too, suggesting to us, "Let us reason together."

And now he rests, and we continue to run, seeking for all our people the happiness that he envisioned. We will go on.

And as we strive for these goals and struggle in the face of seemingly endless dead ends, we will recall LYNDON BAINES JOHNSON; we will recall his strivings and frustrations.

He will always be with us.

Hon. Brock Adams
OF WASHINGTON

Mr. Speaker, the deaths of Presidents Truman and JOHNSON coming so close upon one another were a shock to the Nation. The sudden death of LYNDON JOHNSON was particularly sad, as his vision of what America should be is needed now more than ever.

It is fitting that we should pay tribute to him in the House of Representatives where he began his long career of public service. It was a career marked by triumph and by criticism, by the closest of election victories and later by the greatest presidential landslide in our history. President JOHNSON was a giant of a man, a man of passionate conviction, a strong and dominating leader. Like all such men, his life was one of controversy. The closing years of his public career were overshadowed by the tragedy of the war in Vietnam. It was this war which made him give up public office—a personal abdication made in the search of peace. Now at last, the dark night of that war seems to be lifting. It is a bitter irony that he did not live to see the signing of the cease-fire agreement.

The death of a man who was so much a part of our lives for so long brings us up short. The anger and the passions of the past are burnt away, and we can look at the whole man as he was.

Taking office in the worst of circumstances, upon the death of President Kennedy. LYNDON JOHNSON brought to the Presidency a vision of America as the "Great Society" which it should be; he brought a deep human concern for the people who make up America. To him they were not a "silent majority," but living human beings whose hopes and fears he understood.

President JOHNSON will have many memorials, but his greatest monument will be the human programs enacted under his leadership—civil rights, the war on poverty, and Federal aid to education. These are the deeds for which he would wish to be remembered, and for which history will remember him. As the Johnson years recede into the past, it is this commitment to humanity which will stand out.

LYNDON JOHNSON was a man of Texas, a homeland he loved and from whence he drew his strength. But much as he loved Texas, he was not a regional or parochial man. He was the President of all Americans, and he strove to bring us together, to join with an another in the fight for a better life for every citizen. He asked us to care for the poor, the deprived, for those who only needed a chance to prove their own worth. He asked us to provide a society with careers open to the talents of everybody.

It was moving to hear at his funeral ceremonies the wonderful hymn, based on an old spiritual, "In Christ, There Is No East or West. In Him, No North or South." For LYNDON JOHNSON there was no east or west or north or south, but only the United States of America seeking to become the great society of which its founders had dreamt. He, and we, have not achieved that society. But in LYNDON JOHNSON, his family, and his countrymen, can point with pride to a man who in his life as a public servant tried to build an America that would match our dreams and hopes. In the history of this Nation, President JOHNSON will rank as one of our great Presidents.

Hon. Carl D. Perkins
OF KENTUCKY

Mr. Speaker, the news that former President LYNDON B. JOHNSON is dead in Texas brings sadness to those who love this country. For in a unique way, larger than life, he seemed to embody the traditions, the robust frontier vigor, and the determination to move ahead that have characterized the development of the American Nation.

Leadership was as natural to LYNDON JOHNSON as breathing and eating are to ordinary men. Within his heart he carried a generator that propelled him forward with the drive of a torpedo boat. For him, idleness and reasonless pause were simply intolerable. When there were things to be done—and he constantly saw things to be done—he wanted to be up and doing them.

We are still only 4 years removed from his Presidency, and that is far too close to see it in the perspective of history. The vapors of emotion, personal involvement, and political differences distort the image of the man and of his stewardship. But personally, I have little doubt as to the ultimate historical judgment on LYNDON JOHNSON as President—one of the great humanitarian statesmen of all time.

Mr. Speaker, I do not think of him merely as President. He was truly a man of the Congress. He cut his legislative teeth in this very Chamber, and he went on to become a master of the Senate. In the 184 years since the first Congress met in 1789, until these days when the 93d Congress is organizing itself, LYNDON JOHNSON has had few, if any, peers as an American legislator.

He felt at home in the Congress, and he relished a kind of brotherhood with those with whom he served here, a closeness that did not fade when destiny removed him from the legislative to the executive branches of Government.

Books have been written, and will continue to be written, giving minute details of his activities as a legislative leader, and I need not recite those accomplishments to Members who know them well.

LYNDON JOHNSON loved the Presidency. But I have a feeling that, if it were his to choose, the accolade he would like most would be to have his portrait hang here in the Capitol as one of the great U.S. Senators of all time; and I hope the other body will shortly see that such an honor is bestowed.

In these brief remarks, I could not possibly cover, or even list, all of the accomplishments of his tenure as President. The scope is as broad as the universe.

But, Mr. Speaker, I like to think of LYNDON JOHNSON as the Education President. During his time in the White House, and as a result of his leadership, this Nation made decisions and initiated action that will be felt in education for many generations to come.

Perhaps chief among these was the decision to move ahead with the massive Elementary and Secondary Education Act of 1965. That was the act in which we were finally able to cut the knot that had hampered our efforts to involve the Federal Government in the financing of childhood education. Title I of that great landmark legislation was based upon the JOHNSON determination that no child in America, no matter what the income level of his parents, no matter what the color of his skin, should be deprived of a good education.

That act has paid untold dividends to the Nation in the few short years it has been in operation, and its potential for the future is unlimited.

I can think of no more fitting memorial to LYNDON JOHNSON than to see that this act is extended and its funding provisions strengthened this year, so that we can move ahead with the work already begun.

The roll is long and overpowering. The Higher Education Act of 1965. The Higher Education Facilities Act. The landmark amendments to the Vocational Education Act. The National Vocational Student Loan Insurance Act of 1965. The revitalizing of the Library Services and Construction Act. The Adult Education Act of 1966. The great program of education for handicapped children in title VI of ESEA. These are but a few, but they suggest the enormous scope of the work done in the field of education during LYNDON JOHNSON's time in the White House.

Those were great years. May their greatness be repeated for our children.

Hon. Robert McClory
OF ILLINOIS

Mr. Speaker, I appreciate this opportunity to join in tribute to the late President LYNDON B. JOHNSON. All of us who had an opportunity to be acquainted with him must share in some measure the loss which is felt throughout our Nation at this hour—and which is felt so deeply within the family circle characterized by close and sensitive ties.

Mr. Speaker, I feel fortunate that I enjoyed a personal as well as a social contact with President JOHNSON. This contact was enhanced when my constituent, Pat Nugent, son of Mr. and Mrs. Jerry Nugent of Waukegan, Ill., became the husband of Luci Johnson. I was privileged to be one of the few Members of this House who attended the wedding and White House reception for Pat Nugent and Luci Johnson at that time. In addition to his parents, many of Pat Nugent's relatives and friends from the Waukegan area were in Washington for the occasion and were entertained at my home as part of the nuptial activities.

Mr. Speaker, in addition to the personal and social relationship which President JOHNSON had with many Members of the Congress, his intimate contacts on subjects of official business are unsurpassed in modern history. His personal interest in the Congress and his individual efforts in securing support of measures which he proposed account in large part for the enormous success which he had in the enactment of domestic legislation.

I was privileged to take an active part in the revision of our immigration laws which President JOHNSON dramatized in a bill-signing ceremony in New York with the Statue of Liberty as a backdrop. It was also my privilege to support actively the Voting Rights Act of 1964, which resulted in expanding the voting franchise to millions of black Americans—and has resulted in the large increase in black officeholders particularly in our Southern States.

Mr. Speaker, I have no intention of recounting the legislative and other related events with which I associated President LYNDON JOHNSON, and which come to mind at this time. Instead, I prefer to recall the times when President JOHNSON and his family occupied the White House. Their warm hospitality and outgoing and friendly behavior, as the First Family of our Nation, endeared them in a very personal way to Democrats and Republicans alike. It is the personable, friendly, compassionate LYNDON JOHNSON whom I recall in this hour of reflection. And it is to his immediate family that I extend this expression of great respect and deepest sympathy—to Lady Bird Johnson, to Pat and Luci Nugent and to Lynda and Chuck Robb. My wife, Doris, joins in these sentiments.

Hon. Frank Horton
OF NEW YORK

Mr. Speaker, as we eulogize the late LYNDON B. JOHNSON, a sense of humility pervades this great Chamber. Certainly it will be difficult for us to capture in words the awesome qualities of LYNDON JOHNSON, both as a man and as a President.

These Halls of Congress have seen few men as powerful and effective as LYNDON JOHNSON. He was, in the truest sense, a parliamentary master. His legislative genius was read quickly by his Senate colleagues, who choose him as their party leader while only a freshman Senator. From that moment, he would shape the course of our country for years to come.

LYNDON JOHNSON assumed the Presidency under tragic circumstances. Those of us who sat in this Chamber in 1963 will not forget his moving address to a stunned nation. His primary motivation was to provide continuity and leadership to a country whose President had been struck down. His own words were "let us continue" and he mustered all the powers of his office and of his own being to accomplish that task. What he did accomplish was extraordinary—in education, housing, medical care, environmental protection, and civil rights. In this final category, in particular, LYNDON JOHNSON is credited with accomplishing what perhaps no other man could. The four landmark civil rights laws that bear his signature, including the Civil Rights Act of 1964 and the Voting Rights Act of 1965, have become his most lasting memorial.

The Vietnam war was an agonizing experience and, in this pause for tribute, it is not comforting to think of that costly conflict in relation to LYNDON JOHNSON. History did not make its final judgment in his own lifetime. But in death, even his sharpest critics gave thanks for all the good he had done.

LYNDON JOHNSON's tenure as President coincided with my early years of service in the House. He was unusually accessible to Members of Congress, regardless of their seniority or political party. I met with him on many occasions and came to know him well. He was a kind and considerate man and I cherish having known him and his remarkable wife, Lady Bird.

Hon. Joseph M. McDade
OF PENNSYLVANIA

Mr. Speaker, the Nation has been saddened in the past 6 weeks over the death of two of our former Presidents, Harry S Truman and LYNDON BAINES JOHNSON, President JOHNSON was a man whose whole life was devoted to public service. He began his career as a teacher in his home State of Texas. He was elected to the Congress of the United States and then elected to serve a larger constituency as a Senator from the State of Texas. He served as Vice President to the late John F. Kennedy and no one will forget the difficult burden that was placed upon him when President Kennedy died so tragically at the hands of an assassin.

President JOHNSON was a man of courage and a man of stature. He was above all a man who had the great burden of this Nation's leadership thrust upon him and he accepted that burden. I extend to his beloved widow and his two fine daughters my own deep personal sympathy for the loss of the man who was outstandingly a splendid husband and father.

Hon. Wm. Jennings Bryan Dorn
OF SOUTH CAROLINA

Mr. Speaker, first I want to compliment my good friend and colleague in the well, the distinguished gentlemen from Texas (Mr. Pickle), for the eloquent eulogy which he delivered during memorial services in the rotunda of the Capitol.

Mr. Speaker, at 5:33 p.m. eastern standard time on Monday, January 22, 1973, the stout heart of this great American ceased to beat. The mortal life of America's 36th President, LYNDON BAINES JOHNSON, had ended where it began in his beloved Texas hill country from which he drew his indomitable strength.

All America was deeply shocked and saddened by the sudden and untimely death of President JOHNSON. This great President translated the dreams of a generation of political leaders into an administration of action that will be remembered in history as one of our most exciting eras of achievement.

President JOHNSON believed in America; in America's dedication and ability to provide justice for all, in America's role as a world leader, and most importantly, he believed in the people of America. His hopes and dreams for these people will only be fully appreciated in the years to come.

LYNDON JOHNSON more than any man understood the legislative processes of the Congress. He understood the committee system and the intricacies of congressional interaction—the work of Congress. He worked closely with the departments and agencies of Government to achieve his goals and objectives. He believed in education—and much landmark education legislation was enacted during his administration. He believed in assuring the elderly of adequate medical care—and medicare was enacted. He believed in assisting rural and urban areas in coping with their problems—and legislation to assist small towns, rural and metropolitan areas was enacted which has provided much assistance throughout America. He believed in helping the "little man" and he championed increased incomes for the working people throughout the United States. He had great respect for those who defended this Nation on the world's battlefields—and in veterans' circles throughout our great land, his administration was referred to as "the era of the veteran."

It was my great personal privilege to be associated with LYNDON JOHNSON, beginning in the 80th Congress. He became one of the outstanding leaders of the Senate and he worked in great harmony with President Eisenhower to help keep America strong and vigilant. I had the pleasure of campaigning with him in 1960 and later in 1964 with his lovely wife, Lady Bird. As we stand here today to eulogize President JOHNSON so do all Americans. The black people throughout my congressional district believe LYNDON JOHNSON did more than any President since Abraham Lincoln to eliminate the hardships and inequities which this great minority of our society experienced.

Mr. Speaker, America will always be grateful for LYNDON JOHNSON's strength that enabled him to impart to America a strong sense of continuity and national purpose in the dark days following the tragedy that elevated him into the White House in 1963. LYNDON JOHNSON spent his life in service to his fellow man. From his early years as a schoolteacher, through his Presidential years and later as an elder statesman, he worked to help humanity. Few men were as aptly suited for this task as LYNDON BAINES JOHNSON, and history will note that few men have ever met the task so well. The years will be lonely without him.

Mr. Speaker, Mrs. Dorn joins me in extending our heartfelt sympathy to Mrs. Johnson, her two daughters, the grandchildren and other members of the family upon their great personal loss.

Hon. William A. Barrett
OF PENNSYLVANIA

Mr. Speaker, I am certain history will record LYNDON BAINES JOHNSON as one of America's great men and great Presidents. A man of humble beginning, who never forgot that beginning, even though he attained the highest honor that the people of the United States can bestow upon an individual, that of President of the United States.

History will surely record that he was a most able legislator and legislative leader without peer; that he was dedicated to the best interests of our Nation and our people, rising above political party and ideology if need be. And, if history is fairly and accurately written, will depict him as the man he was, full of compassion and understanding for his fellow man; dedicated to the principles upon which this Nation was founded, the principles of equality and justice.

The legislative record during his years as Senate leader and the legislative accomplishments by the Congress during his term of office as our 36th President will ever stand as a monument to him; to his earnest and sincere desire to improve the quality of life and standard of living for the people of our Nation.

I truly believe that of LYNDON BAINES JOHNSON it can be said, he was a giant among men; he not only dreamed of what should be but ardently sought to make those dreams real.

Hon. Lester L. Wolff
OF NEW YORK

Mr. Speaker, I rise to join with so many of my colleagues in the Congress, as well as national leaders and statesmen the world over, to pay tribute to the memory of President LYNDON BAINES JOHNSON and to offer our sympathy to his wife, children, and grandchildren.

As one looks back over President JOHNSON's political career—his service in both the Senate and the House, his key role as Senate majority leader, his vigorous Vice Presidency, and, of course, his assumption of the Presidency on that tragic day in November almost a decade ago— one cannot help but stand in awe at the accomplishments of this great leader.

I was fortunate to know the President, and, despite our differences on the war in Vietnam, came to value him as a close friend. He fought hard to gain approval of his programs and he devoted his energies constantly to attain the ideal of freedom for all—a concept upon which this country was founded.

It undoubtedly took rare political courage for President JOHNSON to advocate his Great Society programs. When he was first assessed as a potential President, few people would have guessed that he would be responsible for the broadest series of landmark-pioneering social welfare and civil rights legislation ever enacted in a single President's term of office. The various civil rights acts, Federal aid to education, the Voting Rights Act, and other laws passed during his years in the White House have irrevocably altered the social order of this Nation.

President Nixon in announcing the ceasefire agreement in Vietnam said that none would have wanted this peace more than President JOHNSON. I think that he also wanted the domestic tranquillity that our Constitution calls for in its Preamble. LYNDON JOHNSON spent his entire political life fighting for peace in America based on freedom and equality for all people in this Nation. When we finally reach that goal, historians will record that President LYNDON JOHNSON made a monumentally important contribution toward its achievement.

Hon. Ray Thornton
OF ARKANSAS

Mr. Speaker, the tributes which we are offering today to our late President LYNDON JOHNSON will not add to, or take from his stature as a great President and leader.

The impact of his dynamic vision has resulted in significant historical accomplishments which words can only recall. What we speak now more nearly reflects the effect his life had upon us who remain.

Let us be counted among those who are dedicated to those ideals of personal dignity and justice which characterized his contributions as our President.

He was a good man and a great leader of our country. Once he decided a course of action was right, he pursued it full speed ahead.

He translated many of our Nation's highest ideals into reality.

History will write final judgments on the basis of events which have yet to unfold—but we know he spoke and acted according to what he believed was best for the people of this land which he loved and served.

All of us must feel less secure because of his passing, for we no longer have the benefit of his counsel to inspire us to deeper humanity and to warn us of perils which may not be seen from any other vantage point.

Hon. Joseph P. Addabbo
OF NEW YORK

Mr. Speaker, as the Nation and the world mourns the passing of former President LYNDON BAINES JOHNSON, this House of Representatives is filled with memories of a great legislator, an outstanding President and above all, a loyal American. Many of us in this Chamber were privileged to know President JOHNSON and to work with him and under his leadership. We join the millions of mourners around the world whose thoughts this week are concentrated on the life of this man from Texas.

President JOHNSON's career of public service was long and filled with excitement and activity. He knew the innerworkings of the U.S. Congress as few others ever did and he never wavered in his respect for Congress as an institution and as an equal branch of Government.

President JOHNSON was a giant among men who have been at the forefront of the fight for social progress. It will probably take decades before this Nation fully realizes the extent to which President JOHNSON so changed the face of everyday life in this country. He was truly a man of vision—a man with a dream. His blueprint for a Great Society may not have been perfect but it was an imaginative, bold plan for action which proved that Government need not be idle, passive or helpless in the face of national problems. The Great Society was brought closer by his progressive leadership and millions of Americans have benefited from social programs such as medicare, aid to education, and the war against poverty.

Mr. Speaker, the Nation's Capital has lost a statesman who symbolized the political knowledge and expertise which we in Washington strive to equal. His understanding of the country and the feelings of the people was the cornerstone of his success in educating and leading the American public. He understood the people of Texas as well as the Eastern Establishment and he worked to mold a vast consensus which could move the status quo and bring about social change.

I shall always remember President JOHNSON as a man who caused more real change, true social reform, in a few years than I have seen in Washington or the Nation over the past generation. It is understandable that history will need many more years to evaluate the Johnson years, but we can make a more immediate evaluation of the man. He was a great American President and a fascinating and compassionate human being. I join my colleagues in extending personal sympathies to Mrs. Johnson and the family of our late President.

Hon. William Lehman
OF FLORIDA

Mr. Speaker, it is with profound sorrow that we gather here today in recognition of the late President LYNDON JOHNSON. The Nation has lost the last of its former Presidents, and a truly great leader.

Perhaps more than any other President since Abraham Lincoln, Mr. JOHNSON moved social justice further. He was a man of conviction, and fearless and resolute in his pursuit of what he believed in.

The Great Society was his goal; the beneficiaries were to be all Americans, but in particular the poor, the old and the disadvantaged. During his terms in office the Nation saw the creation of medicare, the war on poverty, the Higher Education Act, the Elementary and Secondary Education Act, and the Civil Rights Act of 1964.

The war that tore apart America has ended. Let us hope that history will be able to look beyond the tragic circumstances of the war and judge President JOHNSON in the light of his other far-reaching programs which have given so much to all Americans.

Hon. Don Fuqua
OF FLORIDA

Mr. Speaker, fate decreed that LYNDON B. JOHNSON would serve in this Nation's highest office in one of the most turbulent periods in our history. It was a time of unrest, a time of violence, and yet it was a time when we made significant advances to eliminate many of the causes of those very problems of the future.

It is not incumbent upon me to judge his record. It has been too short a period and that will be for history to determine.

Yet, my personal observation is that LYNDON JOHNSON was a man who really cared about his fellow man. It was his lot to lead this Nation at the time of our greatest involvement in Vietnam, and it turned out to be the greatest tragedy for a man of peace.

In that pursuit, this Nation was misled. He had great support at the outset, but that support immediately dwindled the moment that it was no longer the popular thing to do. I know he felt stunned at the rapid turn of events, but he never shirked his responsibility.

If LYNDON JOHNSON had had his way, he would have liked to have presided over this Nation in a time of peace, a time when he could have spent all of his boundless energies in pursuit of solutions to social problems in the mold of the man he greatly admired, Franklin D. Roosevelt.

LYNDON JOHNSON was the finest steward to succeed a fallen leader in history. He tried to complete the dream of John F. Kennedy, and then he started to fulfill a few of his own.

This Nation is going to be richer for that service. Time is needed for us to reflect on what he stood for, what he tried to do, and what he really accomplished.

It is unfortunate that there was not enough time between his term of office and his death for some perspective to be shown to that record.

He had some of that Harry S Truman presence about the Office of the Presidency. Mr. Truman was to live to see his named placed in the pantheon of heroes before he fell. LYNDON JOHNSON was not to be granted that privilege.

One of the things I liked so much about Mr. JOHNSON was the manner in which he treated Dwight D. Eisenhower. These acts on the part of Mr. JOHNSON were personal and deeply appreciated by the Eisenhowers and President Nixon.

LYNDON JOHNSON would probably agree with me that in Lady Bird Johnson, we had one of our finest First Ladies. Whatever the trial, whatever the tribulation, she was the rock that held fast.

Once he said that while others had often failed him, Lady Bird had never done so. It would have pleased him to know that the Johnson women did not fail him in death.

The quiet dignity of Mrs. Johnson greeting those who came to pay their respect was a moving experience. She is a great lady.

We have lost a leader. I do not dwell on the fantastic record he established in the Senate of these United States. I do not labor over the war nor the legislative accomplishments of his Presidency.

To me, the most memorable phrase he ever uttered is that it is easier to try to do right than it is to know what is right.

As I look out my window at the Capitol and see the flag at half-mast, I know that I cannot say today how history will judge him. But for those of us who had a chance to know him, we know full well that this was a man whose prayer and purpose was to do right.

Hon. Benjamin S. Rosenthal
OF NEW YORK

Mr. Speaker, the death of President Johnson is a deep personal loss to the Nation. In domestic affairs, he was a great leader, a great American, and a great human being.

He was an energetic and mercurial man. But his goal was constant. He was fervently dedicated to the betterment of his country and its people. He said:

This is the richest and most powerful country which ever occupied this globe. The might of past empires is little compared to ours. But I do not want to be the President who built empires, or sought grandeur, or extended dominion.

I want to be the President who educated young children to the wonders of their world.

I want to be the President who helped to feed the hungry and to prepare them to be taxpayers instead of tax-eaters.

I want to be the President who helped the poor find their own way and who protested the right of every citizen to vote in every election.

I want to be the President who helped to end hatred among his fellow men and who promoted love among the people of all races, all regions, and all parties.

LYNDON JOHNSON helped. He knew poverty firsthand, and he tried to eradicate it. His first full-time job was teaching and he never forgot the need for education. He loved the land of his birth and he fought to rid the air and streams of pollution.

By habit and birth Mr. JOHNSON was a man of Congress. To him the essence of government was the passage of legislation and the purpose of legislation was to insure equal justice, opportunity, and civil rights for all Americans. Under LYNDON JOHNSON's stewardship America made rapid progress toward these goals.

He was a big man. He knew power and he knew how to use it. But, of all his Texas-style excesses, one was by far the most abundant—his compassion and his appreciation for the dignity of man.

President JOHNSON was a doer. He worked hard, spoke to hundreds of people every day and steered through the Congress dozens of important bills. His legacy is his legislation. Civil rights, medicare, aid to education, voting rights, immigration reform, model cities programs, rent subsidies, minimum wage hikes, antipollution programs, antipoverty programs, and consumer protection.

But, LYNDON JOHNSON did more than legislate to make the Government a government for, of, and by the people. He listened too. On a wall in his Senate office hung his father's addage, "When you're talkin', you aint learnin' nothin'."

He tried valiantly to heal the wounds of the Nation. Rather than amputate a segment of society he wanted to bring us all together. His goal was reconstruction "with justice for all and malice toward none." His Nation's problems were his personal heartaches.

Hon. Dante B. Fascell
OF FLORIDA

Mr. Speaker, I join our colleagues in mourning the sudden and untimely death of our former President, LYNDON BAINES JOHNSON.

Although President JOHNSON had a history of heart trouble, he worked tirelessly and unendingly for what he believed was best for America. In the finest sense of the word, LYNDON JOHNSON was one of the most political men of our time. Yet, he voluntarily ended his career in an effort to achieve the peace we all so desperately wanted.

His accomplishments in domestic programs were numerous and brilliantly achieved. He turned his dream of a Great Society into specific actions on civil rights, medicare, housing, job opportunities, special education for the disadvantaged, parks and recreation areas for all our citizens, and a thousand other improvements for our country.

Probably no leader in our history cared so much and did so much for the achievement of civil rights and the equal opportunity for all citizens than LYNDON JOHNSON. This was one of his primary concerns in Congress, as Vice President and as President. It continued to be one of his major interests even after he left the White House.

One of his last public appearances, made against the advice of his doctors, was a civil rights symposium, in which he insisted on participating.

One of the most tragic aspects of his death is that it comes so close to the time when it finally appears that we may realize the peace in Southeast Asia over which he agonized. It was President JOHNSON who, after giving up his own career to remove any doubts whatsoever about his effort, first brought the North and South Vietnamese, the Vietcong, and the United States together at the conference table.

We will all miss having the benefit of his wise and willing counsel. Had he lived, he would have continued to contribute much to our Nation. LYNDON JOHNSON has earned a high place in history.

Hon. Daniel J. Flood
OF PENNSYLVANIA

Mr. Speaker, I am proud to say that LYNDON JOHNSON was a friend of mine. We served together when he was a Member of the House; we worked together on legislation when he was a majority leader in the U.S. Senate; and we joined together when he was President to create new programs in the fields of labor, health, education, and welfare.

On that terrible day in Dallas nearly a decade ago when John Fitzgerald Kennedy was assassinated, this man of courage, commitment, and compassion vowed that we should continue, and we did.

LYNDON JOHNSON made the dreams of John Kennedy into reality. For this alone, we should mourn him. But more than that LYNDON JOHNSON made the dreams of the poor and the sick and the aged and the minorities a reality, too.

Medicare, Federal aid to education, better housing, conservation including the battle against pollution, headstart, the job corps, model cities, Appalachia, and civil rights are among the programs that exist today, because LYNDON JOHNSON was a master legislative technician, the best I ever knew. He seemed to be able to make the impossible—possible. LYNDON JOHNSON was a man who never forgot the need for a good education, who never forgot that the missing government is to do for the people that which they cannot do for themselves.

History shall judge him, of course, but I am sure its verdict will cause us to mourn him even more.

With the passing in December of Harry Truman and the death on January 22 of LYNDON JOHNSON, this Nation for the first time in many years now has no living former Presidents. It gives one a sad and empty feeling.

Hon. Charles H. Wilson
OF CALIFORNIA

Mr. Speaker, he said:

To reach for the moon is a risk, but it is a risk we must take.

LYNDON B. JOHNSON was a President who never hesitated to take every possible risk in an effort to help his fellow man. While the risk of Vietnam proved his nemesis, the ones he took on other fronts of American society—health, housing, education, and equal opportunity—brought bountiful rewards to us all.

Believing that America must continue the Revolution of 1776, he worked uncompromisingly to secure independence for all through equal rights and equal opportunity. He literally wrote the chapter on civil rights, feeling rightly that an end to discrimination in America would prove our greatest strength both at home and abroad.

Never one to forget his humble origins and the deep impressions he received as a teacher in a rural school, LYNDON BAINES JOHNSON thought that "the classroom—not the trench—is the frontier of freedom now and forevermore." And from his belief that "it is in the soil of ignorance that poverty is planted," he worked tirelessly both as U.S. Senate majority leader and as President to secure equal education for all.

His achievements in education and civil rights were monumental. A great believer in the democratic system, his vision of America was one of great compassion and humanity. And, from his years of top-level experience in the House and Senate, he became a masterful and pragmatic politician, understanding that "if you're in politics and you can't tell when you walk into a room who's for you and who's against you, then you're in the wrong line of work." Indeed, his keen acumen about politics enabled him not only to initiate but to work effectively with Congress in passing a truly great legislative program.

But the lingering war in Southeast Asia cast the shadow which obscured his domestic accomplishments. Ironically, his death was to occur on the very eve of the negotiated settlement to which he had devoted the last few years of his Presidency. A lion of a President LYNDON B. JOHNSON had great courage in electing to forego a second term in the belief that only by exempting himself from candidacy could he keep the Vietnam conflict from evolving into a political issue.

So, in remembering LYNDON BAINES JOHNSON, let us not dwell upon his tragedy, but rather on his great love for this country and its people and his overriding concern for their welfare.

My deepest condolences go out to Lady Bird Johnson, undisputably a magnificient First Lady, and to the lovely and valiant Johnson daughters. The support of his loyal and devoted family got LYNDON JOHNSON through many a dark night, and I know that his towering memory will give his family a similar strength in the difficult and sad days ahead.

Hon. Frank Annunzio
OF ILLINOIS

Mr. Speaker, I rise today in tribute to LYNDON B. JOHNSON, 36th President of the United States.

I had the honor of knowing LYNDON JOHNSON personally and supported him in all of his major domestic legislative undertakings. I joined with the President in these efforts, not only because he was the leader of our party, but because I considered these efforts to be just and right.

I shall always remember LYNDON JOHNSON as a humble human being. Yet, along with his humility, he possessed tremendous courage and the ability to get things done. President JOHNSON was a great man, because he tried. He faced problems head-on, and tried to solve them fairly with dispatch, and with compassion. Because of his energy and conviction, he was amazingly successful.

LYNDON JOHNSON was President at a time in the history of our Republic when great social and technological changes were compelling us all to change our patterns of thinking. Since Mr. JOHNSON was bigger than life in everything he did, he was the catalyst which forced us all to reevaluate the way we think about ourselves and our country. President JOHNSON was a great leader and a great American. His death is a tremendous loss to our Nation.

Mrs. Annunzio and I extend our deepest sympathy to President JOHNSON's wife and family during this most difficult of times.

Hon. Tom S. Gettys
OF SOUTH CAROLINA

Mr. Speaker, the passing of former President LYNDON B. JOHNSON leaves a void in the lives of all Americans in general and in many of us in particular.

Indeed, he was a public servant of the first magnitude, as well as a formidable legislator. His ability to bring Members of both Houses together to support important legislation was phenomenal. He truly was the President of all the people of all the States and though they differed on innumerable occasions, he could and did meld them into majorities to both support and pass major milestones in legislation.

He was a modern Horatio Alger in that this truly self-made man came from the most humble of economic beginnings. He rose to become a Member of the House of Representatives, the leader of the Senate, Vice President of the United States, and a powerful President, filling out the unexpired term of our martyred President John F. Kennedy and then he was elected in one of history's greatest votes of confidence, by a trusting electorate.

Much of his proposed legislation, although controversial at the moment, was passed and signed into law. Former President JOHNSON was a man years ahead of his time.

He was a man of purpose, who believed in the theory that a purpose is a fantasy unless acted upon to its fullest.

The American people naturally will always differ in their individual assessments of all people and all things, including their evaluation of President JOHNSON's policies. Since freedom of thought and speech is a fundamental right, no one questions their process, but time will prove he was a man of charity and a man who loved his fellow man.

No one will ever charge him with not wanting peace in the world at large, but in Indochina most of all. He inherited, to some extent, this war so far away, yet he tried for peace under every sincere procedure known by both his staff and his office.

My deepest sympathies go out to his family. May their knowledge of our heartfelt loss soften the blow they have received.

Hon. J. J. Pickle
OF TEXAS

Mr. Speaker, it is with deep sadness, yet great respect, that I again take this opportunity to mark the passing of our late President, the Honorable LYNDON BAINES JOHNSON.

Courage, compassion, concern, strength, unselfishness, and honesty, and above all a dedication to get the job done, mark the best qualities of LYNDON B. JOHNSON.

To his countrymen and to the world he came to symbolize the potential of mankind and of a nation.

With superb natural skills as a politician, legislator, and public official he had one consuming drive in life—a fierce desire that our ideas, programs, and actions serve all the men and women of this Nation.

Hon. Dale Milford
OF TEXAS

Mr. Speaker, this is my first opportunity to have the privilege of addressing the House of Representatives. Normally a freshman steps into the well for his maiden speech with the hopes of swaying the Nation on some great issue. My mission today will be to console the Nation on the loss of a great man.

Unlike most of my colleagues, I did not know President JOHNSON personally. I never had the privilege of experiencing his warm handshake or receiving one of his friendly slaps on the back.

Like the majority of this Nation's citizens, I knew President JOHNSON from his career in Government service, a career that took him through both Houses of the Federal Government and into the Presidency.

A citizen forms an attachment for his leader in the same manner that he forms attachments for his immediate family. Our President is closely associated to our father. In our immediate families we often disagree with our father, and even temporarily have squabbles with him. But we maintain our respect and our feeling of warmth.

Our citizen attachment to President JOHNSON and his long years of Government service followed these same patterns.

During his lifetime, for example, many of us called him conservative; many of us called him progressive; there were even a few of us who called him radical. But there are a few things that all the people of my district know to be true. He was great; he was Texan; and we loved him. Therefore, we, as citizens, feel the same sense of loss as that of his immediate family.

Hon. Ray Roberts
OF TEXAS

Mr. Speaker, the man who probably did more for America than anyone since Franklin Roosevelt has passed away. LYNDON BAINES JOHNSON, 36th President of the United States devoted his life to the service of his country. He was a schoolteacher, a congressional secretary, and then he was appointed by his idol, President Franklin Roosevelt, to head up a program in Texas that would make it possible for young people to work part time, go to school, or to learn a trade.

It was my privilege to join him when he was Director of the National Youth Administration in Texas.

I knew him as a young idealist who drove himself from daylight till dark to try to do more for the young people of Texas than could be done elsewhere. It was from this position that he was elected to Congress. He was an inspiration to me from the day I met him until his death.

He quickly became the protege of Speaker Sam Rayburn and one of the favorites of President Roosevelt. He earned his spurs early in Congress when he was selected in his third term to head up the Democratic congressional campaign. Not only did he hold the House for the Democrats, he increased their membership.

As a Senator, he was equally outstanding and became majority leader of the Senate. Throughout his legislative career his philosophy was contained in the biblical exhortation. "Come now, and let us reason together." During this time he was without peers in his ability to find a basis for agreement among disagreeing Members.

As President, LYNDON JOHNSON passed more landmark legislation to help the underprivileged than any President we have ever known. He was

saddled with a war he did not start and could not end. His tremendous success in other fields led most Americans to believe he could do anything he wanted to do, and, therefore, they were critical of the fact he did not end the war.

LYNDON JOHNSON was a great man—great in stature, great in heart and great in ideals for his beloved country. Surely America has lost one of her great leaders, and I have lost one of the greatest friends I ever had.

I extend my deepest sympathy to Mrs. Johnson, Linda Bird and Luci, their husbands and children.

Hon. Omar Burleson
OF TEXAS

Mr. Speaker, observation of history suggests that all great leaders have had much in common. It seems to me that former President LYNDON JOHNSON had an amalgam of characteristics exhibited in many of our modern day statesmen, both in and out of government.

It is not surprising that this appears to be the case since he virtually grew up under the tutelage of such men as Franklin Roosevelt, Sam Rayburn, John Nance Garner, and others who directed the affairs of this Nation during times of change and under varied circumstances which occurred during the formative period of President JOHNSON's political life.

As LYNDON JOHNSON became a national legislator, first as a Member of this U.S. House of Representatives and then the U.S. Senate, he, too, left an imprint on events of that time. Later, as Vice President and then as President, he led this Nation with the great energy and ambition with which he was so greatly endowed.

There were differences of opinion on issues, which are bound to occur between men, but his devotion to what he believed was always something anyone could admire.

I prefer to remember his strong unyielding conviction that this Nation must be strong in its ability to defend itself and to ally those nations who sought our assistance in maintaining their independence.

The ability to anticipate events and shape policy accordingly was always an amazing performance by President JOHNSON. He had vision, he had dreams, and he had the courage to institute actions to bring them to the greatest possible fruition.

As is the case of all great public figures, only time will make it possible to fully appraise the leadership he gave this Nation. This seems to be a characteristic of our Nation as a people but one thing is already proved, and that is that he was a leader.

I join my colleagues in extending sympathy and condolence to Lady Bird and the other members of the Johnson family and hope that they may have the greatest possible comfort with the passing of the shortest time. They can, of course, do so in the knowledge of the great service he rendered and the type of husband and father he was to them.

Hon. Robert G. Stephens, Jr.
OF GEORGIA

Mr. Speaker, on January 24 in the rotunda of our Capitol, a solemn and impressive memorial ceremony was held as the body of President LYNDON B. JOHNSON was brought in to lie in state as a last farewell tribute to him, the President, who had served so long and well in this building as a Member of both Houses of Congress.

As Mrs. Johnson and the President's family gathered there with Members of the House and Senate, with President and Mrs. Nixon, and with friends and former Cabinet members of the Johnson administration, a magnificent eulogy was delivered by President JOHNSON's Secretary of State, Dean Rusk, now professor of international law at the University of Georgia in my home town of Athens, Ga. Mr. Rusk had the privilege of being selected to make this memorial speech from among all the friends and official family of the Johnson times.

The only other address delivered was a fine personal tribute delivered by the gentleman from Texas, Mr. J. J. Pickle, President JOHNSON's own Congressman.

In order to preserve the memorial speech of Secretary Rusk because of its sentiments and also as a part of the historical events of our era, under permission previously obtained I insert the eulogy in the Record at this point:

REMARKS MADE BY DEAN RUSK AT A MEMORIAL SERVICE FOR PRESIDENT LYNDON B. JOHNSON

JANUARY 24, 1973.

A home on the bank of the Pedernales in the beautiful hill country of Texas, surrounded by his beloved family and the friends with whom he so fully shared his warm and generous spirit—.

A home in this place where we are gathered today, in the Congress, which was his life for so long, filled with friendships enlivened by that political debate which is the lifeblood of a free society, but friendships cemented by the common task of insuring that the public business somehow would go forward at the end of the day.

A home for more than five years at the summit of responsibility, of responsibility and not necessarily of power—for he, as other Presidents, understood that many expectations and demands were addressed to him which were beyond his constitutional reach or, indeed, beyond the reach of our nation in a world community where we might persuade but cannot command. These were years of awesome burdens, but burdens lightened by the fine intelligence and the natural grace and the personal devotion of the First Lady who was always at his side.

And now he returns to the Pedernales to a home among the immortals, that goodly company of men and women whom we shall forever cherish because they were concerned about those matters which barred the path to our becoming what we have in us to become. More than a thousand years ago, in a simpler and more robust age, perhaps we might have known him as Lyndon the Liberator, for he was determined to free our people in body, mind and spirit.

A few strokes of the brush cannot portray this man to whom we offer our affection and respect today. As for me, I would begin with his deep compassion for his fellowman, a compassion which was shared by the Congress and resulted in the most extraordinary legislative season in our history.

Who can forget that remarkable evening of March 15, 1965, when President JOHNSON addressed a joint session of Congress on voting rights and other civil rights? It was perhaps his finest single message.

You will remember that, after recalling his days as a teacher of poor Mexican-American children back in 1928, he said, "It never even occurred to me in my fondest dreams that I might have the chance to help the sons and daughters of those students and to help people like them all over the country."

And then, with eyes which bored into the conscience of all who heard him, he said, "But now I do have that chance, and I'll let you in on a secret—I mean to use it. And I hope you will use it with me."

And then he went on to disclose in a very frank way what some of his deepest hopes were. Congressman Pickle has already quoted those hopes. One may give these ideas any name or epithet one might choose. They did not evolve out of some empty intellectual exercise. They were not the product of shrewd political calculation. His colleagues knew them as a volcanic eruption from the innermost being of his soul when the responsibility for leadership finally became his own.

Many have said that LYNDON JOHNSON was demanding upon his colleagues and personal staff. Indeed he was. And demanding upon the Congress and the American people and many a foreign leader as well. But he was most demanding upon himself and stubbornly resisted the admonitions of his associates to slow down. There was so much to do, and there was so little time in which to get it done.

President JOHNSON sometimes deprecated his own background in foreign affairs. Actually he brought great talents and a rich experience to this aspect of the Presidency in November 1963. As Senate Majority Leader throughout much of the Eisenhower years, he was necessarily and deeply involved in the widest range of legislation affecting foreign and defense policy.

When he became Vice President, President Kennedy asked him frequently to make foreign visits and consult with foreign leaders on matters of major importance—not merely a tourist's visit.

He absorbed briefings in a most expert fashion, and with a powerful intellect went directly to the heart of the issues under discussion. And as many present know, he was always formidable in negotiation or persuasion.

He had a special ability, perhaps learned in the Senate, to begin his consideration of a problem by putting himself in the other fellow's shoes, in an attempt to understand which answers might be possible.

He had a personal code of relations among political leaders which did not permit him or his colleagues to engage in personal vilification aimed at foreign leaders, however deep the disagreement might appear to be.

Today's writers are inclined to discuss LYNDON JOHNSON almost solely in terms of Viet-Nam, and such questions as whether he did too much or too little in that tragic struggle. The historian will take a broader view and weigh such things as the Consular and Civil Air Agreements with the Soviet Union, the Non-proliferation Treaty, our space treaties, his East-West trade bill, the beginnings of the SALT talks, and many other initiatives aimed at building the peace.

He had a very special and affectionate feeling for the nations of the western hemisphere. He used to say to us, "This hemisphere is where we live, this is our home, these are our neighbors. We must start with our own neighborhood."

Mr. President, last evening you made some moving remarks about President JOHNSON in your brief address to the American people. We congratulate you on the substance of that address and give you our best wishes for the weeks and months ahead. I mention two points which you made about LYNDON JOHNSON. That President JOHNSON was a man of peace and would have welcomed the peace which seems now to be opening up in Southeast Asia. How true. And he would, indeed, have joined you, Mr. President, in paying tribute to those millions of gallant and dedicated men in uniform whose service and sacrifice opened the way for the peace which is before us.

In his last State of the Union Message to the Congress, his final sentence was, "But I believe that at least it will be said that we tried." Ah, yes, he tried, with reckless disregard for his own life.

And then, in the final chapter of his book, when he was reflecting upon how it looked to him as he returned to that ranch which he loved so much, his final sentence was, "And I knew also that I had given it everything that was in me."

As time passes, the world will increasingly acknowledge that the "everything" that was in him was a very great deal, and that men and women all over the earth are forever in his debt.

Mr. Speaker, the President of the United States, LYNDON JOHNSON, was close to the people of Georgia and close to my district because his family came from our county in Georgia and went from there to an adjacent county and then from there to Texas. We felt especially close to LYNDON

JOHNSON because of the leadership he had given when the county needed that leadership. We felt close to President JOHNSON because of his friendship for our late beloved Senator Richard B. Russell. Senator Russell and Senator JOHNSON at that time were the two great powers of influence in the Senate of the United States. We also felt very close to President JOHNSON because of the heart he showed when young Bobby Russell, one of the associate justices of our supreme court died. Bobby had been up here as a page in the Senate, and President JOHNSON, the President of the United States, put down his busy schedule and came down to Georgia to attend the funeral of Bobby Russell in Winder, Ga.

So it is with appreciation that I come here at this time and thank the gentleman for letting me participate in these memorial speeches for President JOHNSON. Again I thank the gentleman.

Hon. J. J. Pickle
OF TEXAS

Mr. Speaker, at this point in the Record I insert the text of the eulogy delivered by the Honorable W. Marvin Watson, former Postmaster General of the United States and a former member of President JOHNSON's staff. His speech was a moving and inspirational message for all Americans. The eulogy follows:

PRESIDENT LYNDON B. JOHNSON—EULOGY BY HON. W. MARVIN WATSON

He was ours, and we loved him beyond any telling of it.

We shared his victories and his defeats.

In victory he taught us to be magnanimous—in defeat he taught us to be without hate—to learn—to rally—to accept the challenge and to try again.

He believed that good men together could accomplish anything, even the most impossible of dreams. No matter who his opponent, he constantly sought to find that touchstone within the soul of every man which, if discovered, would release the impulse for honest and fair solution. Hate was never in this man's heart.

Each of you has your own memories of this man who served for 37 years in this city. I had the honor of being with him through the final four years of his Presidency—in those great moments of triumph when the American people endorsed him so strongly—in those magnificent hours when he stood before the Congress of the United States and led the way to the passage of laws long overdue that would lead to justice long denied—and in that darkening twilight when, as a man seeking peace, he was forced to continue a bitter war to honor our country's commitment to a small, far-off ally.

I watched the gray come into his hair.

I saw each deep line etch itself into his face as he gave all at his command to lead our country through the turmoil which surged around us.

I watched him as he used his great gift of persuasion to convince a Southern Senator that the time had come for the Civil Rights Act—I watched him formulate, secure passage and sign into law the most comprehensive legislative program in education, housing, conservation and health of any President in history—I watched him in the Situation Room at the time of crisis during the Six Day War when only his ability, his knowledge, and his sheer courage helped to keep that conflict from erupting into a wider confrontation.

I sat with him through those long nights as he endured the agony of Vietnam, as he sought the key to peace, and as he waited for word of men whom he had ordered into battle. Each was a human being to him, not a statistic; each was a name linked with wives and parents and children—he cared for people, not for numbers.

So desparately did he want a just and lasting peace— so much did he want us to reason together—so much did he yearn that man's goodness would triumph over man's evil—so often as friend turned to political foe, did he nod with sad understanding and pray that in the years to come, the sacrifices he was making would be worthy of the American people and serve ultimately as a firm platform on which to build a better world.

And through it all, I saw him earnestly seek God's wisdom for his decisions, for this was a man with a strong belief in the Almighty.

President Nixon, as you so eloquently stated in your message informing Congress of President JOHNSON's death, it was his "noble and difficult destiny to lead America through a long, dark night of necessity at home and abroad." If he could have chosen other circumstances in which to be President, perhaps he would have. But, America has a capacity to call forth the leadership it must have in those hours of its greatest need. We had Abraham Lincoln when he was needed. We had Franklin Roosevelt when he was needed. History will record that in the seventh decade of the 20th century, America had LYNDON JOHNSON when he was needed.

When you remember him, remember him please for two things—his devotion to his country—and his restraint.

So often in his Presidency, dissension escalated into violence. Yet always, no matter how critical the situation, his inner faith in the people came to the fore and his restraint in the uses of power permitted the people to confront each situation and overcome it utilizing the inherent rights of free men.

Those of us who loved him take comfort in the knowledge that before he died, he could see the dawn of domestic tranquility and of foreign peace which he gave so much of his great heart to bring about. The structure of peace which President Nixon, with great distinction and determination, is building in the world today will rest upon a foundation laid in loneliness and stubborn courage by LYNDON JOHNSON.

This man's restless, searching heart began to give out long before January 22nd. He gave so much of himself to so many that it is wondrous that God, in His grace, granted him four years to enjoy his retirement in the hill country he so deeply treasured.

Not for him the easy way.

Not for him any halfway measures.

He was a tall man of giant character, and when he committed himself, he committed himself totally. And he asked his countrymen to do the same.

He asked those who had much to be concerned for those who had least.

He asked us to live up to our national promise.

He asked us to be worthy of our heritage.

He asked us to be true to ourselves.

But, he never asked more than he was willing to give— and what he gave was good enough to confirm and advance the progress of the nation he served.

LYNDON JOHNSON loved a woman, and she was his greatest joy and his greatest comfort. He loved his children and his grandchildren and to see them together was a heartwarming experience, for it transcended normal devotion.

And coupled with that he loved each of us, sometimes with wry amusement at our failures, often with sharp words at our imperfections, but always with a sweeping and generous understanding of our frailties. The dimensions of this man were vast.

He is gone from us now—and this afternoon we shall take him home and he will be forever a part of the hill country.

Last September, I had the opportunity to be with him when he spoke of America and of the future.

He knew then that he might not see another autumn, but this was not a man who welcomed or needed sympathy.

Years from now, when historians appraise him, his speech that day could serve as the cornerstone of their research—for it reflected the true LYNDON JOHNSON. He gave much of himself to it, and it might well be his epitaph. He said:

"With the coming of September, each year, we are reminded as the song says, that the days are dwindling down to a precious few—the green leaves of summer will begin to brown—the chill winds of winter will begin to blow—and before we are ready for the end to come, the year will be gone.

"As it is with the calendar, so it sometimes seems to be with our country and our system. For there are those among us who would have us believe that America has come to its own September—and that our nation's span as mankind's last best hope will be done."

President JOHNON continued:

"But I live by the faith that with each passing day we are always approaching nearer to the beginning of a new springtime and it is by that perspective that I see our country now.

"No nation can be more than the visions of its people. America cannot be more than we believe ourselves capable of becoming.

"I want to open the soul of America to the warm sunlight of faith in itself . . . faith in the principles and precepts of its birth . . . and faith in the promise and potential of its people."

That was LYNDON BAINES JOHNSON, the 36th President of the United States of America.

The years will be lonely without him.

Mr. Speaker, at this point I insert the remarks by the Honorable John B. Connally, former Treasurer of the United States, which was a eulogy delivered at the graveside at the LBJ

Ranch. Mr. Connally was one of the young men who joined the President's staff in the late 1930's and was "one of his boys" and has given a life of dedication and devotion to the President.

[From the Austin Statesman, Jan. 26, 1973]

"How Can a Few Words Eulogize a Man Such as He?"

(By Hon. John B. Connally)

We lay to rest here a man whose whole life embodied the spirit and hope of America.

How can a few words eulogize a man such as he?

Not in a purely personal way, although President and Mrs. Johnson had a profound effect on my life, on Nellie's and the lives of our children, just as they had on the lives of many of you within the sound of my voice.

Not in a dispassionate way, because none who knew him could speak dispassionately of him.

And not in words of great elegance and adornment, simply because he would not have wanted that.

Lyndon Johnson spoke plainly all of his life. He spoke to the hearts of people. The wellspring of his thoughts and words and deeds was always the fundamental character of the plain people he loved and whose dreams and aspirations he tried so hard to bring to reality.

Eloquent praise and heartfelt words of sympathy have poured forth since last Monday afternoon when we learned this great heart had stilled. The world has a fallen leader and owes him much honor.

But I feel today it is these plain people he loved—the silent people—who mourn him the most.

He gave them all he had for forty years.

He gave them his incredible energy, his matchless legislative mind, and his restless devotion to the ideal that his country's grasp should always exceed its reach . . . that nothing was impossible where there was a determined will.

He was one of them. He never forgot it, and they will never forget him.

Lyndon Johnson was one of three presidents to be born in this century. But this hill country in 1908 was not much different from the frontier his father and mother had known.

The comforts and amenities were few, the educational opportunities were determined by the quality of a single teacher or a handful of teachers, and man's fortunes were dictated by the amount of rain or the heat of the sun or the coldness of the north wind.

Yet a child's dreams could be as wide as the sky and his future as green as the winter oats, because this, after all, was America.

Lyndon Johnson made his dreams come true because he saw the real opportunity of this land and this political system into which he was born. He never doubted he could do it, because he always knew he could work harder than anyone else, sustain his dedication longer than anyone else and renew his spirit more completely than anyone else no matter how serious the setback or even the defeat.

Thus he rose from these limited beginnings to the zenith of power, and as he so often said with a mixture of awe and pride, "I guess I've come a long way for a boy from Johnson City, Texas."

But with all of his strengths Lyndon Johnson cannot be viewed as a man above men, a mythical hero conquesting all before him.

In a sense, his life was one of opposition—of conflicting forces within him trying to emerge supreme.

The product of simple rural surroundings he was thrust by his own ambition into an urbane and complicated world.

Born into a Southwestern, Protestant, Anglo-Saxon heritage, he found his native values challenged constantly in the political and social climate which enveloped him.

Reared and educated without benefit of a more worldly existence, he thirsted for the knowledge that would propel him to the heights in the life he chose for himself.

Some criticized him for being unlettered and unsophisticated when in truth he was incredibly wise and incredibly sophisticated in ways his critics never understood, perhaps because he always dealt not with things as they should have been, but as they were.

He dealt with basic human qualities and basic human reactions.

He was uninhibited by hypocrisy or false pride. He was not afraid to let his feelings show.

It is said that in some ways he was an insecure man. Of course he was. He knew he was not endowed with the kingly virtues of always being right; he tried merely to do his best to discover what was right.

He recognized his own shortcomings far more than many of his detractors recognized theirs. He never hesitated to ask for help and he understood better than most the meaning of loyalty and mutual affection among friends and associates.

The same insecurities existed in Lyndon Johnson that exist in all of us. His strengths and his weaknesses were universally human qualities, shared by people everywhere who have also dreamed of the mountaintop, each in his own way.

President Johnson cared for people, no matter where they lived in this world or their color or their heritage.

He showed this in public ways too numerous to list. What is more important, he showed it in private ways when the world was not looking.

Not long ago he visited the ranch of a friend in Mexico and discovered a small rural schoolhouse for children in the depths of poverty.

When he returned to Austin he and Mrs. Johnson gathered dozens of small wind-up toys, medicine, clothing and other items for those children, and when he went back to Mexico he took those things with him and he had his own Christmas celebrations with those children.

So we have the vision of a former president of the United States, perhaps down on his knees, surrounded by youngsters from another land, whose language he did not speak; demonstrating for them how to wind up a 25-cent toy.

Somehow, I think that's how Lyndon Johnson would like best for us to remember him.

The tens of thousands who have filed past his bier and the tens of millions who mourn him from afar—these are the people who understand who he was and what he was and how he thought, because he was one of them.

I think they would know of his frustrations of leaderships, his impatience, the occasional temper, sometimes the sharp tongue, but always the overriding courage and determination of this complex man.

Surely they would know of his anguish over sending men to war when all he wanted was peace and prosperity and freedom. It seems ironic on this day that his predecessors began the war in Southeast Asia and his successor ended it. It was his fate to be the bridge over the intervening chasm of conflict that swept this country and the world. But he accepted that role without flinching, and no one would be happier today, no one would be more appreciative of the beginnings of peace and the president who achieved it, than the president who worked so long and so unselfishly for the tranquility that eluded him.

It is fashionable among some to refer to LYNDON JOHNSON as a tragic president.

But I believe history will describe his presidency as tragic only in the sense that it began through tragedy, for his service was not one of tragedy but one of triumph.

It was a triumph for the poor, a triumph for the oppressed, a triumph for social justice and a triumph for mankind's never-ending quest for freedom.

Along this stream and under these trees he loved he will now rest.

He first saw light here. He last felt life here. May he now find peace here.

Hon. John J. McFall
OF CALIFORNIA

Mr. Speaker, we are here today to memorialize LYNDON JOHNSON.

It is fitting that we do so in this Chamber where Mr. JOHNSON first came 42 years ago.

He knew the Congress as no man ever will. First as a doorman to this room, then as assistant to his Congressman, next as Congressman, and as we so well know, as Senator, Vice President, and President.

The Nation has lost a great leader. The poor, the black, the aged, the sick have lost a champion. I have lost a friend.

Most of us here today supported LYNDON JOHNSON at one time or another. I am proud to have supported him often, and willingly, both domestically and in foreign affairs.

This man's legislative accomplishments were legion. Ideas and social programs that had languished in the Congress for years were placed on the books during his 5 crowded years in office.

And we could do his memory no greater disservice at this time than to allow the systematic dismantling of his social visions and accomplishments.

Medical care for the elderly and the poor had been discussed since the first days of social security. They now have it. We must not take it away.

Rights of the minorities to be treated fairly were discussed since the days of the Civil War. They now have many rights; they will have more, until we all are truly treated equally. We must not take it away.

Aid to education was a dream of many. LYNDON JOHNSON made it a reality in a series of landmark educational measures. We must not take it away.

The training and opportunity for jobs has long been a national necessity. LYNDON JOHNSON made it a source of national pride. We must not resort to callous economic programs whose victims are those whose greatest need is a fair chance at a productive job.

A strong and vital nation, with pride and performance on its commitments was LYNDON JOHNSON's goal. We must not become a weak and impotent nation. He would not have allowed it.

These, and many, many more were the goals and dreams and accomplishments of LYNDON JOHNSON—for himself, perhaps, but really for the people of this Nation.

For he loved the people. When he worked for education, he thought of the individual children who were denied an equal choice. When he worked for voting rights, he thought of the citizen who was denied his rightful voice in government. When he worked for social security and medicare and jobs, he thought not of great programs, but of the individual who had to be given his fair chance, but was denied.

LYNDON JOHNSON's life touched every American. The improvements he dreamed of and fought for and accomplished will be his living monument.

He once said:

I have devoted my time on this earth to working toward the day when there would be no second-class citizenship in America, no second-quality opportunity, no second-hand justice at home, no second-place status in the world for our ideals and benefits.

As I joined his family and friends on his burial day in his beloved Texas hill country, my thoughts turned to how few of us have such great goals and how fewer still accomplish any of them.

He did it all.

Hon. James R. Jones
OF OKLAHOMA

Mr. Speaker, I approach this, my first speech as a Member of this body, with mixed emotions. On the one hand, I am very honored to be able to pay tribute to the man, LYNDON B. JOHNSON, who gave me and scores of other young men and women in the United States an opportunity to serve this country and who also renewed in us a dedication and love for this country.

It also is a sad occasion, because by our tributes we acknowledge that the wisdom, and wit of LYNDON JOHNSON, and the love which LYNDON JOHNSON had for America must rest as a part of our history.

I feel I had a somewhat special relationship with President JOHNSON, which at times extended to employer-employee; at times to man to man; father-son and President-citizen. Particularly during the last 4 years of his Presidency, as a member of his White House staff, I had a rare opportunity to observe this human being who happened to be our President, from early in the morning in the President's bedroom, when he went over the casualty reports and the situation reports worldwide and in Vietnam, to late at night when he usually left the troubles of the Presidency sometime around midnight or thereafter.

I had the opportunity to observe this human being in many moments of pressure and in many times of relaxation. My admiration for him as a private person and as a public being only grew with exposure. He was a genuine, warm, decent man for whom I will always have profound fondness, respect and love.

I remember LYNDON JOHNSON for many things, because he was a man who cared, not in the abstract, but a man who cared for people in human terms. He did not measure his Presidency, nor did he measure his life, by the pieces of legislation which he passed. He measured it by what that legislation and what his works did for people. He had landmark legislation, which this Congress helped him pass, in the field of education. But he did not put it in terms of, "Here is a piece of legislation." He put it in terms of Mexican-American children he had taught as a young man. He put it in terms of an opportunity for all the children of this country, regardless of their backgrounds, to have a chance to get the tools to do for themselves, to share the full opportunities of this country.

He did not look upon his great legislation that he passed in the field of health care, such as Medicare, as just another bill the historians will look at. I remember in Beaumont, Tex., one time in a nursing home, when a lady looked up to him and said, "Mr. President, you have given me pride, you have given me dignity," and that is what he wanted to give his fellow human beings.

He demanded excellence both of himself and of those around him. In many of those long days in the White House, we would be exhausted at the midnight hour from the demands that he had placed on the staff. When you went home, you really realized what he had done for you. He had allowed you to push yourself beyond the capabilities and the abilities that you thought you had, into that pursuit of excellence which he demanded of himself and of the country.

He wanted peace probably more than any single thing. I think that was the single, most important reason why he chose not to run for reelection in 1968.

He loved this country and he loved those who built the country, the constructors, and not those who tore it down. Those people he could not understand.

He was a private man and yet he belonged to the public. He was a humorous man. He was a forgiving man. He was an understanding man.

I remember his wit. One Saturday evening after a particularly long week in which he was going back to the mansion for a private dinner. He invited a particular Member of Congress, who had been vocally critical of him, to have dinner with him and his family. A member of his family said:

Why would you do that? He is your enemy, he is saying all those nasty things about you. Why don't you enjoy dinner with your family?

And he replied:

If I did not have dinner with my enemies, I might be dining alone.

He was a witty man. He was an understanding man. He was a man who loved the power of political office, and mostly what that power would do for the country.

I remember the night before President Nixon was inaugurated in 1968. Mr. JOHNSON had a group of the special assistants and their families in the yellow oval room of the White House, and in what was a most moving experience he recalled the history of America that he had personally participated in. He encouraged all of us to try to be bipartisan in our support of those who would lead us in our lifetimes.

He did have a special relationship with and a special feeling for the Presidency.

Mr. Speaker, I ask unanimous consent to include in the Record at this point some comments from an essay by John Steinbeck which bear upon what America does about its Presidents and what it feels toward its Presidents.

The relationship of Americans to their President is a matter of amazement to foreigners. Of course we respect the Office and admire the man who can fill it, but at the same time we inherently fear and suspect power. We are proud of the President, and we blame him for things he did not do. We are related to the President in a close and almost family sense; we inspect his every move and mood with suspicion. We insist that the President be cautious in speech, guarded in action, immaculate in his private and public life; and in spite of these imposed pressures we are avidly curious about the man hidden behind the formal public image we have created. We have made a tough but unwritten code of conduct for him, and the slightest deviation brings forth a torrent of accusations and abuse.

The President must be greater than anything else, but not better than anyone else. We subject him and his family to close and constant scrutiny and denounce them for things that we ourselves do everyday. A Presidential slip of the tongue, a slight error in judgment—social, political or ethical—can raise a storm of protest. We give the President more work than a man can do, more responsibility than a man can take, more pressure than a man can bear. We abuse him often and rarely praise him. We wear him out, use him up, eat him up. And with all this, Americans have a love for the President that goes beyond loyalty or party or nationality; he is ours, and we exercise the right to destroy him.

Mr. Speaker, as has been said during these tributes to Lyndon Johnson, Mr. Johnson learned about Government from two men— Speaker Sam Rayburn and President Franklin Roosevelt. He was generous with this knowledge and gave me a rare opportunity to learn. I am pleased to see that former Congressman Ed Edmondson from whom I also learned so much is in the Chamber today to pay his respects to our mutual friend, Mr. Johnson, and the Johnson family. In conclusion, Mr. Speaker, I would just point to another essay I read which stated that in America we honor our mediocre Presidents during their lifetimes and we honor our great Presidents after they have departed.

I feel, on behalf of myself and my wife Olivia and all those who had the privilege of working with President Johnson that the honors due him for his greatness and his contributions to this country and to his friends are just now beginning to come home. We will miss him very deeply.

Hon. Barbara Jordan
OF TEXAS

Mr. Speaker, the death of Lyndon B. Johnson diminished the lives of every American involved with mankind.

He was a great man and a great President of the United States. Historians may regard that judgment as premature. But those of us who felt the power of his compassion and were the beneficiaries of his legislative prowess and effectiveness cannot await the historian's judgment. We know now and see clearly that the fact of Lyndon B. Johnson's life and work stripped the Federal Government of its neutrality and made it the actor on behalf of America's old, poor, and black citizens.

The depth of Lyndon B. Johnson's concern for people cannot be quantified. It was big and all encompassing. Old men straightened their stooped backs because he lived. Little children dared look forward to intellectual achievement because he lived.

Black Americans became excited about a future of opportunity, hope, justice and dignity during his Presidency. Lyndon B. Johnson reminded this country shortly before his death that the problem of being black in a white society remains and that the problem of unequal opportunity cannot be overcome until unequal history is overcome. He wanted America to get on with the business of removing the vestiges of racial discrimination wherever found.

The record of the Johnson Presidency provides us with real and hard evidence of his commitment to equality for all men. There is no need to repeat it here for a quick glance at the laws of the United States enacted from 1963 through 1968 provide an authentic account.

The legacy of Lyndon B. Johnson is a legacy of hope for defenseless Americans—a hope born in the decade of the sixties—a hope which must not be allowed to die in the decade of the seventies.

Lyndon B. Johnson left us a legacy of courage and commitment.

Let us today resolve to protect and defend this inheritance. He was counting on us and we must not let him down.

Hon. James C. Wright, Jr.
OF TEXAS

Mr. Speaker, as is always the case when a great man dies, journalists during the past 2 weeks have been recounting the incidents and events, large and small, that help us understand Lyndon Johnson as a distinguished lawmaker, as a President, and as a man.

Since my tenure in Congress coincided in part with Lyndon Johnson's service in the Senate and later in the White House, I came to know him fairly well. He was my friend, a truly monumental person, and a man whom I believe history will treat far better than some of his contemporaries have treated him.

It would be folly to try to paint even a rough word portrait of LYNDON JOHNSON in these few minutes, because he was above all an enormously complex man. There are, however, little scraps of recollection that give illuminating insights into at least certain phases of his personality, his hopes, and his dreams.

My first exposure to LYNDON JOHNSON date back to 1941. Senator Morris Sheppard of Texas had died and there was a special election to fill his vacancy in the Senate. LYNDON JOHNSON, then a young Congressman from central Texas, sought the post. For most Texans, it was the first we had heard of this driving, thrusting personality who was to loom so large in the history of our State and of our Nation.

Mr. JOHNSON was not successful in that bid for higher office. He barely missed winning election to the Senate that year. My most memorable recollection of him at the time was his publicly stated promise, those few fateful months before Pearl Harbor, that if it ever became necessary to send American boys overseas in a foreign war, LYNDON JOHNSON would leave his seat in the U.S. Senate and go with them.

When Pearl Harbor came—in the words of President Roosevelt, "A day that will live in infamy"—Congressman JOHNSON made good his promise. Of all Members of the House and Senate, he was the first to enlist in the service of his country. He left the Halls of Congress and accompanied members of my generation to the South Pacific where he participated in combat action against the Japanese, earning the Silver Star for gallantry.

For some who find it easy to attribute selfish motives to every deed of decency and kindness, LYNDON JOHNSON's championing of the oppressed and the dispossessed may have seemed nothing more than "politics." Those who knew him as a person know better. I recall from the days immediately following the hostilities of World War II an occurrence in which the body of a Mexican-American boy was returned and he was denied burial by the bigoted rules which governed his hometown cemetery in south Texas. It was LYNDON JOHNSON who pointedly and publicly exposed the barrenness of the blind and unthinking prejudice of that community when he arranged for the body of that young man to be buried with honors at Arlington National Cemetery. With

LYNDON JOHNSON, it was not "politics." It was conviction.

One small incident took place on an airplane en route to Texas only a year or so after he had recovered from his first heart attack in 1955. As the plane droned westward from Washington, Mr. JOHNSON and I talked about the racial unrest that was then festering in Texas. Because of his work in behalf of civil rights legislation, Senator JOHNSON was being accused in some quarters of being a turncoat—a traitor to the Southern cause—a tool of the NAACP. One fellow who had been listening to the conversation asked the Senator what he was going to do about this accusation. This fellow asked:

Don't you think you will have to deny it?

I will never forget Mr. JOHNSON's reply. He said:

No, I'm not going to demagogue on that issue. If I have to prove that I hate Negroes in order to win, then I'll just not win.

He told us there was a Negro girl who brought him coffee in the majority leader's office every morning. He said,

I'm not going to have to look away when she comes in for being ashamed of something I've said.

Then, recalling his battle to recover from the heart attack, he told me:

When I lay in that hospital bed I thought of a lot of things. A man doesn't occupy this earth forever. I don't know when I'll die, and I hope it won't be soon. But I'm not going to die with that on my conscience.

A man indeed does not occupy this earth forever. When death struck LYNDON JOHNSON in the privacy of his bedroom all his friends could be certain that his conscience was not haunted by anything he had failed to do in the field of human rights.

LYNDON B. JOHNSON was a big man and he moved on a big stage. He was big in compassion for his fellow man, and big in his ambitions for the betterment of our Nation.

He wanted to wipe out poverty, to end racial injustice, to conquer space, to establish a genuine and lasting peace in Southeast Asia—and he wanted to do them all at once.

The wonder is not that he failed to accomplish all of his goals. The wonder is that he was able to accomplish so many of them.

LYNDON JOHNSON was above all a generous man. He was impulsively generous on occasion with his friends, and often more generous than

many ever realized in his appraisal and personal
treatment of political foes.

More than this, he was generous with himself.
Abundantly, almost wantonly, he spilled out his
time and effort and energy. In the days of his
Presidency, it was almost as though he were
haunted by the limitations of time. There was so
much to be done, and so little time in which to
accomplish it.

Some who were closer to Mr. JOHNSON than
I in the last few months of his life have expressed
privately the feeling that he may have had a
premonition of death. I have no knowledge of
that nor any reliable insight. But I recall with
vivid clarity the last conversation I had with
Mr. JOHNSON. We were having lunch in his suite
in the library which was his endowment to the
University of Texas. The former President was
relaxed. He spoke with pride of his family, his
children and grandchildren, the opportunities for
service that had come his way, the relative comfort and material abundance which had been his
privilege. And then, almost as in a self-pro-
nounced benediction, he said, "I am content."

Many have called LYNDON JOHNSON the greatest legislative leader in our history. He was a
great politician, no one can deny that, but he was
also a great humanitarian with a deep compassion and respect for his fellow man.

He did more than the country ever realized or
appreciated and accomplished less than his own
dreams. He wanted a "Great Society" but unlike
so many who want to improve the country, he
devoted a lifetime to doing something about it.
For LYNDON JOHNSON the "Great Society" was
not just a dream; it was a way of life.

Hon. Teno Roncalio
OF WYOMING

Mr. Speaker, we have witnessed the passing of
a mighty man and a great leader; of this there is
no doubt.

The people of my State knew him and loved
him and remembered him with great warmth
and admiration as a result of his many visits to
our State, not in behalf of himself, but always
to fight the good fight for his party and his country and to acclaim the good works of our own
U.S. Senators, the late Senator Joseph C.
O'Mahoney and our incumbent Senator Gale W.
McGee.

Mr. Speaker, I can think of no more fitting remarks in memory of our late President than the

words of Bernie Horton, editor of the **Wyoming
Eagle**, recalling the tremendous assistance that
great man gave to the Nation and to Wyoming's
public servants.

Mr. Speaker, I would like to ask unanimous
consent, if I may, that my remarks be followed
by the editorial of the Wyoming Eagle of January 23, 1973.

LYNDON B. JOHNSON

Wyoming has lost another friend.

His name: LYNDON JOHNSON, 36th President of the
United States. Mr. JOHNSON died yesterday of a heart
attack.

Many Wyomingites may remember LYNDON JOHNSON
when he came to Cheyenne in 1952 to deliver a free-
swinging political speech in behalf of his long-time friend,
the late Sen. Joseph C. O'Mahoney.

Others may remember him in 1958, when he told
Wyomingites that, if they elected Gale W. McGee to the
United States Senate, he, as majority leader in the Senate,
would see to it that McGee would be appointed to the
powerful Senate Appropriations committee. McGee was
elected and he was appointed to the appropriations committee the day he walked into the Senate.

Some of us will remember talking to LYNDON JOHNSON
in Los Angeles, in 1960 when he was running for President. He ended up as running mate to the late President
John F. Kennedy, and much of the credit for their victory was due to his efforts.

LYNDON JOHNSON came to Cheyenne again, in July,
1963, to speak at a giant appreciation dinner in honor of
Wyoming's senior Senator McGee. More than 1,250 persons from all over Wyoming turned out for the occasion.

On that day, Mr. JOHNSON granted this writer an exclusive interview, perhaps the last exclusive interview he was
to grant for many years. He was Vice President, at the
time, and a few months later he was to become President
following the tragic events that transpired in Dallas, Tex.

LYNDON JOHNSON even rode in the Cheyenne Frontier
Days parade, one year. Remember him? Cowboy hat and
all perched on the back of a stagecoach?

Some may have thought differently.

But we thought LYNDON JOHNSON was one of the most
approachable, down-to-earth men we have ever interviewed.

He answered our questions with candor and sincerity.
It seemed to us that, even as Vice President, he was dedicated to making this a greater nation—a nation with
concern for all.

President JOHNSON was scheduled to return to Cheyenne
on Nov. 4, 1966, but was forced to cancel because of a
serious illness.

Some Wyoming Democrats may remember LYNDON
JOHNSON when he was nominated at the 34th National
Democratic Convention at Atlantic City, Aug. 24–27,
1964.

Some, who are interested in politics, will remember
his landslide victory that year. He won 486 electoral
votes to only 52 for his opponent.

Some may remember the vast number of social and
economic reforms he brought about as President, especially during the months immediately following the death
of President Kennedy.

But we strongly suspect that millions of Americans,

including the citizens of Wyoming, may remember most vividly the address LYNDON B. JOHNSON gave on a Sunday evening, March 31, 1968.

At the very close of a 30-minute speech on Vietnam, during which he announced he was ordering an immediate and unilateral scaling down of American bombing of North Vietnam as "the first step in what I hope will be a series of mutual moves toward peace," Mr. JOHNSON declared:

"I shall not seek and I will not accept the nomination of my party for another term as your President."

That was his way of underscoring the United States' sincerity in seeking to end the war in Vietnam. It eventually was to bring the communists to the conference table. Few times in history has a President, or any other leader of a major international power, placed the welfare of his nation and the struggle for the ideal of peace so clearly and dramatically ahead of his own political ambitions.

Among other things, President JOHNSON may go down in history as the President who gave up his own political future in favor of national unity and a sincere hope for peace.—Bernie Horton, Editor.

Hon. J. J. Pickle

OF TEXAS

Mr. Speaker, I insert in the Record at this point the text of a commentary by Nicholas von Hoffman entitled "A Big, Big Man," which article appeared in the Washington Post edition of January 24, 1973:

A BIG, BIG MAN

(By Nicholas von Hoffman)

Ah, LYNDON, you're not cold yet and they're calling you great. That's what happens when one politician dies: The rest of them call him great, but, LYNDON, you deserve better than patriotic hagiography. You were better than the eulogistic junk they're saying at the memorial services.

LYNDON, you got your teeth into us and we got our teeth into you. Those five years of you in the White House were a barroom brawl, and, just four years ago almost to the day, when we staggered out of the saloon, dusty and bloody, we didn't hate you anymore. We understood better how you got us into Vietnam than how Nixon got us out and we liked you more, you cussed, cussing, bullheaded, impossible, roaring, wild coot.

You had your credibility gaps and your silent, sullennesses, but we read you. Oh, man, LYNDON, did we know you! You were the best and the worst of ourselves, the personification of our national deliriums. You were always so completely, so absolutely you. Kennedy had Pablo Casals to play for him, Nixon's got Pat Boone to pray for him, but you, LYNDON, you had Country Joe and the Fish singing songs soaked in four-letter words at you.

They're not bringing it up at your funeral, but you had a famous dirty mouth. By most accounts the only man in the history of the White House who could cuss better than you was Andrew Jackson. We on the outside knew how to make obscenity a tool of eloquence, too. We could recognize you, not as a Great American, but as an Ameri-

can man. But you did your own hating and your own cussing, not like these stiffs they've got in there now who import Sinatra and the dregs of Las Vegas to call people filthy names for them.

That wasn't your style, LYNDON. You let it all hang out; but then, man, even when we hated you most, we knew you at least had something. Your dogs had names and you pulled their ears. No official court photograph animal for you to have its picture taken as you asked the mutt's name. Sure, you could be gross. Getting your picture taken in the hospital bed, pulling up your pj's so we could all see the scar on your belly, and they still whisper around Washington that you used to receive ambassadors from foreign countries stepping out of the shower bath nikked as a jay bird, as they say where you came from.

And, still you kept your dignity. Maybe because everything you did, good, bad, indifferent or just funny, was so big. You were Andy Jackson's boy. Immoderate and big. No rein on yourself. They say even after the second heart attack you couldn't bring yourself to quit smoking.

LYNDON you were immoderate, and greedy. You outdid all the rest of us hungry Americans for reaching out and grabbing, fingers always stretched for grasping, but now they're saying after your death that you divided America, left her all split and bleeding. It is true that if ever a man had a reach which exceeded his grasp, it was you, you wicked old devil, but you redeemed this country even while dropping us, plop!, in the middle of the Vietnam Big Muddy.

You fought our Second Civil War and carried out our Second Reconstruction. The credit has gone to John Kennedy but he doesn't deserve it. He had the speechwriters to say fair, promising things, while he and his brother appointed racist judges to the federal bench. LYNDON, it isn't fair to you that Jack Kennedy's picture should be tacked up on the walls of so many poor black homes, Kennedy who regarded blacks as but another pressure group to be tricked or placated.

But some of us remember. Some of us who were in a room in the public housing project across the street from Brown's Chapel in Selma, Ala., that night you talked to a joint session of Congress in your rich, half-southern accent and we saw you on TV say to them, "We shall overcome." LYNDON, you did your best to overcome. Where Jack Kennedy reacted with official indifference to what happened to black people, you shook and threatened the federal bureaucracy from the FBI to the Department of Agriculture to make them redeem the pledge of equal protection.

Much of what you started is being abandoned, discarded and attacked, and much of it ought to be. You were so impulsive. You tried to solve social problems like a drunken hardware wholesaler trying to snag girls in a Paris nightclub. You drank so much of the social betterment bubbly the nation woke up with a hangover, but God bless you for it. Every right-living nation ought to go on that kind of a drunk every so often, and even if you went about it the wrong way, you got us thinking about what we should be doing. Your Medicare and Medicaid aren't exactly winners, but thanks to you our people will have the health protection.

You were a big 'un, LYNDON. We're going to miss you, you old booger, and we're going to know, regardless of official proclamations, you deserve better than to be saluted, left at half-mast and forgotten.

Mr. Speaker, I would ask unanimous consent to insert in the Record at this time the texts of speeches delivered on the campus of the University of Texas on January 25, 1973, as follows: the remarks by Mr. Dick Benson, the student president of the University of Texas at Austin; the remarks of Dr. Stephen H. Spurr, president of the University of Texas; and the remarks of the Honorable Charles Alan Wright, chairman of the faculty senate of the University of Texas.

Mr. Speaker, these remarks were given before a large audience at the university, the university which houses the L. B. J. papers, and I am pleased to have them inserted at this particular point:

SPEECH BY DICK BENSON

(Student President at the University of Texas at Austin)

Within the confines of statehood, diplomacy and politics there exists a nearly infinite variability of approach. The subtle weave of events, ideals, information and mankind is so enormously complex and chaotic as to defy definitive analysis of exact description. Approach, or method, becomes then a matter of projection—of arraying the chaos of the world out there to conform with inner assumptions, drives and goals. Of this LYNDON JOHNSON was a master—he carried his milieu both within and without and the strength of his world demanded the attention of those around him—extending outwards to encompass the population of an entire nation.

For those who demand absolutes, politics is a hard road to travel. Those who survive it, like President JOHNSON, are able to endure the void, the chaos, they have the force of will to create from nothing a field of endeavor and inhabit it.

Johnsonian politics besides being earthy and regional was primarily composed of people—inordinately human, the content and structure of his epoch were made up of distinct personalities—in itself, a great contribution. Government exists of and by men only—we not only man, but also create its machinery. To understand this takes sometimes, a substanital leap of faith by those hard-pressed by the system. A personal man as president is a friend or enemy—a person and a personality—infinitely more distinct and valuable than the programed blandness of the scientifically determined and unobjectionable middle of the road.

Composed as they are of human thoughts, I am recently impressed by the ability of events to elude the grasp and manipulation of man himself. Surely, when faced with that situation, leadership acquires a whole new kind of loneliness.

Sometimes intention and event do not coincide and we are often not justified in exacting personal judgments on situations well beyond our comprehension. History in total is not the conscious product of any one man's mind. President JOHNSON's intentions were impeccable in his own moral frame. His life and works were not egotistical but rather the natural extension of an audacious and challenging existence.

I met and knew him briefly for a total of some four to five hours spread over two occasions but those impressions confirm these thoughts. His preoccupations primarily concerned the problems of race, hunger and education. With two others, I first encountered President JOHNSON in the front yard of his ranch. During the ensuing conversation he was asked this question: assuming the apparent goodwill and intelligence of most of the world's leaders, why did war, strife and famine girdle the planet? He was perplexed and could not produce a simple answer but to him it was an issue to consider and not one to be written off as simply beyond man's comprehension—he wanted and tried to understand what probably no person in the world does understand. Presumptuous and in the style of the President but necessary—very necessary for those who care to sustain the terribly tenuous state of peace.

President JOHNSON, just because of his style, would never have selected this statement to end a speech of his own but the Poet Rilke also seems to have known the magnitude of what it is to create a historical world and live in its consequences:

"These things that live on departure understand when you praise them: fleeting, they look for rescue through something in us, the most fleeting of all. Want us to change them entirely within our invisible hearts, into . . . endlessly, into ourselves. Whosoever we are."

❧

SPEECH BY STEPHEN H. SPURR

(President, the University of Texas at Austin)

All of the proper things have been said about LBJ by those most qualified to say them: his largeness of character, his mastery of the art of politics, his leading role in the betterment of American education, and his deep commitment to enlarging the opportunities of ethnic minorities. I can speak personally only of his last year and a half and only of his relationship to our University.

President JOHNSON was fond of telling how he was shamed into going to Southwest Texas State by his parents, and how he was taken in there warmly, and how he came to maturity and ambition through his college experience. His gratitude to his alma mater was great, and his commitment to higher education derived from this crucial turn in his own life.

The University of Texas was, of course, his wife's alma mater. Here he was persuaded to place his presidential papers, and here he gave his blessing and support to having a new and special School of Public Affairs established in his name.

In my dealings with him, I found him deeply respectful of the University community, strongly supportive of our efforts to build a better university, and careful not to intrude in any way on our academic processes. When I came to campus he told me that he respected the presidency of the University as he did the presidency of the country: that he'd never offer advice, but that he'd give it if asked; and that he would never intrude himself on campus but that he was available if wanted. When I hesitantly asked if he would open the Congress of Black Professionals in Higher Education, he countered with the offer to give a major speech if I wanted him to—and he did—although he had to get up at 4:00 in the morning to keep his promise, and although the strain of the effort may have contributed to the heart attack he suffered two days later.

I shall remember best, however, his final moment at the recent civil rights symposium. We knew a disruption was planned, but President JOHNSON would not be deterred. He mounted slowly and painfully to the podium, and stopped to swallow a nitro-glycerin pill to ease the pain before giving his closing remarks. When an uninvited speaker tried to force his way through the secret service to the platform to serve his demands, we could see the President come to life. He seemed literally to grow in stature, to glow, and to fill the room. With one gesture he called off the guards and with another he took the black minister to his bosom. Giving the podium to the speaker, he listened patiently and then delivered a calming, folksy, and wise discourse that left us all—black and white, conformists and dissenter alike, knowing that we had been for a moment in the presence of true greatness. That is how I shall remember him.

ᕦ

SPEECH BY CHARLES ALAN WRIGHT

(Chairman of the Faculty Senate, the University of Texas at Austin)

Members of an academic community have reason to be grateful for the life and career of LYNDON JOHNSON. He was devoted to the cause of education and did much that will be of permanent benefit to higher education generally and to this University in particular. President Spurr will address himself to some of these things. Rather than duplicate what he will say, I would like to reflect with you briefly on the great office that President JOHNSON occupied for more than five years.

In my judgment the most significant original contribution the Framers of our Constitution made to the science of government was in Article II, in which they vested all executive power "in a President of the United States of America." Unlike some of the other novel concepts of the Framers, such as federalism, which have not been much copied elsewhere, their concept of a single officer who is both head of state and head of government and who is chosen by the people for a limited term has been widely adopted throughout the world and has been immensely successful in our own country.

In Moussorgsky's opera "Boris Gudonov," there is a great aria in which Tsar Boris sings "Mine is the highest power." A 17th Century Tsar of All the Russians had great power—but his power was puny compared to that exercised by a President of the United States. The very existence of civilization on this planet may turn on his wisdom, his good sense, his coolness, and his courage, as he makes hard decisions in international crisis in which a nuclear holocaust is a possibility. The President must also several times a day bear the heavy responsibility of resolving issues that are less dramatic but that will have great impact, for good or ill, on "domestic Tranquility" and "the general Welfare." What Chief Justice Vinson described as "the broad executive power granted by Article II to an officer on duty 365 days a year" gives the President considerable room to shape the future course of our nation.

This awesome power is vested in one man. When Congress or the Supreme Court act, the responsibility is shared among those who are in the majority. When the President acts, he acts alone. He can and does listen to wise advisers, but only he can make the decision. In President Truman's phrase, "The buck stops here."

We choose our President in hotly fought elections. His margin of victory may be sweeping, as was President JOHNSON's in 1964, or very thin, as was that of the ticket on which he was chosen Vice President in 1960. But from the moment he takes office, he is President, not of a party, but of all the people. The hopes and aspirations all of us have for our country are wrapped up in one lonely man who has sworn that he "will to the best of my Ability, preserve, protect and defend the Constitution of the United States."

Mark well the phrase, "to the best of my Ability." The Framers made the President, within the area assigned to him, omnipotent, but they could not make him omniscient. Given the complexity of the issues with which he must deal, it is hardly surprising that every President in our history has made some decisions that, with the benefit of hindsight, were wrong and others that caused great controversy when they were made and that can only finally be appraised in the long judgment of history. President JOHNSON was no exception. But we were reminded in the ceremony yesterday in the Capitol rotunda that President JOHNSON closed his final State of the Union message by expressing his hope that it could be said of his administration, "We tried." He closed his memoirs by saying "I gave it all I had." That is all that the Constitution requires. It is all that a free people can properly ask of their chief executive.

The Framers lived in a time of emperors and kings, hereditary monarchs who still exercised significant power. It is a tribute to their genius that they could conceive of an officer more powerful than the mightiest king, yet answerable to the humblest citizen. It is a tribute to that representative product of the sturdy democratic traditions of the Texas Hill Country whom we remember today that he was able to meet the demands of that great office so tragically thrust upon him. All of us, whether we be Republican or Democrat, integrationist or segregationist, hawk or dove, must be grateful for President JOHNSON's service to our country and for his conscientious effort, through five extraordinarily difficult years, to provide, to the best of his ability, wise leadership for the country he loved so well.

Mr. Speaker, I also ask unanimous consent to insert an article by the Honorable Horace Busby, who formerly was a member of President JOHNSON's staff, and who indeed came to Washington in the early 1940's to become a member of his staff at that time. The article is entitled "This Country Isn't Over the Hill" . . . Then L. B. J. Was Gone."

[From the Los Angeles Times, Jan. 28, 1973]

"THIS COUNTRY ISN'T OVER THE HILL" . . .

THEN L. B. J. WAS GONE

(By Horace Busby)

On Sunday, Dec. 31, 1972, at my home in the Washington suburbs, I was awakened early in the morning by the telephone. When I answered, a Secret Service agent at the LBJ Ranch in Texas announced: "President JOHNSON is calling."

Over 25 years, countless days had begun in much the same way, for men and for all other former assistants from the early years whom LYNDON JOHNSON liked to call "my boys." Whatever his office—congressman, senator, Vice President or President—he was awake at dawn, thinking out his strategies to surmount what others deemed insurmountable.

Once his plans were set, he reached for the telephone and oblivious to the hour, began launching his characteristic counter-attack on the approaching day. The pattern lingered on in retirement.

If the call was typical, his manner on this morning was not. He did not banter casually. Speaking crisply and, it seemed, rather hurriedly, he went directly to his point.

"I've called," he said, "about two things."

Out of old habit, I picked up a pencil and prepared to take notes. He did not continue. I heard him lay down the telephone—I assumed on the medicine table beside his bed—and there were sounds of glasses clinking and water being poured. A minute or more passed before he spoke again.

"I'm swallowing these nitroglycerine pills," he said matter-of-factly, "like a goldfish gulping crackers."

Of late, his health had become an increasing concern While he did not always take kindly to inquiries about that subject, I ventured a question anyway, asked how he had been feeling.

"Just fair," he replied. "I'm trying to get in better shape so the doctors will let me go to Mexico next month and rest up in the sun. But it's not good."

The answer was unexpected. Only the previous day, news accounts reported President and Mrs. Johnson's attendance at memorial services in Austin for 16 teen-agers from the city who died in a holiday traffic tragedy. I had assumed his presence at those services meant his health must be improved.

When I began mentioning the news reports, however, he immediately bridled. He apparently suspected that I meant to reproach him—as others around him had been doing in recent weeks—for attending too many funerals, each of which seemed to take a deep emotional toll. He cut my comment short.

"Now, Buzz," he said firmly, "you've got to understand those families all live in south Austin."

In the context of his career, that was explanation enough. Since 1937, when he first ran for Congress, LYNDON JOHNSON had never fully come to terms with Austin's proud old family elite—"the better people," as they were known in the class-conscious New Deal era—who lived in the palatial homes of north Austin.

They resented him politically and were contemptuous of him socially: He was born wrong, schooled wrong, had wrong friends, wrong interests and wrong style. But across the river, in the modest homes of south Austin, where the "little people" lived, he always had the votes.

That schism marked the man from the beginning to the end of his public life. While the fires within him had long been banked, now an ember began to glow hot inside.

"Those people," he said with sudden intensity, "are my people. When nobody else was with me, they stood by me. When they hurt, I hurt. Nothing"—he repeated the word twice more—"is ever going to keep me away from them in times like they're going through."

I said no more about funerals.

After a moment, he turned the conversation, raising the subject of the Vietnam cease-fire negotiations.

"I think they've got it," he said, "or they will have it soon. I just pray to God they can make it stick."

He continued on, repeating concerns he frequently expressed for what might happen next in other Asian lands. Although his comments were not optimistic, he was talking now about national concerns and his mood

brightened noticeably and the horizons of the conversation expanded to Congress, the new Cabinet appointments, economic policy.

"Be sure," he told me, "to meet Barbara Jordan." The newly elected black congresswoman from Texas greatly impressed him. "She's one of the best to go up the pike from down here in a long time," he said.

Other such directions came tumbling out as he went along. There were two editorial page articles in recent issues of the Washington Post and he wanted me to read, "think about," and send him a memorandum of comment.

He would like to have any statistics I could find about black voting in the 1972 national elections. The indicated low turnout of both blacks and 18-year-olds was, he thought, "a damn disgrace." When he returned from Mexico in March, he added, "we've got to get some smart people together and try to figure out something to change that before the next election."

In this mood, he skipped to another pet project. He was trying, he reported, to raise $1 million to fund a guest lectureship program at the Johnson Library in Austin. But he was dissatisfied with the current "crop" of lecturers touring the campus circuit.

"Some of those faces," he said, "are getting pretty old and tiresome. Their needles have been stuck for 10 years. Aren't there any new and exciting thinkers"

I began suggesting some Washingtion figures, but he interrupted. "Hell," he said, "nobody there has enough charisma to fill a small phone booth, except Kissinger, and he's always someplace else."

I laughed, of course, at this flash of his typical humor, and he ran through a list of other names, offering similar succinct comments on each. Then, serious again, he added another assignment.

"While I'm gone," he said, "talk to some good people up there and get some names of lecturers who can really shake up things. These kids on campus aren't fired up like they ought to be."

This talk reminded him of another campus matter. He had been invited, he reported, to deliver the commencement address at the University of Virginia when his son-in-law, Charles Robb, received his law degree this spring.

"That's an old school, a fine school," he commented, "and I want to make the best speech of my life. Remember," he went on, "when Thomas Jefferson wrote his own epitaph, he asked that his tombstone say he was founder of the University of Virginia."

The mood was upbeat, even soaring. This had become a typical early morning LYNDON JOHNSON conversation. Abruptly, though, he left the telephone once again as he had done at the beginning of the call. When he resumed, nothing was said to explain the interruption, but he returned to his opening remark.

"One of the things I wanted to say," he began, "is that I am very pleased with what we've been able to accomplish these last four or five months."

This had special significance. Over most of his period in retirement, LYNDON JOHNSON had severely restricted activities that might thrust him back into the public eye. Invitations to speak, lecture or contribute articles to periodicals were rejected without being considered.

"Whatever I say," he had argued, "they'll twist it around to say that I'm criticizing the President. I'm not mad at anybody. I don't want to fight with anybody. The only way to stay out of scrapes is to stay where I belong on the ranch."

Family and friends, though, believed this isolation worked against his health. For more than 30 years, LYNDON JOHNSON lived with and thrived on the tension and trauma at the center of national affairs. He was further away from that milieu now than at any time since he was 21 years old.

With some conspiracy and much complicity, various associates began working together after his spring heart attack, edging him back toward a more active public role. He continued to resist through the summer. At the start of start of September, however, he abruptly changed, for what reason I do not know.

He accepted an invitation to speak at the Scott and White Clinic in Temple, Tex. From the ranch, he called me in Washington and asked if I could come down and work with him on what he wanted to say.

"I would like to get some things off my chest," he explained.

When I arrived at the ranch, he almost seemed to be waiting at the door. I was hardly inside before he picked up a favorite cap and headed outside, saying, "Come on, we need to take a long ride."

For hours we rode together over the ranch. A Secret Service agent trailing behind. He said nothing about the speech. Instead, he reviewed in minute detail—more, I thought, for his interest than mine—his systematic effort "to get things in order for Bird and the girls."

Family business properties were being disposed of, the ranch itself was being deeded to the government for public use, other relatives for whom he felt responsibility were being moved into appropriate career opportunities.

The ride continued through the morning and into early afternoon. Reluctantly, it appeared, he said he had to return to the house. "If I don't get my oxygen and my sleep," he explained, "I begin to feel it in my chest."

At his request, I followed him into the bedroom. He changed into pajamas, spent a few minutes adjusting the oxygen controls and finally slipped under the covers. Holding the oxygen mask in one hand, he began "dictating" what he wanted to say, gesturing as he did so with the other hand.

"This country isn't over the hill," he said. "We aren't on the skids. This is a just country. It's a beautiful country. All this moaning and complaining isn't true, isn't right and it isn't leadership."

He went on at exceptional length, stopping only when he felt, as he described it, "a little pinching" in his chest. Then he turned out the light and I went away to compose the first draft.

When I sat at the typewriter, I knew I had received two messages that morning—one was LYNDON JOHNSON's message about the country, the other was a distinct message about himself.

The best speeches—or, at least, the best lines in speech texts—usually compose themselves. The message about himself composed the first lines of this text.

"With the coming of September each year, we are reminded, as the song says, that the days are dwindling down to a precious few. By the calendar, we know that soon the green leaves of summer will begin to brown; the chill winds of winter will begin to blow; and—before we are ready for the end to come—the year will be gone."

It was late that night before LYNDON JOHNSON read the draft. He penciled through it extensively, far more than usual, and he read it aloud—to me, to Mrs. Johnson, to the ranch foreman.

When we were alone in the office, he read the first lines aloud for still another time.

"That's just right," he said. "That's just the way I wanted it."

On that December morning, three weeks ago, it was this speech—if not those lines—that was uppermost in his mind.

"As I look back on it," he said, "I think it was that Temple speech that turned things around. I think the things needed to be said and you just wouldn't believe how kind people are in their letters about it."

This time, though, his mood was not melancholy. Things had turned around. He wanted, he said, to get "really active this year."

"After the inauguration," he explained, "we'll have four years behind us and I think I can speak up a little more. I've got some programs up there they are kicking around and I'd like to go more places and see more people again."

It was very good news. Whatever concerns had formed during portions of the conversation seemed to be meaningless. After a month in the sun, he would be eager to go to work once more.

He paused in his conservation. "I told you I had two things to tell you," he said, 'but I can't seem to remember the other." He lingered over it a bit longer, then dismissed it: "It'll come to me later."

That was all. "Thank you for everything," he said, and he was gone.

Mr. Speaker, President JOHNSON was a generous man. Those of us who have worked closely with him all these years know that he had an immense heart that overflowed with gratitude when good things were done for him or for his programs.

Though he drove his staff hard, he never asked them to put in long or short hours, but rather to "get the job done." He matched their hours with double time because he was totally committed to accomplishing whatever task was before him. Many times when the pressure was intense to get the job accomplished, the President would pause to highly compliment his staff members or to hug them or to otherwise bestow gifts upon them. He realized that his efforts would amount to nothing if he did not have a dedicated and loyal group of people working for him.

It is true that he sometimes used sharp words and kindly scolded some of his staff of friends, but it was always a justifiable apprehension.

The story is legend, however, that he always returned that dedication and that kindness ten-thousand fold. His close friends knew that for every act of kindness given to President JOHNSON or to his family or program, it would be returned many times over because he would literally shower his gratitude and affection on them.

I was once a Capitol policeman here assisting Mrs. Johnson when the President went to the far reaches of the South Pacific in World War II.

Because I had one job as a member of his staff and another job as a Capitol policeman, he knew that I was putting in long hours. It had to be done at that time and all of us were glad to make sacrifices. After his return from the service and in all the years thereafter, he constantly referred to the fact that he would never forget that I would come to the Capitol and hold two jobs just to help run the congressional office. In meetings large and small, he has bestowed thanks and credit to me for that early dedication. He never forgot his early or old friends.

Anyone who reads the Record and might study these remarks will know that there are thousands upon thousands of instances where the President has individually bestowed upon his friends his love and affections and blessings.

Some people tend to picture President JOHNSON as a hard-driving, forceful juggernaut of a man who swept toward his destiny with unrelenting fervor. It is true that he knew that he must apply himself and he did so with all of his body and soul. But the other side of LYNDON JOHNSON is that he was warm and compassionate. There were times when he would be so overwhelmed with acts of kindness that he would be in tears himself. When he could help a young student or a child achieve some special consideration, that seemed to pump new spirit into his soul and he would walk on a cloud for hours or days at a time.

If he heard of someone on his staff were having illness or difficulty, he would not make a phone call or write a letter, but instead would see that an airplane was made available to fly him or a member of his family to Mayo Clinic if need be. If a dear friend was being married, he would drive or fly hundreds of miles if he could. Or if a close friend was to be buried, he tried to go personally to pay his last respects.

Few people realize how much money he would bestow on his family or his staff or his friends when he wanted them to make a special trip or wanted them to have relaxation or entertainment.

Some of the most pleasant evenings spent in this lifetime by countless friends have been those times when we could visit individually in the quiet of the evening reminiscing and recalling the good and hard times. The President could tell country stories with a strong and forceful point and it was at these moments he was perhaps at his best. He was warm and considerate and had such a keen insight into human nature that his recollections would be so much like people that the person listening could actually visualize and enjoy an America marching forward into the years.

Mr. Speaker, the constant theme of President JOHNSON's service is the essential fact that he worked for the people. Having been raised in the hard, dry, caliche country of central Texas and having to scrape out an education and a living, President JOHNSON always knew that there were a lot of people who needed help.

When he became a Congressman and later a Senator and then President, he never lost sight of the fact that government was an instrument to help people who could not help themselves. He visualized government as a means of providing essentials to the downtrodden and underprivileged so that they might have hope and faith in their government. He sincerely believed that government was for the people, and he used that power perhaps more than any President we have had. Some say that he was a "populist" President and perhaps the last of the populist-type of Presidents. If "populist" means that government is supposed to do things for people, then that is an apt description of President JOHNSON.

President JOHNSON was the great persuader. He was America. He was big, robust, driving, doing, living, loving, daring, but doing great things during his life. He was easily the most colorful, lovable man of our times, although a controversial man at times. But he was a big man, generous to a fault, who loved his friends whom he had around him at all times.

LYNDON JOHNSON never ate alone at his dinner table, friends always shared his blessing.

He gave his life to public service.

Hon. Dan Rostenkowski
OF ILLINOIS

Mr. Speaker, on this occasion, I would like to join my colleague from Texas, the Honorable Wright Patman in paying tribute to our late President LYNDON BAINES JOHNSON.

With the passing of any prominent public figure, the American tradition for eulogy and ceremony has become so commonplace as to have taken away much of its original meaning. It has been the custom to overly salute those who have passed on and hail their achievements far beyond their worth.

As a result of the American penchant for canonization, it is often difficult to truly evaluate the real man—his achievements and his shortcomings. But in the case of LYNDON BAINES JOHN-

SON, we are indeed fortunate to have a yardstick with which few can dispute. For, although he has been eulogized by friend and foe alike, it is the latter that holds the true key.

As columnist Kenneth Auchincloss said in Newsweek:

Death withheld from him the favors it has granted other Presidents; that extra measure of devotion that falls to those who die in office, such as John Kennedy and Franklin Roosevelt, or the benevolent respect accorded those, such as Dwight Eisenhower and Harry Truman who outlive the memory of all but their most ardent enemies. LYNDON JOHNSON died with many of his old foes still arrayed against him, and his place in history far from clear.

Thus, LYNDON BAINES JOHNSON must be viewed without the tragedy that has so often muted criticism, or the time which so often mitigated it.

But, as a longtime friend and admirer of the late President, I am indeed heartened to see so many of those who opposed him or his policies during his life identify so strongly with him now. I think particularly of the youth of our Nation. A generation of young people who matured in the controversial sixties—a generation that saw their President as a symbol of the war they did not like and did not understand. This generation can now identify with the man for they can see him as he really was. They can now see the one quality above all others, that LYNDON JOHNSON possessed. They realize that even when they disagreed with him, he was doing what he thought was best. That even when they disagreed with him, he was himself. And, they respect that. In a time when national leaders are looked upon as aloof and having a disdain for the common man, our young people can look to the days of LYNDON JOHNSON and remember, whether he was with you or against you, you know it—for this man did not walk the fence.

As this young generation of the sixties turns into the leaders of the seventies and the eighties, they will remember the LYNDON JOHNSON of the civil rights and the voting rights. But even when they think of that war, I am sure they will remember the night in March of 1968 when LYNDON JOHNSON was big enough to relinquish what he had worked a lifetime to achieve. All this, in the mere hope that it would bring that frustrating conflict to a quicker close. No man would have hailed the announcement that peace was indeed at hand more than the President who had passed on but a day earlier.

My memory of LYNDON JOHNSON will always be that of the man as a doer. When he took charge, the reins were in firm control. He was a very decisive person who knew how to get the job done.

It is well known that the dreams of John F. Kennedy were the programs of LYNDON JOHNSON. In my opinion, his record of social legislation is unsurpassed by any President in this century in its sweeping impact on so many phases of American society. The right of the poor, and the right of the elderly to decent health care, were not rights until LYNDON JOHNSON pushed his medicare and medicaid through Congress in the mid-1960's. And the rights of minorities to buy a home where they choose or the right to vote for their public officials did not become realities until LYNDON JOHNSON's Civil Rights and Voting Rights Acts of 1964 and 1965.

Thus, it is a unique tribute to the man that he will not have to wait for years to pass before history will look kindly on him. He does not need us to build monuments to him, for he has left his own. For, it is a rare man whose opponents will look back upon his achievements and say he has guaranteed the rights and bettered the opportunities of generations of Americans yet unborn. LYNDON BAINES JOHNSON was such a rare man.

Hon. Paul Findley
OF ILLINOIS

Mr. Speaker, President JOHNSON will be remembered in history for his effective leadership for voting rights and other programs to improve opportunities for blacks. As no President since Lincoln, LYNDON JOHNSON exerted the full leadership of his office to advance the equality of all Americans. Like Lincoln, his efforts in the field of civil rights, as in Vietnam policy, divided the Nation deeply. The years of his presidency were scarred with bloody protest marches, riots, and public outcries against moving too far, too fast on behalf of human rights. Like Lincoln, LYNDON JOHNSON kept this faith. To use his own earthy phrase, he "hunkered down" when the protests of some whites beat down over his head. Unswervingly he stuck to the guiding principle that gave birth to this Nation, that all men are created equal.

This achievement, so true to the spirit of America, will be honored even when time dims the memory of Vietnam.

Hon. John A. Blatnik
OF MINNESOTA

Mr. Speaker, LYNDON JOHNSON dominated the legislative landscape in his lifetime as he will command a quarter century of historians' writings.

When I came to Congress in 1947 he was already a driving force in the Senate. Even then, his rise seemed foreordained, from majority leader of that body, to Vice President, to the most powerful office in the land.

And he, of all Presidents, was as big as the office.

He charted the most far-reaching record of achievement in American history, both as Senator and as President. Like the man himself, his legislative accomplishments are larger than life, and have changed forever the course of the Nation's history.

Driven by compassion for the least fortunate; convinced that America would not work in theory or practice until every citizen was brought into the great consensus he sought, he put the full force of his energy and determination behind creation of the Great Society as he did behind the Civil Rights Act of 1964, and the Voting Rights Act of the following year.

He asked more of us than we dreamed we had; and forced, cajoled and persuaded the 88th, 89th, and 90th Congresses to join him in history.

LYNDON JOHNSON was a vibrant, vital man of boundless energy, intolerant only of those whose involvement in the world was circumscribed by a shrug. He drove himself relentlessly, and demanded the same total dedication and commitment from those around him.

But beneath the rough exterior I knew him as a kind, compassionate, humanitarian person. His instincts were correct; the love of country that put them into action was real. If the results of some of the Great Society promises have not fulfilled our expectations, it is incumbent upon us to put them right.

The Nation has lost a great leader, the land has lost a giant. History has gained a man who will grow with time as his record is measured against passing generations whose lot is immeasurably improved by his years in the Senate and White House.

Hon. Edward J. Derwinski
OF ILLINOIS

Mr. Speaker, President LYNDON JOHNSON shouldered a heavy responsibility during his term of office, and it has been duly noted by many Members this afternoon that his untimely death can well be traced to the pressure that he felt in the White House.

We remember him not only as the 36th President, but also as a House and Senate Member and a leader during his days in the legislative branch.

It is unfortunate that so much of the review of his career centers around the controversy of the Vietnam period. President JOHNSON was an imaginative President, and an imaginative Member of the House and Senate. Certainly, the success he achieved in politics and government was the result of his determination, the hard work that he put into his assignments, and his willingness to shoulder great responsibility.

His loss, coming so soon after that of former President Truman, deprives our Nation of the wise counsel that a respected senior statesman can give. He will be missed in that sense. He deserves the respect and appreciation of all Americans for the steadfast fashion with which he faced his awesome responsibilities.

On behalf of Mrs. Derwinski and myself, I express to Mrs. Lady Bird Johnson and the other members of the Johnson family our deepest sympathy.

Hon. Morris K. Udall
OF ARIZONA

Mr. Speaker, I would like to join my colleagues in expressing the sorrow we all feel in mourning the untimely death of former President LYNDON BAINES JOHNSON.

Throughout his long career in public service, LYNDON JOHNSON served the Nation with distinction—as Congressman, as Senator, as Vice President and as President. As floor leader of the Senate and later as 36th President of the United States, LYNDON JOHNSON was a man of action, a man who put less stock in rhetoric than in accomplishment. His deep love of the Congress and his keen understanding of the legislative process enabled him to shape his dreams into realities. As President, LYNDON JOHNSON recommended 200 major measures to the Congress. Of these, 181 were passed into law. Let us look at some of these accomplishments for a moment:

1964, Passage of the Civil Rights Act.

1964, Passage of the Economic Opportunity Act.

1965, Passage of the Voting Rights Act.

1965, Passage of the Social Security Amendments.

1965, Passage of the Elementary and Secondary Education Act.

1965, Passage of the Department of Housing and Urban Development Act.

1966, Passage of the Demonstration Cities and Metropolitan Development Act.

President LYNDON JOHNSON started more programs for social progress than any other Chief Executive in our history. He sought to care for the sick through medicare and medicaid; he sought to make life more tolerable for the elderly through increases in social security; he sought to educate the young through tripling money for schools; he sought to provide equal rights and dignity for all men with legislation that advanced the cause of civil rights more significantly than any measure since the Emancipation Proclamation.

Mr. Speaker, it is politically fashionable these days to belittle the accomplishments of these Great Society programs. One reads in the press, and one hears from this administration, that these programs, although noble in inspiration, did not really help people. One reads that these programs raised the hopes of the downtrodden without answering their needs. I do not agree. All one has to do is to think of the pride of a black American who, after two centuries of disenfranchisement, votes for the first time. All one has to do is think of the relief of a sick old man who finally receives hospital care; all one has to do is think of the feeling of accomplishment of a Job corpsman who has just received his first paycheck.

Mr. Speaker, President JOHNSON had his faults, but his sentiments were the right ones. Perhaps nowhere are his basic beliefs stated more clearly than in a speech delivered to a joint session of Congress on March 15, 1965. In that speech he said:

I want to be the President who educated young children to the wonders of their worlds. I want to be the President who helped to feed the hungry and to prepare them to be taxpayers instead of taxeaters.

I want to be the President who helped the poor to find their own way and who protected the right of every citizen to vote in every election.

I want to be the President who helped to end hatred among his fellow men and who promoted love among the people of all races and all regions and all parties.

I want to be the President who helped to end war among the brothers of this Earth.

The tragedy of LYNDON JOHNSON's death is that he died before a cease-fire in Vietnam had been announced. But, in so many other areas, what President JOHNSON wanted he achieved. LYNDON JOHNSON wanted, more than anything else, to help people—especially the poor, the sick, the oppressed—those people too weak to help themselves. When future historians look back at this era I believe LYNDON JOHNSON will be remembered as he would want.

Hon. Robert N. Giaimo
OF CONNECTICUT

Mr. Speaker, former President LYNDON JOHNSON was an imposing figure on the world's landscape throughout the decade of the 1960's. From modest origins he became a congressional aide, a Congressman, a Senator, an effective Senate majority leader, Vice President of this Nation and, in the tragic aftermath of President John Kennedy's death, President by succession and again by virtue of his genuine landslide victory in 1964.

LYNDON JOHNSON brought to full fruition the work of the Roosevelt era, promoting the civil rights of the disenfranchised and the poor, working for the economic, educational, housing, and health advancement of all Americans through Federal action.

It is fashionable now, of course, to note the disappointment and the expense that have followed in the wake of the ambitious variety of Federal programs begun or dramatically enlarged under LYNDON JOHNSON. It is said that programs and Federal money could not buy education, health, or security; neither could they guarantee good housing or outlaw discrimination.

Such a mood of examination should not neglect to note, however, the accomplishments of LYNDON JOHNSON as a legislative leader and as President. The enormous positive accomplishments of the programs passed in that era and implemented through the past decade should not be disregarded.

LYNDON JOHNSON's dream for the Nation were large and ambitious, and his accomplishments as a man matched his dreams. He led this Nation into a time of unparalleled government efforts to improve the lives of all Americans. Medicare, civil rights legislation, voting rights laws, medical research programs and aid to education—all of these are lasting tributes to the man and his dreams.

As an architect, planning the Great Society in America, LYNDON JOHNSON was humane and compassionate; as the builder of an ideal Nation, his energies and skills seemed to have no limit. For those efforts and for the legacy he leaves in a more humane and concerned government, we are all in his debt.

Hon. Charles B. Rangel
OF NEW YORK

Mr. Speaker, the death of our 36th President, LYNDON BAINES JOHNSON, was a tragedy for most of the world. But nowhere was this tragedy felt more deeply than by the poor and minority Americans for whom L. B. J. showed unparalleled concern.

Despite his failure to achieve the peace he longed for in Vietnam, he will live in history as the President who stood with Abraham Lincoln in his concern for the position of the black man in America. While some of his foreign policy decisions may be open to criticism, few Presidents have done as much for those people here in America who needed help the most.

The day that LYNDON JOHNSON announced that he would not again seek the office of the Presidency, he said:

I have not done near enough.

But in the field of civil rights, few men could have done more.

LYNDON JOHNSON believed in the principle of equality for all Americans. As a teacher of Mexican American in his native Texas, he had seen the damage done by discrimination. He knew, as only someone who has observed it can know, the harm that is inflicted by bigotry and injustice.

Six years before he was to become President, LYNDON JOHNSON, as majority leader of the Senate, led the struggle against an attempted filibuster and succeeded in obtaining the passage of the first Federal civil rights bill since Reconstruction. His efforts, more than anyone else in the national leadership, were responsible for the enactment of the Civil Rights Act of 1957. There were those who complained that this act was not

enough, and LYNDON JOHNSON agreed. But it was a beginning, and it was necessary to begin somewhere.

In the first few weeks after that tragic day of President Kennedy's death in 1963, those of us who did not know LYNDON JOHNSON were looking for an indication of what type of President he would become. To a joint session of Congress he said:

Let us continue.

He would soon prove that a person's sense of justice need not have any relation to his birthplace.

It was through the efforts of President LYNDON JOHNSON that the most significant piece of civil rights legislation in our history was enacted, the Civil Rights Act of 1964. This act called for an end to prejudice in not only the areas of employment and public accommodations, but also prohibited discrimination in federally assisted programs.

Yet it was LYNDON JOHNSON who realized that the job was not completed, that millions of black Americans were still denied their birthright in this democracy, the right to vote. He came to Congress in 1965 and had the courage to say, "we shall overcome" while the eyes of the Nation were on Selma, Ala. His desire to let all the people have a voice in our Government resulted in the Voting Rights Act of that same year. The act removed literacy tests and other discriminatory procedures as criteria for registering to vote.

Hon. Shirley Chisholm
OF NEW YORK

Mr. Speaker, the smile on the face of a Job corpsman who has just received his first job, the expression of happiness displayed by the mother of a Headstart child, and the pride seen in a black American who after 100 years of disenfranchisement votes for the first time—all serve as the greatest memorial to the man from Texas—LYNDON BAINES JOHNSON.

The untimely loss of this great President of the "Little People" is deeply felt by us all. The fact that he rose from the reactionary Southern resistance to the challenges of change—to become the greatest innovator of social change in modern America indeed marks the true greatness of President JOHNSON.

LYNDON JOHNSON was a unique man, a rare man who realized that the force of freedom is a never ceasing and unstoppable force. He was a southerner, but yet refused as President to be bound by the tragedies of section hatred and regional perceptions.

There have been and will continue to be many comparisons made between President JOHNSON and his colleague in the Presidency, Abraham Lincoln. Many of these comparisons are valid. But a quality which Mr. JOHNSON possessed singularly was the ability to do what was right on the sole grounds that it was right.

His administration should not be remembered for the great amount of social legislation it produced and initiated as law. But rather it should be remembered, not in the annals of history, but in the lives of our people as having served as an agent of freedom's mission and a commander in this Nation's war with itself.

While it is customary to mark the passing of our national leaders with tribute and praise— LYNDON JOHNSON authorized his own tribute by his steadfast determination to take his high office to the people and thereby allow them to govern. This tribute now serves and shall forever serve as a measuring stick for all of those who shall hold the Presidency of this land.

Most importantly, it allowed Federal marshals to supervise registering and voting procedures in those counties where the Attorney General deemed it necessary.

Despite the success of his efforts to obtain legislation that guaranteed the constitutional rights denied to black Americans and other minorities throughout American history, President JOHNSON had the wisdom to realize that the long, hard journey toward equality had not ended because these rights were won, but had just begun. He realized that it does a man no good to win the right to eat in the restaurant or sleep in the hotel of his choice if his economic condition prohibits him from affording the meal or the room. So LYNDON JOHNSON conceived the Great Society programs to wage war on poverty, and in so doing provided hope and a means out of the depressing cycle of poverty for thousands who before knew no hope and felt that their Government did not care. The Economic Opportunity Act and the other programs of the Great Society such as medicare and Federal aid to education are tributes to LYNDON JOHNSON's compassion for his fellow man.

It was during LYNDON JOHNSON's administration that for the first time, blacks were appointed to important posts in the Federal Government.

Because of LYNDON JOHNSON, a black man now sits on this Nation's Highest Court.

In 1968, LYNDON JOHNSON signed into law two more important pieces of legislation: a Jury Selection Act and a Fair Housing Act.

In 1963, speaking at Gettysburg, Pa., 100 years after Lincoln's Gettysburg Address, Vice President JOHNSON said:

Until justice is blind to color, until education is unaware of race, until opportunity is unconcerned with the color of men's skins, emancipation will be a proclamation not fulfilled in fact, to that extent we shall have fallen short of assuring freedom to the free.

We would all do well to remember his words.

Hon. James M. Collins
OF TEXAS

Mr. Speaker, there have been many inspiring statements written about LYNDON B. JOHNSON. One of the finest statements was the editorial written by Dick West who is the editorial director for the Dallas Morning News. This excellent editorial has some plain-spoken facts about our great plain-spoken President. President JOHNSON was a man of action and it is interesting to see the comments from West about LYNDON JOHNSON in action. Many times it has been said that LYNDON B. JOHNSON was the most colorful personality in the history of Texas. Dick West in the News describes some of these characteristics.

L. B. J.: HIS INFLUENCES AND TALENTS

(By Dick West)

AUSTIN.—Two questions went through my mind as I filed past the flag-draped casket holding the body of former President LYNDON B. JOHNSON: Who and what were the great influences in his life? And what talents or qualities did this complex man, who roamed the Pedernales and ruled the Potomac, use to the fullest?

As to influences: You have to start with Lady Bird, whom he loved deeply but who has talents of her own which helped him greatly: "Sometimes I feel like a bald eagle," he told me once at the ranch as we rode around in his Continental, "I am too aggressive. I want to soar too high, Bird, bless her, has a way of bringing me back to earth."

You include next his parents. His father "worked the laziness out of me," JOHNSON recalled. "He would yell out from the kitchen and tell me to get out of bed—that every boy in town had a head start on me. He was a taskmaster. He taught me the value of attending to details— and, brother, that came in handy about 40 years later when I sat in the President's office. He was big on the meaning of responsibility. Once he said, 'Son, you'll never know what it means to be a father until you are a father.' "

While JOHNSON's father stressed perspiration, his mother lent inspiration.

It was she who made him get an education, who channeled his muscle, energy and drive into higher spheres of endeavor. "I guess if it hadn't been for her," he confided, "I would have been just a clerk in the Highway Department. My daddy made me get up and go. But she was the spark who first got me to thinking where to go."

And then there was the late Speaker Sam Rayburn of Bonham. In the living room at the ranch, there used to be a big picture of Mr. Sam, and JOHNSON loved to sit under it in his favorite chair. He would lean way back in it as he philosophied and talked gently—then lunge forward, arms out wide, as he made a telling point.

Mr. Sam taught him the parliamentary process on Capitol Hill. Mr. Sam taught him how to line up votes in the Senate, Mr. Sam, when LYNDON got down in the dumps, "got me up again." Mr. Sam took him off one day and said, "LYNDON, you've got to get a thicker hide. You let too many little things bother you. This is a rough place to operate. It'll drive you crazy if you let it—and you are by nature sensitive and lovable, striving in a place where you at times can't be sensitive and lovable. There are a lot of s.o.b.'s who'll cut your insides out if you let them."

There was Alvin Wirtz, attorney and Texas state senator in the late 1930s. "Many men have been my teachers, but one stands out above the rest—Alvin Wirtz. He taught me the most about the one element in politics that matters the most—the people."

JOHNSON and Wirtz once met with some private utility executives in an effort to persuade the larger companies to extend power to small farmers in rural areas. At one point, LBJ got mad and told one of the utility presidents to "go to hell."

Wirtz took him off to the side, "Listen, LYNDON, I've been in this business a long time. You felt like a hero talking that way in front of your consumer friends, but your speech broke up the meeting. It left us back where we started. If I have learned anything in all these years, it is this: You can tell a man to go to hell, but you can't make him go."

As to talents and qualities, the two in my opinion which contributed the most to JOHNSON's success were a tremendous reservoir of energy and an uncanny knack of persuasion. He was born with the first; he developed the latter.

He once admitted that the margin he had over other men was his capacity to work harder than they do. He waked up around 7:30 in the White House, worked two hours in bed, entered the oval office in the west wing around 10. After a swim, lunch and nap, he began a "second day" at 4:30 in the afternoon and often labored until midnight—maybe later if he had to attend some official function.

When JOHNSON decided on a political career, the private business world lost the greatest salesman in history. He talked, argued and persuaded his way into the Senate's top leadership. In his earlier years he would become angry and impatient; later he learned the wisdom and art of reasoning without being unreasonable.

One time at a social function he met Sen. Frank Church of Idaho, who had just made a bitter speech against JOHNSON's Vietnam venture.

"Frank," he said, "that speech wasn't a bit helpful."

"Im sorry, Mr. President, the headlines exaggerated what I said."

"Frank, the headlines are all that people read."

"But, Mr. President, I didn't go any farther than Walter Lippmann."

"Well, Frank," the President shot back, "the next time you need money to build a dam in Idaho, you'd better see Lippmann."

The last time I visited the former president at the ranch, I noticed he had mellowed. He was more reflective, he was calmer, definitely more complacent and philosophical about disappointments and frictions of the past.

As I got in the car to head for Dallas, he stuck his head in the window for a final farewell.

"Your paper has been rough on me at times in the past," he commented in a tone of forgive-and-forget. Then he lowered his head, grinned and quipped: "And you know, there were times I had it coming."

Hon. Silvio O. Conte
OF MASSACHUSETTS

Mr. Speaker, I am grateful for this opportunity to honor the memory of our distinguished 36th President and one of the most powerful legislators ever to labor under the dome of the Capitol, LYNDON BAINES JOHNSON.

LYNDON JOHNSON in many respects seemed larger than life. He was a big man, an imposing man, a man who reflected the size and greatness of his beloved home State of Texas.

He was born near Johnson City, Tex., in 1908. After graduating from Southwest State Teachers College in 1930, he got a job teaching school. But the role of an educator is not the one that LYNDON JOHNSON chose to play for a lifetime. Rather, a career of public service as an elected representative of the people called him.

He came to Washington in late 1931 and here he remained until 1968. He left a mark on this city, in this Chamber where he served from 1937 to 1948, in the Senate where he distinguished himself as majority leader, and in the White House where he planned for a Great Society for all Americans.

My fondest memories of LYNDON JOHNSON will always be of his leadership in the area of civil rights. We worked together, taking the great strides toward achieving equality of opportunity for all people.

He told us, in a joint session of the Congress that "We Shall Overcome" and led us to passage of landmark civil rights legislation.

Although he presided over a divided Nation in his last months in office, I believe it is important to remember his unifying plea, "Let us continue" as this country stood numb and profoundly grieved at the death of a young and vigorous President.

Finally, it was the war in Vietnam that lead to LYNDON JOHNSON's decision in 1968 not to seek, once again, the highest office in the land. He may certainly be considered one of the casualties of that tragic conflict.

The awesome responsibilities of the Presidency put a great strain on the heart, even a heart as big as LYNDON JOHNSON's. On January 22, with the knowledge imparted to him by President Nixon that the Vietnam war was, at last and mercifully, over, LYNDON JOHNSON died at his ranch in Texas.

I join with my colleagues in mourning the passing of this dynamic legislator, industrious chief executive and eminent elder statesman. I extend my deepest sympathy to his remarkable wife, Lady Bird, and his entire family.

Hon. Tom Steed
OF OKLAHOMA

Mr. Speaker, it is still hard for all us to realize that LYNDON JOHNSON is no longer here. And in truth, in the measures for which he was responsible which are changing for the better the lives of so many, he will always be here.

He is widely recognized as the outstanding legislative craftsman of our time, the greatest majority leader of the Senate ever. Never before has a single individual had impact like his not just at one end of Pennsylvania Avenue but both.

President JOHNSON was one of the truly great Chief Executives our country has had. If only he could have lived another 10 years. He deserved time to enjoy the retirement he had earned, and time to see how, with the test of the years, people will value his efforts ever more, as happened with President Truman before him.

Others more eloquent will describe his achievements. I want to say a few words of my own experience with the man whom I am privileged to have had as friend.

In 1935, when I first came to Washington as assistant to Congressman P. L. Gassaway of Oklahoma, the New Deal was at its flood tide. One of the first people with whom I became acquainted was LYNDON JOHNSON, who shortly became assistant to Congressman Richard Kleberg of Texas. Those were days of frantic legislative activity. But at that time each House Member had a staff of only two, and the Capitol Hill community had not grown too big for people to generally be acquainted. President JOHNSON and I came from similar agrarian southwestern backgrounds. We were born only about 200 miles apart in central

Texas, although my own family soon moved to Oklahoma.

We had an organization on the Hill then called the Little Congress, and LYNDON JOHNSON was elected as its President, with me among his supporters.

LYNDON JOHNSON was always mindful of people, thoughtful, interested in individuals. Of course, he could lose his temper, as everyone knows, but that was in his zeal for action and was quickly submerged in his basic kindness.

He remembered the little thing as well as the big ones. Even in his White House years he could and did remember to call his birthday greetings to me and others. He was never too self-important to pay due notice to staff people, on the Hill and elsewhere, to let them know that he knew about and valued their work. If genius is an infinite capacity for detail, he had it.

We developed a sentimental attachment. Even after he went back to Texas he never failed on election night to use his fabled ability to reach anyone on earth by telephone, and he would always find me and get the results of my campaign direct.

As chairman of the Legislative Appropriations Subcommittee I saw a good deal of him during the White House years. And my appreciation of his stature consistently grew.

One of the incidents I remember best occurred when I sat on a White House meeting during the crisis following the seizure of the *Pueblo*. The crew of 81 was held by the North Koreans.

Someone urged a hard-line, drastic military response despite the threat that would involve to the lives of the crew. In effect, he said:

It's only 81 men, and the honor of our Nation is at stake.

The President almost ran across the room in his anger to shake his fist at that man and said:

Don't you ever say that to me. I would crawl on my belly before I'd give up the life of one of those men. If we do not cherish the life of one man we have lost everything that counts.

Subsequently, he did what was necessary to bring those men back.

One of my fondest memories of him is of the time in 1960 when he flew to my hometown, Shawnee, Okla., to speak during the climatic period of the presidential campaign. He had spoken many times that day, traveling all the way from Washington State to Oklahoma and going on to Texas the same evening. He was tired, but he gave that crowd everything he had. The response was terrific, and he threw away his prepared text for 15 minutes of impromptu delivery. Those who were present would not forget it. It was the greatest political rally ever for our town. In a front page editorial January 24, Ross Porter, Publisher of the Shawnee News-Star, recalled it:

SHAWNEE REMEMBERS L. B. J.

The sudden death of former President LYNDON JOHNSON, Monday, in his beloved Texas ranch home may have saddened the world, but it solemnly shocked a multitude of friends in his neighboring Oklahoma.

LBJ was a good neighbor to Oklahoma and many of his closest longtime friends here, for almost four decades, had learned to depend upon his friendship and loyaly and they cordinally reciprocated in typical Sooner fashion. LBJ never forgot that.

Here is one example. When the Kennedy-Johnson ticket ran into trouble late in October 1960, LBJ, the vice-presidential candidate who had campaigned the entire country, was so exhausted and distressed after a California trip that he was ready to "throw in the towel" and return to the Texas ranch. He had made a commitment however to speak for his political friends in Shawnee, Oklahoma.

With stark political defeat staring at the ticket, he nonetheless would honor that speaking commitment, even though in a small Oklahoma town.

Arriving at Shawnee airport, from the west coast after dark, on a rainy Thursday night, LBJ discovered what he always later recalled as, "the turning point in the campaign came at Shawnee, I knew then we could win the election."

A very large motorcade met him at the airport and paraded to the Municipal Auditorium, where an overflow crowd of 3,000, wildly cheered almost everything he said.

He returned to the Texas ranch that night a happier man, more convinced of victory by the Shawnee reception. Ten days later the ticket won over Richard Nixon, by the smallest victory—which required several days to officially determine the outcome, that Kennedy and JOHNSON had indeed won the election.

About three years later, Kennedy was assassinated in Dallas and LYNDON JOHNSON became President of the United States for the next five years.

President Richard Nixon, who talked frequently with LBJ, will miss his experienced judgment and wise counseling in the gigantic tasks which confront each president of the United States.

LYNDON JOHNSON always remembered Shawnee and Shawnee will always remember that friendly hard working country boy neighbor from Texas, whom we all called, "LBJ."

He really was "something else," and we believe, history will say so.—RP

Among the best tributes that I have seen was one from a University of Oklahoma student, Randy Splaingard, night editor of the Oklahoma Daily, who wrote this, in part, about the reaction there to the news of his death:

EULOGY TO LYNDON JOHNSON

"About JOHNSON? Wasn't that something?

We talked about it a few minutes—about his greatness as a humanitarian, a world leader, a vibrant down-to-earth man who will go down in history as one of America's greatests.

"Anyone who ever visited his presidential library in Austin can't help but realize how great he was," I said.

"By the way, have you heard they've been having some trouble with that building? The marble's cracking, I think," she said.

"You know, think how symbolic it would be if they would label those cracks "Vietnam." There it would stand—an eight-story monument of fine marble, one of the most impressive buildings in the world, marred by cracks, as only the war in Vietnam marred his five years in office," I thought out loud.

It was nearing 7:30 p.m. and "Maude" again came on at her worst. Soon it was time to return to work and put out a front page.

News of his death was still coming over the wire sporadically, squeezed between the Supreme Court's abortion ruling and the progress of the Paris peace talks.

I sat down to a blank front-page dummy. "JOHNSON gets the top of the page," I thought, "It can be no other way."

I sat there trying to busy myself. I could do little until an adequate story on JOHNSON came over the wire. Finally, more than an hour later it did—and I went to work.

Steve Howland, assistant managing editor, had located a couple of pictures of JOHNSON for my use. A symbolic double black box was drawn on the dummy sheet, the story was fitted, and the picture sized.

It was time to write a headline. "How do you summarize LYNDON JOHNSON's life in 28 letters?" I thought. I sat back and reminisced a short while.

I thought of that dark rainy Friday in November 1963 when sixth-grade classes were proceeding as usual in my Catholic elementary school in Collinsville, Ill. The parish priest suddenly entered the room, and solemnly said, "Let's all kneel down and pray. The President's been shot and killed."

And I remember watching television with the rest of my family for three continuous days. I remember the end of JOHNSON's somber statement upon first arriving in Washington, D.C., as President—"I ask your help and God's."

I remember hearing of the violence in Selma, Ala., and seeing the picture of JOHNSON shaking hands with Dr. Martin Luther King upon signing the Civil Rights Act of 1965.

"Dr. King wasn't the only one who had a dream," I thought.

I recalled writing a letter to him soon after that and receiving a warm one from him in return, along with a five-by-nine black and white portrait of his family. Of course it was a stock letter with a stamped signature, but nevertheless I was impressed.

He was the President.

I remembered his presidential address when for the first time he referred to the "police action" in Vietnam as a "war." As a 13-year-old, I naively thought, "It'll all be over by the time I'm draft age."

I recalled reading letters in Ann Landers' column from persons engaged with the President's treatment of his dogs.

I remembered my grandparents' Social Security increases and their registering for Medicare. I remembered someone calling him "education's best friend."

And I remember "I am not seeking and will not accept the nomination of my party for another term as your President."

So how do you sum it all up in 28 letters?

"Well," I thought, "you use his phrase—'Great Society.' That will be his most lasting gift to this country."

And so the headline was quickly formed—" 'Great Society' President dies."

That seemed to say it all.

I finished the rest of the front page, and approved the others to appear in the next morning's issue. I left Copeland Hall near midnight—about two hours later than usual. But then, it wasn't an ordinary night.

As I walked through the parking lot to my house, I noticed its stillness. Not a car passed along Elm as I made my two minute jaunt.

And I remember thinking, "Let the world stand still for a moment."

LYNDON JOHNSON was dead, and I felt a little less human because of it.

Randy Splaingard.

Another perceptive evaluation came from Jack Reese, executive editor of the Norman Transcript:

COME, LET US . . .

Every President lives, the late LYNDON BAINES JOHNSON told Congress in 1969, not only with what is, but with what has been and what could be.

Within the framework of these circumstances and the varied personalities of the leadership at his disposal, he sees the hope of a better America, a world at peace, a country aware of its own destiny.

He was reminding the men and women with whom he had had such long association as a legislative leader that the great events of any Presidency are shaped by many forces, controlled and uncontrolled.

Strong Presidents, it has been observed, "store up trouble for themselves and their successors."

This is what happened to President JOHNSON, and not solely because of Vietnam, the high price tag which has been attached to a distinguished career in government.

Not many can forget that sad day in November 1963 when a nation, stunned by incredible events, focused its eyes on a new leader, one uniquely equipped by legislative experience, tutored by masters of the political game.

President JOHNSON's ascendancy to power came at one of the moments in history which had been building for at least two decades. The tragedy of the Kennedy assassination served as a kind of catalyst to great hopes.

The unusually active 89th Congress, elected with Mr. JOHNSON in 1964, proceeded to approve legislation that had been stalled for as long as 20 years.

Major laws enacted in 1965 included medical care for the aged under Social Security; aid to primary and secondary schools; immigration reform; protection of Negro voting rights; excise-tax reduction; aid to urban areas, and others.

This burst of activity in a single session led seasoned Washington observers to compare the 89th Congress with the 73rd Congress of 1933-34 (the first two years of Franklin Delano Roosevelt's administration) and the 63rd

Congress of 1913-14 (the first two years of the Woodrow Wilson administration).

The second session of the 89th Congress was notably less productive than the first. And the 90th Congress displayed outright hostility to presidential proposals, even though both houses were controlled by the President's party.

Mr. JOHNSON's experience was far from unique. Every activist president has been accused of being domineering; most have been succeeded by men who took a more cautious approach to the exercise of executive power. Thus, Lincoln was succeeded by Grant; T. R. Roosevelt by Taft; Wilson by Harding; Truman by Eisenhower.

The split within the Democratic party which rejected Mr. JOHNSON had started in the early 1950s when he was the overseer of a Senate which did not reflect in its geographical and ideological makeup the national Democratic party. Forces outside and inside his own party moved Mr. JOHNSON along a historical path which led to the Presidency.

President JOHNSON was an enigma to many. He, indeed, listened to his own drummer. Some who observed him claimed that he had neither deep commitment nor firm philosophy in his handling of domestic or foreign affairs and that he was guided by a kind of frenzy to prove himself as a great President.

Be that as it may, but we believe he did have a firm commitment to his dream of a Great Society, one which it may be said a hundred years from now, that "by working together we helped to make our country more just, more just for all of its people, as well as to insure and guarantee the blessings of liberty for all of our posterity."

That is what President JOHNSON hoped for—but he believed that future historians, for whatever other judgment they might make, would agree that he tried—and tried hard.

It was my honor to be a member of the House delegation to the graveside services at the Johnson family cemetery there across the Pedernales River from Stonewall. He is back there for good now in the hill country whose name will always be linked with his—under the vast dominating sky of the Southwest that can almost command you to look into infinity. The dark, twisting beauty of the live oaks is there, and the little river with its stones and its turtles. His birthplace is only a few hundred feet away. This is the setting that produced LYNDON JOHNSON, and from many others, similar yet always different throughout the land has come the spirit that has made our country.

He was confident that the turmoil of our times is not just the decline of the old but the turbulent birth of the new. With some of his strength of will and devotion, we can try to do as he did and help make that true. He met his measure of success, that people will live a little better for his having been here.

Hon. Abraham Kazen, Jr.
OF TEXAS

Mr. Speaker, today we honor a man who was our friend, our leader, our inspired and determined President. He lived with energy and dedication throughout his life. Every American shares in the heritage he left, his performance in this House, in the Senate, in the White House. We share the loss with his devoted wife and family; we share the pride that our lives were touched by his.

I choose first to say that he was a friend because that word meant so much to him. He never used it lightly; it was for him a term of approval and appreciation. He knew that he marched in the vanguard of his company, but he never felt that he marched alone. And he was grateful for the friendship of others.

I do not need to recite the contributions of his leadership, the progressive legislation that he guided to enactment, the compassion of his achievements. History records them, and I am sure that history will record him as one of the most able Presidents of our Nation. And I shall never forget his relentless effort to do what was best, how time and again he said:

It isn't hard to do what's right; what's hard is knowing what is right to do.

He was fortunate to have a great lady as his wife and constant counselor. Mrs. Johnson served the Nation as well as her husband as, time after time, he labored to know what was right to do. It is recorded that on the night of March 31, 1968, when he startled the world by announcing he would not seek reelection, Mrs. Johnson was the first to speak to him as that television address ended. She said three words: "Nobly done, darling." How much those words say about LYNDON and Lady Bird Johnson.

So as we said farewell to him for the last time, the men and women who spoke and sang at the services, here at the Capitol and in the National City Christian Church as well as at the family burial plot, lifted their voices for all of us. We shared together a grief relieved by pride that our lives had been touched by LYNDON JOHNSON.

None was more touching than words quoted at the church by W. Marvin Watson, friend and aide to the late President. They were words spoken by LYNDON JOHNSON himself last September, at the 75th anniversary observance of the Scott and White Hospital in Temple, Tex. As Marvin Watson said last week, the words might well be LYNDON JOHNSON's epitaph. President JOHNSON said:

With the coming of September each year, we are reminded, as the song says, that the days are dwindling down to a precious few . . . the green leaves of summer will begin to brown . . . the chill winds of winter will begin to blow . . . and before we are ready for the year to end, the year will be gone.

As it is with the calendar, so it sometimes seems to be with our country and our system. For there are those among us who would have us believe that America has come to its own September . . . and that our nation's span as mankind's last best hope will be done.

President JOHNSON continued:

But I live by the faith that with each passing day we are always approaching nearer to the beginning of a new springtime and it is by that perspective that I see our country now.

No nation can be more than the visions of its people. America cannot be more than we believe ourselves capable of becoming.

I want to open the soul of America to the warm sunlight of faith in itself . . . faith in the principles and precepts of its birth . . . and faith in the promise and potential of its people.

So spoke LYNDON JOHNSON. And Mr. Watson concluded:

That was LYNDON BAINES JOHNSON, the 36th President of the United States of America. The years will be lonely without him.

I cannot disagree, but I must add that the years of his leadership, his calling us to action, will live on. Each of us, in a small way, must keep the faith of LYNDON JOHNSON. We may strive to do better; he would not have wanted us to do less.

Hon. Romano L. Mazzoli
OF KENTUCKY

Mr. Speaker, it is indeed ironic that LYNDON BAINES JOHNSON, who in life was a veritable lightning rod for controversy and criticism, should in death evoke such a widespread and spontaneous sense of national loss and grief.

In the Presidency, as well as in the Congress, LYNDON JOHNSON was a wielder of power, a strong, larger-than-life figure, who made no apologies about his determination to get his own way.

The American people, in their great wisdom, are wary of the powerful. This no doubt accounts for the fact that President JOHNSON's style, during his years in the White House, made him a popular target for criticism.

Yet in the retrospect, which comes untimely in the wake of death, the Nation more fully grasps the measure of LYNDON JOHNSON's greatness. It is true that he was a man greatly enamored of power. But, the power of LYNDON JOHNSON was the power of getting things done. It was not the power of brute force, so much as it was the power to strike a positive compromise, the power to forge a legislative solution to problems deemed impossible of solution by lesser men.

But, most significant of all, in our memories of LYNDON JOHNSON as a man of power, is the fact that he wielded his greatest power for the sake of the powerless. The mark of President JOHNSON's greatness is his record of accomplishments in behalf of the poor, the sick, the aged and the disenfranchised.

The nature of political power is such that, all too often, those who are strongest and most influential are best able to command the attention of Government.

At the peak of his political power, LYNDON JOHNSON turned his attention and opened his ears to the needs of our weakest and least influential citizens.

That explains the long lines of saddened citizens who waited hours in the cold to pay their respects when President JOHNSON's body was laid in state in this Capitol.

And, it explains why the only truly fitting memorial which this Congress can pay to President JOHNSON is to do our utmost to see that his programs for the poor and the needy are perfected and continued and brought to full fruition.

Thank you, Mr. Speaker.

Hon. Don Edwards
OF CALIFORNIA

Mr. Speaker, I join with my colleagues today in mourning the death of a great leader. LYNDON JOHNSON understood intimately the potential for leadership vested in the Office of the Presidency. Never was that understanding more clearly demonstrated than in his commitment to securing civil rights for all Americans.

LYNDON JOHNSON knew that the fear and suspicion which divided black from white, poor from rich, uneducated from educated, would not easily be overcome. But he also knew that the President could provide the leadership necessary to mend such divisions.

Shortly before his death in an interview with Walter Cronkite, LYNDON JOHNSON spoke of the responsibilities he had faced. He said:

When I became President, and realized that I was the leader of the country and that I was the President of all the people and all the people were looking to me to correct the inequalities, inequities and injustices and there was something that I could do about it, I concluded that now that I had the power, I was going to use it every way I could.

JOHNSON used his power well. During the 6 years of his administration, LYNDON JOHNSON produced 440 pieces of major legislation, the largest portion of which was aimed at eradicating social injustice.

The Civil Rights Act of 1964, the Voting Rights Act of 1965, the Fair Housing Act of 1968, these were laws which opened the way to equal rights for millions of Americans. Yet, these laws were not enacted without significant opposition. For years, discrimination against nonwhites had become a way of life in both the North and the South. LYNDON JOHNSON took it upon himself to reverse the trends of that discrimination.

I remember sitting in this great hall when President JOHNSON came to address a joint session of Congress in March 1965. He came that night to speak to us of what he called the American promise. That promise, he told us, rested on the right of every American "to be treated as a man equal in opportunity to all others." At issue was the right to vote for millions of Americans who had been disenfranchised solely because of the color of their skin. LYNDON JOHNSON appealed in that speech to the best instincts of Americans. He told us what was right, and he told us as legislators what would be expected of us.

The civil rights laws of the 1960's brought about change. Coupled with legislation in health, education, and public employment, those civil rights laws spelled progress for many disadvantaged minorities.

That progress was sometimes slow and painful, but there was always the reassurance that the President of the United States had committed the resources of the Nation to seeing to it that the goal of equality would be attained.

For the last 2 years, I have served as chairman of the Civil Rights Oversight Subcommittee in the House Judiciary. During that time, I have come to know well the impact of our civil rights laws. And I have come to appreciate, too, how crucial is the role which Presidential leadership plays in the enforcement of those laws. LYNDON JOHNSON understood that prejudices were not easily given up, but he had faith in the American people's sense of justice. That faith led us out of the shadow of our own fears.

I can think of no more fitting epitaph for LYNDON JOHNSON than what he said of his own goals:

> I want to be the President who educated young children to the wonders of their world. I want to be the President who helped feed the hungry and to prepare them to be taxpayers instead of taxeaters.
>
> I want to be the President who helped the poor to find their own way and who protected the right of every citizen to vote in every election.
>
> I want to be the President who helped to end hatred among his fellow man and who promoted love among the people of all races and all regions and all parties.

Mr. JOHNSON, you were such a President.

Hon. Tennyson Guyer
OF OHIO

Mr. Speaker, LYNDON B. JOHNSON was a man unique in our time. From frontier obscurity he rose to international prominence. As President of the United States during one of the most trying periods in our national history, he magnified both his name and his office.

The man from Texas established a new brand that the world will not forget. LBJ was not just a brand for ranch identification. LYNDON JOHNSON put that brand on legislation that brought light to millions who had lived in darkness. That brand brought new freedom, new opportunity, and new identity to minorities who had all too long dwelt in the valley of despair.

LBJ was a hallmark in American political life. It stood for a man who stood for many innovations for people. Yes, it cost him something. Yes, it likely shortened his life. Yes, it carried with it, the thorns of frustration, the sting of rebuke, and placed him all too often on an island of loneliness. LYNDON JOHNSON was a tall man. History says he was the second tallest of all our Presidents. But Mr. JOHNSON was tall in the saddle, tall on human rights, tall in bluntness, tall in action, and tall in courage. There is an empty saddle in the old corral, but LBJ is enshrined where generations unborn may see and know—in the hearts of those he loved, and in the garden of American remembrance.

Hon. Julia Butler Hansen
OF WASHINGTON

Mr. Speaker, I join with my distinguished colleagues in this House in expressing my sorrow, regret, and deep sense of loss at the death of our very beloved late President LYNDON B. JOHNSON.

I had the privilege of knowing him first as a U.S. Senator, second as Vice President, and, finally, as President. But I am proudest of having had the privilege of knowing him as a great, thoughtful, and compassionate citizen of the United States.

Many of you have known him much longer, so I cannot add to those memories. But, I would like to talk, just for a moment of LYNDON JOHNSON the great human being—the man who cared. To do this, I repeat a personal incident.

A very few days after President John F. Kennedy's death, when LYNDON JOHNSON, the new President, must have been at his busiest, my mother passed away. I, with members of my family, had left for the West for her funeral when the White House called my office and asked for me. My secretary who answered presumed that it was a White House staff member speaking and explained that I had already left. The voice on the telephone said, "This is LYNDON JOHNSON. I wanted to express my personal sympathy." Needless to say my secretary was astonished and astounded and said later, "The President himself cared."

I returned from my mother's funeral a few days before Christmas and, like other House Members who were then working on the Russian wheat problem late into the Christmas season, received the gracious invitation to the White House for coffee and fruit cake. Because of the circumstances, I did not quite feel like a social affair and called the White House. They were most gracious.

Two months later President and Mrs. Johnson had one of their delightful, informal parties for House Members. During the course of the evening the President talked with me and his first words were:

> I can't begin to tell you how deeply I sympathize with you on the loss of your mother. It was my mother who shaped my life and I shall miss her forever.

While this is a simple personal experience, it shows the great quality and depth of LYNDON JOHNSON's compassion for human beings. This is but one example among the undoubted thousands of times he remembered and cared for people and their problems. He cared not just for Members of Congress, but all people—the black, the white, the tired, the sick, and the poor.

A budget may now seek to erase LYNDON JOHNSON. But no budget nor legislation can ever erase the compassionate understanding which began Headstart, VISTA volunteers, Community Action programs, medicare, kindergartens, aid to education, and art and beauty for the many. Within millions of homes in America there is some memory that LYNDON JOHNSON passed their way with a message of hope and understanding for their circumstances and problems.

I also salute his courageous and gracious wife who worked and continues to work to make this Nation reflect the beauty which is inherently America at her best.

Mr. Speaker and my distinguished colleagues, I join you in sending any deepest sympathy to Mrs. Johnson and her family. I feel privileged and grateful to have shared a part of the unforgettable Johnson years.

Hon. Joe L. Evins
OF TENNESSEE

Mr. Speaker, today the flags over the Capitol are flying at half-mast in memory of LYNDON BAINES JOHNSON, the 36th President of the United States.

We have all participated in cermonies in the rotunda of the Capitol and at the National City Christian Church here in Washington, and have heard the beautiful and eloquent eulogies of our colleague, Congressman J. J. Pickle, from Texas; the Honorable Dean Rusk, who served with President JOHNSON as Secretary of State; Mr. Marvin Watson, the President's close associate and assistant in the White House; and the Rev. Dr. George R. Davis, pastor of the National City Christian Church, which President JOHNSON attended while in Washington.

These and other tributes and editorials on his passing were moving and beautiful. I should like to take this opportunity of adding my own tribute to this great man and close friend who served the Nation so faithfully and well—both in the Congress and in the White House.

Certainly I was shocked and saddened by the news of the passing of LYNDON B. JOHNSON. He was my personal friend and I felt extremely close to him.

LYNDON JOHNSON had the greatest legislative record of any President I have known—legislation passed during his administration has been compared to the famous "90 days" of President Franklin Roosevelt's administration as he responded to the challenge of the depression.

LYNDON JOHNSON more than any man I have known understood the legislative processes of the Congress. He understood the committee system and the intricacies of congressional interaction—the work of Congress.

His legislative success was a compound of this knowledge, his awareness of the Nation's problems, and his determination to attack these problems with all the force he could muster with the aid of Congress.

Although it may appear fashionable in some quarters to cast aspersions on the Federal career service, President JOHNSON was a Federal career man and he worked with the departments and agencies of Government to achieve his goals and objectives.

He believed in education—and much landmark education legislation was enacted during his administration.

He believed in assuring the elderly of adequate medical care—and the medicare legislation he sponsored has provided this assurance as a matter of right to the poor and needy.

He believed in helping the "little man" directly—rather than in the "trickledown theory"—and legislation which he championed has increased the incomes of the working people throughout America.

He believed in assisting rural and urban areas in coping with their problems—and legislation to assist small towns, rural areas and metropolitan areas has provided much assistance throughout America.

President JOHNSON's list of legislative accomplishments defies definition and comparison.

He thought big—like the man he was and the State of Texas, the State of his origin. And he was a dynamo as he translated his thoughts and dreams into action and reality.

As the first southern President since the Civil War, he accomplished more to assure equal rights for all Americans than any President since Abraham Lincoln.

LYNDON JOHNSON had the common touch—a sensitivity for people. He loved people and identified with them. He wanted all Americans to share in the good life.

As he once remarked:

I believe every American has something to say and under our system a right to an audience.

I believe achievement of the full potential of our resources—physical and human—is the highest purpose of governmental policies next to the protection of those rights we regard as inalienable.

I recall that on one occasion during a campaign swing through Tennessee in 1964 on leaving the airport at Nashville, the President, rather than heading directly for the city chose to detour to greet people who were crowded behind a fence hoping to catch a glimpse of him.

I also recall that as we were returning to the airport after a hard day of campaigning, I pointed out an important constituent among the throngs along the highway. I suggested that he wave to this friend but instead he ordered the driver to stop the car, then bounced out and went over to this constituent, shaking his hand and giving him a warm and enthusiastic greeting.

This was the personal style of campaigning that President JOHNSON loved and that was his trademark—and he made a lifelong friend and supporter of the man he stopped to greet.

While President JOHNSON was in office, I was invited to the White House frequently to participate in bill-signing ceremonies or for receptions, dinners and briefings.

Following his retirement from the Presidency, we corresponded on occasion and he obviously enjoyed maintaining his contacts with old friends in Congress.

Upon leaving the White House in January of 1969, he wrote to me a warm personal letter in which he said:

In this, my last week in office, I am stirred by memories of old battles—and old friends who stood at my side throughout them all.

You are one of those friends.

My admiration and affection for you will never diminish.

I thank you and I salute you.

Sincerely,

LYNDON JOHNSON.

I value and treasure this letter among my most prized mementos.

Although President JOHNSON, when he left the Presidency, had had a number of heart attacks—the first when he was majority leader of the Senate—we, his friends, had hoped that, with the burdens of the Presidency off his shoulders, he would live a long life in retirement.

He lived a full, rewarding life and his work had been completed. His achievements and accomplishments are now history. The Vietnam conflict which he worked to end is drawing to a close.

His administration will stand in history as a monument to social and domestic progress at home and to a strong defense of freedom abroad.

I was deeply saddened by the passing of this great friend, and my wife Ann joins me in expressing our deepest and most heartfelt sympathy to Mrs. Johnson—Lady Bird—and other members of the family in their loss and bereavement.

Because of the high regard and respect of my colleagues and the American people for this great President, I place in the Record herewith copies of editorial eulogies from the Washington Post and Washington Star-News.

The editorial eulogies follow:

[From the Evening Star and the Washington Daily News, Jan. 23, 1973]

LYNDON BAINES JOHNSON

He was six-foot-three and everything about him—his ability his high sense of national purpose, his towering rages—seemed somehow slightly larger than life. Now he is gone at the age of 64, the second former President to die within a month.

The very memory of LYNDON BAINES JOHNSON, thrust into the presidency by an assassin's bullet, is so freighted with partisan feeling that it must remain for another generation of Americans, immunized by time from the contagion of emotion to assess fairly the man and to judge impartially his presidency.

When that day comes, when the Vietnam conflict—like the Spanish Civil War which stirred the conscience of another generation—has become an issue to bring the flush of passion only to the cheeks of old men, we believe that the man from the Pedernales will be counted among this country's near-great presidents.

Historians will record that the first Southern president since Reconstruction engineered the Civil Rights Bill of 1964 (the first in more than 80 years), outlawing racial discrimination in public facilities, employment and union membership and giving the attorney general new powers to enforce Negro voting rights and to step up the pace of school desegregation. They will remember that, while he committed large numbers of U.S. troops to a conflict on the Asian mainland, he kept us out of nuclear war. This and much else in the fields of civil rights, housing and health did JOHNSON, who was perhaps the most consummate politician in modern American history, make part and parcel of our children's heritage.

And yet, at the last, he failed—or believed himself to have failed—withdrawing himself from contention in the 1968 election, leaving the country and his party weary and divided.

The roots of that failure are manifold and difficult to trace. Was it, as he insisted, too close to Appomattox for the country as a whole to accent and appreciate a Southern president, to believe in his vision of "the Great Society"? Was it inevitable, in a rising tide of bitterness and disaffection, that John F. Kennedy's successor should be struck down by the tumbling ruins of Camelot? Did he simply fail to gauge correctly the mood of the country when he vowed to nail that Vietnam coonskin to the wall? Was there some fatal and concealed flaw in his character which prevented him from dealing effectively with the burgeoning crisis of the races?

A little of each of these factors perhaps, contributed to the downfall and bitterness of a man whose personality so vividly reflected the brashness, drive, optimism, and acquisitiveness of his native state. Those good qualities and those defects which he brought to the presidency, in fact, may well have been the inevitable outgrowth of his state and regional heritage.

When time cools the passions of the moment, it will be remembered that he served his state and country, as congressman, senator, vice president and President for 31 consecutive years, and that if he did well by LYNDON JOHN-SON, dying a multimillionaire, he also tried to do well (and often succeeded) by Texas and the United States.

To a certain extent the measure of statesmen can be calculated by the passions they arouse among their contemporaries. Churchill and De Gaulle, for instance, were nothing if not controversial. In this respect, the hostility of his foes makes the big Texan look like tall timber indeed among the scrub growth which forested much of the political hills of America in our times.

LYNDON JOHNSON was a big man and a big President.

$\approx$

[From the Washington Post, Jan. 24, 1973]

LYNDON BAINES JOHNSON

The public lifetime of LYNDON BAINES JOHNSON spanned almost four decades. It was a period marked not just by the development of certain powerful currents in American thought, but also by an eventful reappraisal of where those currents had led. Thus, much which had been considered desirable, necessary and even holy in Mr. JOHN-SON's political youth had fallen into disrepute by the time that he left office. "Internationalism" had come to be known as "interventionism" by many, its painful and costly effects haunting the nation in seemingly unendable war. And the vital and generous impulses that had animated Mr. JOHNSON's commitment to domestic legislation from the New Deal through the Great Society had come to be seen by many as obsolete and outworn habits of mind which caused as many troubles as they cured. At the airport sendoff that January day in 1969, when LYN-DON JOHNSON's homebound plane vanished into the clouds, his longtime friends and colleagues were left with more than an eerie feeling of the suddenness and totality with which power is relinquished in this country. The summary departure of this man who had been the larger-than-life center of ambition and authority in government for five years, also seemed symbolically to end a self-contained chapter in the nation's political development.

It was an era characterized both domestically and in foreign policy terms by an assumption of responsibility—national responsibility—for the welfare of the poor, the rights of the mistreated, the fairness of the way in which we distribute our wealth and the general well-being and stability of countries all over the world. Of Mr. JOHNSON's participation in all this—as a Congressman, Senator, Vice President, and President—it must be said that his impact was so profound that there is hardly a case in which the nation was either blessed or victimized by this particular 20th century passion for responsibility for which

LYNDON JOHNSON himself was not largely responsible. Like indifferent lovers for fractious offspring, a nation can often take things for granted or seem only to notice when it has been wronged. The death of Mr. JOHNSON may serve momentarily to pull us back from these perspectives, to remind us that much which we now expect from our government and our society as a matter of course—black voting rights, care for our elderly and our ill—came to us very recently and largely by courtesy of LYNDON JOHNSON.

The simple, inescapable fact is that he cared—and that it showed. Being in all ways larger than life-sized, he cared about a lot of things: his own political fortunes, his image, and his place in history, for of course he was vain. But he was consistent; all of his appetites were king-sized. So he cared about people with the same enormous intensity. In fact, a fair case can be made that one set of appetites fed on the other; he struggled and wheedled and hammered and cajoled for political power because he yearned powerfully to do great and good things and that is what he wanted the power for.

This was at once the strength and the weakness of LYNDON JOHNSON, for while this tremendous force was more often than not irrestible over the years, both as Senate Majority Leader and President, it was, like everything about the man, very often excessive. It could bend the political process to his will, and to good effect. But it could also bear down too hard, so that the system cracked under his weight. A master at the instrumentality of events, he could use a Selma or an assassination to lever a civil rights law or a gun control bill through Congress. But he could also use a minor gunboat skirmish in the Gulf of Tonkin to produce a resolution from Congress giving overwhelming support to a war effort whose true nature was never revealed in terms which could be expected to prepare either the Congress or the public for the sacrifice that both would later be expected to accept.

Neither LYNDON JOHNSON's memory nor his place in history, we would hope, is going to turn entirely, or even primarily on the war that grew out of that resolution; for Vietnam there is blame enough for all concerned, over four administrations and a good number of Congresses. Confined and carried along by earlier commitments, counseled by the men recruited by his predecessors, unchecked by Congress, Mr. JOHNSON plunged on, overstating, over-promising, over-hoping, over-reaching. But if his time in office marked the big Vietnam escalation, it also will be remembered for the fact that he, by implication and by painfully difficult decision, moved toward the end of his term to acknowledge a great miscalculation—widely shared in, let it be said—which is not something incumbent Presidents are given to doing. Reluctantly, grudgingly, but effectively, he turned the war effort around, abandoning "graduated response" as the method of choice, and bequeathed to his successor a greater opportunity than he himself inherited to move toward disengagement and a re-definition of the mission in realistic terms.

When Harry Truman died a few weeks ago at the age of 88, he died the beneficiary of a gift LYNDON JOHNSON was not to receive: 20 years had passed since the embattled and much maligned Mr. Truman had held office so that time and change and hindsight vastly altered the view people had of him. Mr. JOHNSON was never lucky in this regard. His each and every achievement from his Senate years on seemed to be followed or accompanied by some series of events that spoiled the glory of the moment.

Still, we do not share the notion, now being advanced (sometimes with bitterness) of how unfair it was that he rarely received the recognition he deserved in his lifetime for the good and also great things he did—or that the criticism of his handling of the war unfairly overshadowed all the rest. He would, we suspect, have a wryly humorous view of all this—much as he craved to be well-loved and well-remembered—because he was too shrewd, not to say cynical a student of human and political nature not to have been amused by these efforts by those who served him badly from time to time to revise the record in his (and their) favor. LYNDON JOHNSON must have known that he did not need to be helped into history.

Hon. Edward I. Koch
OF NEW YORK

Mr. Speaker, today the country mourns the death of a great leader and a great American President.

In this hour of LYNDON JOHNSON's passing, let us put aside the disagreement that many of us had with him over Vietnam. He was a man with great courage and fortitude, a man who did what he thought was right, misguided though some of his decisions may have been.

At home LYNDON JOHNSON had the courage and compassion to grapple with some of the most difficult problems of our times: poverty and racial discrimination. He did not retreat from these challenges; indeed, he pursued them with great vision and determination. History will most fondly remember LYNDON JOHNSON for his civil rights legislation and for the commitment the Federal Government made under his leadership to improving the quality of life for all Americans.

LYNDON JOHNSON was a big man in every regard: in stature, in energy, in vision, in capacity, and in compassion. He was a man who embodied almost every human quality in such magnitude that he will be remembered not only for what he did but for the man he was and the dimensions of his leadership.

We all remember the many pictures of the man in the Oval Office who often looked tired and haggard. But, that craggy face reassured us that a man was in the White House who knew and cared about what was going on in the Federal Government and in the country.

It is tragic that LYNDON JOHNSON should have died before the signing of a peace accord settling the Vietnam conflict that through the months of his administration had become so personally consuming and finally his political nemesis.

Within the past month we have lost two great men our country has known. Let this be a period in which we reaffirm our resolve to meet the ideals on which our country was founded.

Mr. Speaker, in remembering President JOHNSON today, my sympathy goes to Lady Bird, Lynda, and Luci and the rest of the Johnson family who gave him such support and comfort during his years in Washington and in his retirement.

Hon. John E. Hunt
OF NEW JERSEY

Mr. Speaker, it is both tragic and ironic that former President LYNDON B. JOHNSON passed away yesterday, on the eve of peace in Vietnam. It was during his administration that the United States brought power to bear on the North Vietnamese in an effort to bring them to the bargaining table. It was during President JOHNSON's administration that Paris became the center of attention when it was announced that peace talks would begin.

One could not help but feel while watching the news last night that it was ironical that the Majestic Hotel in Paris was being prepared for the signing of the peace treaty ending the conflict in Vietnam. It was in this same hotel, in that very room shown last night, that the first hurdle to clear in the talks was the seating arrangement. This was just the first of many frustrations President JOHNSON would suffer in bargaining with the North.

He was indeed a casualty of the war.

Because of his efforts to deal with the Communists and the war with a strong hand, he was snubbed by his own party at the convention in 1968. But now, in retrospect, he, more than anyone else at the time, knew the best way to deal with his adversaries was through strength not weakness.

The war reached its fullest fury under JOHNSON, but it was he, and he alone who had to assume the consequences of difficult decisions, decisions which can only be made by the Commander in Chief.

History may yet prove him right.

Hon. Dominick V. Daniels
OF NEW JERSEY

Mr. Speaker, on January 22, 1973, at 5:33 p.m., death took from us LYNDON BAINES JOHNSON, the 36th President of the United States, almost 4 years to the day from the time he left the White House.

Mr. Speaker, I have already conveyed to Mrs. Johnson my own personal condolences in which Mrs. Daniels joins with me. In addition, I would like to publicly convey the deep and profound sorrow of the people of Hudson County, N.J., at the passing of this towering figure.

Few men dominated the age in which they lived as LYNDON BAINES JOHNSON. In every sense of the word he gravitated toward center stage in every forum in which he performed—as a Member of this House, the Senate, as Vice President, and as President. It is cliche to say that he was larger than life, but no other expression describes his relationship with the world in which he lived.

The tragedy of the Vietnam war has largely obscured the record of LYNDON JOHNSON in domestic affairs, but historians placing events in context will, I am sure, judge the accomplishments of the 89th Congress as the great monument to LYNDON JOHNSON. All of us who served in this body during the years 1965 and 1966 will never forget the nature and kind of leadership supplied by the White House.

It is perhaps a little ironic, but there were few places where LYNDON JOHNSON—the man of the arid plains of south-central Texas—was loved more than in my own Hudson County, N.J. But our people loved him for what he did for the poor, the urban, the black, the Spanish, and all Americans who needed help. His 5 years in the White House raised a new hope for millions, and those millions weep today for their champion.

Benjamin Disraeli once wrote that—

The spirit of the age is the thing that a great man changes.

LYNDON JOHNSON viewed in this light met the test of greatness for he, more than any other man of our time, or any time, led the fight for freedom for black Americans. A product of the segregated Southland, he fought to extend the franchise to millions of black Americans. Through his championship of the great Civil Right Acts of the 1960's, black Americans were led out of peonage and brought into the mainstream of American life. Truly, he changed the spirit of the age.

Mr. Speaker, LYNDON JOHNSON now moves from the contemporary stage to the historical and I know that history will view him as one of the great men of the century. I know that we shall not see his like again. May Almighty God bless LYNDON BAINES JOHNSON and may perpetual light shine upon him.

Hon. Kenneth J. Gray
OF ILLINOIS

Mr. Speaker, America is blessed not only with the quality of her institutions, but the quality of the men who guide her destiny. My dear friend, LYNDON BAINES JOHNSON, was truly a man who knew what America needed and he gave his all to fulfill the hopes and aspirations of millions of Americans.

The congressional district I represent in southern Illinois is a much better place today because this great President had compassion for our needs and put his broad shoulder to the wheel in helping us build a greater southern Illinois. He signed bills providing for better housing, better health care with new hospitals and nursing homes, economic development programs that are now providing thousands of new jobs, clean air and clean water, millions of dollars to provide retraining and a greater educational program from Headstart to postgraduate courses at our great Southern Illinois University, lakes and recreational facilities, superhighways, medicare, social security benefits, and many other benefits too numerous to mention. Yes, Mr. Speaker, when we were fighting desperately to locate the most modern Federal penitentiary in the world at Marion, Ill., LYNDON JOHNSON ignored pressure from all sides and stood with us in guiding this important legislation through the Senate after it had passed the House of Representatives.

Mr. Speaker, the Nation will not only mourn the absence of LYNDON JOHNSON, but we shall miss his clear and penetrating judgments. LYNDON JOHNSON had a real understanding, love and warmth for his family and his fellow man. I think when the history books are written concerning his long period of service in the Congress and in the Presidency, his sterling character, personality, and dedication will rank with the greatest Presidents of all time.

Mr. Speaker, when I saw Mrs. Johnson standing in the rotunda at the service, all I could say was—

I am sorry. You have my sympathy.

I wanted to say more but I am sure I speak for everyone in the Nation when I say that we were all saddened beyond words at the passing of such a great leader. LYNDON JOHNSON was "our kind of people," never too busy to give attention to the ignored; to those in despair, he gave hope; to those in need, he gave help; to the minorities and black, he gave equalization.

Yes, Mr. Speaker, he is gone but he has left behind a legacy and a challenge to us. His good works will stand as a lasting memorial that will be much taller than any monument we could erect.

The entire Gray family, my congressional staff, and the people of the 24th Congressional District of Illinois join me in extending deepest sympathy and prayers to Mrs. Johnson, the daughters, and their families. We thank them for sending this giant of a man our way.

Hon. Richard Fulton
OF TENNESSEE

Mr. Speaker, few men in history have seen fortune and circumstance elevate them to the heights of power and responsibility as did the late LYNDON BAINES JOHNSON only to suffer the tragedies which fate can impose.

And yet I am convinced that this Nation has never had a political leader or President who was more dedicated to the improvement of the life of all our people, particularly those among us who have been in one way or another disadvantaged, or more personally dedicated to the search for world peace.

That LYNDON JOHNSON suffered reverses and made mistakes in pursuit of these noble goals cannot be denied. Yet his accomplishments were legion and many will survive him as a living memorial to all that is good in America and to the worthy greatness to which we justly aspire.

He now belongs to history and it is for the future to judge him. Yet there are millions of Americans today whose lives are somewhat richer and fuller because of the labors of LYNDON B. JOHNSON. For these persons he is justly a great figure.

I am confident that history will regard President JOHNSON highly as a man of great courage who was driven by worthy compulsion to make the great American dream a reality for all Americans and as a man who guided this Nation into a war of tragic consequence not in search of vain glory but in the quest of peace.

Hon. Howard W. Robison
OF NEW YORK

Mr. Speaker, remembering as I do the force and vitality of LYNDON JOHNSON of some 5 or 6 years ago, it is difficult to believe that he is dead.

He was a tower of strength, as majority leader in the Senate for so many years and, then, if the greatness of a President can be measured in terms of success in engineering his programs through an often-reluctant Congress, he was surely one of the greatest of our modern-day Presidents.

Mr. JOHNSON and I often disagreed, but I always saw him as a sincere advocate of America's "little people," and particularly of America's poor and disadvantaged. He constantly wanted to move our Nation forward and his "great society," programs for doing so—no matter how controversial some the same still are—stand as a landmark of Presidential concern.

The tragedy of Vietnam became—and remains—his own personal tragedy. One has to wonder how much that tragedy shortened his life, even as it shortened his political career.

The loss of our only two surviving ex-Presidents within the span of 1 month is a cruel blow to the Nation. It points up again, I think—no matter how late now to consider it—the necessity for our finding some way to continue to use their experience, perhaps as members "emeritus" of the Senate, after they leave office. I hope we will give our attention to that need—as a memorial of sorts to both Harry Truman and LYNDON JOHNSON.

Hon. Patsy T. Mink
OF HAWAII

Mr. Speaker, all Americans are deeply saddened by the sudden death of our beloved former President, the Honorable LYNDON BAINES JOHNSON.

Those of us who were his colleagues during LYNDON JOHNSON's long and distinguished service in the Congress have special reason to mourn his loss. His fellow Members of Congress knew well his great legislative ability, his leadership, and most of all, his tremendous personal qualities.

LYNDON JOHNSON's accomplishments during several decades of public service loom large on the rich tapestry of American history which he helped to fashion. As a Member of Congress, he raised the legislative branch to a pinnacle of power and influence that it has not achieved since. As President, he received the greatest electoral mandate in history. As an American, he captured the support and admiration of perhaps more of our people than any other recent leader.

President JOHNSON won this widespread respect because he was truly a man of the people. More than anything else, he envisioned government as a helping hand for the poor, the sick, the hungry, and the needy. He saw Federal programs as providing the means, through education of the individual, job training, and providing equality of opportunity, whereby the people could be given the means of helping themselves. His great society, and the programs to achieve it, were based on a respect for individualism and personal achievement.

To attempt to list even his major accomplishments in a brief manner is a certain injustice, but LYNDON JOHNSON is perhaps best known for such landmark programs as the war on poverty, the 1964 Civil Rights Act which covered public accommodations, hiring practices, and voting rights, the medicare program for our older citizens, and our most important education bills such as the Elementary and Secondary Education Act of 1965 which was the first general school assistance law in U.S. history. Among other portions of his legislative program was the bill creating the Department of Housing and Urban Development in 1965; the Immigration Act of 1965 which eliminated the national origins quota system; the Wholesome Meat Act of 1967; the Truth in Lending Act of 1968; the Land and Water Conservation Fund Act of 1964; the Wilderness Act of 1964; the 1968 Civil Rights Act which prohibited discrimination in the sale or rental of housing; and the Fair Labor Standards Amendments of 1966. This is a legacy of governmental achievement which would be exceedingly difficult to emulate.

It was incongruous, to say the least, that this man who so believed in human worth should have become involved in a war so little understood by his countrymen. President JOHNSON did not start the war, nor was he able to end it. I am convinced that he sought with all his heart to stop the conflict, but this goal proved as elusive as the social uplift for which he so valiantly strived. More because of the war than anything else, our country was unable to muster the resources required to achieve the ambitious and imaginative program mapped out by President JOHNSON to achieve his domestic ends.

Let history record that here was a man of destiny denied, a figure of epic proportions whose hopes for all mankind were stymied by concerns that go deep into our culture and heritage. It was not enough to reach for the stars, when our roots remained in a clay that was all ours, and seen as indisputably superior to all else. In this, LYNDON JOHNSON fell victim to a national pride that would not accept a lesser role on the world stage, even at the price of abandoning the dream which made us best.

Let the future spell out the lesson of this paradox. For now, it is enough to know that in LYNDON JOHNSON we had a President who embodied the conflicts so inherent in our own society, and whose achievements may be measured by his unprecedented attempt to make it great.

Hon. Charles E. Bennett
OF FLORIDA

Mr. Speaker, the country has lost a great leader in the passing of President LYNDON JOHNSON. I served with him in Congress and always found the door open at the White House while he was there. He used to phone me at home in the evening and talk with me about matters before the country and we have corresponded since his retirement. So this great loss to the country and to the world is a keen loss to me personally. History will properly list him as one of our greatest Presidents.

Hon. Ralph H. Metcalfe
OF ILLINOIS

Mr. Speaker, it is with more than a heavy heart that I learned about the death of former President LYNDON BAINES JOHNSON.

In the course of less than a month this country has lost two of the greatest leaders that it has ever had. Without a doubt, LYNDON JOHNSON worked harder than most men alive to help all minorities attain their rightful equality. Added to this is the fact that he had more compassion and more understanding than the other leaders of this country, especially at a time when compassion and understanding were needed and very necessary. It is not as though he listened like many politicians at the time did; he acted. He worked to present a positive program to the people; something not to placate them, but something constructive, positive.

LYNDON JOHNSON was a man who came up through the ranks, so to speak. He started as a teacher in Texas, something he was exceptionally proud of. He was elected to the House of Representatives in Washington. It was there that he learned the ins and outs of politics as we have come to know it today. He left the House for the Senate where he was an effective Senator, whip, and majority leader, always with the people in mind. From the Senate to a sectionally balanced ticket headed by John Kennedy and, after that tragedy, to the Presidency.

One of the characteristics of Mr. JOHNSON all the way through his political career was that he worked, and those around him felt the aura of this constant work.

In one of the small ironies of his life, it should be noted that one of the last things that he did was to have the Conference on Civil Rights in Texas as his Presidential papers on that subject were opened up to the scrutiny of scholars. There are very few national leaders that I know of who could lay claim to the title of leader in the field of civil rights; Mr. JOHNSON could, but I never recall him doing it.

His Great Society program was a constructive response to the needs of his fellow man. The Civil Rights Act of 1964 and the Voting Rights Act were enacted, because President JOHNSON was firmly committed to equality and because this President was committed to action where there was inequality. He was a man who used the Presidency to exercise the moral leadership in time of crisis.

Mr. JOHNSON was humble in origin, and he was strong in will and spirit. He will be missed by those who love people; those who care about people. He was a man whose wisdom and knowledge will be sorely missed in this country and around the world. He understood the needs of the people and did his utmost to meet these needs. A great leader and a great person—we all will miss this uncommon man and great President.

Hon. Melvin Price
OF ILLINOIS

Mr. Speaker, the death of LYNDON BAINES JOHNSON takes from us a man who spent a lifetime seeking the American dream for all people. A man of boundless energy, talent, and persistence LYNDON JOHNNSON dreamed big dreams for the American people and devoted his public career toward the realization of a great society.

In many ways LYNDON JOHNSON was larger than life. Big of frame, deep of mind, LYNDON JOHNSON came out of Texas like a duster, full of frontier restlessness and energy. Powerful, assertive, and determined LYNDON JOHNSON saw to it that more progressive legislation was enacted during his Presidency than any President in American history.

Education, human rights, economic development men are but several of the legislative enactments that LYNDON JOHNSON saw fashioned into law. Benefiting the American people these legislative programs epitomized LYNDON JOHNSON's belief that the Government should work for the people.

My association with LYNDON JOHNSON goes back to the days when he served as Speaker of the Little Congress, an organization of congressional aides devoted to the realization of the New Deal legislative process and worked long and hard for the goals of his idol, Franklin D. Roosevelt. From that day until the day of his death, LYNDON JOHNSON never lost sight of his main objective: utilize the full powers and resources of the Government for the people of America.

It was my pleasure to serve in the Congress with him as a member of the House Armed Services Committee and later as a member of the Joint Committee on Atomic Energy.

Few men have ever come to the Presidency with as much training as LYNDON JOHNSON. Legislative aide, governmental official. Member of the House of Representatives, Member of the Senate, Senate majority leader, and Vice President, LYNDON JOHNSON was a proven political leader. He understood how the political process could be used effectively for the development of enlightened public policy. No man personalized the Presidency more than LYNDON JOHNSON.

An era has passed with LYNDON JOHNSON's death. Though caught in the cruel wash of the Vietnam war, it was LYNDON JOHNSON who started the Paris peace talks. His devotion to the cause of peace stood second to none. He removed himself from politics in the belief that it, his action, would give peace a chance to work. Ironically, his death came as the cease-fire agreement in Vietnam emerged. Fortunately, he was aware of the coming peace before his death.

In death LYNDON JOHNSON will remain big as he did in life. His career, his spirit, his endless quest for peace and fulfillment will remain forever etched in the American memory of great Presidents. A great patriot who loved his country and was not ashamed to show it, LYNDON JOHNSON gave his life to a cause he believed in: The right of human dignity for all Americans.

Hon. Donald M. Fraser
OF MINNESOTA

Mr. Speaker, the man we honor in this special order once served in this House. LYNDON BAINES

JOHNSON described himself as "a child of Congress."

I would like to believe that it was, in part, because he was "a child of Congress" that he rose above the circumstances of his birth, as we must, expanding himself beyond his parochial, Texas-centered concerns.

But whether or not his service in the Congress aided President JOHNSON in overcoming, it is clear that he did. Born and raised in Texas, Mr. JOHNSON went on to shepherd through the Congress more civil rights legislation than any President who served before or after him.

Those of us who were Members of the 89th Congress saw for ourselves that his efforts were not limited to civil rights measures, but included other landmark social welfare laws also aimed at benefiting the entire Nation. But to me, and to many other Americans, President JOHNSON's effort to end what he described as "the one huge wrong of the American Nation"—the denial of black America's civil rights—is his greatest contribution to this Nation.

In the 10 green volumes containing the public papers of President JOHNSON, there are innumerable evidences of the President's commitment to equal treatment for all Americans, of his concern for those Americans who for whatever the reason need their Government's help if they are to share fully the benefits of American society.

His belief was not that every American problem could be solved in Washington—this was and is an impossible task. But President JOHNSON did recognize that many ills of our society would persist and grow worse if left unattended. Some local and State governments either could not or would not address some of these problems—civil rights was only the most obvious example.

The President knew that the fundamental problems of poverty and color in our society do not evaporate—except in the observer's mind—if they are ignored. They become more complex and concentrated and more difficult for future generations—our children's—to ameliorate or solve.

And President JOHNSON did not believe we could solve our problems by throwing dollars at them. But he knew that problems are not solved without effort. And this effort always requires human and material resources if it is to succeed.

President JOHNSON's ideas evolved, Dean Rusk pointed out during services for the President at the Capitol, from "a volcanic eruption from the innermost being of his soul." These eruptions could lead to error though only good was intended. But the eruptions in behalf of the domestic well-being of the American people were sound and well directed. Just as important, for the President was above all human and fallible, and no one contends his actions were always without error, the President gave to the poor and less affluent of this country a sense that he was committed to progress for all—and they saw evidences of the progress.

He used his national pulpit to assure the afflicted. While he was himself a major beneficiary of the American social and economic system and an unashamed advocate of the free enterprise system, he did not concern himself only with those who share in the benefits of the status quo. He recognized that many still wait in line.

In closing I want to quote briefly from President JOHNSON's June 4, 1965, commencement address at Howard University: "To Fulfill These Rights." His words still have relevance 8 years after they were delivered and they bear repeating and demand action if we are to progress as a nation.

But, more importantly, on this occasion, by illustrating President JOHNSON's commitment to progress for the least advantaged in our society, these words record again his hopes for every member of our society:

"TO FULFILL THESE RIGHTS": COMMENCEMENT ADDRESS AT HOWARD UNIVERSITY, JUNE 4, 1965

This graduating class at Howard University is witness to the indomitable determination of the Negro American to win his way in American life . . . But for the great majority of Negro Americans—the poor, the unemployed, the uprooted, and the dispossessed—there is a much grimmer story. They still, as we meet here tonight, are another nation. Despite the court orders and the laws, despite the legislative victories and the speeches, for them the walls are rising and the gulf is widening. . . . There is no single easy way answer to all of these problems.

Jobs are a part of the answer . . . Decent homes in decent surroundings and a chance to learn—an equal chance to learn—are part of the answer.

Welfare and social programs better designed to hold families together are part of the answer.

Care for the sick is part of the answer.

An understanding heart by all Americans is another big part of the answer . . . But there are other answers that are still to be found . . . [I]t is the glorious opportunity of this generation to end the one huge wrong of the American Nation, and, in so doing, to find America for ourselves, with the same immense thrill of discovery which gripped those who first began to realize that here, at last, was a home for freedom.

All it will take is for all of us to understand what this country is and what this country must become . . .

Hon. William A. Steiger
OF WISCONSIN

Mr. Speaker, the death of LYNDON BAINES JOHNSON leaves a considerable void to all who knew him. President JOHNSON, as has been said many times in the past few weeks, was a giant of a man, a larger-than-life figure we will always remember.

LYNDON JOHNSON was perhaps the ultimate creature of Congress, with a better understanding of the workings of Government and the uses of power than any other man in recent history. When Mr. JOHNSON was Senate majority leader and Sam Rayburn was Speaker of the House, Congress played a more proper role in our "checks and balances" system. His departure, I think, was a factor in and of itself in the decline of Congress.

President JOHNSON was a massive man who when he made a mistake it was massive and who when he moved to correct a wrong he gave it all he had. Millions of Americans benefit directly from the hundreds of laws he pushed through Congress. His vigorous efforts on behalf of his measures was a major factor in Congress' passage and implementation of them.

It is tragic that many remembrances of President JOHNSON have dwelt on his role in the Vietnam war. He did make the decisions, based on the advice of his expert advisers, which did involve us more in the conflict. But he took every action—including the sacrifice of his own political career in March 1968—in the hope of achieving a just peace. President Nixon rightly spoke of Mr. JOHNSON's dedication to peace during his speech announcing the settlement in Southeast Asia.

What will stand as more of a tribute will be his efforts on behalf of the disadvantaged. As Senate majority leader, as Vice President, and then as President, he performed valiantly to erase the barriers condemning many of our fellow citizens to second-class citizenship. History books will, I am sure, list his accomplishments along with Mr. Lincoln's in discussions of the fight for justice, equality, and opportunity for all Americans.

I shall always remember fondly President JOHNSON, Mrs. Steiger and I both shall treasure the opportunities made available to us in our first 2 years in Congress to be at the White House with the President and his family. Most especially, Mrs. Steiger joins with me in expressing our deepest sympathy to Mrs. Johnson, to Lynda and Chuck Robb, and all the other members of the Johnson family.

LYNDON JOHNSON cared—and cared deeply—for his fellowman. And he put this concern into action. His example is a legacy for the ages.

Hon. Edward G. Biester, Jr.
OF PENNSYLVANIA

Mr. Speaker, our Nation now mourns the passing of another President, LYNDON JOHNSON. We will miss the wisdom and perspective he shared with us, and the absence of his presence is a loss we cannot measure but which we will surely feel.

His early life knew hardship and struggle, and his political upbringing was steeped in rural populism, the Great Depression and the New Deal. From these early experiences, LYNDON JOHNSON developed a natural and powerful concern for the weak and the poor. Despite their differences in personality and style, I am struck by the similarities I see in the lives of LYNDON JOHNSON and Harry Truman and the passing of an era their deaths represent. In their passing we may have seen the last of our Presidents who lived and practiced what they learned in that singular and decisive period of American history.

LYNDON JOHNSON saw politics as the art of compromise and the possible. Being the man he was—forceful, strong, fervent—he realized accomplishments others would not have been able to achieve. The Civil Rights Act of 1964 and the Voting Rights Act of 1965 were turning points in our Nation's commitment to provide justice and opportunity for all its people.

The impact that legislation has had is staggering; yet equality remains a goal and not a reality. LYNDON JOHNSON's dedication to this struggle is underscored in one of his last public statements in December at the civil rights symposium at the Lyndon Baines Johnson Library in Austin. At that time he concluded his impromptu remarks with the following:

> We know there is injustice. We know there is intolerance. We know there is discrimination and hate and suspicion, and we know there is division among us.
>
> But there is a larger truth. We have proved that great progress is possible. We know how much still remains to be done. And if our efforts continue, if our will is strong, if our hearts are right, and if courage remains our constant companion, then, my fellow Americans, I am confident we shall overcome.

The Johnson years told us much about our-selves and our Nation. Their successes and fail-ures will be instructive as we continue to grapple with the persisting problems of society. We will learn from the mistakes of those years, but let us never forget the achievements LYNDON JOHNSON won for all the American people.

Hon. Lloyd Meeds
OF WASHINGTON

Mr. Speaker, I appreciate this opportunity to speak of the achievements of the late President LYNDON B. JOHNSON.

President JOHNSON was the first President un-der which I served in the House and as such re-tains a special place in my memories. Shortly after my appointment to the Committee on Education and Labor in 1965, Congress passed the Elemen-tary and Secondary Education Act of that year.

President JOHNSON's key role in passage of this first Federal aid school bill made apparent to me his sincerity and dedication as a friend of educa-tion. In that same congressional landmark year, the hand of President JOHNSON helped mightily in approval of medicare, the Higher Education Act of 1965, and the Appalachian Regional De-velopment Act.

I think President JOHNSON's place in history is assured by his support of vital social legislation and the creative work by the 89th Congress that cast his and our ideals into legislation.

Above all else, his role in civil rights deserves praise. President JOHNSON recognized division by race in this Nation as a potentially destructive force. His efforts to abrogate this force are best illustrated by strong support of the 1964 Civil Rights Act and the 1965 Voting Rights Act.

These and the earlier human rights bills he supported may eventually make possible a viable society in this Nation.

His foresight into the consequences of remain-ing a separate but unequal society, combined with his leadership and understanding of the legisla-tive process, resulted in an opening of doors that was long overdue. It is fitting that his last major address was to a gathering concerned with human rights.

If all our human problems were not overcome in LYNDON JOHNSON's lifetime it was not for lack of his trying.

Hon. Robert D. Price
OF TEXAS

Mr. Speaker, the American people have wit-nessed a most remarkable month—first with the passing of former President Harry S. Truman on December 26, followed by the reinauguration of President Richard Nixon on January 20, and now again with the passing of another former Presi-dent, LYNDON B. JOHNSON.

January was a month of mixed emotions—Americans both celebrated and mourned. We looked with anticipation to the future and yet paused to contemplate the past.

LYNDON B. JOHNSON was no ordinary man. Re-gardless of whether one agreed or disagreed with his policies, JOHNSON was a man of incredible strength and endurance. His steadfastness which was often a target for his detractors nevertheless gave Americans a sense of security and continuity during a time so wrought by strife and emotion.

Although ascending to the Presidency through an act of fate not expected or awaited, LYNDON B. JOHNSON carved his own record, and set into motion the most comprehensive domestic legis-lative program in history. LYNDON B. JOHNSON, a fellow Texan and political protege of the im-mortal Sam Rayburn, will have a place in history. We today are too close in time as his contemporar-ies to truly measure the significance of his pres-ence upon the course of national and world affairs.

But LYNDON B. JOHNSON can never be doubted in his great faith in the American system. To all citizens, regardless of political party, he beck-oned to the call of a task yet unfinished. And of that work which is good, he said, "Let us con-tinue."

Hon. Jonathan B. Bingham
OF NEW YORK

Mr. Speaker, I am glad to join with my col-leagues in paying tribute to the late LYNDON BAINES JOHNSON, 36th President of the United States.

I had the honor of serving under President JOHNSON from the time he assumed the office until March of 1963. At that time I was the U.S. Representative on the Economic and Social Coun-cil of the United Nations. One of Mr. JOHNSON's first acts as President was to come to the United

Nations and address the General Assembly. This was a way of expressing his great interest in and support for the U.N., as well as a method of assuring the world of the continuity of U.S. foreign policy following the tragic death of President Kennedy.

I also had the great privilege of being a Member of the Congress during the 89th and 90th Congresses. There is no doubt that the record of domestic legislation written during those years, especially in 1965, in response to the leadership of President JOHNSON was one of the most remarkable in the history of the Nation.

President JOHNSON knew how to get action out of the Congress. He was unfailingly courteous, hospitable, and friendly, but he was also a hard taskmaster. He never let up in his efforts to press the Congress for constructive action.

While I differed with President JOHNSON in regard to his Vietnam policies, I never had any doubt that he was acting as he believed to be in the best interests of the country.

I cannot conclude these remarks without paying a brief tribute to Mrs. Johnson. She was—and is—an inspiration to all of us. Her dignity, her friendliness, and her intense interest in many important programs, especially the beautification of our country, were truly remarkable. We all extend to her and her family our deepest sympathy in their great loss.

Hon. Donald W. Riegle, Jr.
OF MICHIGAN

Mr. Speaker, all Americans feel a sadness and sense of loss at the sudden death of former President LYNDON JOHNSON. More than any President in recent times he had a deep faith in—and concern for—working people. His strong emphasis on human problem solving gave the country leadership and direction. While his Vietnam war policies were regrettable—his full commitment to equality and human rights was a source of national inspiration.

Above all, LYNDON JOHNSON was a human being—a man who loved his fellowman—and I feel his loss in a personal way. I am proud to have known him—and to have served 2 years in Congress while he was President. My prayers and thoughts are with his family.

Hon. James G. O'Hara
OF MICHIGAN

Mr. Speaker, it is with a sense of profound sadness over the loss of a great leader and an indomitable fighter for the rights of man that I rise to join with my colleagues today in paying tribute to the memory of LYNDON BAINES JOHNSON.

Since I came to this body, in 1959, it has been my privilege to serve under four Presidents. None of them executed the duties of his office with greater passion and persuasion than LYNDON JOHNSON. He battled untiringly for those causes in which he believed—the causes of civil rights, education, full employment, and the rest—and because of his leadership, we made the greatest strides toward these goals that have been made in our lifetime.

It was my privilege to serve as a soldier in LYNDON JOHNSON's army during the great legislative struggle that culminated in the enactment of the Voting Rights Act of 1965. The President was not content merely to issue a manifesto concerning the urgent need for this legislation which would give the franchise to American citizens long denied their rights, because of the color of their skin. He was not content merely to exhort his troops to do battle in the cause of simple justice: Instead, he fought side by side with us throughout the battle in the halls of this great national legislature. All of us who participated in the struggle can be proud of what we accomplished in enactment of the Voting Rights Act. But all of us who participated in that struggle are also aware that victory well might have eluded our grasp, had it not been for LYNDON JOHNSON's efforts.

It is particularly timely, Mr. Speaker, to recall the working partnership which existed between President JOHNSON and the Congress—in this and other legislative milestones which were placed along the road to a greater society during his stewardship in the White House. We could wish today for the same kind of interaction between the legislative and executive branches.

It is a tragedy of history that the Johnson administration was marred by the fact that we became more deeply involved in a war in Southeast Asia which was, to a large extent, President JOHNSON's legacy from his two predecessors in the White House, and a war, in turn, which raged on for 4 long years after LYNDON JOHNSON retired to private life. It is a tragedy, because that war and its consequences, both at home and abroad, have diverted the people's attention from LYNDON JOHNSON's role as the great activist in the White House.

President JOHNSON was a man with faith in America and with a dream about what its people could accomplish. Not content with merely dreaming, he dared to make those dreams come true—and our lawbooks now are studed with landmarks to his challenge to the American people, and to their response to that challenge to their greatness and their better nature. It is my hope, and one I believe is shared by the majority in this body and the majority of the American people, that those great social programs of the Johnson years not be dismantled now.

Mr. Speaker, history will vindicate the memory of LYNDON BAINES JOHNSON. I believe it will stamp him as one of the great Presidents of this century—a man who was truly a partner with the people, and with their elected representatives, in achieving progress toward a better society. I hope we will live to see other Presidents with his cooperative spirit, and with his concern, his compassion, and his capacity for social progress.

Hon. J. J. Pickle

OF TEXAS

Mr. Speaker, LYNDON JOHNSON was an extraordinary man. I think it might be fitting today to relate one of the stories that appeared in the Washington Post the day after this great man passed away. It was a story told by Mr. James Rowe, who had been one of Mr. JOHNSON's friends through the years, and he related the story of a phone call that the then Congressman JOHNSON made. He called home and talked to Mrs. Zephyr Wright, his cook. He told her that he was having five guests in for dinner, and she had to fix five good steaks, and that he would be there in about an hour. And before she could tell him that she did not have any red coupons, which were necessary during those days of food rationing, he had already hung up. Zephyr then called Mrs. John Connally and told her that she had to have some red coupons; that the Congressman said he was going to bring five folks home for dinner, and she did not have any coupons, and could she borrow some from Mrs. Connally? Mrs. Connally said:

Zephyr, I don't have any red coupons, and if I did I wouldn't give them to LYNDON because that man has got to learn that he is just like anybody else.

And Zephyr said:

Yes'm. I know, Mrs. Connally. I know he is just like anyone else, and you know that he is just like anyone else, but he doesn't know it, and I'm not going to be the one to tell him.

Mr. Speaker, this extraordinary man has given his life to Americans. Our country will be improved for ages to come because of the goodness and the dedication of this great man from the hill country of central Texas. We do appreciate his great service. We love him and his family, and we are proud to join today in tributes which, in just a small measure, might be an expression of appreciation for the good things he has done for America, and for the people of America.

Mr. Speaker, I ask unanimous consent that I may include the following editorials on the life and character of the late President LYNDON BAINES JOHNSON.

[From the Austin Statesman, Jan. 26, 1973]

MINISTER SAYS HE LEARNED COURAGE, FAITH FROM
L. B. J.

(By Harry Provence)

WASHINGTON.—"LYNDON my servant is dead, now therefore arise . . ."

So did LYNDON BAINES JOHNSON's minister, Dr. George R. Davis, paraphrase Joshua I, Jehovah's command to Moses' successor, in the final Washington tribute to the former president Thursday morning in National City Christian Church.

"LYNDON JOHNSON was my minister," Dr. Davis told the crowd that packed his house of worship and overflowed all around Thomas Circle in the heart of the nation's capital.

"He taught me grace under pressure, courage, faith . . . he showed me how religion can be a part of daily life . . ."

Dr. Davis recalled two examples of LYNDON JOHNSON's leadership, the first when he took over the presidency after the assassination of John F. Kennedy and the second when he handed over the office to Richard Nixon. Never has there been a more graceful transfer of power in our history, Dr. Davis said.

. . . mourners, including President and Mrs. Nixon, to "arise to the tasks set before us by LYNDON B. JOHNSON."

Mr. JOHNSON was an honorable elder of National City Christian Church and a frequent worshipper at its services. "I know I shall see LYNDON JOHNSON again in heaven." said the minister.

Marvin Watson, business executive, former postmaster general and one-time White House assistant to LBJ, eulogized the memory of the 36th President of the United States:

"We shared his victories and his defeats.

"In victory he taught us to be magnanimous . . . in defeat taught us to be without hate . . . to learn . . . to rally . . . to accept the challenge and try again.

"He believed that good men together could accomplish anything, even the most impossible of dreams. No matter who his opponent, he constantly sought to find that touchstone within the soul of every man which, if discovered, would release the impulse for honest and fair solution. Hate was never in this man's heart," said Marvin Watson.

The former White House aide recalled that "I watched him formulate secure passage and sign into law the most comprehensive legislative program in education, housing and conservation and health of any president in history . . . I watched him in the situation room at the time of crisis during the six days war when only his ability, his knowledge and his sheer courage helped to keep that conflict from erupting into a wider confrontation . . ."

Watson echoed the theme sounded Wednesday by Rep. J. J. Pickle in the ceremony in the Capitol rotunda: "He was a tall man of giant character, and when he committed himself, he committed himself totally. And he asked his countrymen to do the same.

"Those of us who loved him take comfort in the knowledge that before he died, he could see the dawn of domestic tranquility and of foreign peace which he gave so much of his great heart to bring about. The structure of peace which President Nixon, with great distinction and determination, is building in the world today will rest upon a foundation laid in loneliness and stubborn courage by Lyndon Johnson," Watson said.

The gray stone church began to fill an hour before the 10 a.m. funeral service. Admission was by invitation and the crowd overflowed the pews to line the walls on three sides in metal chairs.

Bright television lights made the floral wreaths and sprays more vivid, the flag over Mr. Johnson's casket glow, the cerise and white vestments of the 50-voice church choir glisten.

Leontyne Price, world's premier coloratura soprano, arrived from Los Angeles, where she had given a concert the evening before and thrilled the crowd with her singing of "Take My Hand, Precious Lord" and "Onward Christian Soldiers." The latter selection was one requested by LBJ in a conversation months ago with Mrs. Johnson.

The choir presented "The Church's One Foundation," "A Mighty Fortress Is Our God," with the congregation joining in that hymn. The concluding anthem was "Once to Every Man and Nation."

Loudspeakers carried the words and music of the service to the several thousands of citizens standing behind security barriers in the vicinity of the church. A bright sun softened the temperature which had dropped far below freezing during the night.

The small balcony in the vaulted church bulged with reporters, cameramen and a tangle of wires, switchboards and other gear needed to serve the television network crews. It was a scene of quiet confusion upstairs.

Two Red Cross vans came to the church to serve coffee and chocolate and cookies to the relays of metropolitan policemen, reporters and armed service sentries who took up their stations at daybreak.

The Red Cross volunteers had been on duty all night attending to the needs of men, women and children who shivered in line outside the Capitol awaiting their turns to walk past the casket of the former president. Several of the children suffering from the cold were taken to nearby hospitals by Red Cross workers, they reported. Numerous adults in the night-long vigil required first aid from the bitter temperature, the Red Cross ladies said.

At the conclusion of the funeral in the church, the same servicemen who had acted as pallbearers from the time the Johnson cortege reached Washington bore the casket to a funeral coach for the motorcade to Andrews Air Force Base. As they carried the casket up the aisle, Mrs. Johnson on the arm of retired Maj. Gen. James Cross of Austin led the mourners in a slow walk behind the body of LBJ. Again Mrs. Johnson paused to shake hands with President and Mrs. Nixon and to blow a kiss to the first lady.

From Andrews AFB the Johnson funeral party flew to the LBJ Ranch for burial services in the Johnson family cemetery on the banks of the Pedernales River.

❧

[From the Dallas Morning News, Jan. 24, 1973]

Larger Than Life, L. B. J. Retained Humanity

(By Max Frankel)

New York.—He was larger than life, almost a caricature of the Texas caricature that he could never shake, but he never lost his humanity because with Lyndon Johnson, everything was really personal.

The war that overwhelmed his years in the White House was personal—a test of endurance against Ho Chi Minh, which he acknowledged having lost in the end, no matter who actually won the spoils of battle.

The Great Society was personal, because a lackluster education in his own life had saved him from shiftlessness and he deemed learning of any kind to be forever more the way to get ahead in this world.

The civil rights laws that he wanted as his monument were, in the end, highly personal, because they were drawn on the testimony of his Negro cook and her humiliations whenever she traveled without reliable food or lodging between Washington and the Texas ranch.

And even politics, the business in which he excelled and in which he took such great pride, was to him only a personal, fact-to-face thing. If he had talked George Meany into acquiescence on a point, he thought he had won over all of American labor. If he had conquered Richard Russell on a budget matter, he thought he had won over the Southland.

In this fashion, he had been able to encompass every issue and every center of power in his years as majority leader of the Senate. But from the White House, even his huge reach fell short and his incredibly hard work and keen mind felt often overwhelmed.

REPLACING THE PRINCE

Insecure, despite his size and force, LBJ felt from the moment of John Kennedy's death in Dallas that the nation would never accept his Southern speech and rural manners as a replacement for the slain prince.

So he clung to the Kennedy men and boasted of their Ph.D. degrees and he was afraid, even after his landslide election in 1964, to bring his own men to the capital.

And he could not comprehend, to the moment of death, how so many Kennedy partisans around the country could turn against him because of a war in which he felt he had taken the counsel of his predecessor's cabinet and aides.

So he took it personally. He thought he saw a plot to promote yet another Kennedy and he thought he saw his fate as being merely the caretaker between two Kennedy administrations and he hated the thought and all who made it seem so real.

VINDICATION

In his own mind, he felt certain that history would bring vindication. Historians would see, he thought:

A southerner, who brought the blacks to the ultimate legal equality—with their own seat on the Supreme Court and a court that ruled in their cause.

A conservative kept alive in politics by conservative votes for Texas interests, who made the war on poverty an elaborate concern of the federal government.

A wartime leader who was governed to the end by respect and occasionally even compassion for his "enemy," who really wanted to extend the Great Society to the Mekong River and who systematically refused to whip the nation into an anti-Communist frenzy.

A backwoods boy of modest learning, who gave what seemed to him the disrespectful establishment figures of the East the scope and mandate for great social works.

That is how he also saw himself. He confronted antagonists to the end, always hoping that reason and short ideals and long conversations—really monologues—could find a compromise for every conflict.

Although overcome by a bitter war and the hatreds that it spawned throughout the country, LYNDON JOHNSON remained a man who hated conflict and who feared confrontation for himself and his country.

He made the joint chiefs of staff testify in writing that he should really stand the siege of Khe Sanh.

He made all his diplomatic advisers commit themselves in writing to the advice that he really go to meet Soviet Premier Kosygin at Glassboro, N.J.

He weaned from his wife, Lady Bird, a written recommendation that he ride into battle against Barry Goldwater in 1964 and that he should buck the battle for reelection in 1968. He never really did want to stand alone.

"Well," he said to a newsman on the morning after his surprise announcement of intended retirement in 1968, "do you still believe in the First Amendment?" He thought free speech and free assembly had destroyed him but he went on to confess that he believed in the First Amendment.

He wanted everyone with him all the time and when they weren't, it broke his heart.

⸙

[From the San Antonio Express, Jan. 25, 1973]

L. B. J. WORKED HARD FOR PEACE

(By David Lawrence)

WASHINGTON.—It is unfortunate that LYNDON BAINES JOHNSON didn't live long enough to see the end of the Vietnam war which he had tried so hard to get.

For JOHNSON came into office as the 36th President of the United States when the military involvement of this country in Vietnam had already been instituted during the administrations of Presidents Kennedy, Eisenhower and Truman.

LYNDON JOHNSON's efforts to make peace in Vietnam were continuous, though he found it necessary to increase American forces from about 15,000 when he took office in 1963 to more than 500,000 when he left the White House in January 1969.

President JOHNSON had halted the bombing of North Vietnam in 1968, when "peace talks" were began. The country was surprised at his announcement on March 31, 1968, that he would not seek or accept renomination. His hope was that some progress might be achieved toward a peace settlement during the rest of his term, but it turned out that the North Vietnamese were not negotiating seriously.

JOHNSON got the support of Congress in 1964 when two United States destroyers were attacked by North Vietnamese torpedo boats in the Gulf of Tonkin. Immediate retaliatory action was taken, and Congress answered the President's call for war powers by passing a resolution giving him authority "to take all necessary measures to repel any armed attack against the forces of the United States and to prevent further aggression."

President JOHNSON offered as early as September 1967 to stop all bombing of North Vietnam if this would "lead promptly to productive discussion." But North Vietnam refused.

Looking back over at least ten years of war in Vietnam, it will be found that the United States was honoring its commitments made in the Southeast Asia Treaty, which was ratified by the Senate in 1955. The Vietnam issue was regarded by the chief executives in three administrations as the fulfillment of the pledge to help nations of Southeast Asia which were victims of aggression.

Nevertheless, JOHNSON was under frequent criticism from "antiwar" groups and from members of Congress who left the pressure to terminate the draft and relieve hundreds of thousands of young men from having to go into military service.

While LYNDON JOHNSON made every effort to obtain a settlement with the North Vietnamese, the Communist side in the war was adamant. Military aid to North Vietnam from Red China and the Soviet Union was substantial from the start.

If LYNDON JOHNSON could have lived to read the text of the agreement which will be signed and to learn of the plans for the return of prisoners and withdrawal of all American forces, it would have been one of the most satisfying moments of his life. When peace is achieved, the record will show that he worked hard to attain that goal.

People forget what happened only a few years ago. Many of them, especially the "antiwar" groups, seem not to remember that the Vietnam war was not started under President Nixon. Nor do they realize that he has been carrying out the obligations of the United States in the treaty of 1955 to protect sovereignty of a small nation.

The "antiwar" movement seems to be based upon objections to all war no matter what the consequences are and what the risks would be if aggressors are allowed to grab territory and deny millions of people their rights in freedom.

While there have been many eulogies for LYNDON JOHNSON, his handling of the Vietnam war, especially as he strove to stop the bloodshed, will be regarded as a demonstration not only of his dedication to peace but of his loyalty to the cause which brought the United States into the Vietnam conflict.

The huge sacrifices made will always remain an exhibition of the humanitarianism of the United States.

&

[From the San Antonio Express, Jan. 25, 1973]

L. B. J.: GLORY, TRAGEDY

(By James Reston)

WASHINGTON.—Both the glory and the tragedy of LYNDON JOHNSON was that he believed utterly in the romantic tradition of America.

He believed in the Congress and the church, in that order; in Main Street and Wall Street, in the competitive state and in the welfare state—in all of it part of the time and some of it all of the time: All the dreams and realities and myths, from Horatio Alger to Lord Keynes, no matter how contradictory.

In other words, he was a symbol of this confusing time in America—a little nearer to the old spirit of Frederick Jackson Turner's American frontier than most of his fellow countrymen, but also a little nearer to the folks who had been left behind when the frontier and battle moved to the cities.

JOHNSON was not only sure of the greatness and supremacy of his country, but of his own ability to persuade the Congress after the death of John Kennedy, that it must pass his Civil Rights Bill of 1964 and his Equal Voting Rights Act of 1965, and prove that the Congress was equal to the promises of the Constitution and the Bill of Rights. These are his monuments.

In Washington, he knew every card in the deck, but in the world, he didn't. He knew very little about Vietnam.

* * * * *

He was very close to Gen. Eisenhower. When Ike was president and JOHNSON was the Democratic majority leader of the Senate, JOHNSON never opposed him on foreign affairs. We fight at home, LYNDON said, but when we go overseas, he's my president.

And yet, one of the very odd things in this tragedy of human and political relations, is that President JOHNSON after he got into the White House, paid little or no heed to Gen. Eisenhower's judgment on Vietnam.

Eisenhower's views about Vietnam were well known in Washington at that time. JOHNSON had heard them all years before when Vice President Nixon, Secretary of State John Foster Dulles, and the chairman of the Joint Chiefs of Staff, Adm. Radford, had argued for American intervention in Vietnam during the French crisis at Dien Bien Phu.

Ike said then, what he wrote in his book later, that the political situation in Saigon was weak and confused, and that, without strong political and popular support, American intervention was unwise.

"Willingness to fight for freedom, no matter where the battle may be," Ike wrote, "has always been characteristic of our people, but the conditions then prevailing in Indochina were such as to make unilateral intervention nothing less than sheer folly."

JOHNSON wasn't thinking about President Eisenhower, much as he admired him, when President Kennedy was assassinated. If the evidence of his own book is accurate, he wasn't even thinking about himself.

Certainly he was not concentrating on changing the whole policy. He was focusing on the death of Kennedy, on carrying on Kennedy's policies, on political loyalty, as he saw it, so he plunged deeper into the war, and it destroyed him in the end.

The journalists tried to deal with all this at the time, and even at JOHNSON's death, but it is beyond us. Like Kennedy and Nixon, he is a subject for a great psychological American novel.

But JOHNSON was different. He left a broken record, triumphant at home and tragic in Vietnam, and like most presidents, his policies will be judged by the historians.

The difference is that LYNDON JOHNSON was a great talker, one of the last of the old southern and frontier storytellers of the age.

He didn't leave the real story in his documents in his library at the University of Texas, but in the memories of his friends, companions and political adversaries in Washington.

He loved the camera. No president collected more photographs of himself and his visitors than JOHNSON, but the tape recorder was really the instrument he should have used.

For he gave himself to his visitors, and historians will never be able to sort out the glory and tragedy, unless they somehow manage to collect the stories, listen to the tape recorders and forget the television, which was his downfall, and somehow hear him talk endlessly about his problems, his cunning contrivances, his feeling for the Congress, his love of his country, and particularly his affection for his lovely and remarkable wife, and his hardscrabble land in Texas.

&

[From the Dallas Morning News, Feb. 1, 1973]

L. B. J. RECALLED AS VISIONARY

(By Carl Rowan)

WASHINGTON.—How shall I remember LBJ?

I think of a man I had scarcely met, poking his index finger against my chest one sultry day in Saigon in 1961 and saying: "Mr. Roe-ann, you don't know me. But one of these days you're gonna discover that I'm a goddamn sight more liberal than most of these so-called liberals you've been cottoning up to."

And I shall remember that when the public mood turned mean and ugly in America and lesser liberals ran with the mob, LYNDON JOHNSON remained true to his decent convictions.

I shall remember LBJ as a man driven to success, a man who didn't know how to take it easy, whether ordered to by his doctor or begged to by the Secret Service.

There was that incredibly hot day in some unbelievably dusty villages on the outskirts of Agra, India, when he kept whispering to me: "Stay close to me—right by my shoulder." He was nurturing the illusion that I was some kind of expert on India just because I had written a book about it!

PUMP TALK

I gasped as I tried to stay near him as he plowed through the grasping crowds. As I wiped my sweaty forehead with the front of my hand and my parched lips with the back of it, I asked myself: "Is this a man who has suffered a massive heart attack?"

When the pace slowed to a hotel room and a cool scotch, all JOHNSON wanted to talk about was the cheap water pumps (he thought they were Fairbanks-Morse) that he used to know as a boy in Texas. He wondered why the hell the U.S. couldn't get some of them into India so the people in these villages could have water.

I remember his telephone call on March 15, 1965, asking if I would sit with his wife and daughters while he delivered his address on the Voting Rights Act to a joint session of Congress. That was the speech—the last touches written by him on the way to the Capitol as he cursed the slowness of his speechwriters—in which he startled millions of Americans by using the emotional slogan, "We shall overcome."

And after that speech I remember sitting with him in his living quarters as the White House operator fanned out long distance calls all over the land.

"How did I do?" JOHNSON kept asking. He was a man who meant it when he talked about bringing Americans together, healing the nation's wounds, making this a land of equal opportunity. He wanted so badly to be reassured that what he had done that night was courageous, and good for all America.

Yet, I remember LYNDON B. JOHNSON as one of the most complicated men I ever met. He could seem petty, even mean, about trifling things and then display the broadest vision about the human needs of men and nations.

JOHNSON was at heart a sentimentalist—the kind of man who would weep in San Antonio during the 1964 campaign when an aged black man stood in the back of a pickup truck at a shopping center and said: "I'm a black man, born two blocks from this spot. I never dreamed I'd live to see the day when a Mexican congressman (Henry B. Gonzalez) would introduce me so I could ask you to vote for a white Texan for President."

And JOHNSON would dismiss his tears with the comment that "a man ain't worth a goddam if he can't cry at the right time."

I always felt that a lot of JOHNSON's toughness, even ruthlessness, was part of his effort to hide his sentimentality.

I felt that he waded deeper into Vietnam, and for a longer time than his instincts and intellect dictated, because he never wanted the Joint Chiefs of Staff to think they had a sentimental sissy in the White House. He seemed to want to say to Gen. Curtis LeMay: "I don't puff a 1-foot cigar, but I'm as tough as you are."

IRONY, TRAGEDY

There is special irony and tragedy in the coincidence that the war that killed JOHNSON politically should be grinding to a close just as the fates snuffed out his life completely.

There is double irony in the fact that he died on the eve of a White House campaign to erase much of the "Great Society" whose foundation JOHNSON built.

We have had our truce in the war on poverty; we have our moratoriums on federal subsidies for housing for the poor and middle classes; we have had vetoes of education bills and public works projects. We are told not to ask what government can do for us, but what we can do for ourselves.

There will be more of this. But not in four years nor 40 will they erase all that LYNDON JOHNSON did to change this society—not any more than they have been able to erase the mark of Franklin D. Roosevelt.

Maybe it's a little girl sleeping in a nightgown that won't go up in flames at the slightest spark—because JOHNSON believed in consumer protection; maybe it's a "hillbilly" girl who in June will become the first of her family ever to graduate from college—because JOHNSON insisted that higher education be put within reach of all; maybe it's a black family, walking into a motel in Mississippi tonight where in years past they would have been chased away—because JOHNSON wanted a public accomodations act sincerely enough to browbeat Congress into passing it.

When the Vietnam war and the passions around it become but memories, millions of Americans will look anew at what has been happening inside America this past decade. And they will adjudge LYNDON JOHNSON a great president.

✦

[From the Congressional Record, Jan. 6, 1973]

A HISTORIC MOMENT IN AUSTIN

(Speech by Hon. J. J. Pickle of Texas in the House of Representatives, January 6, 1973)

Mr. Pickle. Mr. Speaker, on December 11 and 12 of last year, a truly remarkable and prestigious gathering was held at the LYNDON BAINES JOHNSON Library in Austin, Tex.

These were the days of the Civil Rights Symposium, marking the opening of the papers dealing with civil rights of President LYNDON JOHNSON's administration.

I was fortunate enough to attend the symposium. The meeting was a meeting of leaders—strong leaders of a good cause.

During the 2 days, one figure dominated the mood, dominated the resurgence of commitment to create a society of equal opportunity.

This man was President LYNDON JOHNSON.

It is appropriate that the last issue of Life of December 29, 1972, carried the best account of those 2 days in Texas.

In his last column on the Presidency for Life, Hugh Sidey caught superbly the moment—its dignity and vitality.

✦

ONE MORE CALL TO REASON TOGETHER

(By Hugh Sidey)

LYNDON JOHNSON savors each day for its meaning and joy, his battered heart frequently sending out signals of pain to let him know that it can't keep up. In the past year he has finally adjusted to this twilight world, melting off about 20 pounds, carrying a pouch full of nitroglycerin tablets and holding that restless soul of his in check. Well, almost in check.

Several months ago, when JOHNSON and his staff began planning symposiums for the Lyndon Baines Johnson Library at the University of Texas, it was JOHNSON himself who insisted on a session dealing with civil rights.

So a fortnight ago they came by jet and auto and bus through an ice storm to be in Austin with "the President" again, one of the few times in the last four years that the men and women who carried the civil rights banner for two decades had assembled. There were some new faces among them, but the focus was on men like Hubert Humphrey, Roy Wilkins, Clarence Mitchell and former Chief Justice Earl Warren. They showed up with more wrinkles than they used to have, more gray hair and a lot more discouragement. From the beginning of the two-day meeting it was plain that civil rights no longer had a clear national leader. Nor could anyone perceive any sympathy for the cause in the White House.

L.B.J. put on his tan rancher's twill and his cowboy boots and came in from the country, sitting silently through the first day's meetings, the fatigue growing on him. That night he went to the reception for the 1,000 guests. The strain took its toll. For JOHNSON the rest of the night was filled with pain and restlessness. His doctors suggested, pleaded, ordered him to give up his scheduled address the next day. He ignored them. He put on his dark-blue presidential suit and those flawless polished oxfords and came back the next morning.

He didn't take a seat in the auditorium but, with a worried Lady Bird at his side, watched the first two hours' proceedings on closed-circuit TV in the anteroom. Near noon he walked slowly to the podium. In a low but steady voice he talked eloquently for 20 minutes. "Until we overcome unequal history, we cannot overcome unequal opportunity," he said. "But to be black in a white society is not to stand on equal and level ground. While the races may stand side by side, whites stand on history's mountain and blacks stand in history's hollow. . . . So I think it's time to leave aside the legalisms and euphemisms and eloquent evasions. It's time we get down to the business of trying to stand black and white on level ground." Even in that short plea there was pain, and JOHNSON reached for one of his pills, munching in front of everybody. It was something he rarely does.

When he was done he acknowledged the applause and stepped off the stage to take a seat in the auditorium. Then squabbling broke out among the black factions, and one of the participants read an indictment of Richard Nixon and his administration.

LYNDON JOHNSON sat for a few minutes in the midst of it. Then, just as if he were back in Washington, he moved. The fatigue of the night before seemed to drop away, the old adrenalin machine pumping back into action. Going to the microphone, with his hands molding the air, he delivered one of his sermons on brotherhood and reason, flavoring it with one of those marvelous stories about a backwoods judge and the town drunk, reminiscenses of when he arrived in Hoover's Washington and the bonus marchers were driven down Pennsylvania Avenue.

"Now, what I want you to do is go back, all of you counsel together," he said, "that soft, kind way, just cool and push off wrath, indulge, tolerate, and finally come out with a program with objectives. . . . There's everything right about a group saying, 'Mr. President, we would like for you to set aside an hour to let us talk,' and you don't need to start off by saying he's terrible, because he doesn't think he's terrible. . . . While I can't provide much go-go at this period of my life, I can provide a lot of hope and dream and encouragement, and I'll sell a few wormy calves now and then and contribute."

When all that human juice clattered out over the wire, the memories begin to rise, of the lean, youngish LYNDON JOHNSON in 1957 leading the United States Senate to pass the first Civil Rights Act in 82 years. It was near midnight, and the tension was so thick you could slice it, but the majority leader just stood there on the floor, calmly counting his votes.

Then there were those later nights, when L.B.J. was President. He would talk about how he ceased to be just a man from the South and had become a leader for all of America. The old tales would roll out—about what

it was to be a black and never sure as you traveled if you would find a decent place to eat or go to the bathroom; or how he knew what it was like to be a Mexican-American child in the Depression, rummaging in the garbage cans for food.

Another night: it was in New Orleans during the 1964 campaign when JOHNSON stood on a street corner in the harsh neon glare, white Louisiana state officials clustered around him, and shouted out his message of hope and equality to the blacks who stood below him. And then in his 1965 civil rights address to Congress, in the place he loved most, among the men he liked best, he sounded the most poignant refrain of the time: "We shall overcome."

No wonder his heart is scarred today. It has been a long and anguished journey, with a long way left to go.

In the auditorium in Austin, the ovation that followed JOHNSON's appeal washed away the controversy, for a moment. People came to the stage and crowded around him as he tried to leave. They were all reaching for a bit of the old magic. But nobody got so much of it as Mr. Youngblood, a thin, aging black who used to wait on tables in Austin's ancient Driskill Hotel, where JOHNSON sweated out election night returns. The former President and the former waiter stood there for a few seconds gripping hands, and if any questions lingered about what LYNDON JOHNSON had tried to do for his country, they were answered right then.

Hon. Yvonne Braithwaite Burke
OF CALIFORNIA

Mr. Speaker, Roger Wilkins, editorial writer for the Washington Post has written an exceptionally sensitive and perpective tribute to LYNDON B. JOHNSON.

Mr. Wilkins, one of the fine young black writers of today, was very close to the former President in his capacity as Director of Community Relations, Department of Justice.

He has put into writing some of my feelings as well as the feelings of many of my colleagues and constituents concerning the former President's lasting contributions toward the advancement of equal opportunity for all Americans.

The article follows:

BLACK PERSPECTIVE ON L. B. J.: THE HOPE, THE HEART, THE LIFT

(By Roger Wilkins)

Black people spend their lives measuring white men. It's a matter of survival. Bosses, friends, teammates, enemies, cops and cab drivers all get the calibrated treatment. Men you don't know can hurt you badly, so you measure them. But, how do you measure a restless mountain?

You can't, but out of a lifetime of habit and necessity, you try. The first sightings were full of prejudice. He was from Texas and he talked that way. He wheeled and dealed and, even though two civil rights bills—in 1957 and 1959—passed the Senate while he was majority leader, it seemed from afar that he was always trying to trim them down, not to get them through. Just that and no more was enough to elicit total agreement with Joe Rauh, who, upon hearing on the convention floor in Los Angeles that John Kennedy had picked LYNDON B. JOHNSON as his running mate, shouted, "Say it ain't so, Jack."

Then there were the years of idleness and the nasty "Whatever happened to . . . ," jokes around Washington. But it filtered back from Gettysburg, in the summer of 1963, that LYNDON JOHNSON had made a hell-for-leather civil rights speech—shouting hoarse, waving his arms, the whole bit. Prejudice still didn't allow us to enlarge the frame. And then Dallas and the extinction of Camelot and this tall Southern stranger was in the chair. God help us.

In the oval office, the mountain began to move. Driven by his own furies and wrestling with the fates, he was a wonderous sight to see. He began to talk about his hopes for America as he pushed his bills through the Congress. When he talked about poverty and civil rights in 1964, the measuring process was still going on and one heard his words, first with disbelief and then with the suspicion that maybe you'd been wrong. Then, suddenly you had his measure. Despite instinctive distrust, despite Camelot lost and despite regional prejudice, this was a man who really wanted to change things. His briefing papers on civil rights and poverty came straight from his past and from his heart.

This as a man who could sound entirely believable when he told you that he intended to finish what Lincoln had begun. So he pulled the throttle out some and got us the Civil Rights Act of 1964 and the Economic Opportunity Act. The next year, after the brutality at the Edmund Pettis bridge at Selma he pulled the throttle full out. He went to the well of the House, asserted that he was committed to gaining full freedoms for minorities, proposed the Voting Rights Act of 1965 and shouted at the Congress and the nation. "We shall overcome." And he got that voting rights legislation and kept on coming. He took Thurgood Marshall off the 2nd Circuit Court of Appeals, made him Solicitor General and then put him on the Supreme Court. He took a black Assistant Secretary of Commerce named Andrew Brimmer and made him a governor of the Federal Reserve system and he put Robert C. Weaver in his cabinet.

And still he kept on coming. He went up to Howard University and began the most incisive and sympathetic analysis of the situation of black people in this country that any President has ever made: "In far too many ways American Negroes have been another nation: deprived of freedom, crippled by hatred, the doors of opportunity closed to hope." And he would end his analysis with a poetic promise, "The Scripture promises: 'I shall light a candle of understanding in thine heart, which shall not be put out.'

"Together, and with millions more, we can light that candle of understanding in the heart of all America. "And, once lit, it will never again go out."

And for a while, it looked like maybe he could go a long way toward keeping his promise. There were some problems. The Mississippi Freedom Democratic Party's attempt to inject some fairness and elemental justice into the 1964 Democratic Convention fell short of the mark, summer rebellions were beginning in the cities and Vietnam somehow wouldn't go away. But, compared to the momentum of the movement with its

powerful and driving ally in the White House, these were just specks on the horizon. He could still gather the greatest power and brains in the civil rights movement in the East Room of the White House and implore them—shouting, arms flailing and the force seeming to come straight from the Texas earth—to plan "night and day" how they together could "fulfill these rights." He would be Lincoln.

But it was not to be. Vietnam got larger, cities burned intensely, blacks became angrier and the young were sometimes rude. He could still, in the bleak death-filled summer of 1967 make clear to his people in purple language that he didn't want his troops killing black people in the streets of Detroit—and they didn't. But it had all begun to close in on him: Robert Kennedy, Eugene McCarthy, Rennie Davis, Rap Brown, Stokeley Carmichael and that wispy little fellow puffing away on his Salems in Hanoi just wouldn't go away. The last months were not good ones. The tiger was flailing about for a peace that would not come and blacks found that their ally had turned his back and was distracted by a war 12,000 miles away.

Still, after his presidency, blacks knew who he had been. An angry young soldier in Vietnam would say for Wallace Terry's record, "Guess Who's Coming Home": "JOHNSON was OK. He always came on with a heavy heart." And, he always did. Right up to the end. In the summer of 1972, he could bear hug a black former aide—estranged since a disagreement over the Kerner Report issued in the bad days of 1968—and promise that he still had a shot or two to deliver on civil rights. And in December, 1972, he would tell a black economist that they had to get together to figure out how to get the banks to put some money into poor peoples' pockets.

In the same month, he could propel a failing body up onto a stage and tell his audience and the nation, "To believe that the essence of government lies with unceasing concern for the welfare, dignity, decency and innate integrity of life for every individual, regardless of color, creed, ancestry, sex or age." And, he would conclude by saying, "Yes, there is injustice. Yes, there is intolerance. Yes, there is discrimination and hate and suspicion and division among us.

"But there is a large truth. We have proved that great progress is possible. We know how much still remains to be done. and if our efforts continue, if our will is strong, if our hearts are right and if courage remains our constant companion, then, my fellow Americans, I am confident that we shall overcome." The hope, the heart and the lift were still there, but the body was almost gone—and soon, so was he.

On LBJs last day in Washington, Mrs. Whitney Young sat near the rear of the church as did Mrs. Martin Luther King Jr. Near the front Thurgood Marshall and Roy Wilkins sat together—heads in muffled conversation. Leontyne Price stood and sang. "Precious Lord, Take My Hand." It was a time to know how far we had come and how much it had cost. And, it was time to cry for a beloved mountain.

Hon. Edward R. Roybal
OF CALIFORNIA

Mr. Speaker, it is indeed sad that even as our flags fiy at half-mast in memory of former President Truman our last surviving Chief Executive, LYNDON BAINES JOHNSON, has been taken from us also. We, as a nation, were totally unprepared for the suddenness with which death came to this outstanding American, and our grief is heartfelt and deep.

A powerful legislator from the very beginning, LYNDON JOHNSON was a commanding figure in both the Congress and the White House. He did a tremendous job in the Senate and his record as President of the United States was no less glowing.

Although he himself attained the ultimate in American political ambition, he never forgot those with whom he shared the common denominator of a "humble background." He had a special empathy with the poverty-stricken and the disadvantaged, and he worked constantly to give substance to his concern for these people, their future and their share in the American dream. Insofar as proposing and enacting legislation in the field of domestic reform, he surely numbers among our greatest Presidents.

At the time he took office he made the remark that:

> Government has an obligation to match the promise of American opportunity with action.

These were no idle words on the part of the President—the Johnson administration was truly an administration of action. Through his able leadership, ideas and social programs that had previously languished in Congress were changed into legislative realities in just 5 short years. His record of accomplishments is massive in number and impressive in scope and covers the entire spectrum of life in our society. His was an era of great domestic achievement—an era in which the American dream seemed near to fruition.

LYNDON JOHNSON, perhaps more than any other President, has made an indelible mark on this country's social progress. The legislation that he authored will stand as a reminder of the immense good that can be done.

Hon. John C. Kluczynski
OF ILLINOIS

Mr. Speaker, there are some men in history for whom no conventional eulogy is wholly adequate. LYNDON BAINES JOHNSON was one of these, a man larger than life and possessed of those qualities of courage and loyalty which are fundamental to the survival of this great Nation which

he loved. LYNDON JOHNSON was a profoundly political being: He enjoyed the drama of politics, and he participated wholeheartedly in the political process. At the same time, he was never a merely partisan leader. Rather, his ultimate concern—as he was to prove to friend and to foe alike—was the well-being of America and the cause of a just and lasting peace.

Wrote Owen Meredith:

> That Man is great and he alone, Who serves a greatness not his own.

So it was with President JOHNSON, whose true and enduring greatness lay in his dedicated service to the best interests of the American people.

Called unexpectedly to the highest office in the land by the tragic death of President Kennedy, he brought to the deliberative councils of the Executive all the rich resources of his many years of congressional experience, years in which he provided a leadership respected and effective.

As President, he was able to heal the distress and anxiety which the events of November 1963, aroused among our people and in the world community. Moreover, in that spirit of confidence and determination, he turned boldly to further legislation in such areas as civil rights and poverty, championing as he had done in his first days in Congress the cause of equal rights and economic justice for all Americans of every race, creed, and color.

His vision was that of Franklin Roosevelt, and he labored without stint to achieve the American dream. The heartbreaking frustration which dogged his search for peace in Southeast Asia generated bitter controversy, which he felt deeply. Perhaps the saddest aspect of his long and remarkably distinguished career was the way in which his quest for a settlement in Vietnam eluded his best efforts.

Nevertheless, the spirit with which he sacrificed his own personal concerns, directing the attention of all to the continuing search for an effective, honorable peace, contributed immeasurably to the ultimate achieving of that goal.

Centuries ago, Seneca counseled:

> Admire those, if thou art a man, who attempt great things, even though they fail.

LYNDON JOHNSON attempted great things, and in many areas met with extraordinary success. He leaves a legacy of brilliant service and great accomplishment. Already, the bitter debates which clouded his last days in the White House have begun to fade, and we are able to see him in a clearer light and in the perspective of his whole career and of his times.

Shrewd, vivid, colorful, toughminded, and tenderhearted, President Johnson now takes his place in the annals of America. We may be confident that the sober judgment of history will vindicate his life. May the great compassion which animated his idealism continue to motivate all Americans as together we seek a nobler commonweal.

Hon. James C. Corman
OF CALIFORNIA

Mr. Speaker, while we mourn with deep sorrow the death of Lyndon Baines Johnson, today in this House and in the Congress he loved so much, we properly commemorate his life and his brilliant leadership as our President.

His Great Society—a dream born many years ago in the heart of this uncommon man because of his concerns for a better world for the poor, the sick, the aged, and especially for black Americans, those hapless victims of racial injustic—bore the fruits of medicare for the aged, the war on poverty, the Elementary and Secondary Education Act, creation of Equal Opportunity Commission. There were many more achievements that uplifted those of our citizens who had been denied so long what most of us have always taken for granted. But to me, his most important legacy to this Nation was his ability to translate racial equality into the laws of our land.

Today, because of Lyndon Johnson, a black person walks with dignity into any public facility in the country. In that part of America where he was formerly denied the right of franchise, a black person goes confidently into a voting booth to cast his ballot for a candidate of his choice. He now sits in the orchestra, if he so wishes, of a theater, a movie house, a concert hall, where formerly he had been ushered to the balcony, reserved for blacks only. A black student may apply to the college of his choice and is considered for admission only on the basis of his qualifications. The right to job opportunities and job protection are no longer denied to a black American. A street in any suburb in the country will today find black families living in decent homes next to their white neighbors—restrictive covenants are gone. And, best of all, black children and white children are being educated together so that they can know one another as Americans, and together

learn the wonders of their own country and of the world.

On a memorable evening of March 15, 1965, President Johnson came to this floor to deliver in joint session a special message to the Congress— "The American Promise," he called it, and his opening words were—

I speak tonight for the dignity of man and the destiny of democracy.

He came to say that he would send to the Congress for consideration a law which was designed to eliminate illegal barriers to the right to vote— that most precious right every American has, except those Americans to whom it had been refused for over 100 years because of the color of their skin.

In perhaps one of the greatest speeches ever given in this House, President Johnson spoke of the striving of American Negroes to secure for themselves the full blessings of this land. He said:

Their cause must be our cause too. Because it is not just Negroes, but really it is all of us who must overcome the crippling legacy of bigotry and injustice. And we shall overcome.

The great, rich, restless country can offer opportunity and education and hope to all: black and white, North and South, sharecropper and city dweller. These are the enemies: poverty, ignorance, disease. They are the enemies and not our fellow men, not our neighbor. And these enemies too, poverty, disease and ignorance, we shall overcome.

In many, many ways, his American promise has been kept. Much we have overcome. The legal barriers tumbled down with the enactment of the Civil Rights Act of 1964, the Voting Rights Act of 1965, and the open housing legislation of 1968. But, there remains a long road ahead to reach what Lyndon Johnson perceived to be his most urgent imperative. "I want to be the President," he said that night in 1965, "who helped to end hatred among his fellow men."

What greater tribute can we pay to Lyndon Johnson—What greater offer can we make to his memory—what greater good can we do for America—than to pledge ourselves that this, too, "we shall overcome"?

Hon. Dawson Mathis
OF GEORGIA

Mr. Speaker, the beginning of my service in the House of Representatives did not come until 2 years after the Johnson administration had ended and Mr. Johnson had returned to Texas.

Therefore, I am unable to say that I had the opportunity to work with LYNDON JOHNSON on matters of legislative importance to our country; but as a newsman prior to my election I did have the opportunity to follow his service and decisions as President.

It might be appropriate to mention that on the date of Mr. JOHNSON's death, I learned of his passing from newsmen who wanted a statement of my reaction. My statement as reported by the Atlanta Constitution is as follows:

> President JOHNSON was a man of great intelligence and determination. From my knowledge of him, he was one of the greatest students of American government, and used his knowledge of government and his talent of persuasion to become one of the greatest movers of ideas in this Nation's history. While I personally disagreed with many of the positions he advocated, I had the highest respect for his ability. He was a giant of mid-twentieth century politics and he will be missed.

Mr. Speaker, I wish to also say that I had the highest regard, too, for Mr. JOHNSON's No. 1 supporter, Lady Bird Johnson, as she ably carried on her responsibility as First Lady, and seeing her standing strongly during the days of final tribute to our fallen leader was just as we had come to expect.

LYNDON JOHNSON made his mark as a statesman, husband, father, and as a great American. He stood tall and did what was expected of him.

I consider it a privilege to join my colleagues in the House of Representatives paying tribute to our former President, LYNDON B. JOHNSON.

Hon. Parren J. Mitchell
OF MARYLAND

Mr. Speaker, it is with great sadness in my heart that I rise to address my colleagues on this solemn occasion. For our Nation has lost a great leader, a man of wisdom and courage, a man of uncommon breadth of vision. He was a man both complex and simple, both proud and modest, who in his brief lifetime both came a long way and accomplished a great deal. He touched a great many people. He was former President LYNDON BAINES JOHNSON.

It is ironic that I, a black Congressman, should rise here today to speak in praise of our Nation's first southern President in 100 years. But in light of the past decade, the tumultuous 1960's, it is not at all surprising. For there are none in this Chamber so young that they do not recall the dark days before the civil rights movement. Those were the days when everywhere could be found signs designating different public facilities for black and white. Those were the days when peaceful demonstrations in the South were met with legalized savagery, including police dogs, fire hoses, and electric cattle prods. Those were the days when any worker in the civil rights movement courted violent death, and the names Evers and Goodman and Chaney and Liuzzo, and Schwerner were etched into the national consciousness. Those were the days when millions of taxpaying Americans, because they were black, were excluded from the right to vote by poll taxes and unfairly applied literacy tests. The most basic right of a democracy was denied by an act of the most blatant racism.

And not only were the black and other minorities ignored and repressed, but the poor were invisible as well. Millions of Americans of all colors went to bed hungry every night and nobody knew let alone cared. In the ghettos, and in the mountains of Appalachia and on the reservations, millions of American youth found life a deadend street without hope. For them, inadequate education lead to sterile jobs or quite often no jobs at all. For them life itself became a boring routine of failure.

LYNDON BAINES JOHNSON did not change all this. That would have been impossible for he had neither the power nor the time. What he did do was to bring to bear the great prestige of the office of the Presidency, to commit the honor of the Nation, to the huge task of eradicating poverty and racism. He adopted the rhetoric of the civil rights movement and promised millions of hopeless people that "we shall overcome." He appointed the first black to the Cabinet and the first black to the Supreme Court. And he brought forth from the Congress three landmark pieces of civil rights legislation.

With the Public Accommodations Act, he took down the separate signs for the races all across the Nation, and opened up public facilities for all. With his open housing bill he outlawed illegal restrictive covenants against minorities. But his most important congressional accomplishment was the Voting Rights Act. With the help of Federal registrars, millions of disenfranchised southern blacks were able for the first time to register and vote. "If everyone has an equal chance at the ballot box," he said, "the rest will take care of itself."

LYNDON B. JOHNSON was not a perfect man, and I will not rehash here the controversy of his last years. I disagreed with him over the tragic conflict in Indochina. But LBJ, despite all this, was a great man and a great President. He cared for all the people.

He will be sorely missed.

Hon. James M. Hanley
OF NEW YORK

Mr. Speaker, almost 2 weeks ago, I stood at the graveside of a great and noble man. As the final taps were rendered and the final salute fired, I felt a tremendous sense of loss. LYNDON BAINES JOHNSON was a great man and a great President. He had a compassion and a drive that knew no limits. He had an understanding of the people as few men ever had.

LYNDON JOHNSON was a big man in physical stature; but he was bigger still in ambitions and his hopes and dreams for America. At times it almost seemed as though he was dragging us to the stars and moon in search of social perfection and social equality. Yet his idealism was tinted with the realism of a man who had grown up in the rough and tumble of American politics. It was here that he achieved his greatest goals. No President in the history of our Nation shaped, directed, and saw to fruition more good social legislation than this man.

LYNDON JOHNSON was accused of having a heavy hand but I can recall many hours at the White House during my first years as a Member of Congress talking and suggesting legislative programs while he listened patiently and earnestly. He was often attacked as one desirous of power but he did more for the powerless, the wretched, and the disinfranchised of this Nation than any predecessor. He was accused of vanity, yet never once did he forget the humble trappings of his youth. The mark of LYNDON JOHNSON is stamped indelibly into the fabric of our Nation.

I will miss him, his family, friends and colleagues will miss him. More importantly, however, the little people of this Nation whom he loved so much will miss him. God rest him, and console his lovely Lady Bird and the family.

Hon. Joe Skubitz
OF KANSAS

Mr. Speaker, there are so many still in Congress who knew the late President LYNDON B. JOHNSON "back when" that in adding my own humble tribute, I hesitate to interject a personal note.

I had been a staff member in the other body when the young Senator JOHNSON burst upon the Senate. I use the term advisedly, for unlike any of his entering colleagues, Senator JOHNSON was a fresh breeze, a Senator who one of his colleagues described—he has got more ideas than a hound dog has fleas.

With it all, he remained within the proprieties; he did not offend his elders by showing off on the floor; he conducted himself in such a way that he was welcomed in the inner club, the members of which formulated the decisions and carried them into execution. In the shortest of possible times, he was a member of his party's policy committee, carrying out assigned functions patiently but with a determination that marked him as a comer, a man to be reckoned with in the affairs of this Nation.

It is significant to add that this view was shared by members of the opposite party, of which I am a member. Republican Senators whom I served and others whom I knew intimately were of the same opinion. Older Senators, conservatives who had their qualms about some of the New Deal programs, were taken by the young Texan's knowledge, ready wit, and polite deference.

When he was named majority leader, one of the youngest in service as a Senator to achieve such an honor, his colleagues respected him for one great quality—his willingness to work at being a Senator. When he was learning the ropes in the policy committee, he was in his own office early and on the floor promptly at noon. He spent long hours legislating, studying the bills and familiarizing himself with parliamentary procedure. He continued that practice as leader. He frequently knew more about any bill than did the sponsor and he knew more about why a particular Senator should be for or against it than did the Senator himself.

I have spent nearly 30 years on this Capitol Hill, pleasant, rewarding and hard-working years. I have seen hundreds of Members of this and the other body come and go. I have thrilled to the oratory of a Borah, a Hiram Johnson, and a Tom Connally, to the sagacity of a Burton K. Wheeler, to the unflagging effort of a young Bob LaFollette, to the consumate ability of a Richard Russell, to the political astuteness of an Arthur Vandenburg and to the integrity of a Robert Taft. None had the ability to command, to persuade, to cajole and influence his fellows that LYNDON

BAINES JOHNSON had; none had the single-minded determination to tackle a project and see it through to victory that the man from Texas exhibited on countless occasions.

My own words of praise are circumscribed, Mr. Speaker, by my inability to command the English language to my purpose. I should like, therefore, to call to my aid an editorial from the January 23 issue of the New York Times which, in my judgment, is perhaps as warm and yet definite a tribute to the late President. I include it to be printed at this place in the Congressional Record:

[From the New York Times, Jan. 23, 1973]

L. B. J.

The shocking news of the death of LYNDON B. JOHNSON will sadden every American, regardless of party, who reveres the Presidential office. Coming so soon and so suddenly after the loss of Harry S. Truman, the only other living ex-President, Mr. JOHNSON's death leaves a sorrowful void in the American scene.

A giant in physical stature, overpowering in his personal approach, an intense and driving extrovert who nonetheless was in some ways a peculiarly private person, LYNDON BAINES JOHNSON was the most paradoxical of all American Presidents.

Convinced for many frustrating years that no man from the South could be nominated, much less elected, in his lifetime, LYNDON JOHNSON nonetheless won the largest percentage of the popular vote ever accorded a Presidential candidate in modern history.

A man who, once in office, aspired only to educate the nation's young, feed its hungry, lift up its poor, promote equality and "end war among the brothers of this earth" finished his political career five years later, discouraged, trapped and bogged down in one of the most unpopular wars in the country's entire history. Many who had been his political friends and supporters forgot his magnificent contributions to the national good and held him almost solely culpable for the war he did not start but might have stopped.

A tempestuous and mercurial man, Mr. JOHNSON provided his critics with fuel to spare. They said he was flamboyant, that he lacked "style," particularly in contrast to his graceful predecessor. They said he was a manipulator, as indeed he was, "wheeler and dealer," which in a sense a President must be if he is to get action on his program. They said his talk was often crude, a charge sometimes made against Lincoln; that he was vain and, worst of all in some circles, "corny." There is enough on the record to substantiate such criticisms. But there is more than enough on the record to dwarf them in the final summing up.

Wrung out as the country was in the days following the assassination of President Kennedy, few Americans could have been unmoved by the emphasis in the new President's first speech to Congress: "We have talked long enough in this country about equal rights. We have talked for 100 years or more. It is time now to write it in the books of law."

He persuaded Congress to do just that, with the most substantial civil rights bill in a century. And to provide medical care for the aged, to give massive Federal financial aid to the elementary and secondary schools of the nation, to raise the minimum wage, launch a major housing program and make a start on what has now become a crusade to clean up the country's air and water. This and more—extraordinary legislative record as it was—was to be only the beginning of the JOHNSON advance toward the "Great Society," following in the tradition of F.D.R.'s New Deal.

Tragically, LYNDON JOHNSON had given little attention as Senate Majority Leader to the intricacies of foreign policy. He came to the Presidency imbued with the simplicities of the postwar years—specifically that there was a monolithic world power called Communism which had to be kept from spreading wherever it could be stayed without bringing on a major war.

A few months of limited military action in Vietnam seemed to him, as it had seemed to President Kennedy, one of the more obvious cases in point. And the quagmire that was to destroy thousands of American troops ultimately destroyed the political life of LYNDON JOHNSON as well.

Wanting almost pathetically to be loved, as his hero Franklin D. Roosevelt had been loved in his time, President JOHNSON felt instead the sting of vilification. Tough and sinewy, he was yet sentimental and felt all the more what he conceived to be not principled differences, but betrayal by his friends.

Yet, sensitive though he was, he stood stubbornly by the course he thought was right—until the political instinct that was the breath of his life persuaded him that the majority he had enjoyed in 1964 had possibly evaporated. Then this man who had lived for power and enjoyed its exercise yielded it up with hardly more than a murmur. And even his severest critics conceded that nothing so became him in office as the leaving of it.

In this age of instant history, with the bitterness of the Vietnam war still unabated, the life of LYNDON B. JOHNSON will no doubt be recorded with more passion than perspective. Future historians should find that life as rich in achievement as in colorful contradiction.

Hon. Chet Holifield
OF CALIFORNIA

Mr. Speaker, the strength and power of America lies in the hands of the common man. It is from his ranks that its greatest leaders emerge. It is the workingman who holds the latent power in America—a power that is most effectively translated by those leaders who are drawn from the masses.

Such a leader was President LYNDON BAINES JOHNSON. LYNDON JOHNSON was not only a great man, he was an honest man, with an intense love of all human beings; the poor, the sick, the handicapped, the underprivileged, and those against whom discrimination was directed.

He once recalled:

I have followed the personal philosophy that I am a free man, an American and a public servant, and a member of my party in that order, always and only.

Until justice is blind to color, until education is unaware of race, and until opportunity is unconcerned with the color of men's skins . . . emancipation will be a proclamation . . . which falls short of assuring freedom to the free.

When he saw suffering, President JOHNSON looked to the government for the cure and in most cases he provided, if not a cure, an improvement and a bridge to hope for those previously without hope.

LYNDON JOHNSON will be remembered for many things during his long political career. For those of us who knew him personally, his physical presence was overwhelming, his dynamic energy brought forth the Great Society, the national war on poverty, and the greatest efforts toward equal rights and equal opportunities in history.

These Halls have seen few men as powerful and effective as LYNDON JOHNSON. He was first and foremost, a parliamentary expert. No arm of government was a stranger to him. He held every high elective office at the Federal level; Congressman, Senator, Vice President, and President. Where weaker men may have hesitated President JOHNSON acted, letting praise and criticism come his way. He knew that, above all things, the President must endure the loneliness of having the very last word.

LYNDON BAINES JOHNSON will be remembered by historians as a man who declared total war on poverty, deprivation, disease, and ignorance with every fiber of his being, while suffering criticism because he stuck to the course he believed right. As President JOHNSON himself once remarked:

Our democracy cannot remain static, a prisoner to the past . . . Government itself has the continuing obligation—second to no other—to keep the machinery of public participation functioning smoothly and to improve it where necessary so that democracy remains a vital and vibrant institution.

LYNDON JOHNSON will be sorely missed by his friends and colleagues, but long remembered by every American for whom his goal was to make democracy a reality.

Hon. J. J. Pickle
OF TEXAS

Mr. Speaker, the employee strike against the Penn Central Railroad has once again focused attention on the problems of mass transportation and freight traffic in the United States, and which makes us appreciate even more the strong interest and effective action which the late President LYNDON B. JOHNSON displayed.

As a member of the Senate Commerce Committee, JOHNSON studied the difficulties involved in transporting people and goods within the Nation. As President, he created the Department of Transportation, in recognition of the crucial role which the Federal Government must play in making transportation more efficient in this vast and rapidly changing country.

I take this opportunity to insert into the Record an editorial from *Traffic World* summarizing the late President's accomplishments. Those in the transportation industry, as well as the rest of us, have good reason to mourn his death.

The editorial follows:

THE LATE L. B. J.—TRANSPORTATION PROTAGONIST

Among the men who in this twentieth century have served as Chief Executives of the United States of America, none displayed more interest in or concern about the needs of suppliers and users of transportation services in this country than LYNDON BAINES JOHNSON, the thirty-sixth President, who died in the late afternoon of January 22 of a heart attack, en route to a San Antonio hospital, after having been stricken at his home on the LBJ Ranch, near Johnson City, Tex.

One important result of President JOHNSON's recognition of the essentiality of healthy transportation media to the nation's well-being was the enactment, in October, 1966, of the legislation that established the Department of Transportation as a new Cabinet department in the U.S. government. Operations of this department (the DOT) began on April 1, 1957, with Alan S. Boyd, therefore Under Secretary of Commerce for Transportation and, in the years 1961 through 1965, chairman of the Civil Aeronautics Board, as the first Secretary of Transportation. Most members of the transportation community regarded Mr. Boyd as a "natural" for the top office in the new department; it's doubtful that anyone else could have done a better job than he did as head of the DOT in the first four years of its existence.

It was in the memorable transportation message he sent to Congress on March 2, 1966, that President JOHNSON made these declarations, among others:

". . . America today lacks a coordinated transportation system that permits travelers and goods to move conveniently and efficiently from one means of transportation to another, using the best characteristics of each. . . .

"The United States is the only major nation in the world that relies primarily upon privately owned and operated transportation. That national policy has served us well. It must be continued. . . .

"We must coordinate the various functions of our transportation agencies in a single coherent instrument of government. Thus policy guidance and support for each means of transportation will strengthen the national economy as a whole.

"I urge the Congress to create a Cabinet-level Department of Transportation. I recommend that this department bring together almost 100,000 employes and almost $6 billion of federal funds now devoted to transportation."

Such a department, President JOHNSON averred, would "serve the growing demands of this great nation, . . . satisfy the needs of our expanding industry and . . . fulfill the right of our taxpayers to maximum efficiency and frugality in government operations."

Our acquaintanceship with the late President from Texas dated back to his service, after election to the U.S. Senate in 1948, as a member of the Senate interstate commerce committee. We noted that in the committee hearings he chose to be a listener rather than a speaker. In later years, however he issued more statements and made more public utterances about transportation problems and proposed remedial measures than had been placed on record by any of his predecessors in the Presidency.

He sought and obtained enactment of a substantial number of legislative proposals affecting transportation, in his five years as President. Those enactments included, in addition to the act establishing the Department of Transportation, the so-called "incentive per diem" act of 1966, and an act creating a board of arbitration to make a final and binding determination for settlement of the work-rules dispute between the railroads and rail employe unions.

From some of the bound volumes of Traffic World for the years 1964–1967 we have selected a few "quotes" from statements made by President JOHNSON on the dates indicated:

January 27, 1964: ". . . The many basic inequities among the various modes of transportation must be removed, if the travelers and shippers are to have available a wide choice of low-cost and high-quality transportation services. Our tangled transportation policies must be reformed. . . ."

January 25, 1965: "If the nation is to have a truly efficient system of transportation, we must revise the traditional government programs of regulation and operation subsidies and place greater reliance upon the forces of competition. . . . My proposals for charging users of government (supported) transportation services a greater share of the costs incurred in their behalf are consistent with this objective.

July 20, 1965: "It remains surprising and even shocking that about 80 per cent of our business firms have never yet entered into foreign trade. I think this represents a great wasteland of unfilled opportunity that is open. I hope that over the next 10 years we can increase three or four-fold the number of American shippers who sell goods abroad."

May 26, 1966 (on signing the freight car per diem bill (S. 1098) enabling the ICC to include incentive elements in the setting of freight car daily rental charges): "The freight car shortage is only a symptom of our larger transportation challenges and opportunities. The bill I sign today is not a cure-all, or the final answer. It is but a part of the total effort we are carrying out in many fields to use transportation in better and more effective ways."

At the time he signed the incentive per diem bill, President JOHNSON shared with many others the belief that this was the best available means of spurring action by the carriers themselves to increase or "stretch" the freight car supply. But perusal of the summaries, elsewhere in this issue, of the U.S. Supreme Court's opinion in an incentive per diem case and of a speech made by ICC Commissioner Rupert L. Murphy on January 23, in Fargo, N. Dak., reveal that the freight car shortage problem remains far from being solved. Presently there seems to be no better approach than the good old one advocated by Commissioner Murphy, namely, that there be a blending of efforts by shippers, carriers and regulators to reach "the common goal" of maximum efficient use of the available car supply.

Hon. John B. Anderson
OF ILLINOIS

Mr. Speaker, I am deeply saddened by the death of former President LYNDON B. JOHNSON. I came to this body in the same year Mr. JOHNSON took office as Vice President and served here during his Presidency from that tragic day in November 1963 through 1968. As a member of the Republican Party I often had occasion to oppose the President's programs, but I nevertheless held him in the highest respect as a man of vision, commitment, and determination. We shall remember him in the Congress as a man of great personal warmth and proven leadership abilities. Even as President he remained a creature of the Congress and this was reflected in the mutual flow of respect and courtesy between the White House and the Hill.

Mr. Speaker, I think I shall best remember President JOHNSON as a man of deep commitment to the cause of civil rights—a man who provided strong and single-minded leadership in this area during the great civil rights battles of the sixties. When he echoed the words of the late Dr. Martin Luther King, Jr., in pledging, "We shall overcome," you knew he spoke from the heart. Perhaps the greatest living tributes to the Presidency of LYNDON B. JOHNSON are the monumental civil rights acts on the books today as a result of his efforts and deep commitment, and I was deeply honored to be a participant in the signing of the Civil Rights Act of 1968, having played a small part in its passage. I carried away from that ceremony the image of a President possessing a sincere conviction and deep devotion to the dream of a better life and equal opportunity for all Americans, and that image remains with me today.

Hon. John J. Rhodes
OF ARIZONA

Mr. Speaker, in the death of LYNDON BAINES JOHNSON, America has lost one of its most illustrious sons. LYNDON JOHNSON truly came from the soil of America, and brought to the high station in life he achieved all of the loyalty and patriotism which can come only from a great love for our land and its people.

Mr. JOHNSON was a leader in every sense of the word. As majority leader of the U.S. Senate, I think it is possible that he will be regarded by history as one of our most effective legislative leaders. As Vice President, he was industrious and productive, all the while being completely loyal to his President and his country. As President of the United States, LYNDON JOHNSON went through some of the most troublesome times in our recent history. He always did his duty as he saw it, and did not shrink from making difficult decisions. He was a strong President in every sense of the word.

LYNDON JOHNSON was very considerate to the Members of the House and the Senate. He seemed to enjoy our company, as few Chief Executives have. The evenings at the White House were prized by all Members of the Congress, and the briefing sessions, which were frequently dominated by the personality of the President himself, were informative. I valued these associations, both as a Congressman and as an individual.

My State of Arizona will never forget that it was in LYNDON JOHNSON's administration that the long-planned central Arizona project was finally authorized. It was a proud moment for me and my colleagues from Arizona when we were allowed to stand at the side of President Johnson as he affixed his signature to this law which was so important to us and to our State.

Texas, America, and the world will miss LYNDON JOHNSON. To Mrs. Johnson and to her two fine daughters and their families, Mrs. Rhodes and I extend our deep sympathy.

Hon. O. C. Fisher
OF TEXAS

Mr. Speaker, our former colleague Wint Smith, of Kansas, served here with much distinction. He served with LYNDON JOHNSON and knew him well. He recently sent me a copy of a eulogy of the former President which I desire to include in my remarks.

It will be recalled that President JOHNSON did not choose to seek a second full term in the White House. At that stepping aside, hopefully, the war in Vietnam might be brought to an earlier end.

The eulogy by Mr. Smith follows:

THE LATE LYNDON B. JOHNSON

(By Wint Smith)

Whenever a President or ex-President of the United States dies almost everyone stops and thinks about this loss to our country and tries to assess his worth for the common good and his future historical stature.

LYNDON B. JOHNSON's death—coming as it did in the midst of world-wide news of the so called peace settlement in Vietnam—did not receive the full assessment that his death would ordinarily have received. This is not to say his death was not fully appreciated by all the news media. His funeral from the Capitol of the United States was most impressive and deserved by any man who has been President of the United States.

Perhaps no President in our history tried as hard as he did to rectify some of the injustices that he felt had long been left undone. No one was ever elected with a greater majority than he up to the time of his election; no one ever tried any harder than he to achieve social justice.

But no President was ever so overwhelmingly elected by his Party and at the end of his four year term driven from his office by those that had elected him. Being forced from office was as tragic as Churchill's defeat at the end of World War II by the unappreciative British voters after Churchill had led the world through the dark days of Nazi German domination to a victory in June 1945. Yet he was forced out of office by an ungrateful people largely due to facts beyond Churchill's control, just as the Vietnam-Kennedy war he inherited.

LYNDON B. JOHNSON was buried along side an unknown little river—not mentioned in song or story—by the slow moving, sometimes almost dry Pedernales lined with live oak and mesquite trees. Many of our Presidents lie along side of America's famous rivers such as the Potomac and Hudson. LYNDON JOHNSON came back to the land of his birth. Buried among his ancestors who for two generations before him earned their living with their hands when things were created by hands and not by machines.

LYNDON B. JOHNSON rose to the highest pinnacle of fame and fortune. This rise was achieved by his own struggle and ability along with deep knowledge of human nature and with the ability to be in the right place at the right time—when the sun would break through to shine on the favorite area. No one in Texas would dispute the fact that LYNDON JOHNSON was the most astute politician ever developed in Texas and that of course includes Sam Rayburn of Texas, Speaker of the House, who served longer as Speaker than any other man in history. And of course he was ahead of Jack Garner, Vice President of the United States and also Speaker of the House of Representatives.

LYNDON JOHNSON was never very far from the heart and soul of his beloved hilly Pedernales River country. He knew the details of the early schools, the country ceremonies, the funerals and the marriages. He knew how his neighbors made their living, the sports, hobbies and past-times, and he full well knew that many of these customs and neighborhood values had disappeared.

We in this rural crossroad area should remember a few facts about LYNDON B. JOHNSON, because he will be the last elected President of the United States who grew up in such a rural country atmosphere. LYNDON JOHNSON knew what the smell of an afternoon rain can do to a parched, drought stricken countryside. He knew the daily duties of an early country farm life—milking cows, shutting farm doors, pulling weeds and cutting cockle burrs. He knew what the sound of a howling, thieving coyote meant when the chicken house door had not been closed at dusk.

He also knew that all Texas men of means wore White Stetson hats. He also knew what this hat meant. Any tall lean Texan wearing a White Stetson hat, clad in high heeled boots could walk into any Texas Bank and pay for the cattle he bought without a letter of credit. LYNDON JOHNSON also knew that the White Stetson hat was a symbol of courage and honesty made famous by the Texas Rangers who enforced the Law from the Rio Grande to the Oklahoma border. These white hatted Rangers were to Texas what the Red Coated, broad brimmed hatted Canadian Mounties were to the people of Canada.

Perhaps some of you saw the grave side ceremonies at the little country cemetery; you heard the guns; you heard the final rites; you heard Taps played by the Army Bugler. But stop here for a moment—to me, this was the most impressive part of all the ceremonies in connection with the Johnson funeral.

LYNDON JOHNSON's ancestors fought on the side of the South during the Civil War. Just after the Civil War started and the North had been defeated in their first battle of Bull Run, Julia Ward Howe, sister of Henry Ward Beecher, one of the leading Pulpit Preachers and Orators of his day and the most vehement exponent of destroying slavery, came to Washington from Boston to visit her brother. In the evening she walked from her hotel and saw the camp fires of the Union soldiers guarding Washington. She returned to her hotel and wrote the "Battle Hymn of the Republic", which song became the official song of the Union Army and has since been sung by millions of patriotic Americans, and strangely enough, is still very popular with all people. Yet it was written for a cause—abolish slavery and unite America.

The opening lines state:

Mine eyes have seen the glory of the coming of the Lord.
He is trampling out the Vintage where the grapes of
        wrath are stored . . .
and the Closing lines of the poem are
As he died to make men holy, let us die to make men
        free
While God is marching on.

Yet from a little country cemetery on the banks of the Pedernales in the scrubby hills in Texas this song was sung at the request of LYNDON JOHNSON as the closing rites of his funeral.

The writer can think of no more fitting tribute to the memory of one who sincerely tried to make men free. LYNDON JOHNSON knew what the song said and what it had meant in other troubled times of American history.

Hon. William G. Bray
OF INDIANA

Mr. Speaker—

For God's sake, let us sit upon the ground,
And tell sad stories of the death of kings.

The poignant lines from "Richard II" are appropriate. For the second time in thirty days the American Republic mourns the death of a former President.

The President is but one man. The Presidency is many men. The American Republic is over 200 million people. But, somehow, in a manner none can fathom, our 200 million coalesce into that one man, and the symbol he is. When our Presidents die, in office or out of it, no matter the circumstances, something is gone from our national life and national soul. And something is gone from each of us, too.

And now the final drum taps have sounded for LYNDON JOHNSON. One man—watching him, you could hear the jingle of spurs, the clump of boot heels on the floor, the creak of saddle leather, and feel the frenzied excitement and hear the rolling drumfire of a mustang at full gallop, hooves striking sparks from the flint. For over 30 years he ranged across the American political scene with a two-fisted stride that was in the best tradition of the frontier from which he came, which he loved, and of which he was so proud.

It may be the supreme irony that the fates decreed one of our saddest and most tragic hours to be LYNDON JOHNSON's finest. He came to the Presidency at a time when the Nation was in the indescribable shock and trauma caused by an assassin's bullet. For us, the sudden passing of a Chief Executive is a twisting, wrenching thing. Continuity and stability are hallmarks of our National Government, and of our way of life. They were replaced by fear, confusion and uncertainty. Only one man—the new President—can offset this. And LYNDON JOHNSON did.

How many knew, as they watched President Kennedy's funeral procession go through the streets of Washington, and as they saw LYNDON JOHNSON marching with it, that the Secret Service had begged him not to expose himself? There had been one assassin already; were there more? He brushed them aside; he knew what was expected of him and what his duty was:

I would rather lose my life than be afraid to risk it.

A President had been murdered, but the country would go on. Waves crashed against the rock, but the rock stood firm. The foundations of the Republic were secure.

Now, an eagle lies under the stone. There is a vacant and lonely place against the sky. History will judge; we cannot. But, whatever is finally written about LYNDON JOHNSON in the annals of the American Republic must have on the pages bright, clear and large, the words "Courage—Devotion—Patriotism."

LYNDON JOHNSON never gave his country any less. No country could ever ask for more.

"And now these waiting dreams are satisfied;
From twilight to the halls of dawn he went;
His lance is broken; but he lies content
With that high hour, in which he lived and died.
And falling thus, he wants no recompense,
Who found his battle in the last resort;
Nor needs he any hearse to bear him hence.
Who goes to join the men of Agincourt."

Hon. John H. Dent
OF PENNSYLVANIA

Mr. Speaker, I want to join my colleagues today in mourning the passing of a good man and a great American, LYNDON BAINES JOHNSON.

As a Congressman and a Senator, and as President of the United States, LYNDON JOHNSON embodied the ideals of this Nation and the ideals of humanity. There is no need to recount his specific accomplishments here; suffice it to say that in his 30 years in public office, he did more good for more people than any of us have done in a lifetime. I say this because, of all the Presidents in this century, LYNDON JOHNSON had the singular distinction of being the one who had the keenest grasp of what the goals of our form of government are and how to translate these goals from the sterile words of the Constitution into true meaning for all Americans.

The Founding Fathers used the inclusive phrase "we the people" to define who is protected by constitutional rights. But, for so many years, "we the people" too frequently meant those who were wealthy, those who were enfranchised, those who were white, and those who were in control of the powers of the U.S. Government. For the Lyndon Johnson years, "we the people" referred to each individual in this country, be he rich or poor, black or white, powerful or powerless.

The legacy of LYNDON JOHNSON has assured us and our posterity that the application of laws under the Constitution will be made fairly and equally. His legacy has assured each American that he or she would have an equal opportunity to seek and achieve the American dream of success and happiness. His legacy has assured each person in this country that he will have the opportunity for an education equal to that of his peers. His legacy has assured those who were powerless that the Government of the United States would extend a helping hand to them so that they could indeed help themselves.

Yet, for all the glory of the Johnson years, the story of his Presidency ended in personal frustration and disappointment. Perhaps this was because LYNDON JOHNSON believed too strongly in the greatness of America; he believed that there were no bounds to what America could accomplish in the world. It was a contagious belief, one which we in Congress felt ourselves.

Yet, as we worked together to achieve those goals of justice and equality for all Americans, we both failed to recognize that the escalation in the Vietnam war would delineate the boundaries of our Nation's greatness.

For this reason, LYNDON JOHNSON's detractors are several; yet history is certain to vindicate his name, for decades from now, when the pain and suffering of the Vietnam war have waned, the groundwork which he laid for freedom in America will live on and continue to be strong.

We mourn the passing of this great man for we knew him in life as a true friend. So, too, we mourn for him as a symbol of the ideals which our country holds so dear. Let us pray to God that our Nation is blessed in the future with leaders who have the ability and foresight of LYNDON BAINES JOHNSON.

Hon. Charles C. Diggs, Jr.
OF MICHIGAN

Mr. Speaker, I share with my colleagues and my fellow Americans a deep sadness at the death of LYNDON BAINES JOHNSON, a President who, through his great concern and great courage, initiated and fought for the most far-reaching legislation in the field of civil rights and social opportunity in the past century in America.

I had the privilege of serving in the Congress at the time when Lyndon Johnson was pursuing his distinguished career as a brilliant and forceful leader of the Senate, when he served under John F. Kennedy as Vice President, and when he brought his skills, knowledge, and experience to the White House as President. His love for this land and all its peoples was limitless; his untimely death is a loss for all Americans.

Hon. Elizabeth Holtzman
OF NEW YORK

Mr. Speaker, I wish to join my colleagues in mourning the passing of LYNDON BAINES JOHNSON. His Presidential leadership on behalf of domestic reform must be considered one of the high watermarks in the annals of American social history. In a time when we are confronted by callous disregard for the problems of the unemployed, the ill-housed and the under-educated, we must remember his courageous efforts to better the life of all Americans and hope that it will inspire us in our own struggle to achieve meaningful social change and equal opportunity for all.

Hon. Gene Snyder
OF KENTUCKY

Mr. Speaker, reflecting on the death of LYNDON JOHNSON, it would be useless and disingenuous for me to praise him as someone I followed and supported in the majority of his programs or presidential endeavors. I did not. We disagreed, and—as opponents are wont to do—we often disagreed vehemently.

And, yet, I feel that I must acknowledge that his death leaves me sorrowlul. He was a worthy and energetic opponent—a man who stood up to you when he thought you were in the way of something he thought was right. I still do not think that many of the things President JOHNSON proposed were right as solutions to the country's ills, but I have never doubted that he was sincere in proposing them—nor do I doubt that he thought they would be best for the Nation. One must admire the tireless way in which he worked to see them become reality.

He was a leader—a dynamic, vigorous, forthright leader of men. I did not follow his lead most of the time in his legislative programs, but I am proud to have followed him in seeking the best for our Nation. In his love of America, in his desire to do what was best for her, LYNDON BAINES JOHNSON was unsurpassed.

I mourn his loss to us—and to the Republic.

Hon. Robert L. F. Sikes
OF FLORIDA

Mr. Speaker, the death of former President LYNDON B. JOHNSON brings shock to all America. Somehow it seems inconceivable that this stalwart and tall son of Texas could be taken from us so early in life.

History will be the final judge of President JOHNSON. He came to the Presidency under con-

ditions he did not want, struggled through more than 5 years of the most trying times in American history, and left the White House under conditions other than those of his own choosing.

It has often been said that LYNDON JOHNSON was a big man—big in all that he undertook and all that he did. He was large in physical stature, immense in his compassion for the least of us, and he stood second to none in his love of country.

I believe it is safe to say that President JOHNSON's dream for America was one of justice for all people. Yet, he launched his quest for the Great Society at a time in history when its goals were not to be allowed. Instead of harmony at home and peace abroad, the President found division at home and war in Asia. He exerted every ounce of his being to ending both division and war, but as the war continued, division grew at home. Some of those for whom he did the most and risked the most were the most critical of his efforts.

Finally, in what must go down as one of the highly patriotic acts in our proud history, LYNDON JOHNSON stepped down from the Presidency in a final effort to bring our Nation together. He was not to live to see his hopes fulfilled. At the time of his death, our Nation still is divided, although not as sharply as before, but peace at long last is at hand. It is a greaty pity that he was not to hear and to enjoy the official ending of the war which brought him so much personal grief.

No President in modern times has assumed office under more trying conditions, nor has a President used his own personal strength so vigorously to bind up the Nation's wounds. There were those who took advantage of his dreams and who abused his trust, and sometimes the results compounded the Nation's problems.

Now he has been taken from us, almost 4 years to the day from the time he departed this city for his beloved Texas. For only the third time in our Nation's history, we find ourselves without a living former President. President Nixon and many others have relied on the counsel and the wide experience of the former President, and I am certain that his help was gladly given to all of them for the sake of our country.

All of us who knew LYNDON JOHNSON grieve with his family for their loss and we grieve that our Nation must go forward without the towering patriotism and abiding love the gentleman from Texas had for America.

Hon. James A. Haley
OF FLORIDA

Mr. Speaker, it is with a deep sense of humility I add my own remarks to the growing tribute to our late President, LYNDON BAINES JOHNSON. Once again our country finds herself without the wisdom and advice of a living former President. Yet we can still look to the life of President JOHNSON for guidance in meeting the needs of this country today.

His assumption of the Presidency on one of the United States darkest days made him the first southern President in over 100 years, yet he transcended the politics of regionalism and sought first what was best for the Nation. He used his great leadership in conjunction with the Congress to lead the Nation, reaffirming the strength and vitality of our great people and the stability of our political system.

President JOHNSON was probably one of the most easily accessible Presidents for Members of Congress to see. He was a man of strong convictions, but he was also a man who listened to many voices. While many of his programs were controversial, he at least had the courage to present and support them.

It will take time for people to fully recognize and analyze his many good qualities, but I think history will judge him kindly.

Hon. Joseph P. Vigorito
OF PENNSYLVANIA

Mr. Speaker, it was an honor and a great privilege to have served as a Congressman for 4 years under such a great President as LYNDON JOHNSON.

He was a man and President for all the people and he exhibited this throughout his life, especially in fighting for strong civil rights and social legislation.

The 89th and 90th Congresses, of which I was a part, will long be remembered by Americans for the many landmark measures that were passed at the prodding of President JOHNSON.

Many Congressmen, including myself, supported JOHNSON during his administration when he sent measure after measure to Capitol Hill because the time was right for legislation to improve our social and economic life.

President JOHNSON can best be remembered for his strong stand during the 1964 election campaign for aid to senior citizens in the form of Medicare.

At last, a segment of America which had contributed so much, were being compensated for their work in building the country. LYNDON JOHNSON saw the inequities in the form of poor health care for the elderly and was able to get the innovative legislation passed in the 89th Congress, of which I was a Member.

LYNDON JOHNSON was a great leader both in the Senate during his days as majority leader and during his 5 years as President. While in the Senate, JOHNSON came to know the intricacies and skills of the legislative process which made him one of the greatest legislators of our time.

This special skill became more apparent during the 4 years I was in Congress while he was President. It was one of the most productive years in terms of legislation signed into law.

JOHNSON will be especially remembered when he became President during a time of national tragedy and grief. He took over the reins of power of this country and brought the Nation back to normalcy after a trying period in American history. I can think of no one more qualified to take the leadership of this great country at such a critical moment.

LYNDON JOHNSON chose to carry on the hard work of John Kennedy and the ideas of such great men as Franklin Roosevelt and Harry Truman as he molded his administration programs for the period of the 1960's.

Many great things were accomplished during the Johnson years. Americans from every background will recall LYNDON JOHNSON as a man of courage and determination. He will have a place in history among our greatest leaders.

Hon. B. F. Sisk
OF CALIFORNIA

Mr. Speaker, I join today with my colleagues in paying tribute to our 36th President, LYNDON BAINES JOHNSON.

His loss has a deep meaning to me. I feel that the Nation as a whole mourns his death with equal depth. To me LYNDON JOHNSON was indeed a big man who rose up to meet the challenges which might have gone unresolved by one without his character.

This man's accomplishments were many; they have been elaborated on already. His deeds were brought about by an uncanny insight and the determination to overcome stumbling blocks, regardless of their size or stature.

My first direct contact with the legislative ability, particularly the persuasive ability of LYNDON JOHNSON, came when I was a member of the Select Committee on Space. Shortly after October, 1957, the initial flight of a sputnik forced this country into an emotionally charged space program. Speaker Rayburn directed the committee's effort at writing the Space Act and establishing NASA. Leo O'Brien of New York and I, added a rather substantial amendment to the proposed legislation. The amendment met with considerable opposition in the Senate, and leading the fight was the Senate majority leader, LYNDON B. JOHNSON.

At the suggestion of Mr. O'Brien, we arranged a luncheon with Mr. JOHNSON to see if we could work out our differences. We did meet. We did compromise. And, for the first of many times, I was allowed to see the great legislative ability and persuasive know-how of LYNDON JOHNSON.

The outcome of the meeting was predictable. Mr. JOHNSON's practical approach to the differences led to a compromise, which at that time moved the project forward toward the goal we were all seeking. It is this type of ability that allows progress, and LYNDON JOHNSON was a master of the art of compromise.

The measure of the man was again vividly shown to me in 1960 when some of my California colleagues and I attended the Democratic Convention as Johnson delegates. As a group we worked very closely with him on his campaign. We felt and saw the pressures building, on Mr. JOHNSON as well as ourselves. When John F. Kennedy was selected as the party nominee, LYNDON JOHNSON showed another one of his rare gifts. He willingly accepted the nomination as vice president, and, in my opinion, this was done for love of country and dedication to the party— the high principles in which he believed.

Needless to say many felt his position as majority leader of the Senate was more powerful than that of the Vice-Presidency, but LYNDON JOHNSON did his job, and he did it well.

The same was true again after he assumed the Presidency. Again, to cite an occasion, let me go back to the troubled times surrounding the passage of the Elementary and Secondary Education Act. As a member of the House Rules Committee, I and some of my colleagues were invited to

the White House to discuss in broad terms the controversy surrounding the legislation. It was a great personal honor for me to be there. It was in this meeting where some of the very necessary understandings were reached in the manner in which the act was promulgated.

In this particular instance I had the experience of realizing that indeed LYNDON JOHNSON had a rather short fuse; but, at the same time, he had the capacity to control his temper and thereby make his point under what were sometimes very trying circumstances.

Later in his career, I watched the agony he suffered over Vietnam. But at no time could I not believe that he was carrying out the policies which he believed to be in the best interests of this country.

I became fully convinced that no man was more dedicated to bringing about peace in Vietnam than President JOHNSON. His entire life and full effort during the latter part of his tenure as President was devoted to that cause. He sought, as I think most of us did, peace with honor.

LYNDON BAINES JOHNSON was a doer of great deeds. He always had a goal. He fought hard. And he fought hardest for that in which he believed and for the things which would improve the lot of all Americans. In the course of accomplishing this oftentimes difficult task he stepped on toes and he took steps which became controversial. But, I firmly believe his heart was in the right place and his singlemost objective was to serve all the people and improve the conditions of all the people.

To Lady Bird, the Johnson daughters and their husbands, and to the grandchildren I offer my deepest condolences.

Hon. John P. Hammerschmidt
OF ARKANSAS

Mr. Speaker, I am burdened with great grief that the flag of our Nation again flies at half-mast on the loss of one of America's outstanding leaders—LYNDON BAINES JOHNSON. As I join with citizens from coast to coast in rejoicing that a peace agreement has been signed to end hostilities in Vietnam and our prisoners of war are heading homeward, I am saddened that our former Chief Executive who had so sincerely endeavored for peace could not be with us to see the culmination of this goal.

If Mr. JOHNSON could not be among us to rejoice this long-sought peace, it is heartening to me to realize that he has left the United States and the world with a legacy of accomplishment in establishing the principle of equality of mankind and equal opportunity for all. From his early days in the U.S. Congress, LYNDON JOHNSON fought with complete dedication and determination to remove social and economic barriers to make way for an open chance at a better way of life for all citizens.

Those who never met with Mr. JOHNSON and were not deeply touched with his personal charm will still profit from his landmark programs to move America toward a truly Great Society. I am among the fortunate many who have lasting impressions of personal experience with L. B. J.

I recall my first trip to the White House to see the President. I had received an appointment to talk with him about impoundment of highway funds and to tell him of adverse effects involving deterioration of roadbeds in the State of Arkansas.

Being the first Republican since Reconstruction from Arkansas ever to make that trip down to the White House, I had apprehensive feelings about the reception I would receive. It was then that I learned of the President's real political and governmental understanding. I immediately felt the warmth of his personality and deep concern for problems we discussed. Incidentally, probably not because of my visit, substantial funds which had been impounded were restored within the week for continuation of the interstate system.

I am confident that history, in an objective or analytical treatment of the Johnson administration, will proclaim Mr. JOHNSON as an outstanding President with extraordinary vision and leadership ability. Despite criticism of many Great Society and war on poverty legislation, these programs were launched toward common national goals and constituted a major step in meeting our critical needs.

The Civil Rights Act of 1964 set a precedent which, for years to come, will continue to unlock doors to progress for our country's disadvantaged and minority groups. Enactment of the Elementary and Secondary Education Act of 1965 marked the first time that Congress had approved legislation which authorized funds for general use in elementary and secondary schools. I have seen, during my tenure in Congress, this act enable major achievements in strengthening education and upgrading instruction throughout the Third District and the State of Arkansas.

As President, JOHNSON expressed strong conviction on the Government's obligation to insure that our older citizens are able to live a full and useful life in their later years. In this regard, he sought and received congressional passage of The Older Americans Act.

The elderly and the disabled throughout the Nation are now more adequately cared for due to the medicare program. The passage of the Social Security Amendments of 1965 climaxed a 20-year fight for a Federal health insurance program for the aged.

In addition to contributions for social programs, we must also attribute JOHNSON's leadership to enactment of economic development, water pollution, highway beautification, and veterans' legislation—all of which constitute a base for our current legislative activities.

My colleagues in Congress found that Mr. JOHNSON had an understanding and receptive ear, although he did not always agree. He was, however, a man with true and deep concern over the welfare of his fellow man. I consider it an honor to have had the opportunity to come into Congress during the Johnson years and learn his great depth of understanding and dedication to make this Nation a better place for us all.

Hon. Harold R. Collier
OF ILLINOIS

Mr. Speaker, it is hard to realize that LYNDON B. JOHNSON has left us, barely 9 years after that tragic afternoon when he suddenly assumed the heavy burdens of the greatest office on earth.

Having spent almost his entire adult life in the service of the legislative establishment, first as an employee, then as a Member of this great body, later as a Member of the other body, and finally as Vice President he entered the White House well qualified to lead the Nation through some of its most difficult years. A broad acquaintanceship with those who serve in the Congress, a great familiarity with the legislative process, and a detailed knowledge of what he was convinced were the needs of the people all combined to make him one of the greatest practitioners of the legislator's art. There has never been a greater lobbyist for the causes in which he believed than LYNDON BAINES JOHNSON.

It is regrettable that, having laid down the burdens of high office while still in the prime of life, he was destined to enjoy but a short retirement. During his 64 years he lived life to the full, striving mightily, first on behalf of his community, later as his horizons broadened, on behalf of Texas, the Nation, and the world.

Mr. Speaker, LYNDON JOHNSON was devoted to his family, to the political philosophy to which he subscribed, and to the country which he served well during war and peace. May he rest in peace and may God comfort his loved ones.

Hon. Thomas P. O'Neill, Jr.
OF MASSACHUSETTS

Mr. Speaker, LYNDON BAINES JOHNSON, a leader of unshakable courage and personal integrity, launched our Nation on a course of sweeping domestic reform, but foundered on the war in Vietnam. Now, he belongs to the ages, yet his monumental domestic achievements will endure to posterity.

President LYNDON BAINES JOHNSON did not envision a good society; he enacted a program of social and economic progress that would create a great society in which all men were really equal; in which the aged would have proper medical attention; in which the people would have more parks and open spaces for recreation; in which the Government would take the lead to clean up air and water pollution; in which every American would have the essentials of life—enough food, a decent home, and adequate clothing.

Though LYNDON JOHNSON's dreams of wiping out poverty and social injustice were not brought to fruition in his lifetime, they were realistic goals. His many accomplishments in domestic reform speak fully for themselves and have taken their rightful place in the archives of our Nation.

Mr. Speaker, I place in the Record the following articles which appeared in the Boston Globe and Boston Herald American:

[From the Boston Globe, Jan. 23, 1973]

JOHN MCCORMACK REMINISCES ABOUT "A TRUE AND GREAT FRIEND"

(By Lucinda Smith)

John W. McCormack, former speaker of the House of Representatives, reminisced last night about LYNDON B. JOHNSON, his close friend for 36 years.

McCormack referred to Mr. JOHNSON as "the President" and "LYNDON" as he told of the years they spent together in Washington, beginning in 1937 when Mr. JOHNSON took a Texas congressional seat.

In 1964, for the first 14 months of Mr. JOHNSON's term after President Kennedy's death, McCormack was second in line for the Presidency.

McCormack last night said: "During that period we were very, very close. The President kept me informed at all times. I sat in on meetings of the Joint Chiefs of Staff, at the President's invitation; and I was constantly briefed by the President on matters of concern."

McCormack added: "Of course we were always very close well before that time. We were friends in the House and Senate, and we would talk over legislation of importance, such as the Civil Rights Bill."

Mr. JOHNSON, McCormack and the late Sam Rayburn, a lifelong friend to the Johnson family in Texas and Speaker of the House before McCormack, were constant companions in Washington during Rayburn's terms of office.

"The friendship between the three of us was very, very close," McCormack said last night.

He remembered the first meeting between Rayburn and Mr. JOHNSON:

"The President told me this story," McCormack said, "while he (Mr. JOHNSON) was sick in the hospital once, an earlier sickness than his heart attacks . . . he was unconscious at one time. On the day he woke up, there was a man sitting beside him, beside his bed, and the man was half-asleep himself with a cigarette in his hand—the cigarette all burned out.

"His eyes were closed . . . this is what LYNDON told me. 'When I woke up.' the President told me, 'this man beside my bed woke up too. I said: Who are you? The man looked at me and said, I'm Sam Rayburn. I served in the Texas Assembly with your father. He was my closest friend.'

"'If I had a son who was sick in another city, your father would be by my son's bedside. And there was Sam Rayburn beside my bed.' Apparently, it was the first time they met," McCormack said. "I think it's a touching story."

McCormack also told of the last time he talked with Mr. JOHNSON. "About three weeks ago," he said, "I called him, and he wasn't in, and then he called me back. We spoke for awhile, as we often do." The occasion was McCormack's 81st birthday.

Last night McCormack said: "I am profoundly shocked to learn of the tragic death of President LYNDON BAINES JOHNSON. I extend to Mrs. Johnson and his daughters my heartfelt sympathy and sincere condolences in their great loss and sorrow. LBJ was a great American President whose eminent role in the critical moment of the world's history and whose firm determination that peace and justice and honor should prevail in the world will insure his place in history. LBJ will long be remembered, too, as a great legislator and as the President who advanced the cause of civil rights more so than any other American. LBJ's contribution to the field of education was the most remarkable contribution in history.

"Under his leadership greater advances were made in education than under all the other Presidents since our country began. This has been overlooked in my judgment, and his achievement in this field should be recognized. LBJ despite some thoughts to the contrary, had a dynamic and warm personality. He had a true sincerity in his belief, and he had an indomitable will. He led the American people strongly and surely in an unbalanced world. LBJ was a leader who belonged to the American people. Now he too, like President Truman, belongs to the ages. It is with deep emotion that I must say that I have lost a true and great friend. America has lost a great leader."

[From the Boston Herald American, Jan. 23, 1973]

YOUNGEST TO HOLD POST: L. B. J. SKILLED SENATE LEADER

WASHINGTON.—Whatever the verdict of history on the Presidency of LYNDON B. JOHNSON, he will be remembered as one of the most skilled leaders ever to serve in the Senate.

He was elected minority floor leader by Senate Democrats in 1953 when he was 44, the youngest man ever chosen for the post. He had served just four years in the Senate and 12 in the House.

During the first year he sat across the aisle from "Mr. Republican", Senate Majority Leader Robert A. Taft, another giant in the history of Senate leadership. Taft died in the summer of 1953. The Democrats regained control of Congress in the 1954 elections, and JOHNSON served as majority leader during the last six years of the Republican Eisenhower administration.

JOHNSON may have learned something from Taft's mastery of the Senate, but he learned more earlier as a protege of his fellow Texan, Speaker Sam Rayburn, and the late President Franklin D. Roosevelt. He had won White House favor as the only Roosevelt supporter among a number of candidates running for a House vacancy in 1937.

It was in 1955 that he repudiated a fragment of the Taft political philosophy that "The business of the opposition is to oppose" and told fellow Democrats that they must place responsibility above partisanship. And he once wrote that he was an American first a Democrat second and a Texan third.

As the dominant figures in the Senate and House from 1955 until JOHNSON became vice president with John F. Kennedy in 1961, the Texas team seemed a strange combination. Rayburn was short, gruff and taciturn. The tall rangy JOHNSON was talkative, flattering and not disposed to let a potential supporter forget favors.

Despite his skills, JOHNSON had his critics inside and outside Congress who called him an arm-twister and a wheeler-dealer.

Both JOHNSON and Rayburn were ready supporters of President Dwight D. Eisenhower on foreign policy issues, although JOHNSON sometimes grumbled privately that the Chief Executive was responsible for foreign policy and should not ask for a vote of confidence from Congress on some issues in that field. As President, he often resorted to those same tactics himself.

Although there never was a breach between JOHNSON and Eisenhower, they disagreed on domestic policies and economics, especially after the 1957 recession.

Installed in the Senate leadership with Southern support, it was JOHNSON who first led the Senate in cracking Southern filibusters against civil rights bills—in 1957 and 1960—that brought the measures to votes without cloture.

Relatively modest measures to break Southern barriers to voting by blacks, they led to passage of the more sweeping civil rights bills of 1964 and 1965.

By Texas standards, JOHNSON was liberal. The labor movement was eager, when JOHNSON was the Democratic nominee for president in 1964, to forget his House vote to override President Harry S. Truman's veto of the Taft-Hartley labor bill in 1947.

In private conversations in the Senate, he never seemed to share the dislike of Truman and Rayburn for the then-vice president and now President Richard M. Nixon.

Hon. Phil M. Landrum
OF GEORGIA

Mr. Speaker, the genius of leadership is manifest in a variety of talents. Some leaders are aggressive; other are benevolent and kind. Some are ideological; others are pragmatic. Some lead by superior intelligence and others through pure inspiration, and sometimes one leads with sheer, boundless physical energy.

Our history is replete with names of great leaders who possessed one or more of such talents. Of the 35 other Presidents who have served our Nation, each of them certainly had a large share of these personal traits. But no one, in my judgment, possessed all of these qualities to the degree of President LYNDON JOHNSON.

He was able to identify the problems of the ordinary American because he was an ordinary American, but he had the extraordinary capacity to lead whether he was on the banks of the Pedernales with the one-room school teacher of his boyhood or at the highest level of our society with industrial giants, ministers of foreign governments and all of the potpourri that is the human element of governments.

Certainly he made mistakes. Like the shortstop who goes after every ball hit in his direction, one comes along occasionally that no one, however capable, can field. But in identifying our problems and offering solutions as he saw them, he not only demonstrated his great powers of discernment and superb qualities of leadership, but he pointed up the human weaknesses characteristic of a nation of free people and through this made tremendous contributions toward the identification and improvement of our problems and the strengthening of the fibers that go to make us what we are.

Some say it is too early to judge his accomplishments, but I say that it is better for his contemporaries to judge by what he did and what he caused us to do than it is to leave it to history. LYNDON JOHNSON was a restless, concerned citizen, a splendid Congressman, a superb Senator and leader of that body, an extremely helpful and cooperative Vice President and, in terms of leading our Nation to recognize its problems and move toward their solutions, LYNDON JOHNSON was a great President.

This is our judgment now, and history can certainly do no less.

Hon. J. J. Pickle
OF TEXAS

Mr. Speaker, one of the most moving and eloquent resolutions ever passed by any State legislative body was passed last week by the Texas Legislature. It is a resolution paying its high regard to the life and accomplishments of our former President LYNDON BAINES JOHNSON. The resolution—House Concurrent Resolution 35—was signed by the Governor of our State, the Honorable Dolph Briscoe and Lt. Gov. William Hobby and Speaker of the House Price Daniel, Jr.

Mr. Speaker, I commend this resolution to the entire membership of this body because I think it is a graphic and moving description of the life of this great man, and I therefore include this resolution in the body of the Record at this point:

HOUSE CONCURRENT RESOLUTION 35

Whereas, A Life which was devoted to Honour and its Country, is no longer ours.

With the death of President LYNDON BAINES JOHNSON on January 22, 1973, Texas and the Nation lost one of its most distinguished sons and the World one of its greatest leaders. The loss is felt across the "flaming ramparts of the world."

Who can look back upon the public services and exalted virtues of the deceased, without exclaiming in the anguish of despair . . . "Is he, too, numbered among the silent dead"? He who bore the anguish and travails of a war against aggression, to which he succeeded, is gone to the realms of eternal peace; and

Whereas, History already has built around him a name and a fame that will light the pathway of generations yet unborn for centuries to come. Patriotism and admiration will not let us forget his mighty stroke of compassion for his fellowman and his unswerving devotion to duty. His talents were employed on the side of righteousness and at whose approach oppressed humanity felt a secret rapture. It was thus that he sometimes soared so high and shone with a radiance so transcendent "as filled those around him with awe and gave to him the force and authority of a prophet." President JOHNSON lived a life characterized by splendid manhood—crowded with deeds and crowned with honours. He was superb in his effort to attain the goals which he aspired. His actions vitalized the principle that "they fail, and they alone, who have not striven"; and

Whereas, This tall Texan—large as Texas herself—a son of the picturesque and enchanting vistas of the Hill Country, which he dearly loved, coursed by the cool, clear waters of the meandering Pedernales River, inspired by the rugged land from which he sprang and in which his roots were laid deep, rose to the pinnacle of world fame upon the precepts and examples taught and set by his fond and loving mother, Mrs. Rebekah Baines Johnson, and his distinguished father, Honorable Sam Ealy Johnson, Jr. with encouragement from his loyal helpmeet of 38 years, the lovely "Lady Bird" Johnson; and

Whereas, Following his graduation from Southwest Texas State Teachers College, now Southwest Texas State University, at San Marcos in February, 1927, he taught school at Cotulla, Texas, before becoming an aide to the late Honorable Richard M. Kleberg, Sr., then United States Representative from Kingsville, thereby launching a public and political career spanning nearly 40 years of continuous, constructive service to his country and to the world. After serving as Director of the National Youth Administration in 1935, he was elected to the United States House of Representatives in 1937, in which he served with dedication to the ideals of his friend, President Franklin D. Roosevelt. Following a period of "seasoning" in the House, under the leadership of Speaker Rayburn, familiarly known as "Mr. Sam", with an interlude of courageous service in the United States Navy during World War II, he was elected to the United States Senate in 1948. By dint of hard work, coupled with his innate ability, his training, his skills and energy, he became the Majority Whip in 1950. Senator JOHNSON was chosen as Majority Leader in 1953, in which capacity he distinguished himself and demonstrated his dynamic leadership with his policy of "reasoning" together. He was called the "most powerful man" in America, as he guided the Democratic-controlled United States Senate through a period of responsible cooperation with the Republican administration of President Eisenhower. It has been said that "JOHNSON was the Senate and the Senate was JOHNSON"; and

Whereas, With his acceptance of the nomination of his Party and his election to the Vice Presidency in 1960, Mr. JOHNSON served in that office with dignity, honour and loyalty while carrying out numerous missions and responsibilities delegated to him by President Kennedy. Whatsoever his hand found to do, he did it with all his might.

The leadership of our country passed into the capable and experienced hands of President JOHNSON when President Kennedy succumbed to the assassin's lethal messenger. There was hope and assurance for America midst the sadness of the hour. His legislative, diplomatic, political and native abilities provided him with the experience and valuable knowledge peculiar to the Office of President of the United States, gained from his close association with Presidents Roosevelt, Truman, Eisenhower and as the "right arm" of President Kennedy, available to no other man on the American scene, to lead our country; and

Whereas, Among the many and varied proposals which became the law of the land during his administration are to be found greatly increased Federal Aid to Education, Medicare and Medicaid, the 1964 Civil Rights Act, the 1965 Voting Act, the War on Poverty, to mention some. While President JOHNSON's public service was fraught with controversy—a characteristic of strong-willed and determinded, dedicated men—nevertheless, his noblest motive was the public good. It may be said of him that he made many friends and lost very few. He made many enemies of the right kind and kept them all. He said that he could not prescribe a formula for success, but that the formula for failure is to try to please everybody. His success was due, largely, to his constancy of purpose; and

Whereas, President JOHNSON, like former President Truman, was plagued by a foreign conflict during which he strove to preserve the integrity of our treaty commitment, negotiated by a former administration and affirmed by subsequent action of the Congress with the adoption of the "Gulf of Tonkin Resolution." He believed that if America reneged on her agreement it would imperil many other nations and, consequently, jeopardize the peace of the world. He never wavered in his desire and efforts to bring about an honourable peace. President JOHNSON was, in his day, a muchly maligned man. He knew that blatant demagoguery and a scurrilous press must be tolerated and borne by patriots. Comfort, however, could be found in the words of General Washington who said that "Real patriots who resist the intrigues of the favorite, are liable to become suspected and odious; while its tools and dupes usurp the applause and confidence of the people to surrender their interests"; and

Whereas, President JOHNSON's courage and patriotism were never more genuinely demonstrated than when, on March 31, 1968, he offered himself a willing sacrifice to the good of his country hopefully to end the Vietnam War with his decision not to become a candidate for reelection; and

Whereas, His private virtues, his public services, his great abilities, involuntarily excite the warmest feelings for him. In all the private relations of life he was honest, faithful, generous and humane and his heart was the seat of manly virtue.

His public services were many—splendid and great. His memory is enshrined in the esteem and affection of his contemporaries and will be consecrated by the gratitude of his country to future ages; and

Whereas, He may have had failings. On these let the tear that pities human weakness fall; on these let the veil which covers human frailty rest, since posterity is incurious bout the minor faults of its heroes; and

Whereas, President JOHNSON was married to Miss Claudia Alta Taylor, familiarly known as "Lady Bird" on November 17, 1934, to which union was born two charming daughters, Lynda, now Mrs. Charles S. Robb of Charlottesville, Virginia, and Luci, now Mrs. Patrick J. Nugent of Austin, Texas, both of whom gave joy and delight to their doting father. President JOHNSON not infrequently said that the charming, intelligent and understanding companionship of "Lady Bird" profoundly influenced his course and career; and

Whereas, He was beloved by his friends, endeared to his family; the statesman, the patriot, is gone. At the fall of such a man, grief is silent and eloquence muses elogiums which cannot be expressed. He has left us the remembrance of his greatness. As the gigantic figure that envelops men within the folds of his dark mantle, and even with the robe drawn about him, President JOHNSON seems so unshrouded that:

"Nothing can cover his high fame but heaven;
No pyramids set off his memories
But the eternal substance of his greatness;
To which I leave him"; and

Whereas, This Concurrent Resolution was prepared at my request by Honorable Dorsey B. Hardeman, a former member of this body, a long-time member of the Senate and a friend of President and Mrs. Johnson for more than 30 years; now, therefore, be it

Resolved by the House of Representatives of the 63rd Legislature of the State of Texas, the Senate concurring, That they express their abiding sympathy to Mrs. Johnson and the surviving members of the family, and their admiration and gratitude for the life and contributions of the man whose simple dignity consisted not in possessing honours but in deserving them by his faith and his works through which he brought joy to his Creator; and, be it further

Resolved, That copies of this Resolution be forwarded to Mrs. Johnson and her daughters; to President Nixon and to all members of the Texas delegation in the Congress of the United States, by the Clerk of the House of Representatives, under the Seal of the House, and that the members of the House of Representatives and of the Senate devote this day to pious contemplation, suitable to the melancholy event which it commemorates and that pages in the respective Journals of each House of the 63rd Legislature of the State of Texas be set aside for preserving this Resolution in memory of President JOHNSON in the knowledge that men's homage and their love shall never cease to follow him.

Mr. Speaker, on January 25, the Honorable Homer Thornberry, judge of the U.S. Court of Appeals, Fifth Circuit, delivered a most moving and eloquent memorial for President LYNDON JOHNSON to a joint session of the Texas Legislature.

Judge Thornberry was a long-time and dear friend of President JOHNSON. When President JOHNSON was elected to the U.S. Senate in 1948, Judge Thornberry was elected to take President JOHNSON's congressional office for the 10th District of Texas. Judge Thornberry served ably in that office until 1963 when he resigned to take a place on the Federal court. At that time, I succeeded Judge Thornberry as the Congressman for the 10th District.

But Judge Thornberry's contacts with the Johnson family go back even farther, far in 1923. Judge Homer Thornberry was a page in the Texas House of Representatives where Sam E. Johnson, the father of LYNDON B. JOHNSON, served as a member.

I know for a fact that Judge Thornberry knew our mutual friend President LYNDON JOHNSON as well as anyone in America, and I know President JOHNSON admired and respected Homer Thornberry as much as anyone in America. I thus insert in the Record at this time, Mr. Speaker, a copy of Judge Thornberry's remarks to the Texas Legislature:

ADDRESS BY THE HONORABLE HOMER THORNBERRY

For I, the Lord thy God, will hold thy right hand, saying unto thee, fear not: I will help thee.

I first came to this chamber officially in 1923, employed as a page in the 39th legislature, in which the Honorable Sam E. Johnson, father of LYNDON BAINES JOHNSON, served as a representative; I came again in 1937 to serve as member of the House in the 45th legislature. I returned because of the high honor you have bestowed on me by inviting me to participate with you in honoring the memory of our friend and neighbor.

No mortal words which I might say here can add to the illustrious memory of the great and magnificent LYNDON B. JOHNSON.

When the news of his passing reached us, there came a solemn and sober moment in the lives, not only of those of us who knew him and loved him, but in the lives of countless people throughout this Nation and the world who never knew him personally.

While we are staggered by an overwhelming loss, a new sense of values takes charge of our minds and hearts.

LYNDON JOHNSON was one of the most thoughtful persons I ever knew. He understood what it meant to be a good neighbor, LYNDON JOHNSON *was* his brother's keeper.

That great heart, which finally failed him, prompted him time and again to provide succor and relief to a multitude of friends—in time of bereavement, illness, or financial need.

Many times he and his noble wife, Lady Bird, were the *first* to provide love and consolation or the solution to a critical problem. Compassionate beyond belief, he was a friend to every man—in every city, in every village, in every mansion, in every hotel—encompassing the globe.

He had a warm sense of humor. He was a picturesque story teller. Time and time again, we have heard him tell a down-to-earth story to illustrate an important point. I think he would want me to say this. He was the most superb domino player I've ever known. I give personal testimony—I never won a game!

In that rugged hill country just west of here he developed the strength of character, the courage, the vision, the sense of realism, the compassion which enabled him to perform with effectiveness the tasks of his office.

He understood the principle—so often overlooked and forgotten—that the art of politics is the art of achieving the possible. He truly believed there was more good than bad in every person.

LYNDON JOHNSON has been rightly called a skilled political and legislative leader, unexcelled and unequalled. He was recognized as leader of his political associates. Now, in retrospect, we recall the many times in this nation's history he rose above the partisan and political differences of the moment to fight with courage and wisdom for the security of our country and the enduring freedom of men, women, and children everywhere. One of the greatest periods of our history unfolded under his leadership, both in the Congress and the White House. As President, he once said, "I would like to be remembered as the President who helped those unable to help themselves."

In his first address before the Joint Session of Congress, November 27, 1963, President JOHNSON said, "we will carry on the fight against poverty and misery, ignorance and disease—in other lands and in our own."

From that moment, he moved directly to the solution of age-old problems which have assailed mankind in our beloved country.

He sought removal of barriers and limitations which have humiliated fellow Americans.

Can we ever forget that speech to a Joint Session of Congress on March 15, 1965, when he said, "their cause must be our cause, too. Because it is not just Negroes, but really it is all of us, who must overcome the crippling legacy of bigotry and injustice. And we shall overcome." No other President has said words like those. Having said them to us, no one of us in this living America will ever be the same.

He sought the elimination of poverty and ignorance from sections of our Nation.

He sought the building of a great society for all America.

He sought to accomplish, through every possible avenue, peace on earth.

We mourn—and yet we rejoice—for LYNDON BAINES JOHNSON was triumphant in the eyes of those who shared the drama of his vision.

Other Presidents had dreams and aspirations which momentarily seemed lost in defeat.

Abraham Lincoln dared to believe in a viable citizenship for the enslaved.

Woodrow Wilson envisioned nations banded together in a quest for peace; he was scorned by his own countrymen.

Always there are those who would doubt, deny, or diminish. We have seen and heard indications that the great society is no longer viable.

The great society is no tangible, physical institution which can be closed down over night. It exists in the hearts of us all—never to be forgotten. Like a seed which germinates to full fruition, the great society will continue its undying influence.

Some have said his was an impossible dream, but "he fought for the right—without question or cause—to right the unrightable wrong."

These words well could have been written for him,

"I know that if I'll only be true to this glorious quest
    That my heart will be peaceful and calm when I'm laid
        to my rest
And the world will be better for this
That one man, scorned and covered with scars,
Still strove with his last ounce of courage
To reach the unreachable star."

We mortals say in the words of the poet—"Mr. President, 'approach thy grave like one who wraps the draperies of his couch about him and lies down to pleasant dreams.' "

For now, LYNDON BAINES JOHNSON has gone to "join that innumerable caravan that moves to that mysterious realm."

An immortal voice must be saying, 'well done thou good and faithful servant. Inasmuch as ye have done it unto one of the least of these, my brethren, ye have done it unto me."

Farewell, great spirit! LYNDON BAINES JOHNSON now belongs to the ages.

Hon. Claude Pepper
OF FLORIDA

Mr. Speaker, the passing of LYNDON BAINES JOHNSON from the American political stage, of which he has been a vital part from his entry into the House of Representatives and which he to a large extent had dominated for decades, ends not only the personal career of a man but an era in American politics. LYNDON JOHNSON and I became associated when the clouds of war were gathering over Europe and we both were working with President Roosevelt to try to avert the war and to prepare America for the storm of war which might hit us. I then felt the magic of this man and the depth of his feeling for his country. We often met at the home of a mutual friend, also a Texan—from Austin—publisher of many southern newspapers, a man who like ourselves was supporting the President's efforts—Charles Marsh.

Our association continued through the years as our friendship deepened. I was his colleague for awhile in the Senate. I saw him from time to time while I was out of the Congress when he was majority leader. In my first campaign for the House in 1962 he came to Miami Beach as Vice President and spoke at a testimonial dinner for me with his usual warmth and moving eloquence. I worked with him from time to time while he was in the White House. I supported him with happy zeal in his great domestic program and in his efforts to conclude the war in a manner that would realize our objectives and honor the cause of freedom in the world.

As President he did me many favors and we often talked of our mutual friend, Charles Marsh. Once when I was at the White House he exhibited his usual thoughtfulness of others by saying:

Tomorrow is Charles Marsh's birthday, send him a wire.

Earlier, while he was Vice President, after Charles Marsh had suffered a stroke, he sat on one side of Marsh's bed and I on the other as we rekindled our friendship for this old friend. We kept up our correspondence after he left the White House. As President and after his retirement whenever I had a testimonial occasion he sent a gracious telegram. So to my wife, Mildred, and to me the passing of President JOHNSON is the loss of a dear and cherished friend as well as the loss of a noble leader.

As a Representative LYNDON JOHNSON was a close friend of President Roosevelt and worked intimately with the President in the support of his many programs for domestic progress and peace in the world. He exhibited at that early stage of his political career the warmth of personality, the deep dedication to the public interest, the diligence and the determination to achieve great deeds which characterized his whole political life. In a little while after he came to the Senate the same keen intelligence, sound judgment, deep feeling for people, and skill in parliamentary procedure and congressional work gained him recognition.

Before long he became the youngest majority leader in the history of the Senate and, as leader, he not only led but in a fine sense dominated the Senate for all the many years that he was there. Under his leadership the Senate responded with a friendly accord and with wholehearted cooperation as it had never done before in the history of this Nation. That achievement was a rare feat in the political history of this country.

Yet, Senator JOHNSON achieved this degree of support from the Senate by an intensity of labor, singularity of purpose, and a degree of dedication to his task also never equaled in the annals of American public life. One of his close confidants told me a while before the Senator left the Senate that he was concerned about the Senator's health if he remained majority leader in the Senate because, as he put it, "Senator JOHNSON works days, nights, Sundays, holidays—all the time—at the job of majority leader." It was his consuming passion and purpose.

Probably President JOHNSON would have had better success in his race for the Presidency if he had devoted more time to his campaign and less to his duties as Senate majority leader. But his sense of duty to the Senate and to the country would not allow him to do that, whatever his personal political sacrifice.

As majority leader of the Senate, President JOHNSON, departing from some of his past, induced the Senate to support civil rights legislation which it had never before enacted. Senator JOHNSON, still the young, zealous, Democratic liberal who caught the eye of President Roosevelt, also led the Senate to the adoption of many other great humanitarian programs. The same love of country and patriotism which led him to be the first Member of Congress to join the armed services in uniform at the beginning of World War II moved him to take the lead in supporting the foreign policy and program of President Eisenhower when he thought it was good for America and for the world. He was too big an American to allow political party differences with President Eisenhower to deter him from serving his country in the Senate as he had gallantly done in uniform.

It was a rather shocking transition for Senator JOHNSON to move from the dynamic activity of the Senate into the necessarily subordinate position of Vice President. Yet, he served his President as Vice President with that same fidelity and loyalty which he would have extended to him had he remained Senate majority leader. He took the roles assigned him and discharged his duties with characteristics competence and zeal. He and his beloved and remarkably able and exceptionally talented wife, Lady Bird, became a great part of the Kennedy team and both at home and abroad they rendered distinguished and memorable service to the Kennedy administration and to America.

When the awesome responsibility of the Presidency fell upon the shoulders of LYNDON JOHNSON he revealed that humility and, yet, that strength which are the attributes of greatness. He determined to carry on the program of his fallen President and he did, with consummate skill and unrelenting determination so that he was able to feel in his conscience that whatever immeasurable losses the country had sustained in the passing of its revered and beloved young President, at least he had assured the country that the President's program would not suffer but became the law of the land. In the ensuing years of his Presidency, President JOHNSON led the Congress to enact, and the country to approve, a volume of legislation unequaled in the history of America, save in the stirring, unparalleled 100 days of President Franklin D. Roosevelt when he took the leadership of America as it stood upon the brink of dissolution and collapse.

This program of President JOHNSON securing the rights of all of our people to enjoy the rich inheritance of everything that was best in America, assuring education, health care, better homes, indeed a richer life, for the masses of the people of this country, I venture to say, will never be excelled however long the glory and grandeur of this great republic may last. He followed the idealism of Franklin Roosevelt, the practical wisdom of Harry Truman, the romantic vision of John F. Kennedy in extending the hand of the Federal Government to the disfranchised, to the poor, to the ill, to the homeless, to the ignorant, to all those who needed help and with that great Federal hand he lifted up the people of a nation to walk on higher ground. I said the passing of LYNDON JOHNSON ended an era; for now we see his successor as President brazenly proposing to abolish those programs, to remove that hand of warm Federal help to those millions who had so gratefully clasped it. Yet, what LYNDON JOHNSON, like Franklin Roosevelt, did for America shall never be lost nor will any President ever be able

to remove it from the goals and dreams of American life.

There are many who lament President JOHNSON's deepening involvement in Southeast Asia. Yet, to him, tragic as has been the cost of our participation in that endeavor, American help to South Vietnam was still the act of an America which was willing to raise its hand, and if necessary its sword, to defend the victim of brutal aggression, to help the little man to resist the cruel tryranny of the big and the powerful who would rob him of his inheritance of freedom. The spirit that led LYNDON JOHNSON deeper and deeper into Vietnam was the same spirit that led Woodrow Wilson and Franklin D. Roosevelt to defend the freedom of Western Europe against the tyranny and the Kaisers' and of Hitler's aggression. It was the same spirit that prompted the United States to save little Cuba at the beginning of this century from foreign and cruel domination.

It is the same spirit that has made America traditionally the friend of the needy—the Nation that held up the bright light of freedom as the right of all men everywhere in the world. Happily, our participation in that conflict is now nearing an end and, we are led to believe that the ideals and aims that led President JOHNSON heavily into that contest are going to be realized. But what we have done in that war in the opinion of the peoples of the world in retrospect will I believe be regarded as in character for America, tragic as has been its cost.

And now LYNDON JOHNSON is a part of American history and of the annals of the world. He is now a memory—indeed a legend. For LYNDON JOHNSON was the kind of a man who becomes a legend; powerful in physique, strong in character, unswerving in courage, indefatigable in labor he was one of the giants of his time. Nature made him so from the beginning and he only became what nature had fitted him to be and to do.

And so the long light of his life and deeds will ever stretch across all this great land, north and south, east and west, and indeed will illuminate the world. He towered above men in his deeds as he did most men in his stature. In every sense of the word LYNDON JOHNSON was a big man. He walked in seven league boots across his time; he ascended the mountain tops in his career. He laid his loving hand upon innumerable hearts and heads; he quickened the Nation to a keener conscience and he stirred many men to heroic deeds.

Those of us who were privileged to see him laid to rest amidst the interlacing boughs of those protecting five-oaks above the little cemetery established by his forebears, beside whom he now sleeps, a short distance from where he was born and went to his first school and where he lived his last years, were touched as one seldom is by the strength and courage of a loving wife and children, the beauty of the scene, the lovely solemnity of the occasion, the moving eloquence of the tributes paid him, the inspiration of the songs sung and the hymns played and by a sort of spiritual feeling that he had done his work and now he lay down to rest. He had come home to the bosom of nature which he loved and to the arms of his God whom he so deeply revered. As one turned away from the scene he heard ringing in his heart the words uttered by Anthony over the body of the fallen Brutus upon the field at Philippi when he said,

His life was gentle and the elements so mixed in him that nature might stand up and say to all the world, this was a man.

Hon. James J. Howard
OF NEW JERSEY

Mr. Speaker, all Americans, and especially those who were here in Washington during the "Johnson years" will deeply miss the late President. His strong leadership, his enormous sense of compassion and humanity, and his great drive to insure a better life for all Americans, combined to make this man a monumental figure in our time.

He will remain with us, however, in the effects of his efforts; in the programs he molded into being to help those less fortunate in our society; in his very basic belief that together we can do great things.

I personally found LYNDON JOHNSON an inspiration as I came to Washington and watched this man move through the Congress and the executive agencies, persuading, cajoling, molding, and developing programs and concepts which he felt would lead this Nation to a higher standard of ethical and national greatness. I did not always agree with him, but even in those areas where one did not agree, one had to deeply admire his courage and strength of character.

Mr. Speaker, I believe one of the most sensitive recollections I have read about our former President over these past weeks was written by Mr. Carl Rowan, and appeared in the Washington Post. I include it at this point in the Record:

ONE MAN'S MEMORY OF LYNDON B. JOHNSON

(By Carl T. Rowan)

How shall I remember LBJ?

I think of a man I had scarcely met, poking his index finger against my chest one sultry day in Saigon in 1961 and saying: "Mr. Roe-ann, you don't know me. But one of these days you're gonna discover that I'm a goddamn sight more liberal than most of these so-called liberals you've been cottoning up to."

And I shall remember that when the public mood turned mean and ugly in America and lesser liberals ran with the mob, LYNDON JOHNSON remained true to his decent convictions.

I shall remember LBJ as a man driven to success, a man who didn't know how to take it easy, whether ordered to by his doctor or begged to by the Secret Service.

There was that incredibly hot day in some unbelievably dusty villages on the outskirts of Agra, India, when he kept whispering to me: "Stay close to me—right by my shoulder." He was nurturing the illusion that I was some kind of expert on India just because I had written a book about it.

I gasped as I tried to stay near him as he plowed through the grasping crowds. As I wiped my sweaty forehead with the front of my hand and my parched lips with the back of it, I asked myself: "Is this a man who has suffered a massive heart attack?"

I remember his telephone call on March 15, 1965, asking if I would sit with his wife and daughters while he delivered his address on the Voting Rights Act to a joint session of Congress. That was the speech—the last touches written by him on the way to the Capitol as he cursed the slowness of his speechwriters—in which he startled millions of Americans by using the emotional slogan, "We shall overcome."

And after that speech I remember sitting with him in his living quarters as the White House operator fanned out long-distance calls all over the land.

"How did I do?" JOHNSON kept asking. He was a man who meant it when he talked about bringing Americans together, healing the nation's wounds, making this a land of equal opportunity. He wanted so badly to be reassured that what he had done that night was courageous, and good for all America.

Yet, I remember LYNDON B. JOHNSON as one of the most complicated men I ever met. He could seem petty, even mean, about trifling things and then display the broadest vision about the human needs of men and nations.

JOHNSON was at heart a sentimentalist—the kind of man who would weep in San Antonio during the 1964 campaign when an aged black man stood in the back of a pickup truck at a shopping center and said: "I'm a black man, born two blocks from this spot. I never dreamed I'd live to see the day when a Mexican congressman (Henry B. Gonzalez) would introduce me so I could ask you to vote for a white Texan for President."

And JOHNSON would dismiss his tears with the comment that "A man ain't worth a goddam if he can't cry at the right time."

I always felt that a lot of JOHNSON's toughness, even ruthlessness, was part of his effort to hide his sentimentality.

I felt that he waded deeper into Vietnam, and for a longer time, than his instincts and intellect dictated because he never wanted the Joint Chiefs of Staff to think they had a sentimental sissy in the White House. He seemed to want to say to Gen. Curtis LeMay: "I don't puff a one-foot cigar, but I'm as tough as you are."

There is special irony and tragedy in the coincidence that the war that killed JOHNSON politically should be grinding to a close just as the fates snuffed out his life completely.

There is double irony in the fact that he died on the eve of a White House campaign to erase much of the "Great Society" whose foundation JOHNSON built.

We have had our truce in the war on poverty; we have our moratoriums on federal subsidies for housing for the poor and middle classes; we have had vetoes of education bills and public works projects. We are told not to ask what government can do for us, but what we can do for ourselves.

There will be more of this. But not in 4 years nor 40 will they erase all that LYNDON JOHNSON did to change this society—not any more than they have been able to erase the mark of Franklin D. Roosevelt.

Maybe it's a little girl sleeping in a nightgown that won't go up in flames at the slightest spark—because JOHNSON *believed* in consumer protection; maybe it's a "hillbilly" girl who in June will become the first of her family ever to graduate from college—because JOHNSON *insisted* that higher education be put within reach of all; maybe it's a black family, walking into a motel in Mississippi tonight where in years past they would have been chased away—because JOHNSON wanted a public accommodations act sincerely enough to browbeat Congress into passing it.

I shall remember him as a man who, for all that Simon Legree posture he could assume, truly respected integrity of viewpoint. I shall never forget the time in India when he was irked at me for two or three days because I disagreed on a policy matter. JOHNSON returned from a session with Jawaharial Nehru and, apropos of nothing, said to me:

"You were right, goddammit, you were right."

As I fumbled for a modest reply he poked me in the chest and said, "Let me tell you something: It never hurts to get knocked down a few times for standing up for what you believe."

He walked perhaps 20 paces away, then turned sharply to shout: "But you'd know that, wouldn't you? Cause you've been getting knocked down all your life."

I knew then that, whatever else they might say, LYNDON JOHNSON was a man.

Hon. Barry M. Goldwater, Jr.
OF CALIFORNIA

Mr. Speaker, Mrs. Almena Lomax of Canoga Park, Calif., is a constituent of mine, and a reporter-staff writer for the San Francisco Examiner.

After the death of former President JOHNSON, Mrs. Lomax wrote an article that was included in the Examiner's coverage of President JOHNSON's death. She was uniquely qualified to write this piece, as she drew upon personal experience.

The article speaks for itself, and I would like to present it now:

WHAT JOHNSON DID FOR THE BLACKS

(By Almena Lomax)

Nine years ago is ancient history to young militants straining against the tensions of racial discrimination, oppression, and inequality of opportunity in urban ghettos today.

But nine years ago, July 2, 1964, LYNDON BAINES JOHNSON cut the ties of a bondage which were but one step removed from actual slavery, giving American Negroes the greatest push forward since Abraham Lincoln signed the Emancipation Proclamation 101 years before.

To any Negro who remembers pre-1964 America, LYNDON JOHNSON will always be regarded as the second Emancipator.

An instance in my life and that of my family will perhaps vividly illustrate this.

AUTO TRIP

On the night of July 2, 1964, I and my children were driving through Texas, running into detour after detour as we tried to reach Austin where there was a Negro-owned motel.

To any Negro traveling through the South and largely through the North before that day, getting to the Negro motel, hotel or the home of a friend, was important as the mode of transportation. Otherwise, one would find oneself spending the night in his car, or in a bus, railroad station or airport, all of which I have done because there was "no room in the inn" for a person of my race.

MONEY TALKS

San Franciscans are largely ignorant of this because money was usually as important as race in determining where a person could eat or sleep in this city.

But in Los Angeles where I grew up, married and reared six children, only famous concert artists like Marian Anderson could stay in downtown hotels, and then they had room service, until former Gov. Edmund G. Brown signed the 1958 fair employment practices law as his administration's first order of business.

The law didn't "take," however, in Southern California past San Bernardino and motorists usually went very fast through border towns like Blythe, called "a little bit of Texas" because, racially-speaking, it was a little bit of Texas.

LBJ RANCH

On that July 2 in 1964, traveling through Texas, we came to the gates of the LBJ Ranch.

It was almost midnight and the four youngest children were asleep, piled one on top of the other in the back seat.

My eldest daughter, Michele, alternated sleep with plucking her eyebrows—"My last touch with reality," she would say archly—throughout the five days of what was known as "another of Mother's journeys to the beginning."

There were five of them; I crossed Texas, all 880 miles of it 10 times in four years, either covering the civil rights struggle and trying to live down there where a responsive chord was struck in me, where, northernbred, though Texas-born, I had, and have, deep feelings that it all began for me down there.

As Michele burrowed sleepily into the shoulder of my eldest son, Michael, he looked angrily and sleepily at the big double gates of the LBJ Ranch and said, "I bet he's sleeping behind those very gates.

"We ought to knock on the door and ask him, 'Is you is, or is you ain't the President of all the people and where in this God-forsaken state can a black man lay his head?' "

MORE THAN DECENT

A little ways on, Michael, then 16 and nowhere near a militant, spoke again.

"Look, Mother," he said, "I'm not going to drive all over Austin looking for THE Negro Motel. I'm sleepy. You pull into the first half-way decent-looking motel you come to."

As the saying goes, I had heard the man.

I pulled into the first motel I came to when we reached Austin—it was more than half-way decent-looking, and Michael untangled his long legs from Michele's and we went into the office.

The clerk seemed to jump as he turned to face us in response to my "Good evening" but he replied, "Good evening."

Inwardly, I discounted that. White southerners will be polite even when they are doing something as monstrous as denying you a glass of water because of your race.

"I would like two connecting double rooms with two double beds for me and my family." I said.

"Yes, mam," he said promptly, and I could hear the tension drain out of my son's body.

I and the girls slept late, but the three boys got up and went swimming in the motel pool.

And all the little white children's parents called them out of the pool—but that had happened to the boys in Blythe where we had stayed overnight for car repairs.

When we had dressed and paid the bill to a blandly courteous clerk, we went to the coffee shop for brunch.

Enroute, I noticed Michele buy a copy of the Austin paper, take one look and fold it over quickly, with what I called her "Queen Nefertiti smile" of mystery on her face.

DINERS STARTLED

Inside the coffee room, several forkfuls of the blue plate special went past the holders' mouths into thin air as we sat down, but the waitress appeared promptly and willingly enough with the menus.

After we had ordered, Michele handed me the newspaper and I opened it.

"President Signs Civil Rights Act," the headline read. "Austin Will Resist."

From Austin on, that was a trip!

We decided on a first rate meal, rather than the fruit, carrots, candy, and soft drinks travelers between Negro accommodations customarily bought at grocery stores and gas stations after the shoe boxes of home-prepared lunch gave out on expeditions such as this.

We drove to the best looking motel in Beaumont, went into the dining room, and sat down while a white man led his family out, cursing "niggers" all the while.

The little blonde, bedizened waitress was a sport, however, and served us with a mixture of respect, satisfaction. and subdued excitement in her face.

V FOR VICTORY

After we were all set up and "boarding to beat the band," as Michael said, the Negro cook and dishwasher came and stood in the doorway and watched us, holding their fingers in the V-for-Victory sign, broad smiles on their faces.

In the five trips to Tuskegee, Eufaula, and Mobile, Ala., Albany and Atlanta, Ga., and back to Los Angeles, between 1961 and 1965, my kids integrated most of the restrooms of the gas stations on Highways 80 or 90.

They had a system. The youngest boy, who has my mother's blue eyes and auburn hair, would go first and get the "white key." Then his browner brothers would follow.

GIRLS, TOO

The youngest girl, who has the Mexican-Indian coloration of her paternal grandparents, would get the "white key" to the ladies' room, and her sisters would follow.

I have the strongest kidneys of man or beast and once drove from Eufaula, Ala., on the Georgia state line, across Alabama, Mississippi and to the Negro motel in Monroe, La., without moving from the driver's seat.

That was the Negro's lot before LYNDON JOHNSON, after watching George Wallace's mounted troopers ride women down on the Alabama River bridge to Selma, rared back and signed the greatest civil rights package—equal accommodations, voting rights, school desegregation, equal job opportunities—in the history of this country into law.

SIT-IN

In 1961, I and my children sat-in a Greyhound bus depot cafeteria in Big Spring, Tex., because the proprietor wouldn't serve us unless we went to the dingy lunch counter outside, reserved for Negroes.

Only July 8, 1964, thanks to LBJ, I and my family ate without incident in one of the finest French restaurants in Mobile.

When Martin Luther King was buried and I covered his funeral, I stayed in the finest hotel on Atlanta's famed Peachtree Street.

NEGRO TOWN

In 1961, when we went to Tuskegee, a predominantly Negro town, the downtown drugstore removed its seats rather than seat Negroes. The voting rolls were composed of dead, moved and infant white. Today, the town has a Negro mayor and a mixed City Council.

All of this came about because of LYNDON JOHNSON, a man who agonized, prayed, cried out, "Lord, let this cup pass me by," but then arose from his knees a bigger, stronger man and went before Congress and pledged, "We shall overcome."

Hon. Louis Stokes
OF OHIO

Mr. Speaker, I want to thank the distinguished gentleman from Texas, the dean of the House, for taking this special order to allow us to pay our respects to the late President JOHNSON.

LYNDON JOHNSON's record of service to the people of this country is unmatched. His years in the Congress were marked by a compassion for the common people of the Nation and by his exceptional skills as a legislator. Having risen to the leadership of the Senate and having sought his party's nomination for the Presidency, LYNDON JOHNSON accepted the vice-presidential nomination. He served brilliantly in that office and was extraordinarily well prepared for the awesome responsibilities of the Presidency.

As President, he directed his attention and all of the powers of his office for the cause of economic and social justice. It is not necessary to recount the major innovations in domestic programs which were created under his leadership. For the first time in our history, we had a President who put the needs of minority, poor, and disadvantaged people ahead of all other national priorities. His commitment to economic and social justice never flagged, and he used all of his talents as a leader to mobilize the Nation to build his visionary Great Society.

President JOHNSON understood, perhaps better than any other white political leader, the needs of black Americans. He listened to black leaders and to black people, and he dedicated himself to their cause.

Of all of his accomplishments, he was proudest of his civil rights legislation. With his passing we have lost a powerful ally, but more important we have lost a dear friend.

His memory will endure but it is up to us to build upon the programs he created. He recognized that his task was not finished. In his memory, we can do no less than our very best to bring about the economic and social justice for which he labored.

Hon. Clement J. Zablocki
OF WISCONSIN

Mr. Speaker, the recent passing of former President LYNDON B. JOHNSON was a tragic loss shared by all Americans. President JOHNSON was truly a formidable leader—a dynamic, vigorous, and forthright leader of men.

President JOHNSON came to the Presidency under conditions he did not desire or enjoy. Therefore as the first southern President in over 100 years he transcended the politics of regionalism and sought first what was best for the people of our Nation. Under his great leadership and with the cooperation of Congress he reaffirmed the strength and vitality of the American people and the stability of our political system. Certainly one of the high points of his public career was his "we shall overcome" speech on civil rights delivered to a joint session of Congress in 1964. It electrified the audience and gave a dramatic emphasis to JOHNSON's own commitment to civil rights—a commitment which had been previously questioned because of his southern background.

From my experience in Congress, President JOHNSON was one of the most easily accessible Presidents for Members of Congress to see and consult with. I recall an occasion during the early 1960's in which JOHNSON, then still the Vice President, was planning an appearance at a dinner in Milwaukee. In preparation for the event, he called together the entire Wisconsin delegation for our advice and counsel. After he had spoken his piece about what the visit was to accomplish he went around the table and asked each person to his views on the upcoming event. This episode epitomized his "let us reason together" approach and his reliance on local advice and counsel in his efforts to serve the people. On difficult and controversial matters he summoned congressional leaders usually on a bipartisan basis to consult and "reason together."

President JOHNSON firmly believed in the American dream—justice and equality for all Americans. In his quest to fulfill that dream, he launched the Great Society. Instead of progress and harmony at home, however, President JOHNSON was faced with seemingly irreconcilable division at home and a war in Asia. In an attempt to avert the growing division at home and to bring about an end to our involvement in Asia, President JOHNSON voluntarily declined to run for the Presidency in a final and courageous effort to bring our Nation together again.

At the time of his untimely passing, our Nation is still divided and responsible and effective leadership is still lacking although peace apparently seems to be at hand. It is a real pity that he was not able to hear the official ending of the war which brought him so much personal anguish and grief.

No President in modern times has assumed office under more unenviable conditions, nor has a President given so much of himself in spirit and in body to solve our Nation's problems. I am sure that the American people and history will remember LYNDON JOHNSON as one of our greatest leaders.

Mrs. Zablocki joins me in expressing our deepest sympathies to Mrs. Johnson and the family.

Hon. Wilbur D. Mills
OF ARKANSAS

Mr. Speaker, in the passing of LYNDON BAINES JOHNSON, the Nation has lost not only its remaining former Chief Executive, it has also lost a great public servant and a true friend of the people.

LYNDON JOHNSON first came to Washington in 1931 as a secretary to a Congressman. He left Washington in 1969 upon his retirement from the Presidency of the United States. During that 38-year period, he indelibly inscribed his mark on the pages of U.S. history. As a congressional staffer, Member of the House, U.S. Senator, majority leader of the Senate, and finally as President of the United States, he served this Nation well and faithfully.

Perhaps no other era in the life of this country has been as eventful and challenging for those in positions of leadership than these past four decades, encompassing the Great Depression, World War II, the Cold War, the Korean conflict, unprecedented domestic social upheaval, and Vietnam. LYNDON JOHNSON never shirked the awesome responsibilities that fell on his shoulders during these times. He gave the Nation his very best during his active public service and continued to serve as a source of sound advice and good counsel for this Nation and its leaders during his retirement years on his beloved ranch along the Pedernales River.

We all mourn the passing of this strong leader and great statesman from our midst.

Hon. Frank M. Clark
OF PENNSYLVANIA

Mr. Speaker, history will record the late LYNDON B. JOHNSON as a great President, a great humanitarian, and a forceful leader of his Nation in a time of great crisis.

As a Member of the House and as majority leader of the Senate, LYNDON JOHNSON was a zealous guardian of the rights and prerogatives of the legislative branch of our Government. As President, he respected the legislative processes.

Although he was known as a rough and tough politician who knew how to get results when toughness was needed, he was a great persuader whose sincerity was convincing. He was self-sacrificing to the extent that he voluntarily gave up the most powerful office in the world—that of President—when he failed to obtain a just and lasting peace in Vietnam.

LYNDON JOHNSON was the champion of the little man and the underprivileged and he pushed through Congress a mountain of legislation to help them. He fought for justice and equality for all Americans. It can truly be said that LYNDON JOHNSON, the man and the leader, was as big as his native State of Texas.

Hon. Olin E. Teague
OF TEXAS

Mr. Speaker, the Texas State Legislature on February 20, 1973, unanimously adopted a house concurrent resolution on the late LYNDON BAINES JOHNSON, 36th President of the United States which I desire to place in the Record at this point:

HOUSE CONCURRENT RESOLUTION No. 35

Whereas, A Life which was devoted to Honour and its Country, is no longer ours.

With the death of President LYNDON BAINES JOHNSON on January 22, 1973, Texas and the Nation lost one of its most distinguished sons and the World one of its greatest leaders. The loss is felt across the "flaming ramparts of the world."

We can look back upon the public services and exalted virtues of the deceased, without exclaiming in the anguish of despair . . . "Is he, too, numbered among the silent dead"? He who bore the anguish and travails of a war against aggression, to which he succeeded, is gone to the realms of eternal peace; and

Whereas, History already has built around him a name and a fame that will light the pathway of generations yet unborn for centuries to come. Patriotism and admiration will not let us forget his mighty stroke of compassion for his fellowman and his unswerving devotion to duty. His talents were employed on the side of righteousness and at whose approach oppressed humanity felt a secret rapture. It was thus that he sometimes soared so high and shone with a radiance so transcendent "as filled those around him with awe and gave to him the force and authority of a prophet." President JOHNSON lived a life characterized by splendid manhood—crowded with deeds and crowned with honours. He was superb in his effort to attain the goals to which he aspired. His actions vitalized the principle that "they fall, and they alone, who have not striven"; and

Whereas, This tall Texan—large as Texas, herself—a son of the picturesque and enchanting vistas of the Hill Country, which he dearly loved, coursed by the cool, clear waters of the meandering Pedernales River, inspired by the rugged land from which he sprang and in which his roots were laid deep, rose to the pinnacle of world fame upon the precepts and examples taught and set by his fond and loving mother, Mrs. Rebekah Baines Johnson, and his distinguished father, Honorable Sam Ealy Johnson, Jr. with encouragement from his loyal helpmeet of 38 years, the lovely "Lady Bird" Johnson; and

Whereas, Following his graduation from Southwest Texas State Teachers College, now Southwest Texas State University, at San Marcos in February, 1927, he taught school at Cotulla, Texas, before becoming an aide to the late Honorable Richard M. Kleberg, Sr., then United States Representative from Kingsville, thereby launching a public and political career spanning nearly 40 years of continuous, constructive service to his country and to the world. After serving as Director of the National Youth Administration in 1935, he was elected to the United States House of Representatives in 1937, in which he served with dedication to the ideals of his friend, President Franklin D. Roosevelt. Following a period of "seasoning" in the House, under the leadership of Speaker Rayburn, familiarly known as "Mr. Sam", with an interlude of courageous service in the United States Navy during World War II, he was elected to the United States Senate in 1948. By dint of hard work, coupled with his innate ability, his training, his skills and energy, he became the Majority Whip in 1950. Senator JOHNSON was chosen as Majority Leader in 1953, in which capacity he distinguished himself and demonstrated his dynamic leadership with his policy "reasoning" together. He was called the "most powerful man" in America, as he guided the Democratic-controlled United States Senate through a period of responsible cooperation with the Republican administration of President Eisenhower. It has been said that "JOHNSON was the Senate and the Senate was JOHNSON"; and

Whereas, With his acceptance of the nomination of his Party and his election to the Vice Presidency in 1960, Mr. JOHNSON served in that office with dignity, honour and loyalty while carrying out numerous-missions and responsibilities delegated to him by President Kennedy. Whatsoever his hand found to do, he did it with all his might.

The leadership of our country passed into the capable and experienced hands of President JOHNSON when President Kennedy succumbed to the assassin's lethal messenger. There was hope and assurance for America midst the sadness of the hour. His legislative, diplomatic, political and native abilities provided him with the experience and valuable knowledge peculiar to the Office of President of the United States, gained from his close association with Presidents Roosevelt, Truman, Eisenhower and as the "right arm" of President Kennedy, available to no other man on the American scene, to lead our country; and

Whereas, Among the many and varied proposals which became the law of the land during his administration are to be found greatly increased Federal Aid to Education,

Medicare and Medicaid, the 1964 Civil Rights Act, the 1965 Voting Act, the War on Poverty, to mention some. While President JOHNSON's public service was fraught with controversy—a characteristic of strong-willed and determined, dedicated men—nevertheless, his noblest motive was the public good. It may be said of him that he made many friends and lost very few. He made many enemies of the right kind and kept them all. He said that he could not prescribe a formula for success, but that the formula for failure is to try to please everybody. His success was due, largely, to his constancy of purpose; and

Whereas, President JOHNSON, like former President Truman, was plagued by a foreign conflict during which he strove to preserve the integrity of our treaty commitment, negotiated by a former administration and affirmed by subsequent action of the Congress with the adoption of the "Gulf of Tonkin Resolution." He believed that if America reneged on her agreement it would imperil many other nations and, consequently, jeopardize the peace of the world. He never wavered in his desire and efforts to bring about an honourable peace. President JOHNSON was in his day, a muchly maligned man. He knew that blatant demagoguery and a scurrilous press must be tolerated and borne by patriots. Comfort, however, could be found in the words of General Washington who said that "Real patriots who resist the intrigues of the favorite, are liable to become suspected and odious; while its tools and dupes usurp the applause and confidence of the people to surrender their interests"; and

Whereas, President JOHNSON's courage and patriotism were never more genuinely demonstrated than when, on March 31, 1968, he offered himself a willing sacrifice to the good of his country hopefully to end the Vietnam War with his decision not to become a candidate for re-election; and

Whereas, His private virtues, his public services, his great abilities, involuntarily excite the warmest feeling for him. In all the private relations of life he was honest, faithful, generous and humane and his heart was the seat of manly virtue.

His public services were many—splendid and great. His memory is enshrined in the esteem and affection of his contemporaries and will be consecrated by the gratitude of his country to future ages; and

Whereas, He may have had failings. On these let the tear that pities human weakness fall; on these let the veil which covers human frailty rest, since posterity is incurious about the minor faults of its heroes; and

Whereas, President JOHNSON was married to Miss Claudia Alta Taylor, familiarly known as "Lady Bird" on November 17, 1934, to which union was born two charming daughters, Lynda, now Mrs. Charles S. Robb of Charlottesville, Virginia, and Luci, now Mrs. Patrick J. Nugent of Austin, Texas, both of whom gave joy and delight to their doting father. President JOHNSON not infrequently said that the charming, intelligent and understanding companionship of "Lady Bird" profoundly influenced his course and career; and

Whereas, He was beloved by his friends, endeared to his family; the statesman, the patriot, is gone. At the fall of such a man, grief is silent and eloquence muses eulogiums which cannot be expressed. He has left us the remembrance of his greatness. As the gigantic figure that envelops men within the folds of his dark mantle, and even with the robe drawn about him. President JOHNSON seems so unshrouded that—

"Nothing can cover his high fame but heaven; No pyramids set off of his memories; But the eternal substance of his greatness; To which I leave him"; and

Whereas, This Concurrent Resolution was prepared at my request by Honorable Dorsey B. Hardeman, a former member of this body, a long-time member of the Senate and a friend of President and Mrs. Johnson for more than 30 years; now, therefore, be it

Resolved by the House of Representatives of the 63rd Legislature of the State of Texas, the Senate concurring, That they express their abiding sympathy to Mrs. Johnson and the surviving members of the family, and their admiration and gratitude for the life and contributions of the man whose simple dignity consisted not in possessing honours but in deserving them by his faith and his works through which he brought joy to his Creator; and, be it further

Resolved, That copies of this Resolution be forwarded to Mrs. Johnson and her daughters; to President Nixon and to all members of the Texas delegation in the Congress of the United States, by the Clerk of the House of Representatives, under the Seal of the House, and that the members of the House of Representatives and of the Senate devote this day to pious contemplation, suitable to the melancholy event which it commemorates and that pages in the respective Journals of each House of the 63rd Legislature of the State of Texas be set aside for preserving this Resolution in memory of President JOHNSON in the knowledge that men's homage and their love shall never cease to follow him.

Hon. Louis Frey, Jr.
OF FLORIDA

Mr. Speaker, President LYNDON BAINES JOHNSON revealed his traits of leadership by serving his Nation well in many varied and difficult times.

Surely, the most trying of the many years of public service were his last.

Those years, of course, were spent downtown—down Pennsylvania Avenue from this magnificent Capitol where his kind of politics was the practical and where his ability to get a bill through a balky Congress was well known by all.

Mr. JOHNSON took over the Presidency at a troubled and trying time—the Nation's leader had been slain and America was at war with an enemy it did not quite recognize.

President JOHNSON wrestled with the war daily, almost hourly while at the White House, and he kept in close touch with President Richard Nixon after he retired to Texas where it is said he often thought of the war and of the divisiveness it threatened to bring to America.

He learned of the nearness of peace in Vietnam only a few days before his death at his beloved ranch in the Texas foothills. We can be sure his joy at the news was not colored by thoughts of partisan politics, for LYNDON JOHN-

son, when it came down to the line for his country, was able to rise above that kind of politics.

Hon. Bo Ginn
OF GEORGIA

Mr. Speaker, the beginning of this year brought deep sorrow to our Nation with the death of LYNDON BAINES JOHNSON, our Nation's last living former President.

It was my great personal honor to have known LYNDON JOHNSON during the years of his Presidency. Although I extended my deepest sympathy to the Johnson family at the time of his death, I would like today to take this opportunity to join with the many other Members who have expressed, in the forum of the House, their sorrow at the passing of this outstanding man and public leader.

President JOHNSON was a friend of Georgia and of Georgians. During his 12 years in the House, he worked closely with our own distinguished Representative Carl Vinson in Mr. Vinson's efforts to bolster our national defense.

Upon his election to the Senate, Mr. JOHNSON formed an early friendship with the man I consider to be one of the greatest Senators in our Nation's history—Senator Richard B. Russell. When Senator Russell declined to accept the post of Senate whip in 1951, the position was opened to LYNDON JOHNSON, and his election to that position launched his rapid advancement within the leadership of the Senate.

The friendship of Senator Russell and LYNDON JOHNSON endured for decades, through Mr. JOHNSON's career in the Senate and then through all the years of his service as Vice President and as President.

LYNDON JOHNSON was a politician in the very highest sense of the word, a master of putting together a consensus and a skilled leader in the tactics of the legislative process. He understood the responsibilities of Members of Congress and he held them in respect.

I remember LYNDON JOHNSON as a warm and remarkable man, a man of enduring compassion and the willingness to take on any task and fight for what he believed to be right. He had an astounding ability of persuasion, and he used this ability to establish some of the most far-reaching programs in the history of our Government.

His decisions were based upon many things— his faith that the people of America would realize their promise and potential of equality for all, and his faith and trust in God's wisdom and guidance.

But the thing I remember most about President JOHNSON was his advice to new Members of Congress. He told them to always "vote for the people." I believe that LYNDON JOHNSON lived up to that promise, and I believe there can be no better epitaph for him than, "LYNDON JOHNSON, the man for the People."

Hon. William R. Cotter
OF CONNECTICUT

Mr. Speaker, many years will pass before historians can make the historical assessments of the life and Presidency of LYNDON BAINES JOHNSON. However, each person in this country can and should record his fresh and personal opinions of this great man, so that future historians will have the benefit of our perception of his great worth.

It was with a deep sorrow that I learned of the passing of LYNDON JOHNSON. This country lost not only a great leader; we lost a compassionate American. All those who had been sick and could not get medical care; all those who had been hungry and could not get food; all those who had been discriminated against and could not gain equality, all of these people lost a man who had fought all his life to aid them. LYNDON BAINES JOHNSON grew up in poverty and came to Washington in the midst of the depression. And from the days of the New Deal to the days of the Great Society, he worked to help those people, the forgotten Americans. As a Senator and as President LYNDON JOHNSON was a mover and a shaker. He moved this country to a closer commitment to its people in order to make the promise of America a reality. He shook from the Nation's laws all remaining forms of the racial discrimination which had scarred our history.

Let us not be content to honor LYNDON JOHNSON in words and memorials. Instead we must honor this man by continuing the commitment which he began. In his own words, "Let us continue."

Some have said that the death of LYNDON JOHNSON symbolically marks the end of the "can do" attitude that has characterized the American people. I hope that it will not die, but instead he channeled to serve the basic human instincts that characterized the life of LYNDON JOHNSON and the history of this great Nation.

Hon. Robert N. C. Nix
OF PENNSYLVANIA

Mr. Speaker, several weeks ago the Nation buried a national leader whose towering presence dominated political life for more than two decades.

LYNDON B. JOHNSON has been acclaimed by political leaders throughout the United States as one of the most powerful men in Congress while serving as a Senator and he will go down in the annals of history as a President who managed to put more social legislation through Congress than any other President since Franklin D. Roosevelt.

Mr. JOHNSON's skill in managing Congress both before he became Vice President and afterward when he was President, probably was unsurpassed in American history. His accomplishments on behalf of the minorities were a case of forcefully striking the iron while it was hot.

His programs intended to improve the position of the Nation's poor, its children, and its aged, particularly benefiting black Americans.

President JOHNSON was a big-hearted, loyal, impatient man. As a result of what he accomplished, the Nation, hopefully, will never again revert to the complacency which existed before, with regard to the poor and the black.

LYNDON JOHNSON had a dream; it was a dream of a society in which men are truly equal in opportunity and dignity. Every American begins life from the same starting line.

Whatever his faults, he was unique and a man who loved his fellow man. His presence will be missed and he will not be forgotten.

Hon. Shirley Chisholm
OF NEW YORK

Mr. Speaker, the smile on the face of a Job Corpsman who has just received his first job, the expression of happiness displayed by the mother of a Headstart child, and the pride seen in a black American who after 100 years of disenfranchisement votes for the first time—all serve as the greatest memorial to the man from Texas—LYNDON BAINES JOHNSON.

The untimely loss of this great President of the little people is deeply felt by us all. The fact that he rose from the reactionary southern resistance to the challenges of change—to become the greatest innovator of social change in modern America, indeed, marks the true greatness of President JOHNSON.

LYNDON JOHNSON was a unique man, a rare man who realized that the force of freedom is a never-ceasing and unstoppable force. He was a southerner, but yet refused as President to be bound by the tragedies of sectional hatred and regional perception.

There have been and will continue to be many comparisons made between President JOHNSON and his colleague in the Presidency, Abraham Lincoln. Many of these comparisons are valid. But a quality which Mr. JOHNSON possessed singularly was the ability to do what was right on the sole grounds that it was right.

His administration should not be remembered for the great amount of social legislation it produced and initiated as law. But rather it should be remembered, not in the annals of history, but in the lives of our people as having served as an agent of freedom's mission and a commander in the Nation's war with itself.

While it is customary to mark the passing of our national leaders with tribute and praise— LYNDON JOHNSON authored his own tribute by his steadfast determination to take his high office to the people and thereby allow them to govern. This tribute now serves and shall forever serve as a measuring stick for all of those who shall hold the Presidency of this land.

Hon. Don H. Clausen
OF CALIFORNIA

Mr. Speaker, I rise to join my colleagues in the House today in paying my personal respects to former President LYNDON BAINES JONHSON.

As we all know, the term "untimely passing" is often used at times such as this. Never, in my judgment, however, have those words been more fitting or had truer meaning than does the "untimely passing" of this man from Texas who gave nearly four decades of his lifetime to public service. With just 36 more hours of life, LYNDON JOHNSON would have learned that the peace he so desperately sought in Southeast Asia had finally become a reality.

I would like to believe that, given his knowledge of the situation and the turn of events during those last 48 hours before his passing, LYNDON JOHNSON knew that an end to America's involvement in Indochina had been realized.

I say this because it is my firm belief that no person on earth wanted an end to the war which he, too, inherited, more than did LYNDON JOHNSON. And, there is no doubt in mind that he was as much of a casualty of the Vietnam war as were those who served there because his agony and deep sense of frustration was as great, and perhaps greater, than their own.

LYNDON JOHNSON, as a Member of Congress and as our Chief Executive, participated in and was a leader throughout the period from the New Deal to the Great Society. His legacy in the field of domestic legislation and human rights is unparalleled in the annals of modern government and to him must go the credit for such landmark laws as the Civil Rights Act of 1964, the Housing and Urban Development Act and a host of new Federal programs dealing with education, aid for the indigent, economic opportunities, and voting rights.

In August of 1969 I was able to suggest and play a part in bringing the Nixon and Johnson families together for the formal dedication of the Redwood National Park in my congressional district. It was a day that will never fade in my memory of the man we all knew as L. B. J. Its purpose was not only to bring these two first families together on what I believe will be a historic day for the redwood empire of California, but to recognize Mrs. Johnson's unselfish and untiring work on behalf of preserving and enhancing our national heritage. It was also President JOHNSON's birthday and speaking without notes or a prepared text, he spoke not of his years in Congress or the White House, but of his deep sense of gratitude that people still cared enough to honor him in this way.

That was the last time I was to see President JOHNSON—a man as tall as the giant redwood trees that held him in awe that warm summer day in 1969. As was said of him in an editorial in the Washington Post:

The simple, inescapable fact is that he cared—and that it showed.

Hon. Frank J. Brasco
OF NEW YORK

Mr. Speaker, LYNDON BAINES JOHNSON never did anything by halves, and even those who opposed him will admit that, Mr. Speaker. He lived life to the hilt, using great ability to do great things.

His vision of America was a western populist's, tinged with the Deep South in more than a peripheral manner. One of the finest tributes to this President was that he rose above sectionalism when the times called for it, and the laws on our statute books proclaiming equality for all Americans will forever testify to his labors.

He was a leader at a time when we needed it, whether it be in the Senate or in the White House. Legislation moved through the Upper Chamber under his hand in a workmanlike fashion, although a few egos got trampled in the process.

L. B. J. grew to understand the give and take of Congress and of our legislative system. If ever someone was educated in the legislative branch of Government to lead the executive branch, it was this man.

When Jack Kennedy was foully murdered, he instinctively did the correct thing to keep the Government of this country viable and moving. He gave us continuity in a time of unparalleled turbulence. And from that short, hectic era emerged some of the finest pieces of domestic legislation in this Republic's history.

For an exciting time there, progress could be measured in miles rather than inches, as a responsive Congress gave this impatient President what he felt was needed to make the American dream viable for all of us, especially those who had been shortchanged over the course of our history.

Many did not agree with him. Others disliked him. But no one could be neutral about this President, who was truly of America's basic essence. History will have to judge in the end what the true balance really is. LYNDON JOHNSON is dead now, but he will not be forgotten.

Not by the people he tried to help. Not by those who got a fresh start in life because of one of his programs. Not by those who saw tangible evidence that their Government cared through for them to reach out in a variety of ways.

Every imprint he made was a huge one, in keeping with his heritage and personal way of life. Many of those marks are on America to stay for good, one way or another. He was not a sophisticated man in the drawing room sense of the term, and perhaps that was a great source of his strength. America, no matter how a few may try, will never be a drawing room society, replete with the trappings and pretensions of aristocracy. LYNDON JOHNSON understood that, because he reached out to those he came from; the man and woman who are salt of the earth—the man and woman, if you please, who make America move and prevail.

LYNDON JOHNSON did not labor in vain. He lifted millions of our people to a better plane of existence. And he believed in this Nation and its promise. And he did his level best, his damndest, if you will to lift our society in a material and spiritual sense. Who dares to claim that he failed? His like shall not pass this way again.

Those boots are one of a kind. He shall be remembered with warmth and respect. History shall be both fair and kind to him. He was, in his own way, a friend to all those who shared his love for our Nation and its ideals.

Hon. Bob Eckhardt
OF TEXAS

Mr. Speaker, the whole tapestry of words fashioned upon President JOHNSON's death still did not adequately depict the real man who fascinated this Nation for a quarter of a century and tried to move it in the direction of a great society. Nor can the words I speak here do so. The satisfaction he sought in life, and which this country grants him unanimously in death, is that of being the one man who advanced civil rights in this century as no other since President Lincoln.

Reporters, intellectuals, historians, and colleagues have written countless words about LYNDON JOHNSON. None stated so well what he was striving for as did a young black man from the South named Lafayette Haynes. Mr. Haynes wrote a column for the Boston Globe about his feelings concerning the death of President JOHNSON. Mr. JOHNSON would have appreciated it. He would have been so proud to know that a young man who is too young to remember his efforts in 1957 in passing the first civil rights bill in a century would benefit and grow from his efforts and would one day write so perceptively about them.

Mr. Speaker, I submit Mr. Haynes' article which appeared in the Boston Globe shortly after the President's death:

HE DARED AS NO OTHER FOR BLACKS

(By Lafayette Haynes)

I never personally knew LYNDON JOHNSON, but in many respects I was part of his history.

I never really had a concern for the war in Vietnam when all the white kids at my school were protesting JOHNSON's escalation of the war through bombing.

Now I am older and my views of Vietnam have changed considerably, but I would not venture to measure the greatness of LBJ or his flaws on the war. But as a Southerner and a black man there are measurements of feeling that LYNDON JOHNSON had a great deal to do with.

When John Kennedy was killed in 1963, most of the black kids my age were scared to go to a hamburger stand because we didn't expect all those northern liberals to come speeding down to Baton Rouge to keep us from getting our asses kicked after their leader had died.

LYNDON JOHNSON was sworn in and there was no doubt in my mind that the rednecks were back in business.

I was wrong. To the rednecks LYNDON JOHNSON was just as much a "pinkie commie" as his proper talking predecessor. And while whites north and south were trying to divert JOHNSON's civil rights effort, blacks were getting angry and challenging everything the President said we had a right to do.

At one point I and a few of my high school teammates had the audacity to tell L.S.U. we had a right to have football scholarships.

Blacks had reached a point where nothing could deny them their right to be "whatever in the hell they wanted to be." In retrospect it is difficult to say if going to a burger stand and having your food spit on or sitting in your car and having a group of white youths speed by shooting the finger at you, were important.

But it was important. And underneath the surge of black Americans was this sullen talking Texan telling white America it had perpetrated injustices on black Americans.

JOHNSON more importantly translated to the southern white man that he, the southern white, for social justice to be evident, would have to lead America. JOHNSON's efforts left him alone holding the country together when no other white dared take the steps he did for black America.

What is left of JOHNSON's legacy is left in places in the South where men never had any difficulty in saying what they felt about each other. A great part of the legacy is an honesty LYNDON JOHNSON felt was rooted in white southerners to make the dream of equality true for all men in America.

When I sat in the president's office at Southern Methodist University in 1968 protesting injustices, I asked myself as I do now what led me to waste my energies fighting rednecks in the heart of Texas.

It was probably because LYNDON JOHNSON had made it a part of my own destiny; a necessary element in resolving this nation's race issue. An issue LYNDON JOHNSON raised because he was a sincere American, but also a deeply rooted southerner who refused to turn his back on it.

JOHNSON was the kind of man I could look at and in a slow drawl call a "son of a bitch" and expect a warm handshake.

It is different when you are a southerner because insult becomes a salutation of manhood.

Hon. Thomas M. Rees
OF CALIFORNIA

Mr. Speaker, all of us mourned the death of President LYNDON JOHNSON. Whether we agreed with him or not, we were continuously impressed with his boundless energy in assuming the great responsibilities which he had, not only as President of the United States; but as Senate majority leader and before that as a Member of the House. It is tragic that the impossible situation of Vietnam has blurred our vision of the accomplishments and the greatness of this man. The ideals he fought for as an officeholder, he also fought for as a retired President.

In his last speech in Austin, Tex., in January, speaking not from prepared notes, but from his heart, he again reached the conscience of Americans:

To be black—to one who is black—is to be proud, to be worthy, to be honorable. But to be black in a white society is not to stand on level ground. While the races may stand side by side, whites stand on history's mountain and blacks stand in history's hollow. Unless we overcome unequal history, we cannot overcome unequal opportunity. That is not—nor will it ever be—an easy goal to achieve.

Much of what has been done during the last 20 years to bring our country together and to mold our citizenry into a cohesive whole bears the mark of LYNDON JOHNSON. He shall not be forgotten, for the good that he accomplished will long remain with us.

Hon. Harley O. Staggers
OF WEST VIRGINIA

Mr. Speaker, Dante wrote:

Be as a tower, that, firmly set
Shakes not its top for any blast that blows.

The age which seems to be passing into history has been an age of strong men. Strong men inevitably polarize public opinion. They arouse bitter antagonism or strong loyalties. The antagonists are seldom sure whether their opposition is directed against the man or against his acts.

But, says Walter Lippmann:

The man must die in his appointed time. He must carry away with him the magic of his presence and that personal mastery of affairs which no man, however gifted by nature, can acquire except in the relentless struggle with evil and blind chance. Then comes the proof of whether his work will endure, and the test of how well he led his people.

The towering figure of LYNDON JOHNSON has passed untimely from the scene. No longer can his physical presence create passionate resistance or blind acceptance. Already there is beginning to emerge a clearer picture of the relentless pressures which brought American society to the boiling point in the age of Johnson. In the words of Lowell:

It is out of that inaccessible tower of the past that Longing leans and beckons.

For Longing must understand and evaluate the stresses of the era in which President JOHNSON moved and which he, in large part, resolved and restructured into a viable society. In the half century which covered the career of LYNDON JOHNSON, the fountains of the great deep were broken up, and new ideas surged to the surface. Those ideas were in conflict with the social and economic wisdom of the past. Were they indeed evil, as many argued, or were they an enlargement of the American dream?

The world in which our children are born today is almost as far removed from the world which their grandparents knew and endured or loved, as the case may be, as are the Middle Ages of European history. Is it necessary to itemize the social changes which are firmly established in everyday life—civil rights, social security, the extension of the franchise, distribution of the products of industry? Or achievements in the world of science and industry? Or in the field of health service? I would not so fret you.

If, however, full and complete lists of all changes which have come to benefit men of all ranks and classes were made, it would be found, I believe, that LYNDON JOHNSON's name would be found in undeviating support of all.

Wise statesmen are those who foresee what time is bringing, and endeavor to shape institutions and to mold men's thoughts and purposes in accordance with the change that is silently surrounding them.—Morley

Such a leader lifts his times out of the limits of the night and brings them into the light of true acceptance of our common humanity. "To endure is greater than to dare," writes Thackery. "To tire out hostile fortune; to be daunted by no difficulty; to keep heart when all have lost it; to go through intrigue spotless; to forego even ambition when the end is gained—who can say this is not greatness?" "Amid life's quests, there seems only one worthy one: to do men good."

This is the tribute I would offer with the utmost sincerity to the memory of President LYNDON JOHNSON whose name will illuminate the proudest pages of history as the years pass into centuries. I am honored to have been a member of LYNDON JOHNSON's host of admirers. I am proud that I have been privileged to support him in his efforts to build a better America.

LYNDON JOHNSON is no longer with us in the flesh. But his warm personality hovers over us like a protecting spirit. I was his friend, and I did not have to guess it. Perhaps the surest evidence of greatness is the ability to win a wide circle of enduring friends. To such a circle I am happy to belong. When all animosities have been dissolved by time, I am sure that circle may include most loyal Americans.

Hon. Charles A. Vanik
OF OHIO

Mr. Speaker, LYNDON JOHNSON, our 36th President, was a man uniquely endowed with the virtue of impatience. He was impatient with the racism which poisons our national spirit. He was impatient with all forms of intolerance. He was impatient with economic injustice which keeps millions in this country living in poverty. He was impatient with the prejudices which prevent some of our citizens from living with dignity and humanity. Above all, LYNDON JOHNSON was impatient with our national complacence. He could not understand how a country so rich could deny to some of its citizens a full measure of that richness.

He was a person impatient with the illness of American society. Only his ideal, Franklin Delano Roosevelt, exceeded his monumental program of social gains—the Civil Rights Act, medicare, the education programs, and Headstart.

But LYNDON JOHNSON's Great Society was not merely a conglomeration of legislative programs. LYNDON JOHNSON's dreams have become our dreams; his goals, our goals. In 1965, President JOHNSON addressed the commencement class at Howard University with these words:

Our earth is the home of revolution. In every corner of the continent, men charged with hope contend in ancient ways in the pursuit of justice. They reach for the newest of weapons to realize the oldest of dreams, that each may walk in freedom and pride, stretching his talents, enjoying the fruits of the earth.

I was with President LYNDON JOHNSON at the signing of the medicare bill in the Truman Library in Independence, Mo., and I never saw a happier man. If it were not for the Vietnam war, he might have entirely succeeded in winning the war against poverty and intolerance.

As for now, even the tragedy of Vietnam cannot obscure the essential humanity of the man. Historians will debate for years his role in that conflict; but we should not allow this debate to detract from the contributions that LYNDON JOHNSON made to all Americans. Without the efforts of

LYNDON JOHNSON, millions of aged would be without medical care; millions of blacks would remain in the political back waters; millions of poor children would be deprived of the opportunity to overcome their disadvantage through a program of preschool education; and millions of other young citizens would be deprived of continuing their education beyond the secondary level.

In the end we should look at the life of LYNDON JOHNSON as an ideal to which we must continually rededicate ourselves. His words will serve as an inspiration to us in our time of doubt, our hour of despair. His call will be remembered by all men devoted to the elimination of human suffering.

Hon. Ella T. Grasso
OF CONNECTICUT

Mr. Speaker, LYNDON BAINES JOHNSON, the man, is gone from us, but his great achievements remain a living monument of dedicated service to the Nation and people he loved.

He had great gifts and a vision of what the Nation and world should be. His powers of persuasion, his shrewdness, and skill at engaging compromise which long ago became legendary made him one of the great leaders and legislators of his day. As Congressman, Senator, majority leader, Vice President, and President, he proved himself to be a dedicated public servant.

LYNDON JOHNSON was a towering physical presence. That presence was still more towering when measured by his vitality and dynamism, courage, and spirit. And let us not forget his abiding compassion that encompassed the world. LYNDON JOHNSON was a man who was committed to the emancipation of the downtrodden and the freedom of the oppressed.

In 1964, the President said that he wanted "a happy nation, not a harassed people—a people who are fearless instead of fearful—men . . . concerned always with the wants and needs of their fellow human beings." He showed that this was his credo as he pressed for the 1964 Civil Rights Act which made public accommodations truly public by opening them to all Americans regardless of color. "We have talked long enough in this country about equal rights," he said in his first speech to Congress as President. "We have talked for 100 years or more. It is time now to write it in the books of law."

Again, his devotion and drive played a significant role in achieving the 1965 Voting Rights Act which assured every citizen the right to vote for the candidate of his choice, and the 1968 Fair Housing Act which gave every individual, regardless of color, the right to live in any house he could afford. Communications established between the White House and Congress paved the way for landmark legislation in the fields of education and housing for the poor, help for the disadvantaged and the elderly. Medicare has been a godsend to millions of our older citizens. Also, it was President JOHNSON who began the present urgent drive to clean up the country's water and air.

LYNDON JOHNSON has returned to the banks of his beloved Pedernales where he began a remarkable life rich in achievement. Indeed, the catalog of his domestic accomplishments is proof positive that under his leadership visions did not remain dreams; they became concrete realities bringing Americans closer to true freedom than ever before.

Hon. William R. Roy
OF KANSAS

Mr. Speaker, LYNDON JOHNSON loved this land with a fierce Texas passion.

This love led him into public life and motivated him to achieve great things for his fellow countrymen.

His place in American history is secure. Often through sheer force of will, he rewrote the domestic programs of our Government and provided millions of Americans with better health care, better education, better housing, better nutrition, better recreation, an a better life than they had ever had before.

In health care, for example, much of the work that we in Congress do today is but an elaboration and enlargement on basic programs enacted during the Johnson years.

He was a President from the South, but he fought vigorously on behalf of equal rights for all the citizens of this Nation.

The Civil Rights Act of 1964, the Voting Rights Act, Federal aid to education and medicare are fitting memorials to his Presidency.

He was a great American. And if he did not achieve the Great Society that he so diligently sought, he brought the United States closer to that dream than we have ever been.

Hon. James W. Symington
OF MISSOURI

Mr. Speaker, as one who was privileged not only to know President LYNDON JOHNSON for many years but also to work with and for him for a considerable period of time, I wish to join my colleagues in expressing great sorrow at his loss and great thanks for his life.

There is little that I can add to the outpouring of reminiscences and proud recollections of his titanic public career. There is so much that each of us has to be grateful for that he gave to his State, his country and the world.

So I would like to share simply one vivid memory of the man at his best. We were bidding farewell to President Cemal Gursel of Turkey who had been here for treatment in 1966. President Gursel was unconscious and suffering from a terminal illness. It was the desire of his government and his family that he should die on Turkish soil. President JOHNSON learning of this immediately authorized the use of Air Force One for this purpose. The President attended the subdued ceremonies at the airport and noticed President Gursel's adopted child weeping to one side of the plane and unattended. He went to her side and conducted her gently to the plane with his arm around her, giving consoling words of comfort.

When all the captains and the kings have departed and the memory of their great works begins to recede this is the man I feel should be remembered by us all as indeed I know he forever will be by those who knew and loved him the most, his incomparable widow and devoted and loving children.

Hon. Al Ullman
OF OREGON

Mr. Speaker, I rise to pay tribute to a great leader, the 36th President of the United States, LYNDON BAINES JOHNSON. As a Congressman, Senator, majority leader of the Senate, Vice President, and President, everything he did was based on his feeling of what was best for the Nation. He was a totally dedicated American.

The tragedy of his Presidency was that he wanted to be a great peacetime President and the architect of a great society. But fate and history made him a wartime President. And the final irony was that he died 1 day before the settlement of the terrible war that defeated him.

I met briefly with LYNDON JOHNSON just 2 weeks before his death. We were attending the memorial service for Hale Boggs in New Orleans. Despite differences we had over the war and whether we could have guns and butter, I will always remember his tremendous capacity for compassion and his ability to get along with and lead his peers.

LYNDON JOHNSON will, of course, be remembered for many great achievements. As a Southern Senator, he negotiated the compromises necessary to achieve enactment of the 1957 Civil Rights Act. As President, he signed four landmark civil rights bills into law—the 1964 Civil Rights Act, the Voting Rights Act of 1955, the Jury Selection Act of 1968, and the Open Housing Act of 1968. His leadership helped bring medicare in 1965, aid to elementary education, Federal antipollution laws, and many other major pieces of domestic reform.

History will list his achievements, but his accomplishments are best expressed in the changes he brought to the lives of so many—the aged who may live out their lives a little more comfortably, the disadvantaged children who may receive a better education, black citizens who may exercise their right to vote. Though many may enjoy these benefits unaware of the man who engineered them, his influence, nevertheless, cannot really die.

Hon. Delbert L. Latta
OF OHIO

Mr. Speaker, I would like to associate myself with the remarks of my colleagues on both sides of the aisle who have expressed their sorrow at the passing of LYNDON JOHNSON.

To those of my persuasion, who opposed him on many issues while supporting him on others, President JOHNSON will be remembered as a superb legislative tactician. His breadth of experience and intimate knowledge of the legislative process, gained through his many years of service in both the House of Representatives and the Senate, served him effectively when he became Chief Executive.

Political life is not without its ironies, and no better example of this in recent years can be found than in the pressures of events surrounding President JOHNSON's latter days in office.

Despite resounding domestic legislative triumphs, it was his steadfast pursuit of what he conceived to be the best interests of the United States in the Vietnam conflict which led to his voluntary retirement from public life. How gratifying it must have been, shortly before his death, for him to have had the personal assurance of President Nixon that peace with honor was at hand.

I want to join all my colleagues in expressing my sincere sympathy to his widow, Lady Bird Johnson, and to his daughters and their families.

Hon. John W. Wydler
OF NEW YORK

Mr. Speaker, President JOHNSON, in my opinion, will go down in history as a great and good man and as an outstanding President of our Nation. History, I believe, will treat him most kindly and he deserves that treatment. I first met him as a freshman Member of Congress, when he, as Vice President, invited me and my wife to his home. It was an indication of the type of hospitality he was always famous for, and that first party was the best one I ever attended in Washington. During his years in the White House I disagreed with him on many occasions, but found him a strong man and one who made no secret of his direction or intentions. His relationship with the Congress was magnificent, for he was of the Congress himself and understood it and its membership well. I will always be glad that some of the years I spent as a Member of Congress were spent while he was the President of our Nation.

Hon. Richard C. White
OF TEXAS

Mr. Speaker, undoubtedly, President LYNDON B. JOHNSON will be treated more kindly by history than he was by some of his contemporaries. History will eventually recognize him as the singularly accomplished leader that I have always known him to be.

My own personal observation of him was that he was a man of great intellect, character, and integrity, far beyond that for which he was accredited by many Americans or by the journalists who were misled by his style. The accent of his Texas rearing misled those who equated his outward easy-going Texas demeanor and drawl with dawdling performance. His mind could assimilate complex and diverse facts into a plan of overt action.

LYNDON JOHNSON reserved intense loyalty for those who had served him or had proven their friendship to him. He also knew his detractors and made allowances for them on the chessboard of his career.

Few men in public office can boast the personal achievements and landmark legislation that is the legacy of President Johnson. His successes have been comprehensively cataloged in the many eulogies authored in his memory. In domestic affairs, his Presidency is unsurpassed—accomplished through the same relentless personal effort that characterized his famed tenure as Senate majority leader. In international affairs, I would stress that it was President JOHNSON who opened avenues to closer accord with those countries which were traditionally antagonistic. It was he who paved the way to future peace and successful foreign policy.

The accomplishments of his domestic and international efforts have been clouded by the sad involvement of our Nation in the Vietnam conflict.

It is perhaps for another era to judge whether he and other Presidents who followed the same course were right or not. Regardless of future judgment, he followed courageously the path he thought was best despite public criticism.

A number of us know why President JOHNSON chose not to run for his second term. It had nothing to do with a fear that he might be rejected, and few believe he could have been defeated. Having suffered the unhappy experience of knitting together a Nation whose President had died in office, LYNDON JOHNSON did not want to put this Nation, or a successor to himself, through the same traumatic situation for a second time in the same generation. He was well aware of his own health problems and he realized the chances of living through a second full term were not good.

Beside him throughout his adult life was one of the finest women who has ever accompanied her husband through the trials of public life. He and Ladybird Johnson formed a superb team to the lasting advantage of this country. She is a lady of great depth whose stature will also grow with developing history.

The accolades that have been extended to President JOHNSON and his family are genuine and well deserved. Of one thing I am also certain: No one will ever review his record and accomplishments without feeling the excitement and the movement which surrounded all he did. To him life was action and he lived.

Hon E de la Garza
OF TEXAS

Mr. Speaker, memories of LYNDON JOHNSON will abound as long as there are those around who touched the perimeter in which this great man lived.

One who knew him well and served him diligently for years was Booth Mooney—well-known author, newspaperman, and President JOHNSON's executive assistant while he was democratic floor leader in the Senate.

One of the Nation's finest newspapers, the Detroit Free Press, mindful of the Mooney connection with then Senator JOHNSON, asked him to do the main piece on a special section the paper put out after the President's untimely death. This is such a tender, understanding article that all who ever knew President JOHNSON would want to read it—and I would want to share it.

Mr. Speaker, here is what Booth Mooney wrote about the man whose first biography, "The LYNDON JOHNSON Story," he wrote:

LYNDON BAINES JOHNSON: AUGUST 27, 1908– JANUARY 22, 1973

(By Booth Mooney)

LYNDON BAINES JOHNSON was always a man in a hurry.

Before he assumed the presidency, he had served 12 years in the United States Senate and 12 in the House of Representatives. Earlier, as a young congressional assistant, he witnessed, and on the fringes participated in, the first 100 days of Franklin D. Roosevelt. He entered the House as one of FDR's favorites.

He experienced the trying and sometimes traumatic years of Harry S Truman's regime, the quiet and confident years with Dwight D. Eisenhower, the too-few years of hope culminating in anguished tragedy with John F. Kennedy and finally, his own administration, which ended for him and the country with a deep sense of frustration.

Running all the way.

LYNDON JOHNSON came into the world on Aug. 27, 1908, on a farm in the rugged hill country of Texas, the first of five children born to Samuel Ealy and Rebekah Baines Johnson. His father was a member of the Texas legislature, so LYNDON was exposed to talk of politics from an early age.

After graduating from high school and Southwest Texas State Teachers College, he taught school for a year before going to Washington in 1931 to become secretary to a newly elected congressman, a family friend, Rep. Richard M. Kleberg.

In the capital city, he benefitted from the friendship of Rep. Sam Rayburn, who had served in the Texas legislature with his father. Rayburn was rising to a position of great power in Washington.

Arthur C. Perry, an old Washington hand who at that time was secretary to Senator Tom Connally of Texas, recalled that the newcomer made an immediate impact on the group of established congressional secretaries.

"I remember when Dick Kleberg brought LYNDON around to our office and told me he wished I would teach his new secretary everything I knew and show him how to find his way around Washington," Perry said. "LYNDON started asking questions as soon as he knew my name. He followed the same procedure with everyone else he met. He set out to learn all he could and learn it fast."

"You never had to tell him anything a second time," Perry said. "This skinny, 6-foot-3 boy was as green as anybody could be, but within a few months he knew how to operate in Washington better than some who had been here 20 years before him."

After Roosevelt was elected President in 1932, Rayburn brought his young fellow-Texan into contact with key men in the New Deal and eventually with the President himself.

Elected a member of the House on April 10, 1937, he was reelected for five successive terms. In 1941 he was a candidate for the U.S. Senate in a special election, but did not win. It was the only election he ever lost.

On Dec. 8, 1941, as war was declared between the United States and Japan, JOHNSON, a member of the Naval Reserve, asked to be placed on active duty. He was the first member of the House to go into uniform. He served for eight months, with the rank of lieutenant commander, before FDR ordered all members of Congress in military service to return to their duties in Washington.

In 1948 JOHNSON entered the Texas Democratic primary as a candidate for the U.S. Senate. He won the nomination by a majority of only 87 votes out of more than a million cast, and there were cries of fraud. But his nomination prevailed, and in the general election he defeated his Republican opponent by a two-to-one majority. On Jan. 3, 1948, he became a member of the Senate.

Assigned to a major committee, the one on Armed Services, the freshman senator gave close attention to the state of the nation's military establishment. In 1950, as the Korean police action began, he introduced and the Senate passed a resolution establishing the Preparedness Investigating Subcommittee.

JOHNSON became its chairman and conducted a series of investigations of defense costs and efficiency.

These investigations brought him to national attention for the first time. They also earned the respect of senior members of the Senate, in particular such southern veterans as Richard B. Russell and Walter George of Georgia, and this was most important to a young senator. It meant he was being accepted in the Senate's "inner club."

A side effect of Dwight D. Eisenhower's sweeping 1952 victory was the defeat out in Arizona of Senate Democratic leader Ernest McFarland. When the Democratic senators no longer a majority, met in their first-of-the-session conference in Washington in January 1953, JOHNSON was unanimously elected floor leader. At age 44, he was the youngest man ever to be named to that position by either major party.

The Democratic Party was disorganized, deeply in debt, and without effectual national leadership. A schism had long existed between the southern and northern wings. Recriminations over the manner in which the losing presidential campaign had been waged were still being hurled back and forth.

JOHNSON set out to quiet the quarreling and to bring unity among his Senate Democrats. He succeeded. His tactics embraced a potent mixture of full consideration of all points of view, tact, persuasion, a policy of giving freshmen senators choice committee assignments, thus assuring their support of his leadership—and personal hard work.

At times he conducted business on the run—literally.

One afternoon, a staff member recalled, he and the senator left the Senate Office Building to go over to the other side of the Capitol to record a radio broadcast. JOHNSON's car was parked no more than a dozen feet from the door of the building. But he literally sprinted the short distance. It was that way with everything he did.

"LYNDON," his wife complained, although not bitterly, "acts like there's never going to be a tomorrow."

JOHNSON was reelected to the Senate in 1954, after having piled up a three-to-one majority over his opponent in the Democratic primary. In that year Democrats regained control of both houses of Congress, and he advanced from minority to majority floor leader in the Senate.

Friend and foe alike agreed that he turned in a dazzling performance in this role.

The "Johnson treatment" became a joyous byword in the congressional cloakrooms and at Washington cocktail parties. The gossips revelled in telling each other stories about JOHNSON—the compulsive talker, the waver of arms in the air, the wheeler-dealer of politics, the operator who could turn on charm and voice implied threats with equal facility. All to get the job at hand done.

He drove himself and his Democratic colleagues—and at times his Republican colleagues as well—in a way not previously known in the august Senate. And he became the most powerful majority leader in the history of that institution.

Much of his strength grew out of the fact that he was, in the largest sense, nonpartisan. He cooperated fully with the Republican President Eisenhower.

One of his notable achievements was to bring about passage of the first civil rights bill to get through the Senate since Reconstruction. That feat came in 1957 at a time when racial unrest was rising throughout the nation.

JOHNSON and House Speaker Sam Rayburn consulted with Eisenhower to an extent unknown to few Democrats and perhaps to no Republicans. The two men from Congress often journeyed to the White House, a mile distant, to talk informally over drinks with the President. These easy sessions, nobody pressuring anybody else, paved the way for congressional approval of more than one important legislative measure.

JOHNSON poured greater physical energy into his job than any other man on Capitol Hill. Even after he suffered a massive heart attack in July 1955, he bounced back after a reasonable period of convalescence. He shed 45 of his 220 pounds and, six months after the attack, returned to work. And he worked as long and hard as ever.

His great success as Senate majority leader led to widespread mention of JOHNSON as a possible Democratic presidential candidate. He was Texas' favorite son at the party's national convention in 1956.

It was not until 1960, however, that he made a serious bid for the nomination. It failed. He received 409 votes for President on the first and only ballot at the Los Angeles convention. John F. Kennedy was the choice of most.

On the following day, July 14, JOHNSON was nominated for vice president by acclamation, having been personally chosen by Kennedy as a running mate. The Kennedy-JOHNSON ticket was elected in November by the closest popular vote margin of any presidential election up to that time in the 20th century.

The years JOHNSON served as vice president were trying for the vigorous Texan. The glamorous Kennedys and their court were the rage in Washington. JOHNSON out of style, did not have enough to do. He spent much time in unaccustomed and uncomfortable loneliness in his richly appointed office.

A compassionate newspaper correspondent recalled an hour-long visit there with the vice president. No one waited to see him in the anteroom, the newsman reported. He received precisely one telephone call during the hour the visitor was present. It was a painful letdown for a man who thrived on excitement, action and achievement.

The situation changed with stunning abruptness.

On a Friday afternoon, Nov. 22, 1963, John F. Kennedy became the fourth American President to die at the hands of an assassin. From the window of a warehouse in Dallas, a sniper fired two bullets in the President's head and body as the Chief Executive rode through the streets of the Texas city.

Ninety-nine minutes later, JOHNSON, his face heavy with grief, took the oath of office as President. The brief ceremony, with his wife and Mrs. Kennedy beside him, was held on Air Force One as it sat on the runway at Love Field in Dallas.

Flown immediately to Washington, JOHNSON spoke briefly at the airport in a message carried to the shocked nation by television.

This is what he said: "This is a sad time for all people. We have suffered a loss that cannot be weighed. For me it is a deep personal tragedy. I know the world shares in the sorrow that Mrs. Kennedy and her family bear.

"I will do my best. That is all I can do. I ask for your help and God's."

The new President moved swiftly to calm the fear that Kennedy's assassination had created. He was at once reassuring and commanding. He set the tone by entreating, "Let us continue," and the country responded.

"I have a feeling," JOHNSON wrote a friend, "that the tragedy of Nov. 22 marked a turning point in American history. The dissension in our land will, hopefully, give way to a new unity—a new reasonableness that will mark the beginning of an era of progress."

The year of 1964 was supremely LYNDON JOHNSON's.

Congress, responding to the leadership of a man regarded by its members as one of their own, set a legislative record that is not likely soon to be matched. Measures affecting civil rights, voting, taxes, medical care, immigration, schools, environmental pollution, and other legislation designed to alleviate the country's problems were whipped throught the legislative body and signed into law by a triumphant President.

Ebullient was the word for the President in those happy and fruitful months. Everything seemed to be going his way as he plunged zestfully into the job for which he had been in training all his adult life.

In that year of glory, JOHNSON also became President in his own right. He campaigned as no man seeking the presidency had ever done before him. He loved every minute of it, tearing into his speeches as if they were so many juicy steaks, plunging into adoring crowds to "press the flesh" of every hand that could reach him, shouting over a bullhorn as he drove through city streets, "Yawl come to the speakin'."

On Nov. 3, 1964, he defeated Barry Goldwater of Arizona by 42,121,085 popular votes to 27,145,161. He carried all but six states. It was the most one-sided result of a presidential election since 1936.

JOHNSON was inaugurated for a full term on Jan. 20, 1965. Shortly afterward, things began to fall apart.

At home and abroad, Americans found themselves confronting problems that loomed large and menacing. They soon began to blame the President.

JOHNSON had talked soothingly about any difficulties in foreign lands during his reelection campaign in particular downplaying the seriousness of fighting in Vietnam. He had promised that American boys would not be sent "nine or ten thousand miles away from home to do what Asian boys ought to be doing for themselves."

But U.S. involvement in Vietnam escalated. Live telecasts from bloody battlefields brought the war into the homes of horrified Americans, and American casualties mounted. The Senate Foreign Relations Committee and its chairman, William Fulbright, were raising critical questions.

Closer to home, an uprising in Santo Domingo caused the President to dispatch U.S. forces into the Caribbean for the first time since 1927. The initial popular approval of his move soon turned to general dismay.

Right at home, the civil rights movement reached a turning point. In Selma, Ala., for the last time, blacks and whites were joining together in massive protest. Violence replaced marching and demonstrations. The Watts riots showed a clear and ominous change in the racial picture. Other riots scarred Detroit and other cities.

Dissent on college campuses mounted over the ever-increasing bloodshed in Vietnam. A cruel and unfair chant was born: "Hey, hey, LBJ, How many babies did you kill today?"

Along with everything else, the President was now having trouble with a recalcitrant Congress. He was trying to move too fast, his critics said. His reply was: "I have so little time." The sympathy and sentiment he had commanded after Kennedy's assassination were running out. He needed time—more time than was to be given him.

His boasted—and effective—consensus was gone by the latter part of 1966. Republicans scored substantial gains in the fall congressional elections.

In the White House, LYNDON JOHNSON suffered. The Great Society of which he had dreamed and preached was dissolving before his eyes. Press criticism was widespread.

One bright spot amidst this was the wedding in the White House, of the younger Johnson daughter, Luci. Her father wore striped pants and a cutaway, something he had not even done for his inaugural.

The revolt against Administration policies developed into direct political action in the presidential election year of 1968. The President was challenged in the primaries, first by Eugene McCarthy, then by Senator Robert F. Kennedy. The Democratic party reeled under the internecine warfare.

The assassinations of another Kennedy and of Dr. Martin Luther King, the leading Negro advocate of nonviolence, threw the nation into more turmoil. Unbearable tension found an outlet in renewed rioting, burning of whole sections of cities, including the nation's capital, and other mass acts of violence.

Even before the deaths of Senator Kennedy and Dr. King, JOHNSON had arrived at a decision about his future course. On March 31, 1968, speaking over national television, the President announced that he was calling a halt to the bombing of North Vietnam and beginning a process that he hoped would lead to an end to U.S. engagement in the war.

Then he had more to say. He said in a single sentence. "I shall not seek and I will not accept the nomination of my party for another term." A large tear formed and rolled down his furrowed cheek.

Two days after this announcement, JOHNSON met with a small group of intimate friends to give them, as he said, "a fuller and personal explanation" of his action, which had stunned them as it had the nation.

"I'm just fed up to here," he said, placing his big hand at his neck, "with the way things have been going."

His tone was thoughtful, not self-pitying.

"I think I've done more for the Negro people than any President since Lincoln," he continued. "And what happens? Negro militants precipitate riots and all the liberals say it's my fault.

"No administration has ever done more for education. But students boo the mention of my name and accuse me of killing babies.

"I was always taught to believe that love of country is a good thing. But patriotism isn't 'in' these days. I wake up in the morning and read in the papers that 50 or 63 American boys have been killed in Vietnam— And then I turn on TV and some senator or other is making a speech saying I'm to blame and we ought to just turn Asia over to the Communists.

"It looks like this country is badly divided and I've become a symbol of the division. I hope that by getting out of the race I can make moves during the next nine months without being accused of political motivations. I'm not going to come out for anybody for the Democratic nomination. I'm going to be working for the country the best way I can, and I hope you-all will help me."

During his last months in the White House, he continued his search for peace. His concern for the country had not lessened. Having made his decision about his future, however, he was more relaxed, calmer, than he had been in years.

He was the old-time LYNDON when he gave a dinner party on the White House lawn one mid-summer evening for several hundred old friends, many of them Texans. In a long, rambling after-dinner speech, made without notes, he managed to mention by names, and with reference to some personal incident of the past, scores of his guests, bringing guffaws and shouts of approval from the uninhibited assemblage. It was a virtuoso performance, wholly in the LBJ tradition.

Peace did not come, and he left the White House on Jan. 20, 1969.

Four years later, one day after JOHNSON's death at his ranch on Jan. 22, 1973, a truce in Vietnam was announced by President Nixon.

This writer's last contact with President JOHNSON was on Sept. 9, 1969, when I paid a visit at the ranch. As we talked about the matter on which I had come, he drove over his acres in the well-publicized white Lincoln Continental.

He looked the part of a rancher, wearing a khaki shirt hanging outside khaki trousers, cowboy boots, and a blue, long-billed golfer's cap which he clearly treasured.

He drove—fast on paved roads, slowly over grass-covered furrows—with his left arm curved around the steering wheel, half-turned in his seat to face me. Occasionally he stopped to give instructions to ranch hands.

"I'm just trying to be suggestive," he told me, "and not give orders. But," he added, "Damn it, they're sure bollixing things up with the way they're spraying those cattle."

One would have thought he had never left the ranch as he rode over the land he loved. He was completely engrossed, as always with the immediate task at hand. That was LYNDON JOHNSON.

Hon. Leslie C. Arends
OF ILLINOIS

Mr. Speaker, LYNDON BAINES JOHNSON was an extraordinary man—an extraordinary Congressman, an extraordinary Senator, an extraordinary President.

I served with LYNDON JOHNSON in the House of Representatives. I worked with him when he was in the Senate and while he was in the White House. His remarkable capacity for leadership was always evident.

When he set objectives, he was not to be deterred in trying to reach them. While I saw him at work in many settings, I especially recall observing him in bipartisan leadership meetings. He was a master in any debate or discussion—always a forceful factor to be reckoned with. I was able to cooperate with him on several occasions. Yet, no matter how much we might have disagreed—and we did from time to time—I could never find myself in diminished respect of him.

It was especially interesting to witness LYNDON JOHNSON as Senate majority leader and former Speaker of the House Sam Rayburn in action together. Both of them clearly exemplified a philosophy which they most certainly must have shared—"To be leaders, you must lead!"

I was in attendance at President JOHNSON's burial in Texas. Being there for that service, I could truly understand why LYNDON BAINES JOHNSON loved his native Texas, his beautiful home along the Pedernales, and the people who weer his neighbors. It was from there that he drew his great strength, the strength which made him a skillful leader whose indelible print is left upon history.

Hon. J. J. Pickle
OF TEXAS

Mr. Speaker, the activities the late President LYNDON B. JOHNSON fostered for the benefit of people during his years in the White House are well known to us all.

They are built on a foundation of people-concerned programs he fostered throughout his public life, some of which are not so well known.

One area which received much of his careful attention was water—a crucial issue in many parts of his home State of Texas.

The executive director of the Texas Water Development Board, Mr. Harry Burleigh, paid tribute recently to President JOHNSON's efforts in the field of water throughout his public career.

I should like at this time to reprint Mr. Burleigh's statement in the Record as follows:

THE EXECUTIVE DIRECTOR'S REPORT

(By Harry P. Burleigh)

The Texas water fraternity lost one of its friends with the death of former President LYNDON B. JOHNSON on January 22 of this year.

The former President loved his State. He loved its people. More importantly, he exercised his leadership in a manner that left a stamp on our State of a nature that will endure in perpetuity and may in the long run be one of the more significant memorials to him and his career. This occurs in the many water projects and water programs he fostered and furthered in the interest of Texas. As a national leader he understood better than any other the catalytic relationship between orderly water programs and economic growth and he expressed this knowledge in purposeful programs. His interest in water matters endured throughout his entire political career from the time he was elected to the House in 1937, to the Senate in 1948, as Senate Majority Leader, and later as Vice President and subsequently as President.

Mr. JOHNSON took many actions that related to Texas water affairs. Some of the more significant include:

A directive in 1949 to the federal water agencies to determine how their technical resources could more effectively assist Texas in development of its water resources.

Publication in 1953 of Senate Document 57, 83rd Congress: "An Appraisal of the Texas Water Problem." The document was preliminary in nature—often the subject of controversy—but for the first time it sharply directed attention to the intricate relationship between unused water of Texas to the State and national economies in a time of rapid economic growth.

Creation, through the Congress, in 1958 of the United States Study Commission. Directives to the Commission were based upon a full awareness of the basic sovereignty of Texas over its own water, and for the first time integrated into a single group the collective capabilities and skills of a number of federal water agencies and the skills and leadership of the various Texas river authorities to common goals. The report of the Study Commission later provided a solid base for the water plan for Texas published by this Board in 1968. Importantly, it represented intergrated views of several levels of government.

Throughout the entire decade of the 50's and later, solid support for appropriations to federal agencies concerned with water matters in Texas.

Late in the 50's, directives to the Corps of Engineers and the Department of Interior to fully cooperate with the then Texas Board of Water Engineers on formulation of the first statewide water plan.

In 1962, a directive to the Bureau of Reclamation and the Corps of Engineers to make a reasonable apportionment of their efforts in Texas as between them. This was done.

Strong support for many individual Texas projects now serving the Texas economy. Among them the Canadian River project, the first totally municipal water supply project to be constructed by the Bureau of Reclamation; Falcon; Amistad; and a host of others.

The preceding are examples. Others could be set forth. In their aggregate implementation Mr. Johnson left a stamp on his beloved Texas that may be in the final analysis his most enduring eulogy.

In the years ahead, Mr. Johnson will be favorably judged for many accomplishments: progress in civil rights, progress in education, progress in social welfare, and other areas. The water fraternity will respect his memory because of his profound knowledge of what intelligent use and control of water meant to the public weal and for the capability to translate that knowledge into practical programs and projects.

He will be missed.

Hon. John J. Rooney
OF NEW YORK

Mr. Speaker, the untimely passing of former President Lyndon Baines Johnson took a titan from our midst. It is with a heavy heart that I pay tribute to his memory and achievements. It was my privilege to count Lyndon Johnson as a friend and for many, many years we worked together toward a mutual goal.

Lyndon Johnson was already a Member of the House of Representatives in June 1944 when I joined this distinguished body. In 1949 he became a Member of the other body where he later became my counterpart for many years in that body as chairman of the Senate Appropriations Subcommittee for the Departments of State, Justice, the Federal judiciary and related agencies. My skills were sharpened from the experience of facing Lyndon Johnson across the appropriations conference table. Our friendship and cooperative efforts continued as he became majority leader of the other body, Vice President, and then President. I shall always cherish the memories of our long years of friendship and association.

From that sad moment in Dallas, Lyndon B. Johnson was destined to carry on his shoulders the responsibilities of the Presidency of a growing, thriving, troubled Nation. Responsibilities from which he never shirked, even in the face of adversaries who would accept nothing but their ideology. The affection which Lyndon Johnson earned from his countrymen is perhaps unique in that it only became fully acknowledged by his death.

The chroniclers have provided us with the full record of Lyndon Baines Johnson and there is little we can add to the accolades he has received from the Nation and the world. We can only urge all men to work toward continued accomplishments in the tasks he laid before us and at which he exerted his energies. No tribute to the memory of Lyndon Johnson can surpass the knowledge that whatever history says of his leadership—in war and peace—the people whose lives were made fuller and richer will remember his record of legislative achievements in their behalf.

Lyndon Baines Johnson died as he had lived, a symbol of what man can do in the face of adversity. Unflinchingly he fought the certainty of death with the same audacity he confronted the trials of life. Nowhere will it be possible to fully record for historians the total sense of loss felt by us by Lyndon's death. His death cast a shadow on the hearts of people everywhere, even of those who failed to see him as their friend and benefactor.

Mrs. Rooney and I are grateful that we had the pleasure of association with Lyndon Johnson and his lovely wife, Lady Bird, and their daughters, and they have our sympathy and prayers in their loss.

Hon. Bob Casey
OF TEXAS

Mr. Speaker, as we pay tribute today to the late President Lyndon Baines Johnson, we are also paying tribute to the American way of life.

The well-known history of the humble origins of the Texas farm boy to the leader of the most powerful and prosperous Nation in the history of the world is indeed an inspiration to all the youth of our country. He was living proof that it can be done.

Mr. Speaker, such a career and productive life does not just happen. LYNDON B. JOHNSON throughout his life gave tremendous credit, which I am sure was justified, to his mother and father and his devoted wife, Lady Bird. However, L. B. JOHNSON, the boy, and L. B. JOHNSON, the man, were imbued with the determination to succeed.

This determination was combined with an endless source of energy. He worked harder than any other person ever associated with him which, in my opinion, was his most outstanding characteristic.

LYNDON JOHNSON also loved people and wanted to serve and help his fellowman.

History will record him as one of our Nation's most outstanding leaders. He was a servant of the people, and there is no doubt that he is one of America's greatest Presidents.

This big man, this great man will truly be missed but he will be remembered by all the people not only of this Nation but throughout the world. We who were privileged to know him more closely and to treasure him as a personal friend have many fond memories to help us bear this loss.

Mr. Speaker, my family and I extend our deepest sympathy to the lovely, charming Lady Bird Johnson and her daughters on the loss of their deeply beloved husband and father. We wish them to know that in some way we are sharing this loss with them. By the same token, we are sharing with them their pride in LYNDON BAINES JOHNSON's greatest accomplishments. They will stand forever as a monument to his public service.

Hon. Fred B. Rooney
OF PENNSYLVANIA

Mr. Speaker, from the heart of America he came upon the national political scene, becoming the most masterful and effective legislator in memory. By fate he was elevated to the Presidency, becoming the impetus for some of the most-far-reaching social legislation in America's history. Because of circumstances in Vietnam which he could not control, however, he left a deeply troubled and tragically divided country when he stepped down from the Presidency.

LYNDON BAINES JOHNSON was a man of many talents, but those of us who served in the Congress while he was President saw him at his best—as a successful pilot for the significant

measures he steered through the legislative process. His years in both the House and Senate were highlighted by his success in learning the ropes—in throwing all his weight behind a measure when the time was right, in compromising when a bill could be saved from extinction in an acceptable form, or in backing off to fight another day when he was certain of overwhelming defeat. Throughout the years of the Eisenhower Presidency from his leadership position in the Senate, LYNDON JOHNSON was the focal point for the programs of the entire Democratic Party and he proved he could do an extremely effective job.

When he chose to accept the Vice Presidential nomination, he embarked on a new course, largely abandoning his manipulative role in legislative matters and calling upon his deeper reserves of statesmanship. During this period, he was involved in many special projects which would later become the cornerstones of his own legislative program—equal opportunities for minorities in education, housing, and job opportunities, and the special problems of the poor and the elderly.

Although he was overshadowed by the style of his predecessor, he competently handled the crisis when President Kennedy was tragically assassinated and provided the stability the country needed to calm its fears. His legislative proposals dealt with the areas of his special concerns. With the assistance of those skills which had served him as a most effective Democratic majority leader, he now steered through Congress social legislation of monumental proportions.

The Civil Rights Act of 1964, the Voting Rights Act of 1965, and the Housing Act of 1968 established his place for all time in the forefront of the fighters for equal rights for all Americans. These were probably the achievements of which he felt the most proud. It was of equal rights for all Americans that he was speaking at the last public appearance before his death. He recognized how much still needs to be done in this area and was urging that others continue the effort.

The war which LYNDON JOHNSON set out to fight was the "war on poverty." Using the observations he made during his vice presidential years as the basis for his legislative program, he sought to make government more responsive to the needs of the poor people in this country. The Economic Opportunity Act, passed in 1964, created many programs which dealt with the problems of poverty for the first time in a comprehensive manner.

The war in Vietnam, however, stalled the domestic legislation and crippled JOHNSON's effectiveness as opposition grew in the Congress and in the Nation as a whole. From the Gulf of Tonkin resolution to the optimistic military predictions of the early end of American involvement to the opposition to the war within his own party, LYNDON JOHNSON's last several years in the office of the Presidency were almost totally overshadowed by the Vietnam war. History will be the final judge of that controversy but it was certainly kind that he knew before his death that the peace which had eluded him had finally come.

Of the evaluations history will make of the man, I think the most significant will be that he had a compassionate concern for his fellow man and a compelling desire to halt the wrongs of injustice. I consider myself privileged to have known him and to have served during the period of the "Great Society."

Hon. John Brademas
OF INDIANA

Mr. Speaker, there can be no question that LYNDON B. JOHNSON was one of the most extraordinary public figures in American history.

A Member of the House of Representatives, majority leader of the Senate, Vice President and, finally, President of the United States—LYNDON JOHNSON brought a combination of energy and intelligence and compassion to his responsibilities unusual to find in any person.

Everyone who came to know the late President will have his own recollections of him.

But, Mr. Speaker, I remember particularly the visit President JOHNSON made to my hometown of South Bend, Ind., in early 1964 to survey the impact on our community of the shutdown in late 1963 of the Studebaker automotive plant. And I continued to be grateful for the assistance he provided to help the people of St. Joseph County recover from that economic blow.

And I remember as well, Mr. Speaker, another visit President JOHNSON paid to my district, to the small community in Elkhart County, of Dunlap, which had been devastated by a tornado, and I recall with continuing appreciation the comfort the presence of the President of the United States meant to the citizens of that small community.

In terms of President JOHNSON's leadership on crucial national issues, I am sure that what most impressed me—and many others—was the depth of his commitment to improving education and health for the American people, to the eradication of the curse of poverty in a wealthy land, and to the translation into reality of the American dream of equality of opportunity for all citizens, regardless of their race or color, their religion or national origin.

We all know, Mr. Speaker, that the great tragedy that afflicted the Presidency of LYNDON JOHNSON was the war in Vietnam.

But no matter our views on the war, all Americans can, I believe, applaud LYNDON JOHNSON and pay tribute to his memory for his remarkable and gifted leadership in so many ways to make a better nation for all our people.

Hon. Wayne L. Hays
OF OHIO

Mr. Speaker, in the death of LYNDON JOHNSON our country has lost one of its most eminent citizens and statesmen; and, I believe, one of its greatest political geniuses. I shall not detain the House by narrating the transactions of his full and useful life. His distinguished services as a Representative, Senator, Vice President, and President are inseparably connected with our Nation's history. In all of these high positions he exhibited a wisdom and patriotism which have made a deep impression upon the grateful hearts of his countrymen. His thoughts and his actions have already been published to the world in written biography, in congressional debates and reports, in the Journals of the two Houses, and in the pages of American history. They have been commemorated on memorials erected in his honor, as well as plaques and medals struck in tribute. But the thoughts and actions of my late friend have also become identified with the immortality of the human mind, and will pass down from generation to generation as a portion of our national inheritance, incapable of annihilation so long as genius has an admirer, or liberty a friend.

Imperishably associated as his name has been for nearly twoscore years with every great event affecting the fortunes of our country, it is difficult to realize that he is indeed gone forever. It is difficult to feel that we shall see no more his noble form within these walls—that we shall hear no more his patriot tones, now rousing his countrymen to vindicate their rights against all foes—foreign and even domestic—now imploring them to preserve concord among themselves. We shall see him no more. The memory and the fruits of his services alone remain to us. Amidst the general gloom, the Capitol itself seems desolate, as if the genius of the place had departed. Already the intelligence has reached almost every quarter of the Republic, and a great people mourn with us, today, the death of their most illustrious citizen. Sympathizing, as we do, deeply, with his family and friends, yet private affliction is absorbed in the general sorrow. The spectacle of a whole community experiencing the loss of a great man, is far more touching than any manifestation of private grief.

And now we are commanded to render back to Texas one of her most illustrious sons. Tenderly he will be committed to the soil that banks the Pedernales River in that area of the Lone Star State which gave him birth. A part of him will not be returned, as it is not ours to give. It belongs to the Nation he loved, to mankind, to freedom, to civilization—to the Ages.

Mr. Speaker, the Nation has lost a leader, the world has lost a man with compassion for all mankind and I am sad at the loss of a friend.

Memorial Tributes

IN THE

Senate of the United States

IN EULOGY OF

Lyndon Baines Johnson

In the Senate of the United States

JANUARY 23, 1973

The Chaplain, the Reverend Edward L. R. Elson, D.D., offered the following prayer:

Eternal Father, in whom we live and move and have our being, quiet our hearts in grateful memory of Thy servant LYNDON BAINES JOHNSON.

We give Thee thanks for his great and good life and for the enduring legacy of his leadership. We thank Thee for his legislative skills, his executive talents, and his enduring statesmanship in the affairs of the whole world. We thank Thee for his devotion to civil rights and human justice, his passion to help the poor, the undereducated, the ill, and those of limited opportunity.

We thank Thee too for his warm friendship, his outgoing good will, his love of the public arena, his ardor in the contest, his steadfastness in fulfilling this Nation's pledges to other nations, his dignity in victory, his quiet patience under criticism, his transcendent devotion to his country, and his abiding faith in Thee.

We beseech Thee, O Lord, to put within us the same high motives to lift the life of all people to its highest and best and to carry forward the vision of a great society in the likeness of Thy promised kingdom.

Grant to those who mourn, the healing of Thy grace and the comfort of Thy Holy Spirit.

Through Jesus Christ, our Lord. Amen.

Mr. Mansfield. Mr. President, on behalf of the distinguished Senators from Texas (Mr. Tower and Mr. Bentsen), and the joint leadership, the distinguished Senator from Pennsylvania (Mr. Scott) and the Senator from Montana, now speaking, I send to the desk a resolution and ask for its immediate consideration.

The President pro tempore. The resolution will be stated.

The assistant legislative clerk read as follows:

SENATE RESOLUTION 24

Resolved, that the Senate has heard with profound sorrow and deep regret the announcement of the death of Honorable LYNDON B. JOHNSON, a former President of the United States, and a former Representative and former Senator from the State of Texas.

Resolved, That in recognition of his illustrious statesmanship, his leadership in national and world affairs, his distinguished public service to his State and his Nation, and as a mark of respect to one who has held such eminent public station in life, the Presiding Officer of the Senate appoint a committee to consist of all of the members of the Senate to attend the funeral of the former President.

Resolved, That the Senate hereby tender its deep sympathy to the members of the family of the former President in their sad bereavement.

Resolved, That the Secretary communicate these resolutions to the House of Representatives and transmit a copy thereof to the family of the former President.

The President pro tempore. Is there objection to the present consideration of the resolution?

There being no objection, the resolution was considered and unanimously agreed to.

Mr. Mansfield. Mr. President, I now yield to the distinguished senior Senator from Texas (Mr. Tower).

Mr. Tower. Mr. President, I know that all of us today are deeply saddened and it is difficult for us to say what is on our hearts at this moment.

The 36th President of the United States was a Texan—and in every good sense of the word. He was a superb leader in the Congress of the United States. He was an able President. He confronted the critical and fast moving events of his day with the determination to make decisions that would serve the greatest good for the greatest number of people.

I spent a good part of my adult life as a political adversary of President Johnson, but it was characteristic of the man that he was able to maintain warmth and to extend the right hand of friendship even to those who opposed him.

He was a man who had a forgiving nature, who never carried a grudge—a man who never became dissolved in any sense of bitterness or frustration. I can say that he was my friend.

I had the opportunity to visit with him personally only a short time ago. There arrived at my desk yesterday morning a warm and friendly letter from him, inviting me to come and see him again.

I am profoundly sorry that he was taken from us at this time in his life when there was so much more in the way of good counsel and advice that he could have given to many of us, and so much more teaching that he could have done for our young people, in whom he had such a deep and abiding interest.

We shall sorely miss him. Those of us who are Texans can think better of ourselves because we come from a society that produced Lyndon Baines Johnson.

Mr. Mansfield. Mr. President, I now yield to the distinguished Senator from Texas (Mr. Bentsen).

Mr. Bentsen. Mr. President, I know of no President of the United States who cared more deeply for the people. I know of no President who worked harder for them. They have lost a great champion and I have lost a personal friend. I shall miss him.

Lyndon Baines Johnson was a leader among men. He was a man of great energy, a man of vigor, a man of courage, and a man of total commitment.

I only wish he could have had the longevity of President Truman so that he could have been viewed in the dispassionate eye of history apart from this bloody war and the passions it has aroused. I think, then, that the contribution this man has made to our society would have been better understood.

He was a man of great intellect, a man who could grasp problems and reduce them to their simplest terms, a man who, apart from great political rhetoric, could illustrate the individual

problem so that a person would identify and relate to it and understand it.

I wish that personality could have extended over the television medium. Time and time again, I have seen the persuasive powers of this man exercised in small groups of people. When he got through telling the problems of the young black trying to make his way in life, and some of the obstacles he had to overcome, I have seen the tears come to the eyes of hardened, tough, cynical men as they better understood the problem, and they became proponents of what he was trying to accomplish.

He was a poor boy, who never forgot that once he was a poor boy, and he understood the problems of the poor. He was a man who was concerned for the sick and wanted to see that they had a chance for medical attention.

He was a man who believed that every man and boy in this country should have the full opportunity of education. He was interested and concerned in our youth.

He had a respect for this body and for the House. He understood Congress and the role it should play under our Constitution.

He had a respect for the Presidency. More than anything else, he wanted to discharge that responsibility in a way that did justice to that great Office. I know how much he appreciated the way President Nixon treated him after he was no longer President.

I think President Johnson also grew in stature, continued to grow, after he left the Presidency, for the manner in which he discharged his responsibilities as an ex-President. He could have been a carping antagonist for the Presidency, but he was not. He tried to contribute in every way he could to the enormous responsibility that Office holds and to its present incumbent.

We have lost a great leader in this country, and the people have lost a champion.

Mr. Mansfield. Mr. President, before I yield to the distinguished Republican leader, on behalf of both of us I send to the desk a message which I ask to be read.

The Vice President. The clerk will read a message from the President of the United States.

The assistant legislative clerk read as follows:

To the Congress of the United States:

It is my sad duty to inform you officially of the death of Lyndon Baines Johnson, the thirty-sixth President of the United States.

His loss is especially poignant for all of us who knew him and worked with him in the House and Senate. It was there that he first became a legend and there that he began to influence our destiny as a great Nation.

Yet LYNDON JOHNSON's legacy extends far beyond his years in the Congress. He was a man of fierce devotion and love. He was devoted to his family. He was devoted to the cause of freedom and equality for his fellow man. And as President, he was devoted in a very special way to the land he loved.

The whole story of the Johnson years in the White House remains to be told, and history has yet to make its judgment. But millions of Americans will always remember a bitter day in November, 1963, when so many of our people doubted the very future of this Republic, when so many were stunned at the very idea that an American Chief of State could be assassinated in this age, and so many abroad were fearful about the future course of the American democracy. And LYNDON JOHNSON rose above the doubt and the fear to hold this Nation on course until we rediscovered our faith in ourselves.

If he had done no more, his place in history would have been assured. But he did much more, and his role then was not a high-water mark but a hallmark. For it was his noble and difficult destiny to lead America through a long, dark night of necessity at home and abroad. He had the courage to do what many of his contemporaries condemned him for, but what will surely win warm praise in the history books of tomorrow.

RICHARD NIXON,
THE WHITE HOUSE, *January 23, 1973.*

Mr. Scott of Pennsylvania. Mr. President, I had the honor of knowing and being a friend of LYNDON JOHNSON for all of these past 32 years, and in that period I have enjoyed his kindness and often his confidence. I have seen him mount to heights of exultation, and I have seen him in the bitterness of despair.

During all this time, he walked among men, and he was with them and of them. His spirit soared on the wings of eagles to reach the goals to which he aspired. His voice roared aloud for the causes for which he believed. He fought for his convictions.

He was among the most persuasive of men. He was, above all, a friendly, human individual; and visits with him here and in the White House were always occasions for fond and happy memories.

I recall particularly when I was much beleaguered in 1964, and President JOHNSON appeared in Pittsburgh, where any word of disparagement on his part might have changed my entire future career. But, far from doing this, he was scrupulously considerate and extremely fair in his judgments. He did nothing of a political or partisan nature which would have worked to the disadvantage of one who had stood in opposition to him in some matters, who had stood in support of him in others.

I am glad that I rose, when he became President, to indicate my support of his foreign policies. I did it no matter how difficult it might have been at times, but I did it because I believe that a President is entitled to that kind of bipartisan support.

I know that he relied upon the confidence of the country in what he sought to do. When he thought at one bitter moment that the confidence of the country had veered and that people had turned their heads from him and hardened their hearts, he made the most difficult decision a man can make: He decided not to be a candidate for the Presidency. That was the act of a big man; it was the act of a great man; it was the act, above all, of a very strong man who loved his country and who had lived to see a return of that confidence and a continuance of that affection and a recognition that, indeed, his name will go into history—this 36th President of ours—as one who deserved well of the Republic.

We honor his memory, we mourn his passing, we express our warm and deep condolences to his beloved wife and to his family, and we hope, as is written in the Book of Common Prayer, that he will now have peace at the last.

Mr. Mansfield. Mr. President, death can, at times, be delayed but, in the end, cannot be avoided. Within the past month, two former Presidents of the United States, Harry S Truman and LYNDON BAINES JOHNSON, have left their existence here on earth. Both were Senators of the United States. Both were Vice Presidents of the United States. Both, through the death of others, became Presidents of the United States and, then, in their own right, became Presidents again.

It was my privilege to work with these men but most closely with LYNDON BAINES JOHNSON. I served with him for 4 years as the assistant majority leader when he was majority leader of the Senate. I succeeded him as majority leader when he became Vice President in 1961 and continued in that capacity throughout his Presidency.

We were in friendly and fairly close contact for those many years. As President, LYNDON JOHNSON was the head of the executive branch and, as the majority leader, I was the representative of the Senate. As might be expected, we did not always agree but at no time did our disagreements impair the civility of our relationship.

LYNDON JOHNSON came from humble origins but he was not a humble man. Rather, he was a man of great pride and his Presidency was a Presidency which bore the hallmark of this pride. We shall not see his like again, nor shall we see the kind of legislative program which was enacted in response to his determined leadership in the pursuit of equal opportunity for all Americans.

Insofar as proposing and enacting legislation in the field of domestic and social reform, LYNDON JOHNSON was, in my judgment, the greatest of Presidents. Historically, his record in that respect will emerge as superior to any other President or any combination of Presidents. He was in the tradition of Franklin D. Roosevelt, the man he so much admired, and his dream of a great society of free men will be his enduring monument in the history of this Republic.

Mrs. Mansfield, our daughter Anne, and I wish to extend our deepest condolences and sympathy to Lady Bird Johnson, one of the outstanding First Ladies of this Republic, to the Johnson daughters, Lynda and Luci, and to all their families in this hour of sorrow and bereavement. May his restless soul find peace.

Mr. Muskie. Mr. President, with all my colleagues I am deeply saddened by the sudden death of LYNDON JOHNSON. We have lost a statesman and a friend. LYNDON JOHNSON served with extraordinary ability in this body for 12 years, as a representative of his beloved State of Texas, and as majority leader.

He proved here that he was a master in the art of the possible, but he also demonstrated that he had dreams, and had the courage and talent to make many of those dreams reality.

After the tragedy in Dallas, LYNDON JOHNSON was thrust without warning into the Nation's highest office. He met the challenge with characteristic energy, vision, and remarkable strength of leadership. And, he presided with great personal dignity over the most tumultuous and troubling period in recent American history.

LYNDON JOHNSON was a man of great feeling for his fellow human beings. He saw Americans ringed into ghettos of difference, of prejudice, of ignorance, and he demanded a better quality of life for every American. LYNDON JOHNSON's dreams were large—we were to have not just a new society, but a great society. And, as the most politically experienced President and party leader in this Nation's history, LYNDON JOHNSON was able to produce the most far-reaching social legislative program since the New Deal. He initiated manpower training for the unemployed, medicare for the elderly, and low-cost, fair housing for minorities. Declaring war on poverty, he mobilized forces of young and old to improve the lives of millions of Americans. With special determination, LYNDON JOHNSON announced, "We shall overcome"—and obtained the strongest civil rights bill in our Nation's history.

His tragedy, and ours, was the war which seems only now hopefully to be ending. But the war can never eclipse his solid achievements in strengthening the fabric of American life. I join America in mourning the loss of a statesman and a friend who was in so many ways larger than life, and will remain so in our memories.

Mr. Allen. Mr. President, the sudden death of President LYNDON JOHNSON shocked the Nation, and all the more so coming as it did so soon after President Truman's death. President JOHNSON fought hard to promote programs to bring a better life to all of our people but his accomplishments have been obscured by the tragedy of the Vietnam war which caused such a division among our people. It is regrettable and ironic that he did not live to see the end of the Vietnam war which now seems so near. After Vietnam has become only a tragic memory, history can make a more accurate assessment of his role in history.

Mr. Humphrey. Mr. President, as we all know, yesterday our Nation was saddened and shocked by the news that the 36th President of the United States, LYNDON BAINES JOHNSON, had passed away.

Mrs. Humphrey and I mourn the loss of a dear friend and the Nation mourns the loss of a remarkable man and leader who struggled to bring dignity and hope to all of the American people.

LYNDON JOHNSON's public life was filled with controversy because he was a man who cared, a man of action, and a man of decision.

He will be remembered most kindly not by the

high and mighty, but rather by those whom society had forgotten or ignored.

He was a strong man, as we know, and yet he cared for the weak and the sick.

He was a country school teacher who in his public career dedicated his energies and talents to the cause of education for every American.

He was man of compassion for the elderly and of concern for the young.

I believe no man gave more to the struggle for human rights, nor asked more of us in the battle against racism and discrimination, than President JOHNSON.

He was a President who saw America as the guardian of freedom throughout the world, and he acted accordingly.

Above all, LYNDON JOHNSON believed that our country could build a society of opportunity and justice. He believed that America could do whatever needed to be done.

He drew strength, understanding, and purpose from his dear and lovely wife, affectionately known to all of us as Lady Bird Johnson, and his devoted family. So to them today we convey, as a very personal message, our heartfelt sympathy, and with that family we share a very great loss.

Mr. President, I know that the Senate will take sufficient time to pay adequate tribute to President JOHNSON. My remarks today are brief and very personal, because it was my good fortune to know this man in all the facets of his life, both public and private.

He will be missed. He was an unusual man, and to share in his fellowship and work alongside him in public life was both an exciting and demanding experience. I consider that to serve with him in the Senate and to serve alongside him as Vice President could not be compared to a tranquil, soft Caribbean cruise, but rather to a storm-tossed voyage across the North Atlantic. But it was a journey worth making.

The reward of public life is the privilege to know great, unusual, remarkable, and gifted men and women. I have had many rewards based on that standard, but none was more generous, more meaningful, or more rich than the reward of being a companion, a colleague, an associate, a fellow Senator, a friend, and a Vice President with LYNDON BAINES JOHNSON.

Mr. Brooke. Mr. President, I am saddened by the death of LYNDON JOHNSON. He assumed the Presidency in the tragedy of Dallas and left in the turmoil of the Vietnam war. Tragedy and turmoil now cloud the triumphs that marked the Johnson years.

I believe that history shall record that President JOHNSON did more to redeem our Nation's promise of equal protection under law, than any other American in history. His legacy in law, the Civil Rights Act of 1964, the voting Rights Act of 1965, and the Civil Rights Act of 1968, are an inspiration for us to continue, in his words, to assure "freedom to the free."

On Memorial Day 1963, then Vice President JOHNSON spoke at Gettysburg. I shall always remember his words. I shall never forget that for 5 years he matched his brave words with forceful action. His words and his deeds will endure in the hearts and minds of millions of Americans who found new hope in his Presidency and new opportunity in his programs.

Mr. President, LYNDON JOHNSON's remarks at Gettysburg inspire us still, and I can think of no more appropriate tribute to him than to repeat today his words:

On this hallowed ground, heroic deeds were performed and eloquent words were spoken a century ago.

We, the living, have not forgotten—and the world will never forget—the deeds or the words of Gettysburg. We honor them now as we join on this Memorial Day of 1963 in a prayer for permanent peace of the world and fulfillment of our hopes for universal freedom and justice.

We are called to honor our own words of reverent prayer with resolution in the deeds we must perform to preserve peace and the hope of freedom.

We keep a vigil of peace around the world.

Until the world knows no aggressors, until the arms of tyranny have been laid down, until freedom has risen up in every land, we shall maintain our vigil to make sure our sons who died on foreign fields shall not have died in vain.

As we maintain the vigil of peace, we must remember that justice is a vigil, too—a vigil we must keep in our own streets and schools and among the lives of all our people—so that those who died here on their native soil shall not have died in vain.

One hundred years ago, the slave was freed.

One hundred years later, the Negro remains in bondage to the color of his skin.

The Negro today asks justice.

We do not answer him—we do not answer those who lie beneath this soil—when we reply to the Negro by asking, "Patience."

It is empty to plead that the solution to the dilemmas of the present rests on the hands of the clock. The solution is in our hands. Unless we are willing to yield up our destiny of greatness among the civilizations of history, Americans—white and Negro together—must be about the business of resolving the challenge which confronts us now.

Our nation found its soul in honor on these fields of

Gettysburg 100 years gao. We must not lose that soul in dishonor now on the fields of hate.

To ask for patience from the Negro is to ask him to give more of what he has already given enough. But to fail to ask of him—and of all Americans—perseverance within the processes of a free and responsible society would be to fail to ask what the national interest requires of all its citizens.

The law cannot save those who deny it but neither can the law serve any who do not use it. The history of injustice and inequality is a history of disuse of the law. Law has not failed—and is not failing. We as a nation have failed ourselves by not trusting the law and by not using the law to gain sooner the ends of justice which law alone serves.

If the white overestimates what he has done for the Negro without the law, the Negro may underestimate what he is doing and can do for himself with the law.

It is empty to ask Negro or white for patience, it is not empty—it is merely honest—to ask perseverance. Men may build barricades—and others may hurl themselves against those barricades—but what would happen at the barricades would yield no answers. The answers will only be wrought by our perseverance together. It is deceit to promise more as it would be cowardice to demand less.

In his hour, it is not our respective races which are at stake—it is our nation. Let those who care for their country come forward, North and South, white and Negro, to lead the way through this moment of challenge and decision. . . .

The Negro says, "Now." Others say, "Never." The voice of responsible Americans—the voice of those who died here and the great man who spoke here—their voices say, "Together." There is no other way.

Until justice is blind to color, until education is unaware of race, until opportunity is unconcerned with the color of men's skins, emancipation will be a proclamation of emancipation is not fulfilled in fact, to that extent we shall have fallen short of assuring freedom to the free.

Mr. Proxmire. Mr. President, no man since Abraham Lincoln did more to overcome America's central problem of racial discrimination than LYNDON JOHNSON. As Senate majority leader he led the first successful assault on a U.S. Senate that had become the citadel of resistance to the achievement of equal rights for blacks. As President, he completed that fight by winning the enactment of laws that provided equal opportunity for all Americans for jobs, education, housing, and in all places of public accommodation.

He also made noble beginnings in challenging the poverty that has always plagued millions of Americans.

Like all of us he had shortcomings, made his mistakes, suffered his failures. But he was a man of compassion, who was fiercely proud of this country and its people and did his best to help it became the Great Society of which he dreamed.

Mr. Robert C. Byrd. Mr. President, LYNDON B. JOHNSON achieved the highest office to which an American can aspire. In his lifetime, he was the confidant and friend of men and women, from the highest to the lowest, in every corner of the globe. He was a man of immense strengths and of immense compassion.

LYNDON JOHNSON loved his country, and spent his life in its service. History will record his triumphs and his tragedies, but to those of us in this Chamber who know him as a colleague and as a friend, he will always remain a towering figure in his time.

Though he may be best remembered as a President, LYNDON JOHNSON, in his heart, was a man of the Senate. He had a deep and abiding faith in this body, and in its place in the past and future history of this Republic. His achievements as the majority leader are too well known to require elaboration; suffice it to say that it is quite possible that the years LYNDON JOHNSON spent in the Senate, might well have been the happiest and most satisfying of his life.

This historic Chamber has known great men in the past, and will see other great men in the future. LYNDON BAINES JOHNSON has his place among them.

MESSAGE FROM THE HOUSE

A message from the House of Representatives by Mr. Berry, one of its reading clerks, communicated to the Senate the intelligence of the death of Hon. LYNDON BAINES JOHNSON, former President of the United States of America, and transmitted the resolution of the House of Representatives (H. Res. 152) relating thereto.

The message announced that the House had agreed to a concurrent resolution (H. Con. Res. 90) authorizing the remains of former President LYNDON B. JOHNSON to lie in state in the rotunda of the Capitol, in which it requested the concurrence of the Senate.

Mr. Robert C. Byrd. Mr. President, I ask the Chair to lay before the Senate a message from the House on House Concurrent Resolution 90.

The Presiding Officer (Mr. Bartlett) laid before the Senate House Concurrent Resolution 90, which was read as follows:

HOUSE CONCURRENT RESOLUTION 90

Resolved by the House of Representatives (the Senate concurring), That in recognition of the long and distinguished service rendered to the Nation and to the world by LYNDON B. JOHNSON, Thirty-sixth President of the United States, his remains be permitted to lie in state in the rotunda of the Capitol from January 24 to January 25, 1973, and the Architect of the Capitol, under the direction of the Speaker of the House of Representatives and the President pro tempore of the Senate, shall take all necessary steps for the accomplishment of that purpose.

Mr. Robert C. Byrd. Mr. President, I ask unanimous consent for the immediate consideration of the concurrent resolution.

The Presiding Officer. Is there objection?

There being no objection, the concurrent resolution (H. Con. Res. 90) was considered and unanimously agreed to.

Mr. Mansfield. Mr. President, I have received some tentative information, which will have to be finalized, to the effect that those who intend to go to Texas for the final rites for former President LYNDON BAINES JOHNSON will likely have to leave an hour and a half earlier than the time for the services to be held at the National City Christian Church in Washington. Further information will be announced as soon as it can be obtained, but so far we are operating in the dark.

WEDNESDAY, *January 24, 1973.*

PRAYER

The Chaplain, the Reverend Edward L. R. Elson, D.D., offered the following prayer:

Eternal Father, we lift our hearts to Thee in thanksgiving for the tidings of peace and reconciliation. Guide us through this day Thy Holy Spirit that the tributes of affection and gratitude for Thy servant LYNDON BAINES JOHNSON may be to Thy glory and the honor of this Nation. May the words of our mouths and the meditations of our hearts be acceptable in Thy sight, O Lord our strength and our Redeemer. Amen.

Hon. Lloyd M. Bentsen
OF TEXAS

Mr. President, today is a somber day for all Americans.

With the death of LYNDON JOHNSON the country has lost one of its strongest leaders, the disadvantaged one of their greatest champions, and I have lost a dear friend. LYNDON JOHNSON's humanity will, in my opinion, be his greatest legacy. His humanity encompassed all men and it included the flaws that we all share. But it was a humanity that carried him through a life of political power without allowing him to forget those who had no power. It was a humanity that

enabled him to enjoy the ultimate ambition of American political life while remembering those who never shared in the abundance and success that we know as Americans.

In the terms of the Texas hill country—"He never forgot his beginnings," and the memory of those beginnings provided us with a legacy of social programs that cover the entire spectrum of life in our society.

LYNDON JOHNSON translated the dreams of a generation of political leaders into an administration of action that will be remembered in history as one of our most exciting eras of domestic achievements.

LYNDON JOHNSON felt that the poor, the black, the aged, the Mexican American, and the Indian were Americans, who continued to face severe handicaps in language, jobs, education, health, and housing opportunities.

For they had sought, but too often had been denied, the dignity of well-paid labor. They had sought, but often had been denied, the proper tools of education for their children. They had sought—but had suffered often because of it—to maintain their own proud traditions in a free society where differences should be respected and cultural diversity honored.

LYNDON JOHNSON was well acquainted with the problems of the poor and the disadvantaged, for he had taught Mexican-American children in the public schools of south Texas. It was here and then that he developed a deep compassion and understanding for the Spanish speaking, who, like many other minority groups, have often had to turn to government to protect their rights and encourage their advancement.

When he became President, LYNDON JOHNSON said:

Government has an obligation to match the promise of American opportunity with action—in employment, a decent wage, better education, improved housing, improved community facilities, and the guarantee of civil rights which every American expects.

The man's legislative accomplishments were legion. Ideals and social programs that had languished in the Congress for years were placed on the books during his 5 crowded years in office.

LYNDON JOHNSON knew his years in the Presidency were limited, and he also knew that given the nature of Congress and the realities of public opinion, he would have to act swiftly. And so he did.

Medical protection for the elderly and poor had been discussed since the days of social security; he passed the bills creating the medicare and medicaid program.

The precious right to vote had been sought by minorities for decades; the President noted that—

We have been talking about equal rights for a hundred years or more . . . Now it is time to write them into law.

And the Voting Rights Act was signed into law.

Expanded Federal aid to education had been a dream almost brought to fruition by John Kennedy. LYNDON JOHNSON succeeded in passing the Elementary and Secondary Education Act of 1965, the higher education, the Bilingual Education Act, and a series of landmark educational measures.

Our outmoded immigration laws had been decried as a national scandal since the 1920's; LYNDON JOHNSON succeeded in having them changed.

All of these measures and more were not the hasty creation of a man bent on revolutionary social change. They were the measures delayed by inaction, frustration, competing interest groups, and the absence of forceful leadership. And LYNDON JOHNSON provided the leadership and made these ideas into reality.

But it is important to remember that improvements in education, equal rights for our citizens, more humane immigration laws, and the rest of the Johnson program were not abstractions to LYNDON JOHNSON.

When he worked for education, he thought of the individual children who were denied an equal chance, because their schools and their materials did not measure up. When he worked for more adequate medical protection, he thought in terms of the elderly man or woman who cannot pay his medical bills and who is cast away on the fragile mercy of the State.

When he sought voting rights for all, he spoke of the individual who deserves a voice in choosing the direction his Government will take.

It has been said that LYNDON JOHNSON concentrated on the quantity of legislation rather than on the effects of legislation. I could not disagree more. A bill to him was only significant in that it made life better for people, people who were underfed and underemployed, people who were undereducated and who did not receive decent medical care. I have never known a man more intimately involved with the needs of his individual countrymen than LYNDON JOHNSON. And

it is that quality of caring that I remember most vividly.

Mr. President, LYNDON JOHNSON's life touched every American and shaped a future for this country that will be his living monument. He was a lion of a man: He held tenaciously to his convictions and possessed a sense of duty to country that never waivered.

He was a restless, impatient man who found too fews hours in a day and too little done at each day's end. He is at rest now and the memory of his time here will be a personal treasury for me and a source of pride for his countrymen.

He once said:

I have devoted my time on this earth to working toward the day when there would be no second-class citizenship in America, no second-quality opportunity, no second-hand justice at home, no second-place status in the world for our ideals and benefits.

That could well be his epitaph.

Mr. President, I ask unanimous consent that a most perceptive article which appeared in The Kansas City Times on Wednesday, January 24, 1973, written by Joe Lastelic, entitled "Man in a Stetson Who Rose to the Top" be printed at this point.

[The Kansas City Times, Wednesday, January 24, 1973]

MAN IN A STETSON WHO ROSE TO THE TOP

(By Joe Lastelic)

Washington—A personal letter from LYNDON B. JOHNSON arrived on my desk Monday afternoon. An hour or so later, at suppertime, I learned he was dead.

His letter was in answer to my request that he write an article for our Sunday magazine Star, on his associations with Harry S. Truman, to be published in May to commemorate Truman's birthday anniversary.

"I will be glad to try my hand at preparing something," he said. "I am pleased to have this opportunity."

Mr. JOHNSON said he would be leaving at the end of this month for a vacation and sent his best wishes to my family and me. He signed the letter L.B.J.

I was elated, as were my editors in Kansas City. Now that project must be forgotten, and all of us are deprived of what would have been a wonderful story.

I had asked for a special favor, and he wanted to grant it. That was LYNDON BAINES JOHNSON. He liked to do things for people. That explained his record of social welfare legislation to help the poor, the sick, the ignorant, those discriminated against. It explains why he remained convinced that the war in Vietnam was a fight to help a small nation and its people from being overrun by communism.

His friend, former President Truman, had lived long enough to see his old critics become admirers. JOHNSON did not. He did more in the fields of education and civil rights, for poor people and old people, than most presidents. But the awards, accolades and compliments from them were sparse. The war overshadowed all he had accomplished.

I remember a day when JOHNSON, then vice president, spent a long time cajoling the late Sen. Edward V. Long of Missouri on the Senate floor. Later I asked Long what JOHNSON was trying to sell.

"He wanted me to vote for that bill," Long said. "I told him I couldn't—my people wouldn't like it. He told me: 'Ed, people won't remember how you vote. It's the favors that count.' "

I met LYNDON JOHNSON in the 1960 campaign and traveled with him as a member of his staff every day for three months, covering 42 states and 72,000 miles. In Des Moines I was introduced to him aboard his airplane. He shook my hand, winked, then talked about his love for the little towns we were flying over on the way back to Washington.

In the hill country of Texas where he was born and died, LYNDON JOHNSON, more than anything else, learned about people—their loyalty. He never forgot them in Hye, Fredericksburg, Johnson City, Dripping Springs and all the rest.

"They know when you're sick; they care when you die," he would say in tribute to his neighbors.

It was his proud habit to take any visitor for a tour of the ranch. "This belongs to Lady Bird," he would say. "I'm just a government worker." He drove by the cemetery, where his mother, father and ancestors are buried—and where he will be buried. He took great pride in keeping the family cemetery a beautiful place. He stopped under an oak tree and contemplated the peaceful scene.

He had quit school, he recalled, to the distress of his parents. His father implored him to return to the classroom, to no avail. His mother, wiser, told him he did not have the brains to finish. LYNDON went back to school.

As we drove around the ranch JOHNSON stopped to admire his cattle. He could not resist some politicking. Slapping one on the rump, he said that when Truman was in office he was getting $3 more a hundredweight for his steers than they were bringing then—in the Eisenhower years.

JOHNSON had agreed to run with John F. Kennedy that year, and it was a decision that mystified many. His close friend and mentor, Sam Rayburn, speaker of the House, had counseled against it, though he later changed his mind. So did Sen. Robert Kerr of Oklahoma. So why did JOHNSON do it?

"My party has always been good to me," JOHNSON said. "Everything I have I owe to my party. My party needed me."

He reached into his pocket, pulled out a letter from a longtime friend and contributor and read it. It condemned him for taking the vice-presidential nomination, for "embracing socialism and Catholicism," as the letter put it. JOHNSON folded the letter, put it back into his pocket. Nobody said anything.

DINNER AT THE RANCH

At the dinner table at the LBJ ranch, JOHNSON sat at the head—his guests, his staff, reporters and Texas friends all about him. It was a good table with plenty of food, well prepared in the best country style—steak, corn on the cob, homemade bread, preserves and ice cream; sometimes enchiladas, tamales or other Mexican food; deer sausage mixed with pork for breakfast; incomparable barbecue.

To the distress of Lady Bird he shoveled in his food, lifting a plate of peas to his chin and spooning them in as he dominated the conversation. He might offer a culinary tip. The secret of good chili, he confided, was to refrigerate it, then scoop off all the grease before heating it again.

At the cocktail hour he preferred Scotch with plenty of fresh seltzer water. When he was drinking more than he should, Mrs. Johnson would chide him. "My doctor says that Scotch keeps my arteries open," was the JOHNSON defense. "They don't have to be that wide open," she said with a wifely smile.

He loved his family. He bragged about the women all the time. Often he would call at a store to look at dresses and personally selected some dresses and other items for his ladies. They complimented him on his good taste.

And how he loved desserts. He always wanted a second helping, but his wife and daughters, Lynda and Luci, did their best to frustrate him and keep him on a fragmentary diet. Once he spied a plateful of chocolate cookies just within reach. He pretended not to notice, but his hand moved toward them. Luci stopped him before he could sneak one away. I could not restrain myself.

"Luci," I said, "your father is the most powerful majority leader in the history of the Senate. Why can't he have a cookie in his own house?" JOHNSON laughed. She relented. He took three.

PURSUED PERFECTION

President JOHNSON was a man of perfection. He instructed the men on his staff on how to tie a tie so the knot was a work of art. He wore custom-made shirts, and on a hot day he would change his shirt as he went from rally to rally, sometimes using up a dozen shirts. He always dressed beautifully. The Stetson hat became his trademark.

His secretaries could not erase. Their letters had to be perfect. I took him a stencil once that was ready for the duplicating machine. He saw the spots where correction fluid had been applied. He would not approve it. I made the mistake of saying, "You don't understand"—Trying to explain how a stencil works. The reply was an order: "Redo it." Both secretaries cried.

In his anger (always shortlived) he sometimes made a scene, and his apology to those hurt in such incidents was unique. One day in the White House rose garden after a speech to some visitors, the President stepped from the porch, walked into the crowd and gave one of his secretaries, Willie Day Taylor, a kiss on the cheek. He never said a word.

"What was that for?" I asked her.

"He blamed me for something yesterday, found out today it wasn't my fault, and that's his way of saying, 'I'm sorry,' " she replied.

He looked after details. The fiasco of the Democrats in their campaign last year never would have been allowed in his operation. Because JOHNSON sometimes encountered loudspeakers that did not work, he brought along his own set. Everybody on his staff had to seek out anyone who helped at a campaign stop—from the policeman to cooks to band leaders to elevator operators to the mayor. Everyone got a thank-you note.

He insisted that anybody who wrote a letter to him should receive an answer. That was a requirement even when he was a freshman member of the U.S. House, with little thought of the presidency in mind.

In Chicago one night I was asleep in a motel when L.B.J. knocked at the door. It was 3 a.m

"What are you doing?" he asked, pushing his way into the room. "Sleeping," I replied. "What's George (Reedy) doing" he asked, Reedy, also a campaign aide, groggily sat up in his bed and lit a cigarette. JOHNSON said he wanted to talk.

"How many people will we have in Erie?" he asked of the next airport rally. Gov. David Lawrence had estimated about 6,000, Reedy replied. "I can't go there—Nixon had 15,000 last week," JOHNSON said. "Get the governor."

Despite the early hour Reedy found the governor's administrative assistant and began to explain the purpose of the call. JOHNSON took the receiver, ordered that the county chairmen in surrounding areas be called, buses chartered and every effort be made to get more people to the airport—or he would not show.

"Yes, sir," came the trembling voice from the other end of the line. The Johnson treatment worked. About 13,000 turned out for the rally, and local Republicans, the press and politicians could not figure where so many Democrats came from in a Republican area.

In Johnstown, Pa., the townspeople had presented a box of locally grown apples to the Johnsons. On returning to his plane JOHNSON wanted to know where the apples were. Bill Moyers, who later became JOHNSON's presidential press secretary, went to look for them and returned to confess they were not aboard.

In a measured voice JOHNSON explained his concern. "We insulted those people," he said. "We did not bother to take their gift." He waited for everyone listening to ponder that lack of courtesy, then went on.

"I saw them on the stage, so I asked the ladies if there was an orphanage. I sent the apples with my card to the children." His lecture continued. "Now I know you all are very busy. So I'll take care of the apples. You go do your work."

It was a typical JOHNSON performance that no one involved ever forgot. Nor were any more apples, grapes, flowers, live turkeys or anything else forgotten.

His attention to detail applied to the press as well. He knew the Washington press corps well, having often in his years as senator stayed late with the boys down at the National Press Club bar. Like most politicians, however, he did not understand the role of the press. A critical story would evoke a hurt remark to the writer: "I thought you were my friend."

He played games, delighting in surprising the press and the nation with his announcements. He was accessible, even as President, holding many news conferences and background sessions, granting interviews and inviting reporters to White House social functions.

He could be tough with reporters. Noticing that several had too much liquor to drink aboard his plane, he ordered the bar closed, complaining that the voters could not distinguish the newsmen from his staff and he would be blamed for their excesses. Some still sneaked drinks in the morning by ordering glasses of milk, then lacing the milk with Scotch.

KEEP THEM WRITING

When federal officials investigated why his big Electra airplane landed on his ranch strip in the 1960 campaign in violation of safety rules, the story filled the papers. At the dinner table JOHNSON brought up the subject to his staff.

"Do you know why the press is writing this story?" he asked. He answered his own question. "Because you guys didn't give them anything else to write about."

Unable to sleep one night he saw a light on in another motel room and found a Texas reporter hard at work at his typewriter. The reporter explained he was in need of an overnight story for the first edition the next day, but he was struggling because he had nothing new to say. JOHNSON provided an instant interview—an exclusive. Periodically after that he would pester his press staff: "What do you have for the overnighter for the boys?"

I had an interview with him in late 1967 in which he talked about the forthcoming campaign. He gave no hint that he intended to bow out and talked proudly of his record of accomplishments. His summation seemed like an opening campaign speech. He predicted that Richard Nixon would win the Republican presidential nomination, said Nelson Rockefeller had no chance because of a divorce and dismissed Ronald Reagan, George Romney and Charles Percy out of hand.

A month later he stopped me in the White House lobby.

"Why didn't you send me a copy of that interview I gave you?" he asked, throwing me off guard. "I saw it in the (Congressional) Record because Dick Bolling put it in." The reference was to Rep. Richard Bolling of Kansas City.

"Mr. President, I sent you three copies," I answered in defense.

Shuffling his feet and looking at the floor, he complained: "I'm the last one around here to see or hear anything."

I sent three more copies, and he thanked me with autographed photos taken during our session together.

LYNDON JOHNSON knew how to turn a bad situation to his advantage. At a South Carolina rally some high school boys and girls carried insulting signs calling him a counterfeit confederate. He learned they were being paid $5 each for their time. He answered their signs, then told the park rally: "We're going to tear the masks off of these men who hide behind little boys and girls."

Then turning his eyes heavenward, he prayed: "Father, forgive them, for they know not what they do."

In Dallas the silk-stocking district housewives came to heckle his luncheon and blocked his entry into the hotel. Police had to help JOHNSON and his wife through the hostile Republican crowd that was shouting insults. The Democrats in the dining room were livid, spoiling for a fight. JOHNSON went to the microphone. "I did not believe," he said, "the time would ever come when I could not walk through the hotel corridors of Dallas with my lady."

The story made headlines throughout the nation. Sen. Richard Russell (D-Ga.), who had been sitting out the campaign, rushed to Texas to be part of the Johnson entourage. "Lady Bird is like a daughter to him," JOHNSON explained. "He comes to the ranch, eats her pickled okra and reads his Plato."

The incident fired up the Texas Democrats, and many political commentators to this day are convinced that is what put Texas into the Democratic column. Without Texas, the Kennedy-Johnson ticket would have lost.

On another occasion he went to a luncheon in New York where the Liberal party was considering whether to endorse the Democratic ticket. The Liberals were angry with Kennedy for choosing JOHNSON, a Southerner they perceived as more enemy than friend. His reception was cool. The press waited for him to be chewed up.

"My friends here at the table asked me if I support your platform," JOHNSON began. "I don't know what your platform is. (Long pause) You didn't send me a copy. (Another long pause).

"But if you are for civil rights, for decent housing, for helping the poor, the oppressed, for building this nation, for tearing down the barriers that divide us, I'm for that."

Thus he went from subject to subject. He walked out of the room to a standing ovation, the endorsement of the Liberal party assured.

He laughed about that success for a long time. He loved good stories and liked to repeat them, laughing so loudly at his own punch lines that it became infectious.

COUSIN ORIOLE

At the ranch he made a nightly visit to his counsin, Oriole, his house guests tagging along. In the twilight as he approached the house he would start calling: "Cousin Oriole. Cousin Oriole." Once inside he stretched out on the brass bed, asked her about any subject that came to mind to get her views. Some of the great men of the world were guests in that little house.

JOHNSON teased her a lot, especially about a car he bought for her—which she wrecked.

"There is only one road leading up to and away from this house," JOHNSON would begin. "Nobody drives on this road but Cousin Oriole and the postman—and she ran into his car."

Amid whoops of laughter he would leave while Cousin Oriole chided him for embarrassing her.

An anti-Nixon story revolved around a legendary Texas schoolteacher seeking a job. The school board was divided and so they called him back and asked if he taught that the world was flat or round.

"He needed a job and he needed it bad," JOHNSON would go on. "So he gave a typical Dick Nixon answer: 'I can teach it either way.'"

Away from the campaign trail and especially in the last four years JOHNSON and Nixon were friends, burying any old hatchets left lying around.

Personally LYNDON JOHNSON was generous. He looked upon his friends as extensions of his family. When my mother met him—the first time she ever met a President—he gave her a big hug and a kiss. Children everywhere had his heart. In campaigns he would pass out autographed cards to them. In the trip to Pakistan, where the mortality rate is so high, he was moved to observe, "It would take so little, so little to make the difference between life and death."

That was one reason why he supported foreign economic aid, despite the cries at home to cut it out. In his office he proudly showed off a group of pictures of boys and girls of every race—every one of them named for him.

Having lost his mother and father, he knew the pain of sorrow and took time to write letters of condolence or to telephone a bereaved friend. It seemed he was always going to funerals. He knew what it meant to be lonely, to worry about the future. He had worked hard as a shoeshine boy, a truck driver, elevator operator

and teacher of Mexican children. Wealth came later in life, but those early experiences seared his memory and conscience. He used to say that the Kennedys just did not realize how hard it was to pay a medical bill.

The politician's politician, the wheeler and dealer, the manipulator of power, JOHNSON always was suspect for what he did. It mattered not what his motives, his sincerity, the critics were quick to find fault. When, as vice-president, he rode in the same car in a parade with some astronauts he was accused of horning in.

His critics forgot that when President Eisenhower had pooh-poohed the space program, JOHNSON had let him have it with: "I have my feet on the ground and my eyes on the stars."

His efforts in behalf of the voting rights bills and the landmark civil rights bill of 1964 caused him much trouble. In light of his past record of voting against antilynching laws when he was a Texas senator, he was pressed to explain his change of heart when he became President. Was he indeed sincere about civil rights as President, or was it just for the votes?

"I didn't feel it then as I do now," he said, adding that no matter how many times the critics point to his past mistakes he was on the right course and would continue it. That admission resulted in the subject fading from the news.

One afternoon in his White House living room he talked about Vietnam. How long would the war last? A correspondent wanted to know. The year was 1965.

"How long you gonna live?" JOHNSON shot back.

"I don't know," the reporter replied.

"That's the answer," JOHNSON said.

Even in the closing days of his administration JOHNSON remained steadfast about his role in Vietnam. There were other things he would have changed, he said, but Vietnam was not a mistake. He wanted peace, he wanted to bring the men home—but this nation had to keep its word. The fact that peace eluded him, he said, was his greatest disappointment.

So Sam's son and Rebekah's boy will return to the nation's capital today, to the scene of his failures and successes, to the places where he served his nation. Hardly a day has gone by since he left here without his name entering a reporter's conversation. LYNDON JOHNSON was that kind of a man. His style was so overwhelming, his determination so crushing, you knew he was something special.

Hon. John G. Tower
OF TEXAS

Mr. President, LYNDON BAINES JOHNSON—the 36th President of the United States—was a Texan in every good sense of the word. He was a superb leader in the Congress of the United States and he was an able President. He was a man of great compassion for his fellow man. His enormous energy and his driving ambition consumed him and those around him. He pushed himself beyond his own physical capabilities to get done the job he felt must be done, and this, no doubt, shortened his years here with us.

President JOHNSON confronted the critical and fast moving events of his day with the determination to make decisions that would serve the greatest good for the greatest number of people. History likely will remember him best for his leadership in the field of human rights. He also will be remembered for his great ability in the field of legislation—as a member of both the legislative and executive branches of our Government.

It was characteristic of the 36th President of the United States that he was able to maintain warmth and to extend the right hand of friendship even to those who opposed him. He was a man who had a forgiving nature, who never carried a grudge—a man who never became dissolved in any sense of bitterness or frustration. It is indeed unfortunate that he was taken from us at this time in his life when there was so much more in the way of good counsel and advice that he could have given to many of us, and so much more he could have taught our young people, in whom he had such a deep and abiding interest.

As much as the war in Southeast Asia dominated his Presidency, it is tragically ironic that he was taken from us only hours before an agreement was announced ending that long and costly entanglement. He yearned for peace which eluded him during those lonely years in the White House.

We shall sorely miss him. Those of us who are Texans can think better of ourselves, because we came from a society that produced LYNDON BAINES JOHNSON.

Hon. Hugh Scott
OF PENNSYLVANIA

Mr. President, one of the mysteries of Heaven's design lies in the ironies with which it revises our human scripts.

LYNDON JOHNSON loved people and loved to be with people, and he loved an audience and he entertained an audience; and it is sadly tragic that at the moment of his death he died alone.

He would have liked, I think, some last words to leave with us; I feel that, indeed, he did leave us those last words. From the moment he became President and stood in that somber light on that tragic day in Dallas and said.

I will do the best I can; I ask your help and God's.

He had the last words.

At the very end of his life, in his last appearance as a public man, he said that some Americans stand on uneven ground and that all men aspire to stand on the level, one with another. He ended as he had so many times, using the same refrain, with the words "We shall overcome."

It seems to me that, as always, our friend LYNDON JOHNSON had the last word.

Hon. Russell B. Long
OF LOUISIANA

Mr. President, today we mourn the passing of LYNDON BAINES JOHNSON, a friend to most of us here and the man whom I hold above any American of his time. With all of my colleagues I join in extending sympathy to his widow, Lady Bird, his daughters, and other family relatives.

LYNDON JOHNSON was the greatest legislative leader in our history by any standard. His record of accomplishments is massive in number and impressive in scope.

I remember his words upon leaving the White House:

What really matters is not the ultimate judgment that historians will pass but whether there was a change for the better in the way our people live. I think there was.

The JOHNSON administration recommended 200 major measures to the Congress; 181 of them were passed. Most are still with us today, a body of law designed to benefit all Americans, in every walk of life.

Perhaps his most important legacy to our Nation is his resolution of the age-old quarrels over civil rights and equal opportunity for all. In his first address to the Congress as President he called for the enactment of a strong civil rights bill. He signed it into law in July 1964, 6 months after taking office. It was the most sweeping civil rights bill since Reconstruction days.

Another milestone in his Great Society program was the passage of medicare and medicaid legislation, breaking the impasse over the issue of medical care for the aged. I was privileged to manage that milestone law and probably view it with more emphasis than some. It fit L. B. J.'s philosophy—and mine—to help those who cannot adequately help themselves.

He also broke the years of deadlock over Federal aid to elementary and secondary education, assuring a good education for all our children.

LYNDON JOHNSON tried to correct every evil and injustice known to him. He declared his war on poverty to uplift the lives of so many Americans.

It will be many years before we fully appreciate all he did for this Nation.

As his achievements were greatest in the field of domestic reform, his greatest frustration was in the war in Southeast Asia. Unlike Harry Truman, LYNDON JOHNSON did not live to see vindicated his decision to commit American troops against aggression; but, history may yet prove that this was the wisest, although the most costly and disappointing, experience of his life.

In October 1966 in addressing our troops at Cam Ranh Bay, he said,

> You know what you are fighting against: A vicious and illegal aggression across this little nation's frontier. You know what you are fighting for: To give the Vietnamese people a chance to build the kind of nation they want—free from terror, free from intimidation, and free from fear.

History may show that by resisting aggression in the jungles and rice paddies of Vietnam, LYNDON JOHNSON saved the world from the course of events that could have ended in a war of atomic devastation.

LYNDON JOHNSON began his life 64 years ago in Stonewall, a small town in Texas. At his birth, his grandfather prophetically said:

> He'll be a United States Senator someday.

He was a Senator some day; he was one of our greatest, and it was my privilege to serve with him for many years.

He came to the Senate from the House in 1948, winning the election by only 87 votes, thus earning him the nickname of "Landslide LYNDON." He was a powerful legislator from the very beginning. Before he completed his first term, he became minority leader; and in 1954, when the Democrats regained power, he became majority leader.

From Capitol Hill, JOHNSON assumed the second highest office in the United States. As Vice President not only did he fulfill the traditional constitutional role of the office by presiding over the Senate, he was also chairman of the President's Space Council, headed the President's Commission on Equal Employment Opportunities, and served on the National Security Council.

LYNDON JOHNSON was 55 years old when, in that time of national grief and horror, an assassin's bullet made him President.

He said to the Nation:

> I will do my best. That is all I can do.

Mr. President, he served in the highest office of our country for 5 years and he did his best.

His best was great, indeed, and I believe history will record it as such. LYNDON JOHNSON may well have been our greatest President.

Hon. Mike Mansfield
OF MONTANA

Mr. President, death can, at times, be delayed but, in the end, cannot be avoided. Within the past month, two former Presidents of the United States, Harry S. Truman and LYNDON BAINES JOHNSON, have left their existence here on earth. Both were Senators of the United States. Both, through the death of others, became Presidents of the United States and, then, in their own right, became Presidents again.

It was my privilege to work with these men but most closely with LYNDON BAINES JOHNSON. I served with him for 4 years as the assistant majority leader of the Senate. I succeeded him as majority leader when he became Vice President in 1961 and continued in that capacity throughout his Presidency.

We were in friendly and fairly close contact for those many years. As President, LYNDON JOHNSON was the head of the executive branch and, as the majority leader, I was the representative of the Senate. As might be expected, we did not always agree but at no time did our disagreements impair the civility of our relationship.

LYNDON JOHNSON came from humble origins but he was not a humble man. Rather, he was a man of great pride and his Presidency was a Presidency which bore the hallmark of this pride. We shall not see his like again, nor shall we see the kind of legislative program which was enacted in response to his determined leadership in the pursuit of equal opportunity for all Americans.

Insofar as proposing and enacting legislation in the field of domestic and social reform, LYNDON JOHNSON was, in my judgment, the greatest of Presidents. Historically, his record in that respect will emerge as superior to any other President or any combination of Presidents. He was in the tradition of Franklin D. Roosevelt, the man he so much admired, and his dream of a great society of free men will be his enduring monument in the history of this Republic.

Mrs. Mansfield, our daughter Anne, and I wish to extend our deepest condolences and sympathy to Lady Bird Johnson, one of the outstanding First Ladies of this Republic, to the Johnson daughters, Lynda and Luci, and to all their families in this hour of sorrow and bereavement. May his restless soul find peace.

Hon. John J. Sparkman
OF ALABAMA

Mr. President, I am pleased to have the opportunity to join my colleagues in paying tribute to a man who all of us knew and with whom we all served, former President of the United States LYNDON B. JOHNSON.

LYNDON JOHNSON entered Congress—the House of Representatives—approximately 3½ months after I did. He served on the Naval Affairs Committee; I served on the Military Affairs Committee. We were closely associated. I knew him throughout the years. Our families were friends.

I have always admired LYNDON JOHNSON for the tremendous job he did in the Senate and as President of the United States. I think we never had a majority leader who was more active, more attentive, more aggressive, and more effective than he was. During part of the time, he was the minority leader, and he showed the same interest and the same activity.

As others have pointed out, he sponsored and put through the Senate—and it may well be said that he put through the entire Congress—some of the most helpful legislation we have seeen enacted. He was interested in all general legislation, but he was especially interested in some of the things that were new and some of the things that were special.

I recall, for example, the very active interest he took in the development of the space program. He really took the leadership in that matter.

I recall his activity in the field of small business. He was actively interested in good housing and all the programs for the good of the people generally throughout the United States.

I shall always remember one thing about him. When President Eisenhower was elected, he brought a Republican Congress with him. LYNDON was our minority leader—the Democratic leader—but I recall the stand he took, right in the beginning, that:

We are not going to be an opposition party as such. We are going to do our best to cooperate and make this a good administration.

I recall some of the things that happened in connection with foreign policy and the activity in the Committee on Foreign Relations and the attitude and the results of the expressed attitude of LYNDON JOHNSON.

He was active when he was President, one of the most active Presidents we have had. He came into the Presidency as the result of a great tragedy, but he took hold quickly; and I feel that he did his best to carry out the policies that had been carried along by President Kennedy, with whom he was serving as Vice President.

I recall an appointment that I had with President Kennedy for December 2, 1963. Following his death and the taking over of the Presidency by President Johnson, I called him one day and told him that I had that appointment to talk about a matter of great concern to my State and my part of the country, and that I should like to see him as soon as I could.

He said to me.

Give me a little time, let me get settled in this job, and I will call you.

Not long after that, he did call me. I talked to him about the project in which he was particularly interested, and he suggested an action that we might take. He said it would require $100,000 to carry out what he had in mind, that he had that money available, and that we would not have to call for an appropriation. So the study he proposed was made, and it proved most helpful in the clearance of the project at a later time.

A great deal has been said, and even more will be said, about the war, in which he was so deeply absorbed.

I remember being at the White House on different occasions, when he would have a small group of Members, primarily of the Foreign Relations Committee, to discuss the war with him. Several of us were there on the morning that he made his decision with reference to what has been called an escalation of the war. He spent a couple of hours discussing the different alternatives that might be taken; then he asked for the advice of those present. I believe I never saw any person deeper in anguish or more troubled than he was on that morning in trying to reach the fateful decision that would be for the best interests of the country and for the world as a whole.

I remember when President JOHNSON made his announcement that he would not be a candidate for renomination. I was in my home in Huntsville, Ala. After listening to him, I immediately called him on the telephone and asked him if he really meant that. I said:

Surely you don't mean that.

He said:

Yes, I think it is best.

I have believed all along, from the things that he told me that night, that he believed that his leaving office might make it easier for someone else to come in and solve this difficult problem with which the country was confronted, and to bring peace. I wish he might have lived long enough to know the developments that have just taken place.

We have sustained a great loss in the going of former President LYNDON JOHNSON. Mrs. Sparkman, my daughter, and I all join with our colleagues here in expressing our sympathy to Lady Bird Johnson, to Lynda Bird, to Luci, and to the whole family. We extend to them our deepest sympathy and pray that the good Lord will comfort them and look over them in these difficult times.

Hon. Alan Bible
OF NEVADA

Mr. President, LYNDON BAINES JOHNSON was a dynamic leader whose life touched closely on us all, and there is shock as well as grief at his passing. No one in Congress or across the Nation was prepared for the suddenness with which death came to this great American. Indeed, it is still difficult to believe his unceasing energy has been stilled.

We mourn the departure of a remarkable political leader, a man who will be regarded by history as one of our greatest Presidents. Here in the Senate, where LYNDON JOHNSON left the indelible mark of his forceful personality, we feel a deep personal loss. He was a commanding figure in both Congress and the White House and I cherish the memory of our close friendship which spanned more than two decades. I shall be ever grateful for his wise counsel when I first entered the Senate. He visited Nevada on innumerable occasions, where he gained many lasting friendships. He was never too busy to assist his friends and his party.

President JOHNSON devoted his entire life to public service, starting with a humble teaching position in his beloved Texas and culminating in the Nation's highest office. His public career kept him at the Capital much of his life, but he never lost touch with the people and the land and with his home on the Pedernales.

It was this close touch with the people and the land that made him a great President. And it was

his long service in Congress—an institution he revered— that made him such an effective President. As perhaps no other Chief Executive, he surmounted the legislative and executive division to achieve an unparalleled spirit of cooperation and unity of purpose between the White House and Capitol Hill.

His energy and drive, his zest for the high challenge of national political leadership—all these were legendary. As President he met those challenges headon. His remarkable record of achievement in the areas of human rights and opportunities is unmatched. He worked incessantly against hunger, poverty, illiteracy, and bigotry. And yet this man of peace found himself prosecuting a destructive, bloody, and unpopular war in Southeast Asia. He met the military challenge abroad with the same determination— if not the personal conviction—that marked his pursuit of social goals.

History will remember LYNDON JOHNSON not as a leader in war, but as a crusader for peace and justice. On that basis it will judge him, and it will judge him a President of immense stature and compassion whose mark will always remain on the social progress of our Nation.

It is perhaps fitting that he died close to the people and the land he loved so much. But this does not ease the great sense of loss our Nation feels.

A remarkable leader has gone. There will never be another like him. Our grief is deep.

Hon. John C. Stennis
OF MISSISSIPPI

Mr. President, along with many other Senators, I have a great deal of feeling on this occasion. Our late friend and I had, for years, identical committee assignments in the Senate. On two of those committees we sat side by side for more than 10 years. I know of many of the major decisions he made then, and even more particularly as floor leader of this body.

I was with him a good deal when he was Vice President, and I know much of what he went through as President of the United States. He was a remarkable man. He was, as we know, a man of action, of great ability. He was always up front, where the action was. Not as an eager beaver, as we use that term, but because he liked the action, and he wanted to do things. He was willing to pay the price. He was not afraid and never dodged a problem because it was hard. But I am going to mention particularly two instances that I remember in which he rendered great service to this country in time of crisis; and he was always ready to respond to crises.

The first was at the time of sputnik, when the Soviet Union orbited the first man-made satellite. Most of us in Congress and many people over the Nation were uncertain. I will not say they were afraid, but there was an air of uncertainty. The feeling of the people was not despair, but the deepest concern as to what this event meant and where the United States stood. These questions were asked: "How delinquent, if at all, was the United States in being prepared;" and "What was the potential power of the Soviet Union and its technology;" and "What was our defense, if any?" He held the first hearings on the situation as chairman of the Preparedness Subcommittee of the Armed Services Committee, and I sat right next to him on that committee.

I thought he rendered a tremendous service at that time. The question developed as to whether or not we were going to make space exploration a civilian program or have it under the military, as had been the case with atomic energy a few years before. He cast his thinking, his lot finally, on the idea of creating a separate, nonmilitary agency which we now call NASA.

The creation of a civilian agency and civilian space program was a successful policy. He was closely connected with it during the first years of the program, and it was truly a pioneer work. He rendered great service in the beginning and development of the space program.

Another crisis that tested him greatly, one which was graver than the first, was the tragic death of the late President John Kennedy. In that confusion, turmoil, international crisis, and crisis at home, I think LYNDON JOHNSON showed his worth as a man of tremendous inner courage, steadfastness, and determination. At the same time, he showed the greatest deference to our fallen President and the first family and the grief of the Nation. He was placed in as difficult a position as one could be placed. He had to assemble his thoughts in a matter of a few minutes, take the tremendous burden of being President of the United States, assure the people and pull them together, assure the free world of our course and his course, and also let all nations know that we would be firm.

It was a tremendous accomplishment amidst criticism on the part of some. A lesser man could not have carried that load the way he did. In a very short time things had settled down due largely to his assurances. The assurances came from his conduct and in the way he took charge.

I want to mention another event here that I feel throws some light on our late friend that might have passed unnoticed unless someone had had some special experience with it. Many will remember during the time of his first heart attack he was a very, very ill man for days and weeks. I lived near Bethesda Naval Hospital, and I would go out to see him after he was able to have company. On one visit, we talked about what is now known as the Jefferson Bible. As many will recall, Jefferson clipped out certain parts of the Bible and put them in a little book. This book is now known as the Jefferson Bible. Senator JOHNSON was very much interested in it then. I got one at the bookstore and took it to him.

He read it all and reported back to me. He was already familiar with the Bible. I do not want to be misunderstood. But he did not have knowledge of Jefferson's particular approach. He never forgot that I had given him a Bible. In the heat of controversy surrounding the White House about the war, he would quote something out of that Bible in his efforts to try to persuade a person. That showed the spiritual current that ran through his character and ran through his mind all the time. This feature surfaced when he was under stress and making hard decisions in a crisis of one kind or another.

I think the greatest difficulty he encountered in the White House was in connection with the war. He was unable to do all he wanted to do. He could not overcome that war obstacle during his term. He was surrounded in such a way that a solution could not be found. I do not say it was his failure. He tried hard. I think, most unfortunately, he received some advice from others that turned out ot be based on erroneous facts, particularly in the early years of the war. They were miscalculations of others. He, and any President has to act, at least in part, on the advice and recommendations of others, but the advice and counsel given to the late President as to what could be done under certain circumstances was under a grave error. I state this for the record deliberately, only to make my little comment on the record a little clearer what he was up against. He never made such a claim to me. I never heard him blame anyone. I am not trying to assess blame, but those of us who were close enough to know what he went through and what the facts were know how those miscalculations misfired.

To Lady Bird Johnson, whom I think was one of our truly great First Ladies, and to all the family, Mrs. Stennis and I extend our condolences in their great loss. And may God bless them now and sustain them now and in the years ahead.

Hon. Robert Taft, Jr.
OF OHIO

Mr. President, I join in the tributes to LYNDON B. JOHNSON. He was one of those unique men with great capacity for leadership. His meteoric rise in the Senate was itself testimony to that fact and acceptance of this quality by his colleagues. Of this he was most proud.

In a number of pleasant, personal contacts with him, he appeared to like nothing more than to reflect on his legislative battles in the Senate in which my father was often a strong adversary. But they were adversaries with great mutual respect and friendship, even in disagreement.

This man's strength and dedication to service and loyalty to his American heritage was admired by all. And, with his great legislative skill, they have already earned him great recognition in history, especially through the many great landmark pieces of legislation which were passed during his administration. I refer particularly to the Civil Rights Act, in which I was very active while a Member of the House. I do not believe that measure could have passed without his strong leadership and the support of the White House. This legislation was in the best interest of the Nation.

I remember particularly when our intelligence ship was attacked over North Korea that I made some comments to him with regard to it, expressing disagreement and caution as to what occurred. He then asked me to visit with him and Walt Rostow at the White House to be sure that I had a full understanding of the situation and the national implications involved. This, I think, was typical of him, rising above, and recognizing that others were capable of rising above, a given situation.

Partisan though he could be, he never allowed partisanship to deter him from pursuing courses of action, no matter how difficult, that he felt were in the best interest of the Nation.

He will be remembered as a legend and will be deeply missed for his sound and careful advice that he often offered to those who knew him.

I join in expressing sympathy to Mrs. Johnson and to the entire Johnson family.

Hon. Jennings Randolph
OF WEST VIRGINIA

Mr. President, our feeling for LYNDON JOHNSON goes back a long time. Perhaps of all the Members in this Chamber, I actually knew him first on Capitol Hill. I came to the House of Representatives and was sworn into office in March of 1933, almost 40 years ago. There are only two Members of the Congress, Representative Wright Patman of Texas and the Senator who now speaks, who were Members of the Congress when Franklin D. Roosevelt became the President of the United States of America.

I remember sitting in the House of Representatives on May 13, 1937, when LYNDON JOHNSON took his oath of office after having been elected in a special election on April 10, 1937, from a congressional district in Texas. As I recall, he had 10 or 11 opponents in the primary. He succeeded Representative Buchanan, who had died in office.

I recall that on the next day, May 14, 1937, I sat talking with LYNDON JOHNSON. I had known him as one of the doorkeepers in the House of Representatives. I had also known him as a member of the staff of Representative Richard Kleberg of Texas.

Mr. President, I asked him where he was going to be living. He replied:

You know, with all the thousands of people who are coming into Washington under the New Deal agencies, and with the depression that resulted in no construction of new housing, it is not easy to find a place in which to live.

It was my time to try to be helpful, saying:

I have two friends who have a furnished apartment in Washington. Their names are Edith and Sam Ourbacker. He is with the Social Security Board and has been asked to take over the office in Cleveland, Ohio. They have contacted me and asked if, perhaps, I might know of someone who would like to rent their apartment.

As always he acted at once. He said:

Give me that telephone number.

I did so. He hurried into the Democratic cloak-room and called the Ourbackers. Early that evening he was at their apartment to see whether he would like it and whether their family would like him. He rented that apartment.

I will never forget what he later said to me:

Jennings, I think I will have to give you a finder's fee. I like that apartment. It has a 4-poster canopy bed that is very large, and I can stretch my legs on it.

We have poignant memories that come from earlier or later experiences with LYNDON JOHNSON.

His career, certainly in Congress, and his career in the White House were as one because he was a forceful and dedicated leader in every job he held or place of leadership he attained. I recall very well that he came to West Virginia, a number of times. My able colleague, Senator Robert C. Byrd, who is in the Chamber now, remembers many of these visits. However, before mentioning the three or four times that Senator Byrd and I were able to be with him in our State, I recall that LYNDON JOHNSON said to both of us in 1959 as we were sworn into service in this Chamber:

I want to be considered as the third Senator from West Virginia.

Yes, he was, in a sense, a third Senator from the State of West Virginia. He was very helpful to us.

And the former Vice President of the United States Hubert H. Humphrey, now a Senator again from the State of Minnesota who is in the Chamber at this time, remembers the day, because he was presiding in this Chamber, when the Appalachian Regional Development Act passed the Senate in 1965. I recall vividly the signing at the White House of that important bill.

President JOHNSON said:

This is a measure, I believe, that will help people in the Appalachian region to help themselves.

And it was true. We in Appalachia are better able to help ourselves—and each other.

LYNDON came to visit the State of West Virginia more than a dozen times. He came not only as a candidate for public office, but to be with the people in the hills and valleys of our State, sharing our concerns and hopes.

It was on September 20, 1964, that he came to Morgantown, W. Va., where he was a dedicatory speaker for new airport facilities. Some 25,000 persons were present for that ceremony. The emphasis then was on the development of transportation. He spoke of the movement of people, the movement of products, and the mobility of our Nation, and the closer ties between sections of our great country.

We remember all of the challenging speeches he gave. We remember when he came on September 3, 1966, to talk on another subject in West Virginia.

He journeyed into the hill country—into the mountains—and there he dedicated the beautiful Summersville Lake. He talked about conservation, the preservation of natural resources, the strength of people who came from the land, and he understood what he was talking about, for he was from the land—a man of the soil and the sky. Some 20,000 people gathered from over the hills and out of the valleys to hear that Nicholas County speech.

I remember so very well when the president of Bethany College, now the president emeritus, Dr. Perry Gresham, called and said.

LYNDON JOHNSON, the majority leader of the Senate, is a member of the Christian Church. Bethany College, in West Virginia, is a college of his denomination. We would like to have him come and make the commencement address, and present him with an honorary degree.

On June 7, 1959, he was in Bethany, W. Va., in what we call the Northern Panhandle of our State—a few miles from Wheeling—and on that occasion he talked about the need for education for the children of the United States of America. He talked about those who, for various reasons, had not had the broader opportunities for education which some portions of our population enjoy.

I have not given these incidents chronologically, because I wanted to come to one that exemplifies, in a sense, what is in our hearts today—a yearning for peace. LYNDON JOHNSON wanted that very much for all mankind.

We were privileged to have LYNDON JOHNSON in West Virginia to deliver what we then called the Armistice Day address. It was deep in the mountain country at Welch, in McDowell County, some 18,000 people were to hear him on that occasion as he told of the torment and the tribulation that was in his heart, even then as Vice President, because of the tragedy of the conflict in Southeast Asia. Bob Byrd will remember that we rode from the Mercer County Airport, located near Bluefield, in a helicopter to the Welch area, because of the rugged terrain.

That was on November 11, 1963; he was to undertake the awesome duties of the Presidency of the United States because of the tragedy which befell this Nation with the death of President John Kennedy. He seemed sad on that trip as he thought of brave men who were dying in battle in Vietnam.

I have spoken intimately, but I think that is the only way I would want to discuss LYNDON JOHNSON today. I never saw him stepping from one point to another; he was always striding from one point to another. I never saw him walking; he was always quickly going somewhere. I think that typified his life here on Capitol Hill and in the White House. And he moved the country with him.

I do remember, as do all of us, the civil rights fight in the Senate, when he kept us in session for extended periods because he believed that the filibuster should be broken and that Members of the Senate of the United States should vote on the civil rights issue. Yes, a man from the South, or the Southwest, led the fight.

Sometimes we have forgotten—perhaps even the leaders in that battle—the breakthrough which he made possible. He must never be forgotten for the work done in the area of human rights, nor should he be forgotten for his vital leadership in the fields of education, better health, and decent housing for the people of the United States of America. Sometime in our history people will understand the constructive contributions which he made during his vigorous lifetime. It was not so long in actual years, 64, but he crowded much into those years, always pressing, always working, always thinking, always, above all else—though some might have thought of him as an operator—endeavoring to secure programs to benefit people. He was a humanitarian, because he loved humanity—and helped humanity in dignity.

My wife Mary, and Lady Bird, were dear and cherished friends. She joins me in our sympathy to the Johnson family.

I remember his congratulatory message following our reelection to the Senate in November of last year—remembering, as always, one of the many colleagues with whom he had worked on Capitol Hill and in the White House. I responded, in part by stating:

I often recall the wonderful years I served for and with you in public life.

In an hour or so, the body of LYNDON JOHNSON will be carried into the rotunda of the Capitol.

His spirit, however, will inspire us because his was a boundless spirit that will be captured, if it is ever to be captured, only in American history.

Hon. John O. Pastore
OF RHODE ISLAND

Mr. President, on an occasion as solemn as this, I do not think what we have to say really counts for as much as what we feel. In my heart I feel that I have lost a dear friend.

I came to the Senate in December of 1950. Before that time I had never met LYNDON JOHNSON. But from the day that I did meet him until the day he died, I always cherished his friendship and admired his strength and the power of his character. He was very close to me, and I feel that I was very close to him. He stepped aside as a member of the Joint Committee on Atomic Energy to make room for me, and I have been a member of that committee from that day forward.

I shall never forget, in June of 1964, when I received word from one of the staff in the cloakroom—

The President of the United States is on the phone, and he would like to talk to you.

I picked up the phone and heard him say, "Johnny, is this you?"

I said, "Yes, this is I."

He said, "I want you to make a speech for me at the convention."

I said," What do you mean by that, Mr. President?"

He said, "I want you to make a keynote address."

And he said, "I want you to make a good speech, good for you and good for me."

He asked me on numerous occasions before the convention to show him the speech that I was preparing. I must say that I refused to do so, because I never showed that speech to anyone. I never made that speech before I made it on the floor of the convention in Atlantic City. As I am doing now, I thought the spontaneity of the moment was required for the effectiveness that one expects to give to his utterances.

The first time I made that speech I never recorded it, but it was recorded at the convention even as I made it. When at Atlantic City I had finished speaking, President JOHNSON was on the telephone again from the White House, congratulating me for what I had said on his behalf. I recall vividly what I said on that occasion, that no man in such a short period of time, the 7 months of his succession, had done more for the people of the country than LYNDON JOHNSON.

He was the father of the civil rights movement. For 100 years, we had struggled to carry out the issue of a civil war and the fiat of the Declaration of Independence that all men are created equal, and here was a southerner gifted with the humaneness and the humanity to realize that the color of a person's skin in America should not stand in the way of achieving his aspirations and ambitions. LYNDON JOHNSON fought hard. The first black man on the Supreme Court was appointed by LYNDON JOHNSON. The first time we heard of aid to education by the Federal Government was under LYNDON JOHNSON. It was the dream of President Kennedy, but it was the fulfillment of President JOHNSON.

These are the monuments that will endure as a reminder to all future Americans of what a good-hearted man can do.

In November of 1967, at his invitation, I sat alone with him in the Oval Room of the White House. He told me of his agony, that the war in Vietnam had accelerated to the divisive point that it had, and that he had been unable to unite the country.

He asked me this pointed question: He said:

Johnny, do you think I should step aside?

I looked him straight in the eye—I could not believe what he was saying to me—and I asked:

Mr. President, do you believe that what you are doing is right even though I disagree with you?

He said:

From my heart I believe that what I am doing is right.

I said:

Well, under those circumstances, if you are right, history will record you as being right; but if you are right and you step aside, history might record that you had failed the people of your country.

Frankly, I thought he was pulling my leg. I could not imagine that the President was serious about stepping aside. Yet I sat in the living room of my home with my wife on that night of March 31, 1968, when, at the conclusion of his speech, LYNDON JOHNSON said that he would not seek renomination and would refuse it if it was granted to him by the Democratic National Convention. Then I realized how serious he had been and how deep his personal agony really had been that previous November of 1967.

Yes, he stepped aside so peace negotiations might be advanced. He gave up the Presidency because he loved his country. If LYNDON JOHNSON had run for reelection in 1968, he might not have achieved the overwhelming plurality of votes he received in 1964, but surely, in my heart, I believe he would have been elected.

But he said on that occasion:

If I step aside, maybe North Vietnam will realize that I am sincere and they will come to the negotiating table.

Mr. President, is it not ironic that today, when Henry Kissinger is detailing the agreement that we have achieved on a cease-fire and the termination of hostilities in Vietnam, the body of LYNDON JOHNSON is lying in state in the rotunda of the Capitol of the United States which he loved so intensely.

Perhaps it is prophetic—perhaps it is God's will—that this is the time peace was to come—the end of a war—the end of a life. History will judge the wisdom of his way—but right or wrong I shall remember LYNDON JOHNSON as my friend. He cherished his family. He adored his Lady Bird. He loved his children. A man who has that intensity of love, has love for his fellow man.

LYNDON JOHNSON knew hard times. He was a young man during the depression years of the 1920's. He worked for a dollar a day. He helped the underprivileged and the suffering because he knew suffering. No man can be big unless he learns to be little. When the chips were down, LYNDON JOHNSON had a heart for the little people.

Thus, on the occasion of his requiem today, I cannot find the words to match the greatness of this individual, because the Lord, with all His generosity, has not blessed any person with adequacy of tongue and mind to say fully what is in his heart.

I say it, as simply and as sincerely as I can—even though it be inadequate—that I mourn his passing. My home extends to his home our deepest sympathy.

I pray that God will give the family of LYNDON JOHNSON the strength to remember the years of happiness they spent together. Let this serve as the premise and the promise for their future good fortune, good health, and happiness.

Hon. Claiborne Pell

OF RHODE ISLAND

Mr. President, the news of the death Monday night of President LYNDON JOHNSON saddened me very deeply, for the world seems an emptier place without his immense energy.

LYNDON JOHNSON was a true leader of men during the 31 consecutive years that he served his State and his country as a Congressman, Senator, naval officer, Vice President, and President.

Guided by his deep compassion and concern for the problems of all our people, he directed his driving force toward improving the quality of life for our people.

The list of his legislative accomplishments, both in the Congress and as President, seems limitless. So many of the programs that we almost take for granted today would not be on the lawbooks were it not for his singular determination and his masterful skill as a legislator.

He was a man who put less stock in rhetoric than in accomplishment. He told us that we as a Nation had talked too long about equality of opportunity for all our citizens. He sought action and he saw to it that we passed the most comprehensive civil rights bill in 100 years.

He sought and obtained action in other fields: medical care for the aged, a higher minimum wage, a major new housing program, and a start toward cleaning up our polluted environment.

And he provided the impetus for a massive infusion of Federal funds into our elementary and secondary schools, programs that I have had the opportunity to oversee for the past 4 years.

No matter what may have been our views on various subjects, I never failed to admire his determination to do what he thought was right for the people who had chosen him as their leader.

LYNDON JOHNSON was a big man who thought in big terms. The world today is a smaller place without him.

My wife and I extend all our sympathy and condolences to his lovely wife and family.

Hon. James O. Eastland

OF MISSISSIPPI

Mr. President, even as we mourn the loss of Harry Truman—accomplished Senator and great President—we suffer yet another lessening in the thin ranks of America's giants of this era.

LYNDON JOHNSON—Senator without peer, President awaiting history's assessment of his labors—is no longer with us.

It seems to me fitting and proper that Texas placed this man on the national stage and the international scene. One of our largest States gave us a leader almost larger than life.

President JOHNSON was, in every sense, a big man. His goals, his desire to serve his country and her people, his hopes for a better future for mankind, his unwavering faith in that future, were all on a towering scale.

None of us in this body can ever forget that LYNDON JOHNSON stood here and symbolized the title of Senator. He was a driving, striving, tireless leader, and he gave real meaning to the honored concept of "the loyal opposition"—a meaning carried forward in outstanding fashion by our present, distinguished majority leader.

He reached out his strong hand to a Chief Executive from our other great political party, and he contributed mightily to the effective functioning of this Government during the Eisenhower years.

When he sought—and lost—the presidential nomination, the breadth of his talent was, of course, recognized by President Kennedy. He became, as always, a working member of the Kennedy team and served with a loyalty that testified to the depth of his character.

When tragedy overtook us—when an assassin struck down John Kennedy and crisis was thrust upon us—LYNDON JOHNSON met and measured up to that gravest of tests.

He assumed the burden of the Presidency. He took the reins firmly and courageously and spoke to the American people, saying, with a calm and steady faith in them, and in the way of freedom, "Let us continue."

Continue we did—and as we will—under leadership selected by our citizens—until the end of time.

LYNDON JOHNSON cast a giant shadow across America and across the earth. It is a sad shadow today because of his passing. However, I believe that in the decades ahead it will be a sheltering shadow for men—here and everywhere—against the evils that beset mankind. I believe this land and the world are better because he tried so very hard to make them better.

If we who knew him and worked with him—and against him, at times—would raise up a monument to President JOHNSON, I suggest that it might be done here, in the Senate he loved with all his heart.

Let us, in this Chamber, salute him by continuing in the work we are in—the work he gave a lifetime to—the ongoing task of dedicating all of the strength and whatever talent we possess to fashioning a brighter tomorrow for each American and for everyone on this earth.

Hon. Thomas J. McIntyre
OF NEW HAMPSHIRE

Mr. President, no President since Abraham Lincoln bore the barbs of criticism and the strings of abuse with more grace than LYNDON JOHNSON.

This proud and sensitive man must have had his moments of bitter anguish, must have had his moments of despair, must have had his share of heartbreak as he watched his monumental accomplishments for this country sullied and disdained in the wash of disenchantment over a war that deceived both predecessors and successor—and many of us in this very Chamber.

But let us look behind this greatest tragedy of our times, a tragedy now, thank God, about to end, and remember once again what LYNDON JOHNSON really was, what LYNDON JOHNSON did for us.

When John F. Kennedy was taken from us in November of 1963, it remained for LYNDON JOHNSON to restore our national spirit and renew our determination.

I wonder, Mr. President, if there was any other man in Government at that time who had the will, the courage, and the skill to set this Nation back on its feet and start it moving again.

And 1 year later a landslide victory at the polls gave him the mandate he needed to start building the Great Society, on the leading edge of the New Frontier.

He accepted that mandate, and in the next 3½ years he started more programs for social progress than any other administration in our history.

He sought to care for the sick through medicare and medicaid, to feed the hungry through food stamps and surplus food, to secure the golden years which landmark increases in social security, to educate the young through a tripling of Federal money for schools, to give to the able-bodied through manpower training and vocational rehabilitation, to provide equal rights and human dignity for all men with civil rights legislation that advanced the cause more significantly than any measure since the Emancipation Proclamation.

Let us think about that legislation for a moment: voting rights, elementary and secondary education, higher education, model cities, rent supplements, minimum wage, the Department of Housing and Urban Development, the Department of Transportation, Job Corps, VISTA, food stamps, a host of antipoverty measures, food for freedom.

Now, Mr. President, it is politically fashionable these days to belittle the accomplishments of these nobly inspired Great Society programs. And perhaps the critics are right. Perhaps it is, indeed, true that legislation alone, money alone, will not cure our social ills.

But this conclusion, even if valid, cannot, shall not, dull the luster of LYNDON JOHNSON's intent.

This son of the Southwest believed, truly believed, in America's promise for every man—and he worked, as best he knew how, toward that end.

He was brought down, finally, by a war that deceived him, and by the flames of rising expectations that he himself had kindled with the very highest of purpose.

Mr. President, 144 years ago Alexis de Toqueville wrote something poignantly appropriate to any consideration of LYNDON JOHNSON. De Toqueville wrote:

Only great ingenuity can save one who undertakes to give relief to subjects after long oppression. The sufferings that are endured patiently as being inevitable, become intolerable the moment it appears there might be an escape. Reform then only serves to reveal more clearly what still remains oppressive and now all the more unbearable. The suffering—it's true—has been reduced. But one's sensitivity has become more acute.

And so it was with LYNDON JOHNSON, Mr. President. He began to lift the oppression of bigotry minorities bore so patiently for so many years. He began to lift the oppression of poverty which millions—white and black—endured as inevitable.

But in so doing, he acutely sensitized those who had suffered before in silence. So along with hope, came frustration and turmoil.

From those on the right with a pathological resistance to change, LYNDON JOHNSON was criticized for even raising these hopes. From his critics on the left, he was condemned for not righting the wrongs of centuries in 4 short years.

But history will be kind to LYNDON JOHNSON, Mr. President. History will be kind, because history does not perceive with tunnel vision. History will see a big picture of a very big man, a very great President.

May he rest in the peace he so richly deserves.

Hon. Strom Thurmond
OF SOUTH CAROLINA

Mr. President, today we are here to eulogize a man who, had he never served his country beyond his service in the Senate, would still be regarded as a distinguished figure in American history. During his tenure in this body, LYNDON JOHNSON made the Senate a focal point of government and politics on the national scene. He was a man of purpose who believed those purposes useless if not acted upon. With great skill, determination, and courage, he became a master of the legislative process and his stamp was firmly placed on the Senate and the laws which emanated from it. Where opportunity existed, he seized it; where no opportunity was apparent, he created it.

Although LYNDON JOHNSON would have made his place in history with his record as a U.S. Senator, he later brought the same impressive abilities and qualities which served him so well as a member of the legislative branch to the Presidency.

Mr. President, it is only natural that students of government, and indeed the American people, will differ in their individual assessments of President JOHNSON's policies. That, after all, is the premise upon which this country was founded. It is my opinion that history will judge LYNDON JOHNSON as a man, as a Senator, and as a President far more charitably than many of his contemporary critics.

I believe it will be seen that he accepted the responsibility thrust upon him, that he made the decisions required of him, and that he did not retreat when lesser men might have. While reasonable men disagree as to the wisdom of his policies, reasonable men of good will, I believe, agree that our country has lost a giant of a man.

Mr. President, my deepest sympathies are with his gracious and dedicated wife, Lady Bird, and to the members of his family. Let us hope our concern for them and their loss will be a comfort to them.

Hon. Frank E. Moss
OF UTAH

Mr. President, for those of us who served with LYNDON BAINES JOHNSON in the Senate, and who worked with him during his White House years to achieve a more equitable measure of human decency for all, his passing leaves a great void. He was always one of us in a special sort of way.

He towers over his times as a colossus—a man who was larger than life size almost from the beginning of his public career. He was an outstanding Representative and an outstanding Senator. The consummate legislative skill with which he operated as majority leader in the Senate has seldom been surpassed, or equalled, in our history. And no President ever worked harder, or with more compassion, to obtain his goals.

It was in the field of domestic legislation that he leaves his greatest legacy. He used his understanding of the legislative process to drive through Congress measures which produced the most substantial advance in civil rights since the time of Lincoln, and spelled the end of an apartheid society in America. It was his leadership which helped us achieve Federal aid to education, medicare, and medicaid, some of our best anti-pollution programs, a revised concept of immigration, the Teacher Corps, and increased assistance to the least of us—the poor—through a series of programs to help them help themselves.

More than anything else LYNDON JOHNSON wanted to help people—and more than anything else he did just that.

That he could not end the war in Vietnam and bring peace to Southeast Asia was a heavy affliction to him. He sought only for the people of South Vietnam the freedom to choose their own destiny, and he hoped for them the benefits of a democratic way of life. It was a noble aspiration, and one which most people of America shared with him. When he found his objective was out of reach, under the terms the Nation had set for itself in the war in Vietnam, he sought to end the hostilities. That he could not, and did not do so, was his greatest agony. He lived with that agony to the end of his days, and it is a bitter irony of fate that he died on the eve of a cease-fire in Vietnam. No one would have been more grateful for last night's news than LYNDON BAINES JOHNSON.

LYNDON JOHNSON was my friend and colleague. He was also a great friend of the State I represent. I recall one incident, especially. Legislation to clarify the status of the relicted lands around Great Salt Lake had passed the 89th Congress, after extensive consideration and debate. Its enactment was most important to Utah. It reached President JOHNSON's desk with a recommendation for a veto from his legal advisers. I discussed the bill with his staff and appealed to the President to sign it. Shortly before the deadline for taking final action on the bill, I received a call from President JOHNSON at his ranch in Texas. I was in Utah. He read to me the veto message prepared for him. The defect noted in the bill was that Federal interests were subjected to State action. In our conversation, the President, ever ready to find a way to get things done, said that an amendment to protect the interests of the Federal Government would satisfy the deficiency in the bill. I promised I would promptly introduce in the Senate such an amendment. So, in a spirit of trust and friendship, the President signed the Great Salt Lake bill. Thereafter, my amendment was introduced and enacted promptly by the Congress.

LYNDON JOHNSON proved that night to me that he was willing to walk the extra mile to get a bill of immense importance to the people of my State. He was, indeed, President of all of America—of all of the people.

The world mourns the passing of this compassionate, forceful, wise, and dedicated leader. Phyllis joins me in expressing deepest sympathy to his charming and gifted wife, Lady Bird, for whom we have the warmest feeling of friendship, and to his two attractive daughters. Their loss is immense, because a great man is gone. But they will live in the glow of his greatness for the rest of their lives.

Hon. George D. Aiken
OF VERMONT

Mr. President, I come from a rural State, and in the loss of President LYNDON B. JOHNSON, I do not hesitate to say that the rural areas and the agricultural areas of America have lost one of the best friends, if not, indeed, the best friend, they ever had in the White House.

LYNDON JOHNSON was human.

He had human virtues and he made human mistakes occasionally, but his loyalty to the people of this country could never be questioned.

I recall many a time when the farm people of America were in difficulty or faced a crisis.

Under such circumstances, I found that I could call him at any time, day or night, even before breakfast, and he would respond with action appropriate to averting the danger.

I could go on reciting incident after incident where his prompt action kept the people of our country out of difficulty.

In the field of foreign policy he made enemies who rejoiced in making charges against him.

This was particularly true in the case of our involvement in Indochina.

And I disagreed with him from time to time myself, but I will say here and now that whenever, in my opinion, he made a mistake he thought he was doing that which would shorten our military involvement in Southeast Asia.

I know that he always hoped to bring that conflict to an early close.

I know, too, that he contemplated giving our aid for reconstruction work even in North Vietnam after the turmoil was over.

Probably I saw more of LYNDON B. JOHNSON than any other President under whom I served.

I worked with him on domestic matters.

I know his sympathy for the needy people of America and, above all else, his loyalty to his flag and his country.

I never knew anyone else just like him and my wife, Lola, and I extend our deepest sympathy to Lady Bird, Lynda, and Luci during this period of sadness.

Hon. Hubert H. Humphrey
OF MINNESOTA

Mr. President, when great men pass on, it is most fitting to talk about their legacies to the Nation; and when great men pass on, men who have enriched one's life with the gift of their friendship, then the remarks concerning that individual take on a very special meaning.

I have been a very fortunate man. Life has been good to me. The rewards of my life have been in the treasured friendships that have come from the Members of this body, neighbors, associates back in my home State, and, above all, the men and women of fame and responsibility who from time to time cross the path of our lives.

I came to the U.S. Senate in 1949, as a Member of the 81st Congress. Another Member of that Congress was LYNDON BAINES JOHNSON, the then junior Senator from the State of Texas. Senator JOHNSON was no newcomer to Washington, however, in 1949. He had been a Member of the House of Representatives. He had worked as an aide to a Congressman. He had been employed on a congressional staff. He knew Capitol Hill and he knew all the prominent people of this interesting city on the American scene.

He always took pride in saying that Capitol Hill was his second home. If there were any two areas of this Nation that he loved, they were the hill country of Texas, his home, his ranch, Johnson City, and Capitol Hill. He was, every inch of him, a Member of the Congress of the United States, even in the days when he served in the Presidency.

But I remember so well that LYNDON JOHNSON, as a Senator in that year of 1949, seemed to know the powerful people in this city.

I was a newcomer to Washington. My background in politics had been as mayor of Minneapolis. Frankly, I knew no one here except what I had read about them. Within the first 2 weeks of my being in the Senate, LYNDON JOHNSON took time to visit with me. He called on me at the office, we visited in this cloakroom right off the Senate floor.

I can say to my colleagues that I was a very lonesome young Senator in those days. This body was much different than it is now. There were rigid lines of division, not only on the basis of party and region and ideology, but also seniority and position. Freshmen Senators were not given important assignments. Freshmen Senators were told not to speak. I am generally considered as one who is rather loquacious, but, Mr. President, I did not speak a word in this body until April 1949.

It was a different Senate—a very different Senate—but there was a young Senator who was not young to Washington, to experience in this city, who was a protege of Franklin D. Roosevelt, an intimate friend of the respected Speaker of the House, Sam Rayburn, an associate of the then senior Senator from Texas, Tom Connally, a man who knew distinguished Senators such as Richard Russell and Walter George of Georgia and Harry Flood Byrd of Virginia, just to mention a few. And it meant so much to me that this man cared enough just

to say hello to a young Senator from Minnesota, a man he had never met, and, for no particular reason, to want to take time to be friendly.

That was the beginning of our relationship, and that relationship developed over the years. Many was the time that I was privileged to go to his home here in Washington to meet his young daughters, to be with his marvelous and wonderful wife, Lady Bird Johnson, to meet his friends. Yes, I always knew that he was an unusual man.

When you come to talk about a man of the quality of LYNDON JOHNSON—Congressman, Senator, Vice President, and President—we generally try to make it look as though, somehow or other, here was the perfect man. But LYNDON JOHNSON would be the last person to want this record to so appear. He was a very human, earthy strong, outgoing, forceful, relentless in pursuit of his objectives. He was a total political man, giving of himself to politics, if it were possible, 24 hours a day, 7 days a week. He was a man of ambition, he asked much from others and gave much. He understood that the purpose of knowledge was action. LYNDON JOHNSON was a man who understood people and things, not an intellectual, but a man of great commonsense and understanding. And he was surely not a modest man, but I say he knew his capacity. He had faith in himself.

He also had an unlimited faith in this country and its ability to do anything that needed to be done. He was, as I said here yesterday, an unusual, unique, remarkable individual. You could not label him, Mr. President.

I remember when we came here, you were either a liberal or a conservative. You were either a reactionary or a progressive. You were either a notherner or a southerner. That is the way it used to be. How many times I heard LYNDON JOHNSON say he was first a free man, then an American, a public servant and a member of the Democratic Party and in that order. His respect for this Senate was an article of faith with him. But above all, while he was from the Southwest and he was a Texan and he was a Democrat, he reminded us that what he really was was an American; he knew neither North nor South, East nor West, in that sense. He quoted frequently from Sam Rayburn, who often reminded his colleagues in the other body, and this country, of the necessity of thinking in terms of this Nation rather than in terms of groups or segments or regions or sections.

I can remember the columnists and the writers and the commentators trying to put a label on LYNDON JOHNSON. What was he? Who was he? How would you classify him? It is so much easier around here, particularly for the purposes of contemporary history, to be able to put a person in a slot or column, to compartmentalize him. He defied all of them. He was far too complex a personality to submit to easy description. Here was a man from the South who led the fight from the Capitol and the White House for civil rights. Here was man from the South who in 1957 and 1960 helped put through Congress the very first legislation in the field of civil rights. Here was a man from the South who refused to sign the Southern Manifesto.

We tend to forget those facts. Those were days when you were really almost compelled by party politics, if you were from a certain region of this country, to line up with the prejudices and parochial attitudes of that region. LYNDON JOHNSON was proud to be a Texan, and he would let you know about it. He was not always the silent man, and he surely was not the most suave and sophisticated in his approach. He would tell you bluntly he was from Texas and, as far as he was concerned, that was it.

He talked with great pride of having a vision about this country that was far greater than any State, community, or section. He was inspired by Franklin Roosevelt. Many was the day he would tell us in intimate conversation about when he first met Roosevelt.

I think he was so pleased that he was looked upon in the public print and by the public as one of the young Members of Congress in those days, in the late thirties and the early forties, who shared in Roosevelt's fellowship and trust. He was a New Dealer in that sense. However, again it was not 100 percent. Again, you could not put a label on him.

LYNDON JOHNSON had the most amazing set of friends. In this body, possibly the closest friend was the esteemed and revered late Richard Russell. They were intimate friends. This I know. Yet they did not always vote alike. And surely in the days of his Presidency, President JOHNSON recommended many things that Richard Russell could not support. But the same man who was a friend of Richard Russell was also a friend of Herbert Lehman, that marvelous, humanitarian, the beloved Senator from New York. The very first person from the Senate who came to the bedside of LYNDON JOHNSON when LYNDON was stricken with a heart attack was Herbert Lehman. LYNDON JOHNSON never forgot that.

The same man who was a friend of Harry Flood Byrd, Sr., the very essence of what we call American political conservatism, shared the friendship of a man who used to stand in this Chamber, a man by the name of Senator Wayne Morse, the maverick and the progressive.

Mr. President, I was fortunate to be one of LYNDON JOHNSON's friends. And in those days in the Senate, he sort of looked to me as a kind of bridge between what he called the liberals—and he even used to refer to them and use the term "bomb throwers." We all know that he had a way of needling you and putting you on, and that was just his way.

Many was the time that I discussed with him many matters relating to the policy committee. I remember one time when he said to me, "Who would you like to recommend?" I do not want to go into details because it is rather personal. However, the recommendation was made and the appointment was made.

I can remember in 1953 when LYNDON JOHNSON called me when I was visiting in New York City with Adlai Stevenson. At that time he said to me: "I want you to get off the Committee on Agriculture and Forestry and the Committee on Labor." They were the two committees that meant more to me than almost anything in Congress at that time. He said: "We want to put you on the Foreign Relations Committee, and we also want to have Mike Mansfield on it."

I said: "I can't do that."

He said: "We have already discussed it. I have been speaking with Sam Rayburn, the Speaker, and we have been talking about adding some new faces on the Committee on Foreign Relations."

I do not think I need to tell you, Mr. President, that he was a very persuasive man. There was hardly a Member of the Senate here who did not have to have his lapels repaired from time to time after a session with LYNDON JOHNSON. I want to talk about my friend, LYNDON JOHNSON, as he was. There was hardly a Member of the Senate who served in this body who did not have to have his ears patched up from time to time as a result of having spoken with LYNDON JOHNSON.

How many of us remember how he would come over and talk to us. I used to say that he knew more about every individual Member of this body than J. Edgar Hoover or a psychiatrist. He was a master in the art of politics, particularly in the legislative body. Many people did not like it because many people do not like to be known that well. He not only knew the Senators, but he also knew their families. He knew all about them. And he was a considerate man.

Many a Senator will remember how former Senator JOHNSON used to call a member of his family who was ill or how he would call the Senator's wife and explain that the husband could not be home that night because the Senate was going to have a late session.

Mr. President, I have a storehouse full of stories that I could tell about LYNDON JOHNSON's capacity for compassion and human understanding.

I shall never forget the time that the late Theodore Francis Green walked out of this Chamber after talking with former Senator LYNDON JOHNSON. LYNDON JOHNSON was occupying a seat about where the Senator from West Virginia (Mr. Robert C. Byrd is sitting now. And dear Senator Green said to LYNDON: "I have to go to a very important meeting. Would you consider handling this little voting rights bill for servicemen for me. If you can take care of it for me, it will help me so much. It is noncontroversial."

This happened to be a night on which Mrs. Johnson expected her husband at a particular affair at the Australian Embassy. That meeting meant a great deal to them because he had been in Australia during the war, and they had friends there that they were supposed to meet.

A bitter argument went on over this little bill of former Senator Green's, and we were here until 11 o'clock at night. When LYNDON JOHNSON got home, his wife asked him why he had not been able to leave. He said to her, "You must understand that we have a job to do in the Senate." She said, "Is that right?"

He said, "One of the most important Members of the United States Senate wanted us to be there for a bill."

She said, "Who was that?"

He said, "It was that beloved man, Senator Theodore Francis Green."

There were even times that this shrewd, remarkable man could be outmaneuvered by a man who seemed so quiet and modest as the late Theodore Francis Green.

We could fill this Record with stories about this man's contribution to our Nation.

LYNDON JOHNSON could be angry. He could take a bite out of you as big as a Texas T-bone steak. Yet, the very next day he would throw his arms around you as though you were a long-lost brother.

I can remember many times when there were reports that there must be some problems existing between the President and Vice President. That only indicated that they did not understand the man in the White House.

When I happened to get public criticism on a matter, I could be sure of getting sympathy from the President.

I knew the man very well. And I really miss him. Many of us here knew him very well. And in a real sense we talk of him in the present because we remember him so well.

I was on a television show with Joe Califano yesterday. And we were talking about LYNDON JOHNSON. The telephone rang, and I said: "Joe, don't you be surprised if he is calling."

Many of us remember the calls we used to get when he was our leader and when he was our President. The telephone was not an electronic instrument. It was an extension of his body. It was an instrument of persuasion. He was a master of the use of the telephone.

Mr. President, there are just a few reflections. I thought I would add a little human touch today, because I shall write about him in the years to come. And I shall write about him as he was.

This was a very strong, powerful, dedicated, and able human being. I repeat that he was a master of the art of colloquy and the art of politics.

So when we talk about the legacies that people leave, I want to talk about the legacy of LYNDON JOHNSON. History books are full of legacies of great men of politics. They speak, for example, of Washington's legacy of independence as the father of our country; of Jefferson's legacy of freedom as the author of the Declaration of Independence, and of his passionate dedication to education.

They speak of Lincoln's legacy of the Union preserved, with justice for all; of Wilson's legacy of peace and international order; of Franklin Roosevelt's legacy of hope and compassion; of Harry Truman's legacy of reconstruction for a war-ravaged world; of the remarkable decisiveness and courage of John Kennedy's legacy of dynamism, of a new generation at the helm of government and power.

So it is well to ask, what will be the legacy of LYNDON JOHNSON?

Well, that legacy will be recorded in the history books; and, by the way, any real, truly objective evaluation of a strong and great man is never possible by his contemporaries. No President who has ever served this country well has been judged fairly by his contemporaries. Lincoln was not popular in his day. Neither was Jefferson nor Jackson. There were people who abhorred and denounced Woodrow Wilson, and there were the Roosevelt haters who became almost a cult. I remind the Members of this body that when Harry Truman left the Presidency, he was one of the most unpopular men who ever left Washington, D.C. He departed from Union Station almost by himself, he and his beloved wife, Bess.

Very few great men are popular in their time; and we will never be able to get a truly objective judgment of Lyndon Baines Johnson at this hour, in this day. It will require the refinement of time to filter out the dust of minutiae, in order to find the solid rock of character and accomplishment.

But it will come. And I predict we will see that Lyndon Johnson's legacy is a living one. In fact, it is here now. It is the legacy of a black or a brown child who will never have to face a segregated hotel or restaurant; who, in this time of our life, can walk tall and strong as a free man or woman—a child who will never have to live in a society that has been divided by law on the basis of race.

It will be the legacy of universal suffrage for all: rich, poor, black, and white. How well I remember President Johnson saying to me that the one thing that we must do for black people is guarantee them their precious right on the vote. He said, "Until they have that, they will always be living at the sufferance of someone else. The way to make the powerless powerful is to give them the precious right of the vote, and protect that right." And he led the fight in this body for the right to vote, and not only for the right, but for the protection of the right to vote. I shall never forget that joint session of Congress when the President came to us with the Voting Rights Act, when he took those words of Dr. Martin Luther King, Jr., as he ended that message by saying, "We shall overcome." The Voting Rights Act alone has changed America.

It will be the legacy of hope for more than 20 million elderly Americans that they can have greater security in their final years. Yes, Lyndon Johnson would have changed the life of this Nation if he had done nothing more than to see through this Congress the passage of medicare. And he did not forget, by the way, that medicare was initiated originally by Harry Truman. Where did he go to sign the bill? To Independence, Mo., in the presence of the man who pioneered the idea, Harry Truman.

The legacy of Lyndon Johnson will be the legacy of an education for every boy and girl in this country. He was a schoolteacher who never forgot that education was the key to opportunity, a man who knew that civil rights was meaningless in ignorance; a man who knew that there was no human dignity in ignorance. And, as has been said from this floor today, he moved mountains to pass the Elementary and Secondary Education Act. Federal aid to education died in Congress year after year on the anvil of either race or religion. We would pass it here, and it would be killed in the House of Representatives, or it would pass the House of Representatives and be killed here, one or the other. But Lyndon Johnson rose above that, and we have today massive infusions of Federal funds to the educational structure of this country. We have all the little children in project Headstart. There are hundreds of thousands of parents today who will remember Lyndon Johnson because their child got a chance in a Headstart class.

There is a young man, who is heavyweight champion of the world today, by the name of George Foreman. He got a chance in a Job Corps camp. George Foreman traveled with me in 1968 for more than a month in my campaign. His wife lives in the Twin Cities, and he is a friend of mine. George Foreman, a clean-cut American youth, the Olympic boxing champion, who stood in Mexico City after he won the heavyweight boxing championship in the Olympics proudly holding that little American flag. George Foreman will never forget Lyndon Johnson. Regrettably, Lyndon Johnson lived to see the closing of some Job Corps camps.

There are thousands of people in the ghettos who got their first chance under the program known as VISTA, and the youth opportunity centers that opened across this land. I traveled with this program to every one of the major cities of this land, Mr. President, President Johnson sent my wife and I to the ghettos of Philadelphia, Chicago, New York, Cleveland to open up programs that we dared to ask the country to undertake.

Yes, the legacy of Lyndon Johnson is a living one. It is the legacy of economic opportunity for hundreds of thousands who needed help and assistance. He was the man who had the courage to declare war on poverty; and I remember all the smart ones in this city who said, "He will never do it." I wonder how many Senators know that a special task force report had been prepared and that in the so-called inside communities of Washington where they really figure out everything in advance that generally does not happen the betting was about 10-to-1 that LYNDON JOHNSON would never act on the report that had been made, which came forth with the recommendation for the creation of the Office of Economic Opportunity. The war on poverty; I helped draft some of the provisions of that bill. LYNDON JOHNSON dared to try.

These are some of LYNDON JOHNSON's living legacies, which are today more vauluable than any page in history. There are so many others, including the first moves in the field of environmental control. And let us not forget at all times, he pledged more to those who had less. Yes, he was a populist. He was the farmer's friend. He had the trust of the working people.

I can recall serving with him as Vice President when, at the White House, men of industry and of labor would be brought together at the same table because President JOHNSON believed in partnership, in cooperation, and not in confrontation.

There is so much to be said, and today we cannot say it all.

Finally, let me point out that it is tragic that in light of major accomplishments in the domestic area that President JOHNSON's administration has been marked in the public view primarily by the tragic war in Vietnam. He told us many times that he did not seek a military victory, that he sought only to prevent the success of aggression, that he sought only to see to it that force should not determine the future course of a people, that he sought only to protect the right of self-determination.

Only history will judge all of this war. But we know now that it lasted too long and most of us wish it had never happened.

But, Mr. President, I think I am in a position to tell this body that no man agonized more over the war in Vietnam than the man who was President then, LYNDON JOHNSON. I am sure that one of the reasons he is not with us now is due to the hours of pain, worry, and anguish that he endured because of that war.

I heard the distinguished Senator from Rhode Island (Mr. Pastore) speak of the message of the President of the United States, when he decided he would not be a candidate for reelection. I recall that he had said, "I do not think I will ever run again." I never believed him, because all of us in politics resign about once a month, only we are so worried that someone will take us up on it, but we got so frustrated and discouraged.

But I remember, on March 31, 1968, Mrs. Humphrey and I were at home, and I had been asked by President JOHNSON to represent the United States in Mexico City at the signing of a treaty to prohibit the stationing of nuclear weapons of mass destruction in Latin America. I had interested myself in that subject matter when I was a Senator. He came to me that day—he had been to church—and he said, "I need to talk to you." We sat down, and he read to me the message that I knew he had been working on the week before, which was primarily a message about the economy and the war. And then he read me the paragraph that said he would not seek reelection, that he would not accept the nomination if it were offered to him, nor would he run. I urged upon him not to make that statement.

I said, "Mr. President, you can be reelected. It will be difficult, but you can be reelected. What is more, no one is better capable of carrying out what you want than you yourself."

I shall never forget when he told me that the main reason he was taking that action was he knew, if he had to stand for reelection, that his motives would be questioned as he sought peace in Vietnam, that he would be under suspicion and, more significantly, he would have to give time to the campaign that he should be giving to the search for peace. He said, "I have made up my mind." Then he said something else. He said, "Hubert, a campaign is an arduous and exhausting experience. I have not had the best of health. For me to undertake another campaign might be too much."

Then he said, "The men in my family have not lived long." How well I remember that.

Well, Mr. President, as I have said two or three times these past days, the conference in Paris that made possible the agreement which the President of the United States announced last evening, was initiated by LYNDON JOHNSON. It was on October 31, 1968, that he stopped the bombing. It was during the summer of 1968 that he encouraged and was able to get the representatives of North Vietnam and South Vietnam to come to the conference table in Paris.

I know, too, that he was as disappointed as I was when President Thieu of South Vietnam, during the first part of November 1968, had indicated for a while that he would not come to the conference table.

But the forum—yes indeed, the table that made possible the negotiations was, in a sense, constructed by the man we mourn today.

I believe that history will also note that this man set the course for better relationships with the Soviet Union. I want my colleagues to know that he gave instructions to his Cabinet that we should not speak in cold war terms. Not once during those years did President JOHNSON use the rhetoric that was so customary in many places in this country concerning the Soviet Union.

He diligently prepared the way for the strategic arms limitation talks which we entered into in 1969. He would have initiated those talks but for the fact that the Soviet Union moved in to attack Czechoslovakia in August of 1968.

Furthermore, Mr. President, I remember the order to his Cabinet that we should speak with great respect of the President of the Republic of France, Charles de Gaulle, that he did not want us to engage in the oratory and the rhetoric of division.

There were many other things, Mr. President, that were accomplished during those days.

As we look to the future, as we look to Asia, remember that the Asian Development Bank, that program for the economic reconstruction of Asia, was a part of that administration.

So, Mr. President, the legacy of LYNDON JOHNSON is to be found in the faces of children today who have better health, because he cared; to be found in the smiles on the faces of senior citizens who needed medical care and can get it now, because he cared.

The legacy of LYNDON JOHNSON is to be found in the schools and colleges of this land whose programs he so greatly strengthened. In the legacy of LYNDON JOHNSON is to be found the fact that hundreds of thousands, yes, millions of impoverished people were recognized for the first time by their Government as being worthy of attention and help.

I want to say, while the time is mine, that we are not going to turn back from that course of humanitarianism and the enrichment of human resources. I am not going to let this day of remembrance of LYNDON JOHNSON be just a testimonial to the man.

I say to every Senator who has spoken of him today: Remember what he stood for. As efforts are being made to weaken the programs of health, education, and child care, to weaken programs to clean up our cities and make them livable again, remember that a testimonial to a dead President, honoring him for what he did but failing to stand up in the days to come for what we need and for what he fought for would be so unfortunate and so false.

I mourn the loss of my friend. Mrs. Humphrey and I have been very sad these days. There is no way to express this sorrow except to say unashamedly that tears have filled our eyes. Our sadness is, of course, but a little, compared with the grief of that lovely family.

The reward of public life is the privilege to know great, unusual, remarkable, and gifted men and women. I have had many rewards based on that standard, but none was more generous, more meaningful, or more rich than the reward of being a companion, a colleague, an associate, a fellow Senator, a friend, and a Vice President with LYNDON BAINES JOHNSON.

Hon. Sam J. Ervin, Jr.
OF NORTH CAROLINA

Mr. President, this is an occasion on which we are reminded, once again, of the poignant words of the Persian poet:

For some we loved, the loveliest and the best
That from his Vintage rolling Time hath prest,
Have drunk their Cup a Round or two before,
And one by one crept silently to rest.

Those of us who were privileged to serve in the U.S. Senate with LYNDON JOHNSON as majority leader mourn his passing. We recognize that he was a big man physically and that he was a big man in all other aspects. I shall not undertake to review at any great length his achievements as a public figure.

As the distinguished Senator from Minnesota (Mr. Humphrey) has just stated, LYNDON JOHNSON was of the earth, earthy. He was quite a human individual. As a public figure, he was more of a man of action than he was a philosopher. As a consequence, he was more concerned with political objectives than he was with basic constitutional or governmental principles.

I had the privilege of knowing him when he was a Member of the House from Texas, back in

1946. As the majority leader of the Senate, after I came to the Senate, he gave me several important assignments, such as serving on the committee to study the censure of Senator Joseph McCarthy, and the committee to investigate improper activities in the labor-management area, and membership upon the Commission on Intergovernmental Relationships. After he became President, he appointed me to membership on the National Commission.

I like to think of LYNDON JOHNSON as a friendly, loving human being. His great achievements in the realm of public affairs have been recounted, and will be recounted, by others.

LYNDON JOHNSON had the uncanny capacity of making anyone with whom he had contact feel that in LYNDON JOHNSON's mind, he was one of the greatest of human beings. This won for LYNDON many friends. All of us like appreciation from others.

LYNDON JOHNSON had a genuine love for those with whom he came in contact. He never forgot his personal affection for others. I recall that on one occasion I had the privilege of flying down to North Carolina, where he made a speech and received an honorary degree at Elon College. I asked him for an autograph of the program of the event for my little grandson Jimmy. LYNDON JOHNSON never forgot Jimmy. Every time he saw me after that, he would ask me how Jimmy was getting along. That was the kind of man LYNDON JOHNSON was. Although he had some opponents, he was on friendly terms with virtually everyone. I think that of all the men who walked earth's surface during his lifetime, the man he loved most was Sam Rayburn. LYNDON JOHNSON would take advice from Sam Rayburn which he would not have taken from any other human being.

When Sam Rayburn was Speaker of the House, LYNDON JOHNSON was leader of the Senate.

I have always thought that perhaps the greatest tragedy that came to LYNDON JOHNSON after he became President was the fact that he did not have Sam Rayburn from whom to seek advice, because Sam Rayburn was a man of great wisdom and vast experience, and all through his life a wise counsellor.

Another great tragedy was the occurrence of the Vietnam war during his administration. I think it can be truly said of LYNDON JOHNSON that he came to the presidency with the vastest experience on the Washington level of any other President. He had served as an aide to a Member of Congress. He had served in the House of Representatives. He had served in the Senate, where he undoubtedly proved himself to be the most effective majority leader in the history of our Nation. He had served as Vice President. He carried all the experience gained in those offices to the Presidency. The fact that the Vietnam war became accelerated and demanded so much of his attention and time and care seriously handicapped in consummating many of his dreams for our country.

I think we can comprehend why some men are successful if we know their wives. When I was a student at the University of North Carolina I heard Horace Williams, professor of philosophy, speak to my class on the subject of the kind of girls we ought to marry.

He said we ought to marry a girl who would stand beside us as a tower of strength in good times and bad times, in joy and in sorrow, and in victory and defeat. He also said we should marry a girl who would make for us a good home in which we could find rest and relaxation, as well as inspiration.

LYNDON JOHNSON was most fortunate in that he married a girl who answered to all of those descriptions. I do not think the Nation has ever had a more charming First Lady than Lady Bird Johnson.

She stood by LYNDON at all times. She was his constant inspiration. A great deal of his success, which led from comparatively humble beginnings in Texas to the highest office within the gift of the American people, was due to the fact that she walked beside him and encouraged him. She supported his efforts at all times. She made a home in which he could find such relaxation as so restless a man as LYNDON could find anywhere on earth.

On behalf of my wife, who shares my great admiration and deep affection for Lady Bird Johnson, and myself, I wish to extend to Lady Bird Johnson our deepest sympathy in the irreparable loss which she and our country have sustained.

Hon. Gale W. McGee
OF WYOMING

Mr. President, I shall take the minute we have before we go elsewhere to call the attention of

Senators to the richness and the warmth of the remarks of the Senator from Minnesota (Mr. Humphrey), who added more chapters of understanding to the history of this great American, LYNDON JOHNSON, than I think have been available to most of us until now.

I would only wish that more had been able to attend his remarks at the time.

I would like to reserve the privilege, Mr. President, of injecting the remarks that I have been collecting at a more leisurely moment, but to urge my colleagues to address themselves to Hubert Humphrey's very wide-ranging and very deeply moving reminiscences of his associations with LYNDON B. JOHNSON.

Hon. Norris Cotton
OF NEW HAMPSHIRE

Mr. President, as I sought to put into words my own feelings as we all join in paying tribute to former President LYNDON JOHNSON, I suddenly realized that for the first time in all my years here, I was speaking not only of a departed President and world leader but also of a personal friend. In company with my colleagues, I had on many occasions met and conferred with the first three Presidents under whom I served, but LYNDON JOHNSON was the first President whom I could honestly call a warm personal friend. He was a Member of the House of Representatives when I entered it but quickly departed to the Senate. From 1954 when I came to the Senate, I served under him as majority leader, as Vice President, and as the President of the United States.

LYNDON JOHNSON was a powerful floor leader. He was not necessarily greater or more effective than other floor leaders before and since, but he was different. LYNDON JOHNSON was dramatic in whatever role he appeared. It was his nature, and he could not help it anymore than he could control the shape of his head or the color of his eyes. Had he been a man of lesser intellect and abilities, he might have been called flamboyant. None of us will ever forget his dynamic personality so clearly displayed in the place where he was at his best—the Senate. We remember how he used to persuade and cajole us as he moved about, putting his hand on our shoulder, straightening our tie, while he confided to us what he was seeking to accomplish on some particular occasion and how we could help. We remember him

equally well in moments of deep tension when he moved the Senate by his eloquence and sometimes even stormed at us. He was a man of many moods—passionate, forceful, harsh, humorous, sympathetic, and kind. But in the end he was our friend in those days of intimate association and, as such, will always live in our hearts. Despite political and partisan differences, I always supported and never criticized him in his darkest days in the White House. That remains my solace and comfort today.

Others may analyze his leadership as President of the United States, his role in world affairs, his successes, his failures, and his place in history. I choose on this sad day to remember him, affectionately, as my friend who was kind and helpful to me when I came here as a freshman Senator and who continued his kindness through all the years since.

Over whatever seas he is sailing
  Whatever strange winds fan his brow,
What company rare he's regailing,
  I know it is well with him now.
And when my last voyage I am making
  May I go, as he went, unafraid,
And, the Pilot that guided him taking,
  May I make the same port he has made.

Hon. Edward M. Kennedy
OF MASSACHUSETTS

Mr. President, so long as the story of America is told, LYNDON JOHNSON will be remembered as one of our Nation's greatest public servants. Throughout a lifetime of dedicated service to his country, he was an outstanding Congressman, Senate majority leader, Vice President, and President. He was a loyal Vice President to President John F. Kennedy. He had the deep respect and affection of my brother, and I shall never forget the many, many private kindnesses he showed to all the members of our family over the years.

As President, his brilliant leadership on the Civil Rights Act of 1964 and the Voting Rights Act of 1965 has earned him a place in the history of civil rights alongside Abraham Lincoln. And his immense efforts to help the poor, the sick, and the oppressed stand out as landmarks of America's concern for those too weak to help themselves. The Great Society, of which he dreamed and for which he worked, still endures in the hearts and minds of all who believe in equality and social justice in America, and who share his faith that "We shall overcome."

Today, as we celebrate his life and mourn his death, we also celebrate the advent of the peace he sought in Indochina. As the long years of national sacrifice and tragedy and bitterness over the war now pass, we see more clearly the immense achievements of President JOHNSON in so many areas. Now, he belongs to history, and history will record him as one of our finest leaders. Without him, America is the poorer.

Mr. President, so that these proceedings may reflect some of the enduring monuments to LYNDON JOHNSON's greatness, I ask unanimous consent to include in these remarks the texts of the Civil Rights Act of 1964 and the Voting Rights Act of 1965, together with the statements made by President JOHNSON when he signed these measures into law. I also ask unanimous consent to include the text of his address, "The American Promise," delivered to Congress on March 15, 1965. That address, one of the most eloquent and inspiring by any President, contains the famous passage that stated his faith in the promise of America so well:

This great, rich, restless country can offer opportunity and education and hope to all: black and white, North and South, sharecropper and city dweller. These are the enemies: poverty, ignorance, disease. They are enemies and not our fellow man, not our neighbor. And these enemies too, poverty, disease and ignorance, we shall overcome.

❧

CIVIL RIGHTS ACT OF 1964

(88th Congress, H.R. 7152, July 2, 1964)

An act to enforce the constitutional right to vote, to confer jurisdiction upon the district courts of the United States to provide injunctive relief against discrimination in public accommodations, to authorize the Attorney General to institute suits to protect constitutional rights in public facilities and public education, to extend the Commission on Civil Rights, to prevent discrimination in federally assisted programs, to establish a Commission on Equal Employment Opportunity, and for other purposes.

Be it enacted by the Senate and House of Representatives of the United States of America in Congress assembled, That this Act may be cited as the "Civil Rights Act of 1964".

TITLE I—VOTING RIGHTS

SEC. 101. Section 2004 of the Revised Statutes (42 U.S.C. 1971), as amended by section 131 of the Civil Rights Act of 1957 (71 Stat. 637), and as further amended by section 601 of the Civil Rights Act of 1960 (74 Stat. 90), is further amended as follows:

(a) Insert "1" after "(a)" in subsection (a) and add at the end of subsection (a) the following new paragraphs:

"(2) No person acting under color of law shall—

"(A) in determining whether any individual is qualified under State law or laws to vote in any Federal election, apply any standard, practice, or procedure different from the standards, practices, or procedures applied under such law or laws to other individuals within the same county, parish, or similar political subdivision who have been found by State officials to be qualified to vote;

"(B) deny the right of any individual to vote in any Federal election because of an error or omission on any record to requisite to voting, if such error or omission is not material in determining whether such individual is qualified under State law to vote in such election; or

"(C) employ any literacy test as a qualification for voting in any Federal election unless (i) such test is administered to each individual and is conducted wholly in writing, and (ii) a certified copy of the test and of the answers given by the individual is furnished to him within twenty-five days of the submission of his request made within the period of time during which records and papers are required to be retained and preserved pursuant to title III of the Civil Rights Act of 1960 (42 U.S.C. 1974–74e; 74 Stat. 88): *Provided, however,* That the Attorney General may enter into agreements with appropriate State or local authorities that preparation, conduct, and maintenance of such tests in accordance with the provisions of applicable State or local law, including such special provisions as are necessary in the preparation, conduct, and maintenance of such tests for persons who are blind or otherwise physically handicapped, meet the purposes of this subparagraph and constitute compliance therewith.

"(3) For purposes of this subsection—

"(A) the term 'vote' shall have the same meaning as in subsection (e) of this section;

"(B) the phrase 'literacy test' includes any test of the ability to read, write, understand, or interpret any matter."

(b) Insert immediately following the period at the end of the first sentence of subsection (c) the following new sentence: "If in any such proceeding literacy is a relevant fact there shall be a rebuttable presumption that any person who has not been adjudged an incompetent and who has completed the sixth grade in a public school in, or a private school accredited by, any State or territory, the District of Columbia, or the Commonwealth of Puerto Rico where instruction is carried on predominantly in the English language, possesses sufficient literacy, comprehension, and intelligence to vote in any Federal election."

(c) Add the following subsection "(f)" and designate the present subsection "(f)" as subsection "(g)":

"(f) When used in subsection (a) or (c) of this section, the words 'Federal election' shall mean any general, special, or primary election held solely or in part for the purpose of electing or selecting any candidate for the office of President, Vice President, presidential elector, Member of the Senate, or Member of the House of Representatives."

(d) Add the following subsection "(h)":

"(h) In any proceeding instituted by the United States in any district court of the United States under this section in which the Attorney General requests a finding of a pattern or practice of discrimination pursuant to subsection (e) of this section the Attorney General, at the time he files the complaint, or any defendant in the proceeding, within twenty days after service upon him of the complaint, may file with the clerk of such court a request that a court of three judges be convened to hear and determine the entire case. A copy of the request for a three-judge court shall be immediately furnished by such clerk to the chief judge of the circuit (or in his absence, the presiding circuit judge of the circuit) in which the case is pending. Upon receipt of the copy of such request it shall be the duty of the chief judge of the circuit or the presiding circuit judge, as the case may be, to designate immediately three judges in such circuit, of whom at least one shall be a circuit judge and another of whom shall be a district judge of the court in which the proceeding was instituted to hear and determine such case, and it shall be the duty of the judges so designated to assign the case for hearing at the earliest practicable date, to participate in the hearing and determination thereof, and to cause the case to be in every way expedited. An appeal from the final judgment of such court will lie to the Supreme Court.

"In any proceeding brought under subsection (c) of this section to enforce subsection (b) of this section, or in the event neither the Attorney General nor any defendant files a request for a three-judge court in any proceeding authorized by this subsection, it shall be the duty of the chief judge of the district (or in his absence, the acting chief judge) in which the case is pending immediately to designate a judge in such district to hear and determine the case. In the event that no judge in the district is available to hear and determine the case, the chief judge of the district, or the acting chief judge, as the case may be, shall certify this fact to the chief judge of the circuit (or, in his absence, the acting chief judge) who shall then designate a district or circuit judge of the circuit to hear and determine the case.

"It shall be the duty of the judge designated pursuant to this section to assign the case for hearing at the earliest practicable date and to cause the case to be in every way expedited."

TITLE II—INJUNCTIVE RELIEF AGAINST DISCRIMINATION IN PLACES OF PUBLIC ACCOMMODATION

SEC. 201. (a) All persons shall be entitled to the full and equal enjoyment of the goods, services, facilities, privileges, advantages, and accommodations of any place of public accommodation, as defined in this section, without discrimination or segregation on the ground of race, color, religion, or national origin.

(b) Each of the following establishments which serves the public is a place of public accommodation within the meaning of this title if its operations affect commerce, or if discrimination or segregation by it is supported by State action:

(1) any inn, hotel, motel, or other establishment which provides lodging to transient guests, other than an establishment located within a building which contains not more than five rooms for rent or hire and which is actually occupied by the proprietor of such establishment as his residence;

(2) any restaurant, cafeteria, lunchroom, lunch counter, soda fountain, or other facility principally engaged in selling food for consumption on the premises, including, but not limited to, any such facility located on the premises of any retail establishment; or any gasoline station;

(3) any motion picture house, theater, concert hall, sports arena, stadium or other place of exhibited or entertainment; and

(4) any establishment (A)(i) which is physically located within the premises of any establishment otherwise covered by this subsection, or (ii) within the premises of which is physically located any such covered establishment, and (B) which holds itself out as serving patrons of such covered establishment.

(c) The operations of an establishment affect commerce within the meaning of this title if (1) it is one of the establishments described in paragraph (1) of subsection (b); (2) in the case of an establishment described in paragraph (2) of subsection (b), it serves or offers to serve interstate travelers or a substantial portion of the food which it serves, or gasoline or other products which it sells, has moved in commerce; (3) in the case of an establishment described in paragraph (3) of subsection (b), it customarily presents films, performances, athletic teams, exhibitions, or other sources of entertainment which more in commerce; and (4) in the case of an establishment described in paragraph (4) of subsection (b), it is physically located within the premises of, or there is physically located within its premises, an establishment of the operations of which affect commerce within the meaning of this subsection. For purposes of this section, "commerce" means travel, trade, traffic, commerce, transportation, or communication among the several States, or between the District of Columbia and any State, or any territory or possession and any State or the District of Columbia, or between points in the same State but through any other State or the District of Columbia or a foreign country.

(d) Discrimination or segregation by an establishment is supported by State action within the meaning of this title if such discrimination or segregation (1) is carried on under color of any law, statute, ordinance, or regulation; or (2) is carried on under color of any custom or usage required or enforced by officials of the State or poltical subdivision thereof; or (3) is required by action of the State or political subdivision thereof.

(e) The provisions of this title shall not apply to a private club or other establishment not in fact open to the public, except to the extent that the facilities of such establishment are made available to the customers or patrons of an establishment within the scope of subsection (b).

SEC. 202. All persons shall be entitled to be free, at any establishment or place, from discrimination or segregation of any kind on the ground of race, color, religion, or national origin, if such discrimination or segregation is or purports to be required by any law, statute, ordinance, regulation, rule, or order of a State or any agency or political subdivision thereof.

SEC. 203. No person shall (a) withold, deny, or attempt to withhold or deny, or deprive or attempt to deprive, any person of any right or privilege secured by section 201 or 202, or (b) intimidate, threaten, or coerce, or attempt to intimidate, threaten, or coerce any person with the purpose of interfering with any right or privilege secured by section 201 or 202, or (c) punish or attempt to punish any person for exercising or attempting to exercise any right or privilege secured by section 201 or 202.

SEC. 204. (a) Whenever any person has engaged or there are reasonable grounds to believe that any person is about to engage in any act or practice prohibited by section 203, a civil action for preventive relief, including an application for a permanent or temporary injunction, restraining order, or other order, may be instituted by the person aggrieved and, upon timely application, the court may, in its discretion, permit the Attorney General to intervene in such civil action if he certifies that the case is of general public importance. Upon application by the complainant and in such circumstances as the court may deem just, the court may appoint an attorney for such complainant and may authorize the commencement of the civil action without the payment of fees, costs, or security.

(b) In any action commenced pursuant to this title, the court, in its discretion, may allow the prevailing party, other than the United States, a reasonable attorney's fee as part of the costs, and the United States shall be liable for costs the same as a private person.

(c) In the case of an alleged act or practice prohibited by this title which occurs in a State, or political subdivision of a State, which has a State or local law prohibiting such act or practice and establishing or authorizing a State or local authority to grant or seek relief from such practice or to institute criminal proceedings with respect thereto upon receiving notice thereof, no civil action may be brought under subsection (a) before the expiration of thirty days after written notice of such alleged act or practice has been given to the appropriate State or local authority by registered mail or in person, provided that the court may stay proceedings in such civil action pending the termination of State or local enforcement proceedings.

(d) In the case of an alleged act or practice prohibited by this title which occurs in a State, or political subdivision of a State, which has no State or local law prohibiting such act or practice, a civil action may be brought under subsection (a): *Provided,* That the court may refer the matter to the Community Relations Service established by title X of this Act for as long as the court believes there is a reasonable possibility of obtaining voluntary compliance, but for not more than sixty days: *Provided further,* That upon expiration of such sixty-day period, the court may extend such period for an additional period, not to exceed a cumulative total of one hundred and twenty days, if it believes there then exists a reasonable possibility of securing voluntary compliance.

SEC. 205. The Service is authorized to make a full investigation of any complaint referred to it by the court under section 204(d) and may hold such hearings with respect thereto as may be necessary. The Service shall conduct any hearings with respect to any such complaint in executive session, and shall not release any testimony given therein except by agreement of all parties involved in the complaint with the permission of the court, and the Service shall endeavor to bring about a voluntary settlement between the parties.

SEC. 206. (a) Whenever the Attorney General has reasonable cause to believe that any person or group of persons is engaged in a pattern or practice of resistance to the full enjoyment of any of the rights secured by this title, and that the pattern or practice is of such a nature and is intended to deny the full exercise of the rights herein described, the Attorney General may bring a civil action in the appropriate district court of the United States by filing with it a complaint (1) signed by him (or in his absence the Acting Attorney General), (2) setting forth facts pertaining to such pattern or practice, and (3) requesting such preventive relief, including an application for a permanent or temporary injunction, restraining order or other order against the person or persons responsible for such pattern or practice, as he deems necessary to insure the full enjoyment of the rights herein described.

(b) In any such proceeding the Attorney General may file with the clerk of such court a request that a court of three judges be convened to hear and determine the case. Such request by the Attorney General shall be accompanied by a certificate that, in his opinion, the case is of general public importance. A copy of the certificate and request for a three-judge court shall be immediately furnished by such clerk to the chief judge of the circuit (or in his absence, the presiding circuit judge of the circuit) in which the case is pending. Upon receipt of the copy of such request it shall be the duty of the chief judge of the circuit or the presiding circuit judge, as the case may be, to designate immediately three judges in such circuit, of whom at least one shall be a circuit judge and another of whom shall be a district judge of the court in which the proceeding was instituted, to hear and determine such case, and it shall be the duty of the judges so designated to assign the case for hearing at the earliest practicable date, to participate in the hearing and determination thereof, and to cause the case to be in every way expedited. An appeal from the final judgment of such court will lie to the Supreme Court.

In the event the Attorney General fails to file such a request in any such proceeding, it shall be the duty of the duty of the chief judge of the district (or in his absence, the acting chief judge) in which the case is pending immediately to designate a judge in such district to hear and determine the case. In the event that no judge in the district is available to hear and determine the case, the chief judge of the district, or the acting chief judge, as the case may be, shall certify this fact to the chief judge of the circuit (or in his absence, the acting chief judge) who shall then designate a district or circuit judge of the circuit to hear and determine the case.

It shall be the duty of the judge designated pursuant to this section to assign the case for hearing at the earliest practicable date and to cause the case to be in every way expedited.

SEC. 207. (a) The district courts of the United States shall have jurisdiction of proceedings instituted pursuant to this title and shall exercise the same without regard to whether the aggrieved party shall have exhausted any administrative or other remedies that may be provided by law.

(b) The remedies provided in this title shall be the exclusive means of enforcing the rights based on this title, but nothing in this title shall preclude any individual or any State or local agency from asserting any right based on any other Federal or State law not inconsistent with this title, including any statute or ordinance requiring nondiscrimination in public establishments or accommodations, or from pursuing any remedy, civil or criminal, which may be available for the vindication or enforcement of such right.

TITLE III—DESEGREGATION OF PUBLIC FACILITIES

SEC. 301. (a) Whenever the Attorney General receives a complaint in writing signed by an individual to the effect that he is being deprived of or threatened with the loss of his right to the equal protection of the laws, on account of his race, color, religion, or national origin, by being denied equal utilization of any public facility which is owned, operated, or managed by or on behalf of any State or subdivision thereof, other than a public school or public college as defined in section 401 of title IV hereof, and the Attorney General believes the complaint is meritorious and certifies that the signer or signers of such complaint are unable, in his judgment, to initiate and maintain appropriate legal proceedings for relief and that the institution of an action will materially further the orderly progress of desegregation in public facilities, the Attorney General is authorized to institute for or in the name of the United States a civil action in any appropriate district court of the United States against such parties and for such relief as may be appropriate, and such court shall have and shall exercise jurisdiction of proceedings instituted pursuant to this section. The Attorney General may implead as defendants such additional parties as are or become necessary to the grant of effective relief hereunder.

(b) The Attorney General may deem a person or persons unable to initiate and maintain appropriate legal proceedings within the meaning of subsection (a) of this section when such person or persons are unable, either directly or through other interested persons or organizations, to bear the expense of the litigation or to obtain effective legal representation; or whenever he is satisfied that the institution of such litigation would jeopardize the personal safety, employment, or economic standing of such person or persons, their families, or their property.

SEC. 302. In any action or proceeding under this title the United States shall be liable for costs, including a reasonable attorney's fee, the same as a private person.

SEC. 303. Nothing in this title shall affect adversely the right of any person to sue for or obtain relief in any court against discrimination in any facility covered by this title.

SEC. 304. A complaint as used in this title is a writing or document within the meaning of section 1001, title 18, United States Code.

TITLE IV—DESEGREGATION OF PUBLIC EDUCATION

DEFINITIONS

SEC. 401. As used in this title—

(a) "Commissioner" means the Commissioner of Education.

(b) "Desegregation" means the assignment of students to public schools and within such schools without regard to their race, color, religion, or national origin, but "desegregation" shall not mean the assignment of students to public schools in order to overcome racial imbalance.

(c) "Public school" means any elementary or secondary educational institution, and "public college" means any institution of higher education or any technical or vocational school above the secondary school level, provided that such public school or public college is operated by a State, subdivision of a State, or governmental agency within a State, or operated wholly or predominantly from or through the use of governmental funds or property, or funds or property derived from a governmental source.

(d) "School board" means any agency or agencies which administer a system of one or more public schools and any other agency which is responsible for the assignment of students to or within such system.

SURVEY AND REPORT OF EDUCATIONAL OPPORTUNITIES

SEC. 402. The Commissioner shall conduct a survey and make a report to the President and the Congress, within two years of the enactment of this title, concerning the lack of availability of equal educational opportunities for individuals by reason of race, color, religion, or national origin in public educational institutions at all levels in the United States, its territories and possessions, and the District of Columbia.

TECHNICAL ASSISTANCE

SEC. 403. The Commissioner is authorized, upon the application of any school board, State, municipality, school district, or other governmental unit legally responsible for operating a public school or schools, to render technical assistance to such applicant in the preparation, adoption, and implementation of plans for the desegregation of public schools. Such technical assistance may, among other activities, include making available to such agencies information regarding effective methods of coping with special educational problems occasioned by desegregation, and making available to such agencies personnel of the Office of Education or other persons specially equipped to advise and assist them in coping with such problems.

TRAINING INSTITUTES

SEC. 404. The Commissioner is authorized to arrange, through grants or contracts, with institutions of higher education for the operation of short-term or regular session institutes for special training designed to improve the ability of teachers, supervisors, counselors, and other elementary or secondary school personnel to deal effectively with special educational problems occasioned by desegregation. Individuals who attend such an institute on a full-time basis may be paid stipends for the period of their attendance at such institute in amounts specified by the Commissioner in regulations, including allowances for travel to attend such institute.

GRANTS

SEC. 405. (a) The Commissioner is authorized, upon application of a school board, to make grants to such board to pay, in whole or in part, the cost of—

(1) giving to teachers and other school personnel inservice training in dealing with problems incident to desegregation, and

(2) employing specialists to advise in problems incident to desegregation.

(b) In determining whether to make a grant, and in fixing the amount thereof and the terms and conditions on which it will be made, the Commissioner shall take into consideration the amount available for grants under this section and the other applications which are pending before him; the financial condition of the applicant and the other resources available to it; the nature, extent, and gravity of its problems incident to desegregation; and such other factors as he finds relevant.

PAYMENTS

SEC. 406. Payments pursuant to a grant or contract under this title may be made (after necessary adjustments on account of previously made overpayments or underpayments) in advance by way of reimbursement, and in such installments, as the Commissioner may determine.

SUITS BY THE ATTORNEY GENERAL

SEC. 407. (a) Whenever the Attorney General receives a complaint in writing—

(1) signed by a parent or group of parents to the effect that his or their minor children, as members of a class of persons similarly situated, are being deprived by a school board of the equal protection of the laws, or

(2) signed by an individual, or his parent, to the effect that he has been denied admission to or not permitted to continue in attendance at a public college by reason of race, color, religion, or national origin,

and the Attorney General believes the complaint is meritorious and certifies that the signer or signers of such complaint are unable, in his judgment, to initiate and maintain appropriate legal proceedings for relief and that the institution of an action will materially further the orderly achievement of desegregation in public education, the Attorney General is authorized, after giving notice of such complaint to the appropriate school board or college authority and after certifying that he is satisfied that such school board or authority has had a reasonable time to adjust the conditions alleged in such complaint, to institute for or in the name of the United States a civil action in any appropriate district court of the United States against such parties and for such relief as may be appropriate, and such court shall have and shall exercise jurisdiction of proceedings instituted pursuant to this section, provided that nothing herein shall empower any official or court of the United States to issue any order seeking to achieve a racial balance in any school by requiring the transportation of pupils or students from one school to another or one school district to another in order to achieve such racial balance, or otherwise enlarge the existing power of the court to insure compliance with constitutional standards. The Attorney General may implead as defendants such additional parties as are or become necessary to the grant of effective relief hereunder.

(b) The Attorney General may deem a person or persons unable to initiate and maintain appropriate legal proceedings within the meaning of subsection (a) of this section when such person or persons are unable, either directly or through other interested persons or organizations, to bear the expense of the litigation or to obtain effective legal representation; or whenever he is satisfied that the institution of such litigation would jeopardize the personal safety, employment, or economic standing of such person or persons, their families, or their property.

(c) The term "parent" as used in this section includes any person standing in loco parentis. A "complaint" as used in this section is a writing or document within the meaning of section 1001, title 18, United States Code.

SEC. 408. In any action or proceeding under this title the United States shall be liable for costs the same as a private person.

SEC. 409. Nothing in this title shall affect adversely the right of any person to sue for or obtain relief in any court against discrimination in public education.

SEC. 410. Nothing in this title shall prohibit classification and assignment for reasons other than race, color, religion, or national origin.

TITLE V—COMMISSION ON CIVIL RIGHTS

SEC. 501. Section 102 of the Civil Rights Act of 1957 (42 U.S.C. 1975a; 71 Stat. 634) is amended to read as follows:

"RULES OF PROCEDURE OF THE COMMISSION HEARINGS

"SEC. 102. (a) At least thirty days prior to the commencement of any hearing, the Commission shall cause to be published in the Federal Register notice of the date on which such hearing is to commence, the place at which it is to be held and the subject of the hearing. The Chairman, or one designated by him to act as Chairman at a hearing of the Commission, shall announce in an opening statement the subject of the hearing.

"(b) A copy of the Commission's rules shall be made available to any witness before the Commission or required to produce written or other matter shall be served with a copy of the Commission's rules at the time of service of the subpena.

"(c) Any person compelled to appear in person before the Commission shall be accorded the right to be accompanied and advised by counsel, who shall have the right to subject his client to reasonable examination, and to make objections on the record and to argue briefly the basis for such objections. The Commission shall proceed with reasonable dispatch to conclude any hearing in which it is engaged. Due regard shall be had for the convenience and necessity of witnesses.

"(d) The Chairman or Acting Chairman may punish breaches of order and decorum by censure and exclusion from the hearings.

"(e) If the Commission determines that evidence or testimony at any hearing may tend to defame, degrade, or incriminate any person, it shall receive such evidence or testimony or summary of such evidence or testimony in executive session. The Commission shall afford any person defamed, degraded, or incriminated by such evidence or testimony any opportunity to appear and be heard in executive session, with a reasonable number of additional witnesses requested by him, before deciding to use such evidence or testimony. In the event the Commission determines to release or use such evidence or testimony in such manner as to reveal publicly the identity of the person defamed, degraded, or incriminated, such evidence as testimony, prior to such public release or use, shall be given at a public session, and the Commission shall afford such person an opportunity to appear as a voluntary witness or to file a sworn statement in his behalf and to submit brief and pertinent sworn statements of others. The Commission shall receive and dispose of requests from such person to subpena additional witnesses.

"(f) Except as provided in sections 102 and 105(f) of this Act, the Chairman shall receive and the Commission shall dispose of requests to subpena additional witnesses.

"(g) No evidence or testimony or summary of evidence or testimony taken in executive session may be released or used in public sessions without the consent of the Commission. Whoever releases or uses in public without the consent of the Commission such evidence or testimony taken in executive session shall be fined not more than $1,000, or imprisoned for not more than one year.

"(h) In the discretion of the Commission, witnesses may submit brief and pertinent sworn statements in writing for inclusion in the record. The Commission shall determine the pertinency of testimony and evidence adduced at its hearings.

"(i) Every person who submits data or evidence shall be entitled to retain or, on payment of lawfully prescribed costs, procure a copy or transcript thereof, except that a witness in a hearing held in executive session may for good cause be limited to inspection of the official transcript of his testimony. Transcript copies of public sessions may be obtained by the public upon the payment of the cost thereof. An accurate transcript shall be made of the testimony of all witnesses at all hearings, either public or executive sessions, of the Commission or of any subcommittee thereof.

"(j) A witness attending any session of the Commission shall receive $6 for each day's attendance and for the time necessarily occupied in going to and returning from the same, and 10 cents per mile for going from and returning to his place of residence. Witnesses who attend at points so far removed from their respective residences as to prohibit return thereto from day to day shall be entitled to an additional allowance of $10 per day for expenses of subsistence, including the time necessarily occupied in going to and returning from the place of attendance. Mileage payments shall be tendered to the witness upon service of a subpena issued on behalf of the Commission or any subcommittee thereof.

"(k) The Commission shall not issue any subpena for the attendance and testimony of witnesses or for the production of written or other matter which would require the presence of the party subpenaed at a hearing to be held outside of the State wherein the witness is found or resides or is domiciled or transacts business, or has appointed an agent for receipt of service of process except that, in any event, the Commission may issue subpenas for the attendance and testimony of witnesses and the production of written or other matter at a hearing held within fifty miles of the place where the witness is found or resides or is domiciled or transacts business or has appointed an agent for receipt of service of process.

"(l) The Commission shall separately state and currently publish in the Federal Register (1) descriptions of its central and field organization including the established places at which, and methods whereby, the public may secure information or make requests; (2) statements of the general course and method by which its functions are channeled and determined, and (3) rules adopted as authorized by law. No person shall in any manner be subject to or required to resort to rules, organization, or procedure not so published."

SEC. 502. Section 103(a) of the Civil Rights Act of 1957 (42 U.S.C. 1975b(a); 71 Stat. 634) is amended to read as follows:

"SEC. 103 (a) Each member of the Commission who is not otherwise in the service of the Government of the United States shall receive the sum of $75 per day for each day spent in the work of the Commission, shall be paid actual travel expenses, and per diem in lieu of subsistence expenses when away from his usual place of residence, in accordance with section 5 of the Administrative Expenses Act of 1946, as amended (5 US.C. 73b–2; 60 Stat. 808)."

SEC. 503. Section 103(b) of the Civil Rights Act of 1957 (42 US.C. 1975(b); 71 Stat. 634) is amended to read as follows:

"(b) Each member of the Commission who is otherwise in the service of the Government of the United States shall serve without compensation in addition to that received for such other service, but while engaged in the work of the Commission shall be paid actual travel expenses, and per diem in lieu of subsistence expenses when away from his usual place of residence, in accordance with the provisions of the Travel Expenses Act of 1949, as amended (5 U.S.C. 835–42; 63 Stat. 166)."

SEC. 504 (a) Section 104(a) of the Civil Rights Act of 1957 (42 US.C. 1975c(a); 71 Stat. 635), as amended, is further amended to read as follows:

"DUTIES OF THE COMMISSION

"SEC. 104. (a) The Commission shall—

"(1) investigate allegations in writing under oath or affirmation that certain citizens of the United States are being deprived of their right to vote and have that vote counted by reason of their color, race, religion, or national origin; which writing, under oath or affirmation, shall set forth the facts upon which such belief or beliefs are based;

"(2) study and collect information concerning legal developments constituting a denial of equal protection of the laws under the Constitution because of race, color, religion or national origin or in the administration of justice;

"(3) appraise the laws and policies of the Federal Government with respect to denials of equal protection of the laws under the Constitution because of race, color, religion or national origin or in the administration of justice;

"(4) serve as a national clearinghouse for information in respect to denials of equal protection of the laws because of race, color, religion or national origin, including but not limited to the fields of voting, education, housing, employment, the use of public facilities, and transportation, or in the administration of justice;

"(5) investigate allegations, made in writing and under oath or affirmation, that citizens of the United States are unlawfully being accorded or denied the right to vote, or to have their votes properly counted, in any election of presidential electors, Members of the United States Senate, or of the House of Representatives, as a result of any patterns or practice of fraud or discrimination in the conduct of such election; and

"(6) Nothing in this or any other Act shall be construed as authorizing the Commission, its Advisory Committees, or any person under its supervision or control to inquire into or investigate any membership practices or internal operations of any fraternal organization, any college or university fraternity or sorority, any private club or any religious organization."

(b) Section 104(b) of the Civil Rights Act of 1957 (42 U.S.C. 1975c(b); 71 Stat. 635), as amended, is further amended by striking out the present subsection "(b)" and by substituting therefor:

"(b) The Commission shall submit interim reports to the President and to the Congress at such times as the Commission, the Congress or the President shall deem desirable, and shall submit to the President and to the Congress a final report of its activities, findings, and recommendations not later than January 31, 1968."

SEC. 505. Section 105(a) of the Civil Rights Act of 1957 (42 U.S.C. 1975d(a); 71 Stat 636) is amended by striking out in the last sentence thereof "$50 per diem" and inserting in lieu thereof "$75 per diem."

Sec. 506. Section 105(f) and section 105(g) of the Civil Rights Act of 1957 (42 U.S.C. 1975d (f) and (g); 71 Stat. 636) are amended to read as follows:

"(f) The Commission, or on the authorization of the Commission any subcommittee of two or more members, at least one of whom shall be of each major political party, may, for the purpose of carrying out the provisions of this Act, hold such hearings and act at such times and places as the Commission or such authorized subcommittee may deem advisable. Subpenas for the attendance and testimony of witnesses or the production of written or other matter may be issued in accordance with the rules of the Commission as contained in section 102 (j) and (k) of this Act, over the signature of the Chairman of the Commission or of such subcommittee, and may be served by any person designated by such Chairman. The holding of hearings by the Commission, or the appointment of a subcommittee to hold hearings pursuant to this subparagraph, must be approved by a majority of the Commission, or by a majority of the members present at a meeting at which at least a quorum of four members is present.

"(g) In case of contumacy or refusal to obey a subpena, any district court of the United States or the United States court of any territory or possession, or the District Court of the United States for the District of Columbia, within the jurisdiction of which the inquiry is carried on or within the jurisdiction of which said person guilty of contumacy or refusal to obey is found or resides or is domiciled or transacts business, or has appointed an agent for receipt of service of process, upon application by the Attorney General of the United States shall have jurisdiction to issue to such person an order requiring such person to appear before the Commission or a subcommittee thereof, there to produce pertinent, relevant and nonprivileged evidence if so ordered, or there to give testimony touching the matter under investigation; and any failure to obey such order of the court may be punished by said court as a contempt thereof."

Sec. 507. Section 105 of the Civil Rights Act of 1957 (42 U.S.C. 1975d; 71 Stat 636), as amended by section 401 of the Civil Rights Act of 1960 (42 U.S.C. 1975d(h); 74 Stat 89), is further amended by adding a new subsection at the end to read as follows:

"(i) The Commission shall have the power to make such rules and regultaions as are necessary to carry out the purposes of this Act."

TITLE VI—NONDISCRIMINATION IN FEDERALLY ASSISTED PROGRAMS

Sec. 601. No person in the United States shall, on the ground of race, color, or national origin, be excluded from participation in, be denied the benefits of, or be subjected to discrimination under any program or activity receiving Federal financial assistance.

Sec. 602. Each Federal department and agency which is empowered to extend Federal financial assistance to any program or activity, by way of grant, loan, or contract other than a contract of insurance or guaranty, is authorized and directed to effectuate the provisions of section 601 with respect to such program or activity by issuing rules, regulations, or orders of general applicability which shall be consistent with achievement of the objectives of the statute authorizing the financial assistance in connection with which the action is taken. No such

rule, regulation, or order shall become effective unless and until approved by the President. Compliance with any requirement adopted pursuant to this section may be effected (1) by the termination of or refusal to grant or to continue assistance under such program or activity to any recipient as to whom there has been an express finding on the record, after opportunity for hearing, of a failure to comply with such requirement, but such termination or refusal shall be limited to the particular political entity, or part thereof, or other recipient as to whom such a finding has been made and, shall be limited in its effect to the particular program, or part thereof, in which such noncompliance has been so found, or (2) by any other means authorized by law: *Provided, however,* That no such action shall be taken until the department or agency concerned has advised the appropriate person or persons of the failure to comply with the requirement and has determined that compliance cannot be secured by voluntary means. In the case of any action terminating, or refusing to grant or continue, assistance because of the failure to comply with a requirement imposed pursuant to this section, the head of the Federal department or agency shall file with the committees of the House and Senate having legislative jurisdiction over the program or activity involved a full written report of the circumstances and the grounds for such action. No such action shall become effective until thirty days have elapsed after the filing of such report.

Sec. 603. Any department or agency action taken pursuant to section 602 shall be subject to such judicial review as may otherwise be provided by law for similar action taken by such department or agency on other grounds. In the case of action, not otherwise subject to judicial review, terminating or refusing to grant or to continue financial assistance upon a finding of failure to comply with any requirement imposed pursuant to section 602, any person aggrieved (including any State or political subdivision thereof and agency of either) may obtain judicial review of such action in accordance with section 10 of the Administrative Procedure Act, and such action shall not be deemed committed to unreviewable agency discretion within the meaning of that section.

Sec. 604. Nothing contained in this title shall be construed to authorize action under this title by any department or agency with respect to any employment practice of any employer, employment agency, or labor organization except where a primary objective of the Federal financial assistance is to provide employment.

Sec. 605. Nothing in this title shall add to or detract from any existing authority with respect to any program or activity under which Federal financial assistance is extended by way of a contract of insurance or guaranty.

TITLE VII—EQUAL EMPLOYMENT OPPORTUNITY

DEFINITIONS

Sec. 701. For the purposes of this title—

(a) The term "person" includes one or more individuals, labor unions, partnerships, associations, corporations, legal representatives, mutual companies, joint-stock companies, trusts, unincorporated organizations, trustees in bankruptcy, or receivers.

(b) The term "employer" means a person engaged in an industry affecting commerce who has twenty-five or more employees for each working day in each of twenty or more calendar weeks in the current or preceding calendar year, and any agent of such a person, but such term does not include (1) the United States, a corporation wholly owned by the Government of the United States, an Indian tribe, or a State or political subdivision thereof, (2) a bona fide private membership club (other than a labor organization) which is exempt from taxation under section 501(c) of the Internal Revenue Code of 1954: *Provided,* That during the first year after the effective date prescribed in subsection (a) of section 716, persons having fewer than one hundred employees (and their agents) shall not be considered employers, and, during the second year after such date, persons having fewer than seventy-five employees (and their agents) shall not be considered employers, and, during the third year after such date, persons having fewer than fifty employees (and their agents) shall not be considered employers: *Provided further,* That it shall be the policy of the United States to insure equal employment opportunities for Federal employees without discrimination because of race, color, religion, sex or national origin and the President shall utilize his existing authority to effectuate policy.

(c) The term "employment agency" means any person regularly undertaking with or without compensation to procure employees for an employer or to procure for employees opportunities to work for an employer and includes an agent of such a person; but shall not include an agency of the United States, or an agency of a State or political subdivision of a State, except that such term shall include the United States Employment Service and the system of State and local employment services receiving Federal assistance.

(d) The term "labor organization" means a labor organization engaged in an industry affecting commerce, and any agent of such an organization, and includes any organization of any kind, any agency, or employee representation committee, group, association, or plan so engaged in which employees participate and which exists for the purpose, in whole or in part, of dealing with employers concerning grievances, labor disputes, wages, rates of pay, hours, or other terms or conditions of employment, and any conference, general committee, joint or system board, or joint council so engaged which is subordinate to a national or international labor organization.

(e) A labor organization shall be deemed to be engaged in an industry affecting commerce if (1) it maintains or operates a hiring hall or hiring office which procures employees for an employer or procures for employees opportunities to work for an employer, or (2) the number of its members (or, where it is a labor organization composed of other labor organizations or their representatives, if the aggregate number of the members of such other labor organization) is (A) one hundred or more during the first year after the effective date prescribed in subsection (a) of section 716, (B) seventy-five or more during the second year after such date or fifty or more during the third year, or (C) twenty-five or more thereafter, and such labor organization—

(1) is the certified representative of employees under the provisions of the National Labor Relations Act, as amended, or the Railway Labor Act, as as amended;

(2) although not certified, is a national or international labor organization or a local labor organization recognized or acting as the representative of employees of an employer or employers engaged in an industry affecting commerce; or

(3) has chartered a local labor organization or subsidiary body which is representing or actively seeking to represent employees of employers within the meaning of paragraph (1) or (2); or

(4) has been chartered by a labor organization representing or actively seeking to represent employees within the meaning of paragraph (1) or (2) as the local or subordinate body through which such employees may enjoy membership or become affiliated with such labor organization; or

(5) is a conference, general committee, joint or system board, or joint council subordinate to a national or international labor organization, which includes a labor organization engaged in an industry affecting commerce within the meaning of any of the preceding paragraphs of this subsection.

(f) The term "employee" means an individual employed by an employer.

(g) The term "commerce" means trade, traffic, commerce, transportation, transmission, or communication among the several States; or between a State and any place outside thereof; or within the District of Columbia, or a possession of the United States; or between points in the same State but through a point outside thereof.

(h) The term "industry affecting commerce" means any activity, business, or industry in commerce or in which a labor dispute would hinder or obstruct commerce or the free flow of commerce and includes any activity or industry "affecting commerce" within the meaning of the Labor-Management Reporting and Disclosure Act of 1959.

(i) The term "State" includes a State of the United States, the District of Columbia, Puerto Rico, the Virgin Islands, American Samoa, Guam, Wake Island, the Canal Zone, and Outer Continental Shelf lands defined in the Outer Continental Shelf Lands Act.

EXEMPTION

SEC. 702. This title shall not apply to an employer with respect to the employment of aliens outside any State, or to a religious corporation, association, or society with respect to the employment of individuals of a particular religion to perform work connected with the carrying on by such corporation, association, or society of its religious activities or to an educational institution with respect to the employment of individuals to perform work connected with the educational activities of such institution.

DISCRIMINITION BECAUSE OF RACE, COLOR, RELIGION, SEX, OR NATIONAL ORIGIN

SEC. 703. (a) It shall be an unlawful employment practice for an employer—

(1) to fail or refuse to hire or to discharge any individual, or otherwise to discriminate against any individual with respect to his compensation, terms, conditions, or privileges of employment, because of such individual's race, color, religion, sex, or national origin; or

(2) to limit, segregate, or classify his employees in any way which would deprive or tend to deprive any individual of employment opportunities or otherwise adversely affect his status as an employee, because of such individual's race, color, religion, sex, or national origin.

(b) It shall be an unlawful employment practice for an employment agency to fail or refuse to refer for employment, or otherwise to discriminate against, any individual because of his race, color, religion, sex, or national origin, or to classify or refer for employment any individual on the basis of his race, color, religion, sex, or national origin.

(c) It shall be an unlawful employment practice for a labor organization—

(1) to exclude or to expel from its membership, or otherwise to discriminate against, any individual because of his race, color, religion, sex, or national origin;

(2) to limit, segregate, or classify its membership, or to classify or fail or refuse to refer for employment any individual, in any way which would deprive or tend to deprive any individual of employment opportunities, or otherwise adversely affect his status as an employee or as an applicant for employment, because of such individual's race, color, religion, sex, or national origin; or

(3) to cause or attempt to cause an employer to discriminate against an individual in violation of this section.

(d) It shall be an unlawful employment practice for any employer, labor organization, or joint labor-management committee controlling apprenticeship or other training or retraining, including on-the-job training programs to discriminate against any individual because of his race, color, religion, sex, or national origin in admission to, or employment in, any program established to provide apprenticeship or other training.

(e) Notwithstanding any other provision of this title, (1) it shall not be an unlawful employment practice for an employer to hire and employ employees, for an employment agency to classify, or refer for employment any individual, for a labor organization to classify its membership or to classify or refer for employment any individual, or for an employer, labor organization, or joint labor-management committee controlling apprenticeship or other training or retraining programs to admit or employ any individual in any such program, on the basis of his religion, sex, or national origin in those certain instances where religion, sex, or national origin is a bona fide occupational qualification reasonably necessary to the normal operation of that particular business or enterprise, and (2) it shall not be an unlawful employment practice for a school, college, university, or other educational institution or institution of learning to hire and employ employees of a particular religion if such school, college, university, or other educational institution or institution of learning is, in whole or in substantial part, owned, supported, controlled, or managed by a particular religion or by a particular religious corporation, association, or society, or if the curriculum of such school, college, university, or other educational institution or institution of learning is directed toward the propagation of a particular religion.

(f) As used in this title, the phrase "unlawful employment practice" shall not be deemed to include any action or measure taken by an employer, labor organization, joint labor-management committee, or employment agency with respect to an individual who is a member of the Communist Party of the United States or of any other organization required to register as a Communist-action or Communist-front organization by final order of the Subversive Activities Control Board pursuant to the Subversive Activities Control Act of 1950.

(g) Notwithstanding any other provision of this title, it shall not be an unlawful employment practice for an employer to fail or refuse to hire and employ any individual for any position, for an employer to discharge any individual from any position, or for an employment agency to fail or refuse to refer any individual for em-

ployment in any position, or for a labor organization to fail or refuse to refer any individual for employment in any position, if—

(1) the occupancy of such position, or access to the premises in or upon which any part of the duties of such position is performed or is to be performed, is subject to any requirement imposed in the interest of the national security of the United States under any security program in effect pursuant to or administered under any statute of the United States or any Executive order of the President; and

(2) such individual has not fulfilled or has ceased to fulfill that requirement.

(h) Notwithstanding any other provision of this title, it shall not be an unlawful employment practice for an employer to apply different standards of compensation, or different terms, conditions, or privileges of employment pursuant to a bona fide seniority or merit system, or a system which measures earnings by quantity or quality of production or to employees who work in different locations, provided that such differences are not the result of an intention to discriminate because of race, color, religion, sex, or national origin, nor shall it be an unlawful employment practice for an employer to give and to act upon the results of any professionally developed ability test provided that such test, its administration or action upon the results is not designed, intended or used to discriminate because of race, color, religion, sex or national origin. It shall not be an unlawful employment practice under this title for any employer to differentiate upon the basis of sex in determining the amount of the wages or compensation paid or to be paid to employees of such employer if such differentiation is authorized by the provisions of section 6(d) of the Fair Labor Standards Act of 1938, as amended (29 U.S.C. 206(d)).

(i) Nothing contained in this title shall apply to any business or enterprise on or near an Indian reservation with respect to any publicly announced employment practice of such business or enterprise under which a preferential treatment is given to any individual because he is an Indian living on or near a reservation.

(j) Nothing contained in this title shall be interpreted to require any employer, employment agency, labor organization, or joint labor-management committee subject to this title to grant preferential treatment to any individual or to any group because of the race, color, religion, sex, or national origin of such individual or group on account of an imbalance which may exist with respect to the total number or percentage of persons of any race, color, religion, sex, or national origin employed by any employer, referred or classified for employment by any employment agency or labor organization, admitted to membership or classified by any labor organization, or admitted to, or employed in, any apprenticeship or other training program, in comparison with the total number or percentage of persons of such race, color, religion, sex, or national origin in any community, State, section, or other area, or in the available work force in any community, State, section, or other area.

OTHER UNLAWUL EMPLOYMENT PRACTICES

Sec. 704. (a) It shall be an unlawful employment practice for an employer to discriminate against any of his employees or applicants for employment, for an employment agency to discriminate against any individual, or for a labor organization to discriminate against any member thereof or applicant for membership, because he has opposed any practice made an unlawful employment practice by this title, or because he has made a change, testified, assisted, or participated in any manner in an investigation proceeding, or hearing under this title.

(b) It shall be an unlawful employment practice for an employer, labor organization, or employment agency to print or publish or cause to be printed or published any notice or advertisement relating to employment by such an employer or membership in or any classification or referral for employment by such a labor organization, or relating to any classification or referral for employment by such an employment agency, indicating any preference, limitation, specification, or discrimination, based on race, color, religion, sex, or national origin, except that such a notice or advertisement may indicate a preference, limitation, specification, or discrimination based on religion, sex, or national origin when religion, sex, or natonal origin is a bona fide occupation qualification for employment.

EQUAL EMPLOYMENT OPPORTUNITY COMMISSION

SEC. 705. (a) There is hereby created a Commission to be known as the Equal Employment Opportunity Commission, which shall be composed of five members, not more than three of whom shall be members of the same political party, who shall be appointed by the President by and with the advice and consent of the Senate. One of the original members shall be appointed for a term of one year, one for a term of two years, one for a term of three years, one for a term of four years, and one for a term of five years, beginning from the date of enactment of this title, but their successors shall be appointed for terms of five years each, except that any individual chosen to fill a vacancy shall be appointed only for the unexpired term of the member whom he shall succeed. The President shall designate one member to serve as Chairman of the Commission, and one member to serve as Vice Chairman. The Chairman shall be responsible on behalf of the Commission for the administrative operations of the Commission, and shall appoint, in accordance with the civil service laws, such officers, agents, attorneys, and employees as it deems necessary to assist it in the performance of its functions and to fix their compensation in accordance with the Classification Act of 1949, as amended. The Vice Chairman shall act as Chairman in the absence or disability of the Chairman or in the event of a vacancy in that office.

(b) A vacancy in the Commission shall not impair the right of the remaining members to exercise all the powers of the Commission and three members thereof shall constitute a quorum.

(c) The Commission shall have an official seal which shall be judicially noticed.

(d) The Commission shall at the close of each fiscal year report to the Congress and to the President concerning the action it has taken; the names, salaries, and duties of all individuals in its employ and the moneys it has disbursed; and shall make such further reports on the cause of and means of eliminating discrimination and such recommendations for further legislation as may appear desirable.

(e) The Federal Executive Pay Act of 1956 as amended (5 U.S.C. 2201–2209), is further amended—

(1) by adding to section 105 thereof (5 U.S.C. 2204) the following clause:

"(32) Chairman, Equal Employment Opportunity Commission"; and

(2) by adding to clause (45) of section 106(a) thereof (5 U.S.C. 2205(a)) the following: "Equal Employment Opportunity Commission (4)."

(f) The principal office of the Commission shall be in or near the District of Columbia, but it may meet or exercise any or all of its powers at any other place. The Commission may establish such regional or State offices as it deems necessary to accomplish the purpose of this title.

(g) The Commission shall have power—

(1) to cooperate with and, with their consent, utilize regional, State, local, and other agencies, both public and private, and individuals;

(2) to pay to witnesses whose depositions are taken or who are summoned before the Commission or any of its agents the same witness and mileage fees as are paid to witnesses in the courts of the United States;

(3) to furnish to persons subject to this title such technical assistance as they may request to further their compliance with this title or an order issued thereunder;

(4) upon the request of (i) any employer, whose employees or some of them, or (ii) any labor organization, whose members or some of them, refuse or threaten to refuse to cooperate in effectuating the provisions of this title, to assist in such effectuation by conciliation or such other remedial action as is provided by this title;

(5) to make such technical studies as are appropriate to effectuate the purposes and policies of this title and to make the results of such studies available to the public;

(6) to refer matters to the Attorney General with recommendations for intervention in a civil action brought by an aggrieved party under section 706, or for the institution of a civil action by the Attorney General under section 707, and to advise, consult, and assist the Attorney General on such matters.

(h) Attorneys appointed under this section may, at the direction of the Commission, appear for and represent the Commission in any case in court.

(i) The Commission shall, in any of its educational or promotional activities, cooperate with other departments and agencies in the performance of such educational and promotional activities.

(j) All officers, agents, attorneys, and employees of the Commission shall be subject to the provisions of section 9 of the Act of August 2, 1939, as amended (the Hatch Act), notwithstanding any exemption contained in such section.

PREVENTION OF UNLAWFUL EMPLOYMENT PRACTICES

SEC. 706. (a) Whenever it is charged in writing under oath by a person claiming to be aggrieved, or a written charge has been filed by a member of the Commission where he has reasonable cause to believe a violation of this title has occurred (and such charge sets forth the facts upon which it is based) that an employer, employment agency, or labor organization has engaged in an unlawful employment practice, the Commission shall furnish such employer, employment agency, or labor organization (hereinafter referred to as the "respondent") with a copy of such charge and shall make an investigation of such charge, provided that such charge shall not be made public by the Commission. If the Commission shall determine, after such investigation, that there is reasonable cause to believe that the charge is true, the Commission shall endeavor to eliminate any such alleged unlawful employment practice by informal methods of conference, conciliation, and persuasion. Nothing said or done during and as a part of such endeavors may be made public by the Commission without the written consent of the parties, or used as evidence in a subsequent proceeding. Any officer or employee of the Commission, who shall make public in any manner whatever any information in violation of this subsection shall be deemed guilty of a misdemeanor and upon conviction thereof shall be fined not more than $1,000 or imprisoned not more than one year.

(b) In the case of an alleged unlawful employment practice occurring in a State, or political subdivision of a State, which has a State or local law prohibiting the unlawful employment practice alleged and establishing or authorizing a State or local authority to grant or seek relief from such practice or to institute criminal proceedings with respect thereto upon receiving notice thereof, no charge may be filed under subsection (a) by the person aggrieved before the expiration of sixty days after proceedings have been commenced under the State or local law, unless such proceedings have been earlier terminated, provided that such sixty-day period shall be extended to one hundred and twenty days during the first year after the effective date of such State or local law. If any requirement for the commencement of such proceedings is imposed by a State or local authority other than a requirement of the filing of a written and signed statement of the facts upon which the proceeding is based, the proceeding shall be deemed to have been commenced for the purposes of this subsection at the time such statement is sent by registered mail to the appropriate State or local authority.

(c) In the case of any charges filed by a member of the Commission alleging an unlawful employment practice occurring in a State or political subdivision of a State, which has a State or local law prohibiting the practice alleged and establishing or authorizing a State or local authority to grant or seek relief from such practice or to institute criminal proceedings with respect thereto upon receiving notice thereof, the Commission shall, before taking any action with respect to such charge, notify the appropriate State or local officials and, upon request, afford them a reasonable time, but not less than sixty days (provided that such sixty-day period shall be extended to one hundred and twenty days during the first year after the effective day of such State or local law), unless a shorter period is requested, to act under such State or local law to remedy the practice alleged.

(d) A charge under subsection (a) shall be filed within ninety days after the alleged unlawful employment practice occurred, except that in the case of an unlawful employment practice with respect to which the person aggrieved has followed the procedure set out in subsection (b), such charge shall be filed by the person aggrieved within two hundred and ten days after the alleged unlawful employment practice occurred, or within thirty days after receiving notice that the State or local agency has terminated the proceedings under the State or local law, whichever is earlier, and a copy of such charge shall be filed by the Commission with the State or local agency.

(e) If within thirty days after a charge is filed with the Commission or within thirty days after expiration of any period of reference under subsection (c) (except that in either case such period may be extended to not more than sixty days upon a determination by the Commission that further efforts to secure voluntary compliance are warranted) the Commission has been unable to obtain voluntary compliance with this title, the Commission shall so notify the person aggrieved and a civil action may, within thirty days thereafter, be brought against the respondent named in the charge (1) by the person claiming to be aggrieved, or (2) if such charge was filed by a member of the Commission, by any person whom the charge alleges was aggrieved by the alleged unlawful employment practice. Upon application by the complainant and in such circumstances as the court may deem just, the court may appoint an attorney for such complainant and may authorize the commencement of the action without the payment of fees, costs, or security. Upon timely application, the court may, in its discretion, permit the Attorney General to intervene in such civil action if he certifies that the case is of general public importance. Upon request, the court may, in its discretion, stay further proceedings for not more than sixty days pending the termination of State or local proceedings described in subsection (b) or the efforts of the Commission to obtain voluntary compliance.

(f) Each United States district court and each United States court of a place subject to the jurisdiction of the United States shall have jurisdiction of actions brought under this title. Such an action may be brought in any judicial district in the State in which the unlawful employment practice is alleged to have been committed, in the judicial district in which the employment records relevant to such practice are maintained and administered, or in the judicial district in which the plaintiff would have worked but for the alleged unlawful employment practice, but if the respondent is not found within any such district, such an action may be brought within the judicial district in which the respondent has his principal office. For purposes of sections 1404 and 1406 of title 28 of the United States Code, the judicial district in which the respondent has his principal office shall in all cases be considered a district in which the action might have been brought.

(g) If the court finds that the respondent has intentionally engaged in or is intentionally engaging in an unlawful employment practice charged in the complaint, the court may enjoin the respondent from engaging in such unlawful employment practice, and order such affirmative action as may be appropriate, which may include reinstatement or hiring of employees, with or without back pay (payable by the employer, employment agency, or labor organization, as the case may be responsible for the unlawful employment practice). Interim earnings or amounts earnable with reasonable diligence by the person or persons discriminated against shall operate to reduce the back pay otherwise allowable. No order of the court shall require the admission or reinstatement of an individual as a member of a union or the hiring, reinstatement, or promotion of an individual as an employee, or the payment to him or any back pay, if such individual was refused admission, suspended, or expelled or was refused employment or advancement or was suspended or discharged for any reason other than discrimination on account of race, color, religion, sex or national origin or in violation of section 704(a).

(h) The provisions of the Act entitled "An Act to amend the Judicial Code and to define and limit the jurisdiction of courts sitting in equity, and for other purposes," approved March 23, 1932 (29 U.S.C. 101–115), shall not apply with respect to civil actions brought under this section.

(i) In any case in which an employer, employment agency, or labor organization fails to comply with an order of a court issued in a civil action brought under subsection (e), the Commission may commence proceedings to compel compliance with such order.

(j) Any civil action brought under subsection (e) and any proceeding brought under subsection (1) shall be subject to appeal as provided in sections 1291 and 1292, title 28, United States Code.

(k) In any action or proceeding under this title the court, in its discretion, may allow the prevailing party, other than the Commission or the United States, a reasonable attorney's fee as part of the costs, and the Commission and the United States shall be liable for costs the same as a private person.

SEC. 707. (a) Whenever the Attorney General has reasonable cause to believe that any person or group of persons is engaged in a pattern or practice of resistance to the full enjoyment of any of the rights secured by this title, and that the pattern or practice is of such a nature and is intended to deny the full exercise of the rights herein described, the Attorney General may bring a civil action in the appropriate district court of the United States by filing with it a complaint (1) signed by him (or in his absence the Acting Attorney General), (2) setting forth facts pertaining to such pattern or practice, and (3) requesting such relief, including an application for a permanent or temporary injunction, restraining order or other order against the person or persons responsible for such pattern or practice, as he deems necessary to insure the full enjoyment of the rights herein described.

(b) The district courts of the United States shall have and shall exercise jurisdiction of proceedings instituted pursuant to this section, and in any such proceeding the Attorney General may file with the clerk of such court a request that a court of three judges be convened to hear and determine the case. Such request by the Attorney General shall be accompanied by a certificate that, in his opinion, the case is of general public importance. A copy of the certificate and request for a three-judge court shall be immediately furnished by such clerk to the chief judge of the circuit (or in his absence, the presiding circuit judge of the circuit) in which the case is pending. Upon receipt of such request it shall be the duty of the chief judge of the circuit or the presiding circuit judge, as the case may be, to designate immediately three judges in such circuit, of whom at least one shall be a circuit judge and another of whom shall be a district judge of the court in which the proceeding was instituted, to hear and determine such case, and it shall be the duty of the judges so designated to assign the case for hearing at the earliest practicable date, to participate in the hearing and determination thereof, and to cause the case to be in every way expedited. An appeal from the final judgment of such court will lie to the Supreme Court.

In the event the Attorney General fails to file such a request in any such proceeding, it shall be the duty of the chief judge of the district (or in his absence, the acting chief judge) in which the case is pending immediately to designate a judge in such district is available to hear and determine the case, the chief judge of the district, or the acting chief judge, as the case may be, shall certify this fact to the chief judge of the circuit (or in his absence, the acting chief judge) who shall then designate a district or circuit judge of the circuit to hear and determine the case.

It shall be the duty of the judge designated pursuant to this section to assign the case for hearing at the earliest practicable date and to cause the case to be in every way expedited.

EFFECT ON STATE LAWS

SEC. 708. Nothing in this title shall be deemed to exempt or relieve any person from any liability, duty, penalty, or punishment provided by any present or future law of any State or political subdivision of a State, other than any such law which purports to require or permit the doing of any act which would be an unlawful employment practice under this title.

INVESTIGATIONS, INSPECTIONS, RECORDS, STATE AGENCIES

SEC. 709. (a) In connection with any investigation of a charge filed under section 706, the Commission or its designated representative shall at all reasonable times have access to, for the purposes of examination, and the right to copy any evidence of any person being investigated or proceeded against that relates to unlawful employment practices covered by this title and is relevant to the charge under investigation.

(b) The Commission may cooperate with State and local agencies charged with the administration of State fair employment practices laws and, with the consent of such agencies, may for the purpose of carrying out its functions and duties under this title and within the limitation of funds appropriated specifically for such purpose, utilize the services of such agencies and their employees and, notwithstanding any other provision of law, may reimburse such agencies and their employees for services rendered to assist the Commission in carrying out this title. In furtherance of such cooperative efforts, the Commission may enter into written agreements with such State or local agencies and such agreements may include provisions under which the Commission shall refrain from processing a charge in any cases or class of cases specified in such agreements and under which no person may bring a civil action under section 706 in any cases or class of cases so specified, or under which the Commission shall relieve any person or class of persons in such State or locality from requirements imposed under this section. The Commission shall rescind any such agreement whenever it determines that the agreement no longer serves the interest of effective enforcement of this title.

(c) Except as provided in subsection (d), every employer, employment agency, and labor organization subject to this title shall (1) make and keep such records relevant to the determinations of whether unlawful employment practices have been or are being committed, (2) preserve such records for such periods, and (3) make such reports therefrom, as the Commission shall prescribe by regulation or order, after public hearing, as reasonable, necessary, or appropriate for the enforcement of this title or the regulations or orders thereunder. The Commission shall, by regulation, require each employer, labor organization, and joint labor-management committee subject to this title which controls an apprenticeship or other training program to maintain such records as are reasonably necessary to carry out the purpose of this title, including, but not limited to, a list of applicants who wish to participate in such program, including the chronological order in which such applications were received, and shall furnish to the Commission, upon request, a detailed description of the manner in which persons are selected to participate in the apprenticeship or other training program. Any employer, employment agency, labor organization, or joint labor-management committee which believes that the application to it of any regulation or order issued under this section would result in undue hardship may (1) apply to the Commission for an exemption from the application of such regulation or order, or (2) bring a civil action in the United States district court for the district where such records are kept. If the Commission or the court, as the case may be, finds that the application of the regulation or order to the employer, employment agency, or labor organization in question would impose an undue hardship, the Commission or the court, as the case may be, may grant appropriate relief.

(d) The provisions of subsection (c) shall not apply to any employer, employment agency, labor organization, or joint labor-management committee with respect to matters occurring in any State or political subdivision thereof which has a fair employment practice law during any period in which such employer, employment agency, labor organization, or joint labor-management committee is subject to such law, except that the Commission may require such notations on records which such employer, employment agency, labor organization, or joint labor-management committee keeps or is required to keep as are necessary because of differences in coverage or methods of enforcement between the State or local law and the provisions of this title. Where an employer is required by Executive Order 10925, issued March 6, 1961, or by any other Executive order prescribing fair employment practices for Government contractors and subcontractors, or by rules or regulations issued thereunder, to file reports relating to his employment practices with any Federal agency or committee, and he is substantially in compliance with such requirements, the Commission shall not require him to file additional reports pursuant to subsection (c) of this section.

(e) It shall be unlawful for any officer or employee of the Commission to make public in any manner whatever any information obtained by the Commission pursuant to its authority under this section prior to the institution of any proceeding under this title involving such information. Any officer or employee of the Commission who shall make public in any manner whatever any information in violation of this subsection shall be guilty of a misdemeanor and upon conviction thereof, shall be fined not more than $1,000, or imprisoned not more than one year.

INVESTIGATORY POWERS

SEC. 710. (a) For the purposes of any investigation of a charge filed under the authority contained in section 706, the Commission shall be authority to examine witnesses under oath and to require the production of documentary evidence relevant or material to the charge under investigation.

(b) If the respondent named in a charge filed under section 706 fails or refuses to comply with a demand of the Commission for permission to examine or to copy evidence in conformity with the provisions of section 709(a), or if any person required to comply with the provisions of section 709 (c) or (d) fails or refuses to

do so, or if any person fails or refuses to comply with a demand by the Commission to give testimony under oath, the United States district court for the district in which such person is found, resides, or transacts business, shall, upon application of the Commission, have jurisdiction to issue to such person an order requiring him to comply with the provisions of section 709 (c) or (d) or to comply with the demand of the Commission, but the attendance of a witness may not be required outside the State where he is found, resides, or transacts business and the production of evidence may not be required outside the State where such evidence is kept.

(c) Within twenty days after the service upon any person charged under section 706 of a demand by the Commission for the production of documentary evidence or for permission to examine or to copy evidence in conformity with the provisions of section 709(a), such person may file in the district court of the United States for the judicial district in which he resides, is found, or transacts business, and serve upon the Commission a petition for an order of such court modifying or setting aside such demand. The time allowed for compliance with the demand in whole or in part as deemed proper and ordered by the court shall not run during the pendency of such petition in the court. Such petition shall specify each ground upon which the petitioner relies in seeking such relief, and may be based upon any failure of such demand to comply with the provisions of this title or with the limitations generally applicable to compulsory process or upon any constitutional or other legal right or privilege of such person. No objection which is not raised by such a petition may be urged in the defense to a proceeding initiated by the Commission under subsection (b) for enforcement of such a demand unless such proceeding is commenced by the Commission prior to the expiration of the twenty-day period, or unless the court determines that the defendant could not reasonably have been aware of the availability of such ground of objection

(d) In any proceeding brought by the Commission under subsection (b), except as provided in subsection (c) of this section, the defendant may petition the court for an order modifying or setting aside the demand of the Commission.

NOTICES TO BE POSTED

SEC. 711. (a) Every employer, employment agency, and labor organization, as the case may be, shall post and keep posted in conspicuous places upon its premises where notices to employees, applicants for employment, and members are customarily posted a notice to be prepared or approved by the Commission setting forth excerpts from or, summaries of, the pertinent provisions of this title and information pertinent to the filing of a complaint.

(b) A willful violation of this section shall be punishable by a fine of not more than $100 for each separate offense.

VETERANS' PREFERENCE

SEC. 712. Nothing contained in this title shall be construed to repeal or modify any Federal, State, territorial, or local law creating special rights or preference for veterans.

RULES AND REGULATIONS

SEC. 713 (a) The Commission shall have authority from time to time to issue, amend, or rescind suitable procedural regulations to carry out the provisions of this title. Regulations issued under this section shall be in conformity with the standards and limitations of the Administrative Procedure Act.

(b) In any action or proceeding based on any alleged unlawful employment practice, no person shall be subject to any liability or punishment for or on account of (1) the commission by such person of an unlawful employment practice if he pleads and proves that the act or omission complained of was in good faith, in conformity with, and in reliance on any written interpretation or opinion of the Commission, or (2) the failure of such person to publish and file any information required by any provision of this title if he pleads and proves that he failed to publish and file such information in good faith, in conformity with the instructions of the Commission issued under this title regarding the filing of such information. Such a defense, if established, shall be a bar to the action or proceeding, notwithstanding that (A) after such act or omission, such interpretation or opinion is modified or rescinded or is determined by judicial authority to be invalid or of no legal effect, or (B) after publishing or filing the description and annual reports, such publication or filing is determined by judicial authority not to be in conformity with the requirements of this title.

FORCIBLY RESISTING THE COMMISSION OR ITS REPRESENTATIVE

SEC. 714. The provisions of section 111, title 18, United States Code, shall apply to officers, agents, and employees of the Commission in the performance of their official duties.

SPECIAL STUDY BY SECRETARY OF LABOR

SEC. 715 The Secretary of Labor shall make a full and complete study of the factors which might tend to result in discrimination in employment because of age and of the economy and individuals affected. The Secretary of Labor shall make a report to the Congress not later than June 30, 1965, containing the result of such study and shall include in such report such recommendations for legislation to prevent arbitrary discrimination in employment because of age as he determines advisable

EFFECTIVE DATE

SEC. 716. (a) This title shall become effective one year after the date of enactment.

(b) Notwithstanding subsection (a), sections of this title other than sections 703, 704, 706, and 707 shall become effective immediately.

(c) The President shall, as soon as feasible after the enactment of this title, convene one or more conferences for the purpose of enabling the leaders of groups whose members will be affected by this title to become familiar with the rights afforded and obligations imposed by its provisions, and for the purpose of making plans which will result in the fair and effective administration of this title when all of its provisions become effectve. The President shall invite the participation in such conference or conferences of (1) the members of the President's Committee on Equal Employment Opportunity, (2) the members of the Commission on Civil Rights, (3) representatives of State and local agencies engaged in furthering equal employment opportunity, (4) representatives of private agencies engaged in furthering equal employment

opportunity, and (5) representatives of employers, labor organizations, and employment agencies who will be subject to this title.

TITLE VIII—REGISTRATION AND VOTING STATISTICS

SEC. 801. The Secretary of Commerce shall promptly conduct a survey to compile registration and voting statistics in such geographic areas as may be recommended by the Commission on Civil Rights. Such a survey and compilation shall, to the extent recommended by the Commission on Civil Rights, only include a count of persons of voting age by race, color, and national origin, and determination of the extent to which such persons are registered to vote, and have voted in any statewide primary or general election in which the Members of the United States House of Representatives are nominated or elected, since January 1, 1960. Such information shall also be collected and compiled in connection with the Nineteenth Decennial Census, and at such other times as the Congress may prescribe. The provisions of section 9 and chapter 7 of title 13, United States Code, shall apply to any survey, collection, or compilation of registration and voting statistics carried out under this title: *Provided, however,* That no person shall be compelled to disclose his race, color, national origin, or questioned about his political party affiliation, how he voted, or the reasons therefore, nor shall any penalty be imposed for his failure or refusal to make such disclosure. Every person interrogated orally, by written survey or questionnaire or by any other means with respect to such information shall be fully advised with respect to his right to fail or refuse to furnish such information.

TITLE IX—INTERVENTION AND PROCEDURE AFTER REMOVAL IN CIVIL RIGHTS CASE

SEC. 901. Title 28 of the United States Code, section 1447(d), is amended to read as follows:

"An order remanding a case to the State court from which it was removed is not reviewable on appeal or otherwise, except that an order remanding a case to the State court from which it was removed pursuant to section 1443 of this title shall be reviewable by appeal or otherwise."

SEC. 902. Whenever an action has been commenced in any court of the United States seeking relief from the denial of equal protection of the laws under the fourteenth amendment to the Constitution on account of race, color, religion, or national origin, the Attorney General for or in the name of the United States may intervene in such action upon timely application if the Attorney General certifies that the case is of general public importance. In such action the United States shall be entitled to the same relief as if it had instituted the action.

TITLE X—ESTABLISHMENT OF COMMUNITY RELATIONS SERVICE

SEC. 1001. (a) There is hereby established in and as a part of the Department of Commerce a Community Relations Service (hereinafter referred to as the "Service"), which shall be headed by a Director who shall be appointed by the President with the advice and consent of the Senate for a term of four years. The Director is authorized to appoint, subject to the civil service laws and regulations, such other personnel as may be necessary to enable the Service to carry out its functions and duties, and to fix their compensation in accordance with the Classification Act of 1949, as amended. The Director is further authorized to procure services as authorized by section 15 of the Act of August 2, 1946 (60 Stat. 810; 5 U.S.C. 55(a)), but at rates for individuals not in excess of $75 per diem.

(b) Section 106(a) of the Federal Executive Pay Act of 1956, as amended (5 U.S.C. 2205(a)), is further amended by adding the following clause thereto:

"(52) Director, Community Relations Service."

SEC. 1002. It shall be the function of the Service to provide assistance to communities and persons therein in resolving disputes, disagreements, or difficulties relating to discriminatory practices based on race, color, or national origin which impair the rights of persons in such communities under the Constitution or laws of the United States or which affect or may affect interstate commerce. The Service may offer its services in cases of such disputes, disagreements, or difficulties whenever, in its judgment, peaceful relations among the citizens of the community involved are threatened thereby, and it may offer its services either upon its own motion or upon the request of an appropriate State or local official or other interested person.

SEC. 1003. (a) The Service shall, whenever possible, in performing its functions, seek and utilize the cooperation of appropriate State or local, public, or private agencies.

(b) The activities of all officers and employees of the Service in providing conciliation assistance shall be conducted in confidence and without publicity, and the Service shall hold confidential any information acquired in the regular performance of its duties upon the understanding that it would be so held. No officer or employee of the Service shall engage in the performance of investigative or prosecuting functions of any department or agency in any litigation arising out of a dispute in which he acted on behalf of the Service. Any officer or other employee of the Service, who shall make public in any manner whatever any information in violation of this subsection, shall be deemed guilty of a misdemeanor and, upon conviction thereof, shall be fined not more than $1,000 or imprisoned not more than one year.

SEC. 1004. Subject to the provisions of sections 205 and 1003(b), the Director shall, on or before January 31 of each year, submit to the Congress a report of the activities of the Service during the preceding fiscal year.

TITLE XI—MISCELLANEOUS

SEC. 1101. In any proceeding for criminal contempt arising under title II, III, IV, V, VI, or VII of this Act, the accused, upon demand therefor, shall be entitled to a trial by jury, which shall conform as near as may be to the practice in criminal cases. Upon conviction, the accused shall not be fined more than $1,000 or imprisoned for more than six months.

This section shall not apply to contempts committed in the presence of the court, or so near thereto as to obstruct the administration of justice, nor to the misbehavior, misconduct, or disobedience of any officer of the court in respect to writs, orders, or process of the court. No person shall be convicted of criminal contempt hereunder unless the act or omission constituting such contempt shall have been intentional, as required in other cases of criminal contempt.

Nor shall anything herein be construed to deprive courts of their power, by civil contempt proceedings, without a jury, to secure compliance with or to prevent obstruction of, as distinguished from punishment for violations of, any lawful writ, process, order, rule, decree, or command of the court in accordance with the prevailing usages of law and equity, including the power of detention.

SEC. 1102. No person should be put twice in jeopardy under the laws of the United States for the same act or omission. For this reason, an acquittal or conviction in a prosecution for a specific crime under the laws of the United States shall bar a proceeding for criminal contempt, which is based upon the same act or omission and which arises under the provisions of this Act; and an acquittal or conviction in a proceeding for criminal contempt, which arises under the provisions of this Act, shall bar a prosecution for a specific crime under the laws of the United States based upon the same act or omisson.

SEC. 1103. Nothing in this Act shall be construed to deny, impair, or otherwise affect any right or authority of the Attorney General or of the United States or any agency or officer thereof under existing law to institute or intervene in any action or proceeding.

SEC. 1104. Nothing contained in any title of this Act shall be construed as indicating an intent on the part of Congress to occupy the field in which any such title operates to the exclusion of State laws on the same subject matter, nor shall any provision of this Act be construed as invalidating any provision of State law unless such provision is inconsistent with any of the purposes of this Act, or any provision thereof.

SEC. 1105. There are hereby authorized to be appropriated such sums as are necessary to carry out the provisions of this Act.

SEC. 1106. If any provision of this Act or the application thereof to any person or circumstances is held invalid, the remainder of the Act and the application of the provision to other persons not similarly situated or to other circumstances shall not be affected thereby.

Approved July 2, 1964.

✽

(Public Law 89–110, 89th Congress, S. 1564, August 6, 1965)

VOTING RIGHTS ACT OF 1965

An act to enforce the fifteenth amendment to the Constitution of the United States and for other purposes

Be it enacted by the Senate and House of Representatives of the United States of America in Congress assembled, That this Act shall be known as the "Voting Rights Act of 1965".

SEC. 2. No voting qualification or prerequisite to voting, or standard, practice, or procedure shall be imposed or applied by any State or political subdivision to deny or abridge the right of any citizen of the United States to vote on account of race or color.

SEC. 3. (a) Whenever the Attorney General institutes a proceeding under any statute to enforce the guarantees of the fifteenth amendment in any State or political subdivision the court shall authorize the appointment of Federal examiners by the United States Civil Service Commission in accordance with section 6 to serve for such period of time and for such political subdivisions as the court shall determine is appropriate to enforce the guarantees of the fifteenth amendment (1) as part of any interlocutory order if the court determines that the appointment of such examiners is necessary to enforce such guarantees or (2) as part of any final judgment if the court finds that violations of the fifteenth amendment justifying equitable relief have occurred in such State or subdivision: *Provided,* That the court need not authorize the appointment of examiners if any incidents of denial or abridgement of the right to vote on account of race or color (1) have been few in number and have been promptly and effectively corrected by State or local action, (2) the continuing effect of such incidents has been eliminated, and (3) there is no reasonable probability of their recurrence in the future.

(b) If in a proceeding instituted by the Attorney General under any statute to enforce the guarantees of the fifteenth amendment in any State or political subdivision the court finds that a test or device has been used for the purpose or with the effect of denying or abridging the right of any citizen of the United States to vote on account of race or color, it shall suspend the use of tests and devices in such State or political subdivisions as the court shall determine is appropriate and for such period as it deems necessary.

(c) If in any proceeding instituted by the Attorney General under any statute to enforce the guarantees of the fifteenth amendment in any State or political subdivision the court finds that violations of the fifteenth amendment justifying equitable relief have occurred within the territory of such State or political subdivision, the court, in addition to such relief as it may grant, shall retain jurisdiction for such period as it may deem appropriate and during such period no voting qualification or prerequisite to voting, or standard, practice, or procedure with respect to voting different from that in force or effect at the time the proceeding was commenced shall be enforced unless and until the court finds that such qualification, prerequisite, standard, practice, or procedure does not have the purpose and will not have the effect of denying or abridging the right to vote on account of race or color: *Provided,* That such qualification, prerequisite, standard, practice, or procedure may be enforced if the qualification, prerequisite, standard, practice, or procedure has been submitted by the chief legal officer or other appropriate official of such State or subdivision to the Attorney General and the Attorney General has not interposed an objection within sixty days after such Attorney General certifies with respect to any political subdivision named in, or included within the scope of, determinations made under section 4(b) that (1) he has received complaints in writing from twenty or more residents of such political subdivision alleging that they have been denied the right to vote under color of law on account of race or color, and that he believes such complaints to be meritorious, or (2) that in his judgment (considering, among other factors, whether the ratio of nonwhite persons to white persons registered to vote within such subdivision appears to him to be reasonably attributable to violations of the fifteenth amendment or whether substantial evidence exists that bona fide efforts are being made within such subdivision to comply with the fifteenth amendment), the appointment of examiners is otherwise necessary to enforce the guarantees of the fifteenth amendment, the Civil Service Commission shall appoint as many examiners for such subdivision as it may deem appropriate to prepare and maintain lists of persons eligible to vote in Federal, State, and local elections. Such examiners, hearing officers provided for in section 9(a), and other persons deemed necessary by the Commission to carry out the provisions and purposes of this Act shall be appointed, compensated, and separated without regard to the provisions of any statute administered by the Civil Service Commission, and service under this Act shall not be considered employment for the purposes of any statute administered by the Civil Service Commission, except the provisions of section 9 of the Act of August 2, 1939, as amended (5 U.S.C. 118i), prohibiting partisan political activity: *Provided,* That the Commission is authorized, after consulting the head of the appropriate department or agency, to designate suitable persons in the official service of the United States, with their consent, to serve in these positions. Examiners and hearing officers shall have the power to administer oaths.

SEC. 7. (a) The examiners for each political subdivision shall, at such places as the Civil Service Commission shall by regulation designate, examine applicants concerning their qualifications for voting. An application to an examiner shall be in such form as the Commission may require and shall contain allegations that the applicant is not otherwise registered to vote.

(b) Any person whom the examiner finds, in accordance with instructions received under section 9(b), to have the qualifications prescribed by State law not inconsistent with the Constitution and laws of the United States shall promptly be placed on a list of eligible voters. A challenge to such listing may be made in accordance with section 9(a) and shall not be the basis for a prosecution under section 12 of this Act. The examiner shall certify and transmit such list, and any supplements as appropriate, at least once a month, to the offices of the appropriate election officials, with copies to the Attorney General and the attorney general of the State, and any such lists and supplements thereto transmitted during the month shall be available for public inspection on the last business day of the month and in any event not later than the forty-fifth day prior to any election. The appropriate State or local election official shall place such names on the official voting list. Any person whose name appears on the examiner's list shall be entitled and allowed to vote in the election district of his residence unless and until the appropriate election officials shall have been notified that such person has been removed from such list in accordance with subsection (d): *Provided,* That no person shall be entitled to vote in any election by virtue of this Act unless his name shall have been certified and transmitted on such a list to the offices of the appropriate election officials at least forty-five days prior to such election.

(c) The examiner shall issue to such person whose name appears on such a list a certificate evidencing his eligibility to vote.

(d) A person whose name appears on such a list shall be removed therefrom by an examiner if (1) such person has been successfully challenged in accordance with the procedure prescribed in section 9, or (2) he has been determined by an examiner to have lost his eligibility to vote under State law not inconsistent with the Constitution and the laws of the United States.

SEC. 8. Whenever an examiner is serving under this Act in any political subdivision, the Civil Service Commission may assign, at the request of the Attorney General, one or more persons, who may be officers of the

United States, (1) to enter and attend at any place for holding an election in such subdivision for the purpose of observing whether persons who are entitled to vote are being permitted to vote, and (2) to enter and attend at any place for tabulating the votes cast at any election held in such subdivision for the purpose of observing whether votes cast by persons entitled to vote are being properly tabulated. Such persons so assigned shall report to an examiner appointed for such political subdivision, to the Attorney General, and if the appointment of examiners has been authorized pursuant to section 3(a), to the court.

Sec. 9. (a) Any challenge to a listing on an eligibility list prepared by an examiner shall be heard and determined by a hearing officer appointed by and responsible to the Civil Service Commission and under such rules as the Commission shall by regulation prescribe. Such challenge shall be entertained only if filed at such office within the State as the Civil Service Commission shall by regulation designate, and within ten days after the listing of the challenged person is made available for public inspection, and if supported by (1) the affidavits of at least two persons having personal knowledge of the facts constituting grounds for the challenge and (2) a certification that a copy of the challenge and affidavits have been served by mail or in person upon the person challenged at his place of residence set out in the application. Such challenge shall be determined within fifteen days after it has been filed. A petition for review of the decision of the hearing officer may be filed in the United States court of appeals for the circuit in which the person challenged resides within fifteen days after service of such decision by mail on the person petitioning for review but no decision of a hearing officer shall be reversed unless clearly erroneous. Any person listed shall be entitled and allowed to vote pending final determination by the hearing officer and by the court.

(b) The times, places, procedures, and form for application and listing pursuant to this Act and removals from the eligibility lists shall be prescribed by regulations promulgated by the Civil Service Commission and the Commission shall, after consultation with the Attorney General, instruct examiners concerning applicable State law not inconsistent with the Constitution and laws of the United States with respect to (1) the qualifications required for listing, and (2) loss of eligibility to vote.

(c) Upon the request of the application or the challenger or on its own motion the Civil Service Commission shall have the power to require by supena the attendance and testimony of witnesses and the production of documentary evidence relating to any matter pending before it under the authority of this section. In case of contumacy or refusal to obey a subpena, any district court of the United States or the United States court of any territory or possession, or the District Court of the United States for the District of Columbia, within the jurisdiction of which said person guilty of contumacy or refusal to obey is found or resides or is domiciled or transacts business, or has appointed an agent for receipt of service of process, upon application by the Attorney General of the United States shall have jurisdiction to issue to such person an order requiring such person to appear before the Commission or a hearing officer, there to produce pertinent, relevant, and nonprivileged documentary evidence if so ordered, or there to give testimony touching the matter under investigation; and any

failure to obey such order of the court may be punished by said court as a contempt thereof.

Sec. 10. (a) The Congress finds that the requirement of the payment of a poll tax as a precondition to voting (i) precludes persons of limited means from voting or imposes unreasonable financial hardship upon such persons as a precondition to their exercise of the franchise, (ii) does not bear a reasonable relationship to any legitimate State interest in the conduct of elections, and (iii) in some areas has the purpose or effect of denying persons the right to vote because of race or color. Upon the basis of these findings, Congress declares that the constitutional right of citizens to vote is denied or abridged in some areas by the requirement of the payment of a poll tax as a precondition to voting.

(b) In the exercise of the powers of Congress under section 5 of the fourteenth amendment and section 2 of the fifteenth amendment, the Attorney General is authorized and directed to institute forthwith in the name of the United States such actions, including actions against States or political subdivisions, for declaratory judgment or injunctive relief against the enforcement of any requirement of the payment of a poll tax as a precondition to voting, or substitute therefor enacted after November 1, 1964, as will be necessary to implement the declaration of subsection (a) and the purposes of this section.

(c) The district courts of the United States shall have jurisdiction of such actions which shall be heard and determined by a court of three judges in accordance with the provisions of section 2284 of title 28 of the United States Code and any appeal shall lie to the Supreme Court. It shall be the duty of the judges designated to hear the case to assign the case for hearing at the earliest practicable date, to participate in the hearing and determination thereof, and to cause the case to be in every way expedited.

(d) During the pendency of such actions, and thereafter if the courts, notwithstanding this action by the Congress, should declare the requirement of the payment of a poll tax to be constitutional, no citizen of the United States who is a resident of a State or political subdivision with respect to which determinations have been made under subsection 4(b) and a declaratory judgment has not been entered under subsection 4(a), during the first year he becomes otherwise entitled to vote by reason of registration by State or local officials or listing by an examiner, shall be denied the right to vote for failure to pay a poll tax if he tenders payment of such tax for the current year to an examiner or to the appropriate State or local official at least forty-five days prior to election, whether or not such tender would be timely or adequate under State law. An examiner shall have authority to accept such payment from any person authorized by this Act to make an application for listing, and shall issue a receipt for such payment. The examiner shall transmit promptly any such poll tax payment to the office of the State or local official authorized to receive such payment under State law, together with the name and address of the applicant.

Sec. 11. (a) No person acting under color of law shall fail or refuse to permit any person to vote who is entitled to vote under any provision of this Act or is otherwise qualified to vote, or willfully fail or refuse to tabulate, count, and report such person's vote.

(b) No person, whether acting under color of law or otherwise, shall intimidate, threaten, or coerce, or attempt to intimidate, threaten, or coerce any person for voting or attempting to vote, or intimidate, threaten, coerce, or attempt to intimidate, threaten, or coerce any person for urging or aiding any person to vote or attempt to vote, or intimidate, threaten, or coerce any person for exercising any powers or duties under section 3(a), 6, 8, 9, 10, or 12(e).

(c) Whoever knowingly or willfully gives false information as to his name, address, or period of residence in the voting district for the purpose of establishing his eligibility to register or vote, or conspires with another individual for the purpose of encouraging his false registration to vote or illegal voting, or pays or offers to pay or accepts payment either for registration to vote or for voting shall be fined not more than $10,000 or imprisoned not more than five years, or both: *Provided, however,* That this provision shall be applicable only to general, special, or primary elections held solely or in part for the purpose of selecting or electing any candidate for the office of President, Vice President, presidential elector, Member of the United States Senate, Member of the United States House of Representatives, or Delegates or Commissioners from the territories or possessions, or Resident Commissioner of the Commonwealth of Puerto Rico.

(d) Whoever, in any matter within the jurisdiction of an examiner or hearing officer knowingly and willfully falsifies or conceals a material fact, or makes any false, fictitious, or fraudulent statements or representations, or makes or uses any false writing or document knowing the same to contain any false, fictitious, or fraudulent statement or entry, shall be fined not more than $10,000 or imprisoned not more than five years, or both.

Sec. 12. (a) Whoever shall deprive or attempt to deprive any person of any right secured by section 2, 3, 4, 5, 7, or 10 or shall violate section 11 (a) or (b), shall be fined not more than $5,000, or imprisoned not more than five years, or both.

(b) Whoever, within a year following an election in a political subdivision in which an examiner has been appointed (1) destroys, defaces, mutilates, or otherwise alters the marking of a paper ballot which has been cast in such election, or (2) alters any official record of voting in such election tabulated from a voting machine or otherwise, shall be fined not more than $5,000, or imprisoned not more than five years, or both.

(c) Whoever conspires to violate the provisions of subsection (a) or (b) of this section, or interferes with any right secured by section 2, 3, 4, 5, 7, 10, or 11 (a) or (b) shall be fined not more than $5,000, or imprisoned not more than five years, or both.

(d) Whenever any person has engaged or there are reasonable grounds to believe that any person is about to engage in any act or practice prohibited by section 2, 3, 4, 5, 7, 10, 11, or subsection (b) of this section, the Attorney General may institute for the United States, or in the name of the United States, an action for preventive relief, including an application for a temporary or permanent injunction, restraining order, or other order, and including an order directed to the State and State or local election officials to require them (1) to permit persons listed under this Act to vote and (2) to count such votes.

(e) Whenever in any political subdivision in which there are examiners appointed pursuant to this Act any persons allege to such an examiner within forty-eight hours after the closing of the polls that notwithstanding (1) their listing under this Act or registration by an appropriate election official and (2) their eligibility to vote, they have not been permitted to vote in such election, the examiner shall forthwith notify the Attorney General if such allegations in his opinion appear to be well founded. Upon receipt of such notification, the Attorney General may forthwith file with the district court an application for an order providing for the marking, casting, and counting of the ballots of such persons and requiring the inclusion of their votes in the total vote before the results of such election shall be deemed final and any force or effect given thereto. The district court shall hear and determine such matters immediately after the filing of such application. The remedy provided in this subsection shall not preclude any remedy available under State or Federal law.

(f) The district courts of the United States shall have jurisdiction of proceedings instituted pursuant to this section and shall exercise the same without regard to whether a person asserting rights under the provisions of this Act shall have exhausted any administrative or other remedies that may be provided by law:

Sec. 13. Listing procedures shall be terminated in any political subdivision of any State (a) with respect to examiners appointed pursuant to clause (b) of section 6 whenever the Attorney General notifies the Civil Service Commission, or whenever the District Court for the District of Columbia determines in an action for declaratory judgment brought by any political subdivision with respect to which the Director of the Census has determined that more than 50 per centum of the nonwhite persons of voting age reside therein are registered to vote, (1) that all persons listed by an examiner for such subdivision has been placed on the appropriate voting registration roll, and (2) that there is no longer reasonable cause to believe that persons will be deprived of or denied the right to vote on account of race or color in such subdivision, and (b), with respect to examiners appointed pursuant to section 3(a), upon order of the authorizing court. A political subdivision may petition the Attorney General for the termination of listing procedures under clause (a) of this section, and may petition the Attorney General to request the Director of the Census to take such survey or census as may be appropriate for the making of the determination provided for in this section. The District Court for the District of Columbia shall have jurisdiction to require such survey or census to be made by the Director of the Census and it shall require him to do so if it deems the Attorney General's refusal to request such survey or census to be arbitrary or unreasonable.

Sec. 14. (a) All cases of criminal contempt arising under the provisions of this Act shall be governed by section 151 of the Civil Rights Act of 1957 (42 U.S.C. 1995).

(b) No court other than the District Court for the District of Columbia or a court of appeals in any proceeding under section 9 shall have jurisdiction to issue any declaratory judgment pursuant to section 4 or section 5 or any restraining order or temporary or permanent injunction against the execution or enforcement of any provision of this Act or any action of any Federal officer or employee pursuant hereto.

(c)(1) The terms "vote" or "voting" shall include all action necessary to make a vote effective in any primary, special, or general election, including, but not limited to, registration, listing pursuant to this Act, or other action required by law prerequisite to voting, casting a ballot, and having such ballot counted properly and included in the appropriate totals of votes cast with respect to candidates for public or party office and propositions for which votes are received in an election.

(2) The term "political subdivision" shall mean any county or parish, except that where registration for voting is not conducted under the supervision of a county or parish, the term shall include any other subdivision of a State which conducts registration for voting.

(d) In any action for a declaratory judgment brought pursuant to section 4 or section 5 of this Act, subpenas for witnesses who are required to attend the District Court for the District of Columbia may be served in any judicial district of the United States: *Provided,* That no writ of subpena shall issue for witnesses without the District of Columbia at a greater distance than one hundred miles from the place of holding court without the permission of the District Court for the District of Columbia being first had upon proper application and cause shown.

SEC. 15. Section 2004 of the Revised Statutes (42 U.S.C. 1971), as amended by section 131 of the Civil Rights Act of 1957 (71 Stat. 637), and amended by section 601 of the Civil Rights Act of 1960 (74 Stat. 90), and as further amended by section 101 of the Civil Rights Act of 1964 (78 Stat. 241), is further amended as follows:

(a) Delete the word "Federal" wherever it appears in subsections (a) and (c);

(b) Repeal subsection (f) and designate the present subsections (g) and (h) as (f) and (g), respectively.

SEC. 16 The Attorney General and the Secretary of Defense, jointly, shall make a full and complete study to determine whether, under the laws or practices of any State or States, there are preconditions to voting, which might tend to result in discrimination against citizens serving in the Armed Forces of the United States seeking to vote. Such officials shall, jointly, make a report to the Congress not later than June 30, 1966, containing the results of such study, together with a list of any States in which such preconditions exist, and shall include in such report such recommendations for legislation as they deem advisable to prevent discrimination in voting against citizens serving in the Armed Forces of the United States.

SEC. 17. Nothing in this Act shall be construed to deny, impair, or otherwise adversely affect the right to vote of any person registered to vote under the law of any State or political subdivision

SEC. 18 There are hereby authorized to be appropriated such sums as are necessary to carry out the provisions of this Act.

SEC. 19. If any provision of this Act or the application thereof to any person or circumstances is held invalid, the remainder of the Act and the application of the provision to other persons not similarly situated or to other circumstances shall not be affected thereby.

Approved August 6, 1965.

❦

RADIO AND TELEVISION REMARKS UPON SIGNING THE CIVIL RIGHTS BILL

(Broadcast from the East Room at the White House, July 2, 1964, at 6:45 p.m.)

My fellow Americans: I am about to sign into law the Civil Rights Act of 1964. I want to take this occasion to talk to you about what that law means to every American.

One hundred and eighty-eight years ago this week a small band of valiant men began a long struggle for freedom. They pledged their lives, their fortunes, and their sacred honor not only to found a nation, but to forge an ideal of freedom—not only for political independence, but for personal liberty—not only to eliminate foreign rule, but to establish the rule of justice in the affairs of men.

That struggle was a turning point in our history. Today in far corners of distant continents, the ideals of those American patriots still shape the struggles of men who hunger for freedom.

This is a proud triumph. Yet those who founded our country knew that freedom would be secure only if each generation fought to renew and enlarge its meaning. From the minutemen at Concord to the soldiers in Viet-Nam, each generation has been equal to that trust.

Americans of every race and color have died in battle to protect our freedom. Americans of every race and color have worked to build a nation of widening opportunities. Now our generation of Americans has been called on to continue the unending search for justice within our own borders.

We believe that all men are created equal. Yet many are denied equal treatment.

We believe that all men have certain unalienable rights. Yet many Americans do not enjoy those rights.

We believe that all men are entitled to the blessings of liberty. Yet millions are being deprived of those blessings—not because of their own failures, but because of the color of their skin.

The reasons are deeply imbedded in history and tradition and the nature of man. We can understand—without rancor or hatred—how this all happened.

But it cannot continue. Our Constitution, the foundation of our Republic, forbids it. The principles of our freedom forbid it. Morality forbids it. And the law I will sign tonight forbids it.

That law is the product of months of the most careful debate and discussion. It was proposed more than one year ago by our late and beloved President John F. Kennedy. It received the bipartisan support of more than two-thirds of the Members of both the House and the Senate. An overwhelming majority of Republicans as well as Democrats voted for it.

It has received the thoughtful support of tens of thousands of civic and religious leaders in all parts of this Nation. And it is supported by the great majority of the American people.

The purpose of the law is simple.

It does not restrict the freedom of any American, so long as he respects the rights of others.

It does not give special treatment to any citizen.

It does say the only limit to a man's hope for happiness, and for the future of his children, shall be his own ability.

It does say that there are those who are equal before God shall now also be equal in the polling booths, in the classrooms, in the factories, and in hotels, restaurants, movie theaters, and other places that provide service to the public.

I am taking steps to implement the law under my constitutional obligation to "take care that the laws are faithfully executed."

First, I will send to the Senate my nomination of

LeRoy Collins to be Director of the Community Relations Service. Governor Collins will bring the experience of a long career of distinguished public service to the task of helping communities solve problems of human relations through reason and commonsense.

Second, I shall appoint an advisory committee of distinguished Americans to assist Governor Collins in his assignment.

Third, I am sending Congress a request for supplemental appropriations to pay for necessary costs of implementing the law, and asking for immediate action.

Fourth, already today in a meeting of my Cabinet this afternoon I directed the agencies of this Government to fully discharge the new responsibilities imposed upon them by the law and to do it without delay, and to keep me personally informed of their progress.

Fifth, I am asking appropriate officials to meet with representative groups to promote greater understanding of the law and to achieve a spirit of compliance.

We must not approach the observance and enforcement of this law in a vengeful spirit. Its purpose is not to punish. Its purpose is not to divide, but to end divisions—divisions which have all lasted too long. Its purpose is national, not regional.

Its purpose is to promote a more abiding commitment to freedom, a more constant pursuit of justice, and a deeper respect for human dignity.

We will achieve these goals because most Americans are law-abiding citizens who want to do what is right.

This is why the Civil Rights Act relies first on voluntary compliance, then on the efforts of local communities and States, to secure the rights of citizens. It provides for the national authority to step in only when others cannot or will not do the job.

This Civil Rights Act is a challenge to all of us to go to work in our communities and our State, in our homes and in our hearts, to eliminate the last vestiges of injustice in our beloved country.

So tonight I urge every public official, every religious leader, every business and professional man, every working man, every housewife—I urge every American—to join in the effort to bring justice and hope to all our people—and to bring peace to our land.

My fellow citizens, we have come now to a time of testing. We must not fail.

Let us close the springs of racial poison. Let us pray for wise and understanding hearts. Let us lay aside irrelevant differences and make our Nation whole. Let us hasten that day when our unmeasured strength and our unbounded spirit will be free to do the great works ordained for this Nation by the just and wise God who is the Father of us all.

Thank you and good night.

Mr. Vice President, Mr. Speaker, Members of Congress, members of the Cabinet, distinguished guests, my fellow Americans:

Today is a triumph for freedom as huge as any victory that has ever been won on any battlefield. Yet to seize the meaning of this day, we must recall darker times.

Three and a half centuries ago the first Negroes arrived at Jamestown. They did not arrive in brave ships in search

of a home for freedom. They did not mingle fear and joy, in expectation that in this New World anything would be possible to a man strong enough to reach for it.

They came in darkness and they came in chains.

And today we strike away the last major shackle of those fierce and ancient bonds. Today the Negro story and the American story fuse and blend.

And let us remember that it was not always so. The stories of our Nation and of the American Negro are like two great rivers. Welling up from that tiny Jamestown spring they flow through the centures along divided channels.

When pioneers subdued a continent to the need of man, they did not tame it for the Negro. When the Liberty Bell rang out in Philadelphia, it did not toll for the Negro. When Andrew Jackson threw open the doors of democracy, they did not open for the Negro.

It was only at Appomattox, a century ago, that an American victory was also a Negro victory. And the two rivers—one shining with promise, the other dark-stained with oppression—began to move toward one another.

THE PROMISE KEPT

Yet, for almost a century the promise of that day was not fulfilled. Today is a towering and certain mark that, in this generation, that promise will be kept. In our time the two currents will finally mingle and rush as one great stream across the uncertain and the marvelous years of the America that is yet to come.

This act flows from a clear and simple wrong. Its only purpose is to right that wrong. Millions of Americans are denied the right to vote because of their color. This law will ensure them the right to vote. The wrong is one which no American, in his heart, can justify. The right is one which no American, true to our principles, can deny.

In 1957, as the leader of the majority in the United States Senate, speaking in support of legislation to guarantee the right of all men to vote, I said, "This right to vote is the basic right without which all others are meaningless. It gives people, people are individuals, control over their own destinies."

Last year I said, "Until every qualified person regardless of . . . the color of his skin has the right, unquestioned and unrestrained, to go in and cast his ballot in every precinct in this great land of ours. I am not going to be satisfied."

Immediately after the election I directed the Attorney General to explore, as rapidly as possible the ways to ensure the right of vote.

And then last March, with the outrage of Selma still fresh, I came down to this Capitol one evening and asked the Congress and the people for swift and for sweeping action to guarantee to every man and woman the right to vote. In less than 48 hours I sent the Voting Rights Act of 1965 to the Congress. In little more than 4 months the Congress with overwhelming majorities, enacted one of the most monumental laws in the entire history of American freedom.

THE WAITING IS GONE

The Members of the Congress, and the many private citizens, who worked to shape and pass this bill will share a place of honor in our history for this one act alone.

There were those who said this is an old injustice, and there is no need to hurry. But 95 years have passed since the 15th amendment gave all Negroes the right to vote.

And the time for waiting is gone.

There were those who said smaller and more gradual measures should be tried. But they had been tried. For years and years they had been tried, and tried, and tried, and they had failed, and failed, and failed.

And the time for failure is gone.

There were those who said that this is a many-sided and very complex problem. But however viewed, the denial of the right to vote is still a deadly wrong.

And the time for injustice has gone.

This law covers many pages. But the heart of the act is plain. Wherever, by clear and objective standards, States and counties are using regulations, or laws, or tests to deny the right to vote, then they will be struck down. If it is clear that State officials still intend to discriminate, then Federal examiners will be sent into register all eligible voters. When the prospect of discrimination is gone, the examiners will be immediately withdrawn.

And, under this act, if any county anywhere in this Nation does not want Federal intervention it need only open its polling places to all of its people.

THE GOVERNMENT ACTS

This good Congress, the 89th Congress, acted swiftly in passing this act, I intend to act with equal dispatch in enforcing this act.

And tomorrow at 1 p.m., the Attorney General has been directed to file a lawsuit challenging the constitutionality of the poll tax in the State of Mississippi. This will begin the legal process which, I confidently believe, will very soon prohibit any State from requiring the payment of money in order to exercise the right to vote.

And also by tomorrow the Justice Department, through publication in the Federal Register, will have officially certified the States where discrimination exists.

I have, in addition, requested the Department of Justice to work all through this weekend so that on Monday morning next, they can designate many counties where past experience clearly shows that Federal action is necessary and required. And by Tuesday morning, trained Federal examiners will be at work registering eligible men and women in 10 to 15 counties.

And on that same day, next Tuesday, additional poll tax suits will be filed in the States of Texas, Alabama, and Virginia.

And I pledge you that we will not delay, or we will not hesitate, or we will not turn aside until Americans of every race and color and origin in this country have the same right as all others to share in the process of democracy.

So, through this act, and its enforcement, an important instrument of freedom passes into the hands of millions of our citizens.

But that instrument must be used.

Presidents and Congresses, laws and lawsuits can open the doors to the polling places and open the doors to the wondrous rewards which await the wise use of the ballot.

THE VOTE BECOMES JUSTICE

But only the individual Negro, and all others who have been denied the right to vote, can really walk through those doors, and can use that right, and can transform the vote into an instrument of justice and fulfillment.

So, let me now say to every Negro in this country: You must register. You must vote. You must learn, so your choice advances your interest and the interest of our beloved Nation. Your future, and your children's future, depend upon it, and I don't believe that you are going to let them down.

This act is not only a victory for Negro leadership. This act is a great challenge to that leadership. It is a challenge which cannot be met simply by protests and demonstrations. It means that dedicated leaders must work around the clock to teach people their rights and their responsibilities and to lead them to exercise those rights and to fulfill those responsibilities and those duties to their country.

If you do this, then you will find, as others have found before you, that the vote is the most powerful instrument ever devised by man for breaking down injustice and destroying the terrible walls which imprison men because they are different from other men.

THE LAST OF THE BARRIERS TUMBLE

Today what is perhaps the last of the legal barriers is tumbling. There will be many actions and many difficulties before the rights woven into law are also woven into the fabric of our Nation. But the struggle for equality must now move toward a different battlefield.

It is nothing less than granting every American Negro his freedom to enter the mainstream of American life: not the conformity that blurs enriching differences of culture and tradition, but rather the opportunity that gives each a chance to choose.

For centuries of oppression and hatred have already taken their painful toll. It can be seen throughout our land in men without skills, in children without fathers, in families that are imprisoned in slums and in poverty.

RIGHTS ARE NOT ENOUGH

For it is not enough just to give men rights. They must be able to use those rights in their personal pursuit of happiness. The wounds and the weaknesses, the outward walls and the inward scars which diminish achievement are the work of American society. We must all now help to end them—help to end them through expanding programs already devised and through new ones to search out and forever end the special handicaps of those who are black in a Nation that happens to be mostly white

So, it is for this purpose—to fulfill the rights that we now secure—that I have already called a White House conference to meet here in the Nation's Capital this fall.

So, we will move step by step—often painfully but, I think, with clear vision—along the path toward American freedom

It is difficult to fight for freedom. But I also know how difficult it can be to bend long years of habit and custom to grant it. There is no room for injustice anywhere in the American mansion. But there is always room for understanding toward those who see the old ways crumbling. And to them today I say simply this: It must come. It is right that it should come. And when it has, you will find that a burden has been lifted from your shoulders, too.

It is not just a question of guilt, although there is that.

It is that men cannot live with a lie and not be stained by it.

DIGNITY IS NOT JUST A WORD

The central fact of American civilization—one so hard for others to understand—is that freedom and justice and the dignity of man are not just words to us. We believe in them. Under all the growth and the tumult and abundance, we believe. And so, as long as some among us are oppressed—and we are part of that oppression—it must blunt our faith and sap the strength of our high purpose.

Thus, this is a victory for the freedom of the American Negro. But it is also a victory for the freedom of the American Nation. And every family across this great, entire, searching land will live stronger in liberty, will live more splendid in expectation, and will be prouder to be American because of the act that you have passed that I will sign today.

Thank you.

🌱

SPECIAL MESSAGE TO THE CONGRESS: THE AMERICAN PROMISE

(As delivered in person before a joint session March 15, 1965 at 9:02 p.m.)

Mr. Speaker, Mr. President, Members of the Congress:

I speak tonight for the dignity of man and the destiny of democracy.

I urge every member of both parties, Americans of all religions and of all colors, from every section of this country, to join me in that cause.

At times history and fate meet at a single time in a single place to shape a turning point in man's unending search for freedom. So it was at Lexington and Concord. So it was a century ago at Appomattox. So it was last week in Selma, Alabama.

There, long-suffering men and women peacefully protested the denial of their rights as Americans. Many were brutally assaulted. One good man, a man of God was killed.

There is no cause for pride in what has happened in Selma. There is no cause for self-satisfaction in the long denial of equal rights of millions of Americans. But there is cause for hope and for faith in our democracy in what is happening here tonight.

For the cries of pain and the hymns and protests of oppressed people have summoned into convocation all the majesty of this great Government—the Government of the greatest Nation on earth.

Our mission is at once the oldest and the most basic of this country: to right wrong, to do justice, to serve man.

In our time we have come to live with moments of great crisis. Our lives have been marked with debate about great issues, issues of war and peace, issues of prosperity and depression. But rarely in any time does an issue lay bare the secret heart of America itself. Rarely are we met with a challenge, not to our growth or abundance, our welfare or our security, but rather to the values and the purposes and the meaning of our beloved Nation.

The issue of equal rights for American Negroes is such an issue. And should we defeat every enemy, should we double our wealth and conquer the stars, and still be unequal to this issue, then we will have failed as a people and as a nation.

For with a country as with a person, "What is a man profited, if he shall gain the whole world, and lose his own soul?"

There is no Negro problem. There is no Southern problem. There is no Northern problem. There is only an American problem. And we are met here tonight as Americans—not as Democrats or Republicans—we are met here as Americans to solve that problem.

This was the first nation in the history of the world to be founded with a purpose. The great phrases of that purpose still sound in every American heart, North and South: "All men are created equal"—"government by consent of the governed"—"give me liberty or give me death." Well, those are not just clever words, or those are not just empty theories. In their name Americans have fought and died for two centuries, and tonight around the world they stand there as guardians of our liberty, risking their lives.

Those words are a promise to every citizen that he shall share in the dignity of man. This dignity cannot be found in a man's possessions; it cannot be found in his power or in his position. It really rests on his right to be treated as a man equal in opportunity to all others. It says that he shall share in freedom, he shall choose his leaders, educate his children, and provide for his family according to his ability and his merits as a human being.

To apply any other test—to deny a man his hopes because of his color or race, his religion or the place of his birth—is not only to do injustice, it is to deny America and to dishonor the dead who gave their lives for American freedom.

THE RIGHT TO VOTE

Our fathers believed that if this noble view of the rights of man was to flourish, it must be rooted in democracy. The most basic right of all was the right to choose your own leaders. The history of this country, in large measure, is the history of the expansion of that right to all of our people.

Many of the issues of civil rights are very complex and most difficult. But about this there can and should be no argument. Every American citizen must have an equal right to vote. There is no reason which can excuse the denial of that right. There is no duty which weighs more heavily on us than the duty we have to ensure that right.

Yet the harsh fact is that in many places in this country men and women are kept from voting simply because they are Negroes.

Every device of which human ingenuity is capable has been used to deny this right. The Negro citizen may go to register only to be told that the day is wrong, or the hour is late, or the official in charge is absent. And if he persists, and if he manages to present himself to the registrar, he may be disqualified because he did not spell out his middle name or because he abbreviated a word on the application.

And if he manages to fill out an application he is given a test. The registrar is the sole judge of whether he passes this test. He may be asked to recite the entire Constitution, or explain the most complex provisions of State law. And even a college degree cannot be used to prove that he can read and write.

For the fact is that the only way to pass these barriers is to show a white skin.

Experience has clearly shown that the existing process

of law cannot overcome systematic and ingenious discrimination. No law that we now have on the books—and I have helped to put three of them there—can ensure the right to vote when local officials are determined to deny it.

In such a case our duty must be clear to all of us. The Constitution says that no person shall be kept from voting because of his race or his color. We have all sworn an oath before God to support and to defend that Constitution. We must now act in obedience to that oath.

GUARANTEEING THE RIGHT TO VOTE

Wednesday I will send to Congress a law designed to eliminate illegal barriers to the right to vote.

The broad principles of that bill will be in the hands of the Democratic and Republican leaders tomorrow. After they have reviewed it, it will come here formally as a bill. I am grateful for this opportunity to come here tonight at the invitation of the leadership to reason with my friends, to give them my views, and to visit with my former colleagues.

I have had prepared a more comprehensive analysis of the legislation which I had intended to transmit to the clerk tomorrow but which I will submit to the clerks tonight. But I want to really discuss with you now briefly the main proposals of this legislation.

This bill will strike down restrictions to voting in all elections—Federal, State, and local—which have been used to deny Negroes the right to vote.

This bill will establish a simple, uniform standard which cannot be used, however ingenious the effort, to flout our Constitution.

It will provide for citizens to be registered by officials of the United States Government if the State officials refuse to register them.

It will eliminate tedious, unnecessary lawsuits which delay the right to vote.

Finally, this legislation will ensure that properly registered individuals are not prohibited from voting.

I will welcome the suggestions from all of the Members of Congress—I have no doubt that I will get some—on ways and means to strengthen this law and to make it effective. But experience has plainly shown that this is the only path to carry out the command of the Constitution.

To those who seek to avoid action by their National Government in their own communities; who want to and who seek to maintain purely local control over elections, the answer is simple:

Open your polling places to all your people.

Allow men and women to register and vote whatever the color of their skin.

Extend the rights of citizenship to every citizen of this land.

THE NEED FOR ACTION

There is no constitutional issue here. The command of the Constitution is plain.

There is no moral issue. It is wrong—deadly wrong—to deny any of your fellow Americans the right to vote in this country.

There is no issue of States rights or national rights. There is only the struggle for human rights.

I have not the slightest doubt what will be your answer.

The last time a President sent a civil rights bill to the Congress it contained a provision to protect voting rights in Federal elections. That civil rights bill was passed after 8 long months of debate. And when that bill came to my desk from the Congress for my signature, the heart of the voting provision had been eliminated.

This time, on this issue, there must be no delay, no hesitation and no compromise with our purpose.

We cannot, we must not, refuse to protect the right of every American to vote in every election that he may desire to participate in. And we ought not and we cannot and we must not wait another 8 months before we get a bill. We have already waited a hundred years and more, and the time for waiting is gone.

So I ask you to join me in working long hours—nights and weekends, if necessary—to pass this bill. And I don't make that request lightly. For from the window where I sit with the problems of our country I recognize that outside this chamber is the outraged conscience of a nation, the grave concern of many nations, and the harsh judgment of history on our acts.

WE SHALL OVERCOME

But even if we pass this bill, the battle will not be over. What happened in Selma is part of a far larger movement which reaches into every section and State of America. It is the effort of American Negroes to secure for themselves the full blessings of American life.

Their cause must be our cause too. Because it is not just Negroes, but really it is all of us, who must overcome the crippling legacy of bigotry and injustice.

And we shall overcome.

As a man whose roots go deeply into Southern soil I know how agonizing racial feelings are. I know how difficult it is to reshape the attitudes and the structure of our society.

But a century has passed, more than a hundred years, since the Negro was freed. And he is not fully free tonight.

It was more than a hundred years ago that Abraham Lincoln, a great President of another party, signed the Emancipation Proclamation, but emancipation is a proclamation and not a fact.

A century has passed, more than a hundred years, since equality was promised. And yet the Negro is not equal.

A century has passed since the day of promise. And the promise is unkept.

The time of justice has now come. I tell you that I believe sincerely that no force can hold it back. It is right in the eyes of man and God that it should come. And when it does, I think that day will brighten the lives of every American.

For Negroes are not the only victims. How many white children have gone uneducated, how many white families have lived in stark poverty, how many white lives have been scarred by fear, because we have wasted our energy and our substance to maintain the barriers of hatred and terror?

So I say to all of you here, and to all in the Nation tonight, that those who appeal to you to hold on to the past do so at the cost of denying you your future.

This great, rich, restless country can offer opportunity and education and hope to all: black and white, North and South, sharecropper and city dweller. These are the enemies: poverty, ignorance, disease. They are the enemies and not our fellow man, not our neighbor. And these enemies too, poverty, disease and ignorance, we shall overcome.

AN AMERICAN PROBLEM

Now let none of us in any sections look with prideful righteousness on the troubles in another section, or on the problems of our neighbors. There is really no part of America where the promise of equality has been fully kept. In Buffalo as well as in Birmingham, in Philadelphia as well as in Selma, Americans are struggling for the fruits of freedom.

This is one Nation. What happens in Selma or in Cincinnati is a matter of legitimate concern to every American. But let each of us look within our own hearts and our own communities, and let each of us put our shoulder to the wheel to root out injustice wherever it exists.

As we meet here in this peaceful, historic chamber tonight, men from the South, some of whom were at Iwo Jima, men from the North who have carried Old Glory to far corners of the world and brought it back without a stain on it, men from the East and from the West, are all fighting together without regard to religion, or color, or region, in Viet-Nam. Men from every region fought for us across the world 20 years ago.

And in these common dangers and these common sacrifices the South made its contribution of honor and gallantry no less than any other region of the great Republic—and in some instances, a great many of them, more.

And I have not the slightest doubt that good men from everywhere in this country, from the Great Lakes to the Gulf of Mexico, from the Golden Gate to the harbors along the Atlantic, will rally together now in this cause to vindicate the freedom of all Americans. For all of us owe this duty; and I believe that all of us will respond to it.

Your President makes that request of every American.

PROGRESS THROUGH THE DEMOCRATIC PROCESS

The real hero of this struggle is the American Negro. His actions and protests, his courage to risk safety and even to risk his life, have awakened the conscience of this Nation. His demonstrations have been designed to call attention to injustices, designed to provoke change, designed to stir reform.

He has called upon us to make good the promise of America. And who among us can say that we would have made the same progress were it not for his persistent bravery, and his faith in American democracy.

For at the real heart of battle for equality is a deep-seated belief in the democratic process. Equality depends not on the force of arms or tear gas but upon the force of moral right; not on recourse to violence but on respect for law and order.

There have been many pressures upon your President and there will be others as the days come and go. But I pledge you tonight that we intend to fight this battle when it should be fought; in the courts, and in the Congress, and in the hearts of men.

We must preserve the right of free speech and the right of free assembly. But the right of free speech does not carry with it, as has been said, the right to holler fire in a crowded theater. We must preserve the right to free assembly, but free assembly does not carry with it the right to block public thoroughfares to traffic.

We do have a right to protest, and a right to march under conditions that do not infringe the constitutional rights of our neighbors. And I intend to protest all those rights as long as I am permitted to serve in this office.

We will guard against violence, knowing it strikes from our hands the very weapons which we seek—progress, obedience to law, and belief in American values.

In Selma as elsewhere we seek and pray for peace. We seek order. We seek unity. But we will not accept the peace of stifled rights, or the order imposed by fear, or the unity that stifles protest. For peace cannot be purchased at the cost of liberty.

In Selma tonight, as in every—and we had a good day there—as in every city, we are working for just and peaceful settlement. We must all remember that after this speech I am making tonight, after the police and the FBI and the Marshals have all gone, and after you have promptly passed this bill, the people of Selma and the other cities of the Nation must still live and work together. And when the attention of the Nation has gone elsewhere they must try to heal the wounds and to build a new community.

This cannot be easily done on a battleground of violence, as the history of the South itself shows. It is in recognition of this that men of both races have shown such an outstandingly impressive responsibility in recent days—last Tuesday, again today.

RIGHTS MUST BE OPPORTUNITIES

The bill that I am presenting to you will be known as a civil rights bill. But, in a larger sense, most of the program I am recommending is a civil rights program. Its object is to open the city of hope to all people of all races.

Because all Americans just must have the right to vote. And we are going to give them that right.

All Americans must have the privileges of citizenship regardless of race. And they are going to have those privileges of citizenship regardless of race.

But I would like to caution you and remind you that to exercise these privileges takes much more than just legal right. It requires a trained mind and a healthy body. It requires a decent home, and the chance to find a job, and the opportunity to escape from the clutches of poverty.

Of course, people cannot contribute to the Nation if they are never taught to read or write, if their bodies are stunted from hunger, if their sickness goes untended, if their life is spent in hopeless poverty just drawing a welfare check.

So we want to open the gates to opportunity. But we are also going to give all our people, black and white, the help that they need to walk through those gates.

THE PURPOSE OF THIS GOVERNMENT

My first job after college was as a teacher in Cotulla, Tex., in a small Mexican-American school. Few of them could speak English, and I couldn't speak much Spanish. My students were poor and they often came to class without breakfast, hungry. They knew even in their youth the pain of prejudice. They never seemed to know why people disliked them. But they knew it was so, because I saw it in their eyes. I often walked home late in the afternoon, after the classes were finished, wishing there was more that I could do. But all I knew was to teach them the little that I knew, hoping that it might help them against the hardships that lay ahead.

Somehow you never forget what poverty and hatred can do when you see its scars on the hopeful face of a young child.

I never thought then, in 1928, that I would be standing here in 1965. It never even occurred to me in my fondest dreams that I might have the chance to help the sons and daughters of those students and to help people like them all over this country.

But now I do have that chance—and I'll let you in on a secret—I mean to use it. And I hope that you will use it with me.

This is the richest and most powerful country which ever occupied the globe. The might of past empires is little compared to ours. But I do not want to be the President who built empires, or sought grandeur, or extended dominion.

I want to be the President who educated young children to the wonders of their world. I want to be the President who helped to feed the hungry and to prepare them to be taxpayers instead of taxeaters.

I want to be the President who helped the poor to find their own way and who protected the right of every citizen to vote in every election.

I want to be the President who helped to end hatred among his fellow men and who promoted love among the people of all races and all religions and all parties.

I want to be the President who helped to end war among the brothers of this earth.

And so at the request of your beloved majority leader, the Senator from Illinois; the minority leader, Mr. Mc-Culloch, and other Members of both parties. I came here tonight—not as President Roosevelt came down one time in person to veto a bonus bill, not as President Truman came down one time to urge the passage of a railroad bill—but I came down here to ask you to share this task with me and to share it with the people that we both work for. I want this to be the Congress, Republicans and Democrats alike, which did all these things for all those people.

Beyond this great chamber, out yonder in 50 States, are the people that we serve. Who can tell what deep and unspoken hopes are in their hearts tonight as they sit there and listen. We all can guess, from our own lives, how difficult they often find their own pursuit of happiness, how many problems each little family has. They look most of all to themselves for their futures. But I think that they also look to each of us.

Above the pyramid on the great seal of the United States it says—in Latin—"God has favored our undertaking."

God will not favor everything that we do. It is rather our duty to divine His will. But I cannot help believing that He truly understands and that He really favors the undertaking that we begin here tonight.

NOTE.—The address was broadcast nationally.

Hon. Adlai E. Stevenson III

OF ILLINOIS

Mr. President, it is said that LYNDON JOHNSON was a difficult man. I suspect that secretly he rather enjoyed that reputation. And now, even in death, he continues to frustrate those who try to capture him in words.

LYNDON JOHNSON was so large he defied normal description. Even those close to him saw only aspects of the man; it was impossible to see the entirety of such an enormous figure. Those of us who knew him only slightly came away with vivid impressions. My foremost impression is of a man whose whole approach to life and politics was always deeply personal, emotional, even sentimental.

To President JOHNSON, politics was never merely a matter of loyalty to abstract ideals. It was a matter of personalities—of real men, their problems, their families, and their lives.

He never thought of his constituents as a vast, faceless mass, to be measured by the Gallup poll and manipulated by Madison Avenue. He saw the American people as individuals and families, in real homes under real rooftops with real hopes and real difficulties. When he talked about them, he described them as "Molly and the babies"— a phrase that to sophisticates seemed naive, but to him represented the people he knew and served.

His approach to his colleagues in politics was similarly human, emotional, and sentimental. His was the politics not of abstractions, but of human encounter: the handshake; the hurried conversation in a hallway; the long, pleading telephone call; the personal favor; the friendly drink; the unexpected gesture of friendship or sympathy. If he was a shrewd and canny political animal, he was also a man who went to weddings and funerals and shed real tears.

To my father, his contemporary in American politics, President JOHNSON was not only correct and courteous, but generous and thoughtful. Though they sometimes differed on issues, they were always friends, who saw themselves as laborers in common for the public good. And after my father's death, President JOHNSON's kindness was directed toward our family. He came to the funeral in Bloomington, Ill. At the height of Mr. JOHNSON's difficulties during the Vietnam conflict, he took time out to unveil a bust of my father in the White House Cabinet Room. And though my father had been a critic of that conflict, the President spoke of him with warmth and magnanimity and showed our family the most genuine courtesy.

LYNDON JOHNSON was a product of the countryside and the small town. He brought to our highest national affairs the virtues of the small town; real, not synthetic emotion, and the human touch.

Others will elaborate upon his public achievements. I will close by offering my warmest respect and sympathy to Mrs. Johnson and all his family, and by quoting Stephen Spender's words about those who "were truly great." Spender speaks of:

Those who in their lives fought for life, who wore at their hearts the fire's center.

LYNDON JOHNSON, in his life, fought for life. And in his tempestuous, achieving career, he stood near the fire's center.

It is tempting to say that losing President JOHNSON is like losing a part of our national landscape. But LYNDON JOHNSON was always too restless and fast-moving to be described as a mere landmark. Losing him is more like losing a part of the weather. We will miss him.

Hon. Warren G. Magnuson
OF WASHINGTON

Mr. President, it is with the deepest kind of sorrow that I stand here today. We are paying our tributes, making our eulogies to a President of the United States. But I have also lost a friend.

It is a lucky man, after a good life, who can count his friends on the fingers of his hands. I am especially lucky, because I always could count LYNDON JOHNSON among mine.

Today, on this day of such mixed emotions, I am luckier than most because I can look back upon good memories and warm times. LYNDON JOHNSON and I came to Congress together more than three decades ago. We served on the same committees and went to war together in the Pacific. It was my great privilege that LYNDON JOHNSON stood up for me at my wedding and my bride's great privilege that Lady Bird Johnson stood for her. Those memories are my treasures now.

Life is not always kind and LYNDON JOHNSON took its thorns with its roses. He presided over this Nation at a time of great accomplishment and of great agony. Only history can be the final judge on those times.

But I have my own personal judgments about President JOHNSON—and there is no doubt in my mind about his place in history. Can any of us on this floor forget those heady days in 1964 when we approved more progressive legislation than perhaps any Congress in history?

It was LYNDON JOHNSON who saw medicare through to passage after two decades of bickering. Millions of Americans will never forget. But it only began there—a stream of accomplishments that uplifted that part of our Nation that had been held down so long.

If there is to be a memorial to LYNDON BAINES JOHNSON, it seems clear to me what that memorial should be. Washington is ripe these days with rumors of the dismantling of the great social programs enacted in the 1960's. Our memorial should be a simple one—to assure that what LYNDON JOHNSON did is not undone, that the memorial he erected is not torn down.

Now that the war that tortured him is all but over, let us turn ourselves to the priorities that LYNDON JOHNSON himself would have established. He set out to build a great society. And, at least he set its foundations.

Which of our Presidents did more for the impoverished, more for the ghetto dwellers and the underprivileged, more for the frustrated and the disenfranchised?

That is his legacy now, and a legacy we should devote our own energies to maintaining. We can, as he would have wished, build our fair and great Nation into a fairer and greater Nation.

Just over 10 years ago, when LYNDON JOHNSON was elevated to the Presidency on one of the saddest days in our Nation's history, he quietly urged: "Let us continue." He would urge the same thing today. As a friend—and as a believer—I make the pledge now to do what I can to continue.

Aside from his beloved land on the Pedernales, this place in which we now stand—the Senate—is the place that gave LYNDON JOHNSON his greatest sustenance. I would hope that here in this Senate his work will go on. Let us, his colleagues, not allow his dream to die. There still is so much to be done.

Hon. Walter Huddleston
OF KENTUCKY

Mr. President, the Nation has lost a dedicated and humane leader. President JOHNSON cared about people and their needs, and this was reflected in a lifetime of public service dedicated to providing his fellow citizens with better education, improved health care, equal rights, a cleaner environment, and many other amenities of the good life.

I believe history will remember LYNDON JOHNSON as one who demonstrated great concern for his fellow man—especially the "little man" born in poverty and want. To demonstrate such concern for the less fortunate is not always politically popular; but that does not deny the moral imperative to do so. That LYNDON JOHNSON sought to fulfill this moral imperative is a tribute to his courage and humanity.

President JOHNSON assumed the high office of President following a national tragedy, and not the least of his many accomplishments was his ability to take hold of the office and carry on the Nation's business during a very trying period. A lesser man might well have been overwhelmed by the magnitude of such responsibilities thrust upon him so suddenly, and in such trying times.

But President JOHNSON took firm hold of the reins of leadership and moved forward to some of his greatest accomplishments immediately after he became President. His leadership led to passage of legislation outlawing discrimination in places of public accommodation, programs to alleviate poverty, medicare and health care for the aged, and a program for improving living conditions in Appalachia.

These are the things for which LYNDON JOHNSON will be remembered. They are his living monuments, and the Nation is highly indebted to him for providing the leadership and determination necessary to bring them about.

It has often been said that LYNDON JOHNSON's happiest days were spent right here in the U.S. Senate. That is easy to understand when you consider his many legislative accomplishments while serving in this body.

We in Kentucky have always felt a close kinship to LYNDON JOHNSON. Although he was a Texan by birth he had roots in Kentucky through both sides of his family. The President's grandmother, Elizah Bunton, was born in Russelville, Ky., and later moved to Texas. His mother was Rebecca Baines, whose maternal grandparents were natives of Kentucky.

But whether he is linked to Kentucky or to Texas, his real constituency was the Nation and he served it well.

I think all will agree that he was a dedicated American, who sought what he thought best for his country and his people. It is hard to ask any more of a public servant, or of man.

Hon. Henry L. Bellmon
OF OKLAHOMA

Mr. President, President LYNDON JOHNSON will principally be remembered by many for his role in the Vietnam war. Such narrow identity overlooks the fact that he was a courageous, effective President who was probably the all-time master of the legislative art.

Throughout his long career, he remained a southwesterner. He maintained his direct, sometimes blunt manner, which sometimes caused him problems after he went to the White House.

While I differed with him on occasion, it is my opinion that history will be kind to the record and the memory of President LYNDON JOHNSON. I feel that our world today would have been a vastly different and less desirable place had he not taken his courageous yet unpopular stand in Southeast Asia and persevered even at the cost of his personal political career.

Hon. Roman L. Hruska
OF NEBRASKA

Mr. President, this Senator notes the passing of LYNDON BAINES JOHNSON, 36th President of the United States, with sorrow and regret. I wish to extend my deepest sympathy to Lady Bird, her two daughters, and their children.

We of the Senate will never forget L. B. J. We will remember him as a man driven to achieve greatness by some inner power. We will remember him as a Senator who was perhaps one of the most skilled statesmen to walk and speak in our Halls and Chambers. We will remember him as a President who could cover 31,500 miles in a 17-day factfinding tour and still remain ready for more work.

He was, indeed, a leader, who as President Nixon has said of him, was a "partisan of principle." Those of us who knew him and sometimes disagreed with him in the Senate can attest to his unfailing principle and devotion to the Republic. He was a man who viewed America's future with optimism.

Although fate has chosen to take him from us at the age of 64, all of us have a responsibility to do justice to his expectations for America. He would have expected no less from us.

We of the Senate shall miss his principle. The Nation shall miss his guidance, expertise, and insight. The passing of a great man is like the stillness after thunder. This Nation is smaller today without LYNDON JOHNSON.

Hon. Walter F. Mondale
OF MINNESOTA

Mr. President, this Nation has suffered a tragic loss in the death of our 36th President, LYNDON BAINES JOHNSON.

We have lost a strong man who, by sheer force of character and ability, exercised unparalleled influence over the history of this Nation in the last quarter century.

As Senate majority leader and President, he worked tirelessly to transform the 14th amendment's commitment to racial equality into a living national purpose.

He sponsored the greatest social reform since the New Deal—medicare, medicaid, and expanded social security benefits for the elderly, aid to public education, a national commitment to end poverty and hunger.

And when he saw that the war in Southeast Asia had irrevocably divided the American people, he stepped aside in an unselfish effort to end the war and to unite the American people.

He left us an unfinished agenda for social justice—an end to hunger and malnutrition; decent housing for all American families; safe working conditions, a fair wage and a secure retirement for working men and women; real educational opportunities, and a chance in life for children of all backgrounds.

We will honor the memory of a man who cared deeply about the lives of the American people, who knew and hated poverty, and who longed for the peace which he tragically did not live to see.

Hon. Harold E. Hughes
OF IOWA

Mr. President, I join with my colleagues and with Americans everywhere in bidding goodbye to a great President and in extending to his lovely wife and family my deepest sympathy.

To me, as to many other Americans, President JOHNSON was an enigma, but I never doubted his greatness, his devotion to his country, his determination to carry out what he believed to be the right things no matter what effort was required.

Having experienced both his generosity and his anger, I can personally attest to the fact that both were king size. We parted friendly relations over Vietnam. It was an honest difference of opinion that I have always regretted, but it had to be. But this in no sense diminished my admiration for this President's colossal record of service to his country—in civil rights, in medical care for the aged, in elementary and secondary education, in housing, in the alleviation of poverty, in raising the minimum wage, in pioneering environmental protection, and in countless other areas.

To me the most remarkable quality of LYNDON JOHNSON as President was not his strength as a decisionmaker, which was undeniable, or his skill as a leader—as in his relations with Congress—which was awesome, but in the fact that I always knew he cared, cared about people and the problems they have, including the run of the mill, the afflicted and the victims of discrimination.

And, of course, he built a mighty edifice of laws and administrative acts built on this capacity to care.

As the country is mourning the loss of this very complex and human President, it is reported that the people value programs he innovated and put through Congress with his incomparable skill and energy are now being dismantled and laid aside.

It appears to be true, but in my judgment, this is only a temporary phase. It is probably true that too much was attempted by the Johnson administration in too short a time to help too many people. But thank God, somebody cared enough to make the effort.

As I see it, the idea of the Great Society is not dead. It will rise again, in a different, more workable and lasting form, because the concept fundamentally is right and just and we are a nation of conscience.

And when this concept lives again, it seems to me that it will be the most splendid memorial that any President could have. It could be written as an epitaph that on a big scale, as with everything else he did, LYNDON JOHNSON cared.

Hon. Philip A. Hart

OF MICHIGAN

Mr. President, President JOHNSON lies in state today just as the war that caused him so much anguish appears to be coming to an end.

History has played a curious trick on us, giving us great cause to rejoice but compelling us at the same time to mourn and sorrow.

The tragedy of this day, January 24, lies in the timing of President JOHNSON's death.

He died almost precisely at the moment when the dust clouds of an unfortunate war appear to be subsiding. And now, as they subside, they reveal—for the first time to many—the memorials that will honor the name of LYNDON B. JOHNSON for many generations.

His true memorials stand among us.

They are those millions of black Americans who now vote because of LYNDON JOHNSON's ceaseless efforts and his devotion to democracy.

They are those millions of Americans who are better schooled today because of his determined pursuit of more educational funds.

They are those other millions who have achieved a greater measure of dignity in their old age because he pressed hard and long for medicare.

Those millions will continue to have a benign effect on the course of the Nation long after the Vietnam war is a footnote in the history books.

When LYNDON JOHNSON left office, he could look across this country and honestly tell himself, "Well, I fixed something."

That is a sentence, I suppose, that many politicians utter to themselves at one time or another. But LYNDON JOHNSON had the record to back it up.

If 30 years ago you had asked American blacks to guess the origin of this century's greatest civil rights President, not many of them would have named Texas.

His fervor for equality was not generated by political need, because I suspect he could have slid through in this area by making encouraging noises and symbolic gestures.

He did not.

He had identified the racial problem as one crucial to the survival of the Nation. And he moved. He moved with all the energy and skill at his command—and that was considerable.

As a consequence, we had the Omnibus Civil Rights Act of 1964. In retrospect, that one does not seem much. Its principal concept—one that seems rather quaintly anachronistic in 1973—was that blacks have the right to eat in restaurants and sleep in hotels.

But it forced the Nation to confront the problem. It set events in motion.

And a year later, President JOHNSON was back to Congress again, this time with the Voting Rights Act. It passed. But when it passed it did not seem as important as the bill that had gone before, for some reason. Perhaps because it was shorter, because it did not have as many titles, because it applied to fewer States.

But I think LYNDON JOHNSON knew what it would do. He knew it would change things, and not just in the South. Its ripples have now been felt in one way or another throughout the country. And I think we are the better for it, the stronger for it.

Late last year, while driving to a vacation in Mexico with two of my sons, the highway took us through a Mississippi town called Fayette.

It distresses me to admit that I could not immediately recall why the name rang a bell. Then, of course, it came. Fayette had a mayor named Charles Evers.

We stopped. We saw the town. We saw the mayor. We heard the history of the first black administration in the community's history. We talked to whites.

And it is reassuring to report that we could find no indication anywhere that democracy is a mistake.

Charles Evers knew who was primarily responsible for that concept of democracy. And he said he had made it a point frequently to call the L. B. J. ranch and thank the man he held most responsible.

As the years pass, we will all have more and more cause to reflect on Mr. JOHNSON's accomplishments. They will be about us for generations. And they will not be mere forgotten milestones on unremembered roads. They will be growing oaks that will soften our landscape and shade us for as far into the future as we can see now.

Yes, we will reflect on his career. And as we do, all of us, I think, will become more and more appreciative that he was here—and that he had the wisdom to fix some things that need fixing.

Hon. Harrison A. Williams, Jr.

OF NEW JERSEY

Mr. President, history is marked by islands of time on which are clustered several events of great magnitude which occur, coincidentally, within historical moments of each other; we are living through one of those time islands now.

Less than 1 month ago, our Nation was deeply saddened at the news that former President Harry S Truman had died. But within weeks of that unhappy time, our spirits were lifted by reports that the awful ordeal in Southeast Asia might soon be at an end. And then, at virtually the same time that the dream of peace was being transformed into reality, we were shocked by the unexpected tragedy of the death of former President LYNDON BAINES JOHNSON.

It is ironic that LYNDON JOHNSON died 2 days after the expiration of what would have been his second term as President. And it is a cruel irony indeed, that his death came shortly before a treaty to end the war in Vietnam was to be finally agreed to. There can be no doubt that LYNDON JOHNSON longed for an end to this war as fervently as anyone in this country.

Mr. President, I know I do not have to remind any Member of this body that LYNDON JOHNSON has left behind him a magnificent legacy of social progress for millions of Americans—and for millions more yet unborn. Virtually his entire life was dedicated to public service; it was a career marked by compassion for human needs, and a fierce dedication to making the promise of America a reality for all Americans.

LYNDON JOHNSON summed up his philosophy of government in a speech he made near the beginning of his full term as President in 1964, when he said:

> I want a happy nation, not a harassed people—a people who love instead of hate—a people who are fearless instead of fearful—men with pride in their ancestry and hope for their posterity—but humble before their God and concerned always with the wants and needs of their fellow human beings.

Mr. President, LYNDON JOHNSON's life in itself was an embodiment of the American experience. His ancestors helped settle the West, and he grew up living close to the land. He started work as a construction worker, went on to become a teacher, and was introduced to National Government as a congressional staff member during the depths of the depression. He went on, of course, to become one of the most powerful leaders this body has ever had, and then to the highest office in American political life.

Those of us who were privileged to serve in the Senate when LYNDON JOHNSON was majority leader, and later when he was Vice President and then President, knew very well that he was a grand master of the political process. The politics he practiced was sometimes rough, usually colorful, and almost always effective. He knew better than any of us how to pass legislation, and he used his skill to its utmost to compile one of the most magnificent legislative records in our Nation's history.

LYNDON JOHNSON knew the needs of average Americans, and the legislation he worked for was addressed to those needs. He was an ardent supporter of the kind of economic reforms begun by Franklin Roosevelt's New Deal, and he was one of the first Members of Congress to recognize the urgent need for legislation to erase discrimination in all phases of American life.

When the tragedy in Dallas left LYNDON JOHNSON heir to the Presidency, he was scrupulously loyal to the programs he inherited from John F. Kennedy. And when he won a great mandate to his own term in the White House, he consolidated his dreams for America in a program he called "The Great Society"; it was a program he described this way:

> The Great Society asks not only how much, but how good; not only how to create wealth but how to use it; not only how fast we are going, but where we are going.

LYNDON JOHNSON was more successful than probably any President—with the possible exception of his hero, F. D. R.—in getting his program enacted into law. As one who was privileged to play some part in achieving passage of that great and visionary program, I can only say that it was a unique and memorable experience. The great legislation on education, civil rights, economic opportunity, health care for the elderly, environmental quality, and housing and urban development, which was passed during those years, stands today as a monument to LYNDON JOHNSON's Presidency.

Mr. President, perhaps the most fitting description we can attribute to LYNDON BAINES JOHNSON is to say simply that he cared deeply about all the people of our country, and did all in his power to make their lives better. I join today with my colleagues in expressing the deepest sense of personal loss at his death, and extending my sincerest condolences to the Johnson family.

Hon. Hiram L. Fong
OF HAWAII

Mr. President, I join my colleagues in paying tribute to former President LYNDON B. JOHNSON, whose sudden death this week at age 64, shocked all of us.

It was my privilege to know LYNDON JOHNSON as majority leader of the Senate, as Vice President, and as President. I was always impressed by his warmth and charm and friendliness to me, and I am deeply saddened by his death. America is the poorer to lose such a dynamic elder statesman. We had hoped to have the benefit of his counsel for many years to come.

To capsulize the life and achievements of this dynamic and complex man through his 31 years of public service in the legislative and executive branches of our National Government is difficult indeed. This we can say: our Nation owes him much.

Certainly those who lived through the horror of the assassination of President John F. Kennedy will always be grateful to LYNDON JOHNSON for the masterly manner in which he promptly and firmly took hold of the reins of government. We could have had chaos and turmoil. Instead we had order and continuity and inspiration. Through his courage, strength, and skill, LYNDON JOHNSON rallied the American people to weather the tragedy an assassin's bullet had inflicted upon us. His conduct and leadership during those difficult circumstances were exemplary.

LYNDON JOHNSON leaves a record of tremendous achievements and some disappointments, the most notable of course his failure to end the war in Vietnam that he inherited. He felt he had done everything he possibly could, including sacrificing a bid for a second elective term, to no avail. Yet it is a mark of the man that he would not settle for a peace that would only be surrender in disguise.

On those other issues that remain unfinished and controversial, only time and future events will give us the necessary perspective and tell us whether he was right or wrong. At this time, however, there is no doubt that in the death of LYNDON JOHNSON, our Nation has lost a leader whose life was marked by enormous energy, vitality, and a capacity for leadership few men possess.

We know he was a master of the legislative process as his effective tenure as majority leader of the Senate attests. And, as President, his knowledge of Congress and Congressmen enabled him to push to enactment a record number of new domestic programs.

The Civil Rights Act of 1964 and the Voting Rights Act of 1965 stand as noble monuments to his tireless work as President in behalf of all Americans.

Imbued with a deep-rooted love of America, he was a man in the familiar tradition of our country, rising from humble beginnings to the highest elective offices in the land. And it is to his everlasting credit that he never forgot his humble origins. Undoubtedly his zeal for wiping out poverty and his strong support of better education for all had their roots in his early life. Those American citizens disadvantaged by color, race, or poverty knew that in LYNDON JOHNSON they had a staunch champion.

Born and raised in the dirt-poor hill country of central Texas, LYNDON JOHNSON knew what it was for people to scratch for a living. But he also knew that in America a person could get an education and work his way up. Throughout his public career, he strove mightily to widen that opportunity for those Americans in need.

LYNDON JOHNSON was a big man from big country. Six feet two inches tall and large of frame, he came from Texas, our largest State until Alaska entered the Union. He thought big. He planned big. His horizons were so big they had no finite limits. He dreamed big dreams for America and he labored tirelessly to make those dreams come true.

It was this capacity for dreaming big and thinking big that enabled LYNDON JOHNSON to embrace enthusiastically the idea of statehood for Alaska and Hawaii. While others clung to a United States of America with only contiguous States, LYNDON JOHNSON saw the feasibility of accepting noncontiguous Alaska and mid-Pacific Hawaii. LYNDON JOHNSON was one of the architects of statehood for Alaska and Hawaii. I am sure I speak for all citizens of Hawaii when I say the people of the 50th State will always have a special aloha for LYNDON JOHNSON.

Just as LYNDON JOHNSON led the drive for statehood for Alaska and Hawaii in 1959, so in 1960, he made possible enactment of legislation to establish in Hawaii the Center for Cultural and Technical Interchange between East and West. He agreed that Hawaii, a crossroads between the United States and Asian-Pacific lands, should be the site of a Federal institution supported by the people of America to promote understanding between our people and our neighbors in Asia and the Pacific. The East-West Center has been in operation for more than a decade in the work he envisioned.

Many years ago, when ground-breaking ceremonies were scheduled for the East-West Center, President and Mrs. Johnson agreed to attend and they invited Mrs. Fong and myself to fly to Hawaii with them and join in the ceremonies. The aircraft assigned us had only two sleeping bunks. President JOHNSON insisted that Mrs. Fong and I take one of the bunks and he and Mrs. Johnson would take the other. We, of course, demurred and tried to persuade them to keep both bunks. But in his customary generous and warm-hearted way, President Johnson would not take "No" for an answer. He and Mrs. Johnson gave up one bunk so that we could be comfortable. It is such acts of kindness that we recall on this sad occasion.

It is little wonder that in 1964, Hawaii gave LYNDON JOHNSON an overwhelming vote of thanks and confidence. In his election campaign, 79 percent of Hawaii's voters cast their ballots for LYNDON JOHNSON.

We in Hawaii are very, very sorry to lose such a staunch friend and we bid him a sad aloha.

My wife Ellyn joins me in extending to Mrs. Johnson, to daughters Lynda and Luci, and to their families our deepest condolences in their bereavement. We know how proud he was of them and how much comfort he derived from their love and loyalty.

Hon. Frank Church
OF IDAHO

Mr. President, the death of former President LYNDON JOHNSON leaves a great void, nowhere felt more poignantly than in this Capital.

For it was in Washington that LYNDON JOHNSON pursued his remarkable career during most of his adult life. And it was here in Washington that his friends were legion, his talents most appreciated and best understood.

As a man, LYNDON JOHNSON was bigger than life; as a Senator, he was bigger than Texas; as majority leader of the Senate, he soon became the second biggest man in the Government. Only the Presidency itself was cut to fit his size.

The irony is that the people never knew LYN-

DON JOHNSON for what he really was, a man of warmth who cared deeply about the dispossessed. The public could not know the private LYNDON JOHNSON, so pungent, volatile, folksy, and sentimental.

I will remember him for these intensely human qualities; for the leadership he gave to good causes such as civil rights; for the landmark legislation he pulled through Congress, medicare for the elderly and better education for the young.

His life, so full of struggle, was buoyed by the constant companionship and encouragement of his faithful wife, Lady Bird. She matched his energies and shared his ideals. To her, their children, and grandchildren, my wife, Bethine, and I extend our heartfelt sympathy.

Though we differed on the question of the war, my regard for LYNDON JOHNSON never faltered. He was a giant of a man, and I will miss him.

Hon. Edmund S. Muskie
OF MAINE

Mr. President, LYNDON JOHNSON was, in many ways, larger than life. In a political career spanning nearly four decades, he exemplified so many of the attributes commonly associated with his beloved State of Texas—flamboyance and pride, coupled with enormous charm and a canny perception of the frailties and strengths of those with whom he worked.

All of us who worked closely with him marvelled at his energy, respected his vigorous dedication and were amazed by his tenacity and persuasive qualities. During his 12 years as majority leader, we could be sure that when LYNDON JOHNSON promised a night-long session, we would be at our desks through the night. He was totally absorbed in his work, and I suspect that if it had been within his power, he would have created 25-hour work days.

His personality enveloped the Senate, and it will be a rare leader who will run the Senate LYNDON's way again.

He proved here that he was master in the art of the possible, but he also demonstrated that he had dreams and the courage and talent to make many of those dreams reality.

After the tragedy in Dallas, LYNDON JOHNSON was thrust without warning into the Nation's highest office. He met the challenge with characteristic energy, vision, and remarkable strength of leadership. And he presided with great personal dignity over the most tumultuous and troubling period in recent American history.

He understood that continuity was vital to the country and the world, vital to demonstrate the durability of our institutions and the stability of our society and our political mechanisms. President JOHNSON's first message to Congress began with ringing:

We shall continue.

And he did continue. His mastery of the intricacies of the Senate and Congress' responsiveness to programs began by President Kennedy provided some momentum, but his ultimate success came for his own deep commitment to the American system and to its political institutions.

LYNDON JOHNSON was a big man: in body, in vision, and in ambition. His ambition stretched far beyond himself to his country. He dreamed not just of a new society, but of a great society, one that dealt justly and shared its riches widely with all its citizens.

The simple, inescapable fact was that this big man cared, and he cared intensely, about the farmer in Iowa, the fisherman in Massachusetts, and the rancher in Texas, and the disadvantaged of all colors, all of whom shared the same hopes and harbored the same fears. It was the task of political leaders, JOHNSON said in 1964, to make Americans aware of their fundamental unity of interest, purposes, and belief. And it was his highest ambition "to satisfy the simple wants of the people." He demanded a better quality of life for those Americans, he saw ringed into ghettos of indifference, of prejudice, of ignorance.

A distinguishing quality of a great free society is its freedom to experiment, freedom to make mistakes, freedom to change direction, to back away from failure and to enlarge on success. President JOHNSON had the courage to risk uncertain results in his determination to find bold new ways of reducing domestic problems of staggering complexity and magnitude—problems stemming from quiet words—poverty—hunger—education—opportunity.

Most importantly, LYNDON JOHNSON made a commitment to those American society had treated unfairly. "We shall overcome," he said. And he put those words into action, enacting sweeping civil rights reforms which America is still building on today in order to make this a truly just society.

When history judges LYNDON JOHNSON, I am certain that that effort will not be forgotten.

All of us who knew him have personal recollections of his unique personality. I came to know his bite and his bark, his warmth and his charm, his icy disapproval and his overgenerous praise. He was the most fascinating human being I have known in my political life.

So many of us shared with him the tragedy of the war which marked his Presidency so indelibly. I was always conscious of his agonizing desire to know what was right; and now history must write the final judgment.

Hon. Ernest F. Hollings
OF SOUTH CAROLINA

Mr. President, I was both surprised and saddened to learn of the untimely passing of LYNDON BAINES JOHNSON. Coming so closely as it does to the death of another of the architects of modern times—Harry S Truman—President JOHNSON's passing leaves a certain silence on our tongues as well as a pain in our hearts. The words to express any judgment on the tumultuous events of the Johnson years come slowly. So close are we to the events themselves that we are denied the luxury of perspective and judgment. It remains for the future to determine the outcome of the many fateful decisions it was LYNDON JOHNSON's destiny to make.

As Congressman, Senator, majority leader, Vice President, and finally President of the United States, LYNDON JOHNSON was a man of true compassion. He cared greatly about people. At the pinnacle of power, he never forgot the underprivileged and downtrodden. Indeed, once he found himself in a position to really make a difference, he bent his every effort to improving the lives of those who needed help. No President was more passionately committed to improving the health and education and housing of the American people. None was more convinced of the essential equality of men. And none did more to insure that every American—regardless of race—enjoyed the blessings of liberty and democracy.

LYNDON JOHNSON was—more than most men— a son of the soil. Time and again throughout his life, he returned to the Texas hill country for sustenance and reinvigoration. From his early experiences with friends and neighbors who had to struggle to survive, he drew his fundamental faith in the goodness of people.

He knew that given a chance, most Americans would work long and hard to vindicate the hopes and dreams of those who built America. He knew the American dream was reality because he lived it.

His experiences as a young man developed in the future President a sincere and intense love of country. LYNDON JOHNSON was a patriot. He was proud of America, and he did what he believed was right for his country. Never a prisoner of party, JOHNSON was—as President Nixon observed so well—a partisan of principle. As majority leader of the U.S. Senate, JOHNSON developed a fine working relationship with President Dwight Eisenhower. It was a case of two men rising above party and dedicating themselves to the greater good.

Many of President JOHNSON's decisions were highly controversial. None, of course, knew this better than the President himself. I think immediately of the tough decisions on Vietnam. The wisdom of some of those decisions will long be debated. But one thing is certain—President JOHNSON made his decisions with the well-being of his country uppermost in mind. When he realized in 1968 that his continuance in office might make it even more difficult to achieve a peace, he decided to forego the Presidency by not running again. It must have been a difficult decision for a proud man to make—but he stuck with it because he believed it was the right thing to do.

Probably my most vivid and enduring memory of the Johnson Presidency is the leadership given in the wake of John F. Kennedy's assassination. In a time of confusion and fear, JOHNSON provided direction and assurance. He assumed the reins of government with confidence; he provided a program; and he immediately got down to the business of first calming—and then moving—a Nation. His address to the Congress just a few days after the assassination is among the most moving and eloquent addresses in all the annals of the Presidency. It did credit to JOHNSON, and JOHNSON did credit to the Nation.

Now, in this Chamber that he loved so much, we mourn the passing of another of the giants. He was a controversial man in difficult times, but LYNDON JOHNSON never recoiled from either controversy or difficulty. He was more than willing to have his case submitted to posterity. He died confident in the belief that history would vindicate his actions. I am sure that history will smile upon much of the JOHNSON legacy, and I

am consoled by the thought that this true patriot kept his confidence and pride in country to the very end. Mr. President, I join the Nation in mourning the passing of LYNDON JOHNSON, and I extend my condolences to the Johnson Family.

Hon. Stuart Symington
OF MISSOURI

Mr. President, those of us who enjoyed the friendship of our late President LYNDON B. JOHNSON knew of his incredible capacity for hard work, his rare natural gift of leadership, his determination to carry out the programs he felt wise and good for the people, especially the little people, of America.

No American, no citizen of any country at any time in history, has ever done more to improve the lot of millions of his fellow men and women.

A large part of his great success as a statesman resulted from his fortunate marriage. The close and inspiring lady who stood by his side for so many years was equally responsible for the love story that has become a saga in the history of the country they both loved so well.

To her, to the daughters he loved so ardently, and to his family, speaking for his legions of friends in Missouri, I extend my heartfelt sympathy.

Hon. John L. McClellan
OF ARKANSAS

Mr. President, LYNDON BAINES JOHNSON is dead—and we are all diminished by his passing. Today, the Nation mourns a lost leader—and I have lost a friend. Coming so soon and so unexpectedly after the death of Harry S Truman, the only other living former Chief Executive, LYNDON JOHNSON's death leaves a sorrowful void in American life.

It is altogether fitting that we pay tribute to him in this Chamber. LYNDON JOHNSON loved the Senate. Here he spent some of the happiest and most rewarding years of his life—as Senator from Texas, member of the Committee on Appropriations, where we served together from 1956 to 1961, majority leader and, finally, as Vice President. Few men have known and understood the heart and mind of this body so well.

Many of us here today knew him as a colleague and were proud to call him our friend. We all have memories of this tall Texan, who often seemed to embody in himself all the exuberance associated with his native State. Sometimes, both as a collegue and as President, we disagreed with him—but I am firmly convinced that none doubted his sincerity or his conviction that whatever he was doing was in the best interests of the American people.

LYNDON JOHNSON's life was a fulfillment of the American dream. When he summoned the Nation to a war on poverty, he knew the enemy at first hand. He had been born in a three-room house in the back-country hills of Texas. When he introduced legislation to improve our schools, it was based upon his own experience. A hard-won education had set him on the path to leadership.

LYNDON JOHNSON was a son of the frontier. This is not so much a geographic place as it is a symbol—a symbol of America's confidence that beyond the moment, over the horizon, the world will be brighter, the future better.

The United States has become a more populous and far more urbanized nation, but LYNDON JOHNSON labored to preserve the heritage of the frontier. Open country, clear skies, clean streams, equality of opportunity, the dignity of the individual, the commitment to justice for all—are derived from this legacy.

LYNDON JOHNSON believed that political unrest, economic uncertainty, and social upheaval have not dulled the values that our historical experience has taught us.

I am reminded of something that LYNDON JOHNSON once wrote in a forward to "The Texas Rangers," a book by his good friend and fellow Texan, Dr. Walter P. Webb, where he recalled that one Ranger had defined courage as "a man who keeps on coming on."

LYNDON JOHNSON said:

You can slow a man like that, but you can't defeat him—the man who keeps on coming on is either going to get there himself, or make it possible for a later man to reach the goal.

In these challenging and perilous times, free men everywhere might profitably consider this motto. We cannot be certain we will reach and fulfill the goals of our society or the ideals upon which our system stands. But we can, by dedication and commitment, be the kind of people who "keep coming on."

Mr. President, LYNDON BAINES JOHNSON was such a man.

Hon. William D. Hathaway
OF MAINE

Mr. President, LYNDON JOHNSON's life was a chronicle of great achievement. Like all men who are doers, he knew the taste of both victory and defeat; of great satisfaction and deep despair.

He will be remembered most for his passionate commitment to social justice; for his efforts to redeem our national pledge of equal justice and protection under law.

While the great personages of the world will eulogize him, the lowly will recall him as one who, with unprecedented zeal, sought to better educate our young; feed our undernourished, improve the condition of our poor, and eliminate the barriers to equal opportunity in our society.

LYNDON JOHNSON envisioned a great society for America, one in which the promises set forth by our Founding Fathers will finally be fulfilled.

This vision is his legacy to us. He pointed the way and led us part way down the path. It is now incumbent on us who labor in these halls he once trod to honor him in the manner most appropriate to this body—by continuing his efforts to build a country "with liberty and justice for all."

Hon. Charles H. Percy
OF ILLINOIS

Mr. President, I join with my Senate colleagues here today and Americans from every part of the country in mourning the death of President LYNDON BAINES JOHNSON. In the short time since the President's death, I have been remembering my personal encounters with him and rereading the accounts of his life—from his boyhood in the Texas hills to the zenith of his career in the White House. In my opinion, no single sentence has captured the whole of the man's personality and accomplishment more effectively than the comment his wife made when she was recounting their whirlwind courtship and marriage. She said:

Sometimes LYNDON simply takes your breath away.

LYNDON JOHNSON's astonishing career in the political arena did, indeed, take away the breath of all who followed it. As a young Congressman, he carefully watched and absorbed the way the political process operates in the Congress. Under the tutelage of such political greats as President Franklin Roosevelt and House Speaker Sam Rayburn, young Congressman JOHNSON developed into the greatest politician of them all.

As he rose through the ranks in the Congress until he became the powerful Senate majority leader, he learned the political art of bargaining and compromise as no other man had done. And as his influence grew, so did his compassion and his understanding of the average citizen and his needs.

There is no need to recount here the circumstances of his accession to the Presidency. But it is good to remember that he presided over the country during that difficult, painful time with an uncommon grace and a strength which enabled all of us to move out of our anguish over President Kennedy's death and move forward to accomplish so much of the program he had hoped to achieve.

LYNDON JOHNSON took the reins of Government and channeled our energy toward solving the massive social problems that had come to a head in the early 1960's. As was his wont, he took on the issues with gusto, sending to the Congress for consideration and action more social legislation than any President had ever offered. Out of this highly productive time came the most important civil rights legislation ever enacted in this country. He saw the need for quality housing and fought for legislation that would make that possible. He knew the needs of the elderly and the poor of this country, and he offered the medicare program as a solution.

It is safe to say that no President, not even his teacher and hero Franklin D. Roosevelt, compiled a greater record of domestic legislation than LYNDON JOHNSON.

It would be less than honest in any discussion of President JOHNSON not to mention the Vietnam war, which was to divide our Nation and end one of the most extraordinary political careers in our history. I, along with many other Americans, am sorry that President JOHNSON did not live to see the end of this war. I did not agree with his policies in Indochina, but I believed him when he said that no man living wished more profoundly for an end to the war than he did.

LYNDON JOHNSON was a powerful man. Although he has been far from the public eye on all but the rarest occasions since he left the White House just 4 years ago, we shall all miss the presence which once dominated our lives. He

was a good man, who did what he believed was right in every situation, both when the public, whose admiration he desired so intensely, was with him and, in the end, when it was turned against him. His devotion to principle should be a lesson to every one of us here.

It took a man of LYNDON JOHNSON's imagination and magnitude to call for the creation of a great society. If he did not see the fulfillment of his dream of a great society; if that dream was shattered by the sheer profundity of the problems all Americans faced; if, indeed, the great society he longed for took second place while he waged a war that fewer and fewer Americans believed was right, he should have—and I deeply hope he did—take pride, great pride, in the fact that he made this country better for his efforts.

Mr. President, Mrs. Percy and our children, to whom the entire Johnson family was always very kind, join me in extending to Mrs. Johnson and her children and grandchildren our deepest sympathy in this time of sorrow. I hope that they can take some measure of comfort in the realization that their unfailing devotion to him was returned in full measure.

Hon. Paul J. Fannin
OF ARIZONA

Mr. President, LYNDON B. JOHNSON was a remarkable man who worked mightily to improve the Nation he loved.

His life itself was a fulfillment of the American dream—from humble origins to schoolteacher to Congressman to Senator to Senate Leader to Vice President to President.

He was—and I say this with greatest admiration and respect—perhaps the most effective politician in recent American history.

For himself and for the Nation he set lofty goals and he had the capacity to bring about the means he believed would achieve these goals.

He sought to wipe out discrimination, to eradicate poverty, to advance medical care, and to improve education in America.

Abroad, he vowed to keep America's commitment to help defend free nations against aggression.

Once committed to these goals, President Johnson remained steadfast even when he was abandoned by former supporters when the going got rough.

As a member of the opposition party I often

differed with President JOHNSON regarding his programs for achieving national goals, but I certainly agreed with him on the objectives.

As President Nixon has observed, it is especially saddening that Mr. JOHNSON passed away on the eve of the announcement that a peace agreement has been reached in Vietnam. President JOHNSON sacrificed his political life in his determination to bring the Vietnam war to a conclusion. It is ironic that on this day when we celebrate the reaching of a peace agreement we also mourn the death of the man who suffered and struggled so long to resolve this conflict.

In my experience with President JOHNSON he was always very cordial. He was a man who lived and enjoyed life to the fullest.

Mr. President, I mourn the passing of this man whose brand is on such a long and important segment of American history. I join the Senate and my fellow Americans in extending condolences to Mrs. Johnson and members of the family.

Hon. Milton R. Young
OF NORTH DAKOTA

Mr. President, this is a sad day for the Senate of the United States. Death has taken one of our great men of this country, President LYNDON BAINES JOHNSON.

He was one who for most of his life served as a devoted, dedicated, and able public servant. He was one of our ablest and best liked majority leaders of the Senate.

President JOHNSON was the most personable and likable President in my time. He was the easiest to contact and visit with. Part of this was because we were so closely associated for many years while he was in the Senate. Following his years as a great leader of the Senate, he was to be elected Vice President of the United States, during which time he endeared himself to Members of the Senate even more—if that were possible.

No President ever was responsible for getting more domestic programs enacted by Congress. He fought very hard for many of them, even though they were not always popular in his own State, because he believed they were right and necessary.

President JOHNSON was the closest to agriculture and rural America of any President I have ever known. He was a man of the soil and this had much to do with his overall philosophy of life.

He succeeded to the Presidency at a most difficult time when we were already halfway into the war in Vietnam. He inherited many top government officials who were very war minded. Largely because of this, he got deeply involved in the war in Vietnam and I cannot help but believe this had much to do with the decisions he later made. I am sure this kindly, considerate man wanted more than anyone to end our involvement in this unpopular war.

I share the sadness of all of the Members of the Senate in the passing of this great man.

I cannot help but feel that history will deal kindly with his long record as a public servant, and particularly in his capacity as President of the United States.

Patricia and I extend our deepest sympathy to his beloved wife, Lady Bird, and all of his wonderful family.

Hon. Bill Brock
OF TENNESSEE

Mr. President, I deeply regret the passing of former President JOHNSON.

While our Nation's flag is still at half-mast in mourning the passing of former President Truman, we have lost another leader.

LYNDON JOHNSON was a unique man of the Congress. While his Nation honored him by electing him Vice President and President, it was in the Senate that his mastery of the political process was displayed most keenly.

Thrust into the Presidency by the tragedy of assassination, he led the Nation through many troubled days. History will record his strength and ability under the most difficult circumstances.

My deepest sympathy goes to his family and many friends.

Hon. Jacob K. Javits
OF NEW YORK

Mr. President, "The greatest civil rights President since Lincoln," said Roy Wilkins of LYNDON JOHNSON. High praise from the head of the NAACP to the first southerner to sit in the White House since reconstruction, but those of us who served in this body during the midsixties and who worked with him to enact landmark civil rights legislation would agree.

President Johnson did not originate the comprehensive 1964 act, he inherited it—the work of many civil rights advocates and the legacy of President Kennedy—he made it his first legislative priority. He urged, pleaded, cajoled, demanded, and implored the Congress—and his commitment and leadership played a large part in winning the votes we needed for cloture and passage. He also provided the moral leadership which moved the American people not simply to accept, but to demand the civil rights revolution of the sixties. The phrase may be cliche now, but those of us who were present at the joint session of Congress on March 15, 1965, will never forget the words of the President still shocked by Selma: "We shall overcome." We knew then, for he had promised in the language of the movement itself, that his commitment was moral as well as political, that he understood personally the cause of the black Americans who had suffered so much and that his determination to see justice done was formidable. We passed the Voting Rights Act, and he enforced it to the hilt.

His initiatives in the war on poverty, his advocacy of medicare and medicaid, the Job Corps, the Headstart program, and his support of large-scale Federal aid to education are all major milestones in American history. They reflect a deep and real concern for people, especially the poor and disadvantaged.

His responsibility in the Vietnam war will be better understood, especially by those who differed with him, as an intense loyalty, according to his lights, to the principle of self-determination of peoples, which he held most dear.

When history is written, I believe the greatest achievements of his administration will be the Civil Rights Acts of 1964, 1965, and 1968. Just last month, in addressing a convocation at the Johnson Library in Austin, President Johnson spoke with pride of these achievements, and with hope for the future of racial harmony in America. When we do achieve complete equality of opportunity for black and white, rich and poor, it will be in large measure due to the progress we made during Lyndon Johnson's Presidency.

Hon. Vance Hartke
OF INDIANA

Mr. President, with the passing of Lyndon Baines Johnson the Nation and the world have lost a most courageous and energetic leader. The final clouded and stormy years of his Presidency cannot belie a life of service to the American people. President Johnson took great strides toward full racial equality for all Americans. He focused our attention on the persistent problems of poverty and left us an enduring dream of a better America. History will long remember President Johnson as one of the powerful political figures in our Nation, but today let us remember him as spokesman for the underprivileged and the neglected.

Hon. Marlow W. Cook
OF KENTUCKY

Mr. President, for the second time in a period of weeks our Nation is steeped in mourning over the passing of a great leader. The sudden and untimely death of former President Lyndon Baines Johnson is a tremendous loss to our great society which he worked so diligently to improve. His contributions to domestic projects in America will have an impact on all of our lives for many years to come.

A forceful leader, Lyndon Johnson was able to set aside parochialism and partisanship as he attempted to apply the doctrines of equity and fairness across the entire spectrum of American society. He met every challenge with dedication and forthrightness and never acted other than to promote the best interests of all people. When finally beset by a nation in turmoil, he chose to dedicate all his energies to the resolution of internal and foreign conflicts rather than to engage in partisan political activity. This was perhaps one of the most difficult decisions ever made by a Chief Executive of the United States. That action typified the devotion to duty which Lyndon Johnson obviously felt. The memory of his leadership and spirit will continue to serve as an inspiration to the American people.

Hon. Daniel K. Inouye
OF HAWAII

Mr. President, the death of Lyndon Baines Johnson marks the passing of a great and a good man and the loss of a personal friend. He left his deep imprint upon this body, upon our Nation's Capital, and upon our country. Lyndon Johnson was a big man who felt strongly about the Senate, about our Government, and about our Nation.

It was also very difficult, if not impossible, not to feel strongly about LYNDON JOHNSON. I did and I liked him, respected him, and admired him. I admired his tremendous energy, knowledge, and drive. But most of all, I admired his deep commitment to the principle of human equality.

The steps which our Nation took under his tireless prodding toward making it possible for all of our people to walk upright in full participation and citizenship truly marked a second proclamation of emancipation. It was, therefore, particularly appropriate that his last major public appearance was to be at ceremonies for the opening of his civil rights papers this past month.

At that time he said:

We know there is injustice We know there is intolerance. We know there is discrimination and suspicion and division among us

But there is a larger truth. We have proved that great progress is possible.

And he added:

We know that much remains to be done.

Despite his achievements in this field of endeavor—achievements unequalled in modern history—LYNDON JOHNSON was not satisfied. A mark of his greatness, and of the depth of his concern, was his unwillingness to rest on the laurels of half-way measures and half-met goals.

And although the road to his envisioned Great Society proved to be a very long and difficult one, it must be said of LYNDON JOHNSON that he had the courage to embark upon it. He not only had the courage to begin that journey but the will to drive ever forward even when the going proved stormy and rough. His was not the dedication of the fainthearted. His was not the patriotism of the summer soldier.

It is my firm belief that the trail which he blazed, the benchmarks to progress which he erected thereon, will remain long and beyond the efforts of lesser men who flee that field of endeavor in a denial of responsibility and in a search for escape from conflict.

LYNDON JOHNSON had a voracious appetite for involvement and for action. As he once remarked:

To hunger for use and to go unused is the worst hunger of all.

While even he was not able to shape all of history's forces to his indomitable will he has left us a rich legacy indeed. Enriched by his presence, warmed by his friendship, we are much saddened by his passing. The Halls of this Congress, the streets of this city, and the highways and byways of this Nation, will not see the equal of this man for many a year.

Hon. Quentin N. Burdick
OF NORTH DAKOTA

Mr. President, words cannot do justice to the accomplishments of LYNDON JOHNSON as Congressman, Senator, Vice President, and President of the United States.

His true monument will not be one of stone. It will be in the way his dreams and achievements touch the daily life of American citizens. Because of LYNDON JOHNSON and his works, our elderly look forward to increased financial security and improved health care; millions of young people can give thanks for better educational opportunities; members of minority groups can hold their heads high; and residents of the most underdeveloped areas of the country have been given some hope for improved lives.

Through the years he held steadfast to his belief that this country was one that should offer opportunity for all people, rural and city, black and white, young and old.

And LYNDON JOHNSON was the true friend of the farmer throughout his career. He had firsthand knowledge of the hazards and problems farmers face. He strongly supported rural electrification, farm commodity price supports, soil and water conservation, and the programs of the Farmers Home Administration. He believed in the development of rural areas and communities as well as the rebirth of urban areas.

The problems of people shaped the course of LYNDON JOHNSON's life and in return his labor and energy and vision helped shape the lives of millions of his countrymen for the better.

We must make sure that these accomplishments are not obscured by the tragedy of a war which he tried vainly to bring to a conclusion.

My heartfelt sympathies go out today to that great lady, Mrs. Johnson, and to her family.

Hon. Howard H. Baker, Jr.
OF TENNESSEE

Mr. President, former President LYNDON JOHNSON was a man of great actions and great expectations. He was one of the most energetic and effective Presidents this Nation has ever known—a skilled legislative leader and a strong

Chief Executive who worked untiringly to translate his beliefs into solid accomplishments.

In both triumph and tragedy, President Johnson was a man satisfied with nothing less than attempting to move the Nation at the same hectic pace he required of himself. He was an ambitious man in the best sense of the word. He set great goals and committed his time and his talents to their fulfillment.

As a champion of the disadvantaged, Lyndon Johnson had few equals. He helped bring about the enactment of the greatest volume of social reform legislation in the Nation's history. He acted boldly and with compassion in the fields of job training, education, poverty relief, health care, civil rights, urban development, and care for the aged. If he fell short of achieving his Great Society, it was not for a lack of good intentions.

President Johnson was a man characterized by his commitments. As Senate majority leader during President Eisenhower's administration, he played an important and responsible role as the leader of the loyal opposition. He was a dedicated partisan who rose above partisanship to meet his commitments to the Nation.

As Vice President under President John Kennedy, Lyndon Johnson was dedicated to an activist role. Serving as an international good will ambassador, Chairman of the National Aeronautics and Space Council, and a spokesman for the National Government, he helped to further elevate the office of the Vice-Presidency.

Thrust into the Presidency at a time of tragedy, President Johnson accomplished a smooth changeover in the national leadership which encouraged and inspired his fellow citizens. He carried out his commitment to the unfinished work of his predecessor and went beyond in attempting to fashion a society dedicated to his concepts of social reform. At the same time, he dedicated himself to other commitments abroad with the same intensity. That he never accepted limitations of what he felt could be accomplished through the exercise of national power was the source of his greatest achievements and his greatest sorrows.

Lyndon Johnson stood by his commitments to what he believed to be the best interests of his Nation, even in time of great national conflict over his foreign and domestic programs. In the end he laid down his career to help seek a peaceful settlement of that most perplexing conflict in Southeast Asia.

The passing of such a renowned national leader is always a somber experience, but it is especially sad at this instance. We are now achieving that peace abroad which eluded President Johnson and which he so sincerely sought when he stepped down.

President Johnson deserves to be remembered as something more than the last casualty of the Vietnam era. With the coming of peace, the Nation will have the opportunity for a more objective evaluation of this man and his administration.

He showed us what could be accomplished through Government action—and what could never be accomplished through Government action. He showed us what Government could do for the people—and we learned what people, and nations, must do for themselves. If we have not yet achieved the Great Society, we can work to build a better society—and perhaps this commitment will be Lyndon Johnson's most fitting memorial.

Hon. Joseph M. Montoya
OF NEW MEXICO

Mr. President, we are gathered today to pay homage to a great man. A man who we all respected and one whom many of us here knew personally.

For all of us, the death of Lyndon Baines Johnson is a profoundly saddening event.

But for me, the death of this great man is especially poignant. I was proud to know President Johnson as a friend. I spent many hours in his company at his home where I learned to know him as a warm and compassionate man.

The public record of President Johnson's administration was a true reflection of the private record of the man.

President Johnson, during a career in public office that spanned more than three decades and reached the apex of American political life, never forgot his humble origins in the hill country of Texas. He never forgot the people back home—and for him "back home" meant all of the United States, while the people meant all the people.

During his long career, President Johnson was often faced with decisions that would make a smaller man shrink away and allow the tides of history to carry him along.

But confronted with the giant and enormously complex problems of America in the 1950's, as

Senate majority leader, and the 1960's as Vice President and President, President JOHNSON took the bull by the horns and sought solutions instead of procrastination. He was a man who recognized that problems must be solved, not merely identified.

His response to the problems facing America was a galaxy of legislation that reflected all the best things in him and his dreams for America.

An end to poverty, equality for all Americans, better social security benefits and increased medical care were goals that motivated President JOHNSON.

These goals sprung from the innermost depths of President JOHNSON. But without his political acumen and plain commonsense, they would have remained little more than goals and dreams for millions of Americans.

The legislation that President JOHNSON sponsored and saw passed stands as a true and honest memorial to him.

Although in recent years, President JOHNSON had lived a private life, he was always ready to offer his wise counsel when it was sought. He stood like rock anchoring an important part of America's social fabric.

My family and the people of New Mexico join with me simply to say to President JOHNSON: Vaya con Dios. We will miss you.

Hon. Henry M. Jackson
OF WASHINGTON

Mr. President, I wish to join my Senate colleagues today in tribute and heartfelt remembrance of LYNDON JOHNSON. It was my good fortune to serve with him in the House as well as here in the Senate and to witness his steady and remarkable growth as a skilled and dynamic legislative leader. As majority leader of the Senate he knew how to get things done. He was a master of the legislative process—he consulted, he urged, he prodded, he beguiled, and the Senate responded. He was the greatest legislative leader in all our history.

I can think of few men who so completely embodied those qualities we think of as quintessentially American. Like America itself, he proceeded on the basis of large dreams, and tried to move the country toward them with boundless energy.

LYNDON JOHNSON assumed the Presidency in a traumatic and difficult hour. But he rose to the challenge. Under his administration, our Nation moved to correct social injustice, improve health care, advance educational opportunity, expand conservation efforts and launch new environmental programs. Tragically, the division in this country over the unfortunate and long-drawn-out Vietnam war tended to obscure LYNDON JOHNSON's great domestic achievements.

Certainly, LYNDON JOHNSON was a controversial figure. But the debate over the wisdom of his policies became for many an opportunity to abandon constructive criticism for harassment and abuse. Few of our Presidents had to endure this kind of purely personal animosity.

It is tragic that LYNDON JOHNSON could not have lived 48 hours longer to see the Vietnam agreement.

LYNDON JOHNSON was a strong man who put his own indelible stamp of leadership on everything he did. I believe history will judge him a great President.

Hon. Peter H. Dominick
OF COLORADO

Mr. President, having served in the House and Senate for 8 years while LYNDON JOHNSON was Vice President and President, I have many bright memories of him and of his lovely wife whether we were in agreement or disagreement on specific issues.

President and Mrs. JOHNSON came to Colorado on one occasion about a year after the 1964 Civil Rights Act had passed with my strong support. We drove through a fine residential area of Denver to which many blacks had moved following the passage by the State Legislature in 1959 while I was serving there. Mrs. Johnson was so pleased with the area and we discussed at length the upward surge which I believe the 1964 Civil Rights Act would insure for the minorities opportunities which we both thought was imperative.

President JOHNSON was a great believer in this wonderful country of ours, he was a man of great vitality and enthusiasm; a man fashioned by the New Deal and still trying to put those ideas into effective programs.

He went out of his way to help all Members of the Senate in the Indochina situation and went to extraordinary length to persuade the membership of the rightness of the course in which he had embarked in Vietnam.

The country will miss his experience and his strength as we continue our course through history.

My deep sympathy is extended to Mrs. Johnson and his fine family.

Hon. Birch Bayh
OF INDIANA

Mr. President, great men do not live placid lives; they never enjoy the luxury of general acclamation. To the contrary, the conditions in which good men are elevated to greatness are inevitably marked by difficult decisionmaking amid sharp disagreement.

LYNDON BAINES JOHNSON was a good man; a compassionate soul who sought power not for itself, but as the means of improving the lot of others.

But he was more than a good man. Without doubt LYNDON JOHNSON was a great man; a courageous individual who did not run from the hard decisions. Instead he was a noble leader who set as his high purpose the goal of sharing among all our people the fruits of our national wealth.

Racial discrimination affronted his deep moral sense that all people, regardless of color, deserved individual dignity and respect. Ignoring the pleas of those who urged him to "go slow," LYNDON JOHNSON moved rapidly and forcefully to extend civil rights to all Americans.

It hurt LYNDON JOHNSON to know that there were children who were hungry in this country and abroad. He sought to feed them, and while welcoming progress never stopped striving to do better.

LYNDON JOHNSON could not accept the existence of poverty in the world's wealthiest Nation. With characteristic forcefulness and conviction he declared war on poverty and sought to mobilize the American people to win that war.

The inadequacy and sometimes prohibitive cost of medical care for older Americans ran counter to LYNDON JOHNSON's conception of what was fair and just. The situation demanded more than lipservice, and LYNDON JOHNSON provided the leadership which made medicare a reality.

LYNDON JOHNSON never took for granted the precious freedom that we are privileged to live with in this Nation. He wanted to prevent any erosion of that freedom, and to share it with others. This required hard decisions, decisions for which he was later vilified by some. There were some of us in this body who disagreed with some of those decisions, but no one who ever knew this great man doubted for an instant the sincerity and high purpose with which he made those decisions.

And those of us who had the opportunity to know LYNDON JOHNSON remember well that his desire for peace was as strong as his desire for justice and freedom. If anyone ever doubted the utter selflessness and decency of LYNDON JOHNSON those doubts were certainly dispelled when he forswore another term as President in the hope that his standing aside might hasten the peace he so desperately wanted to give to his countrymen.

There was much speculation when LYNDON JOHNSON left office about how history would view his Presidency. That speculation has been renewed with his sudden, shocking death.

I know that if history is fair and just, room will have to be made in the litany of great Presidents for LYNDON BAINES JOHNSON.

For the purpose he gave his countrymen;

For the dream of a better life for the poor, the hungry;

For the courage to stand firmly and with unflinching resolve against racial discrimination;

For the commitment to bring decent housing, adequate education, and hope to all Americans;

For the unyielding devotion to democracy and freedom—the ideals we hold most dear;

For all of these things, and for much more, LYNDON JOHNSON unquestionably deserves to be recognized as a great man, indeed, as a great President.

And it would be shortsighted to cite only his Presidency as evidence of his greatness.

In the other body and then in this Chamber LYNDON JOHNSON clearly demonstrated the qualities of decency and courage which were to mark his Presidency. He made his mark and he made it indelible. When, in 1965, President JOHNSON told a joint session of the Congress that "We shall overcome" he was not a newcomer to civil rights. Majority Leader JOHNSON was pushing for civil rights in 1957 when the first modern Civil Rights Act was passed.

The earnestness of his commitment to freedom, manifest in his resolve as President, was evidenced more than two decades earlier when he left the relatively safe Halls of Congress to take a naval commission in World War II. Suffice to say that he was decorated with a Silver Star for personal courage.

Through three decades of public service LYNDON JOHNSON never wavered from his commitment to helping others. He never showed anything but the greatest courage and uncompromising decency.

He was a great man because of that courage and decency. Perhaps, as important in honoring his memory, let us remember that before he was a Congressman, a Senator, a Vice President, a President, before all else LYNDON JOHNSON was a good man.

If I may be permitted a personal note, Mr. President, I am reluctant to let my reflection on this towering personality rest with LYNDON JOHNSON, the public man. Mrs. Bayh and I had the opportunity, for which we will be forever grateful, to know LYNDON JOHNSON and his dear wife, Lady Bird, his daughters Lynda and Luci and their husbands, on a treasured, personal basis.

President and Mrs. JOHNSON had a beautiful marriage; two strong people who gave and took strength and love from each other. The goodness which lay behind the public LYNDON JOHNSON was very much a part of the private LYNDON JOHNSON. And it is shared by Lady Bird. Never have I known anyone who cared so deeply for the well-being of others as did LYNDON JOHNSON. He could personalize and despair over the hunger, hopelessness, and illness of thousands of anonymous people, who for others were only statistics.

The Nation has not only lost a great leader. The community of man has lost a noble soul whose most fitting epitaph may well be, "He cared and he tried."

Marvella joins me in extending to Lady Bird and her daughters a sympathy which is so rooted in our hearts that words are inadequate for its expression. Your loss is our loss; your sadness is our sadness—and the Nation's.

Many memorials will be erected to LYNDON BAINES JOHNSON. But it may be said rightfully that no memorial will be as fitting nor as important as the ultimate victory over the social and human evils whose eradication was his life's work.

Hon. Thomas F. Eagleton
OF MISSOURI

Mr. President, all Americans mourn the passing of LYNDON B. JOHNSON, 36th President of the United States.

It was the fate of this man to stand at the center of one of the more turbulent periods in our history. We are still too close to its promises, its conflicts, and its tragedies to fairly judge his place in history. No doubt, as with other Presidents of stature, his reputation will rise and fall with the changing perspectives of succeeding generations.

But these things we do know.

LYNDON JOHNSON was a large man who dreamed large dreams. He wanted to care for the ill and the elderly. He wanted to educate the young. He wanted to provide decent housing for the poor and training for the unemployed. And he wanted to assure black Americans the rights and opportunities that would enable them to move into the mainstream of our national life.

In short, he wanted to lead the American people into a great and united and just society.

And President JOHNSON acted upon his dreams. No President ever pursued with more vigor and persistence those policies and programs he believed to be right.

As a result he achieved the enactment of the most comprehensive program of social legislation in our history.

Aid to education, civil rights, medicare, low-cost housing, the war on poverty—each of these landmark measures and others bore the stamp of his concern and his determination.

President JOHNSON loved this country, and he spent his life in its service—as Congressman, Senator, Vice President, and President.

For all of this he deserved in life—and deserves now in death—the respect and gratitude of his countrymen.

We will honor him most truly by keeping alive his vision of the Great Society and by preserving and building on the best of what he began.

Hon. Sam Nunn
OF GEORGIA

Mr. President, we are gathered here today for the second time in less than 30 days to pay homage to a fellow Senator who went on to lead our Nation at one of its most troubled times. In both instances, Harry Truman and LYNDON JOHNSON had to step in to lead this Nation upon the untimely death of a President.

LYNDON B. JOHNSON demonstrated to an anxious world that he was a singular man, of unique ability, who had prepared himself to assume the monumental role of Chief Executive at a moment's notice.

Although I have been in the U.S. Senate for only a brief time, I have developed a new dimension of respect and admiration for LYNDON B. JOHNSON. He is revered as the strongest leader in the history of the U.S. Senate.

I received a long telegram from former President Johnson and Lady Bird on the night of my election, reflecting not only his congratulations, but also an intimate knowledge of the campaign in Georgia. His love of political life and his deep consideration for those battling in this arena were prominent among the many traits which made him the most effective legislator in modern history and led him to the zenith of power in this Nation.

History will indelibly record his deep love for this Nation, his total dedication to his fellow man, and his great faith in the future of America.

Hon. Howard W. Cannon
OF NEVADA

Mr. President, it was with great sadness that this Nation received the death of former President Lyndon Baines Johnson. This remarkable man was one of America's most outstanding Presidents, and as we here assembled know and appreciate fully, he was the greatest legislative leader in our history.

The years that President Johnson spent in the White House were troubled years, beset by war and domestic strife. Yet his was a tremendous legacy measured by a distinguished list of accomplishments for the education, the health, and the civil rights of all Americans. Race, regionalism, public education, housing, and medical care found in him a tireless worker for the common good.

Lyndon Baines Johnson was the majority leader when I came to the Senate in 1959 and he was an awesome and inspiring figure during the years we served together in that body. I knew him as a most powerful leader, compiling one of the most successful records in this body.

He knew the intricacies of every piece of legislation that passed through his desk. From his leadership came the passage of the first civil rights bill to pass the Senate in 82 years. On a personal level, he took me under his wing and gave me encouragement as I aimed for committee assignments on which I felt I could most contribute.

Lyndon Johnson will not only be remembered for carrying out with zeal and with force the programs of his predecessor John Fitzgerald Kennedy. He soared even beyond these dreams as he established himself as the greatest proponent of social reform legislation in modern times. And although the tragedy of Vietnam overshadowed in public view his many and great accomplishments in the domestic field, I am convinced history will judge him as having acted with forthrightness and courage in fulfilling our international obligations. It is for this reason that I am especially saddened that Lyndon Johnson could not have lived to see the final end of this long and tragic Indochina war, a cause toward which he aimed every moment during his Presidency.

Hon. Richard S. Schweiker
OF PENNSYLVANIA

Mr. President, I would like to join all Pennsylvanians and all Americans, in expressing the profound loss we feel over the sudden death of President Lyndon B. Johnson.

During his long tenure as U.S. Senator from Texas, Senate majority leader, Vice President, and our Nation's 36th President, Lyndon Johnson made a significant mark in the policies and progress of America.

His sense of compassion for all Americans, his determination to make this country a more decent place for all citizens, and his sensitive sense of social justice resulted in national leadership to move our country forward with important domestic programs. His image of a Great Society included equality and prosperity for everyone, and he utilized his vast governmental experience and leadership to encourage all to join him in this effort.

In carrying on debate over what programs are most effective to accomplish these goals, and over what units of government are in the best position to provide meaningful services to our communities, we must never forget the goals and aspirations that inspired President Johnson to formulate his Great Society programs. Although times and conditions change, the overriding concern for the health and welfare of all citizens remains paramount, and President Johnson's leadership and compassion in this area still stands out as an example for every legislator and every citizen.

In recent years, the memory of the work of Lyndon Johnson has tended to be concentrated on Vietnam, and his involvement in this tragic war. With the ending of this conflict this week, it is particularly appropriate for us to remember the great domestic leadership and social consciousness of President JOHNSON.

The Nation mourns a great humanitarian and a great leader.

Hon. James A. McClure
OF IDAHO

Mr. President, twice in the past month, the American people have endured the tragic death of a former leader. In the case of LYNDON JOHNSON, it is particularly sad that he did not live to see an end to the Vietnamese conflict—the war which plagued his years in the Presidency.

If I were to pick one quality which best characterized LYNDON JOHNSON, the public servant, it would be this: More than any other man in our time, he understood the necessity for cooperation between the White House and Capitol Hill. What achievements history accords the Johnson administration were due almost solely to this quality and his ability to use the political process. First as Senate leader working with a Republican President, then as a President facing a sometimes hostile Congress, he understood the meaning of the words cooperation and bipartisan. Our country is the better for it.

Like all of those in Washington who have viewed the political process and seen its relationship to our personal freedoms, I salute the man who understood it better than anyone else. I also want to express my sadness at his passing.

Hon. Edward J. Gurney
OF FLORIDA

Mr. President, for a man who loves his country, there can be no higher calling than public service. LYNDON JOHNSON loved his country, and for 37 years he served it to the best of his ability— as a congressional aide, a youth program administrator, a Congressman, a Senator, a Vice President and, finally as the 36th President of the United States. While there were some who questioned his policies over the years, which is always true of any strong, dynamic leader, no one could question his dedication, his commitment to doing what he believed was right for America. For this he will be well remembered.

Amidst all the hue and cry about what was wrong with America, President JOHNSON stood for what is right about America—its ideals, its dreams, its hopes, and its commitment to freedom, not only in this country but around the world. At home, he strove to make the American dream a reality, and abroad, he fought to give others a chance to share our dream. His efforts on behalf of the cause of freedom in which he so deeply believed deserve the highest praise.

In remembering him today, we should not forget President JOHNSON's contribution as a Senator and as Senate majority leader. In the latter capacity, he was extremely effective; some say he was the most outstanding in the Senate history. Yet he never let partisanship interfere with what he believed to be the best interests of the country. At times of crisis during the Eisenhower years, LYNDON JOHNSON was there to offer support and to help unite the country.

Indeed, President JOHNSON was a uniter; he pulled the Nation together after the assassination of the late President John F. Kennedy and he gave up the Presidency rather than see the country further divided over the war in Southeast Asia.

I am sure that were he alive, there would be no one happier about what happened at Paris yesterday than President JOHNSON. When the history books are written, I think they will show that his determination to prevent a Communist takeover of South Vietnam laid the groundwork for the honorable settlement that has now been secured.

That is no small accomplishment. Rather, it is a fitting legacy for a man who loved his country—and the cause of freedom—as much as LYNDON JOHNSON. His advice and counsel will be sorely missed.

Mr. Mansfield. Mr. President, on behalf of the distinguished minority leader and myself I send to the desk a resolution and ask for its immediate consideration.

The Presiding Officer. Is there objection to the present consideration of the resolution?

There being no objection, the resolution (S. Res. 34) was considered and agreed to as follows:

Senate Resolution 34

Resolved, That the Sergeant at Arms of the Senate shall take such steps as may be necessary to carry out the provisions of Senate Resolution 24, 93d Congress, agreed to January 23, 1973, and necessary expenses in carrying out such resolution shall be paid out of the contingent fund of the Senate.

Hon. James B. Pearson
OF KANSAS

Mr. President, our Nation has been blessed with able, perhaps extraordinary, men who were capable of stepping into the Nation's highest office in times of crisis and guiding us through troubled times. President LYNDON BAINES JOHNSON was such a man. His courage and leadership were an inspiration to us all in those tragic days of November 1963.

But more importantly, President JOHNSON may be remembered as a strong leader, a man with a vision of a Great Society and the courage to seek it when many thought the challenge overwhelming. As majority leader of the Senate, he left his mark on this body and led it to the passage of vital legislation. As a Commander in Chief, he bore the awesome burdens of the Presidency through difficult years.

His quest for a Great Society brought some of the most far-reaching legislation of our time. The Civil Rights Act, Voting Rights Act, aid to education, open housing, are only the beginning of a long list of legislation enacted during the early years of his administration. Through those laws, he is part of our lives today and for generations to come.

For his strength and consummate political skill, we stood in awe of LYNDON JOHNSON, half fearing, always respecting, his ability to use the powers of his office. His grasp of the political arts and his vast reservoir of energy set the pace for us all during the 5 years of his Presidency. He was a giant of American politics with few equals in this century.

Now is not the time to judge the Presidency of LYNDON JOHNSON. That is a task for the future generations. But let us remind them that LYNDON JOHNSON was a complex man. He was tough, and compassionate. He was willing to hear, but often stubborn. He was a man of his region transformed into a national leader. He was a man of his time leading a new generation. Let the future judge him for all his qualities, and let it judge him kindly.

Mr. President, LYNDON JOHNSON was the first President I knew well and, like all who came into personal contact with him, I shall never forget him. I respected him as a man, as a politician, and as our national leader. I sincerely regret that he passed from this earth on the eve of the end of the war which was the tragedy of his Presidency and our Nation. We shall miss his wise counsel and vision in the years ahead.

Hon. George McGovern
OF SOUTH DAKOTA

Mr. President, for the last time yesterday LYNDON JOHNSON was back in the place where his life in politics began and the triumphs of his Presidency were written into law. Now we try as we must and as best we can to write his epitaph.

The war in Vietnam led to differences between LYNDON JOHNSON and some of us, even within his own party, just as it diminished the hopes and dreams within his own heart. Yet even in the midst of tragedy and division, none of us doubted his overwhelming love for this land. And all of us marveled at the progress he made possible and the programs he passed, without precedent in our time or perhaps any time in American history.

So let us remember the good he did, which was so great.

He told us: "We shall overcome."

And in the beginning, after that moment of crushing loss in Dallas, he helped all of us to overcome our doubts and our despair, so we could move on to finish the work we were in.

He helped America to overcome the bondage of bigotry and prejudice, so all of us could see as he did that the only race that counts is the human race.

He sought to overcome man's ancient and mortal enemies—poverty, ignorance, and disease—not by words, but by the remarkable works he did with us and left to us.

LYNDON JOHNSON was President of the United States, but he was at the same time so much more. He was a healer to the sick, a servant to the deprived, an educator of children, and the second Great Emancipator.

His advances at home may have been dimmed by war abroad, but they were so bright that they still shine forth as an example to the weary and the faint-hearted of how Government may use its power to serve its people. He always called himself a "can do" man; now his memory calls those of us in Government to believe that we can do what compassion and justice command.

The rites yesterday were ordained by tradition. Yet the real measure of this man should be taken not from the praises of the powerful and the famous, but from the feelings of so many ordinary people who are unpracticed in the forms of public mourning.

Who grieves for LYNDON JOHNSON?

Not just Senators, but citizens—the Job Corps graduate who has had and used his chance; the elderly who need no longer choose between their health and their savings; the young children who have been fed and taught because he cared and acted.

LYNDON JOHNSON may not have reached his Great Society, but he left our society greater. Now he has left us. Now it is for us, the living, to hear and heed the message he gave us in the early hours of his national leadership: "Let us continue."

Hon. Hubert H. Humphrey

OF MINNESOTA

Mr. President, I ask unanimous consent to have printed in the Record the moving tribute to President LYNDON B. JOHNSON by Bill Moyers, which appeared in the New York Times on January 26, 1973.

This very personal tribute by a man who knew President JOHNSON so well strikes harmonic chords of reminiscence for many others of us who were proud to be President JOHNSON's friend and associate.

There being no objection, the article was ordered to be printed in the Record, as follows:

ACROSS THE PEDERNALES

(By Bill Moyers)

WASHINGTON.—I was in Minneapolis, filming a public television show with Chippewa Indians, when the radio flashed the news of President JOHNSON's death.

As I walked into the tribal hall, one Indian who knew that I had worked for Mr. JOHNSON, pulled me aside and said: "A mighty wind has been stilled. I'm sorry."

LYNDON JOHNSON struck people that way. Friends, enemies and strangers alike felt the force of his enormous, restless energy. Like the Chippewa's "mighty wind" he could be awesome, capricious and inexplicable—his presence, as Washington learned after 1968, felt even by his absence.

I was drawn to him early. To a generation of ambitious Texans LYNDON JOHNSON was as big as the state itself and just as promising. To a small-town kid with an overwrought Baptist conscience he showed how to get things done in a hurry. We were short on philosophy in Texas, short on history and philosophy, too. On the frontier, which Texas remained until late, life was its own reason for living, action its own justification. And you didn't read a text book on how to climb the greasy pole; you just started climbing. How often I would hear him say: "Don't just stand there, son, get busy."

But power had a purpose for L.B.J. It was the way to deliver the goods. If you shared in the rewards (his mother, he told me, insisted that "If you do good, you'll make good"), so be it; the "folks" were always the real winners. The greatest good for the greatest number, he preached, and the largesse was pouring in; rural electricity, dams, highways, defense contracts, space projects, aerospace plants. "This is what your Government did," he told his hill country friends as he patted a new R.E.A. building as if it were a new-born calf.

His critics smirked when he said that what most people want "is a rug on the floor, a picture on the wall and music in the house." Their criticism bothered him least of all. "Those S.O.B.'s got it all," he said. "The folks I'm talking about don't even have the simple decencies, and they outnumber that slicked-down crowd"—here he would wrinkle his nose as if squinting through pince-nez—"ten million to one."

So I wrote him for a summer job. Later he told me the letter was impertinent, my suggesting that he was out of touch with Texas young voters and offering to help him reach them, but maybe because he had also been brash and not a little cocky when he was 18; he told me to come to Washington, sight unseen.

I flew there aboard an old two-engine Convair, my first trip east of the Red River, and landed expecting to counsel the mighty. Instead I wound up in a tiny airless room so deep in the basement labyrinth of the Capitol that one old Senator who had stashed his mistress in a nearby hideaway got lost coming back from a quorum call and couldn't find her for hours.

I spent my first night in Washington—from 5 P.M. to the following noon—completing my first assignment for LYNDON B. JOHNSON: addressing 100,000 letters to Texas voters one at a time on an ancient machine operated by pumping the right foot up and down, like a sewing machine. I stopped only to go to the bathroom and to assure Senator ———'s girl friend, who kept poking her tearful face in the door to inquire how long quorum calls lasted (I didn't know), that he was certain to return (I didn't know that, either).

I emerged the next day squinting in the light, hobbling on my now-stunted right foot, and wondering how L.B.J. would reward me. I soon found out. "I'm going to promote you to an upstairs room," he announced. I reported there immediately—and got to put stamps on all those letters I had just addressed. Some reward.

Years later I told him how my illusions had suffered those first two days in Washington. "Politics is stamps, spit, and shakin' hands," he said. Then he smiled: "Besides, whom the Lord liketh, He chasteneth." Not quite a literal translation, but I got the point.

Throughout his career LYNDON JOHNSON carried on that kind of love affair with the country, a one-time school teacher from Cotulla, Texas, forever trying to instruct his charges.

He taught us that the country is "peepul," with names, faces and dreams. He came to despise the bureaucracy his own programs created because they started dealing in "categories" and assigning numbers to human beings whose names were Hathie, Joe Henry, Fritz or Betty Lou—people who lived down the road, across the Pedernales. Once he cut an H.E.W. official off in mid-sentence with the outburst: "Goddamit, you make those folks sound like subjects instead of citizens."

Another time he ripped into a group of Government lawyers who had drafted an Appalachian assistance bill. "Who the hell can read this gobbledygook?" he thundered. "But that's a technical document, Sir," one of the men replied. The President gave him a long, merciless stare, then with his own black felt pen he rewrote the establishing clause. "There!" he said, holding the document out before him with a flourish. "Now they'll know down in Morgantown what we're talking about."

As the Manila Conference droned to a close in 1966 the President was handed a draft on the final memorandum of agreement. He was aghast at its flat, sterile, polysyllabic prose: "Come on," he whispered, pulling at my sleeve, and we left without so much as an "excuse me" to the dignitaries around the table. At the door he stopped long enough to whisper to the Secret Service Agent: Don't let one of 'em out until I get back."

In the next room he handed me a pad and his own pen. "Now I want to rewrite that preamble so it can be read in the public square at Johnson City," he said. We labored for an hour while Marshal Ky, President Thieu, Dean Rusk and other assorted, perplexed personages waited in the next room. The President dictated, edited, looked over my shoulder as I added what I could, finally picked up the pad, read silently, nodded, and stalked back toward the conference room. He stopped at the door and, winking at me, said: 'I want you to leak this to Smitty (Merriam Smith of UPI) first. It gets home first that way, and when ol' Judge Moursund reads this he'll know what we're trying to do out here with his money."

He taught us there's no progress without some giving up, that a nation of 200 million will stagnate without compromise. Some people scoffed as he reached for consensus, charging him with trying to please all the people all the time. But to him politics meant inclusion—"Noah wanted some of all the animals on board," he said, "not just critters with four legs." If consent of the governed is essential to democracy, to L.B.J. compromise was its lubricant

On the day I resigned, we rode around his ranch for hours. "You were born over there with those Choctok Indians," he said. "Bet you don't know where the word 'okay' came from."

I didn't.

"Right from the Choctaws themselves," he said. "It meant 'we can agree now, if you aren't so all-fired set on perfection.' " If he had been born in another time, I thought, he would have made his living as a horse trader. Instead, he bent this remarkable talent for getting agreement from disparate men to making things happen. He taught us, after years of stalemate, that the legislative process can function.

Why, then, wasn't he willing to compromise in Vietnam? The irony is, he thought he was. "Well, boys, I've gone the second, third and fourth mile tonight," he said after his Johns Hopkins speech in 1965. He had proposed a multibillion-dollar rehabilitation program for Indochina, including North Vietnam, and he was convinced that it was a bargain Ho Chi Minh couldn't turn down. Another time he made another offer, in secrecy, and Ho again said no. "I don't understand it," he said, with a note of sadness in his voice, "George Meany would've grabbed at a deal like that."

Therein may be the biggest lesson LYNDON JOHNSON may inadvertently have taught us. We think of ourselves as a broad-minded, good-intentioned, generous people, pursuing worthy goals in a world we assume is aching to copy us. "Surely," the logic goes, "all we have to do is offer them what we would want if we were in their place."

This is not a lesson in the limits of power. LYNDON JOHNSON knew better than most the fragile nature of power, its shortcomings, the counter-tides it inevitably provokes. "Hurry, boys, hurry," he would implore his staff after his great electoral triumph of '64. "Get that legislation up to the Hill and out. Eighteen months from

now ol' Landslide LYNDON will be Lame-Duck LYNDON."

He knew the limits of power. What he had to learn the hard way, and teach us as he went along, was something about the limits of perception. What made LYNDON JOHNSON such a unique and authentic figure—half Texas hill country, half Washington—may have also been his undoing. He was so much a creature of those places that he may have shaped the world in their image. And this image would hem him in, causing him to see others as he saw himself. It was this that made him such an American man when the world was in reality reaching for other models.

I don't know, this is conjecture. What I do know is that LYNDON JOHNSON was cut ten sizes larger than any of us. This made him coarser, more intemperate, more ambitious, cunning and devious. But it also made him more generous, intelligent, progressive and hopeful for the country. He was, inside, a soft man—I saw him weep as he watched television reports from Selma, Ala.: "My God," he said, "those are people they're beating. Those are Americans." Inside, I don't think he had what it took to prosecute a war wholeheartedly, and in the end he may yet teach us that democracy just doesn't have the heart for those dirty little wars.

He's gone now, and history will take a fuller measure of the man than those of us who served him. I suspect he would have enjoyed what his fellow politicians are saying about him today. I know he would believe them.

Our own relationship was strained toward the close and he died before the prodigal got home. But he did more for me than any man and I loved him.

Mr. President, I ask unanimous consent to have printed in the Record the eulogy of President LYNDON B. JOHNSON, delivered by W. Marvin Watson.

Mr. Watson's magnificent eulogy was given by him at the National City Christian Church, Washington, D.C. on January 25, 1973, at the official memorial service. The gratitude he so eloquently expressed for all of us needs no elaboration. I thank my friend, Marvin Watson, for speaking with heart and mind about a great President. He has given us insights into the life and works of LYNDON BAINES JOHNSON.

There being no objection, the eulogy was ordered to be printed in the Record, as follows:

PRESIDENT LYNDON B. JOHNSON

(A eulogy by W. Marvin Watson)

He was ours, and we loved him beyond any telling of it. We shared his victories and his defeats.

In victory he taught us to be magnanimous . . . in defeat he taught us to be without hate . . . to learn . . . to rally . . . to accept the challenge and to try again.

He believed that good men together could accomplish anything, even the most impossible of dreams. No matter who his opponent, he constantly sought to find that touchstone within the soul of every man which, if discovered, would release the impulse for honest and fair solution. Hate was never in this man's heart.

Each of you had your own memories of this man who served for 37 years in this city. I had the honor of being with him through the final four years of his Presidency . . . in those great moments of triumph when the American people endorsed him so strongly . . . in those magnificent hours when he stood before the Congress of the United States and led the way to the passage of laws long overdue that would lead to justice long denied . . . and in that darkening twilight when, as a man seeking peace, he was forced to continue a bitter war to honor our country's commitment to a small, far-off ally.

I watched the gray come into his hair.

I saw each deep line etch itself into his face as he gave all at his command to lead our country through the turmoil which surged around us.

I watched him as he used his great gift of persuasion to convince a Southern Senator that the time had come for the Civil Rights Act . . . I watched him formulate, secure passage and sign into law the most comprehensive legislative program in education, housing, conservation and health of any President in history . . . I watched him in the Situation Room at the time of crisis during the Six Day War when only his ability, his knowledge, and his sheer courage helped to keep that conflict from erupting into a wider confrontation.

I sat with him through those long nights as he endured the agony of Vietnam, as he sought the key to peace, and as he waited for word of men whom he had ordered into battle. Each was a human being to him, not a statistic; each was a name linked with wives and parents and children—he cared for people, not for numbers.

So desperately did he want a just and lasting peace . . . so much did he want us to reason together . . . so much did he yearn that man's goodness would triumph over man's evil . . . so often as friend turned to political foe, did he nod with sad understanding and pray that in the years to come, the sacrifices he was making would be worthy of the American people and serve ultimately as a firm platform on which to build a better world.

And through it all, I saw him earnestly seek God's wisdom for his decisions, for this was a man with a strong belief in the Almighty.

President Nixon, as you so eloquently stated in your message informing Congress of President JOHNSON's death, it was his "noble and difficult destiny to lead America through a long, dark night of necessity at home and abroad." If he could have chosen other circumstances in which to be President, perhaps he would have. But America has a capacity to call forth the leadership it must have in those hours of its greatest need. We had Abraham Lincoln when he was needed. We had Franklin Roosevelt when he was needed. History will record that in the seventh decade of the 20th century, America had LYNDON JOHNSON when he was needed.

When you remember him, remember him please for two things—his devotion to his country . . . and his restraint.

So often in his Presidency, dissension escalated into violence. Yet always, no matter how critical the situation, his inner faith in the people came to the fore and his restraint in the uses of power permitted the people to confront each situation and overcome it utilizing the inherent rights of free men.

Those of us who loved him take comfort in the knowledge that before he died, he could see the dawn of domestic tranquillity and of foreign peace which he gave so much of his great heart to bring about. The structure of peace which President Nixon, with great distinction and determination, is building in the world today will rest upon a foundation laid in loneliness and stubborn courage by LYNDON JOHNSON.

This man's restless, searching heart began to give out long before January 22d. He gave so much of himself to so many that it is wondrous that God, in His grace, granted him four years to enjoy his retirement in the hill country he so deeply treasured.

Not for him the easy way.

Not for him any halfway measures.

He was a tall man of giant character, and when he committed himself, he committed himself totally. And he asked his countrymen to do the same.

He asked those who had much to be concerned for those who had least.

He asked us to live up to our national promise.

He asked us to be worthy of our heritage.

He asked us to be true to ourselves.

But, he never asked more than he was willing to give . . . and what he gave was good enough to confirm and advance the progress of the nation he served.

LYNDON JOHNSON loved a woman, and she was his greatest joy and his greatest comfort. He loved his children and his grandchildren and to see them together was a heartwarming experience, for it transcended normal family devotion.

And coupled with that he loved each of us, sometimes with wry amusement at our failures, often with sharp words at our imperfections, but always with a sweeping and generous understanding of our frailties. The dimensions of this man were vast.

He is gone from us now . . . and this afternoon we shall take him home and he will be forever a part of the hill country.

Last September, I had the opportunity to be with him when he spoke of America and of the future.

He knew then that he might not see another autumn, but this was not a man who welcomed or needed sympathy.

Years from now, when historians appraise him, his speech that day could serve as the cornerstone of their research—for it reflected the true LYNDON JOHNSON. He gave much of himself to it, and it might well be his epitaph. He said:

"With the coming of September, each year, we are reminded as the song says, that the days are dwindling down to a precious few . . . the green leaves of summer will begin to brown . . . the chill winds of winter will begin to blow . . . and before we are ready for the end to come, the year will be gone.

"As it is with the calendar, so it sometimes seems to be with our country and our system. For there are those among us who would have us believe that America has come to its own September . . . and that our nation's span as mankind's last best hope will be done."

President JOHNSON continued:

"But I live by the faith that with each passing day we are always approaching nearer to the beginning of a new springtime and it is by that perspective that I see our country now.

"No nation can be more than the visions of its people. America cannot be more than we believe ourselves capable of becoming.

"I want to open the soul of America to the warm sunlight of faith in itself . . . faith in the principles and precepts of its birth . . . and faith in the promise and potential of its people."

That was LYNDON BAINES JOHNSON, the 36th President of the United States of America.

The years will be lonely without him.

Hon. Abraham A. Ribicoff
OF CONNECTICUT

Mr. President, LYNDON BAINES JOHNSON, the 36th President of the United States, was a strong, purposeful, determined man, as idealistic as he was often misunderstood. He felt deeply about America and the American dream of a land where all citizens enjoy equality of opportunity. LYNDON JOHNSON wanted more than anything else to make this Nation a better place for all our people. His accomplishments in health, education, civil rights, and poverty programs will be rated by future historians as the most far-reaching achievements for social progress in this century.

In those first few hours and days of uncertainty that followed the assassination of President John Kennedy, LYNDON JOHNSON moved with skill, confidence, and calm as he assumed control of the Government. He showed a steady, courageous hand to the American people and, in so doing, assured them that their Government and their Nation would persevere. For that accomplishment alone, President JOHNSON earned the deep and everlasting gratitude and respect of the American people. But more work awaited President JOHNSON than to manage the succession of executive power.

Blessed with extraordinary energy, Mr. JOHNSON acted with unprecedented skill in seeking to carry out the domestic policies which had been at the heart of the program John Kennedy and he had been elected on. Given impetus by the landslide election in 1964, President JOHNSON was able to win over heartening majorities in both Houses of Congress and amassed an historic legislative record.

Haynes Johnson of the Washington Post wrote two articles about President JOHNSON that say much about the former President. The articles appeared January 23 and 24, 1973.

Two Washington Post editorials about Mr. JOHNSON are equally interesting. The first appeared January 19, 1969, at the conclusion of the President's term; the second on January 24, 1973, 2 days after Mr. JOHNSON died.

James Reston of the New York Times wrote a perceptive column about President JOHNSON January 24, 1973.

Mr. President, I ask unanimous consent that the editorials and articles be printed in the Record at this point.

[From the New York Times, Jan. 24, 1973]

THE GLORY AND TRAGEDY OF L. B. J.

(By James Reston)

WASHINGTON, January 23.—Both the glory and the tragedy of LYNDON JOHNSON was that he believed utterly in the romantic tradition of America—in the Congress and the church, in that order; in Main Street and Wall Street, in the competitive state and in the welfare state—in all of it part of the time and some of it all of the time; all the dreams and realities and myths, from Horatio Alger to Lord Keynes, no matter how contradictory.

In other words, he was a symbol of this confusing time in America—a little nearer to the old spirit of Frederick Jackson Turner's American frontier than most of his fellow countrymen, but also a little nearer to the folks who had been left behind when the frontier and battle moved to the cities.

Mr. JOHNSON was not only sure of the greatness and supremacy of his country but of his own ability to persuade the Congress, after the death of John Kennedy, that it must pass his civil rights bill of 1964 and his equal voting rights act of 1965, and prove that the Congress was equal to the promises of the Constitution and the Bill of Rights. These are his monuments.

In Washington, he knew every card in the deck, but in the world, he didn't. He knew very little about Vietnam. He was not very comfortable with what he called the "fancypants" characters in the State Department and the Foreign Service, who knew a great deal more than he did about the philosophy and escape-hatch boundaries for guerrilla warfare in Indochina, but he had a strong personal conviction.

It was simply inconceivable to him, with his belief in America's noble purposes, as he saw them, and his belief in military power, money and machines, that any big nation, let alone, as he called it, any "two-bit nation" could carry on for very long.

He was very close to General Eisenhower. When Ike was President and Mr. JOHNSON was the Democratic majority leader of the Senate, Mr. JOHNSON never opposed him on foreign affairs. We fight at home, LYNDON said, but when we go overseas, he's my President.

And yet, one of the very odd things in this tragedy of human and political relations is that President JOHNSON, after he got into the White House, paid little or no heed to General Eisenhower's judgment on Vietnam.

Mr. Eisenhower's views about Vietnam were well known in Washington at that time. Mr. JOHNSON had heard them all years before when Vice President Nixon, Secretary of State Dulles, and the chairman of the Joint Chiefs of Staff, Admiral Radford, had argued for American intervention in Vietnam during the French crisis at Dien Bien Phu.

Ike said then, what he wrote in his book later, that the political situation in Saigon was weak and confused, and that, without strong political and popular support, American intervention was unwise.

"Willingness to fight for freedom, no matter where the battle may be," Ike wrote, "has always been characteristic of our people, but the conditions then prevailing in Indochina were such as to make unilateral intervention nothing less than sheer folly."

Mr. JOHNSON wasn't thinking about President Eisenhower, much as he admired him, when President Kennedy was assassinated. If the evidence of his own book is accurate, he wasn't even thinking about himself. Certainly he was not concentrating on changing the whole policy. He was focusing on the death of Kennedy, on carrying on Kennedy's policies, on political loyalty, as he saw it; so he plunged deeper into the war, and it destroyed him in the end.

The journalists tried to deal with all this at the time, and even at Mr. JOHNSON's death, but it is beyond us. Like Kennedy and Nixon, he is a subject for a great psychological American novel.

But Mr. JOHNSON was different. He left a broken record, triumphant at home and tragic in Vietnam, and like most Presidents, his policies will be judged by the historians.

The difference is that LYNDON JOHNSON was a great talker, one of the last of the old Southern and frontier story-tellers of the age. He didn't leave the real story in his documents at the University of Texas but in the memories of his friends, companions and political adversaries in Washington.

He loved the camera. No President collected more photographs of himself and his visitors than Mr. JOHNSON; but the tape recorder was really the instrument he should have used. For he gave himself to his visitors, and historians will never be able to sort out the glory and the tragedy unless they manage to collect the stories, listen to the tape recorders and forget the television, which was his downfall, and somehow hear his cunning contrivances, his feeling for the Congress, his love of his country, and particularly his affection for his lovely and remarkable wife, and his hard-scrabble land in Texas.

✌

[From the Washington Post, Jan. 24, 1973]

LYNDON BAINES JOHNSON

(By Haynes Johnson)

Perhaps the most poignant aspect of LYNDON JOHNSON's death is that this most public man, who was in his element when surrounded by cheering crowds, died alone, calling for help.

His wife, who had stood by him in every crisis and on whom he relied so much, was away. His daughters, grandchildren, cronies and friends whom he loved to regale with his inimitable stories were absent.

He reached for a phone in his bedroom at 3:50 p.m., we are told, and asked for the head of his Secret Service detail. The agent was in a car at the time, so another agent answered the call. Mr. JOHNSON asked him to come immediately to the bedroom without saying why.

When the agents arrived, they found the 36th President lying on the floor next to his bed, apparently dead.

His death came quietly, in lonely seclusion, after a stormy life played out so largely in public view.

It is that vibrant life that Washington is recalling today as LYNDON JOHNSON's body is borne back to the Capitol he once dominated.

While memories are fresh, and before the stories pale, let one last recollection be recorded. It is an account of the last time many of us at The Washington Post saw LYNDON JOHNSON.

He came to lunch that Tuesday, April 7, 1970. Nearly five hours later he left us all drained, fascinated, enthralled and full of questions that never could be answered or resolved

Probably none of us present that day could successfully capture or reconstruct all the moods, the language, the mobile expressions or the specific points made. It was, at the least, a virtuoso performance He was soft, sarcastic, crisp, commanding, anecdotal, colorful—and in the end confounding as always.

LYNDON JOHNSON was telling us his story, and speaking to his place in history. He was a salesman, and the ex-President came prepared with the goods in the form of stacks of papers marked Top Secret and Top Secret Sensitive. Over and over, he read from the various memoranda, letters and other documents to back up his positions.

In retrospect what was most memorable about his performance was not what he said about the war or other aspects of his presidency. It was the two sides of LYNDON JOHNSON displayed that day that made the most lasting impression.

It was a subdued, somber LYNDON JOHNSON who first appeared. He had only recently recovered from a stay in a San Antonio hospital, where he had been admitted suffering from chest pains, and his initial conversation was all about his health. He had aged dramatically.

"He came in a little after 12:30," Richard Harwood wrote immediately after the long luncheon, "looking less tall, less bulky than I had remembered him. His hair was almost completely white and was growing long in the back in the old-fashioned Southern senator style, the way Mendel Rivers wears it.

"His illness showed in his face, I thought, and from the side his skin had the yellowish-gray look you find on extremely sick men. His hands were mottled with crimson splotches; there was a scab on the back of one finger and lots of freckles, all of which brought images of an old man."

LYNDON JOHNSON's own manner reinforced the impression. He seemed tired, withdrawn, quiet, and appeared preoccupied with problems of his health. He was on a diet of 850 calories a day, he said, and was getting back his strength gradually. There had been quite a bit of pain this time, he said. His trouble really had begun the previous spring when he was working on his ranch.

He liked to get out and take his exercise, he went on slowly. One day he was laying lengths of pipe, lifting and placing them in the mud. Suddenly he became short of breath and began to experience slight pains in his chest. He remembered stopping his work without realizing quite why.

For nearly the next hour at the luncheon, he continued in the same vein. He was the elder statesman, above partisanship.

There was none of the old remembered JOHNSON fire and flash, none of the earthy anecdotes about men and events, he would not comment on Richard Nixon. He preferred to speak philosophically, it seemed, to talk about the memoirs on which he was working each day, to reflect on the higher problems of the presidency (he favored a single six-year term, and he didn't think being a lame-duck President necessarily reduced a chief executive's power).

But gradually his manner and mood changed. He began talking about Vietnam, and suddenly he was more vigorous and assertive. He folded and unfolded his napkin, began leaning forward, rocking back and forth in his chair, speaking first softly and then loudly. Now he was, clearly, LBJ.

To quote Harwood's recollections—one of many we all composed that day—"As he talked he seemed to take on another appearance. The pallor and signs of sickness went away and all of a sudden you were sitting with a vigorous, commanding, strong man whose mind was so clear, so well-organized, so quick that you instantly became aware of the power of his personality, of the ability to dominate and persuade and overwhelm."

Much of what he said that day about Vietnam has since appeared in his book. But what was most fascinating was not what he said about the war and other problems, but how he said it.

LBJ was overpowering. He thumped on the table, moved back and forth vigorously, grimaced, licked his lips, gestured with his arms, slumped back into his seat, switched from a sharp to a soft story, and kept the conversation going from the moment he sat down at the dining table until hours later when his wife called The Post and sent in a note reminding him he should come home and rest.

As he reminisced, going back into his childhood and then on through his entire political career, he became more colloquial and more Texan. His Daddy used to whip him with a razor strap, he said, and "It hurt him more than it hurt me. But that's the kind of thing you have to do in a family." In a way, it was the same thing as being President: there were certain things you had to do that were unpopular, but you did them for the public benefit.

His language, and phrases, were picturesque:

"So I took a cold belly buster . . ."

"Anyone who's smart enought to pour water from a boot . . ."

"And Dick Russell said, "I've been to the duck blind with the man. I know him. I may not agree with him on everything, but he's a good man, he cares for the people, and he'll try to do what's right (referring to his plans to nominate his friend, Judge Homer Thornberry of Texas, to the Supreme Court)."

"Those Laotians can't stop anybody. They just stand around throwing water at each other . . ."

"MacArthur pinned a medal on me for heroism. It looks good on my chest"—here, he fingered the Silver Star citation in his coat lapel—"but it's a good thing they couldn't see what that flight did to my pants."

"Now, I don't want you good people to have a heart attack here at this good table eating this good food. And if any of you has heart trouble, you better take nitro-gylcerine now, because the first person to urge me to halt the bombing was Walt Rostow . . ."

He mentioned his wife, Lady Bird, and said, "She always knew how to handle me," Then he told how he had decided, in advance of the 1964 Democratic convention, that he was going to announce publicly that he would not be a candidate that year. But Bird, he said talked him out of it. She told him, she knew he would like to leave the White House, but that he would miss being where things were happening, and where he had a chance to accomplish everything he had worked for in 30 years of politics.

But that wasn't why he should run, he said she told him. "It would make it seem as though you were running away. Your friends would hang their heads in shame, your enemies would dance and rejoice."

He recalled a story from his early days as a young Texas congressman, Elliott Roosevelt, the President's son, came to him on behalf of electrical power interests in Texas, he said. This was at a time when LBJ was fighting the power companies there.

"I always liked Elliott," he said. "He was a good boy. But they'd got to him, and so he came down there to see me and asked me to ease up on them.

"He said he had talked with his Daddy and his Daddy wanted him to tell me that he agreed. So I said, 'All right, I'll do that, Elliott. But before I do, I want you to do one thing for me, I want you to go back to your Daddy and tell him to write me a letter, in his own hand, saying what he wants, and then sign it.' Well, I could see Elliott wasn't expecting that, I'd kind of roughed him up. So he said, 'Why do you want father to write you a letter? I've already seen him, and he wants you to do this.'

"And I told him, 'Well, Elliott, it's this way: when I do what your Daddy wants and I come back to Texas they're going to run me out of the state. Now the nearest border is 150 miles away and that's over the bridge to Mexico. And I figure I can get to that bridge before they get me, and when I'm half way over, and on the Mexican side, I want to be able to turn around and stop and hold up that letter showing the signature of Franklin Delano Roosevelt so everyone can read it. Like this'."

He held up an imaginary piece of paper, relishing the role he was playing and the laughter it inspired.

LBJ was full of such performances. He acted out various roles. He mimicked people: Clark Clifford sitting up straight and dignified like this (he sat up very straight and very solemnly in his chair and folded his arms over his chest); Hubert Humphrey and HHH's reaction to the news LBJ was going to renounce the presidency in 1968: "I told him not to go off to Mexico, but I guess he didn't believe me." LBJ gave a "hee-hee-hee-hee-hee" rendition to show how silly Humphrey thought the idea.

Finally, after nearly five hours, Lady Bird's note was sent into the dining room asking him to come home, LYNDON JOHNSON became serious. "I want you to know," he said, "no matter how we differ about things, I feel I am at the table of friends, and I want to thank you for letting me come and visit with you."

Here he was, he went on, in the twilight of his years, among good friends. He had one more story to tell. It was one Sam Rayburn used to tell about a small Texas town.

Once, when Rayburn was just beginning as a politician, everyone important in that town had turned him down when he was looking for a place to spend the night—the banker, the newspaper editor, the judge. Finally a little old blacksmith said he would be glad to take Rayburn in for the night. Years later, after Rayburn had become famous and powerful, he came back to that town. Everyone clamored for him, the banker, the newspaper editor, the judge. They all wanted the honor of his staying with them.

No, Rayburn told each to his face, he didn't want to stay with them. But was that little old blacksmith still there. Yes, he was. Bring him to me, Rayburn commanded. When the blacksmith came, Rayburn told him: Jeeter, I'd like to spend the night at your house if you'll have me." The blacksmith did, and kept Rayburn up all night talking. When Rayburn said he had to go to sleep, for he had a busy day ahead of him, tears welled up in the blacksmith's eyes.

"Mr. Sam, I'd just like to talk to you all night."

And that, Lyndon Baines Johnson said, was the way he felt about his friends at The Post.

There were some bitter-end Johnson critics among those of us around that dining table, but when LBJ stood up to begin shaking each person's hand to say good-bye we all spontaneously burst into applause. Some of us had tears in our eyes.

We thought we might never see his likes again. And perhaps we were right.

ↄ⸾

[From an editorial in the Washington Post, Jan. 19, 1969]

Lyndon Johnson's Presidency

They have not been dull, the Johnson years, from the first crisis in Panama to Santo Domingo and South Vietnam, from the wild campaign of 1964 to the triumphs in Congress, the protests on the campus, the riots in the cities and the sudden abdication in 1968. And they have not been unproductive, in their rich yield of civil rights and social welfare legislation. More than anything, perhaps, they have been sad, in the sense that Franklin D. Roosevelt thought of Lincoln as a "sad man because he couldn't get it all at once—and nobody can."

Lyndon Johnson tried, you have to give him that. He brought more raw force and endless energy and craving for accomplishment to the office of President than anyone could ask. Where he succeeded, he succeeded big, in education and civil rights and all the rest. And while it can be said that he also failed big—by not being able to win his way in the war in his time, and by having to acknowledge such a division in the country that he could only carry on in his final year by foreswearing his candidacy for another term—not the least of his legacies to President Nixon is what he himself did to turn the war around and head it in the direction of a gradual American disengagement and a political settlement. Serious peace talking is to begin in Paris this coming week not so much because Lyndon Johnson halted the bombing of North Vietnam in October but because he stared down his generals last March and made the much more difficult decision to refuse them the massive reinforcement of American troops that they were asking for.

If this seems as somewhat negative legacy, there are more than enough that are positive. The list of legislative accomplishments runs on and on from the 1964 Civil Rights Act to rent supplements, voting rights, model cities, medicare, control of water pollution, immigration reform, job training, educational aid. And while some of this was the finishing of unfinished business, well begun his time, some of it broke new ground.

A landmark aid to education act, for elementary and secondary schools, cracked a constitutional and political impasse over church-school relationships, and it was brought into being not by past momentum or by parliamentary manipulation, but through the innovation and sheeer determination of the President. . . .

It is often said of Mr. Johnson that his trouble came from some incapacity to inspire, and thus to lead. He would say, on the contrary, that he was unjustly victimized by Easterners and intellectuals and liberals and the Kennedy people who scorned him for his regionalism and his roughness, his table manners and the twang of his voice. There is truth to both, and also irony, because the sad thing is that his origins are the best thing about him, the thing he has going for him whenever he is himself, and he didn't know it. Or maybe he just wasn't confident enough about it.

Whatever it was, he tried to run the country in the way he ran the United States Senate and it did not work. He wheedled and cajoled and high-pressured and oversold, and seemed to be counting the legislation passed not so much for its contents as its bulk, and this wasn't what people were concerned about. They were worrying about casualty figures and about how the combat troops got to Vietnam in the first place and how they got involved in combat operations when the Secretaries of State and Defense had said they weren't supposed to; they were worrying about how it was all going to end and what it was doing to the country and whether it was worth it, and by the time the Administration got around to leveling a little more on the subject it was too late, because the confidence was gone.

This isn't the whole story by any means but it was a big part of the story of how Lyndon Johnson lost his majority: If he was, like Lincoln, a sad man, he didn't show it and he didn't let it slow him; he was forever driving. He wanted nothing more than to succeed—and he did, in many, many ways. But he wanted support for the war and money for a bigger antipoverty effort and safety in the streets and housing for the poor and education for all our children and medical care for all of the elderly and the love and respect of all the elderly people, and it wouldn't stretch. He wanted to get it all at once and Roosevelt was right: nobody can.

ↄ⸾

[Editorial From the Washington Post, Jan. 24, 1973]

Lyndon Baines Johnson

The public lifetime of Lyndon Baines Johnson spanned almost four decades. It was a period marked not just by the development of certain powerful currents in American thought, but also by an eventual reappraisal of where those currents had led. Thus, much which had been considered desirable, necessary and even holy in Mr. Johnson's political youth had fallen into disrepute by the time that he left office. "Internationalism" had come to be known as "interventionism" by many, its painful and costly effects haunting the nation in a seemingly unendable war. And the vital and generous impulses that had animated Mr. Johnson's commitment to domestic legislation from the New Deal through the Great Society had come to be seen by many as obsolete and outworn habits of mind which caused as many troubles as they cured. At the airport sendoff that January day in 1969, when Lyndon B. Johnson's homebound plane vanished into the clouds, his longtime friends and colleagues were left with more than an eerie feeling of the suddenness and totality with which power is relinquished in this country. The summary departure of this man who had been the larger-than life center of ambition and authority in government for five years, also seemed symbolically to end a self-contained chapter in the nation's political development.

It was an era characterized both domestically and in foreign policy terms by an assumption of responsibility—national responsibility—for the welfare of the poor, the rights of the mistreated, the fairness of the way in which we distribute our wealth and the general well-being and stability of countries all over the world. Of Mr. Johnson's participation in all this—as a Congressman, Senator, Vice President and President—it must be said that his impact was so profound that there is hardly a case in which the nation was either blessed or victimized by this particular 20th century passion for responsibility for which LYNDON JOHNSON himself was not largely responsible. Like indifferent lovers of fractious offspring, a nation can often taken things for granted or seem only to notice when it has been wronged. The death of Mr. JOHNSON may serve momentarily to pull us back from these perspectives, to remind us that much which we now expect from our government and our society as a matter of course—black voting rights, care for our elderly and our ill—came to us very recently and largely by courtesy of LYNDON JOHNSON.

The simple, inescapable fact is that he cared—and that it showed. Being in all ways larger than life-sized, he cared about a lot of things; his own political fortunes, his image, and his place in history for of course he was vain. But he was consistent; all of his appetites were king-sized. So he cared about people with the same enormous intensity. In fact, a fair case can be made that one set of appetites fed on the other; he struggled and wheedled and hammered and cajoled for political power because he yearned powerfully to do great and good things and that is what he wanted the power for.

This was at once the strength and the weakness of LYNDON JOHNSON, for while this tremendous force was more often than not irresistible over the years, both as Senate Majority Leader and President, it was, like everything about the man, very often excessive. It could bend the political process to his will, and to good effect. But it could also bear down too hard, so that the system cracked under his weight. A master at the instrumentality of events, he could use a Selma or an assassination to lever a civil rights law or a gun control bill through Congress. But he could also use a minor gunboat skirmish in the Gulf of Tonkin to produce a resolution from Congress giving overwhelming support to a war effort whose true nature was never revealed in terms which could be expected to prepare either the Congress or the public for the sacrifice that both would later be expected to accept.

Neither LYNDON JOHNSON's memory nor his place in history, we would hope, is going to turn entirely, or even primarily on the war that grew out of that resolution; for Vietnam there is blame enough for all concerned, over four administrations and a good number of Congresses. Confined and carried along by earlier commitments, counselled by the men recruited by his predecessors, unchecked by Congress, Mr. JOHNSON plunged in, overstating, over-promising, over-hoping, over-reaching. But if his time in office marked the big Vietnam escalation, it also will be remembered for the fact that he, by implication and by painfully difficult decision, moved toward the end of his term to acknowledge a great miscalculation—widely shared in, let it be said—which is not something incumbent Presidents are given to doing. Reluctantly, grudgingly, but effectively, he turned the war effort around, abandoning "graduated response" as the method of choice, and bequeathed to his successor a greater opportunity than he himself inherited to move toward disengagement and a re-definition of the mission in realistic terms.

When Harry Truman died a few weeks ago at the age of 88, he died the beneficiary of a gift LYNDON JOHNSON was not to receive: 20 years had passed since the em-

battled and much maligned Mr. Truman had held office so that time and change and hindsight vastly altered the view people had of him. Mr. JOHNSON was never lucky in this regard. His each and every achievement from his Senate years on seemed to be followed or accompanied by some series of events that spoiled the glory of the moment. Still, we do not share the notion, now being advanced (sometimes with bitterness) of how unfair it was that he rarely received the recognition he deserved in his lifetime for the good and also great things he did—or that the criticism of his handling of the war unfairly overshadowed all the rest. He would, we suspect, have a wryly humorous view of all this—much as he craved to be well-loved and well-remembered—because he was too shrewd, not to say cynical a student of human and political nature not to have been amused by these efforts by those who served him badly from time to time to revise the record in his (and their) favor. LYNDON JOHNSON must have known that he did not need to be helped into history.

⚓

[From the Washington Post, Jan. 23, 1973]

JOHNSON PERSONIFIED A NATION'S TRAUMA

(By Haynes Johnson)

LYNDON JOHNSON once said he didn't want everyone to love him, as his enemies often said, he merely wanted them to like him. It was part of his tragedy that he wound up being reviled as no leader since Lincoln. No President ever fell so swiftly from so high a pinnacle.

There had been a time, in the mid 1960s, when history seemed to have set LYNDON JOHNSON on a different course. He had won what was up to that time the greatest political victory in American history. All the old problems on the American agenda—race and regionalism, poverty and public education, medical care and housing—suddenly seemed capable of resolution. The country was unified. Blacks and whites joined hands and marched together. There were no riots, no rancor, no revolution, no dissenters. If it was not a Great Society that was being fashioned, in the typically grandiloquent JOHNSON phrase, at least it promised to be a better one. It was, the wise men said, the beginning of the Johnson Era. They found a good omen in a Southerner leading the nation toward a new day of reconciliation.

Mr. JOHNSON himself had pronounced the theme. 'Come," he said, borrowing from the Bible and the Book of Isaiah, "let us reason together."

When he left office only a few short years later the nation had been cleft in two. LYNDON JOHNSON, the conciliator, the man of consensus, the compleat politician, presided over a nation more deeply divided than at any time since the Civil War. At home, there were riots and the beginnings of a revolution in the streets. Abroad, America was embroiled in the most unpopular war in her history. And Mr. JOHNSON, a man who craved affection and attention, was unable to travel freely in his country without hearing the chant, "Hey, hey, LBJ, how many kids did you kill today?"

Mr. JOHNSON personified the national trauma. He was blamed as both architect and executioner of tragedy. Some Negroes, whose cause he espoused more vigorously than any other President, felt he had abandoned them. The South, from whose soil he sprung, rejected him. The students, whose hearts he wanted more than any group, turned on him as a Judas who took them into "Johnson's war." The conservatives found him too radical, too spend-thrift, the liberals too easily diverted from domestic priorities, too quick to pervert what they presumed to be the ideals of John F. Kennedy.

CERTAIN DISADVANTAGES

From hardly a corner of the country was there a kind word for him.

Had he been a Kennedy he might have chosen a line from Shakespeare to express his lament. LYNDON JOHNSON's response came out of a different milieu.

He blustered, he bellowed, he lashed out at all whom he felt had let him down along the way. The press. The politicians. The Negroes. The South. The Democrats. The American people themselves. Then, in a softer tone, he expressed a different thought.

It was always clear to him, he said after leaving office, that he had "certain disadvantages" that affected his ability to lead the nation: his upbringing, his limited educational advantages, his place of birth, his accent and "the prejudices that exist." He had, he said, a general inability to stimulate, inspire and unite all the people of the country, which I think is an essential function of the presidency."

LYNDON JOHNSON added:

"Now I have never believed that I was the man to do that particular job."

And again:

"I always felt that every job that I had was really too big for me."

As he should have expected, those remarks brought further abuse. To the end, he was not believed.

CONTRADICTORY, COMPLEX, CONFOUNDING

LYNDON JOHNSON, in the popular picture, partly self-drawn, partly cruel caricature, was a monumental egotist with an unbridled passion for power and place. Yet it is also possible to believe he was something else—a man of massive talent, and equally massive insecurities. Looking back on it now, everything he did seemed to fit the pattern.

LYNDON JOHNSON didn't want just a good society, in the term cast by Walter Lippmann in the 1930's; he wanted a *great* society. He did not want to equal his mentor, Franklin Roosevelt; he wanted to eclipse him. He didn't want just to help rebuild Southeast Asia; he wanted to transform it into a grander Europe.

He was contradictory, complex, confounding. He could be cruel and vindictive, kind, and thoughtful. He could weep in public—and did on the day Roosevelt died. He could be vulgar, petty, scheming, conspiratorial—and compassionate and generous. No one who saw him close up could ever forget him.

Every politician wears many faces, probably none more than LBJ. The very initials were so much a mark of the man. The LBJ Ranch, Lady Bird Johnson, Lynda Bird Johnson, Luci Baines Johnson. He even named one of his dogs Little Beagle Johnson.

It was proof, if any more were needed, that the man needed to leave his mark. Some saw it as a sinister manifestation of a deeper psychological problem: He was so vainglorious, so absorbed in himself, it was said, that he could not distinguish issues clearly. Everything came through colored by the complexities of his personality.

Perhaps. Certainly, he was memorable—and bewildering.

CONTRASTING STYLES

That first impression, somewhere in the 1950s, remains indelible. It was a political rally in Washington, dreary in its way, as they all are. All the war horses of the Democrats had turned out: Harry Truman, the former President; Sam Rayburn, "Mister Sam," tough, balding, flinty, somewhat inscrutable Speaker of the House; Averell Harriman, the ambassador who wanted to become President. There were others who wanted to be President, senators all of them—Hubert Humphrey of Minnesota, Stuart Symington of Missouri, John Kennedy of Massachusetts. Then there was LBJ.

He took the podium, leaned forward, and launched into a loud, stem-winding stump speech. He flailed his arms. He pounded his lectern. He shouted until he was hoarse. He leaned forward to watch the crowd. You could see the veins bulging out on his neck. No one was surprised; that was the way the rangy majority leader regaled the faithful in Texas.

Years later, another JOHNSON and another speech. It was his first address to Congress as President. Soft, subdued, almost soulful. Seeing him, it seemed impossible to remember him as ever being anything other than the quiet, fatherly figure he presented that day.

Throughout his presidency those same mercurial glimpses could be seen. They were illuminating flashes between the private JOHNSON and the public one.

His first trip as President was one of those moments. For months after the Kennedy assassination Mr. JOHNSON had remained in the White House, waiting out the transition period between mourning and action. Then, in the early spring of 1964, he took to the country.

He was a force unleashed. Restless, searching, he charged into crowds, grasping hands and beaming at the squeals and screams his presence elicited while his Secret Service men stood by in despair. He moved across the land, from town to city to state, declaring war on poverty and promising to banish it from the nation. Finally, late in the day his helicopter arrived in Inez, Ky., a hamlet tucked away in the Appalachians.

By then, his wife was exhausted. She sat in the car, holding a bouquet of roses, grateful for a moment's respite while her husband charged through the crowds. As he walked forward, shaking hands left and right, he noticed his wife wasn't at his side.

"Where's Bird?" he said in a low tone to a Secret Service agent at his side.

"She's behind us in the limousine, Mr. President."

"Tell her to get out here and walk with me," the President said, still in the same low tone, still moving forward shaking hands.

"She's very tired, Mr. President," the agent began.

"Get Bird out here and tell her I want her to walk with me," the President snapped.

Minutes later, his wife joined him, smiling faintly, still carrying her roses.

LYNDON JOHNSON could be that way.

He also could humiliate some of his closest aides. More than once in the presence of reporters or others in his Oval Office he ridiculed such men as Jack Valenti, his self-effacing assistant.

TEXAS HYPERBOLE

Some of those sessions with Mr. JOHNSON created other lasting impressions. There was the press briefing immediately following the establishment of orders in Santo Domingo. Mr. JOHNSON had dispatched American forces in great numbers to put down what he said was a Communist threat to that small Caribbean island in May, 1965. In the process, he came under sharp criticism for his motives and his actions.

Before the television cameras, he was measured and judicious. In his own office, with no cameras and only reporters present, he was something else.

He snapped his fingers in reporter's faces, his eyes flashing. He pulled what he said were classified documents from his pockets, and read snatches of them to prove his point He pounded the desk. He was bellicose He said things that later proved to be untrue. (It was a case, his aides always explained, of his penchant for "Texas hyperbole.")

It was also a foretaste of later actions that were to have more serious consequences. Mr. JOHNSON, under criticism, reacted with increasing defensiveness. He seemed unable to accept criticism. Privately, and sometimes publicly, he made disparaging remarks about those who opposed him, including some who had been his respected colleagues for years. In time, he lost some of his most valuable counselors and supporters.

As the Vietnam war turned into something no one wanted, a true land war in Asia, and as dissent began to rise at home about American priorities and actions, Mr. JOHNSON reacted with more and more truculence.

It's only a matter of speculation, but many a veteran LBJ observer in Washington came to believe that part of the seeds of Mr. JOHNSON's final fall were sown in the 1964 campaign. It was seductive. He won so great a victory—even greater than the Roosevelt landslide of 1936—that few men would have been able to keep a perspective about their place in the public heart.

Whatever the analysis, one thing was clear. The American people were not following their President. A substantial portion of the public turned on him with a vehemence beyond recollection. An overwhelming majority wanted a change. In 1968, in that most confounding and devasting year in our political history they got it.

MAINTAINED HIS HOLD

To the end, Mr. JOHNSON maintained his hold, if not his power, over the American people. In the most surprising development of that political year, he announced he was withdrawing from consideration as a presidential candidate. His stunning "shall not seek and I will not accept" his party's nomination signaled the finish to his presidency. Before he left office, he set in motion the process of disengagement and ultimate withdrawal from Vietnam that was pursued by his successor, Richard Nixon.

Of LYNDON JOHNSON it can be said that he was a victim of himself—of his excesses, of his flamboyance, of his manner and style, of his penchant for secrecy and manipulation. The public believed him to be a Machiavellian politician, the master of the deal, the biggest political operator of them all.

Yet in a larger sense he was also a victim of circumstances over which he had no control—of the aura of the assassinated young and elegant President, of the resentment of those who were left waiting for the next Kennedy restoration, of prejudice toward Southerners, of the policies of the past that he did not fashion.

History may judge him differently, and more kindly. At the least, he will be regarded as one of the most tragic Presidents.

It may well be that his finest moment came in that time of national tragedy as he assumed the presidency. When the nation was shocked, uncertain, and fearful after John F. Kennedy's assassination, LYNDON JOHNSON was cool, assured, capable. He provided a steady hand as he carried out the difficult process of picking up the threads of government. The way in which he gathered together the various elements was reassuring. He was a model of stability.

Mr. JOHNSON also showed a personal brand of courage then. On that November day when John F. Kennedy was buried on the slopes of Arlington amid a gathering of kings, princes and prime ministers, the President's Secret Service agents urged him not to march in the public procession. They were afraid of another mad assassin's attempt. Mr. JOHNSON brushed the security arguments aside.

"I would rather lose my life than be afraid to risk it," he said.

He walked at the head of the procession from the White House to St. Matthew's Cathedral.

A FEELING FOR PROBLEMS

Mr. JOHNSON, in those early days, led a united nation. Within two years, he was facing the personal attacks that increased in emotion and venom for the remainder of his presidency.

For all the bitterness his presence engendered, for all the anger and outrage that swirled around his time in office, it was easy to overlook other traits in the man. He was, as it was said, melodramatic; in the sneering term, he was a cornball. But he did have a feeling for American problems, for poverty, for problems of the disinherited and disadvantaged, for those who never knew the comforts of society or advantages of a fine education.

During his presidential campaign, he used to draw rude snickers from some when he would say, in his flagrant manner, that he knew something about poverty. He knew what it was to shine shoes and work for a dollar a day. He knew what it was to be hungry.

It seemed incongruous. The big Texan, strong, powerful, a multi-millionaire who lived at the peak and created the image of some potentate of old, surrounded by servants (and some thought sycophants), was anything but a man out of poverty. But he was.

LYNDON JOHNSON had come up the hard way. He did know what it meant to be poor and hungry. The hill country of Texas left its lasting stamp. It was desolate, barren country, a place of rocks and hills and scrub grass and small, gnarled trees, not rich ranch country.

Johnson City, in the valley of the Pedernales River, was a small sleepy, impoverished town. A few buildings, a few stores, a bank, a barber shop—that was all. Dusty and drab.

By the time he was 15, LYNDON JOHNSON began working for a road gang at a dollar a day. His biographers—the real biographers, not the pamphleteers and propagandists who wrote such one-sided accounts of him—have one intriguing period of his life to unravel. When he was still in his teens, LYNDON JOHNSON took to the highways.

EVENTS THAT SHAPED HIM

His formal campaign material only noted that he worked his way west to California by taking odd jobs. He was an elevator operator, a car washer, a handyman in a cafe. Then he worked his was back to Texas. What happened to him on those journeys, what experiences colored his outlook, no one knows. He finally decided, though, as he once recalled, "that there was something to this idea of higher education"; then he hitchiked to San Marcos, Tex., enrolled in Southwest State Teachers College and became a student.

He continued to work his way through school—as janitor at the school, door-to-door hosiery salesman, secretary to the college president.

Even so, he was forced to drop out of school for a year because he didn't have enough money to pay his tuition.

Those events shaped LYNDON JOHNSON in ways that were little understood, or appreciated, later when he became the quintessence of the powerful politician.

Although his critics belittled his style, his accent, his fragrant and folksy expressions (we were going to "nail the coonskin to the wall" in Vietnam), he said; "Get on your horses and get me a plan!" he recalled saying to his Secretary of State, LYNDON JOHNSON was more than a bombastic Texas stereotype. He sensed personal problems, understood and tried to alleviate them.

AN AMERICAN PRIMITIVE

By the time his moment on the stage was passing, Mr. JOHNSON bore the marks of the tumultuous period. He was older, slower, grayer, more subdued. That expressively mobile face, all long lines and creases, wore a somber expression. Later, he would reminisce in a melancholy vein about the ordeal of the presidency—and particularly his personal ordeal over Vietnam.

"The real horror was to be sleeping soundly about 3:30 or 4 or 5 o'clock in the morning and have the telephone ring and the operator say, 'Sorry to wake you, Mr. President.' There's just a second between the time the operator got Mr. (Walt) Rostow in the Situation Room, or Mr. (McGeorge) Bundy in the Situation Room, or maybe Secretary (Dean) Rusk or Secretary (Robert) McNamara, Secretary (Clark) Clifford.

"And we went through the horrors of hell that 30 seconds or minute or two minutes. Had we hit a Russian ship? Had an accident occurred? We have another *Pueblo?* Someone made a mistake—were we at war?"

That was part of Mr. JOHNSON's problems—and part, at least, was of his own making. Not all of the other problems could be laid at his feet.

It was his fate to preside at a time when the old values were changing, when new forces were rising, when society and government were under severe challenge. It was his fate, too, to preside when the old voice of the progressive or populist no longer was adequate to the moment.

He spoke as an American primitive, and left a legacy as an American original. He was both great and gross, full of promise and imperfections. He did more than the country realized or appreciated, and accomplished less than his own dreams.

In that, LYNDON JOHNSON was like America herself.

Hon. Hubert H. Humphrey
OF MINNESOTA

Mr. President, we have observed in the press an outpouring of meaningful comment on the life and legacy of our remarkable former President, LYNDON B. JOHNSON.

I ask unanimous consent that a selection of recent articles and editorials, including the transcript of a CBS news special, be printed in the Record.

I hope that when the bound volume of tributes to President JOHNSON is printed it will be possible and proper that these editorial reflections be included.

[From the Minneapolis Tribune, Jan. 23, 1973]

LYNDON B. JOHNSON

An era died yesterday with LYNDON BAINES JOHNSON. It was already coming to an end in March 1968 when, as president, he said he would not run for re-election. Perhaps, Mr. JOHNSON knew, although he did not admit, that under his presidency the nation had done itself incalculable damage by sliding deep into the Indochina quagmire. "What irony, what tragedy," writes David Halberstam, "for a man who had so little taste for the military . . . who never wanted this particular little war, who had a sense of foreboding about what it might do to his domestic dreams, but could not pull back from what he saw as the forces of history."

To define the era that ended, one need only think back on those who preceded and followed LYNDON JOHNSON in office, and on what he did and failed to do.

He was a political child of Franklin Roosevelt's New Deal. In Congress then and during the Truman years he saw the rise of America to its predominant world role and the rise, too, of federal concern for the black, the poor and the old. Under Dwight Eisenhower he was leader of the loyal opposition in the Senate, cautioning the president against intervention to forestall French defeat in Indochina. As John Kennedy's vice-president, he was never quite at ease among the energetic intellectuals brought into the White House, but he shared the can-do philosophy of the thousand days. He lived to see Richard Nixon take more than four years to end "JOHNSON's war"; to see a revolution in American relations with Russia and China; to see, sadly, a start made in undercutting Mr. JOHNSON's finest achievements.

Every president of the last 40 years has earned a place in history by acts of leadership, Mr. JOHNSON's place is assured by his initiative in social reform. Not only did he say what needed to be done, but—equally important—he had the support and the know-how to push his programs through Congress.

In May 1964 he told students at the University of Michigan: "For in your time we have the opportunity to move not only toward the rich society and the powerful society, but upward to the Great Society . . . It demands an end to poverty and racial injustice, to which we are totally committed in our time. But that is just the beginning."

One thinks of Medicare, the Voting Rights Act, of legislation for an array of urban programs, of the expanded activities of Health, Education, and Welfare. Some of those ideas were too hastily conceived, and some created unrealistic expectations of early success. But they created a needed momentum of social concern backed by a commitment of resources. It is a commitment that neither

Mr. JOHNSON nor, we believe, most Americans would want to see eroded by the executive-branch reaction now in the offing.

Ironically, it is another kind of commitment that marred the Johnson record. He carried the stigma of Vietnam, although he was not the president who first involved Americans in the war. And although he was the president who first said of that involvement, Enough, it is he who rightly was charged with letting American participation grow to devastating proportions.

What died with LYNDON JOHNSON, and maybe before, was the American belief that this country must go any place to defend any ally at any price. In its place has grown the more prudent belief in limitations of American power to which President Nixon alluded Saturday. That should not mean a shirking of international responsibility, only an admission that this country alone cannot act as global guardian.

What grew with LYNDON JOHNSON was the American belief in responsibilities at home. Not all his visions of the Great Society fully materialized, but a surprising number did. As he said in the 1964 Michigan speech, "But that is just the beginning." It is a good way to remember LYNDON JOHNSON.

❧

[From the Minneapolis Star, Jan. 23, 1973]

LYNDON BAINES JOHNSON

So strong was LYNDON B. JOHNSON's personality that even though four years have passed since he left the White House, we still have not been able to perceive clearly his accomplishments. And yet this is natural enough, for JOHNSON was one of those presidents whose personal life and public acts were so interwoven that neither could be understood without the other.

He was part of a pattern that began with Jackson and may very well be ended now: The home-spun, up-from-the-soil politician that was a product of the American frontier. Out of this, each in his own way, came presidents like Lincoln and Truman and below the presidential level scores of senators and congressmen. This was, in wide outline, the Populist tradition, and it is close to Minnesota's own tradition.

It was no accident that the lives of LYNDON JOHNSON and Hubert Humphrey are so closely intertwined.

They represent, as did Harry Truman, the stump-speaking, hand-shaking, down-to-earth, folksy style. In his lifetime this was often ridiculed as "cornpone" but even when JOHNSON was crushed with disappointment and frustration he was never aloof. He was a man of the people and, divided though the country became, he was a man for the people. That was why he found it so hard to understand the miasmic forces and hatred that the war unleashed.

From what perspective we now have it is both significant and ironic that he died as the war was finally ending, no longer "his war" but Richard Nixon's. It is difficult to see now how history will interpret the war he so enlarged in a more benign light, though in the fullness of time it may find some aspects less unforgiveable than we see them now. What is clear is that the war all but destroyed the Great Society. That was not only his, but the nation's tragedy.

But JOHNSON, more Western than Southern although still a man of the South, leaves a magnificent civil rights record, and already in short retrospect the framework of

a progressive and humane domestic program. That he was carrying out the last stages of the Roosevelt revolution is no blemish on that record. He was the epitome of that great surge of humanitarianism. He could do no other.

He understood deep in his soul what was to stand weak in the dust, beset by economic forces over which one has no control. It is another historical irony that he died as President Nixon was seeking to change the fundamental policy putting aside as paternalism the kind of government JOHNSON had felt in his bones was right.

It may be that Nixon will demonstrate that New Deal "big government" is not the solution any more. In JOHNSON's time the spirit, if not always the form, of New Deal, Fair Deal, New Frontier and Great Society government seemed the only answer.

That JOHNSON, whose style was as open as the small town neighborhood, was under the pressure of adversity an angry, at times uncouth and downright mean man, can be forgiven now. He agonized over his mistakes. He was only too human, and the epitaph he deserves is his conviction "that we shall overcome" if we but gather and reason together.

❧

[From the St. Paul (Minn.) Dispatch, Jan. 27, 1973]

LYNDON BAINES JOHNSON

A few weeks ago LYNDON BAINES JOHNSON, the 36th President of these United States, sat in Austin, Texas, at a symposium and listened as old faces and names and some new figures in the struggle for decent civil and human rights in this country, were seen and heard on a podium set up in the Johnson Memorial Library.

Against his physician's admonitions he made a moving speech asking his audience to shake themselves loose from their lethargy and start anew a crusade against race discrimination and bigotry in this country.

When opposing black groups triggered by ultra-militants, some strident voices tried to take over the conference and an open dispute arose, Johnson again rose to his feet and made an impassioned speech in which he urged the assembled group to quit the quarreling, to sit down and reason out a course of strategy, and action to get the human rights movement back on track. While he talked he had to use nitro-glycerine tablets to keep from collapsing—all in the interest of trying to convince leaders that fragmentation and division were suicidal to solid progress and offered no real return in progress.

LYNDON BAINES JOHNSON died the other day. We believe that he never had fully recovered from his physical and emotional effort at Austin at the civil rights symposium. In a large sense, he became a martyr with Martin Luther King, John and Robert Kennedy, to the cause of human rights and decency for all American people.

Just as he picked up Dr. King's cry for peace and victory over bigotry, "We shall Overcome," he died that all people should enjoy the freedom promised by the Bill of Rights. LYNDON JOHNSON knew his days were numbered unless he was very careful about his health, but he felt he had a contribution to make and he felt he had to rally once again those who had led the battle for decency in the Civil Rights Bill, the Voting Rights and other legislation needed to give a large percentage of this nation's population its just rights. He dared to risk his life to do this and Monday he made the Supreme Sacrifice because of what he felt was his duty.

LYNDON BAINES JOHNSON looms larger and larger in our minds as he leaves us. We stand bereft—comforted, however, because there was a man who dared move over with a black man and join him in proclaiming, "We Shall Overcome."

[From the St. Paul (Minn.) Dispatch, Jan. 23, 1973]

LYNDON B. JOHNSON

And then came Vietnam, violent dissent and personal defeat and tragedy. That is about the essence of what could have been a presidential career that would have been viewed by historians as grandly humanitarian and unqualifiedly great.

Without the war LYNDON JOHNSON, who died Monday at the age of 64, would have been given instant recognition as one of our great presidents. The activist southerner bulling through the Civil Rights Act of 1964 would, in itself, have given some guarantee of that.

What will be remembered most by this generation, though, was his widening escalation of the Vietnam war which had, at its worst under him, about a half-million fighting men involved in bloody conflict.

He got us into a major war there through one device or another, superbly confident of his mission and convinced of its rightness. In spite of the outburst of public praise and mourning Monday from friend and seeming foe, it will not be easy to arrive at the easy assessments so predictable at such a time. The Vietnam war was his tragedy and downfall.

He was a man. He had faults. He could be cruel. He could be generous. He was devious. He had a jovial openness. He did what he thought was right but understood and used the force of political clout as few before him.

He became the complete man in retirement, an elder statesman in the best sense of the term. He stayed out of the limelight he had treasured. He developed a mellowness that surprised those who had known him. He did not second guess or whine. We had all wished him a longer, peaceful retirement.

Although there were warnings, his death seemed to surprise us and to come far too soon. Whatever his faults, he was unique and a man who loved his country. His presence will be missed and he will not be forgotten.

[From the Christian Science Monitor, Jan. 24, 1973]

LYNDON BAINES JOHNSON

LYNDON JOHNSON's place in American history is presently obscured by the oppressive cloud of the war he allowed to get big during his presidency and which he was unable to finish one way or another. Yet someday that war will go away and its memory will fade. When that time comes the other LYNDON JOHNSON, who tried so very hard to make his country a better place for all its people, will take over as the more lasting memory of a president who was big of heart and enormous of ambition.

Much of what that other JOHNSON tried to do is under attack right now. The Johnson method is called "throwing money at problems." In the current wisdom that isn't the way to solve problems. Richard Nixon is trying to undo much of what LYNDON JOHNSON launched. And, as such things are perceived today, much of it may have to be reworked and begun again.

The flaw in JOHNSON's work was that he tried to do more in one presidency than any one man could do in the span allotted to him in the White House. Yet, while it was a mistake to overdo, it was also the kind of mistake that springs from goodness and bigness of heart.

LYNDON JOHNSON had a dream. It was the new-old dream of frontier America, a dream of a society in which men are truly equal in opportunity and in dignity. In that dream all Americans—old or young, rich or poor, white or black, Protestant, Catholic, Jew or Muslim—begin the "pursuit of happiness" from the starting line.

To that end LYNDON JOHNSON bullied, cajoled, and maneuvered the Congress into passing the biggest quantity of social legislation since the Roosevelt New Deal, perhaps the biggest quantity attempted in any modern country in such a short span of time. It included civil and voting rights for all, low-cost housing for the poor, rent and welfare for the still poorer and underpriviledged, better education for all, an end to slums in the cities, clean air and clean water, free health services for the elderly.

Had he been satisfied just to achieve that gargantuan program of physical and spiritual renewal for America and the American people he could have gone down in history as one of the truly great presidents. All that he dreamed of doing will someday be done by other men, if at a slower pace. But he tried to do all that and also impose his political ideas and his imperious will on people way off in Southeast Asia whom he did not know or understand. The methods which might work with Congress failed to work on the Vietnamese.

The strain of trying to remake America and the world as well was too much for the country and for the man. He had to hand over the presidency, as he did. He was exhausted by his superhuman efforts.

Everything LYNDON JOHNSON did was done in a big way. He failed big in Vietnam and failed to make all Americans love each other and work harmoniously together. His administration was marked by unprecedented turmoil and strife among Americans. Yet he stirred things up and revived old dreams. In the long run his country will be the better for having been driven, too fast of course, in the right direction by this overly ambitious and oversized human being.

[From the New York Times, Jan. 23, 1973]

A PERSONAL POLITICIAN—JOHNSON PRESSED FOR GREAT SOCIETY AND THE WAR IN A FACE-TO-FACE STYLE

(BY MAX FRANKEL)

He was larger than life, almost a caricature that he could never shake, but he never lost his humanity, because with LYNDON JOHNSON everything was really personal.

The war that overwhelmed his years in the White House was personal—a test of endurance against Ho Chi Minh, which he acknowledged having lost in the end, no matter who actually won the spoils of battle.

AN APPRAISAL

The Great Society was personal, because a lackluster education in his own life had saved him from shiftlessness and he deemed learning of any kind to be forever more the way to get ahead in this world.

The civil rights laws that he wanted as his monument were, in the end, highly personal, because they were

drawn on the testimony of his Negro cook and her humiliations whenever she traveled without reliable food or
lodging between Washington and the Texas ranch.

PERSONAL POLITICS

And even politics, the business in which he excelled
and in which he took such great pride, was to him only
a personal, face-to-face thing. If he had talked George
Meany into acquiescence on a point, he thought he had
won over all of American labor. If he had conquered
Richard Russell on a budget matter, he thought he had
won over the Southland.

In this fashion, he had been able to encompass every
issue and every center of power in his years as majority
leader of the Senate. But from the White House, even his
huge reach fell short and his incredibly hard work and
keen mind felt often overwhelmed.

Insecure despite his size and force, L.B.J. felt from the
moment of John Kennedy's death in Dallas that the nation would never accept his Southern speech and rural
manners as a replacement for the slain prince.

CLUNG TO KENNEDY MEN

So he clung to the Kennedy men and boasted of their
Ph. D. degrees and he was afraid, even after his landslide election in 1964, to bring his own men to the capital.

And he could not comprehend, to the moment of
death, how so many Kennedy partisans around the country could turn against him because of a war in which he
felt he had taken the counsel of his predecessor's Cabinet and aides.

So he took it personally. He thought he saw a plot to
promote yet another Kennedy and he thought he saw his
fate as being merely the caretaker between two Kennedy
administrations and he hated the thought and all who
made it seem so real.

In his own mind, he felt certain that history would
bring vindication:

A Southerner, who brought the blacks to the ultimate
legal equality, with their own seat on the Supreme Court
and a Court that ruled in their cause.

A conservative kept alive in politics by conservative
votes for Texas interests, who made war on poverty an
elaborate concern of the Federal Government.

A wartime leader who was governed to the end by
respect and occasionally even compassion for his "enemy,"
who really wanted to extend the Great Society to the
Mekong River and who systematically refused to whip
the nation into an anti-Communist frenzy.

A backwoods boy of modest learning, who gave what
seemed to him the disrespectful Establishment figures of
the East the scope and mandate for great social works.

That is how he saw himself and how he expected to
be seen in history. He confronted antagonists to the end,
always hoping that reason and short ideals and long conversations—really monologues—could find a compromise
for every conflict.

HATED CONFLICT

Although overcome by a bitter war and the hatreds
that it spawned throughout the country, LYNDON JOHNSON
remained a man who hated conflict and who feared confrontation for himself and country.

He made the Joint Chiefs of Staff testify in writing
that he should really stand at the siege of Khe San.

He made all his diplomatic advisers commit themselves

in writing to the advice that he really go to meet Soviet
Premier Kosygin at Glassboro, N.J.

He won from his wife, Ladybird, a written recommendation that he ride into battle against Barry Goldwater in 1964 and that he should buck the battle for reelection in 1968. He never did want to stand alone.

"Well, Max," he asked an acquaintance on the morning
after the surprise announcement of his intended retirement in 1968, "do you still believe in the First Amendment?" He thought free speech and free assembly had
destroyed him, he believed in the First Amendment.

He wanted everyone with him all the time and when
they weren't, it broke his heart.

[From the Wall Street Journal, Jan. 23, 1973]

LYNDON B. JOHNSON

It is impossible to do justice to LYNDON JOHNSON in the
few moments between his death and the printing of this
newspaper, if indeed it will be possible for any of his
contemporaries to do justice to him ever. Above all he
was a Texas larger-than-life picture, a man whose faults
were parodies of his virtues.

The judgments of President JOHNSON this morning will
be harsh, for it was his fate to preside over this nation in
some of its most wrenching hours. It should not be forgotten, though, that much of this really was fate. He was
handed the presidency, for example, three weeks after
the overthrow of President Diem, an act that did much
to make our commitment to South Vietnam an open-
ended one, and an act that Vice President JOHNSON had opposed. On domestic policy, similarly, the Great Society
may now seem the *reductio ad absurdum* of the liberal
impulse, but in its time those who held that impulse celebrated it as their final victory.

None of which is to excuse LYNDON JOHNSON for any of
his mistakes. It was he who sent the combat troops into
Vietnam. It was he who engineered the ineffectual social
programs. It was he who refused to face the reality of
choice between the two in 1965. And most telling of all,
it was he who lost the confidence of American society—
which, as he and his defenders have suggested, may be
some mark against that society, but is certainly a compelling judgment against the leader of any society.

For all of that, LYNDON JOHNSON was in his day a much
maligned man. He was not the greedy imperialist, but a
man who wanted to help the South Vietnamese and to
defend freedom. He was not the evil-hearted manipulator, but a man who wanted to help the downtrodden
in American society, and who, in some measure, succeeded. If he was the wrong man in the wrong place at
the wrong time, he was a man who wanted to do good.

[From the New York Times, Jan. 23, 1973]

LYNDON BAINES JOHNSON

The shocking news of the death of LYNDON B. JOHN-
SON will sadden every American, regardless of party, who
reveres the Presidential office. Coming so soon and so
suddenly after the loss of Harry S Truman, who had been
the only other living ex-President, Mr. JOHNSON's death
leaves a sorrowful void in the American scene.

A giant in physical stature, overpowering in his personal approach, an intense and driving extrovert who nonetheless was in some ways a peculiarly private person, LYNDON BAINES JOHNSON was the most paradoxical of all American Presidents.

Convinced for many frustrating years that no man from the South could be nominated, much less elected, in his lifetime, LYNDON JOHNSON nonetheless won the largest percentage of the popular vote ever accorded a Presidential candidate in modern history.

A man who, once in office, aspired only to educate the nation's young, feed its hungry, lift up its poor, promote equality and "end war among the brothers of this earth," finished his political career five years later, discouraged, trapped and bogged down in one of the most unpopular wars in the country's entire history. Many who had been his political friends and supporters forgot his magnificent contributions to the national good and held him almost solely culpable for the war he did not start but might have stopped.

A tempestuous and mercurial man, Mr. JOHNSON provided his critics with fuel to spare. They said he was flamboyant, that he lacked "style," particularly in contrast to his graceful predecessor. They said he was a manipulator, as indeed he was, a "wheeler and dealer," which in a sense a President must be if he is to get action on his program. They said his talk was often crude, a charge sometimes made against Lincoln; that he was vain and, worst of all in some circles, "corny." There is enough on the record to substantiate such criticisms. But there is more than enough on the record to dwarf them in the final summing up.

Wrung out as the country was in the days following the assassination of President Kennedy, few Americans could have been unmoved by the emphasis in the new President's first speech to Congress: "We have talked long enough in this country about equal rights. We have talked for 100 years or more. It is time now to write it in the books of law."

He persuaded Congress to do just that, with the most substantial civil rights bill in a century. And to provide medical care for the aged, to give massive Federal financial aid to the elementary and secondary schools of the nation, to raise the minimum wage, launch a major housing program and make a start on what has now become a crusade to clean up the country's air and water. This and more—extraordinary legislative record as it was— was to be only the beginning of the JOHNSON advance toward the "Great Society," following in the tradition of F.D.R.'s New Deal.

Tragically, LYNDON JOHNSON had given little attention as Senate majority leader to the intricacies of foreign policy. He came to the Presidency imbued with the simplicities of the postwar years—specifically that there was a monolithic world power called Communism which had to be kept from spreading wherever it could be stayed without bringing on a major war.

A few months of limited military action in Vietnam seemed to him, as it had seemed to President Kennedy, one of the more obvious cases in point. And the quagmire that was to destroy thousands of American troops ultimately destroyed the political life of LYNDON JOHNSON.

Wanting almost pathetically to be loved, as his hero Franklin D. Roosevelt had been loved in his time, President JOHNSON felt instead the sting of vilification. Tough and sinewy, he was yet sentimental and felt all the more

what he conceived to be not principled differences, but betrayal by his friends.

Yet, sensitive though he was, he stood stubbornly by the course he thought was right—until the political instinct that was the breath of his life persuaded him that the majority he had enjoyed in 1964 had possibly evaporated. Then this man who had lived for power and enjoyed its exercise yielded it up with hardly more than a murmur. And even his severest critics conceded that nothing so became him in office as the leaving of it.

In this age of instant history, with the bitterness of the Vietnam war still unabated, the life of LYNDON B. JOHNSON will no doubt be recorded with more passion than perspective. Future historians should find that life as rich in achievement as in colorful contradiction.

ᡐ

[From the Washington Post, Jan. 23, 1973 (From an editorial in the Washington Post, Jan. 19, 1969)]

LYNDON JOHNSON'S PRESIDENCY

They have not been dull, the Johnson years, from the first crisis in Panama to Santo Domingo and South Vietnam, from the wild campaign of 1964 to the triumphs in Congress, the protests on the campus, the riots in the cities and the sudden abdication in 1968. And they have not been unproductive, in their rich yield of civil rights and social welfare legislation. More than anything, perhaps, they have been sad, in the sense that Franklin D. Roosevelt thought of Lincoln as a "sad man because he couldn't get it all at once—and nobody can."

LYNDON JOHNSON tried, you have to give him that. He brought more raw force and endless energy and craving for accomplishment to the office of President than anyone could ask. Where he succeeded, he succeeded big, in education and civil rights and all the rest. And while it can be said that he also failed big—by not being able to win his way in the war in his time, and by having to acknowledge such a division in the country that he could only carry on in his final year by foreswearing his candidacy for another term—not the least of his legacies to President Nixon is what he himself did to turn the war around and head it in the direction of a gradual American disengagement and a political settlement. Serious peace talking is to begin in Paris this coming week not so much because LYNDON JOHNSON halted the bombing of North Vietnam in October but because he stared down his generals last March and made the much more difficult decision to refuse them the massive reinforcement of American troops that they were asking for.

If this seems a somewhat negative legacy, there are more than enough that are positive. The list of legislative accomplishments runs on and on from the 1964 Civil Rights Act to rent supplements, voting rights, model cities, medicare, control of water pollution, immigration reform, job training, educational aid. And while some of this was the finishing of unfinished business, well begun before his time, some of it broke new ground. A landmark aid to education act, for elementary and secondary schools, cracked a constitutional and political impasse over church-school relationships, and it was brought into being not by past momentum or by parliamentary manipulation, but through the innovation and sheer determination of the President. . . .

It is often said of Mr. JOHNSON that his trouble came

from some incapacity to inspire, and thus to lead. He would say, on the contrary, that he was unjustly victimized by Easterners and intellectuals and liberals and the Kennedy people who scorned him for his regionalism and his roughness, his table manners and the twang of his voice. There is truth to both, and also irony, because the sad thing is that his origins are the best thing about him, the thing he has going for him whenever he is himself, and he didn't know it. Or maybe he just wasn't confident enough about it. Whatever it was, he tried to run the country in the way he ran the United States Senate and it did not work. He wheedled and cajoled and high-pressured and oversold, and seemed to be counting the legislation passed not so much for its contents as its bulk, and this wasn't what people were concerned about. They were worrying about casualty figures and about how the combat troops got to Vietnam in the first place and how they got involved in combat operation when the Secretaries of State and Defense had said they weren't supposed to; they were worrying about how it was all going to end and what it was doing to the country and whether it was worth it, and by the time the Administration got around to leveling a little more on the subject it was too late, because the confidence was gone.

This isn't the whole story by any means but it was a big part of the story of how LYNDON JOHNSON lost his majority: If he was, like Lincoln, a sad man, he didn't show it and he didn't let it slow him; he was forever driving. He wanted nothing more than to succeed—and he did, in many, many ways. But he wanted support for the war and money for a bigger antipoverty effort and safety in the streets and housing for the poor and education for all our children and medical care for all the elderly and the love and respect of all the elderly people, and it wouldn't stretch. He wanted to get it all at once and Roosevelt was right: nobody can.

❧

[From the Evening Star and the Washington Daily News, Jan. 23, 1973]

L. B. J.

He was six-foot-three and everything about him—his ability, his high sense of national purpose, his towering rages—seemed somehow slightly larger than life. Now he is gone at the age of 64, the second former President to die within a month.

The very memory of LYNDON BAINES JOHNSON, thrust into the presidency by an assassin's bullet, is so freighted with partisan feeling that it must remain for another generation of Americans, immunized by time from the contagion of emotion, to assess fairly the man and to judge impartially his presidency.

When that day comes, when the Vietnam conflict—like the Spanish Civil War which stirred the conscience of another generation—has become an issue to bring the flush of passion only to the cheeks of old men, we believe that the man from the Pedernales will be counted among this country's near-great presidents.

Historians will record that the first Southern president since Reconstruction engineered the Civil Rights Bill of 1964 (the first in more than 80 years), outlawing racial discrimination in public facilities, employment and union membership, and giving the attorney general new powers to enforce Negro voting rights and to step up the pace of school desegregation. They will remember that while he

committed large numbers of U.S. troops to a conflict on the Asian mainland, he kept us out of nuclear war. This and much else in the fields of civil rights, housing and health did JOHNSON, who was perhaps the most consummate politician in modern American history, make part and parcel of our children's heritage.

And yet, at the last, he failed—or believed himself to have failed—withdrawing himself from contention in the 1968 election, leaving the country and his party weary and divided.

The roots of that failure are manifold and difficult to trace. Was it, as he insisted, too close to Appomattox for the country as a whole to accept and appreciate a Southern president, to believe in his vision of "the Great Society?" Was it inevitable, in a rising tide of bitterness and disaffection, that John F. Kennedy's successor should be struck down by the tumbling ruins of Camelot? Did he simply fail to gauge correctly the mood of the country when he vowed to nail that Vietnam coonskin to the wall? Was there some fatal and concealed flaw in his character which prevented him from dealing effectively with the burgeoning crisis of the races?

A little of each of these factors, perhaps, contributed to the downfall and bitterness of a man whose personality so vividly reflected the brashness, drive, optimism and acquisitiveness of his native state. Those good qualities and those defects which he brought to the presidency, in fact, may well have been the inevitable outgrowth of his state and regional heritage.

When time cools the passions of the moment it will be remembered that he served his state and country, as congressman, senator, vice president and President for 31 consecutive years, and that if he did well by LYNDON JOHNSON, dying a multimillionaire, he also tried to do well (and often succeeded) by Texas and the United States.

To a certain extent, the measure of statesmen can be calculated by the passions they arouse among their contemporaries. Churchill and De Gaulle, for instance, were nothing if not controversial. In this respect, the hostility of his foes make the big Texan look like tall timber indeed among the scrub growth which forested much of the political hills of America in our times.

LYNDON JOHNSON was a big man and a big President.

❧

[From the Washington Post, Jan. 25, 1973]

ONE MORE CALL TO REASON TOGETHER

(By Hugh Sidey)

Several months ago, when JOHNSON and his staff began planning symposiums for the Lyndon Baines Johnson Library at the University of Texas, it was JOHNSON himself who insisted on a session dealing with civil rights.

So a fortnight ago they came by jet and auto and bus through an ice storm to be in Austin with "the President" again, one of the few times in the last four years that the men and women who carried the civil rights banner for two decades had assembled. There were some new faces among them, but the focus was on men like Hubert Humphrey, Roy Wilkins, Clarence Mitchell and former Chief Justice Earl Warren. They showed up with more wrinkles than they used to have, more gray hair and a lot more discouragement. From the beginning of the two-day meeting it was plain that civil rights no longer had a clear national leader. Nor could anyone perceive any sympathy for the cause in the White House.

L.B.J. put on his tan rancher's twill and his cowboy boots and came in from the country, sitting silently through the first day's meetings, the fatigue growing on him. That night he went to the reception for the 1,000 guests. The strain took its toll. For JOHNSON the rest of the night was filled with pain and restlessness. His doctors suggested, pleaded, ordered him to give up his scheduled address the next day. He ignored them. He put on his dark-blue presidential suit and those flawlessly polished oxfords and came back the next morning.

He didn't take a seat in the auditorium but, with a worried Lady Bird at his side, watched the first two hours' proceedings on closed-circuit TV in an anteroom. Near noon he walked slowly to the podium. In a low but steady voice he talked eloquently for 20 minutes. "Until we overcame unequal history, we cannot overcome unequal opportunity," he said. "But to be black in a white society is not to stand on equal and level ground. While the races may stand side by side, whites stand on history's mountain and blacks stand in history's hollow. . . . So I think it's time to leave aside the legalisms and euphemisms and eloquent evasions. It's time we get down to the business of trying to stand black and white on level ground." Even in that short plea there was pain, and JOHNSON reached for one of his pills, munching in front of everybody. It was something he rarely does.

When he was done he acknowledged the applause and stepped off the stage to take a seat in the auditorium. Then squabbling broke out among the black factions, and one of the participants read an indictment of Richard Nixon and his administration.

LYNDON JOHNSON sat for a few minutes in the midst of it. Then, just as if he were back in Washington, he moved. The fatigue of the night before seemed to drop away, the old adrenalin machine pumping back into action. Going to the microphone, with his hands molding the air, he delivered one of his sermons on brotherhood and reason, flavoring it with one of those marvelous stories about a backwoods judge and the town drunk, reminiscences of when he arrived in Hoover's Washington and the bonus marchers were driven down Pennsylvania Avenue.

"Now, what I want you to do is go back, all of you counsel together," he said, "that soft, kind way, just cool and push off wrath, indulge, tolerate, and finally come out with a program with objectives. . . . There's everything right about a group saying, 'Mr. President, we would like for you to set aside an hour to let us talk,' and you don't need to start off by saying he's terrible, because he doesn't think he's terrible. . . . While I can't provide much go-go at this period of my life, I can provide a lot of hope and dream and encouragement, and I'll sell a few wormy calves now and then and contribute."

In the auditorium in Austin, the ovation that followed JOHNSON's appeal washed away the controversy, for a moment. People came to the stage and crowded around him as he tried to leave. They were all reaching for a bit of the old magic. But nobody got so much of it as Mr. Youngblood, a thin, aging black who used to wait on tables in Austin's ancient Driskill Hotel, where JOHNSON sweated out election night returns. The former President and the former waiter stood there for a few seconds griping hands, and if any questions lingered about what LYNDON JOHNSON had tried to do for his country, they were answered right then.

L. B. J.: A RARE PERSONAL FORCE

(By Marianne Means)

WASHINGTON.—The nation buried last week a retired leader whose towering presence dominated much of American public life for more than two decades.

As LYNDON JOHNSON went to his grave with the national panoply earned by only 37 men in two centuries, his place in history is still a subject of violent argument.

But there is no dispute among those who knew him and dealt with him that the man himself was a rare personal force with almost no outer limits.

He could be anyone, or anything, at any time. He dominated every room he entered within a few minutes. When he told a humorous story, it was a long one. When he gave orders, they were short. Both received the same attention.

GENEROUS WITH PRAISE AND REVENGE

He did not hold any of himself back. It was all there for his friends and his enemies to see and to judge. When crossed, he got revenge if it took 30 years. When served well, he was generous with praise and with his pocketbook.

He was an excellent judge of human nature and it fascinated him endlessly. He loved to tease. He once owned a small automobile equipped to be driven into the water and float, and he delighted in alarming passengers as he plunged off the road into Lake LBJ.

He was a people person, a man who worked out his ideas by discussing them with others rather than poring over tomes of written theories. He never lost his common sense, and his sense of the common man.

He was smarter than almost anybody else, but he contrived to make them forget it. He always warned, "When anyone says he's a country boy, put your hand on your wallet." Then he would laugh and describe himself as a country boy.

His manners were often atrocious. He knew better, but he thought many of the social graces were superficial and he never liked anything to be superficial.

He thrived on adversity and great decisions. Author Theodore H. White once called him "a heavy-duty motor" that functions best when the going is rough but develops a cough when forced to idle.

IMAGINATION OR LYING

He was a ham. He loved play-acting, and the Presidency was a role he played to the hilt. Sometimes he got carried away with his own imagination, and the press refused to call it that but called it lying instead.

He loved plotting and scheming and making people and systems work and produce. He would have made a great puppeteer.

He could be more sentimental than any old maid. He never failed to comment on the beauty of the sunset over Packsaddle Mountain, near his ranch.

He had more intimate friends than most Presidents and they had earned their right to be in his circle by their fierce loyalty to him. So many friends wanted to sit by his coffin as it lay in state in the rotunda that several arguments ensued over who had loved him best.

In the beginning, he had been strong and brave and diligent. And the best politician on Capitol Hill.

In his last years, he had mellowed and thought more about real estate than affairs of state.

But he never lost that special quality of personality which made him unique and which made him a man who will not be forgotten.

❦

SOME FRIENDS OF PRESIDENT JOHNSON (AS BROADCAST OVER THE CBS TELEVISION NETWORK, JANUARY 24, 1973)

Walter Cronkite. Good evening.

We are gathered here not to discuss perhaps the serious side of President LYNDON JOHNSON, but some of the inside of that thirty-sixth President of the United States as seen by men who were very close to him indeed.

May I introduce them to you: Hubert Humphrey, who was his vice president, as you all know, and now, again, senator from Minnesota; Dean Rusk, who was his, as well as President Kennedy's, secretary of State; General William Westmoreland, who was the chief of staff immediately after President JOHNSON and was, for most of President JOHNSON's career in the White House, the commander of our forces in Vietnam; and Harry McPherson, who was counsel to President JOHNSON, wrote many of his speeches, and, therefore, knew him intimately, of course, and a fellow Texan.

Gentlemen, I suppose the cliche that one probably hears most about President JOHNSON and that lives, because those cliches which are true seem to, was that he was bigger than life. To many people he was their most unforgettable character. I'm just wondering if you remember—I'm sure you do—the first time you ever met LYNDON BAINES JOHNSON.

Senator Hubert H. Humphrey. I surely do. I remember him in the United States Senate. I was a very lonesome fellow there. I'd just arrived from Minnesota. Frankly, I didn't know anybody in the Senate. This town of Washington seemed a very different place than Minneapolis. And I was a member of the Eighty-first Congress, 1949. And I heard about a man from Texas that had just barely won an election down there. And his name was LYNDON JOHNSON. And very shortly after we were in the Senate, I believe, Harry, they were calling him "Landslide LYNDON" then . . .

Harry McPherson. That's right.

Senator Humphrey. And, of course, just to even have any jest about anybody—I was so up-tight about being in the Senate and not exactly the most popular fellow at the time having given that civil rights speech up in Philadelphia, as you may recall . . .

Cronkite. Particularly with southerners, I would suppose.

Senator Humphrey. Yes, that's right. But LYNDON JOHNSON was the first man of what we called the southern senators, which I found later on did not properly classify LYNDON JOHNSON, that came on over to me, towering over me, just like, you know, you'd expect him to be, and looking down at me and asking me all kinds of questions about how I got elected and how it was to be mayor of Minneapolis—made me feel important. I liked him. I guess he was about the only one at that time that was really interested in my election. I remember that. I also was impressed by the fact that he knew Sam Rayburn, that he knew men that I'd been told were very important, as they turned out to be—Dick Russell, Walter George and Tom Connally, Harry Byrd, Scott Lucas. He knew all these men. I didn't hardly know the way home, Walter, to be honest with you.

Cronkite. But he also was a freshman senator. Did he come on with that air of importance then, even though he was a freshman, even as you were?

Senator Humphrey. No, it wasn't importance. He was just accustomed to it. As a matter of fact, in your initial greetings with LYNDON JOHNSON, he'd always seem kind of like he was being a little over-modest with you until you got to know him better. I'm sure all of you recall. He'd just sort of always kind of come up to you, kind of—just sort of kind of saddle up to you, you know, and not coming on strong, but showing interest in you.

And I always remember he kind of always looked at you, you know. It wasn't as if somehow that he was looking off in the distance. He was looking right at you and making you wonder whether he was analyzing you, on the one hand, or really had such a great interest in you that he was just really concentrating on you.

Cronkite. That's a rare quality in Washington where most people are looking over your shoulder to see if there's somebody more important that they ought to be speaking to.

Secretary Rusk, do you remember your first meeting . . . ?

Secretary Dean Rusk. Well, I had met Senator JOHNSON very briefly while he was a senator. But I first really came to know him when he became vice president. And I was deeply grateful for the effort which he and Lady Bird made to help out in our relations with other governments, not only here in Washington, but in his travels overseas. And it was obvious that we were dealing with a very strong personality.

I always marveled at the restraint which he showed as vice president, because he was an energetic and powerful man. You talked about his way of coming up to you in a quiet and deprecating fashion. But you and I know, Hubert, that when a man from the farm country starts out by saying, "Well, I'm just a simple farmer" . . .

Cronkite. Watch out.

Rusk. . . . You'd better throw up your pockets . . .

Senator Humphrey. That's right.

Rusk. . . . because you know you're going to be had. [Laughter.]

Rusk. But he was tremendously helpful as vice president, and I'll never forget it.

Cronkite. How about you, General?

General William Westmoreland. Well, I first met him when he was the Vice President. I was the superintendent at the Military Academy at West Point. And he came up to make the graduating address for the class of 1961, I met him at a nearby airfield. And we got in the automobile and proceeded to West Point. It took about twenty-five minutes. And the first comment he made—he said, "General"—he said—"I read my speech coming up in the airplane, and I didn't like it at all" . . .

Cronkite. Had Harry written it?

General Westmoreland. I think Harry wrote it. [Laughter.]

He thought it was a lousy speech. "And I'm thinking about casting it aside and speaking from my heart. And I'd like to have your advice." And I said, "Well, Mr. Vice President, I haven't read your speech, but I do respect your judgment. And if you think it's lousy, I'm sure it is. And I suggest that you follow your instincts and speak from your heart." And he did. And he talked about freedom; freedom in this country, freedom abroad. And at that time, of course, the young cadets and all of us who were pursuing a military career had ringing in our ears President Kennedy's inaugural address where this country would go to any extreme to protect freedom throughout the world. And that was the theme of his address, and it was an inspiring address from the heart.

Cronkite. I'm going to ask in just a second, Harry, about that first remembrance of yours of President JOHNSON. But first of all, I'd like to talk about that speech matter now, because you did write some speeches for him. And I don't know which ones you wrote necessarily. I mean I don't recall offhand. You might be able to refresh my memory on some.

But it seemed to me that it was true about President JOHNSON that he was not very good at reading a speech, that he was tremendous when he went off on his own, like this speech. That was when he began giving that gesture, you know, and he pounded that point home with his left hand. And what did that do to you who wrote speeches for him?

McPherson. Well, it'd make you feel wretched. You could never write as well as he could do extemporaneously. The best speech I ever heard him make was in Abilene, Texas to a group of REA district managers. . . .

Senator Humphrey. Oh, he loved to talk to them.

McPherson. And he loved them.

Rusk. Rural Electrification.

McPherson. That's right. It was early one morning. We were having breakfast with them. He showed up about eight, and he ate two or three bowls of oatmeal as he talked to them. And I guess he talked for two hours. It was absolutely magnificent. He told them why they had a great deal in common with Walter Reuther and other people who wanted low interest rates. And for these farmer electrical managers out there in west Texas, that was rather strange medicine. But it was absolutely superb. It went on for an hour and a half. And no speechwriter could have ever matched it.

Rusk. Yes, it's extraordinary, because in a small, informal group LYNDON JOHNSON could be the most persuasive . . .

McPherson. That's right.

Rusk. . . . and eloquent man in the world, for some reason that I will never understand, when he came onto television and on a formal occasion, he seemed to freeze up. But he was most persuasive in a group like this.

I remember being at a dinner in the White House one evening which he had given to the top business leaders of the country. Probably four-fifths of the economic structure of the country was represented there that evening. And I was sitting at a table with about eight of these people. And President JOHNSON got up and just talked. And after a bit one of my businessman neighbors turned to me and said, "My God, he's going to be elected unanimously."

He was absolutely—the difference between the man in a small group and the man in a formal occasion was really quite extraordinary.

Senator Humphrey. And the sense of humor.

Rusk. Yes.

Senator Humphrey. And every one of his stories that he would tell—and they all were related to the political life of a community or a state or a country. Every one of them had a punch and a twist. And he could mimic. You know, I've often felt that if I could have been his agent, I could have made a fortune. Because, you know, he could mimic anybody, and he could go through all the gyrations of different people that he knew. I wouldn't even dare tell you how—I'm sure he mimicked me many times. But I used to see him mimic some of my colleagues, you know. . . .

Voice. He did.

Senator Humphrey. . . . as he did. I know. I know. No doubt about it. But, you know, I think the reason that he was the way we're describing him is that he had a richness of experience. You know, he wasn't what I'd call a book politician. Everything about his political life was out of an experience. I mean when you talk about REA, that's one of the reasons that we got along good. We were against high interest rates. We both came from the Dust Bowl, so to speak. You know, we were kind of contemporaries of the Depression, admirers of Roosevelt, except, of course, he knew him, and all I did was know about him.

But when he saw farmers, he really felt at home with them, you know, and they could just feel the juices. You know, they knew it. And I used to just—oh, I used to just feel, you know, when I was over there at the White House in the vice presidency—I would think if he could just get out in the country and he could just talk to them like he's talking to us. . . .

Rusk. Yes. Right.

Senator Humphrey. . . . you know, because it was really a talent lost on that TV. But when he was with you, he'd have you rolling in the aisles, if he wanted, and crying the next minute, you know, and you talking about coming down like that. You remember when he used to do this? You'd go out of there; you'd feel like you were punctured.

[Confusion of voices.]

Senator Humphrey. And then he'd get right up on you. You remember, Walter?

Cronkite. Yes.

Senator Humphrey. Well, you know, he was a virtuoso.

McPherson. Well, that's it. When he was in a small group, he could use every device known to man . . .

Senator Humphrey. And he did.

McPherson. . . . moral, immoral, ethical, appeals to country, appeals to self-interest, anything. And one of them would sink home. And he could tell it when it did. And then he would begin driving in on that one.

Cronkite. It must have driven you people who were charged with trying to get the image across nationally in the television and the public speeches absolutely crazy that you couldn't capture this quality. And I'm going to ask you about that in just a minute, Harry. We're going to be right back.

*   *   *   *   *

Cronkite. Harry, presidents are always difficult to talk to. After all, they're the President of the United States. They hold the biggest job in the world. And they become Mr. President. They're no longer LYNDON, or anything else.

How did he take to advice on his public image when you, as a speechwriter, and others around him tried to say, "Look, Mr. President?" Or did you ever try to say, "Mr. President, if you'd only do it this way?"

McPherson. Well, I didn't render a great deal of advice about his public image. But you know, as in everything else, he was a complex man and a various man. On the one hand, he hoped to have a good public image and he was sensitive about it. He raised a lot of Cain with television and the press, because they didn't present him in an image that he wanted to have.

On the other hand, he was extremely realistic about himself. I remember sitting with him one night in the White House as he went over some photographs of himself with various public figures. And there, in one set of photographs, was what I used to call the John Wayne face. It was the face—I can't really make it. But it had the eyebrows going up and the furrows going up into a kind of inverted "V." It was a very sweet face and one that you couldn' believe if you saw it every day of your life. And he said, "Look at that picture." He said, "Have you ever seen anything more hypocritical in your life?" And I said, "No, I really haven't."

[Laughter.]

And he said, "You know, I can't stand that fellow" that he was standing next to. "And everytime I'm with somebody I can't stand, I try to look all the more sincere. And everytime I try it, I look just the worse. And it's a bind I can't get out of. What do you recommend?" Well, what do you recommend to that, because he was really—he was showing how he really felt on his face. And people saw that. And the more he tried to look like a bishop, solemn and sincere and sweet, the more people mistrusted him, because it wasn't really the galvanic personality that he was, full of passion and emotion.

One of the unhappy things for me about this obituary period is that everyone will remember the goodness and the humanity that he had in great measure. But no one will talk about the other side of it, which was also part of his tremendous personality, the capacity to rage and the capacity for mimicry and great fun that was there as well.

Cronkite. Well, it was said that he was very hard to work for! Was that right?

McPherson. Yes and no. He could be very rough on you. He certainly was on me on occasion. On the other hand, he was the most exciting man you can imagine to work for. He was the fastest intelligence I've ever known. He was probably the brightest man I've ever known. He was not an intellectual. He had almost no interest in things in themselves. He had an interest in things insofar as they led to something. But he could put together information and collate it faster than any human being I've ever seen. And that was very exciting to work for.

Cronkite. Well—excuse me.

Rusk. I think it's important to say about LYNDON JOHNSON that he had a passion for performance rather than words. I remember two days after he became President. He picked up the phone and called me and said, "What are we doing about the Alliance for Progress?" And I gave him about two minutes of a typical State Department answer. And he said, 'I'm not talking about that. What are we doing? What contracts are we letting? What projects are underway? What are we doing?" And if you'll look at the record, you'll see that the activities of the Alliance for Progress just went up like that as soon as he became President.

He was always snapping at our heels. He was a tough man to work for. But he was tough on himself. . . .

Senator Humphrey. Right. Very definitely.

Cronkite. I mean his personal relations with those of you, particularly you three—I think, Harry, your relation was rather special, being right in the White House family. But you were secretary of State, you were vice president, you were commander . . .

Senator Humphrey. But I was senator with him too, and that's another dimension . . .

Cronkite. You were what?

Senator Humphrey. . . . When you're senator with him, he was a different man as senator than when that President/Vice President relationship. That's an entirely different relationship. When you were over there in the Senate with him, and when he wanted to get something done, and when he'd call you into his office and he'd explain things to you and he'd tell you what his plans were, and you know that there was more to it than he was telling you, and all that relationship—that was when you were on a first name basis. He was an incredible performer

You talk about demanding things, you know. His sense of timing in the legislative was superb. Lots of us would be wondering, you know, well, when is this going to happen. And we'd think that he wasn't going to do anything and he was dragging his feet. I had a big battle with some of my ADA liberal friends one time about LYNDON JOHNSON. This was when he was in the Senate. Was he a civil libertarian? And I remember President JOHNSON, then Senator JOHNSON, Majority Leader, masterminding a maneuver in the Senate where he put together—Harry, you may recall this—four bills that had been reported out of a committee, all of which would have destroyed the Constitution, any one of them. And every one of them would pass on their own. And cleverly enough, he permitted every one of them to pass and then moved to put them all together in one packet. And he said, when you go out to kill the snake with the hoe, you've got to take its head off. You remember how he used to talk?

Rusk. Yes.

Senator Humphrey. And down—those bills went down the drain.

In the meantime there must have been at least fifteen of my closest liberal friends that said, "You see, I told you. He's betraying you. You've been leading us down," because I would say, "No, it's going to work out all right. You've got to have some faith. He promised me. It's going to work out all right." And each day it looked like it was getting worse and worse and worse. And finally the hour came. And by the cleverest of maneuvers—I still don't know how it was done. But he was a master at the legislative process and the rules of the Senate. Before anybody knew what had happened, those four separate bills, Walter, were in one package, and before you knew what had happened on that, there was a roll call vote. And when the roll was called, the bills were dead as McNamara's goat.

And he walked out and he says, "Tell those liberal friends of yours to have a little faith in me, would you?" You know, he always used to do that. And I said—you know, he used to call my buddies bomb throwers. And Harry, I guess I was kind of a bridge between that part of the Senate and President JOHNSON.

McPherson. You were.

Senator Humphrey. But I trusted him. I used to get mad at him, though, I'll be honest with you about that. You know, he'd work you over sometimes and leave you wondering what was going to happen.

Cronkite. Was that true when you were vice president?

Senator Humphrey. Oh, yes. There was a different relationship. If he were applying the penalty to me then, it was not verbally; it was that I might not just be around for a little while.

But I'll tell you what would happen. All I needed was one news story attacking me for something that I did or didn't do or making fun of the Vice President. Then the next day I'd get a call, and over to the White House I'd come. He'd put his arm around me, and he'd say, "Hubert, let's have lunch." Or we'd have breakfast. And I just tell you, all I needed to do was to have some reporter just give me a real—you know, a real shot, just give me a tough one, and he'd come to my defense; he'd pick me up. And from there on out for at least a week, I'd be the best friend he had, I guess, around there. He'd tell Dean and all of them what a great vice president I was.

Then after that was done for a while, why, I'd maybe be out to pasture a little bit. But my relationship with him was a good one. I can honestly say—and I'm somewhat of a student of vice presidents. I've tried to study the history of them. I think that it's very difficult to be a vice president and a president and to have a friendship. LYNDON JOHNSON himself told me that he couldn't recall any president and vice president over any extended period of time that ever were able to preserve their friendship. When he asked if I wanted to run on the ticket with him in '64, he said, "You know, I hate to ask you, because we're such good friends." And he said, "I'm afraid that if you run with me and we're elected," he said, "that friendships apt to dissolve."

And he reminded me of Truman and Barkley. He said, "You know, there were no two better friends. But within a year after the election, that close relationship kind of dissolved." And we talked out what the possibilities were—this is before the election of '64—and what the ground rules would be. And I think I came out of those four years—I believe I can honestly say that we preserved not only a respect for each other, but a warm friendship.

Cronkite. You had something of an advantage in that LYNDON JOHNSON himself had been a vice president, so he knew . . .

Senator Humphrey. Yes, he remembered that . . .

Cronkite. . . . the other side of the coin.

Senator Humphrey. He remembered that.

Rusk. You know, its a part of the political game in Washington that the staff people around the President get a lot of fun out of poking at the vice president . . .

Senator Humphrey. Yes, they do.

Rusk. But this does not represent the attitude of presidents toward their vice president. President Kennedy had the greatest regard for LYNDON JOHNSON. And LYNDON JOHNSON had the greatest possible regard for you. But that is not the conventional wisdom, because you always have these fellows at the second and third echelons who think it's fun to snipe at a vice president.

Cronkite. Well, but you see, the press does serve a purpose. They wrote a little nasty piece and you got invited to the White House.

Senator Humphrey. Well, listen, Walter, I never ever called him to ask him to see him but what I got (word unintelligible) right quickly from him.

Cronkite. I'm going to ask you, General Westmoreland, in just a moment, if I may, about your relations with the President at the other end of the phone line where you were most of the time in Vietnam with the communications system that you had. Let me ask you that when we come back in just a minute.

* * * * *

Cronkite. General Westmoreland, we were talking about whether President JOHNSON was a tough boss. You must have heard some salty language occasionally, I

guess, at the other end of that communications line to Vietnam, didn't you?

Westmoreland. Walter, I think it's generally accepted that President JOHNSON called me on the telephone once or twice a day. But as a matter of fact, I've never talked to President JOHNSON on the telephone from Saigon to Washington. Although he liked to talk to many people and communicate with a variety of individuals whose opinions he respected, he always dealt with me through the chairman of the Joint Chiefs of Staff, General Wheeler. Now I talked to General Wheeler frequently. And frequently I would get messages from General Wheeler which would reflect the questions of the President. On a few occasions, I received communications over the teletype from the President, but they were normally in terms of, say, giving me bravos and a vote of confidence.

Now, on the other hand, when we conferred in Saigon or in Washington—I saw him frequently—and this was quite different. When I came back to Washington—and I normally stayed at the White House—I would usually get a message, enroute back, asking me to be his guest at the White House. Well, normally I'd made other plans, but I changed them rapidly. And many times Mrs. Westmoreland and I were his guests at the White House. And he would call me at 11:00 at night, and he said "Westy, have you gone to bed?" And I said, "Well, Mr. President, yes. But I'm not totally asleep." And he said, "Well, can you come down to my bedroom." So I would go down and sit at his bedside, and the televisions would be going—and he had usually three or more in his bedroom—and we would talk. Or he would call me up at seven o'clock in the morning. And he says, "Are you up yet?" And I said, "Well, not quite, Mr. President." And he said, "Well, when you get up, please come down and have breakfast with me." So I would get up rapidly and I would go down, and we would have breakfast together. And while having breakfast, he would make half a dozen telephone calls. He would listen to three televisions. He would be conferring with several staff aides. Joe Califano or Cy Vance would be coming in on various matters. And it was a three ring circus. I mean how he could juggle so many balls in the air and keep them all sorted out was absolutely remarkable.

And of course, frequently we met in Hawaii. And Dean, you remember the famous conference we had at a critical stage of the war in February of 1965. And after two days of conference, he made a very emotional speech, which ended up—he says "The time has arrived to pin the coonskins on the wall." Now, this meant something to the Americans, but the Vietnamese were there themselves, and I'm not sure they knew what a coon was, much less a coonskin.

But he was a very energetic man. He projected himself very well. And when you were with him, there were no dull moments.

Cronkite. Did he ever get angry with you in those personal meetings at his bedside or at breakfast? Was he ever . . .

Westmoreland. No, not really. The only time he got angry with me was after the Manila Conference. And Dean, you were there. It had been concluded, and a general agreement had been arrived at between the various nations associated with our effort. It was about eleven o'clock at night. And we were discussing a visit by the President to Vietnam. I recommended Cam Ranh Bay. He said when can you see me. And I said, "Mr. President, it's going to be awfully difficult for me to make the necessary arrangements and provide the security in less than twenty-four hours." And he pounded the desk and he shook his finger at me, and he said, "If you don't want me to come, I won't come. And if I'm going, I'm going tomorrow morning, or nothing."

So I flew back that night. I made arrangements. He arrived on schedule about eight o'clock the next morning, and I had a representation of all the units there at Cam Ranh Bay with a cover plan so that nobody knew where they were going. But they saw the President, and he had a great visit.

Cronkite. That must have been one of the best quick movements of troops since Patton wheeled the Third Army around in the Battle of the Bulge.

Westmoreland. Much quicker than that.

[Laughter.]

Rusk. You know, there's one point, Walter, that affects LYNDON JOHNSON's relations with General Westmoreland. It was not just a great personal confidence and trust in General Westmoreland; but it was a very strong feeling on the President's part about the ordinary GI in the field. That fellow out there, that dogface, was always on his mind. And what he wanted to do was to give that fellow as much support and as much of a chance as possible. And that had contributed a lot to the relations between you and President JOHNSON.

Cronkite. It speaks something of the concern he had throughout the Vietnam war . . .

Rusk. Right.

Cronkite. . . . and expressed in every personal conversation about the concern for that man.

Rusk. Right.

Cronkite. We're going to be back in just a moment for more discussion among the friends of LYNDON JOHNSON.

*   *   *   *   *

Cronkite. We were talking to General Westmoreland about the fact that the one time you recall his blowing up was over a matter of personal arrangements of getting to Cam Ranh Bay. Was that—was that typical of the President? Mr. Secretary?

Rusk. Well, he was very demanding about his personal arrangements. After he became President after the tragic assassination of John F. Kennedy, he was, among other things, under great pressure from the Secret Service not to announce his movements and his presence in advance. And that gave him a reputation of being impetuous. But he did believe that it was up to the State Department to make arrangements with foreign presidents and potentates and princes in a way that would make it possible for him to conduct his business, as he saw it, in the most efficient fashion. And sometimes that got to be very difficult. And he wouldn't let up.

Voices. Yes.

[Laughter].

Rusk. So that he was demanding on that kind of thing. No question about it.

Cronkite. I, you know, had had the great privilege of interviewing him several times since he left office for television, a series we did. And I've selected a couple of quotations from his own words here that I'd like to get your comments on, if I might. I don't want to make any[thing] formal out of this. But on himself, he said once to me: "It's been very clear to me that I had certain serious disadvantages which would ultimately preclude my completing my term as President as I would

like to complete it. Those disadvantages I thought were upbringing, brought up in a poor setting; limited education advantages; geography, where my mother was born, and the prejudices that exist; and, in general, a general inability to stimulate, inspire and unite all the people of the country, which I think is an essential function of the presidency."

Well, that's a terrible statement, it seems to me, in a way, indicating a feeling of inadequacy, a feeling of snobbery on the part of a great number of our people, and perhaps of particular groups. Did he have an inferiority complex, do you think, Harry?

McPherson. Well, I don't know. I think . . .

Cronkite. I mean, because the vision, of course, is just the opposite, basically: a superiority complex, if anything.

McPherson. Well, he had some. And as it was said earlier, he had a feeling of coming in after a very glamorous President, John Kennedy, one who was very much beloved in the Georgetown salons, and that he was something of a bumpkin in their eyes. He had that feeling.

But I thought maybe he misread it. And my own view was that JOHNSON was not a Texas provincial. He was a Washington provincial.

Voice. Yes.

McPherson. This was his town. This was his province. He knew this place like the back of his hand. There is probably no more sophisticated human being in the Twentieth Century in the life and affairs of Washington, D.C. He knew the representatives of power on the Hill, in business and labor, in government, and all the rest of it.

But that's an essential world for a President to know. But if you concentrate on it totally, you may not be able to pick up the vibrations from out there in the states. And I think that was really the provincialism that made it very difficult for him to convey himself to the people.

Senator Humphrey: And don't you think that was true, Harry, particularly in that formative period of his life as a congressman and a senator. When he was the Majority Leader in the Senate, you know, you couldn't get him to travel a great deal. He masterminded the Senate. And that is a task unto itself. At that time, ninety-six, then soon a hundred, individualists. Sometimes we're called prima donnas. But he was able to make that place work and do it both with a Democratic president and a Republican president.

I do think that he had a feeling about, though, you know, that in Washington a Texan from the hill country—I think he maybe even talked himself into that a little bit. And because of the way he worked in the Senate, where it isn't how much oratory you have and it isn't how suave you look; it's how you know how to put the mechanics, the pieces together. The operation of the Senate is like putting a jigsaw puzzle together to get a picture or a pattern. It doesn't make any difference whether you can whistle or sing, or charm or charisma. That stuff doesn't—that just doesn't go there, I mean, because that's a limited clientele that you have. . . .

Cronkite. That dog doesn't hunt. . . .

Senator Humphrey. That dog doesn't hunt. That's right.

[Confusion of voices.]

Senator Humphrey. So this is where he got—this is where he got his reputation with what we call the media or the press corps.

Then, as you say, when he went to the White House

as vice president, you don't make many points as vice president, to be frank about it, with the media. You can't. You're supposed to be second man. You're not front man. You're not making policy pronouncements. You are following the outlines and the guidelines of an administration, and the President is up front.

So during that period of time of the vice president, when he was immensely loyal to Kennedy—and I'm glad you said that, because he really was. And I know, because I was then the majority whip of the Senate. And the things he got us to do over there and how he worked for President Kennedy day after day to get [the] program moving [sic].

But when he became President, that feeling, both on the people that observed him as well as himself, existed for a while. I used to say, just like you said, if we could just get him out there. If I could have brought him out to Minnesota for the Minnesota Editorial Association and turned him loose, like we were talking about, in one of these free-for-all, free swinging, ad lib commentaries of his, he'd have had them in the palm of his hand. He really would have. Whoever he brought into the White House at those dinners—and, by the way, he didn't just bring the rich and the mighty. You know what I liked, Walter. He'd bring in those friends of his from down in Texas. He'd bring in somebody he met in a war. He'd bring in somebody that he just met someplace, and they'd be sitting right there with the big shots, you know . . .

Cronkite. well, a Pakistani camel driver.

Senator Humphrey. Yes, this is how the man was.

McPherson. Right.

Rusk. Let a man from Georgia point out that provincialism turns up in all sorts of places . . .

Senator Humphrey. Yes.

Rusk. I talked to a graduate student some weeks ago who is writing a Ph.d. thesis on the politics of a southern accent. Now there are places in our country which will accept any accent in the world—German, Oxford, Russian, Yiddish—but not a southern accent, because they think that anyone with a southern accent somehow's a little stupid.

Now one of the things that's going to surprise the historians when they get full access to those thirty-one million documents in the Johnson Library will be the intellectual power of this man. But this was concealed . . .

Senator Humphrey. Yes.

Rusk. . . . from some elements in our society by his southern accent and his homily and cornpone stories.

And so I think he was aware of this . . .

Senator Humphrey. Yes, that's right . . .

Rusk. . . . because it is a fact in our society. And this derives from some of the flamboyance and the reactionism of some of the Senators we've had in the last hundred years in our Senate. But this, I think, he felt was a handicap. And who can say that he was wrong.

Cronkite. You said that he was loyal to the Kennedys . . .

Senator Humphrey. Yes.

Cronkite. Senator, but do you think there might also have been some jealously, some resentment, perhaps, on the other hand, of the Eastern establishment, the Ivy League, and so forth?

Senator Humphrey. Yes, I really do. I think that was there.

But I'll tell you something else. Walter—that in terms of the way that that group loved President Kennedy.

President Kennedy was an extremely charming and charismatic man, a remarkable person; very different from LYNDON JOHNSON. They were very, very different personalities. But, of course, they complemented each other.

But I always—I always felt that in order to understand President JOHNSON's kind of politics, you really had to be the kind of a person that had been in the political arena and kind of just wrestled around in the pit of politics. Then you understood it. His politics was glandular, in part, as well as a bright mind and an experienced political person, and with intellectual depth.

I think that the one thing that impressed me first after President Kennedy's assassination—I never will forget sitting with him that night, Harry, when he came back here at Andrews Air Force Base. He called a few of us in. We went over to the Executive Office Building before he went to his home. And he said to us—in a very sober mood, he said, "Look, I not only need your prayers"; he said, "I need your help." He said, "I'm tellin' you, this is—this is—this is more than I can do." And he said, "We've just got to carry through now." And he told us—you know, it really was a kind of a moving, sentimental moment. And he was a very sentimental man.

And then he set out to make sure that every single program that President Kennedy had advocated was passed. And I tell you that I can remember—I think I had more intimate conversations with him about things like this in those days than any other time. I believe he really relied a great deal on me, Harry, if I may say, when I was the majority whip. He thought I'd get things done. I was a can-do man for him. And he used to say to me, "We're going to put through, Hubert, everything that John Kennedy put up to that Congress." He said, "That's going to be my tribute to him. That's what we're going to do. We're going to get everything done." And I'm tellin' you, we did. That's when you really saw the man who was determined to prove not only his loyalty but his dedication.

Then when he went into his own term of office, it was another thing, but with the same kind of dedication and the same kind of demand.

Cronkite. Did he do that, in carrying on the Kennedy program, as a matter of conviction, that he believed that program was right, or as a matter of sentiment, as a matter of the man who had picked up the fallen leader's baton?

Senator Humphrey. Both. Both. I think it's fair to say that Kennedy, President Kennedy, relied on LYNDON JOHNSON a great deal in the formulation of the legislative program, from what I knew at that time, because we used to come to those breakfasts, Harry, you know. And I sat right on the side of the table alongside of Vice President JOHNSON on those Wednesday morning breakfasts. And that's where we really caulked out the legislation and who would do what. So that President JOHNSON was looked upon, in his vice presidency, by President Kennedy as his chief legislative arm, because JOHNSON knew so much about the Congress.

Cronkite. You know, we think of him in domestic policy, but not so much in the foreign policy, and certainly not when he was vice president.

You told me a story, Mr. Secretary, about the Cuban missile crisis. And I'm going to ask you about it in just a minute when we come back.

Rusk. All right.

Cronkite. Secretary Rusk, you told me once that you

thought that President JOHNSON, when he was vice president, had a considerable influence in the Cuban missile crisis.

Rusk. Yes. That story is not likely to be told because it is not in the documentation. But throughout that crisis, he would come over and sit in quietly and informally with the various task forces that were considering the alternatives that were in front of us. He would spend a lot of time with Secretary McNamara and myself and with President Kennedy. His practical wisdom was injected into the discussions in a way that was very important.

And one thing that I will always remember with the greatest gratitude was that the two coolest men in town during that frightful crisis were John F. Kennedy and LYNDON JOHNSON. His role in that crisis, I suspect, will probably never be told. Maybe someday I'll tell it, but it is a very important role.

Cronkite. You know, he was thought of as being mercurial in many ways. But was he, in most crisis, cool, would you say, Harry?

McPherson. Yes. I think he was, the ones that I saw him in the last two or three years of his administration. I think he was cool.

Senator Humphrey. Remember that Six Day War crisis, Dean, down in the situation room . . .

Rusk. Yes.

Senator Humphrey. And the hotline I guess had been used.

Rusk. The Israeli Six Day War.

Senator Humphrey. Yes. The Six Day War in June, '67. And the fleet—he had removed the Sixth Fleet from along the coastline there at Haifa in Israel and got it back deeper in the Mediterranean . . .

Rusk. Right. Right.

Senator Humphrey. And apparently Mr. Kosygin, or one of the Russian leaders, had sent a rather sharp message, that either tell the Israelis to stop or do this, or we'll take whatever action, including military action. And I happened to be at that meeting. That was a very important meeting. And quietly, he told—maybe it was you or Secretary McNamara, one of you—he said, just order the fleet to turn around. And he didn't send back any message to Kosygin, per se, at the time. The Russians understood that. He said, "They'll understand that better than anything I can say." And that fleet that had been coming out of the Mediterranean was wheeled around and didn't need to go very far. And the Russians cooled right away. And there was just no doubt about it. And he was as cool, as they say out home, as a cucumber. He just did it.

Those were days that I saw him face up to tremendous pressures. There were pressures from all sides, domestic and international.

Rusk. He didn't react emotionally . . .

Senator Humphrey. No.

Rusk. . . . to major issues of war and peace. As a matter of fact, he had an extraordinary capacity to put himself in the other fellow's shoes in order to try to understand what was eating on the other fellow. And he was very deliberate and calm about the major decisions which he had to make in those foreign policy questions which involved the possibility of war.

Now there were times he had to act quickly. For example, in the Dominican affair. About two o'clock in the afternoon, our ambassador in the Dominican Republic said, "We don't need the Marines. Don't worry about it."

And then about two hours later, the ambassador came in and said the situation has changed completely; we've got to have the Marines.

Now, you've got to decide that within a couple of hours. You can't send out a bunch of people to do Ph. D. theses on the question. So that when he had to act, he acted. But he always thought about them and did not act in any kind of emotional response.

I mean, this notion that he was moved by hubris, that is false pride, or machismo, or things of that [sort], is utter nonsense. Utter nonsense. Because he recognized the responsibilities which rest upon a President of the United States.

Senator Humphrey. You remember the admonition that he gave every one of us? You mentioned that today in the ceremony at the Rotunda. "To cool the rhetoric." Didn't make any Cold War speeches. The detente that we're talking about with the Soviet Union didn't happen just last week. That was a long process through LYNDON JOHNSON's administration. Dealing with President de Gaulle: constant care. Always I remember that the whole idea was that somehow or another that if you get the rhetoric around [sic], it'll be easier to talk sense; if you'll cool down the verbiage, the adjectives and the rhetoric.

I know that the preparations for those SALT talks were very dear to him, as you know better than anybody else.

Rusk. Well, you'll see from the public record that he didn't let us attack Chairman Khrushchev . . .

Senator Humphrey. No.

Rusk. . . . or later Mr. Brezhnev or Mr. Kosygin, or Ho Chi Minh, or President de Gaulle, or anyone in personal terms, because diplomacy has learned over the last three hundred years that that's not the way you settle problems.

Cronkite. Well, clearly, he was a man who was concerned about what people thought of him. What man isn't, and particularly a man in a leadership role? And it's only human to have been. But he did seem to occasionally carry it to the extreme. He carried those polls around with him all the time, and it didn't take a drop of the hat to show them to you.

[Laughter.]

But he must have felt . . .

Rusk. I bet Hubert carried some polls . . .

Senator Humphrey. I'll tell you, when you're an elective officer, there's nothing that's more cheering to you than a favorable poll.

Cronkite. Well, I was going to say—I was going to say that, did he—among you, did he worry about his image? Did he ever say I'm so sick that I'm misunderstood? Did he wear this on his sleeve? Harry?

McPherson. No, not with me. I don't think I ever heard that. I know that people were brought in from time to time to fix it up, to work on the television image and the rest of it. And surely many of the things he did were done to improve the image. But I never heard him worry out loud about it being a bad image.

Cronkite. Did the Vietnam war—you know, everybody—the common knowledge is that—the common feeling is that it was the Vietnam war that brought him down, that everything else worked well and that this did not. You gentlemen were part of the policy that did that. Do you agree with that assessment? I mean, do you think he was misunderstood on the Vietnam war?

Rusk. This war was his great agony, because there

would not have been, General Westmoreland, a single American in uniform firing a weapon at anyone in Southeast Asia if Ho Chi Minh had kept his men and his arms in his own country.

President Kennedy made the basic decision to intrude American forces out there. And President Kennedy was faced with the terrible Berlin crisis of '61, '62, with the unspeakably dangerous Cuban missile crisis, and the situation in Southeast Asia. President Kennedy and President Johnson didn't want these situations. They were presented to them.

The Vietnam war stood in the way of so many things that Lyndon Johnson wanted to accomplish as President of the United States. And no one wanted peace more than he did.

As a matter of fact, we went into every capital of the world looking for peace, to the point where some of our experienced friends in Europe said to me, "Look, you're trying too hard. You're going to create misunderstandings in Hanoi. You better be quiet for a while . . ."

Senator Humphrey I heard the President of Burma tell that directly to the President of the United States. I don't know whether you're supposed to talk this openly or not. But when the President said to him, "What am I doing that's wrong?"—when President Johnson [sic]—he says "You're asking for peace." And he said, "That's interpreted in our part of the world as a sign of weakness." And President Johnson said, "Look, I'm President of the United States. Our people want peace. And that's what I want."

Rusk. Exactly.

Senator Humphrey. I mean, I remember being taken upstairs that one evening when there was a state dinner. Wasn't it President . . .?

Rusk. Ne Win

Senator Humphrey. Ne Win, yes. And we were talking about it.

Rusk. But this idea that somehow Lyndon Johnson looked upon himself as a bronco-buster, all-out to go gung ho to do somebody in the eye, is a complete misunderstanding of his approach to this problem.

Cronkite. Well, thank you very much, gentlemen, all friends of Lyndon Johnson.

I'll be back in just a moment.

*   *   *   *   *

Cronkite. We've been talking with some friends of Lyndon Johnson. There was one side to the President that all of us knew, or that everyone who met him was vividly aware of, I'm sure, and that was his great pride in his country.

He told me this story during an interview at the LBJ Library. And I think it's an appropriate way to close this hour.

President Lyndon B. Johnson. I heard a president of the University of Minnesota tell this story the other day about the Frenchman that was talking to an Englishman, and he said to him, if I had not been born a Frenchman, I think I would have liked to have been born an Englishman. And the Englishman was—responded and said, well, I think if I had not been born an Englishman, I would have wished to have been born an Englishman.

And that's the way I feel about my country. I'm so glad I was fortunate enough, lucky enough, to be born an American, with our system; that if I had not been born an American, I just really believe that, knowing what I

do about this country and its system, I would have wished to have been born an American.

Cronkite. Thank you, Mr. President.

Announcer. "Some Friends of President Johnson" was recorded earlier tonight in our CBS News studios in Washington.

Hon. J. Bennett Johnston, Jr.
OF LOUISIANA

Mr. President, I am pleased to have the opportunity to join Senators in paying tribute to a great American, Lyndon Baines Johnson.

Mrs. Johnston and I extend our deepest sympathy and condolences to Mrs. Johnson and to the Johnson daughters and their families. Throughout the sad events of the past week the Johnson women were pillars of strength and composure, and our hearts go out to them.

Although I did not have the opportunity to serve with him in Washington, I feel with all Americans the great sense of shock and sadness over the death of President Johnson. His unexpected passing leaves a void in the affairs of a nation which he loved deeply and to which he dedicated a lifetime of service.

Throughout his tenure as majority leader and the 5 tumultuous years of his Presidency, I followed his career with respect and awe—respect for his forthright stands and the office he held; awe of his political acumen and his successes in the Congress.

The Johnson administration provided the leadership and impetus for Congress to enact into law ideas and social programs that had been discussed since the New Deal. Domestic legislation of the Great Society encompassed assistance for the underprivileged, the black, the aged, the Mexican-American, the American Indian and all Americans denied their just share of this affluent society.

His programs included medical protection for the elderly and poor, expanded Federal aid to education, and the eradication of all barriers to the voting booth. The Johnson administration offered the Congress approximately 200 major measures and almost 90 percent of them passed. This body of law touches all Americans in every walk of life.

He brought to the highest office in the land experience without precedent, compassion without parallel, and energy that knew no bounds. He did indeed sometimes seem larger than life, and he had seen more of life than most. Those of us who shared a somewhat common heritage as neighbors and fellow southerners draw special pride from President JOHNSON's untiring efforts to build a better America.

However, history finally assesses the actions of his Presidency. LYNDON JOHNSON's countrymen should always be grateful for the strength that enabled him to impart to America a strong sense of continuity and national purpose in the dark days following the tragedy that elevated him to the White House in 1963.

LYNDON JOHNSON spent his life in service to his fellow man. From his early years as a school-teacher through his post-Presidential years as elder statesman, he worked to help humanity, to correct those injustices that he saw in the world about him. Few men were as aptly suited for this task as LYNDON BAINES JOHNSON, and history will note that few men have ever met the task so well.

Hon. Lee Metcalf
OF MONTANA

Mr. President, on January 24, during the period set aside for eulogies of the late President JOHN-SON, I was unable to obtain recognition before the Senate adjourned to attend the ceremonies in the Rotunda of the Capitol.

I listened to the praise heaped upon President JOHNSON by his former colleagues, and since then I have read tributes to him by people from all over America. These have all been printed in the Congressional Record. I have decided to discard the brief remarks I would have made at that time and substitute the following personal statement.

Everyone who has tried to talk or write about LYNDON JOHNSON is immediately impressed with the breadth and complexity of his life, his per-sonality, and his achievements. Many editorials have commented on this. It is apparent in many of the eulogies that here was a man impossible to label or categorize. A true representative of the great State he represented, his interests, his con-cerns, his temperament was spacious.

First of all he was a superb legislator. As a craftsman he had thoroughly mastered the art. He knew when to press forward—frequently—when to compromise—seldom—and when to courteously and considerately acquiesce to over-whelming odds—almost never. He was a formi-dable foe on the floor of the Senate, in committee, in negotiations. He knew the job of a Representa-tive, of a Senator, of a majority leader of the Senate, and he did these jobs magnificently.

From this Senator's viewpoint, the issues he advocated and for which he used his skill and his power were correct. His instincts were for people, for their right to be free, to vote, to par-ticipate, to be educated. And these things were partially achieved under his leadership. They were, of course, implemented when he became President as they have not been implemented since.

So here was a man of tremendous competence. I came to Congress as a Member of the House of Representatives. I served an apprenticeship under another Texan, Sam Rayburn. These two great legislators are to me the epitome of legislative excellence.

When I was a small boy, one of my heroes was William Travis, the commander at the Alamo. Cool, calculating, and courageous, Travis esti-mated the odds and without bravado decided upon his course and kept upon it despite a realiza-tion of almost certain death. LYNDON JOHNSON was a true descendant of Travis. JOHNSON's great courage was one of the chief characteristics that is most often applauded. JOHNSON as a combina-tion of Travis and Rayburn, was a man to be reckoned with.

JOHNSON was a westerner. He was sometimes brutal, sometimes more forthright than diplomacy would demand. But he was big, he was tolerant, and he was understanding. The critics who point out some personality traits that they deplore fail to understand the men and women who are born to the vastness of the West, who cope with bliz-zards and heat waves, who know mountains and prairies. LYNDON JOHNSON was a true representa-tive of Americans—of all Americans.

As President, his legislative achievements were unsurpassed. Many have dwelt upon his accom-plishments in civil rights, in education, and in housing, but there is not an aspect of American life that has not some JOHNSON imprint.

In the closing years of his administration, Presi-dent JOHNSON was locked in by the war in Viet-nam, an unfortunate captive of that unhappy time. Nevertheless, history will proclaim his essen-tial goodness, his humanity, and greatness of soul.

Of course, Mrs. Johnson, a gracious lady and an affectionate mother, was an example to the women of America. Without Lady Bird our country would be uglier, and Washington would not be the city of blooming shrubs and flowered squares it is today. From the first daffodils and tulips to the last withered chrysanthemums she is responsible for making our Capital City one of the loveliest cities in the world.

Washington is a city with the shortest memory in the world. Most public figures are forgotten as soon as they lose power. Keats desired that his tombstone carry the inscription "Here lies one whose name was writ in water." In Washington, most men and women leave without that much of a ripple. Not LYNDON JOHNSON. He will be long remembered here for his courage, his competence, and his integrity. His achievements will affect the lives of Americans for many years to come and his life will be an inspiration to all men.

I am proud that I knew LYNDON JOHNSON.

Hon. Mike Mansfield
OF MONTANA

Mr. President, I ask unanimous consent that Enrolled House Concurrent Resolution No. 1008 passed by the house of representatives of the first session of the 34th Oklahoma Legislature, the senate concurring, having to do with the passing of our distinguished former President, LYNDON B. JOHNSON, and our distinguished late colleague, Senator LYNDON B. JOHNSON, be printed in the Record.

RESOLUTION OF THE OKLAHOMA STATE LEGISLATURE

(A concurrent resolution noting the life and many accomplishments of the Honorable LYNDON BAINES JOHNSON, 36th President of the United States of America; citing his achievements as a Congressman, Senator, Vice President, and President; noting his compassion and deep concern for his fellow man; expressing the sympathy and condolences of the people of Oklahoma to the family of former President JOHNSON; and directing distribution)

Whereas, on January 22, 1973, the Omnipotent Lord of the Universe did summon his faithful and loyal servant LYNDON BAINES JOHNSON, former Congressman, Senator, Vice President and 36th President of these United States; and

Whereas, it is appropriate that the State of Oklahoma join the remainder of the Nation and the World in recognition of the contributions to mankind made by LYNDON BAINES JOHNSON throughout his years of public service; and

Whereas, Mr. JOHNSON was born on a farm near Stonewall, Texas, on August 27, 1908, graduated from high school in Johnson City, Texas, received his Bachelor of Science Degree from Southwest Texas State Teachers College at San Marcos, Texas, and attended Georgetown University Law School in Washington, D.C.; and

Whereas, Mr JOHNSON taught public speaking in Houston High School from 1930 to 1932, served as secretary to Representative R. M. Kleberg from 1932 to 1935, and was appointed Texas State Administrator of

the National Youth Administration by President Franklin D. Roosevelt in 1935; and

Whereas, LYNDON B. JOHNSON, following the example of his father and grandfather who served in the Texas Legislature, sought and won election to Congress in 1937, and was then reelected to five full terms; and

Whereas, Mr. JOHNSON was elected to the United States Senate in 1948, and was reelected in 1954, becoming his party's whip in 1951 and Majority Leader in 1953; and

Whereas, he was a member of the U.S. Naval Reserve and served in the United States Navy as a Lieutenant Commander in 1941–42, winning the Silver Star for bravery in action; and

Whereas, Mr. JOHNSON was Texas' favorite son for the Democratic presidential nomination in 1956, and was selected as the vice-presidential nominee in 1960; and

Whereas, LYNDON B. JOHNSON proved to be a tireless campaigner during the election and a hard-working Vice President when elected, representing President John F. Kennedy abroad and serving as Chairman of the President's Committee on Equal Employment Opportunity and as a member of numerous advisory boards governing the areas of national security, space and technology, and the Peace Corps; and

Whereas, LYNDON B. JOHNSON succeeded John F. Kennedy in the Presidency on November 22, 1963, and quickly moved to complete the programs he had helped mold as Vice President, including those in the areas of civil rights, antipoverty, tax reduction, national defense, and education; and

Whereas, winning election to a full term in 1964, Mr. JOHNSON, his firm and resolute character further shaped by the crucible of the Presidency, determined to complete the platform of the "New Frontier," and to expand upon its goals many times over through the worthy "Great Society" program, insuring a greater measure of social and economic justice for all Americans; and

Whereas, President JOHNSON guaranteed to all citizens more self-respect and a higher degree of participation in the tasks and benefits of society through the enactment of measures on voting rights, medicare, veterans benefits, social security, minimum wages and rent supplements; and

Whereas, he showed keen foresight and great innovative capacity in new programs for elementary and secondary education, higher education, transportation planning, housing and urban development, model cities, air and water pollution, and development of parks and recreation land—all areas which have the most vital impact upon the quality and style of American life; and

Whereas, the fruits of the foregoing programs could readily be seen in an increased gross national product, a drop in unemployment rates coupled with the creation of over seven million new jobs, and an increase of $180 billion in disposable personal income for the people of this country; and

Whereas, President JOHNSON increased communication and understanding between all the peoples of the world, and gave them an enlarged share of freedom and security through such devices as the Peace Corps, Food for Freedom, the Alliance for Progress, the Nuclear Test Ban Treaty, and a far-reaching space program; and

Whereas, as President, Mr. JOHNSON led the Nation through a period of extreme danger from external enemies, and bore well the difficult burden of leadership of the free world in its fight to resist Communist domination; and

Whereas, President JOHNSON's concern for the well-being of the American people was indicated not only in his writings, including *This America, A Time for Action,* and *The Vantage Point; Perspectives of the Presidency,* but also in his daily actions as a citizen, a party leader and a public official; and

Whereas, no mere listing of the many achievements and proud accomplishments of LYNDON B. JOHNSON can describe adequately his compassion, his goodwill and his proven capability for leadership and growth within the framework of our American democracy; and

Whereas, many Oklahomans were fortunate enough to have known him well, and to have served with him during his long public career, so that it is with the special regard of neighbors and friends that we express our sincere admiration for the achievements of LYNDON BAINES JOHNSON.

Now, therefore, be it resolved by the House of Representatives of the 1st session of the 34th Oklahoma Legislature, the senate concurring therein:

Section. 1. That the State of Oklahoma join the Nation and the World in recognition of the achievements and accomplishments of LYNDON BAINES JOHNSON during his loyal tenure as a public official.

Sec. 2. That the State of Oklahoma and its citizens express their heartfelt sympathy and condolences to the family of former President LYNDON BAINES JOHNSON.

Sec. 3. That this Concurrent Resolution be spread in full upon the pages of the House and Senate Journals of the 1st Session of the 34th Oklahoma Legislature.

Sec. 4. That duly authenticated copies of this Resolution, following consideration and enrollment, be prepared for and sent to:

Mrs. Lyndon B. Johnson, her daughters Lynda and Luci and their families;

The Lyndon B. Johnson Library at the University of Texas in Austin;

The Library of Congress;

President Richard M. Nixon;

Vice President Spiro T. Agnew;

Honorable Mike Mansfield, Majority Leader, United States Senate;

Honorable Carl Albert, Speaker, United States House of Representatives.

Adopted by the House of Representatives the 24th day of January, 1973.

Hon. Hubert H. Humphrey
OF MINNESOTA

Mr. President, I ask unanimous consent that the Congressional Record and the bound volume of congressional tributes to President JOHNSON reprint the order of graveside service and meditation by the Reverend Dr. Billy Graham, at the funeral of President LYNDON B. JOHNSON, January 25, 1973.

FUNERAL OF PRESIDENT LYNDON B. JOHNSON—ORDER OF GRAVESIDE SERVICE (OFFICIATED BY THE REVEREND DR. BILLY GRAHAM, L. B. J. RANCH, STONEWALL, TEX., THURSDAY, JANUARY 25, 1973)

LET US WORSHIP GOD

"I am the resurrection, and the life; he that believeth in Me, though he were dead, yet shall he live:

"And whosoever liveth and believeth in Me shall never die."—(John 11:25–26).

"Let not your heart be troubled, ye believe in God, believe also in Me.

"In My Father's house are many mansions: if it were not so, I would have told you. I go to prepare a place for you.

"And if I go and prepare a place for you, I will come again, and receive you unto Myself; that where I am, there ye may be also."—(John 14:1–3).

THE MEDITATION

Few events touch the heart of every American as profoundly as the death of a President—for the President is our leader and every American feels that he knows him in a special way because he hears his voice so often, glimpses at his picture in the paper, sees him on television, and so we all mourn his loss and feel that our world will be a lonelier place without him. But to you who were close to him, this grief is an added pain because you wept when he wept and you laughed when he laughed. When he was misunderstood you felt his pain and wondered why others had no heart to feel or no eyes to see, but such is the burden, the anguish and the glory of the Presidency.

Here amidst those familiar hills and under these expansive skies his earthly life has come full circle. It was here that LYNDON BAINES JOHNSON was born and reared and his life molded. But the Scripture teaches that there is a time to be born and a time to live and a time to die. LYNDON JOHNSON's time to die came last Monday. The absence of his vibrant and dominant personality seem so strange as we gather on this site. There was a mass of manhood in LYNDON JOHNSON. "He was a mountain of a man with a whirlwind for a heart." He loved his hill country. He often said, "I love this country where people know when you are sick, love you while you are alive, and miss you when you die."

Not long ago President JOHNSON brought me here to this very spot and said, "One day you are going to be asked to preach my funeral. You'll come right here under this tree and I'll be buried right there." In his homespun way he continued, "You'll read the Bible and preach the Gospel and I want you to." And he said, "I hope you'll tell people about some of the things I tried to do."

History will not ignore him for he was history in motion. He will stand tall in the history books that future generations will study. The great events of his life have already been widely recounted by the news media this week. I think most of us have been staggered at the enormous things he accomplished during his lifetime. His thirty-eight years of public service kept him at the center of the events that have shaped our destiny. During his years of public service, LYNDON JOHNSON was on center stage in our generation. To him the Great Society was not a mild dream but a realistic hope. The thing nearest to his heart was to harness the wealth and knowledge of a mighty Nation to assist the plight of the poor. It was his destiny to be involved in a tragic war. It is a mysterious act of Providence that his death came during the same week that a peace agreement was reached. As President Nixon said Tuesday night: "No one would have welcomed this peace more than he."

However, there was another more personal, more intimate and more human side to LYNDON JOHNSON—that his family, neighbors and friends that are gathered here today would know. For example, some of you have seen him load his car or station wagon with children of various racial and ethnic backgrounds and take them on rides or to see the deer running across the ranch. There were hundreds of little things that he did for little people that no one would ever know about. He had a compassion for the underdog.

No one could ever understand LYNDON JOHNSON unless they understood the land and the people from which he came. His roots were deep in this hill country. They were also deep in the religious heritage of this country. President JOHNSON often pointed with pride to a faded yellow letter on the wall of his office written to his great grandfather, like many of his forebears, was a preacher and had led Sam Houston to a personal faith in Jesus Christ. Symbolically it says that LYNDON BAINES JOHNSON had respect for "the faith" that has guided his family, his state and his nation through generations. LYNDON JOHNSON's mother, Rebekah Baines Johnson, who lies here, often read the Bible to her young son.

Within weeks of the time he became President of the United States he said, "No man can live where I live now, nor work at the desk where I work now, without needing and seeking the strength and support of earnest and frequent prayer."

He could have had more excuses than most for not attending church on Sunday. But one of the things for which he will be remembered is that he probably went to church more than any other President.

Some months ago my wife and I were visiting the Johnsons here at the ranch. LYNDON JOHNSON brought me out to this spot and reminded me again that I was to participate in this service. We spoke of the brevity of life and the fact that every man will someday die and stand before his Creator.

There is a democracy about death, John Donne said: "It comes equally to us all and makes us all equal when it comes." The Bible says: "It is appointed unto men once to die, but after this the judgment" (Hebrews 9: 27).

For the believer who has been to the Cross, death is no frightful leap in the dark, but is the entrance into a glorious new life. The Apostle Paul said: "For to me to live is Christ, and to die is gain" (Phil. 1: 21). For the believer the brutal fact of death has been conquered by the historical resurrection of Jesus Christ. For the person who has turned from sin and has received Christ as Lord and Savior, death is not the end. For the believer there is "hope" beyond the grave. There is a future life! As the poet has written:

God writes in characters too grand
For our short sight to understand;
We catch but broken strokes, and try
To fathom all the mystery
Of withered hopes, of death, of life,
The endless war, the useless strife,—
But there, with larger, clearer sight,
We shall see this—God's way was right.
(John Oxenham.)

We do not say goodbye to LYNDON today. The French have a better way of saying it. They say, "Au revoir!"—till we meet again. To you Mrs. Johnson, Lynda, Luci, and other members of the family, it is my prayer that God's grace will be sufficient for you in the days to come. May God grant to each of you a deep satisfaction in the life of one who served his country with such complete dedication. May the God and Father of our Lord Jesus Christ, the Father of all mercies and the God of all comforts, sustain you now and in the days to come.

What he once said about another President we can now say about him: "A great leader is dead. A great nation must move on. Yesterday is not ours to recover but tomorrow is ours to win or lose."

PRAYER FOR THE FAMILY

Our Heavenly Father, who art the dwelling place of Thy people in all generations, have mercy upon us as we are here today under the shadow of great affliction; for in Thee alone is our confidence and our hope.

God of all comfort, in the silence of this hour we ask Thee to sustain this family and these loved ones and to deliver them from loneliness, despair and doubt. Fill their desolate hearts with Thy peace and may this be a moment of rededication to Thee.

Our Father, those of us who have been left behind have the solemn responsibilities of life. Help us to live according to Thy will and for Thy glory—so that when Thou dost call us that we will be prepared to meet Thee.

We offer our prayer in the Name of Him who is the resurrection and the life, even Jesus Christ our Lord. Amen.

BENEDICTION

"Unto Him that loved us, and washed us from our sins in His own blood,

"And hath made us kings and priests unto God and His Father; to Him be glory and dominion for ever and ever. Amen."—(Revelation 1: 5–6).

The God of peace, that brought again from the dead our Lord Jesus, that great Shepherd of the sheep, through the blood of the everlasting covenant, make you perfect in every good work to do His will, working in you that which is well pleasing in His sight, through Jesus Christ, to whom be glory for ever and ever. Amen.

Mr. President, I ask unanimous consent to have printed in the Record—and for purposes of reprinting in the bound volume of tributes to President JOHNSON—the moving eulogy to President LYNDON B. JOHNSON, delivered by the former

Governor of Texas and former Secretary of the Treasury John Connally, as a part of the grave-side service, January 25, 1973.

EULOGY FOR PRESIDENT LYNDON JOHNSON BY JOHN CONNALLY, JANUARY 25, 1973

We lay to rest here a man whose whole life embodied the spirit and hope of America.

How can a few words eulogize a man such as he?

Not in a purely personal way, although President and Mrs. JOHNSON had a profound effect on my life, on Nellie's, and the lives of our children just as they had on the lives of many of you within the sound of my voice.

Not in a dispassionate way because none who knew him could speak dispassionately of him.

And not in words of great elegance and adornment simply because he would not have wanted that.

LYNDON JOHNSON spoke plainly all of his life. He spoke to the hearts of people. The whispering of his thoughts and words and deeds was always the fundamental character of the plain people he loved, whose dreams and aspirations he tried so hard to bring to reality.

Eloquent praise and heartfelt words of sympathy have poured forth since last Monday afternoon when we learned this great heart had stilled. The world has a fallen leader and owes him much honor.

But I feel today it is those plain people he loved—the silent people—who mourn him the most.

He gave them all he had for 40 years.

He gave them his incredible energy; his matchless legislative mind, and his restless devotion to the ideal that his country's grasp should always exceed its reach . . . that nothing was impossible when there was a determined will.

He was one of them. He never forgot it, and they will never forget him.

LYNDON was one of three presidents to-be-born in this century. But this Hill Country in 1908 was not much different from the frontier his father and mother had known.

The comforts and amenities were few; the educational oportunities were determined by the quality of a single teacher or a hand-full of teachers; and a man's fortune was dictated by the amount of rain or the heat of the sun or the coldness of the north wind.

Yet a child's dreams could be as wide as the sky and his future as green as the winter oats because this, after all, was America.

LYNDON JOHNSON made his dreams come true because he saw the real opportunity of this land and this political system into which he was born. He never doubted he could do it because he always knew he could work harder than anyone else . . . sustain his dedication longer than anyone else . . . and renew his spirit more completely than anyone else—no matter how serious the setback or even the defeat.

Thus he rose from those limited beginnings to the zenith of power, and as he so often said with a mixture of awe and pride, "I guess I've come a long way for a boy from Johnson City, Texas."

But with all of his strengths, LYNDON JOHNSON cannot be viewed as a man above men—A mythical hero conquering all before him.

In a sense, his life was one of opposites—of conflicting forces within him trying to emerge supreme.

The product of simple rural surroundings, he was thrust by his own ambition into an urbane and complicated world.

Born into a southwestern, Protestant, Anglo-Saxon heritage, he found his native values challenged constantly in the political and social climate which enveloped him.

Reared and educated without benefit of a more worldly existence, he thirsted for the knowledge that would propel him to the heights in the life he chose for himself.

Some criticized him for being unlettered and unsophisticated when, in truth, he was incredibly wise and incredibly sophisticated in ways his critics never understood; perhaps because he dealt not with things as they should have been, but as they were.

He was uninhibited by hypocrisy or even false pride. He was not afraid to let his feelings show.

It is said that in some ways he was an insecure man. Of course he was. He knew he was not endowed with the kingly virtues of always being right; he tried merely to do his best to discover what was right.

He recognized his own shortcomings far more than many of his detractors recognized theirs. He never hesitated to ask for help, and he understood better than most the meaning of loyalty and mutual affection among friends and associates.

The same insecurities existed in LYNDON JOHNSON that exist in all of us. His strengths and his weaknesses were universally human qualities shared by people everywhere who have also dreamed of the mountaintop each in his own way.

President JOHNSON cared for America. He demonstrated his care not so much in words, although many of those words will endure for as long as freedom endures, but in the goals he set and the deeds he performed.

President JOHNSON cared for people, no matter where they lived in this world or their color or their heritage. He showed this in public ways too numerous to list. What is more important, he showed it in private ways when the world was not looking.

Not long ago, he visited the ranch of a friend in Mexico and discovered a small rural schoolhouse for children in the depths of poverty. When he returned to Austin, he and Mrs. Johnson gathered dozens of small windup toys, medicine, clothing and other items for those children. And when he went back to Mexico, he took those things with him, and he had his own Christmas celebration with those children.

So we have the vision of a former President of the United States, perhaps down on his knees, surrounded by youngsters from another land whose language he did not speak, demonstrating for them how to wind up a 25-cent toy.

Somehow, I think that's how LYNDON JOHNSON would like best for us to remember him.

The tens of thousands who have filed past his bier, and the tens of millions who mourn him from afar—those are the people who understand who he was, and what he was, and how he thought—because he was one of them.

I think they would know of his frustration of leadership, his impatience, the occasional temper, sometimes the sharp tongue, but always the overriding courage and determination of this complex man.

Surely they would know of his anguish over sending

men to war when all he wanted was peace and prosperity and freedom. It seems ironic on this day that his predecessors began the war in Southeast Asia, and his successor ended it. It was his fate to be the bridge over the intervening chasm of conflict that swept this country and the world. But he accepted the role without flinching, and no one would be happier today, no one would be more appreciative of the beginnings of peace and the President who achieved it than the President who worked so long and so unselfishly for the tranquillity that eluded him.

It is fashionable among some to refer to LYNDON JOHNSON as a tragic President.

But I believe history will describe his Presidency as tragic only in the sense that it began through tragedy, for his service was not one of tragedy, but one of triumph.

It was a triumph for the poor, a triumph for the oppressed, a triumph for social justice, and a triumph for mankind's never ending quest for freedom.

Along this stream and under these trees he loved, he will now rest.

He first saw light here. He last felt life here. May he now find peace here.

Hon. Alan Bible

OF NEVADA

Mr. President, like all Americans, the people of Nevada were greatly saddened by the death of former President JOHNSON. Over the years, he visited our State a number of times, and the people of Nevada developed a special affection for him. This high regard is reflected in the tributes paid to President JOHNSON in the Nevada press following his death, and I ask unanimous consent that the following articles and editorials paying final tribute to him be printed in the Record.

[From the Nevada State Journal, Jan. 23, 1973]

THE RISE AND FALL OF LYNDON JOHNSON

The wire services reported Monday that former President LYNDON BAINES JOHNSON died of an apparent heart attack, but his death must have been hastened by a broken heart.

Few American presidents have come into office with greater promise, enjoyed greater initial popularity, accomplished more with their Congressional programs, and then fallen so low in popularity.

His standing with the people was ruined by the nation's impossible position in the Vietnam War.

When he ran for election, a year after he had succeeded to the Presidency, he made the mistake of basing his campaign on what was fundamentally a peace program. At least the voters believed this and he rolled up the greatest vote majority of any presidential candidate in U.S. history.

Once returned to office, apparently on the counsel of his military advisers, he made a command decision to expand the military effort in Vietnam.

The consequences record his political downfall. There was no limit to how much military effort could be expended without productive results. A settlement remained as elusive as ever. The gamble failed, and JOHNSON lost popularity rapidly.

Always keen and analytical in a political situation, he appraised his position objectively, and decided not to seek re-election in 1968. He withdrew in the interests of national unity, showing his immense sense of political responsibility.

The final turn of fate was grossly unfair and unfortunate for him personally for he had been a powerful political figure—one of the all-time great leaders in Congress who was probably as knowledgeable about how government really works as any man ever elected President.

JOHNSON began his career with a marvelous personal mix for a future politician. He appeared to come from modest circumstances, but from the start he had and used extremely influential connections.

With a background of education in a teachers college where he worked as a janitor to get through school, and then two years of teaching plus his natural Texas style, he was disarmingly homespun.

But JOHNSON'S wife was wealthy, and he himself attracted the top politicians in the nation as his own political sponsors from the start.

House Speaker Sam Rayburn took a liking to him, and got President Roosevelt to appoint him as director of the National Youth Administration for Texas, and to take a continuing interest in his political future.

The administrative job set the stage for JOHNSON to get into the U.S. House at a young age where he served for 10 years before being elected to the Senate.

Along the way he developed an interesting formula for political success. He faithfully supported the economic interests of his major backers in Texas, which made him appear a strong conservative. But he voted liberal in every area not directly linked to his economic base at home, gaining liberal support for his career from many quarters.

In the Senate JOHNSON quickly became nationally known to ordinary citizens He became minority leader, then majority leader, and probably demonstrated more practical legislative ability than any other Senator of this century.

A smart, shrewd, complex man, he was a superb strategist. He ran the Senate with an iron hand arousing resentment from his critics and admiration from his supporters.

As President, he made these skills pay off with Congress. He got through Congress the most sweeping civil rights bill since Reconstruction days.

He also got passed the Medicare-Social Security bill, a voting rights act that enfranchised millions of blacks, and got Social Security benefits brought up to date.

Despite all this he was rejected by a people frustrated over the Vietnam War.

In the end, he must have been a good enough judge of history to realize that ultimately, when the Southeast Asian War is seen in perspective, he will be regarded as one of the better American presidents.

Even so, this may have been little solace to a political leader as sensitive as LYNDON JOHNSON, who must have died feeling rejected by the people he gave his whole life's effort to serve.

[From the Reno (Nev.) Evening Gazette, Jan. 23, 1973]

HE WILL ENDURE

A person is allowed a mistake or two in almost any occupation.

Not so in the presidency, though, where a wrong judgment is apt to spell disaster for the country and damage a distinguished political career.

So it was with LYNDON JOHNSON, or so it seems at the present. He had made few errors in his climb to the top, but as President, his luck ran bad.

Dealing with an inherited war, he opted to end it quickly through escalation. It was a point of view strongly advocated at the time by many sound minds both Republican and Democrat.

When it failed and the nation was drawn deep into a long and bitter war, it was the President who bore the blame. That was the end of JOHNSON in the White House and in politics. Had he not bowed out of the office, it is likely that the voters would have chased him out.

Among those who now rage against our role in the war, he is still the villain. Nor, until the conflict is just a distant memory will this be likely to change.

Time, though, will most certainly treat JOHNSON more kindly. There were too many accomplishments in his time, too many laudable aspects of the tall, soft-voiced Texan's character to remain obscured by the shadow of his disaster.

There was the phenomenal career in public service— a long and consistent story of skill in the art of politics and well-earned progress through the ranks of party and office to the presidency.

And, there was the fundamental outlook on life, at least as important to his fortunes as were his considerable ambition and ability.

Nearly all who knew JOHNSON praise him as a man of great personal warmth. His concern for people, particularly the poor and the oppressed, was genuine, they say.

It is reflected in his many speeches and his legislative works promoting the cause of civil rights. And it is apparent in his Great Society program which, even if less than successful, was a sincere effort to improve the lot of the poor, the outcast and the aged.

With the former President's death, his failures will eventually recede into memory as the nation reflects on the man's many strengths.

Most of us will grieve the loss of a great American and a friend to man.

[From the Reno (Nev.) Evening Gazette, Jan. 26, 1973]

THEY SHARED COMMON GOAL

Last spring former President LYNDON JOHNSON wrote to a Sparks man and advised they both must give up heart attacks.

Howard W. Pickering of Sparks had read about one of JOHNSON's attacks, then suffered a mild one himself.

He wrote to JOHNSON in Texas and said his wife, Virginia, told him, "I just wish that President JOHNSON would get well and stop having heart attacks. When he has one, you have one." Pickering wrote, "Mr. JOHNSON, please get well and stop having heart attacks. It's killing me."

JOHNSON replied on May 2.

"Despite the gravity of the content, that letter was so well written that it gave me a chuckle or two . . . and I did appreciate it. I assure you that I will concentrate very hard on taking care of us both.

"There are so many wonderful reasons for living that we just must give up these heart attacks."

Pickering said today he didn't want to make the letter public while JOHNSON was still alive.

JOHNSON's funeral was Thursday.

[From the Boulder City (Nev.) News, Jan. 25, 1973]

GARRETT TELLS MEMORIES OF JOHNSON

The death of LYNDON B. JOHNSON, 36th president of the United States, will be mourned by many Southern Nevadans who will remember his first appearance in Nevada in 1954 at which time he established himself as a man "of the people" in the minds of those who heard him and met him as the principle speaker at the Democratic state convention, according to Elton M. Garrett, of the convention committee.

JOHNSON, then democratic leader of the Senate, in his speech in the Silver Slipper banquet room, read a lengthy telegram which had been sent to President Dwight Eisenhower by himself and Speaker Sam Rayburn of the House of Representatives, in which they pledged the president there would be no opposition in congress to the president's programs purely for the sake of partisan politics when during the election, of senators and congressmen the democrats "took over" control of congress.

"This was a memorable part of the then senator's speech," said Garrett, "and when he was afterward asked for a copy of the telegram he handed it over immediately for reference use in Southern Nevada. He impressed many at that time as being presidential calibre."

The state convention was held in the then new high school gymnasium in Boulder City, climaxed with the dinner in Las Vegas featuring Senator JOHNSON as the speaker.

[From the Nevada State Journal]

NEVADA LEADERS HAIL JOHNSON AS GREAT MAN

Both Democratic and Republican leaders throughout Nevada hailed former President JOHNSON as one of the great men of this century and a great American.

Sen. Alan Bible, D–Nev., said "LYNDON JOHNSON was one of the ablest men I have ever known, and I will cherish the memory of our close friendship which spans more than two decades.

"He was a truly remarkable man who devoted his entire life to serving America," said Bible. "His accomplishments in the Congress and later as President will stand as a lasting tribute to his leadership and vision."

Sen. Howard Cannon, D–Nev., said, "This remarkable man was one of America's most outstanding Presidents and has been a tremendous force in the U.S. Senate for more than a decade. The tragedy of Vietnam overshadowed in public view his many and great accomplishments in the domestic field, but I am convinced history will judge him as having acted with forthrightness and courage in fulfilling our international obligation."

Gov. Mike O'Callaghan, who worked under JOHNSON in

the Job Corp and as western regional director for the office of emergency planning said "JOHNSON's administration resulted in passage of domestic legislation unequalled in history for its humanitarian concern.

"He was great to work for, as you never had to worry about his personal loyalty," said O'Callaghan.

Former Gov. Paul Laxalt, a Republican who was governor during part of JOHNSON's administration said he was saddened by the news of the death. He said "history will record that LYNDON JOHNSON was a very misunderstood President. He was vilified for problems he did not create. As a result he did not receive credit for many social reforms. In my book, he did a good job."

Atty. Gen. Robert List said "JOHNSON will go down as one of the most effective public servants of this century."

List, a Republican said, "Because of his relatively young age, his death came not only as a shock but also as a reminder of the tremendous physical drain which the responsibilities of the presidency bring."

Former Gov. Grant Sawyer said "Although foreign problems, particularly Vietnam somewhat clouded the magnitude of the impact of the Johnson presidential years, history will show that Johnson years produced more dynamic and progressive legislation than any other similar period.

"Time will prove LYNDON JOHNSON as one of the truly great men in the history of this country," Sawyer, now a Las Vegas lawyer said.

Robert Faise, a Las Vegas attorney and former staff assistant to JOHNSON said "This was a loss for free men everywhere. His life was dedicated to his country and to the ideals of democracy and equality of mankind.

"He was often misunderstood, but I am confident history will vindicate the decisions he made for America and prove him to be one of our greatest men."

Phil Carlin, state Democratic party chairman said "The nation has suffered a great loss."

Robert L. McDonald, a prominent Reno attorney and deputy coordinator of JOHNSON's 1964 election campaign in Nevada, was stunned by word of the former President's death.

"I'm just sick," McDonald said. "I knew him well and he was one of the greatest guys in the world. His death is a great loss to the nation."

McDonald, like the nation, had thought JOHNSON was recovering well from last year's serious coronary problems. But after an initial shock subsided he praised the Texan in carefully chosen words.

"I think he will be compared with Harry Truman, who was treated so badly by the press for a number of years," McDonald said. "He will go down in history as a great president."

𝕊

[From the Nevada State Journal]

SWEEPING AWAY—THE COBWEBS

(By Ty Cobb)

Among the Reno people with personal memories of the late President LYNDON B. JOHNSON is Mrs. Toska Slater, who will be 96 next month.

Mrs. Slater owned a parcel of land near the University of Nevada, where the interstate freeway was *"some day"* planned to run through. When the rights-of-way for the highway were being obtained, there was pressure on Mrs. Slater to sell her home and adjacent land.

Which she did.

However, she was reluctant to move out of her home of many years. "I wrote a letter to Mr. JOHNSON, telling him that the home had been sold and the neighbors had moved out—but that there was no sign of any highway being built," recalls Mrs. Slater.

"I got a letter back *so fast!* Mr. JOHNSON wrote it on White House paper. He told me that it was not a federal matter now, but if there was no sign of the highway being built right away, they'd see what could be done."

The upshot of the exchange of letters: They gave Mrs. Slater a lease on the home she had already sold, and she got to live there six more years.

𝕊

[From the Las Vegas (Nev.) Sun, Jan. 23, 1973]

NEVADANS SHOCKED BY DEATH: STATE LEADERS PRAISE L. B. J.

The death of former President LYNDON BAINES JOHNSON, Monday came as a shock to political leaders of Southern Nevada. It was a personal loss for men who knew him while he was a senator, a vice president and then the chief executive of our nation.

JOHNSON's most memorable visit to Las Vegas was a hoopla-filled Oct. 11, 1964, in the middle of one of the hardest-fought presidential elections of the century.

Three thousand Nevadans greeted him at McCarran International Airport; another 9,000 heard his words in the Las Vegas Convention Center.

Uncounted thousands lined the route between hoping for a glimpse of the man hurled into the presidency a year before by the impact of an assassin's bullet.

The President later remembered a warm welcome from Nevada's political leaders, but Nevadans themselves recall a visit from a president who repeatedly broke the ranks of his own Secret Servicemen to increase his contact with the public—physical contact, in the case of two Basic High School majorettes, who he greeted with hugs.

His speech thanked Nevadans for supporting his administration by giving it two Democratic Senators in 1960 while his own home state of Texas had provided him only one ally.

The Las Vegas speech primarily urged Nevadans to reelect Sen. Howard Cannon and promised a continuation of the policies began by the man he succeeded, President John F. Kennedy.

From here he continued to Reno, where he attached to his opponent, Sen. Barry Goldwater of Arizona, a label that was to stick: "A man running against the office of president instead of for it."

JOHNSON, also visited Las Vegas in 1962, while vice president, and participated in a political rally. He was on his way to San Francisco to address the first group of volunteers for the Peace Corps.

He had also visited Las Vegas several times during his years as a Senator.

Both Democratic and Republican leaders hailed President JOHNSON as one of the great men of this century.

𝕊

[From the Las Vegas (Nev.) Voice, Jan. 25, 1973]

NATION MOURNS L. B. J. DEATH

LYNDON BAINES JOHNSON, 64—the 36th President of the United States died of an apparent heart attack Monday afternoon.

L.B.J. was the strongest advocate of Civil Rights ever to sit in the White House. As such he DID more to help Blacks, to have a greater part of the American way of life. His fight for the voting rights act, which was enacted by the 89th Congress was but one of many, many fronts he fought. Most of the Civil Rights legislation of the 60's was passed at his insistance. He fought against poverty—ignorance.

He believed that all men were created equal. Yet he knew many were denied equal treatment. He believed that all men have certain inalienable rights, yet many Americans did not enjoy those rights, all because of the color of their skin.

One of the most important statements L.B.J. made was—He pledged—That if and when he had the power to help the plight of the minorities that he would do so—and he did.

L.B.J. was the greatest champion of the right of Black men and women to have all of the things our Constitution promised. The announcement of his death was sad news for Blacks—for they have lost a leader who marshaled all of this expertise in providing a better way of life.

He believed "that the reason most poor people were poor was that they never got a decent break," all because they were born in the wrong part of the country; or that they were born in with the wrong color skin.

The Civil Rights act of 1964, gave to every American the right to go to school, to get a job, to vote and pursue his life unhampered by the barriers of racial discrimination. But for his strong moral convictions and determination we would not have made the gains we have today.

He knew that each generation must fight to secure—renew and enlarge upon the meaning of freedom.

This is his legacy.

Hon. Gale W. McGee

OF WYOMING

Mr. President, the passing of President LYNDON BAINES JOHNSON is a great loss to our Nation and a deep, personal loss to me.

While I had known of, and about, LYNDON JOHNSON a great many years, he did not come to know me until my mentor, Senator Joseph C. O'Mahoney, asked L. B. J. to come to Casper, Wyo., on my behalf. The occasion was my initial race for the U.S. Senate in 1958. It was at a public meeting in Casper that the then majority leader of the Senate was so bold as to publicly pledge to the Wyoming voters that—

If you send that young history professor to the Senate of the United States, I promise to put him on the most powerful committee in the Senate—Appropriations.

They did, and he did.

Many present at that meeting thought LYNDON JOHNSON's promise was a typical political promise made to all constituencies, no matter what the State. Even I did not believe that the man who made it would have any reason to deliver. However, the moment I arrived in Washington, LYNDON JOHNSON's first public deed on my behalf was to announce the appointment of that young, new, freshman Senator from Wyoming to the Appropriations Committee.

Needless to say, the State of Wyoming has never forgotten that this man kept his word. And personally, from that moment on, I learned to respect the integrity of the man who was my majority leader in my "green years" in the Senate; later, my counselor and father-confessor; and ultimately, my President. But most of all, LYNDON B. JOHNSON was always my friend.

I suppose it would be fair to say that there were many instances and occasions where events drew us more closely together—particularly with members of his family. I recall even yet those warm occasions when his daughters, Luci Baines and Lynda Bird, were organizing young people in the Washington area high schools during national campaigns. I appeared jointly with them and enjoyed the good fun and camaraderie. Or those occasions when Lady Bird and LYNDON seemed to find his greatest comforts in sharing reminiscences with those western Senators with whom he seemed to speak a language much like their own.

No events, however, drew us more tightly together than the crunches of the war in Southeast Asia. It was during those tense and lonely years that the President seemed to become more and more isolated from many of his lifelong friends. A loneliness grew within him that only decision-making at the White House could create or explain. The loneliness of the Presidency must have reached an all-time peak during L. B. J.'s Vietnam years.

The climax of those troubled years is capsulized best by the President's momentous decision on March 31, 1968, not to seek reelection. Some already had reason to suspect that the President preferred to spend his retiring years with his family. But the threatened violence and divided voices of America in that fateful spring of 1968 prompted the President to make one of the most statesmanlike decisions any President has ever had the courage to make—that he would forgo another political race for reelection—one which, in the judgment of some of us, he would have won—because he felt that even in another election victory, the very fact of his presence in the White House would jeopardize the chances for a meaningful peace in Southeast Asia.

Probably more than any other modern President, LYNDON JOHNSON was the kind of political professional who relished political success the most. For him to forgo its prospects and promises in the interests of the well-being of his country says a great deal about the man's selflessness and statesmanship.

The occasion of President JOHNSON's retirement afforded the opportunity for many of us to engage in efforts to summarize his career. At the time he stepped down from the office of the Presidency, I said in a speech on the floor of the Senate—and I now quote from that text:

Mr. McGee. Mr. President, LYNDON BAINES JOHNSON came to Washington as a young man 38 years ago. Shortly he leaves his town, this Capital, this bastion of democracy, as a still young man. He leaves us with the knowledge that he is a vigorous man whose dedication to people will cause him to continue an active life and contribute many more years of service to this country. He leaves us with much more than that, however.

If LYNDON JOHNSON's career had ended at almost any point it would still have stood as a great record of achievement, for he served in five Congresses as a Member of the House of Representatives, was elected three times to the Senate, served as whip and as both minority and majority leader in this body, as Vice President and as President—the highest office this land, indeed this world, has to offer. It is a remarkable record of achievement which President JOHNSON has established. Only a remarkable man could have done it.

For myself, I count myself fortunate to know and to have worked with LYNDON B. JOHNSON, not alone because he has held power, but because he is, as a man aside from the positions of great influence which have marked his career, truly a remarkable person. I know that I am not alone in holding LYNDON B. JOHNSON in great esteem and affection, for he has been a friend to all of us—a dedicated friend to all the people of the United States. We know this whether or not we have agreed with our President on specific issues of the past. He himself, addressing us in his farewell state of the Union speech just this week, said it best:

I hope it may be said, a hundred years from now, that by working together we helped to make our country more just, more just for all of its people—as well as to insure and guarantee the blessings of liberty for all of our posterity. That is what I hope, but I believe that it will be said that we tried.

Certainly, it will be said that LYNDON JOHNSON's leadership of this country was met by turbulence as well as progress, by hate as well as affection, by fear as well as faith. But never will it be said that he gave less than a total effort to doing what, as Chief Executive, he saw as necessary, and I do suspect that 100 years from now historians will agree that this era did see America advance as a just country, just for all its people, and strengthened liberty for the future.

LYNDON B. JOHNSON has a rather special place in the State of Wyoming and in the West in general, not just because he was known to wear boots and raise white-faced cattle on his beloved ranch—though that did not hurt him any—but because he understood us and was, in real measure, one of us. He has enriched our country's democratic tradition immensely. A young man from the Texas hill country, a graduate of Southwest Texas State Teachers College, a teacher himself, he became our leader. And he led us.

Mr. President, I wish LYNDON JOHNSON and the great lady who is his wife and has been such a grand First Lady to all of us, Godspeed as they return to their Texas home.

Mr. President, indeed at the ranch, LYNDON and Lady Bird sought the quiet of their beloved hill country. But even in retirement, the President continued his quest for meaningful answers to the complex problems of humanity. Not for a moment did he rest or desist from driving himself to find better answers or higher ground upon which to resolve the conflicts that his fellow man experienced as they sought to achieve equality, understanding, and tolerance of one another. Even as he departed this world, LYNDON JOHNSON was striving to heal the wounds of this Nation laid open by racial strife and bigotry.

A giant in his own time, LYNDON B. JOHNSON will emerge as a giant on the pages of our Nation's history. The judgment of history will accord him a place of highest honor in our people's memory. For history has a way of sorting out the irrelevent and emotional attacks of contemporaries from the significant and sensitive achievements of one who is a leader. As it was the fate of Woodrow Wilson and Harry Truman, so it will be the fate of LYNDON BAINES JOHNSON.

Loraine joins me in expressing our own deep sense of loss and sympathy to Lady Bird, to Lynda Bird, to Lucie Baines, and their families.

Wyoming's sense of loss is epitomized in an editorial published in the Wyoming Eagle on January 23, 1973. Editorial Writer Bernie Horton opened his remarks by saying, "Wyoming has lost another friend."

I ask unanimous consent that the editorial be printed in the Record.

LYNDON B. JOHNSON

Wyoming has lost another friend.

His name: LYNDON B. JOHNSON, 36th President of the United States. Mr. JOHNSON died yesterday of a heart attack.

Many Wyomingites may remember LYNDON JOHNSON when he came to Cheyenne in 1952 to deliver a free-swinging political speech in behalf of his long-time friend, the late Sen. Joseph C. O'Mahoney.

Others may remember him in 1958, when he told Wyomingites that, if they elected Gale W. McGee to the United States Senate, he, as majority leader in the Senate, would see to it that McGee would be appointed to the powerful Senate Appropriations committee. McGee was elected and he was appointed to the appropriations committee the day he walked into the Senate.

Some of us will remember talking to LYNDON JOHNSON in Los Angeles, in 1960 when he was running for President. He ended up as running mate to the late President John F. Kennedy, and much of the credit for their victory was due to his efforts.

LYNDON JOHNSON came to Cheyenne again, in July, 1963, to speak at a giant appreciation dinner in honor of Wyoming's senior Senator McGee. More than 1,250 persons from all over Wyoming turned out for the occasion.

On that day, Mr. JOHNSON granted this writer an exclusive interview, perhaps the last exclusive interview he was to grant for many years. He was Vice President, at the time, and a few months later he was to become President following the tragic events that transpired in Dallas, Tex.

LYNDON JOHNSON even rode in the Cheyenne Frontier Days parade, one year. Remember him? Cowboy hat and all perched on the back of a stagecoach?

Some may have thought differently.

But we thought LYNDON JOHNSON was one of the most approachable, down-to-earth men we have ever interviewed.

He answered our questions with candor and sincerity. It seemed to us that, even as Vice President, he was dedicated to making this a greater nation—a nation with concern for all.

President JOHNSON was scheduled to return to Cheyenne on Nov. 4, 1966, but was forced to cancel because of a serious illness.

Some Wyoming Democrats may remember LYNDON JOHNSON when he was nominated at the 34th National Democratic Convention at Atlantic City, Aug. 24–27, 1964.

Some, who are interested in politics, will remember his landslide victory that year. He won 486 electoral votes to only 52 for his opponent.

Some may remember the vast number of social and economic reforms he brought about as President, especially during the months immediately following the death of President Kennedy.

But we strongly suspect that millions of Americans, including the citizens of Wyoming, may remember most vividly the address LYNDON B. JOHNSON gave on a Sunday evening, March 31, 1968.

At the very close of a 30-minute speech on Vietnam, during which he announced he was ordering an immediate and unilateral scaling down of American bombing of North Vietnam as "the first step in what I hope will be a series of mutual moves toward peace," Mr. JOHNSON declared:

"I shall not seek and I will not accept the nomination of my party for another term as your President."

That was his way of underscoring the United States' sincerity in seeking to end the war in Vietnam. It eventually was to bring the communists to the conference table. Few times in history has a President, or any other leader of a major international power, placed the welfare of his nation and the struggle for the ideal of peace so clearly and dramatically ahead of his own political ambitions.

Among other things, President JOHNSON may go down in history as the President who gave up his own political future in favor of national unity and a sincere hope for peace.

Hon. Joseph R. Biden, Jr.
OF DELAWARE

Mr. President, unlike my more fortunate colleagues, I cannot claim to have served in Congress with LYNDON BAINES JOHNSON—or even to have seen him. When LYNDON JOHNSON was first elected to the U.S. House of Representatives in 1938, I had not yet been born. When he was elected to the U.S. Senate, where I now sit, I had reached the ripe age of 6, more interested in playing than politicking.

But as my interest in politics developed early, I could not help become interested—and fascinated—by the political professionalism of LYNDON JOHNSON. His mammoth concern for the well-being of impoverished Americans is a permanent and distinguishing mark of his Presidential stewardship. His legislative programs were gargantuan ones, but always we should remember the generous impulses upon which these programs rested. If his stewardship became a "splendid misery," as some have described the Presidency, nevertheless the word "splendid" should be remembered in connection with his Presidency as well as the "misery" of it. If his failures were sometimes larger than life, so were his successes. It does neither him nor his Presidency a disservice to paint him, as an artist once did, another outstanding but earlier President, "warts and all."

Mr. President, I ask unanimous consent that an editorial from the Washington Post of January 24, 1973, which discusses the Johnson Presidency, be printed in the Record.

LYNDON BAINES JOHNSON

The public lifetime of LYNDON BAINES JOHNSON spanned almost four decades. It was a period marked not just by the development of certain powerful currents in American thought, but also by an eventual reappraisal of where those currents had led. Thus, much which had been considered desirable, necessary and even holy in Mr. JOHNSON's political youth had fallen into disrepute by the time that he left office. "Internationalism" had come to be known as "interventionism" by many, its painful and costly effects haunting the nation in a seemingly unendable war. And the vital and generous impulses that had animated Mr. JOHNSON's commitment to domestic legislation from the New Deal through the Great Society had come to be seen by many as obsolete and outworn habits of mind which caused as many troubles as they cured. At the airport sendoff that January day in 1969, when LYN-

DON B. JOHNSON's homebound plane vanished into the clouds, his longtime friends and colleagues were left with more than an eerie feeling of suddenness and totality with which power is relinquished in this country. The summary departure of this man who had been the larger-than-life center of ambition and authority in government for five years, also seemed symbolically to end a self-contained chapter in the nation's political development.

It was an era characterized both domestically and in foreign policy terms by an assumption of responsibility—national responsibility—for the welfare of the poor, the rights of the mistreated, the fairness of the way in which we distribute our wealth and the general well-being and stability of countries all over the world. Of Mr. JOHNSON's participation in all this—as a Congressman, Senator, Vice President and President—it must be said that his impact was so profound that there is hardly a case in which the nation was either blessed or victimized by this particular 20th century passion for responsibility for which LYNDON JOHNSON himself was not largely responsible. Like indifferent lovers or fractious offspring, a nation can often take things for granted or seem only to notice when it has been wronged. The death of Mr. JOHNSON may serve momentarily to pull us back from these perspectives, to remind us that much which we now expect from our government and our society as a matter of course—black voting rights, care for our elderly and our ill—came to us very recently and largely by courtesy of LYNDON JOHNSON.

The simple, inescapable fact is that he cared—and that it showed. Being in all ways larger than life-sized, he cared about a lot of things: his own political fortunes, his image, and his place in history, for of course he was vain. But he was consistent; all of his appetites were king-sized. So he cared about people with the same enormous intensity. In fact, a fair case can be made that one set of appetites fed on the other; he struggled and wheedled and hammered and cajoled for political power because he yearned powerfully to do great and good things and that is what he wanted the power for.

This was at once the strength and the weakness of LYNDON JOHNSON, for while this tremendous force was more often than not irresistible over the years, both as Senate Majority Leader and President, it was, like everything about the man, very often excessive. It could bend the political process to his will, and to good effect. But it could also bear down too hard, so that the system cracked under his weight. A master at the instrumentality of events, he could use a Selma or an assassination to lever a civil rights law or a gun control bill through Congress. But he could also use a minor gunboat skirmish in the Gulf of Tonkin to produce a resolution from Congress giving overwhelming support to a war effort whose true nature was never revealed in terms which could be expected to prepare either the Congress or the public for the sacrifice that both would later be expected to accept.

Neither LYNDON JOHNSON's memory nor his place in history, we would hope, is going to turn entirely, or even primarily on the war that grew out of that resolution; for Vietnam there is blame enough for all concerned, over four administrations and a good number of Congresses. Confined and carried along by earlier commitments, counselled by the men recruited by his predecessors, unchecked by Congress, Mr. JOHNSON plunged on, overstating, over-promising, over-hoping, over-reaching. But if his time in office marked the big Vietnam escalation, it also will be remembered for the fact that he, by implication and by painfully difficult decision, moved toward the end of his term to acknowledge a great miscalculation—widely shared in, let it be said—which is not something incumbent Presidents are given to doing. Reluctantly, grudgingly, but effectively, he turned the war effort around, abandoning "graduated response" as the method of choice, and bequeathed to his successor a greater opportunity than he himself inherited to move toward disengagement and a redefinition of the mission in realistic terms.

When Harry Truman died a few weeks ago at the age of 88, he died the beneficiary of a gift LYNDON JOHNSON was not to receive: 20 years had passed since the embattled and much maligned Mr. Truman had held office so that time and change and hindsight vastly altered the view people had of him. Mr. JOHNSON was never lucky in this regard. His each and every achievement from his Senate years on seemed to be followed or accompanied by some series of events that spoiled the glory of the moment. Still, we do not share the notion, now being advanced (sometimes with bitterness) of how unfair it was that he rarely received the recognition he deserved in his lifetime for the good and also great things he did—or that the criticism of his handling of the war unfairly overshadowed all the rest. He would we suspect, have a wryly humorous view of all this—much as he craved to be well-loved and well-remembered—because he was too shrewd, not to say cynical a student of human and political nature not to have been amused by these efforts by those who served him badly from time to time to revise the record in his (and their) favor. LYNDON JOHNSON must have known that he did not need to be helped into history.

Hon. Hubert H. Humphrey
OF MINNESOTA

Mr. President, I ask unanimous consent to have printed in the Record, so that it may appear in the bound volume of tributes to President LYNDON B. JOHNSON, the remarks of former Secretary of State Dean Rusk at the memorial service held in the rotunda of the Capitol, January 24, 1973.

Many Senators were present at this service and I know I speak for them in commending Secretary Rusk on his speaking so well and eloquently for us.

REMARKS MADE BY FORMER SECRETARY OF STATE
DEAN RUSK

A home on the bank of the Pedernales in the beautiful hill country of Texas, surrounded by his beloved family and the friends with whom he so fully shared his warm and generous spirit—

A home in this place where we are gathered today, in the Congress, which was his life for so long, filled with friendships enlivened by that political debate which is the lifeblood of a free society, but friendships cemented by the common task of insuring that the public business somehow would go forward at the end of the day.

A home for more than five years at the summit of responsibilty, of responsibility and not necessarily of power—for he, as other Presidents, understood that many expectations and demands were addressed to him which were beyond his constitutional reach or, indeed, beyond the reach of our nation in a world community where we might persuade but cannot command. There were years of awesome burdens, but burdens lightened by the fine intelligence and the natural grace and the personal devotion of the First Lady who was always at his side.

And now he returns to the Pedernales to a home among the immortals, that goodly company of men and women whom we shall forever cherish because they were concerned about those matters which barred the path to our becoming what we have in us to become. More than a thousand years ago, in a simpler and more robust age, perhaps we might have known him as LYNDON the Liberator, for he was determined to free our people in body, mind and spirit.

A few strokes of the brush cannot portray this man to whom we offer our affection and respect today. As for me, I would begin with his deep compassion for his fellowman, a compassion which was shared by the Congress and resulted in the most extraordinary legislative season in our history.

Who can forget that remarkable evening of March 15, 1965, when President JOHNSON addressed a joint session of Congress on voting rights and other civil rights? It was perhaps his finest single message.

You will remember that, after recalling his days as a teacher of poor Mexican-American children back in 1928, he said, "It never even occurred to me in my fondest dreams that I might have the chance to help the sons and daughters of those students and to help people like them all over the country."

And then, with eyes which bored into the conscience of all who heard him, he said, "But now I do have that chance, and I'll let you in on a secret—I mean to use it. And I hope you will use it with me."

And then he went on to disclose in a very frank way what some of his deepest hopes were. Congressman Pickle has already quoted those hopes. One may give these ideas any name or epithet one might choose. They did not evolve out of some empty intellectual exercise. They were not the product of shrewd political calculation. His colleagues knew them as a volcanic eruption from the innermost being of his soul when the responsibility for leadership finally became his own.

Many have said that LYNDON JOHNSON was demanding upon his colleagues and personal staff. Indeed he was. And demanding upon the Congress and the American people and many a foreign leader as well. But he was most demanding upon himself and stubbornly resisted the admonitions of his associates to slow down. There was so much to do, and there was so little time in which to get it done.

President JOHNSON sometimes deprecated his own background in foreign affairs. Actually he brought great talents and a rich experience to this aspect of the Presidency in November 1963. As Senate Majority Leader throughout much of the Eisenhower years, he was necessarily and deeply involved in the widest range of legislation affecting foreign and defense policy.

When he became Vice President, President Kennedy asked him frequently to make foreign visits and consult with foreign leaders on matters of major importance—not merely a tourist's visit.

He absorbed briefings in a most expert fashion, and with a powerful intellect went directly to the heart of the issues under discussion. And as many present know, he was always formidable in negotiation or persuasion.

He had a special ability, perhaps learned in the Senate, to begin his consideration of a problem by putting himself in the other fellow's shoes, in an attempt to understand which answers might be possible.

He had a personal code of relations among political leaders which did not permit him or his colleagues to engage in personal vilification aimed at foreign leaders, however deep the disagreement might appear to be.

Today's writers are inclined to discuss LYNDON JOHNSON almost solely in terms of Viet-Nam, and such questions as whether he did too much or too little in that tragic struggle. The historian will take a broader view and weigh such things as the Consular and Civil Air Agreements with the Soviet Union, the Non-proliferation Treaty, our space treaties, his East-West trade bill, the beginnings of the SALT talks, and many other initiatives aimed at building the peace.

He had a very special and affectionate feeling for the nations of the western hemisphere. He used to say to us, "This hemisphere is where we live, this is our home, these are our neighbors. We must start with our own neighborhood."

Mr. President, last evening you made some moving remarks about President JOHNSON in your brief address to the American people. We congratulate you on the substance of that address and give you our best wishes for the weeks and months ahead. I mention two points which you made about LYNDON JOHNSON. That President JOHNSON was a man of peace and would have welcomed the peace which seems now to be opening up in Southeast Asia. How true. And he would, indeed, have joined you, Mr. President, in paying tribute to those millions of gallant and dedicated men in uniform whose services and sacrifice opened the way for the peace which is before us.

In his last State of the Union Message to the Congress, his final sentence was, "But I believe that at least it will be said that we tried." Ah, yes, he tried, with reckless disregard for his own life.

And then, in the final chapter of his book, when he was reflecting upon how it looked to him as he returned to that ranch which he loved so much, his final sentence was, "And I knew also that I had given it everything that was in me."

As time passes, the world will increasingly acknowledge that the "everything" that was in him was a very great deal, and that men and women all over the earth are forever in his debt.

Hon. Lloyd M. Bentsen
OF TEXAS

Mr. President, in this city, there will always be debate about memorials and monuments to

Presidents and other Government leaders. The Washington Star, in a recent editorial, very succinctly and very plausibly, I believe, put this issue in focus as it relates to the late President JOHNSON. I concur with the writer's conclusion, that President JOHNSON is totally deserving of this type of living tribute.

Further, the Star makes a very telling point—When Mrs. Lyndon Johnson does something, the public can depend on it being done in taste and in proper perspective.

Mr. President, I ask unanimous consent that the editorial be printed in the Record.

AN L. B. J. MEMORIAL

No subject under the sun is capable of producing more dissension, and more agonizing debate and more bureaucratic spinning of wheels than memorials to our former presidents. Remember, for example, the furor over those giant slabs of stone proposed in West Potomac Park to memorialize Franklin Delano Roosevelt?

So, too, in the natural order of things, such controversy may well up in regard to the most recently deceased of our chief executives, LYNDON B. JOHNSON.

But perhaps not.

At the very least, in the proposal unveiled the other day, we are off to a good start. The idea, as initiated by Laurance Rockefeller, involves a grove of trees—possibly encompassing a sculpture of the late President—within the park area already named for Lady Bird Johnson on the Virginia side of the Potomac River between the Memorial and 14th Street Bridges.

Nash Castro, a former director of National Capital Parks who is working to advance the proposal, says he already has discussed it with Mrs. Johnson, and quotes the former First Lady as being "touched and moved" by the concept.

Well, we are, too. This city owes an immense debt of gratitude to Mrs. Johnson for the areas of annual flowering beauty which she initiated here—as indeed the nation is indebted to LYNDON JOHNSON for his own efforts in the fields of beautification.. The 150-acre Lady Bird Johnson Park is itself a lovely setting, which could be made more so by an attractive grove of trees.

One more thing is to be said in the idea's behalf: With Mrs. Johnson's personal involvement, there is a good chance that the job would be done right.

It is not our position that a memorial in Washington to every deceased president, especially in view of many of the grandiose proposals that have been advanced in the past, is a necessity. But we think this one would be fitting to the man, and an asset to the city.

Hon. Gaylord Nelson
OF WISCONSIN

Mr. President, history, especially recent history, is a very subjective study. Most of us stand-ing too close to the events and the people involved can only view it as it affected us, as we remember it, how we felt, and whether we disagreed or agreed.

The memory of LYNDON JOHNSON again presents that difficulty. He was magnificently controversial as only great men can be controversial. One could not be ambivalent about the man as Senator, Vice President, or President. Even though he was an accomplished politician who was a master of compromise, he was nonetheless, a man of strong convictions who made the tough, hard decisions when it was necessary to make them.

My personal feelings about him range as broadly today as they did when he was President. We differed completely on the war, and that was a major difference. But I was proud to support his social legislation and be part of an exciting period of legislative history.

Since his death, it has been observed that JOHNSON will be remembered in history as one of the great Presidents, especially in the area of social legislation.

Even though I can only give a very subjective observation, I feel that JOHNSON was one of the great Presidents of this Nation and that his record on social legislation will be difficult to equal.

I have not accustomed myself to the fact that he is dead and that we can no longer call on the experience of his years in Government. The Nation has been cheated by his untimely death. The world lost a compassionate man who did all the things we all do and was human at a time when too few political leaders are human by choice or expectation.

Hon. Alan Cranston
OF CALIFORNIA

Mr. President, the distinguished poet laureate of the State of California, Charles B. Garrigus, has memorialized the passing of two great Americans, Harry S Truman and LYNDON B. JOHNSON.

Mr. Garrigus' eloquent and heartfelt words lyrically honor the spirit and passions of two of our greatest Presidents.

I know my colleagues will want to share these panegyrics with me. Mr. President, I ask unanimous consent that they be printed at this point in the Record.

IN MEMORIAM: LYNDON BAINES JOHNSON

Beside the Pedernales cattle low
And Texas skies are filled with starlight's glow;
The winding waters have a ghostly gleam
As if the stars were floating in the stream.
This is the land where LYNDON JOHNSON grew,
Here live the people LYNDON JOHNSON knew.
This land—this people—shaped what he would do.
Friendly, proud, ambitious in this place.
He marked the course where he would run his race.
What most he sought was exercise of power,
To furnish civil rights as each man's dower.
He believed that what American must be
Would show the world how true democracy
Could guarantee all men their dignity.
This man whom strong ambition lifted high
Became conspicuous in his country's eye.
Proud, persuasive, pompous and profane,
He drove himself and others for our gain.
He knew his trust, his faith, and his desire
Would lift him to the heights where men aspire
To work for service rather than for hire.
Long hours of stress and anguish caused by war
Weakened a heart already strained too far.
He saw so well the twilight of his day,
But walked with cheerful courage all the way.

Remember LYNDON JOHNSON for his cause:
That each man suffers for his neighbor's flaws;
That men find freedom in respect for laws.

IN MEMORIAM: HARRY TRUMAN

Now by Missouri's lonely hickory hills,
A noble civil servant takes his rest.
He was an unpretentious, common man;
And yet his record ranks him with the best.
Salesman, captain, clerk and politician
Are terms that designate a simple man.
He was all of these, but so much more
That history proudly marks the course he ran.
Thrust by cruel chance into an awful task,
He ne'er complained nor wavered in his course.
His duty and his conscience were his guides;
His deep religious faith in God his force.
The common people saw themselves in him,
Saw faith and fear and doubt before the fact;
Saw anger, pride, and pleasure in the game,
Saw victory in the way he dared to act.
In centuries hence across the stage of time,
The world shall see great men pass in review—
Warriors, kings, the leaders of the earth—
Our Man from Independence walks there too.

INDEX

Memorial Tributes in the House of Representatives of the United States

Memorial Tributes in the Senate of the United States